PRAISE FOR *ACCIDENT*

"*Accidental Presidents* is a compelling and that shines a light on unexplored corners ᴏɪ ᴏᴜɪ ᴍɪstory. . . . In his typically engaging and gripping style, Jared Cohen tells us why it is not easy to amend the Constitution and why it should be amended. He explores the complexities of the American Constitution and politics as a gifted storyteller. . . . It will resonate for a long time to come among the scholars and students of American history."

—Washington Independent Review of Books

"While much is known about the two successful accidentals, Roosevelt and Truman, and the partially successful Lyndon, the latter Johnson, much of the book's treasure lies in earlier, lesser-known accidentals."

—*New York Journal of Books*

"What a delightful book and brilliant concept! Jared Cohen treats us to some of the most colorful and momentous episodes in our history when we unexpectedly got a new president. He reveals the historic importance of some lesser-known leaders, such as John Tyler and Millard Fillmore, and highlights the greatness of Teddy Roosevelt, Harry Truman, and Lyndon Johnson. Through their fascinating tales we learn why America is such a resilient nation and our Constitution a living document—lessons very powerful for today."

—Walter Isaacson, #1 *New York Times* bestselling author of
Leonardo da Vinci

"Every single sentence in this books counts."

—Fox News

"Fascinating, compelling, and often alarming. With astonishing story after story, Jared Cohen chronicles the whole pageant of the unsteady, the unready, and the unexpectedly capable. Nearly ten percent of our presidents succeeded because of the deaths of those who chose them mostly out of political expediency to be forgotten number twos. Will we luck out in the future with a surprising Harry Truman or with a wrecker like Andrew Johnson? In God we trust. But read Jared Cohen."

—Sidney Blumenthal, author of *A Self-Made Man* and
Wrestling with His Angel

"Thanks to Jared Cohen. The stories of eight accidental presidents are now all in one grand place. Cohen deserves a medal for performing this public service."

—Patricia O'Toole, author of *The Moralist: Woodrow Wilson and the World He Made*

"History is the most contingent of enterprises, and little has proven more contingent than the nature of the American presidency. In this eloquent and often surprising book, Jared Cohen explores how fate has shaped the office—and all of us. In an age marked by widespread concerns about the character of the person who reaches the pinnacle (by whatever means), Cohen's study is illuminating and resonant."

—Jon Meacham, #1 *New York Times* bestselling author of *The Soul of America: The Battle for Our Better Angels*

"This is a fascinating prism through which to look at American history. . . . It is a well-written fast-paced book that is filled with interesting facts and insights. Anyone who is interested in American history will delight in it."

—Fareed Zakaria, CNN

"A deep dive into the terms of eight former presidents is chock-full of political hijinks—and déjà vu . . . chapters flick at familiar themes: trust busting, scandal wrangling, and brawls that read like highbrow TMZ. . . . The book is also a reminder that, when it came to succession, America's founders basically winged it."

—*Vanity Fair*

"One of the many insights to be found in *Accidental Presidents* is that history unfolds in death as well as in life."

—*The Wall Street Journal*

"Pleasant reading for politics junkies, especially those keen on reading the political winds."

—*Kirkus Reviews*

"Illuminating . . . [a] genuinely interesting history on a topic that has never been addressed in this depth."

—*Booklist*

"Colorful . . . clear and engaging . . . confidently told."

—*Publishers Weekly*

ACCIDENTAL PRESIDENTS

Eight Men Who Changed America

JARED COHEN

Simon & Schuster Paperbacks

NEW YORK   LONDON   TORONTO   SYDNEY   NEW DELHI

Simon & Schuster Paperbacks
An Imprint of Simon & Schuster, Inc.
1230 Avenue of the Americas
New York, NY 10020

Copyright © 2019 by Jared Cohen

First Simon & Schuster trade paperback edition January 2020

SIMON & SCHUSTER and colophon are registered trademarks
of Simon & Schuster, Inc.

For information about special discounts for bulk purchases,
please contact Simon & Schuster Special Sales at 1-866-506-1949
or business@simonandschuster.com.

The Simon & Schuster Speakers Bureau can bring authors to your
live event. For more information, or to book an event, contact the
Simon & Schuster Speakers Bureau at 1-866-248-3049
or visit our website at www.simonspeakers.com.

Interior design by Paul Dippolito

Manufactured in the United States of America

5   7   9   10   8   6   4

Library of Congress Cataloging-in-Publication Data is available.

ISBN 978-1-5011-0982-9
ISBN 978-1-5011-0983-6 (pbk)
ISBN 978-1-5011-0984-3 (ebook)

To my amazing daughters, Zelda, Annabel, and Ingrid,
who with each passing day fill me with joy and happiness

The Presidents on Assassination . . .

*[I stayed up] waiting for important dispatches from the front . . .
[As I dreamed I felt] a death-like stillness about me . . . [and heard]
mournful sounds of distress [and as I entered the East Room,
I saw] a sickening surprise [a coffin guarded by soldiers] . . .
'Who is dead in the White House?' I demanded of one of
the soldiers. 'The president. He was killed by an assassin!'*
—ABRAHAM LINCOLN RECALLING HIS DREAM TO WARD HILL LAMON

*Well, if assassination is to play its part in the campaign, and
I must be the sacrifice, perhaps it is best. I think I am ready.*
—JAMES GARFIELD

*As soon as I am aware of the condition of my beloved
president, I will set about clearing my good name
about having hired an assassin to harm our president.*
—CHESTER ARTHUR TO JAMES BLAINE

*I give you my word, I do not care a rap
about being shot; not a rap.*
—THEODORE ROOSEVELT

*Since you can't control these things [assassination
attempts], you don't think about them.*
—FRANKLIN ROOSEVELT

*I was beginning to realize how little the founding
fathers had been able to anticipate the preparations
necessary for a man to become president so suddenly.*
—HARRY TRUMAN

*If anybody really wanted to shoot the president of the United,
States it was not a very difficult job—all one had to do was get
a high building someday with a telescopic rifle, and there was
nothing anybody could do to defend against such an attempt.*
—JOHN F. KENNEDY TO AN AIDE THE MORNING OF HIS ASSASSINATION

Contents

John Wilkes Booth *On April 14, 1865, the established actor and Confederate sympathizer snuck into the presidential box at Ford's Theatre and assassinated Abraham Lincoln with a single-shot Deringer pistol.* **Charles Guiteau** *The mentally unstable office seeker shot President James Garfield at the Baltimore and Potomac Railroad Station in Washington, D.C., on July 2, 1881. He was hanged on June 30, 1882.* **Leon Czolgosz** *Portrait of the anarchist, who on September 6, 1901, shot President William McKinley in a receiving line at the Pan-American Exposition in Buffalo, New York. He was tried, convicted, and electrocuted on October 29.* **Lee Harvey Oswald** *A former marine who had spent time in the Soviet Union before killing President Kennedy on November 22, 1963. He was shot and killed by nightclub owner Jack Ruby two days later.*

Foreword

"My office renders me so completely insignificant that all Parties can afford to treat me with a decent respect which accordingly they do, as far as I observe, or hear or suspect. They all know that I can do them neither much good nor much harm."[1]

—John Adams as the first vice president

John Tyler, Millard Fillmore, Andrew Johnson, Chester Arthur, Theodore Roosevelt, Calvin Coolidge, Harry Truman, Lyndon Johnson: Eight times a vice president has become president upon the death of his predecessor—history altered by a heartbeat. This is the story of how these eight men, neither the voters' nor their party's choice, dealt with that power and changed history, for better or worse.

These men ascended to the presidency without the Constitution having specified an order of succession. The founders didn't think of everything. They made compromises to get things done, such as giving each state two senators to get the smaller states to sign on to proportional representation in the House of Representatives. Succession was no different, particularly given how little thought had been given to the vice presidency itself. The fact that the country navigated these abrupt transfers of power eight times during a one-hundred-and-twenty-two-year period and amended the Constitution only after John F. Kennedy's assassination in 1963 offers a powerful response to the originalist, or literal, interpretation of the Constitution.

In many cases, the men who came to fill the shoes of dead presidents had been spouses in a marriage of political convenience for a president to win a state or appease a particular constituency. Only five—John Adams, Thomas Jefferson, Martin Van Buren, Richard Nixon, and George H. W. Bush—completed terms as vice president and went on to win the presidency. Their election relieved them of that vice-presidential image of irrelevance. In the eight instances when the vice president succeeded to the office, a set of common challenges made the path to success much harder. Each had to earn the respect of the men loyal to his predecessor, or find a way to discard them. They had to honor the loss while at the same time getting back to governing. All had to find the balance between continuing the policies of the man who was elected (including navigating the ambiguity left behind) and responsibly fulfilling their present duties. Each had to step out of the shadow of his predecessor and earn the presidency in his own right.

Each transition is treated as its own chapter, with the exception of FDR, where the combination of high stakes and certainty of death warrant extra attention. There is no strict pattern that determined performance, although in two of our most extraordinary cases—Abraham Lincoln and Franklin Roosevelt—they made poor choices, given the wartime context. In Roosevelt's case, he got lucky because Harry Truman proved up to the job, the best of the lot other than the great Theodore Roosevelt. Lincoln's vice president, Andrew Johnson, proved the biggest catastrophe of the eight.

One president, Gerald Ford, became both vice president and president without being elected to either position. While coming into both offices on the heels of resignation makes him an accidental president of sorts, this book is about the abrupt transitions that occur when a president dies in office. Such circumstances truly deprive the voters of their choice and have historically imposed expectations on their successors that are different from when Nixon resigned in the wake of Watergate. Ford's transition is also different in that by the time Nixon resigned, presidential succession had been formalized and legal codified with the ratification of the twenty-fifth amendment. Thus, while there is no chapter devoted to Ford, his ascension is given some discussion in the book's final chapter.

We can't understand what a miracle Truman is without understanding both the lackadaisical effort that went into FDR's choice of a 1944 running mate and the extraordinary performance of Harry Truman as president. Truman had big shoes to fill, but so did the other seven. They had their own biases. Most had been excluded from their predecessors' inner circles. Their ambition to make their own mark led them down very different paths. Some rose to the occasion, others failed. The chapters show mixed performances—some started and ended wars, while others accelerated and slowed social progress. Each story also raises questions about how history might have been different had the president survived.

The stories of eight men who became president by accident are remarkable in what they reveal. They are all part of a history of presidential succession which has been frivolous and has left the country exposed to Constitutional crisis or vulnerable to luck and chance. The framers paid little attention to succession and despite eight deaths in office, the matter of succession has been trivialized by voters, candidates, and lawmakers.

William Henry Harrison *became the first Whig president, but died after just thirty days in office. The Constitution was vague on whether the vice president assumes the office, or simply fulfills its duties as "acting president."*

John Tyler *became the nation's first accidental president. He was reviled by the Whigs and kicked out of his own party. He annexed Texas and precipitated war with Mexico.*

CHAPTER ONE

First to Die

Chief Tecumseh[1] had every right to be vengeful. At the age of six, the future Shawnee chief watched a Virginia militia kill his father during the 1774 Battle of Point Pleasant. Just a few years later he bore witness to the violent consequences his tribe would suffer for siding with Britain in the American Revolution. And at twenty-one years old, he joined an unsuccessful resistance movement against settler expansion in Tennessee, only to watch his older brother, Cheeseekau, die in combat. Despite repeated setbacks, he continued fighting, returning to the Midwest in 1794 to fight with the Shawnee in the Battle of Fallen Timbers.[2] But persistence once again failed him as Shawnee battle tactics fell short against an overpowering American military.

As the story goes, it was there at Fallen Timbers that Chief Tecumseh first encountered William Henry Harrison, a young, ambitious aide-de-camp to General "Mad" Anthony Wayne and future president of the United States. At the battle's conclusion, General Wayne leveraged his victory, along with a combination of coercion and bribery, to negotiate the Treaty of Greenville, which ceded more than three million acres of Shawnee land to the American government. Angered by the one-sided nature of the treaty, Chief Tecumseh and his surviving brother, Tenskwatawa— nicknamed "The Prophet"—founded a village called Prophetstown, which they intended to be the epicenter of a larger Native American confederacy that would stem the tide of white settlers who threatened their land. But those plans never materialized, and in 1811, Tecumseh and Harrison found themselves once again facing off, this time in the Battle of Tippecanoe. In that decisive battle, Harrison, who was now an established politician and seasoned major general in the Army, dealt Tecumseh and the Shawnee a devastating blow.[3] Over the course of a generation, the two men grew in stature within their communities, but it was Harrison who found success while Tecumseh came to know only the death and destruction of his people.

As legend has it, a lifetime of animosity led Chief Tecumseh to place a curse on the American presidency. The terms of this curse* stipulated that Tecumseh, "who caused the Sun to darken and Red Men to give up firewater . . . [can] . . . tell you [that William Henry] Harrison will die. And after him, every Great Chief chosen every 20 years thereafter will die. And when each dies, let everyone remember the death of [the Shawnee] people."[4]

While curses and vengeful Indian chiefs make for a colorful tale, the story of the accidental presidents began with the presidential campaign of 1840, which was an unprecedented political spectacle. The election was a rancorous charade that offered just enough games and gimmicks to attract what at the time was a record 80.2 percent of eligible voters.[5] The newly established Whig Party ran the aging retired general William Henry Harrison—nicknamed "Old Tippecanoe"—against incumbent Democrat Martin Van Buren—a Jacksonian Democrat who had the misfortune of taking office five weeks before the country's worst economic crisis in its history. Van Buren's presidency was doomed from the start, and following a barrage of Whig attacks that painted him as an out-of-touch elitist, his prospects for reelection were bleak.

For purposes of the campaign, William Henry Harrison was a simple man born in a log cabin who rose through the ranks of the military to become an American hero. His story was inspiring and offered a remarkable tale of beating the odds at a time when so many people were losing hope. While the hero part was true, the rest of the narrative was a myth; a fabrication meant to present the retired general as Everyman. His wealth and privilege were obfuscated through campaign intrigue so prodigious that presidential elections would never be the same. Whether his story was fact or fiction mattered little as the voters got drunk on the idea of Old Tippecanoe, quite literally, as the campaign hosted hard cider events in log cabins throughout the twenty-six United States. Liquor distributors had a

---

* The curse would make for a powerful historical anecdote, except for the fact that it was a pop fabrication printed in a 1931 edition of *Ripley's Believe It or Not,* which published the absurd story over a century after the alleged curse was issued.

field day and wanted the campaign to last forever. Some, like E. C. Booz, the innovative whiskey distiller from Philadelphia, resorted to shameless tactics such as filling whiskey bottles designed as log cabins and calling it "Old Cabin Whiskey," which some have even credited as the origin of the word "booze."[6] And where alcohol was not sufficient, the Whigs resorted to other measures. Party supporters built gigantic papier-mâché balls to roll from town to town in a public display of support. Music, songs, and dances were choreographed and written. The Whigs produced gimmick after gimmick, avoiding taking a position on any major issue.

In the backdrop of all of this was John Tyler, Harrison's running mate, and the second half of the catchy campaign slogan "Tippecanoe and Tyler Too." He was supposed to be a footnote in history, thrown onto the Whig ticket in 1840 to help carry Virginia, which they lost anyway, and offer a nod to states' rights, which didn't really happen either. He was a pragmatic choice, a national figure with a "dignified southern charm."[7] He had run as a Whig in Maryland and Virginia four years earlier, and he could help bring along southern anti-abolitionists and states' rights zealots.[8] Some argued that he was antinationalist and most (perhaps including Tyler himself) believed that he was a Jacksonian Democrat at heart. But these factors aside, there weren't many viable candidates who would actually accept the job,[9] and time was running out. Despite some rumblings and objections, even the detractors became complacent with the idea of parking Tyler in the vice presidency. What harm could he cause in such an irrelevant position?

The two won a commanding victory on top of an already firm Whig control of the government. The party had 85 percent of the gubernatorial seats, nearly 57 percent[10] of the House of Representatives, 51 percent of the Senate, the majority of state legislatures,[11] and now for the first time, the presidency. Victory gave the Whigs control over eighteen thousand federal appointments, which meant they could kick the Democrats out of the federal government and disperse jobs to party loyalists.[12]

On March 4, 1841, the new president rode into Washington on a train, the first president to do so.[13] For the parade down Pennsylvania Avenue, he climbed atop a white horse—his favorite, "Whitey"—waved to an estimated fifty thousand[14] adoring fans, and then delivered his inaugural address from a podium on the eastern portico of the Capitol.[15] At 8,445 words, the speech lasted an hour and forty-five minutes, the longest in history. It mirrored the campaign in its lack of direction and substance. Some antsy spectators left their seats and ambled around out of sheer boredom, while others stamped their feet to manage the frigid weather.[16]

At sixty-eight, Harrison was the oldest man to win the presidency—later eclipsed by Ronald Reagan and then Donald Trump. Eager to prove that he was able-bodied, the new president braved the brisk weather without a hat, gloves, or overcoat, which appeared to many observers to lead to his catching a mild cold. The cold weakened him, but he was out and about shortly thereafter: as president, he enjoyed strolling around unescorted, proving that he really was a man of the people. Three weeks after the inauguration, however, shortly after returning to the White House after one of his jaunts, he fell ill from what his doctors diagnosed as "pneumonia of the lower lobe of the right lung, complicated by congestion of the liver."[17] By April 4, the president was dead, having served thirty days in office. Despite the original diagnosis sustaining for 173 years, the *New York Times* reported that the true cause of death was more likely enteric fever, which would have been caused by the field of human excrement that, in the absence of a proper sewer system, flowed into a marsh near the White House.[18]* Lying slightly reclined and surrounded by his niece and nephew, three cabinet secretaries, and Reverend William Hawley,[19] Harrison reserved his last words for a cryptic plea to his successor: "Sir—I wish you to understand the true principles of government. I wish them carried out—I ask nothing more."[20]

His successor, however, was nowhere near the president's bedside to hear these words. Harrison was delirious in his final hour and while his words were directed at Tyler, they were in fact spoken to his personal physician, Dr. N. W. Worthington.[21] John Tyler, resigned to the irrelevance of the vice presidency, had already dashed out of Washington the same day as the inauguration to his home in Virginia. Other than an occasional trip to the Senate, he intended to spend his four-year term outside the nation's capital.

There was no precedent for this situation, nor had there been any planning. With the president dead and the vice president several hundred miles away, Secretary of State Daniel Webster mustered the cabinet and insisted that they draft a memorandum for the vice president.[22] Webster

---

* Scientists have argued that the buildup of human waste was also responsible for James Polk's death just three months after leaving office in 1849.

dispatched his twenty-three-year-old son, Fletcher, chief clerk for the State Department, and Robert Beale, the doorkeeper of the U.S. Senate, to deliver the tragic news. The two men took the first possible train to Richmond and chartered a boat to make the final leg of the journey.[23] They arrived at dawn, exhausted and standing before Tyler's home.[24] Webster knocked on the door, but perhaps in his gentlemanly way did not knock loud enough to wake the vice president. Beale, who was the less polite of the two boys, gave the door a good pound until Tyler awakened, came downstairs in shock that someone in this respectful town would disturb his slumber,[25] and answered the door in his pajamas and nightcap. As the story goes,[26] the messengers telegraphed the tragic news with their facial expressions, but remained calm and collected, conveying that they had "been instructed by the Secretary of State to deliver these dispatches to you without delay." Upon reading the letter, Tyler cried, "My God, the President is dead,"[27] and urged the two young messengers to come into his home.

Tyler was disheartened, but remained composed. He was a gentleman with a reserved manner that many mistook for weakness. But he rarely overlooked even the subtlest detail and when reading the letter he noticed a few omissions. The message, which was signed by the entire cabinet, mentioned nothing about Tyler now being president and stopped short of urging his return to Washington. Furthermore, the signatories addressed the letter to "John Tyler, Vice-president of the United States."[28] These were not careless drafting mistakes, nor were they inadvertent omissions. Harrison fell ill in the early weeks of his presidency, but only in the previous week did it appear as though he might die. Preparing for the worst-case scenario, members of the cabinet began debating and deliberating on the implications.

While no official record of these meetings exists, Nathan Sargent, a prominent journalist covering the Whig beat, wrote that the cabinet deliberated on how to address Tyler and concluded that "Mr. Tyler must, while performing the functions of President, bear the title of Vice-President, acting President."[29] Assuming Sargent's account is correct—and it likely is given that the full cabinet signed on to the letter—there were probably two reasons for this: First, these were all Harrison men with a low opinion of both the vice presidency and its current occupant. Second, the Whigs believed in a weak executive and Harrison was a known quantity.

He had pledged a single term and promised to be deferential to the legislature. In cabinet meetings, he subscribed to a process of one man, one vote, whether you were the president or the postmaster general. Tyler was more of a wild card and none of Harrison's men knew how his views and style would manifest themselves. More important, none of them trusted him and, in fact, they probably didn't like him much. They questioned his commitment to the Whig agenda—national bank, internal improvements, weakening of the executive branch, raising the tariff. They knew he kept the outside counsel of a trusted group of Virginia states' rightist confidants.

Tyler woke his wife and children, shared the somber news, ate his breakfast, and called a family meeting. His wife, Letitia, was gravely ill and partially paralyzed, so the future of their seven[30] children weighed heavily on her. The family deliberated and agreed that Tyler should rush to Washington after which two of his children, Robert and Priscilla, would join him the following week. Pending her health, Letitia would follow sometime thereafter.[31]

With the family decisions temporarily settled, Tyler focused on navigating the political complexities of assuming the presidency. In search of wise counsel, he paid a visit to another close friend and Williamsburg neighbor, Nathaniel Beverley Tucker, a law professor at the College of William and Mary.[32] Tyler admired and trusted Tucker both for his legal mind and states' rights advocacy.[33] Tucker was a fascinating character, part legal scholar and part political novelist, whose written works attracted praise from the likes of Edgar Allan Poe.[34] Tucker suggested he honor Harrison's single-term pledge and announce immediately that he would not seek election in his own right in 1844.[35] But Tyler was not ready to declare himself a one-term president—although he gave it serious thought—and instead focused on getting to Washington as quickly as possible, moving into the White House, and meeting the diplomatic corps to demonstrate continuity of government.

The cabinet's letter created a sense of urgency, not because of what it contained, but because of what it didn't. Each passing hour left Tyler exposed to a scenario where the wheels of succession planning would spin without him. Recognizing this, he said farewell to his family and set off for Washington early that Monday.[36] He and his entourage made the journey, an exhausting and emotionally draining 230-mile trip—through a circuitous route combining trains, boats, and carriages—in twenty-one hours.[37] The speed of the journey was not lost on Tyler, who finally checked into Brown's Indian Queen Hotel[38]—a magnificent five-story white structure located at Sixth and Pennsylvania Avenue—at 4:00 a.m. on April 6.[39]

Tyler considered himself president from the moment he arrived in Washington[40] and saw no need to formalize this with a separate oath.[41] He was meant to be a peripheral part of the administration and barely knew General Harrison. According to one contemporary biographer, "what little he did know he did not much like."[42] He had been disgusted by what he perceived to be the deception of the American people through a campaign built on myths and lies. His predecessor served too short a time to leave behind any vision or policies. Left to his own devices, Tyler would simply "follow the light of my own judgment and the prompting of my own feelings."[43] But before charting his own path, he would need to make sure his ascension to the presidency was unquestioned.

John Tyler and the men in his inherited cabinet read the same article in the Constitution and arrived at completely different conclusions about its meaning. The Article II succession clause of the Constitution states: "In Case of the Removal of the President from Office, or of his Death, Resignation, or Inability to discharge the Powers and Duties of the said Office, the Same shall devolve on the Vice President."[44] Nobody was confused about Tyler assuming the duties of the president, but divergent interpretations of "the Same" and "devolve" revealed a gaping hole of ambiguity that bred further confusion around an unprecedented situation. Looser readings at the time concluded that "the Same" refers to both the office and the duties, while the stricter interpretations applied this only to the latter.

None of the original drafters of the Constitution were alive (James Madison was the last to die in 1836) so no one had firsthand accounts of what was intended by the succession clause.[45] The drafters hadn't left much of a paper trail on the matter, mainly because they had little enthusiasm for the idea of a vice president, and in fact, only a few favored the inclusion of a vice president.[46] What limited debate the drafters had over succession was inconclusive. Charles Pinckney of South Carolina and

Alexander Hamilton of New York suggested that should the president die, resign, or be deemed incapable of performing his duties, the president of the Senate should assume the duties of president, pending a new election.[47] There was some discussion about what was meant by an "inability" to perform presidential functions—most notably by John Dickinson of Delaware, who asked, "What is the extent of the term disability[?]"[48] In September 1787, Hugh Williamson, who represented North Carolina at the Constitutional Convention, acknowledged the lack of attention the drafters gave to the nation's second-highest office, suggesting "such an officer as vice-president was not wanted. He was introduced merely for the sake of a valuable mode of election, which required two to be chosen at the same time."[49]

These fragments of debate offered no blueprint for how to handle Harrison's death. Webster and the cabinet sought the counsel of outside experts. They called on William Thomas Carroll, chief clerk of the Supreme Court, to summon Chief Justice Roger B. Taney, who was then in Baltimore. Taney, the temperamental jurist who sixteen years later would write the majority pro-slavery opinion in *Dred Scott v. Sanford*, refused to offer his take on the Tyler question, citing his belief that "the communication from [executive branch] to the [judicial branch] ought to be direct and from the proper origin . . . [and he] did not wish to appear to be intruding in the affairs of the executive branch without a formal request from the cabinet or from John Tyler."[50]

Taney believed his conclusion was the right legal judgment, but he also understood that this was a political lose-lose. As a Jacksonian Democrat, he detested Henry Clay, who at the time served as "Senate leader," although this was not yet a formal elective position.* He understood that if the "Acting President" interpretation prevailed, the government would be handed over to Clay, who as the Whig party leader would have been the actual source of power. Balancing the equation, Taney also had no love lost for John Tyler, who had voted against his confirmation as secretary of the treasury.[51]

It appears that John Tyler knew exactly what he was walking into.

---

* During the nineteenth century, the Senate leader was an unofficial position typically occupied by the chairman of a powerful committee or the party conference. (See U.S. Senate Historical Office.)

Ready to stand firm and meet the controversy, he gathered the Harrison cabinet to state, not debate, that he was president of the United States. Six men joined Tyler at the table: Secretary of State Daniel Webster, Secretary of the Treasury Thomas Ewing, Secretary of War John Bell, Attorney General John J. Crittenden, Postmaster General Francis Granger, and Secretary of the Navy George E. Badger. While the cabinet may have intended to bully or trap Tyler into serving as an "Acting President," the Virginia politician had two things going for him: information and time. A tip from his friend James Lyons about the seriousness of Harrison's illness and the long journey had given him breathing room to plot his move.

That first cabinet meeting lasted from early morning to late afternoon and focused almost entirely on the details of Harrison's funeral,[52] which was scheduled for the following day and was also without precedent. The discussion over funeral details[53] did not overshadow the elephant in the room, which was the question of Tyler's status. As the talk moved from funeral arrangements to other matters, Webster noted that Harrison made all policy decisions by majority vote in the cabinet. His subtle injunction was the bait that Tyler had been waiting for. He took it and without hesitation explained that he would do things differently.[54] "I am the President, and I shall be held responsible for my administration," he told them. "I shall be pleased to avail myself of your counsel and advice. But I can never consent to being dictated to as to what I shall or shall not do . . . when you think otherwise, your resignations will be accepted."[55]

Harrison's men accepted their new president, reluctantly. Webster suggested that Tyler formalize his ascension to the presidency by taking the oath of office, which Tyler agreed to do. William Cranch, the chief judge of the Federal Circuit Court, issued the oath of office and subsequently issued a sworn statement saying that Tyler had appeared before him and "although he deems himself qualified to perform the duties and exercise the powers and office of the President . . . without other oath than that which he has taken as Vice-President, yet as doubts may arise, and for greater caution, [he] took and subscribed the . . . oath before me."[56]

The cabinet was the least of Tyler's worries. His real concern was the Whig Party, which he viewed as a scrappily constructed hodgepodge of politicians who agreed on almost nothing except for their hatred of Andrew Jackson. As the president observed, the cabinet left him "surrounded by Clay-men, Webster-men, anti-Masons, original Harrisonians, old Whigs, and new Whigs, each jealous of the others, and all struggling for the offices." While Tyler was prepared to dismiss his entire cabinet if they didn't fall into line, he also recognized that replacing the cabinet would take time and cause more problems.[57] Furthermore, retaining the cabinet was necessary to keep the Whig Party intact,[58] at least for the time being. There was a continuity of government argument.

The president made his decision regarding the cabinet and was prepared to live with it. He would later regret keeping all of Harrison's men, but he needed early stability and time to fend off two looming challenges: First, William Henry Harrison, in his only act as president, had called for a special session of Congress to be convened on May 31, 1841, to address the immediate financial challenges facing the country. While there was nothing controversial about that decision, Tyler knew that this session would open a Pandora's box of Whig factions. The second challenge was Henry Clay, the fiery Whig party leader who aspired to the presidency and believed he was the real power broker in the Whig-dominated government. Harrison had proven to be more independent-minded than Clay expected[59]—although short of a Manchurian candidate, it is unclear that any president could have met Clay's expectations of allowing him to essentially run the government—but he anticipated greater success at manipulating Tyler. The "Sage of Ashland" was in for a rude awakening.

On April 9, John Tyler delivered a pithy inaugural address. After briefly acknowledging the tragedy of his predecessor's passing, he called for an increase in the size of the Navy, avoidance of public debt during peacetime, stabilization of the currency, and greater scrutiny over abuse of public offices. And in case the audience didn't hear him, he made the last point several times over.[60] Tyler importantly sought to clarify the right of succession in the Constitution. He noted, "For the first time in our history the person elected to the Vice-Presidency of the United States, by the happening of the contingency provided for in the Constitution, has had devolved upon him the Presidential office." Unlike his predecessor, he made no mention of serving one term in office. He referred to himself as "president" and suggested that "in succeeding, under circumstances so sudden and unexpected" there may be some who engage in "assaults" on his administration.[61] The assaults would come but not until the special session.

When the special session convened on May 31, Tyler spoke to a joint session of Congress. Well aware that the skepticism about his inheritance of the presidency continued, he sought to put the issue to rest. "By the provisions of the fundamental law the powers and duties of the high station to which [Harrison] was elected have devolved upon me," he told them; and in the "dispositions of the representatives of the States and of the people will be found, to a great extent, a solution of the problem to which our institutions are for the first time subjected."[62]

Tyler would have been naive to assume that his words alone would muffle the critics. That same day, one of his allies in Congress, Virginia congressman Henry A. Wise, proposed a standard resolution, within which he formalized Tyler's status as *the* president of the United States.[63] A heated exchange followed,[64] led by Congressman John Quincy Adams, a former president. Adams would write in his diary: "[Tyler's assumption of the Office of the President] is a construction in direct violation both of the grammar and context of the Constitution, which confers upon the Vice-President, on the decease of the President, not the office, but the powers and duties of the said office."[65] John McKeon, a congressman from New York, moved to strike "president" and replace it with "vice-President, now exercising the office of the President." He went on to suggest that "a grave constitutional question" had been raised, and it should be put "at rest for all future time."[66] Despite the strong opposition of Adams and McKeon, the Wise resolution passed in the House without any alteration in the wording.[67] The next day, the two senators from Ohio, William Allen and Benjamin Tappan, came out against Tyler's assumption of the presidency. John C. Calhoun, the former vice president and senator from South Carolina, came to Tyler's aid—not surprising since they were both staunchly pro-slavery—and inquired instead about the vacant vice presidency. The debate dragged on for a bit longer until the Senate followed the House in adopting a resolution,[68] voting overwhelmingly, 38 to 8, to recognize John Tyler as the president of the United States.[69]

Passage of the Wise Resolution may have formalized Tyler's presidency, but it did little to stop his critics from mocking him behind his back. He was called everything from "His Accidency" to "usurper." Some, like John Quincy Adams, continued their grumbling, suggesting that if Tyler really was a strict constructionist, as he claimed to be, he would call into question "whether the Vice-President has the right to occupy the President's house, or claim his salary, without an Act of Congress."[70] Tyler remained defiant. Throughout his career, he returned any letter unopened if it addressed him other than as "President of the United States."

Tyler never wavered from his decision. It set a precedent that would pave the way for seven future presidents: Millard Fillmore, Andrew Johnson, Chester Arthur, Theodore Roosevelt, Calvin Coolidge, Harry Truman, and Lyndon Johnson. If Tyler's precedent established a right of succession for future vice presidents, his presidency demonstrated how unexpected ascension to power may change the course of history. While it is true that Tyler fortified the presidency by winning the constitutional arguments over succession,[71] his subsequent policy decisions would lead the country down a very different path and illustrate that abrupt transitions can pivot the country's trajectory.

President Without a Party

Tyler was doomed from the early weeks of his presidency, not because of the controversy over his ascension, but because of Henry Clay's tenacity to get what he wanted. Perhaps the largest personality of his day, Clay was both charming and obnoxious and possessed a unique oratory gift, which often served him well. He was a performer, a man of presence with piercing eyes, high cheekbones, messy long hair that dangled in front of his ears, a dimple in the middle of his chin, and a small back arch in his posture that almost made him look as if he had been genetically designed as a debater. His political and social crafts were legendary and he could navigate both a political labyrinth and royal court with ease and charm. One biographer describes how "no matter how badly he behaved he constantly dazzled people who came in contact with him, even when they differed strongly with him on policy and principles."[72] He liked a good political fight and surrounded himself with drama that he both created and absorbed.

In April 1826, Clay formally challenged Senator John Randolph to a duel, after the latter accused him of "crucifying the Constitution and cheating at cards."[73] He appreciated the power of narrative and like William Henry Harrison he concocted an exaggerated story of his rise from obscurity, even coining the popular term "self-made man,"[74] which he applied to himself. His craft and presence inspired an entire generation of up-and-comers, including Abraham Lincoln, who idolized him. He dazzled crowds, engendered fierce loyalty, and enraged both friends and foes with his frequent and unreasonable demands on them. And when his demands went unmet, as President Tyler would soon find out, he was capable of unleashing an unruly assault on his victims that rarely left them standing.

By the time Clay founded the Whig Party in 1836, he had already held almost every major position of power—speaker of the house, secretary of state, and party leader of the Senate. While he was a difficult personality, his power and influence was unquestioned. But at sixty-four years old, he still had a more ambitious vision for himself that started and ended with the presidency. When he failed to secure the Whig nomination in 1840, he began immediately thinking about 1844, which meant aggregating power under President Harrison. Believing that strong maneuverability was best achieved by retaining his spot in the Senate, Clay turned down a position as secretary of state before being offered the post and advocated instead for his political frenemy Daniel Webster. Webster, who also harbored ambitions of the presidency, was well aware that he was destined to play the role of Clay's understudy in the Senate, and thus viewed the State Department as his own fiefdom[75] through which he could broker a deal with England over the disputed Maine boundary and elevate his status as a statesman.[76]

Following Harrison's inauguration, Clay's plans hit some unexpected bumps in the road. He was surprised to find the mild-mannered general more independent than he had anticipated. President Harrison rejected most of Clay's attempts to install his cronies in government positions and ignored his insistence that political foes be blocked from appointments. But Clay's real wake-up call came on March 11, when the cabinet convened to make a decision on whether to call an extra session of Congress, something that he had strongly advocated. Webster, who was eager to keep Clay on the sidelines as long as possible, urged the president not to consent to a special session of Congress.[77] The six-man cabinet was split down the middle and the president broke the tie with a negative vote.[78] Clay responded hastily with an overzealous letter to President Harrison urging him to reconsider the special session, even including draft language of his reconsideration.[79] The president was furious and responded immediately with accusations of impetuousness. He reminded the senator, "Much as I rely upon your judgment there are others whom I must consult and in many cases to determine adversely to your suggestion."[80]

Clay was apoplectic. He had expected a White House dinner invitation and instead he was left with one of his greatest abasements. He was so rattled by the president's response that a friend found him fuming in solitude, pacing the floor of his room "in great perturbation" while crumpling Harrison's note in his hand. "And it has come to this!" he lamented to that same friend. "I am civilly but virtually requested not to visit the White House—not to see the president personally, but hereafter only communicate with him in writing!"[81] Clay responded to Harrison on March 15, describing himself as "mortified . . . by the implication that [he] had been . . . dictating" and suggested that his "enemies" were "poisoning" the president's "mind towards [him]."[82] He stormed out of town, and overcome by stress he "suffered a physical collapse" by the time he reached Baltimore.[83] Harrison and Clay would never see each other again.

On March 17, President Harrison reversed his position and summoned an emergency session of Congress to meet on May 31, 1841, though not because of Henry Clay's insistence. Secretary of the Treasury Thomas Ewing—who, ironically, Clay had opposed for the position—warned of a runaway deficit exceeding $11 million unless additional revenue was quickly raised.[84] Ewing argued that any hesitation on the part of the president could result in a deepening of the dire economic situation.

The president's death on April 4 complicated Clay's political position. John Tyler was fifty-one years old, making him at that time the youngest man to serve as chief magistrate. Born during George Washington's first term, he represented a generational shift as the first president born in the new United States. Tyler was tall and slender, roughly six feet and somewhat gaunt in his appearance.[85] He was elegant, more than imposing, carrying himself with the grace and sophistication of a proper southern gentleman. While much of his character has been recorded with bias, typically negative, most agree that he was a man of deep conviction, committed to states' rights and a strict constructionist interpretation of the Constitution. He was known to be exceptionally well-read and a lively conversationalist who loathed confrontation, which many mistook for weakness. He was neither flashy, nor overly emotional. He had few vices, mainly the indulgence of light profanity and fine champagnes.[86] More than any other figure of his time, Tyler displayed remarkable resilience in the face of an unprecedented bombardment of critique and slander in the press, including from his own party. During a March 1842 visit to the White House, Charles Dickens described the president as "look[ing] somewhat worn and anxious, and well he might, being at war with everybody—but the expression of his face was mild and pleasant, and his manner was remarkably unaffected, gentlemanly, and agreeable."[87]

Tyler's ascension to power was initially hopeful for Clay, who believed he could reclaim much of the influence over the president that he had squandered with Harrison. He did not believe the young and accidental president would be willing to oppose him and in the early days of his administration, Tyler, who owed much of his good fortune to Henry Clay, even dispensed some spoils to Clay's friends as a demonstration of goodwill.[88] But Clay's restored standing was temporary. Tyler, like his predecessor, had no intention of becoming Henry Clay's puppet.[89]

With or without the popularity of his predecessor, John Tyler had every intention of charting his own path as president. From the moment he took the oath of office, he began reversing much of what Harrison pledged in his brief tenure. He ignored Harrison loyalists who continued urging the new president to honor a single-term pledge. A principled states' rightist, he was opposed to much of the Whig agenda, including a national bank, protective tariff, and internal improvements, all of which he viewed as unconstitutional. Furthermore, his willingness to control patronage as opposed to allowing the legislature—or Henry Clay—to dictate it, meant that he wielded enormous power over congressmen and senators who needed the president to throw jobs to their supporters.[90] And rather than shake up the Harrison cabinet, he undermined it almost completely, stripping them of their equal vote in decision making and seeking outside counsel from a kitchen cabinet that included a slew of Virginia states' righters, mainly Nathaniel Beverley Tucker, Judge Abel Upshur, Congressmen Henry Wise and Thomas Gilmer, and Senator William C. Rives.[91] Much to the chagrin of the existing cabinet, these men would have enormous impact on the president, both influencing and reinforcing his ideology and views on the Whigs' legislative agenda.

Tyler's first few months as president were spent putting out fires, first with the nonsense about whether he could call himself "president," then managing the impending collapse of the Whig Party. He inherited the scheduled special session of Congress, which he felt was premature and which he knew would force a showdown with Clay and his own party over a national bank he believed to be unconstitutional. This was a difficult hand, but even he had no idea what kind of firestorm awaited him. Clay, on the other hand, knew exactly the kind of chaos he wanted to create and while Tyler organized his administration, he began to mobilize the legislature for a fight. He installed proponents of the Whig agenda in the key committees across both the Senate and House and exploited the country's dire economic conditions to coerce members of the Whig Party into either supporting his agenda or living with the country's ruin on their conscience. Clay treated the Whig Party as his personal asset, all geared toward the end goal of making him president. For Clay, supporting the Whig agenda—particularly the national bank—became a referendum on party loyalty, and those who did not comply would be harshly punished.

Tyler would become a political casualty in Clay's ambitious plan to push the national bank through Congress. The president's attempts to compromise with the obstreperous Kentuckian proved futile, with Clay making it abundantly clear that his dogmatic push for states' rights qualifications in the bank plan was unacceptable. For Tyler, his friend turned foe had become politically insufferable and, as had happened with his predecessor, his patience eventually snapped during one of their exchanges: "Go you now, then, Mr. Clay, to your end of the avenue, where stands the Capitol, and there perform your duty to the country as you shall think proper. So help me God, I shall do mine at this end of it as I shall think proper."[92] While Clay sought reconciliation from Harrison, he was prepared to wage war with Tyler. Both men understood that the first battle would be over the national bank.

Political War

When the first national bank bill reached President Tyler's desk, it was met with a swift and unwavering veto, although the president was artful in how he conveyed the message. In particular, he wanted to avoid torpedoing the bankruptcy bill,* which was pending in Congress,[93] and which ran the risk of becoming collateral damage in a political backlash. Just before sending the bill back to Congress with his veto, the president went to Sunday mass and asked God to guide him.[94] Guided by his conscience and some sort of divine reassurance, the president dispatched his private secretary and son, the twenty-two-year-old John Tyler, Jr., to deliver the message to Congress. On August 16, 1841, the young man arrived in the Senate with the veto in hand, navigated the crowds, and brought all business before the Senate chamber to a halt as he read his father's message.[95]

The president's veto message was defensive, devoting a considerable amount of attention to reminding the Senate that he had "opposed a national bank for twenty-five years, in the state legislature, both houses of Congress, and ambiguity forgotten, during the 1840 campaign."[96] He explained that the notion of Congress asserting the "right to incorporate a United States bank with power and right to establish offices of discount and deposit in the several States of this Union with or without their consent"[97] went beyond the limits of Congress's constitutional authority by suggesting that the legislative body has a "superiority of power and control" over the states.[98] As a staunch states' rightist, such a measure weighed heavily on his conscience and thus to bend to the popular will of Congress or his own party "would be to commit a crime which I would not willfully commit to gain any earthly reward, and which would justly subject me to the ridicule and scorn of all virtuous men."[99]

The Democrats were overjoyed by the president's veto. It dealt a devastating blow to the Whig agenda and represented a personal affront to the party leader, Henry Clay, whom Democrats expected to run against—and hoped to defeat—in the 1844 presidential election. That evening, Democratic leaders paraded to the White House to salute the president upon his "patriotic and courageous" action.[100] The meeting between the Democrats and the Whig president became the subject of comedic ridicule by Clay, who just a few days later performed an impromptu satire on the Senate floor with voice impressions so convincing that the entire chamber burst into a bipartisan applause.[101] As the Democrats rejoiced, the Whigs were

---

* Refers to the Bankruptcy Act of 1841, which updated the previous legislation from 1800 and would establish a uniform system of bankruptcy throughout the United States. Statute I, Chap. IX, 27th Congress, session I (1841).

out for blood. Just hours before the veto message was delivered to Congress, John Minor Botts, a Whig congressman from Virginia and mortal enemy of the president, sent an ominous letter addressed to the "coffee house, Richmond"[102] eviscerating the president and suggesting that "Tonight we must and will settle matters, as quietly as possible, but they must be settled."[103]

And settle it they did. Due in part to the publication of the Botts letter, word quickly spread of the president's veto, with angry sentiments on Capitol Hill spreading to the pubs and eventually the streets. By the evening of August 17, a rowdy group of anti-Tylerites got drunk at a local tippling house and sometime between 10:00 p.m. and 2:00 a.m. made their way to the executive mansion. As was reported in the press, these "Whig rowdies, emboldened by spirituous liquids, gathered under the White House portico,"[104] they began to behave like deranged lunatics looking for blood. The belligerent crowd, armed with guns and bugles,[105] blunderbusses, drums, and trumpets,[106] began with shouts, such as "Huzza for Clay!" and "A Bank! A Bank! Down with the Veto!"[107]

As the crowd grew in size, the shouts became more personal and it was reported that the impromptu drunken orchestra "serenaded [the president] and his family with a variety of favorite airs, such as the Rogues March [and] Clear the Kitchen,"[108] which were two particularly obnoxious songs of the era. According to a dispatch from the *Montgomery Advertiser*, the crowd then "forced open the gates in front and rear, stood in the porch and shouted: 'Bah!' 'Hustle him out!' 'Resign, God d[am]n you!' 'Groans for the Traitor!' 'Down with the veto!' 'Cheers for Clay!'"[109] The *Edgefield South Carolina Advertiser* described how this group of "miscreants," emboldened by mob mentality, "committed the most disgusting nuisance on the porch in front of the President's house."[110] Lugging around a "large transparency of the President,"[111] they proceeded to hang and burn the president in effigy, an act that would be repeated throughout the country.[112] The *New York Herald* reported that by the middle of the night the growing decibel level awakened the entire executive mansion, terrifying the already feeble first lady and her children.[113] It was only when a "light appeared in one of the rooms [that a] panic seized the crowd and it hastily departed."[114]

The drunken spectacle surrounding the White House may have been the most visible part of this political storm, but throughout the United

States, reports of similar Whig protests were widely observed, leading to rumors that President Tyler had suffered such an affront to his character that he would resign.[115] But the drunken riots against the president had two immediate consequences, neither of which were thoughts of resignation. First, they led Congress to immediately pass legislation to establish a night police force in Washington,[116] appropriating $7,000 for a fifteen-member Auxiliary Guard to protect against "incendiaries."[117]

Second, the experience being so publicly abraded dealt a meaningful blow to the president's honor and demoralized his presidency. Tyler had expected a backlash from his veto, but he was surprised by the violent opposition. He had failed to appreciate the centrality of a national bank to the Whig platform.[118] The verbal assaults from Clay and Botts, the sozzled mob that descended on his home, the public thrashings, and effigy hangings in multiple states, all served as a direct affront to Tyler's character.[119] It didn't stop either. Even though the riots lasted one evening (although some papers reported multiple nights), the fear within the Tyler household remained, and a steady flow of letters poured in threatening him with assassination.[120]

While drunken Whigs took to the streets, Tyler held out hope that there might be room for compromise to rectify the political deadlock. A second version of the bank bill was in the works, and this time around he insisted on seeing the final language of the bill before it was sent to the House. Despite this insistence, he wasn't shown the bill before it reached the House. The president was irate, particularly with Secretaries Webster and Ewing, who had incorrectly declared that the "new bill conformed to the President's opinions and bore his imprimatur." Once he saw the language, Tyler made it clear that the final form did not suit him, particularly it failed to give the states enough leeway to restrict the branches.[121] This was the precise situation that he wanted to avoid. Tyler, who had been careful to maintain a poker face, was so incensed that he once again broke from strategy and told two House members that "he would have his right [arm cut off], and his left arm too, before he would sign the Bill."[122]

The bill passed in both the House and Senate with relative ease,[123] putting Tyler in the uncomfortable position of having to prove his defiance. He regretted that the bank bill had gotten caught up in partisan politics and felt so strongly about this that he initially included a pledge not to run in 1844 as part of his veto message. After several iterations on the language, however, Daniel Webster and Duff Green, who was another one of the president's trusted confidants, convinced him that he couldn't afford to further weaken his position with the Whigs.[124] With his veto message done, Tyler readied himself for the second battle of a civil war with his own party.

On Thursday morning, September 9, the president dispatched his eldest son, Robert—who, like John Tyler, Jr., also served as a private secretary—to deliver the second veto message to a packed House.[125] Tyler was well aware that this was his second veto in less than two months. The message sought to clarify that he exercised a second veto with legal certainty but political regret. He described himself as having "no alternative" and sought to articulate the two bad options that lay before him, "he must either exert the negative power entrusted to him by the Constitution chiefly for its own preservation, protection, and defense or commit an act of gross moral turpitude. Mere regard to the will of a majority must not in a constitutional republic like ours control this sacred and solemn duty of a sworn officer."[126] In an empathetic appeal, he reminded everyone of the extraordinary circumstances of his ascension, the extra session of Congress, and the haste in which they had taken on the bank issue. He asked, "May we not now pause until a more favorable time, when, with the most anxious hope that the Executive and Congress may cordially unite, some measure of finance may be deliberately adopted promotive of the good of our common country?"[127]

Whereas Tyler's first veto resulted in a drunken and violent mob that could be dismissed as peripheral buffoons, the second veto produced an all-out brawl on the floor of Congress, ironically between different factions of the same Whig Party. It started with Edward Stanly, a southern Whig from North Carolina, who desired a national bank and who loathed any argument that favored states' rights over a strong Union. He stood before the House chamber and "charged" his Virginia colleague Henry Wise with "inconsistency," which must have been the 1841 version of a cheap shot. Wise, who was among President Tyler's closest confidants in Congress and known by many to be the leader of his kitchen cabinet, suggested the two men take their feud outside and settle it like men. Stanly preferred to settle things in the chamber and continued with the insults, this time calling Wise a "liar." Wise had enough and threw the first punch.[128]

What followed was a general hullabaloo.[129] In one detailed account, provided by the *Ohio Democrat*,[130] the House floor was described as having degenerated into a "street fight" with "most of the members rush[ing] to the scene of action, and crowd[ing] round the combatants, some jumping from desk to desk over the heads of other members, and others uttering exclamations of all descriptions such as 'order order,' 'go it Stanly,' 'Give it to him Stanly.'"[131] Stanly grabbed "the collar of Mr. Wise with one hand, and with the other was putting it into his antagonist who was thrown with his back against a desk."[132]

Within minutes, a fight between a few men turned into a brawl. William O. Butler, a veteran of the War of 1812 turned Kentucky congressman, lunged toward Thomas D. Arnold of Tennessee, grabbing him "by the throat, thr[owing] him with the small of his back on the arm of a chair, and chok[ing] him until his tongue protruded down to his cravat."[133] Amidst the chaos, Speaker of the House John White, who would be the main culprit in an even worse brawl on the floor of Congress three years later, screamed for order, but failed. Recognizing that yelling for calm was insufficient, the House clerk "seized the Sergeant at Arms' mace and ran bout the house with the ponderous instrument on his shoulder like a Roman battle axe screaming 'order, gentlemen order.'"[134] That didn't work either. Aaron V. Brown of Tennessee jumped on one of the desks and cried, "For the honor of your country and for the love of God come to order." Others shouted "order be damned" and "go into them—let 'em have it." Hundreds of voices were now vying for airtime, which only contributed to the commotion.

Finally, Thomas Gilmer and George Proffit, a Whig congressman from Indiana, "cleared the desks at a hop skip and jump into the midst of the affray; neighbor clutched neighbor, and they struggled pushed, roared, and cursed each other in perfect desperation." As momentum shifted toward restoring order, "Butler relaxed his gripe of Arnold's throat," Louisiana's John B. Dawson "threw Stanley across his knees," while Dixon H. Lewis of Alabama's "at large" posse* used his big frame and "ponderous arm" to

---

* In the twenty-seventh Congress, Alabama—which didn't achieve statehood until 1819—had five members elected to Congress, who each represented the state "at large." This was partially resolved by the 1840 census, but the five members had already been elected before this could be accounted for.

clear the area and hold back Mr. Wise. As everyone caught their breath, Aaron Ward, a general from New York, screamed, "Gentlemen that wish to restore order take your seats." Amazingly everyone returned to their desks and fixed their clothes. Congressman Wise rose to apologize and everyone quickly moved on.[135]

While members of Congress pummeled each other physically, Tyler's many critics—particularly those aligned with Henry Clay—launched another onslaught of verbal assaults. The Kentucky-born Indiana congressman Henry Smith Lane said, "Tyler was guilty of perfidy and his name could be added to the list of other American traitors: Benedict Arnold, Isaac Hull, and Aaron Burr." And Senator Willie Person Mangum lambasted Tyler as "mad, weak and a traitor."[136]

The president was up against the ropes with no clear remedy to his predicament. Clay, who smelled blood in the water, went for the kill and used a September 9 dinner at the navy secretary's home to orchestrate a mass cabinet resignation. Two days later, on September 11, that plan went into effect. As recounted by Tyler's biographers, from "12:30 to 5:30 P.M., five cabinet officers marched into Tyler's office and laid their resignations on his desk while John Tyler, Jr., the President's secretary, stood by, watch in hand, recording for posterity the exact moment of each resignation." Clay's goal had been to use the decimation of the cabinet as a way to cripple the executive branch, humiliate the president in the wake of his two bank vetoes, and ultimately force his resignation. If Clay's goal was Tyler's resignation, then this plan was tantamount to a coup. With the vice presidency vacant, the next in line to the presidency was Samuel L. Southard, who served as president pro tempore of the Senate and, more important, was a hard-core Clay loyalist.[137]

The president was well aware of Clay's plan and had anticipated the cabinet walkout. His friends James Russell of Pennsylvania and John Taliaferro of Virginia had intimated that the bank bills were designed to provoke presidential vetoes, which Clay believed would trigger a set of events that would destroy Tyler's presidency.[138] Tyler had no intention of resigning even in the wake of a mass cabinet walk-out. Reflecting on the incident in 1844, he wrote, "My resignation would amount to a declaration to the world that our system of government had failed."[139] Still, the timing could not have been worse. The last resignation came in late afternoon that Saturday and Congress had voted to adjourn the following Monday, which left only a small window to reconstitute a new cabinet. Tyler, a strict con-structivist even when inconvenient, held the strong belief that such vacan-cies could only be filled while the Senate remained in session. Following this logic, he would have to move fast or find himself without a cabinet for three months until the next session, a fate that would leave him without anyone at the helm of the various departments and likely force him to resign over his inability to run the government.[140]

Tyler expected and welcomed the resignations, especially since he re-gretted retaining them. He had inherited a cabinet comprised of mostly Clay men, and thus feared intrigue at every turn from his own advisors. The one exception was Daniel Webster, who could deliver a loyal con-stituency of New England supporters and help thwart Clay since the two men were rivals.[141] The president also understood that unlike the other members of the cabinet, Webster was far more torn on whether he should resign. The last thing Webster wanted was to hand Clay a political vic-tory, especially since the two were likely to face off in the 1844 presidential election. Tyler's resigning on anything but his own terms would be tanta-mount to an endorsement of his political rival.[142]

Webster needed the secretary of state platform in order to bolster his own credentials. If he could settle two boundary disputes with England—Maine at the forty-fifth parallel and Oregon at the forty-ninth parallel—and facilitate the dismantling of the Mexican Empire in California, he could claim a major diplomatic victory that would enhance his presiden-tial prospects two years later.[143] But this required navigating a complex dynamic with the president, who was quickly becoming persona non grata with the party and who harbored his own aspirations for the 1844 nom-ination. It was a tricky situation and Webster chose to take it head-on. "Where am I to go, Mr. President?" he asked. The president turned it back to his secretary of state, suggesting, "You must decide that for yourself, Mr. Webster." Continuing the theatrics, Webster declared, "If you leave it to me, Mr. President, I will stay where I am." Tyler was likely relieved, but not surprised. He stood from his chair and leaned forward, gazing into his eyes: "Give me your hand on that, and now I will say to you that Henry Clay is a doomed man."[144]

But if Clay was doomed, so, too, was Tyler. He was now essentially at war with his own party with no hope of rectifying the situation. Eventu-ally the escalating tension came to a breaking point. On September 13, a group of fifty Whig zealots in Congress caucused on Capitol Square,[145] and led by the Whig novelist and congressman John P. Kennedy of Baltimore, they publicly kicked the president out of the party. In their manifesto of excommunication, "the Whig party," they declared, "loathed his action, especially for reviving Jackson's executive tyranny."[146] Clay triumphantly declared that Tyler was now "a president without a party"[147] and the Whig papers—*Richmond Whig, Enquirer, The Lexington Intelligencer,* and *New York Courier*—tore the president apart. They described Tyler as the "Executive Ass," revived labels of "His Accidency," and one paper described him as "a man destitute of intellect and integrity, whose name is the synonym of nihil."[148]

Tyler's excommunication was a blessing and a curse. It was humiliating for the president, but it also unshackled him to do what his party (and predecessor) never would have done. Despite what his opponents assumed would be an impossible task, he reassembled his cabinet with remarkable speed, completing the refurbishment by mid-October. This time around, he would make sure to be surrounded by men who were subordinate loyalists who believed in his legitimacy as president.[149] In a letter to his good friend Thomas Cooper in October 1841, Tyler celebrated his extrication from the trappings of Harrison's cabinet by offering the following description: "Like myself, they are all original Jackson men, and mean to act upon Republican principles." The letter explained that he would require "conform[ity] to my opinions" on all issues.[150]

The Whigs were so busy pummeling the president that they lost their edge in the lead-up to the 1841 elections. The vetoes hurt Tyler, but they also hurt the Whigs, particularly since the vetoes were seen as victories for the Democrats. The party paid a heavy price at the ballot box, losing six of the eight gubernatorial races—in Maine, Georgia, Maryland, Pennsylvania, Michigan, and Mississippi. Outside the gubernatorial races, they had been annihilated in state legislative races that fall, which would have an impact on the Senate, which was elected through state legislatures.[151] To many outside and inside observers, the Whigs appeared to be finished. John Calhoun declared the Whigs "destroyed" and predicted "they can never again rise under their present name, nor on their present issues."[152]

When Congress reconvened on December 7, 1841, Tyler used his annual address and newfound independence to begin expressing an idea that would come to define the rest of his presidency. Buried behind his financial proposals and a multitude of foreign policy issues was a reference to Texas, which was made without sectional reference and with brilliant subtlety. He called out discrepancies in the boundaries with Texas, but quickly pivoted to his observation that, "the United States cannot but take a deep interest in whatever relates to this young but growing [Lone Star] Republic. Settled principally by emigrants from the United States, we have the happiness to know that the great principles of civil liberty are there destined to flourish under wise institutions and wholesome laws."[153]

The Whigs were so hell-bent on destroying Tyler that they completely missed his having telegraphed his next move, which was to use the prize of Texas as a pathway to winning the presidency in his own right. Instead, they were consumed with destroying Tyler's domestic agenda, and as part of this strategy they held the president's budget hostage as a way to coerce him into adopting Whig legislation. This political move boxed the president into a situation where vetoing any Whig legislation meant he would be destroying the country's livelihood.[154] They waited six months before bringing any legislation to the floor and when they finally did in June 1842, Henry Clay and his cohort ensured that any bill they drafted would be unacceptable to the president. The aim was to provoke as many vetoes as possible so they could levy accusations of "perfidy" and "treason" and "executive dictatorship" in response to each veto. This didn't deter the president,[155] who with each veto found his relationship with the Whig Party growing from bad to worse. The Whig leadership even withheld funds for a much needed White House restoration.[156] John Crittenden, a prominent Whig who had served as Tyler's attorney general for his first year as president, wrote, "My wish is to see the Whig party rid of him—rid of the nuisance. Whigs should strip him of all disguise and expose his true character of enmity and hostility."[157]

From Crittenden's perspective, it was not good enough to have just kicked him out of the party; he wanted the president removed from office. His Whig colleagues agreed and by July 19, 1842, began impeachment proceedings against the president[158] for the first time in history. Tyler, who by this time had toughened up and had the bruises to show for it, weathered this new round of abuse with his seasoned pragmatism: "Because I will not go with him [Clay], I am abused in Congress and out, as man never was before—assailed as a traitor, and threatened with impeachment.

But let it pass. Other attempts are to be made to head me, and we shall see how they will succeed."[159]

Tyler had reached a new low point in his popularity. He was hated by the press, hated by the people, and admired only by a small coterie of Tylerites. Millard Fillmore, a Whig congressman from New York who would himself become an accidental president a decade later, snarkingly joked to colleagues, "I have heard of but two Tyler men in this city [Buffalo] and none in the country, and I need not add that both of these are applicants for office."[160] The dislike for him became so widespread that satire became vernacular, some even giving the nickname "Tyler Grippe" to a nationwide epidemic of influenza.[161]

Winning the Presidency in His Own Right

By the spring of 1842, Tyler began to shift his attention away from his congressional battles and redirected it toward the twin goals of annexing Texas and winning office in his own right. He understood that political excommunication made the path to reelection difficult, but not impossible. He still controlled federal patronage and used this privilege to his advantage. With this resource, Tyler embarked on what was dubbed a political "reign of terror," in which he replaced large numbers of Whig officeholders with Democrats.[162] For Democrats, this was a blessed period, but for the Whigs it was disastrous and painful.[163]

Despite Tyler's maneuvering, his path to victory in 1844 would prove more difficult than he expected due to a series of miscalculations. First, he really was despised and he underestimated the full impact three years of media assaults had on the public's perception of him. He had assumed incorrectly that the harsh critiques were a Washington phenomenon and did not permeate the masses. He was out of touch, in part because during his entire presidency he never really spent time with people. He didn't know the voters and made almost no attempts to correct the loathsome image painted by the anti-Tyler press.

Second, Tyler hoped and believed he would be welcomed back into the Democratic Party, which would nominate him for president in 1844. But while the Democrats appreciated and agreed with Tyler's anti-Clay sentiments, they neither trusted nor forgave him for the Whig assault on their candidate's reputation in the campaign of 1840. Tyler mistook their courtship as a vested interest in his career prospects, when the Democrats' real interest was in exploiting his situation to divide the rival Whig Party.

Once Tyler realized he would not be given the nomination as a Democrat, he hoped to peel away enough votes from Democrats and Whigs to ensure that neither party's nominee could muster enough electoral votes to win the election. This would throw the election to the House of Representatives, which could then decide to make him president. This was not far-fetched, given that two elections—1800 and 1824—were decided by the House of Representatives after neither candidate received the required electoral majority. But this, too, was a miscalculation. Tyler lacked a sufficient support base to peel away enough votes to achieve this outcome.

Tyler's future seemed hopeless. By the summer of 1843, the economy began to recover, which allowed the Whigs to make a comeback and rally around Henry Clay. Clay's temporary retirement had afforded him the opportunity to hold court in Kentucky and build his political machinery. The Democrats seemed poised to nominate Martin Van Buren, which meant that a Clay victory was all but guaranteed since Van Buren was unlikely to excite the populace. But the Whigs overestimated both the cohesiveness of their own base and divisions within the Democratic Party.[164]

The president had one more trick up his sleeve. Just as Clay was all but ready to assume victory, the president injected the prospects of annexing Texas into the public discourse. For Tyler, Texas was about his personal political resurrection, although he was more than happy to simultaneously create obstacles for his rivals. Annexation would destabilize both parties by creating tensions between land-hungry Anglophobes and proslavery factions.[165] By this logic, it would offer the president—still without a party—a new political base comprised of southern Democratic expansionists, northern anti–Van Buren Democrats, and southern states' rights Whigs.[166] If that base was large enough, he could form a third party and have a real shot at winning the presidency in 1844.

Texas was a dangerous political issue for everyone except the president, who at this point had little to lose. None of Tyler's predecessors had been supportive of annexation, and by late 1842 there was still no evidence that public sentiments about Texas had changed. Both parties saw Texas as a losing issue, destined to lead whichever candidate dared embrace annexation to alienate either the abolitionist or anti-abolitionist blocs that they desperately needed to win the presidency.[167] Furthermore, both frontrunner candidates—Van Buren and Clay—had made their opposition to annexation known publicly and had no intention of flip-flopping.[168]

Tyler pushed Texas to the front of his agenda, making it so neither party would be able to bow out of the debate. His relentless pursuit of annexation was made easier by the fact that in addition to the reasons related to his political survival, he fundamentally believed in annexation, particularly as a southern slaveholder. Tyler owed much of his political opportunity to slavery and used the sale of slaves to finance his political career. When his father passed away in 1813, the then twenty-three-year-old Tyler inherited his first thirteen slaves, and added more that same year upon his marriage to Letitia Christian.[169] One of those slaves, Ann Eliza (also the slave with whom Tyler had the closest relationship), ended up being sold to fund his run for Senate.[170] He was in a tight spot financially and wrote to his brother-in-law soliciting "as speedy a sale as can be made,"[171] even granting permission to "hand her over to the Hubbard's* for public auction" if he could not secure a neighborhood sale.[172]

If protection of slavery was Tyler's domestic rallying cry, then Anglophobia was his geopolitical raison d'être. He hated and feared England. So deep was his hatred that during a tour of Niagara Falls, he allegedly refused to experience the better view from Canada, lest he stand on British soil.[173] Tyler and his cohorts believed that the British were bankrolling American abolitionists to foment chaos as part of their imperialist intrigue.[174] Abel Upshur, who like Tyler feared the prospect of slave insurrections,[175] concluded in a letter to John Calhoun, "There can be no doubt . . . that England is determined to abolish slavery throughout the American continent and islands if she can."[176]

The president's answer to this British threat—real or perceived—was to annex Texas as soon as possible. In order to do this, he would need to bury the sectional arguments, promulgate a nationalist narrative, and wrap it all in a package of urgency. He also needed to get Texas on board. The Lone Star Republic, as it was known at the time, had enjoyed five years of independence after winning the Battle of San Jacinto in 1836.[177] The

---

* "Hubbard's" refers to Brooke & Hubbard, which was a well-known slave auctioneer.

United States had twice rejected Texas's offer of annexation under previous administrations, first during the Jackson administration and later the Van Buren presidency. In an act of desperation, Texas President Sam Houston began flamboyantly courting a relationship with Britain.[178] In all likelihood, Houston used flirtation with America's chief rival to woo her into the annexation camp—at least that is what he claimed several years later.[179] This subtle message was lost on Tyler, who perceived the advances toward Britain as a real threat. There was also the issue of Mexico, which Tyler viewed as a vehicle for British agitation. By the time the president considered the Texas question, tensions between the United States and Mexico were at an all-time high and Texas was terrified that even entertaining annexation would result in a war with Mexico that they were ill-equipped to win.

Tyler may have wanted to annex Texas immediately, but he also understood that he needed a more tempered approach given the political land mines. His strategy was implemented in phases, beginning with patience. Daniel Webster was still secretary of state and seemed well on the path to successfully negotiating the Webster-Ashburton Treaty, which would resolve the border between Maine and England's colonies to the north. But Webster was anti-annexation and couldn't be counted on to negotiate a treaty with Texas, not to mention that he would likely resign if the president asked him to. This strategy proved wise as Webster completed his own treaty and eventually left the administration on May 8, 1843, to begin exploring his own presidential run. While he would go on to criticize the march toward Texas, his critique from outside was far more manageable than it would have been from within.

Tyler used Webster's exit as an opportunity to further pack his cabinet with Texas annexation enthusiasts. He had already brought in a new secretary of the treasury, John C. Spencer, who was a hard-charging New Yorker and had previously run the War Department. By all accounts, Spencer was ready to do whatever the president asked, including purge those at the Treasury Department in opposition to his plan and to treat annexation as a loyalty oath for all new appointments.[180] Tyler wanted someone similar for secretary of state, a shark who exhibited an even greater yearning for Texas than he had. Abel Upshur, described by Tyler as the country's most "enthusiastic advocate of annexation,"[181] was the perfect man for the job.

Upshur accepted the appointment and joined the administration on June 24, giving the president another key ally in the cabinet. Still, Tyler needed to exercise patience as the polarizing nature of the Texas issue meant that in these early stages, the work was best handled by secret agents who could work outside of the public domain. Such an approach would allow him covertly to set the wheels of annexation in motion. This was not the first time that President Tyler relied on covert action abroad; he was the first president to so robustly deploy such tactics. Beginning in the fall of 1841 he tapped his good friend and advisor, Duff Green, to undertake a series of covert missions to England with the clever cover of a "businessman and industrial promoter."[182] Paranoid that American influencers were stoking the British flame of abolitionism, Tyler tasked Green to subvert American abolitionists,[183] including John Quincy Adams, who, when he learned of this scheme, publicly unmasked Green as Tyler's pro-slavery operative.[184]

Tyler's Texas intrigue relied on similar tactics, but with greater success in keeping a secret. To bring Texas to the table, Tyler ordered Secretary of the Treasury John C. Spencer to draw $100,000 from a secret service contingency fund* and covertly transfer the money to an undercover agent in New York City who would use it to pay for the deployment of a naval force into the Gulf of Mexico. If he wanted to maintain a veil of secrecy, the covert disbursement of funds was the only way to give Texas its requested naval protection against Mexico.[185] This plan hit an unexpected speed bump when, much to Tyler's surprise, Spencer refused, insisting that such an action was illegal. He resigned his post on May 2 the following year.

Covert activities aside, Tyler understood that if he wanted Texas he would need to win over the American public. Any annexation treaty would require two-thirds of the Senate for ratification. Given his relationship with the Whigs, Tyler appreciated that he lacked the ability to jam this through. But if he could change the political tide and elevate annexation to a national rallying cry, he believed the Senate would have no choice but to ratify. This would have the added electoral benefit of

---

* The Secret Service was under the purview of the Department of the Treasury and was primarily responsible for combating counterfeiting. The contingency fund was part of a discretionary budget that the Secretary of the Treasury could draw on.

taking a divisive issue—annexation—and distinguishing himself by making it his, since both the Democratic and Whig front-runners had openly opposed it.

The Texas mission was a tough task. Texas remained skeptical that the U.S. Senate would ratify a treaty of annexation, which would lead them to fend for themselves in a likely war with Mexico. On December 13, 1843, the Texas government let Upshur know that they were uneasy about negotiations, asking why they should risk conflict with Mexico if ratification wasn't guaranteed.[186] Upshur didn't give up. On January 16, 1844, he sent a lengthy message via Isaac Van Zandt, who was the Texas chargé d'affaires in the United States, and attempted to explain away previous American snubs. "The issue had not been understood . . . by the American public," Upshur wrote, emphasizing "that the present chief executive was eager for annexation." The letter went on to highlight the dangers of Texas turning to England, arguing, "The policy of England is purely commercial. Her object is to engross the commerce of the world—by diplomacy, if she can; and by force, if she must. She is bent on destroying slavery. War with her is inevitable. The peace of the civilized world, the destinies of millions in Europe and America depend . . . on the decision of Texas." Upshur insisted that there had been a shift in public opinion on annexation, particularly among northerners, who now are "not only favorable to, but anxious for it," and boasted that they had the two-thirds majority required in the Senate.[187]

Upshur certainly knew how to put an optimistic spin on things. But he also understood that Texas needed security assurances or the treaty would be a nonstarter. Lone Star president Sam Houston had been burned before and understood that any visible attempt to negotiate with the United States of America could invite an attack from Mexico. He insisted that this concern be addressed as a precondition to talks.[188] On January 17, 1844, an overzealous Van Zandt went off script and asked Upshur to deploy Army and naval forces near the border and in the Gulf of Mexico.[189] This placed Upshur in an awkward position as he knew only Congress could authorize this. Whatever Upshur's reply to Van Zandt, the Texan wrote to his government on January 20, 1844:

I am authorized by the secretary of state, who speaks by the authority of the president . . . to say that the moment a treaty of annexation shall be signed, a large naval force will be assembled in the Gulf of Mexico upon the coast of Texas, and that a sufficient number of the Military force will be ordered to rendezvous upon the borders of Texas ready to attack as circumstances may require; and that these assurances will be officially given preliminary to the signing of the treaty if desired by the government of Texas; and that this government will say to Mexico that she must in no wise disturb or molest Texas.[190]

Whether Upshur actually agreed to this or Van Zandt just made the whole thing up, it worked; and on January 20, 1844, Houston told his Congress that annexation was in their best interest.[191] A few weeks later, on February 5, 1844, the Texas Congress approved Houston's program. Following the approval, Upshur made a verbal commitment to the Texans that upon consummation of the treaty, "the President would make a precautionary disposal of troops in the neighborhood of Texas, and employ all the means placed within his power by the Constitution to protect Texas from foreign invitations."[192] With security assurances in place, Houston dispatched General J. P. Henderson to Washington to negotiate the treaty with Van Zandt, but he would not arrive until early March. That delay would prove fatal in more ways than they could imagine.[193]

Princeton Explosion

With the Texas treaty nearly complete, John Tyler finally had reason to bask in glory. The negotiations had been kept secret and he was regaining his confidence about the prospects of winning the 1844 election. The good news coincided with an unrelated celebration of American naval power, which was to take place on board the USS *Princeton*. The "gala on the Potomac"—as it became known—was the most coveted invitation that winter and the nation's capital had been buzzing for weeks with speculation about who was invited. With wind in his sails and plenty to celebrate, the president looked forward to being the guest of honor.

Guests began to arrive at the wharf in Alexandria around 11:00 a.m. on February 28, 1844. One Maryland paper reported, "The sun rose clear and bright, and the town from early in the morning presented a gay and busy scene. Nearly all the carriages were engaged, and freighted with the loveliness, beauty, and grace of the city."[194] The barrage of arrivals showcased the upper echelon of Washington society for all to see: the women dressed in beautiful gowns; the men sported morning suits and top hats; and strapping officers from young lieutenants to decorated generals were decked out in their dress uniforms.

As small boats shuttled the rich and powerful from the docks to the *Princeton,* crowds massed along the river to observe the scene and identify famous guests. By the time the last carriage dropped off its passengers, more than three hundred socialites, legislators, aristocrats, power-hungry ambitious types, diplomatic corps, and decorated war heroes joined the president and all but one member of the cabinet to celebrate America's naval prowess. Of all the guests on board that day—including the president—none attracted more attention than Dolley Madison, the seventy-six-year-old former first lady and widow of the great James Madison.[195] She was a captivating figure—the closest living link to the founding fathers. Her colorful attire and feathered hat transformed her into a statuesque presence that morning.[196]

No expense was spared on the party. While there had been two prior excursions on the *Princeton*—one on January 16 for the president and department heads and the other on January 20 for members of Congress—this was her first time welcoming the public.[197] The entire ship was decked out for the occasion with every rope and yard[198] adorned in flags of countries from all around the world, suggesting that American power was on display for all to see. Just before departure, the Marines offered a twenty-six-gun salute,[199] while the Marine Band played "The Star-Spangled Banner," "Hail Columbia," and "Hail to the Chief."[200]

The ship was magnificent. It was the American Navy's "state-of-the-art nautical wonder," equipped with two twelve-inch guns nicknamed the "Oregon" and the "Peacemaker," each able to fire 225-pound shells up to five miles with a fifty-pound powder charge.[201] The twin guns were the largest in the world, and the guests on board would have the opportunity to be the first members of the public to see them in action.

More than just a magnificent ship, the *Princeton* symbolized an inflection point for America. The perceived threat from Britain still lingered twenty-two years after the War of 1812. President Tyler was particularly vexed by what he believed to be an ongoing and secret British plot aimed at fostering an abolitionist insurgency in the South. In his view and the view of many in his inner circle, America would never truly be independent from Britain unless it could protect its coastline and defend its seas with a world-class navy. The *Princeton* was to be a symbol of that independence and power. In addition to a good party, officials hoped that the greatness of the ship and its two guns would reverberate across the Atlantic in a way that would deter future acts of aggression.

President Tyler had several presidential reasons to celebrate, but he had a more personal conquest that excited him about the journey. David Gardiner, a wealthy former state senator and aristocrat from New York, brought his daughter Julia, whom the widower president had been actively courting since his wife died* and she was barely twenty-four. Undeterred by their thirty-year age difference, Tyler was determined to make Julia his wife. He had already attempted a proposal, but was rebuffed when his would-be mother-in-law interjected on account of what she deemed to be an inappropriate age difference. Mrs. Gardiner's opposition to the proposal also served as a convenient excuse for Julia, who had become a fixture of the Washington social scene. She was fair with a round face. Her hair was often half-up and half-down, curled on the sides and back where it dangled just below her shoulders. And on top of her head, she frequently wore a beaded piece of jewelry that looked like the crown of a young princess. Julia's beauty, wealth, and connections led to an inundation of suitors, of which the president was just one of many. She was "flattered by the president's attention," but it didn't sway her emotions.[202] But the ever-persistent Tyler was determined to prove her wrong and sweep the young Julia off her feet.

The *Princeton* began its short journey just after 1:00 p.m., heading for Fort Washington and Mount Vernon.[203] Just past Fort Washington, the width of the Potomac allowed for sufficient breathing room to fire the Peacemaker.[204] The sailors had erected a kind of scaffolding for the ladies to stand on,[205] so that the jubilant and already tipsy crowds could cheer the sound of the magnificent gun, which had already been fired twice earlier in the voyage. Guests marveled at the rumbling sounds of power that

---

* Letitia Tyler died on September 10, 1842, after suffering a stroke. She was the first first lady to die while her husband was in office.

emanated from the state-of-the-art gun and sent ripples throughout the calm waters of the Potomac. Some on board claimed to have seen the ball bounce at least seven times on the water and some claimed fifteen or sixteen times.[206]

Meanwhile, the lower deck of the ship was transformed into a salon with the finest wines and refreshments.[207] There was insufficient space for the entire party to eat together, so meals were prepared in two shifts, the first of which served mostly women. At around 3:00 p.m. the remaining guests (which included the president)—many of whom were now hungry and drunk—made their way downstairs. Julia straggled behind above deck with her father and presumably some of her suitors, who were always aplenty. The president noticed her absence and sent his official wingman to find her. The emissary enticed the mingling apple of the president's eye with a frivolous injunction: "The President wishes to take you into the collation which is just served. I suppose you will have to obey orders."[208] Charmed, but not won over, the young Julia temporarily acquiesced.

The banquet was worthy of the occasion. The chef on board prepared a delicious lunch of roast fowl and ham,[209] which drew adulation from the crowd. As guests completed their final course, the secretary of state clinked his glass to get everyone's attention and stood to toast the president. Realizing he had grabbed an empty bottle of champagne, he said with some levity that the "dead bodies" must be cleared away before he could begin. Captain Robert Stockton, who was the ship's architect and who seized every opportunity to attract attention to himself, piped up to remind the secretary that "there are plenty of living bodies to replace the dead ones," after which he offered the secretary of state a full bottle.[210] President Tyler, charmed by the exchange, stood up to offer a pithy toast "to the three great guns: the Princeton, her commander and the Peacemaker."[211]

As lunch wound down, Captain Stockton received word that the ship was approaching Mount Vernon, the home of America's first president, and that some of the guests wanted the Peacemaker fired a third time in tribute to the founding father. Stockton, who was initially apprehensive about pushing the gun's limits, agreed when he learned the request came directly from the secretary of the navy. The gun exploded when fired at 4:06 p.m.,[212] shaking the entire ship and leaving behind a dense cloud of smoke enveloping the group on the forecastle.[213] The smoke was heavy, eventually clearing and revealing the devastating situation. The force of the blast sent guests flying backward and so many bodies lay flat on the deck that at first it appeared as if dozens of people were dead. Women's cocktail dresses were drenched in blood and dismembered body parts scattered across the deck. Top hats and bonnets were blown off and landed in the water, creating confusion about whether some passengers had fallen overboard. Gigantic lumps of wrought iron from the cannon's port side flew across the deck, creating a blizzard of shrapnel.[214] Some smaller fragments pierced hats and tails of coats with the trajectory of bullets. "Twenty feet of the ship's bulwark had been ripped away and bodies were strewn everywhere, with bits of flesh scattered about," writes Niall Kelly in "The Forgotten Tragedy." "The acrid smell of gunpowder mixed with the smell of burning flesh hung heavily on the air."[215]

One huge piece of iron landed on Abel Upshur's breast, killing him, and required two sailors to remove it.[216] The blast also killed Secretary of the Navy Thomas Gilmer. These were the two most important officials in Tyler's cabinet. They were the architects of both the president's dreams: the annexation of Texas and the development of a world-class navy. Secretary of War William Wilkins should have also died, but he moved to the other end of the *Princeton* after anxiously expressing distaste for the firing.[217] Virgil Maxcy, the U.S. chargé d'affaires to Belgium; Beverley Kennon, the Navy's chief of construction; and David Gardiner, the former state senator and millionaire father of Julia Gardiner, were among the other distinguished guests who perished in the blast.

Others died as well, including two seamen and Armistead,[218] John Tyler's personal slave. The latter, a "stout black man about twenty-three or twenty-four years old," would have normally been out of sight, but the president granted him special permission to witness the firing. When the gun exploded, he had been leaning against a cannon, which was hit with a large piece of shrapnel. According to an eyewitness account by George Sykes of New Jersey, he survived for "about an hour after—when they came to examine him and lay him out neither surgeon of the *Princeton* nor any other person could discover the slightest wound or injury about him."[219] John Tyler, hardly a champion of equal rights for blacks—dead or alive—offered $200 compensation to Armistead's mother,[220] who was presumably also Tyler's slave.

The scene was unimaginable, with the bodies of Upshur, Kennon, and Maxcy gruesomely dismembered.[221] Gardiner lost both his arms and legs and bled to death,[222] after hanging on for about half an hour.[223] The secretary of state's "arms and legs were broken and his bowels torn out" and "Maxcy's severed arm struck a lady in the head, covering her face with blood and knocking off her bonnet."[224] As several men attempted to come to Maxcy's aid and lay him flat, his other "arm came off about half-way between his arm and wrist."[225] Twenty others were wounded, including Captain Stockton, whose hair was singed[226] and who suffered powder burns. Senator Thomas Hart Benton was knocked unconscious[227] and his right eardrum was punctured. Nine seamen were injured, some severely.[228] And one of the daughters of Postmaster General Charles Wickliffe, who was one of the few women above deck when the gun exploded, sustained light injuries and was fortunately the only woman injured in the blast.[229]

Other notables just barely escaped death. Whig senator from Tennessee Spencer Jarnagin, Democratic senator from Indiana Edward Hannegan, and a handful of foreign ministers were all blown to the floor, and while disoriented they each returned to their feet miraculously unscathed. Senator Samuel Phelps lost all the buttons on his coat, but was unharmed. Thomas Jesup, the controversial general from the Second Seminole War, barely survived after shrapnel from the gun nearly hit his face.[230]

The grief that immediately ensued was pierced in the minds of anyone present that day. The president wept bitterly when he saw the dead bodies of Upshur and Gilmer.[231] Dolley Madison vowed never to speak of the event again, so long as she lived, which was remarkably another five years. Mrs. Gilmer went into a state of shock. She shed not a single tear and instead sat on deck, with her hair disheveled, pale as death, struggling with her feelings with dignity. Her lips quivering, her eyes fixed and upturned, without a tear, only the corners a little moist, soliloquizing: "Oh certainly not!—Mr. Gilmer cannot be dead! Who would dare to injure him! Yes oh Lord, have mercy upon me! Oh Lord, have mercy on me!"[232]

The disaster on board the *Princeton* killed more top U.S. government officials in a single day than any other tragedy in American history.[233] The twin vacancies left by Upshur's and Gilmer's passing were enough to change the course of history, but what's more extraordinary is that President Tyler was not among the dead. By a stroke of luck, William Waller, a young attorney from Williamsburg and the president's son-in-law— married to his daughter Elizabeth[234]—began singing one of the president's favorite Revolutionary War songs, which caused the president to pause on his way to witness the third and final firing of the Peacemaker. Upon hearing the tune, the president excused himself from the crowd, telling those around him, "When I was a young man that was one of the most popular songs in Virginia—and as I have not heard it for 20 years or more I prefer returning to the cabin and listening to it instead of seeing the gun fired again."[235] This proved a life-saving decision for the president and the "large number" of people who followed him below deck.

Tyler was in a joyous mood, singing along with Waller while holding a drink in his hand. Julia Gardiner, who was probably the real reason the president stayed back, was also below deck, although she was busy entertaining the flirtatious advances of John Potter Stockton, the captain's young son.[236] Just as Waller reached a critical line in the song, "eight hundred men lay slain," the Peacemaker was fired on the deck above. The song and the blast were so in sync that those around him rejoiced in cheers.[237] The joy was short-lived, as a loud voice from above deck shrieked that the secretary of state was dead. The president scurried up the ladder and when he reached the scene of the disaster, those who had been killed were already being covered with flags and blankets, while the injured were brought below deck and attended to by physicians.[238]

Tyler's death in office would have sent the U.S. deep into constitutional crisis. Controversy already surrounded his claim to the presidency, and he did not replace himself, since there was no constitutional mechanism for doing so. His death would have left a double vacancy in the nation's two highest offices. Had that happened, today's line of succession would point in the direction of John Winston Jones, who was speaker of the house. But the act of succession was different in 1844. Section 9 of the Presidential Succession Act of 1792 provided that in the event of twin vacancies of the presidency and vice presidency, the president pro tempore of the Senate would serve as "Acting President" until a new election could be scheduled.

That man would have been Willie Person Mangum, a planter from North Carolina who had risen to become president pro tempore of the Senate. He may be lost in the footnotes of history, but he nearly became the nation's first "Acting President" (as it was a leap year, he would have also been the only president sworn in on February 29). His contemporaries observed him to be among the most "astute political leader[s], effective debater[s], and [most] powerful campaigner[s] with personal charm and magnetism"[239] and who rivaled the greatest politicians of his time. Handsome with long features and slight curls that ran along his ears, Mangum was one of the most capable legal and political minds of his era. But at fifty-two years old, with a failed presidential bid from almost a decade earlier, he knew the presidency was not in the cards. Little did he know how close he would come that winter afternoon.

John Tyler's brush with death didn't stop on board the *Princeton*. Just as Julia Gardiner reached the deck, a sailor scurried from the front of the ship saying, "Don't let miss Gardiner forward, her father is dead."[240] Upon hearing this startling news, Julia Gardiner fainted in the president's arms and fell unconscious. As recounted by his grandson, still alive 155 years later,* "The president took her back downstairs, laid her on a bunk and commanded that the ship go to the shore at the nearest dock."[241] By then, additional medical aid was summoned, and the small steam vessel *I. Johnson* arrived to help the grief-stricken passengers.[242] In today's context, the president would have been the first person rushed out of the scene, but then he was just one of the helping hands. He took immediate responsibility for the grief-stricken Julia.

In what became the next chapter in a fascinating love story, Tyler lifted his young crush into his arms and proceeded to carry her down the gangplank from the ship's deck to the *I. Johnson*. The president, thirty years her elder, had to take extra care to balance himself so that they did not fall over the gangplank and into the water, which given the ship's height would have almost certainly killed them both. It was at this moment that Julia regained consciousness, flailing her arms and legs as she woke up confused and in shock. She was disoriented and unaware of who was carrying her, leading to a frantic panic that nearly knocked them both overboard. Such an outcome would have been a tragic irony: She would have been the woman who saved the life of the president by tempting him to stay and have a drink only to inadvertently kill him an hour later. In reflecting back on the event, she later recalled, "I fainted and did not revive until someone was carrying me off the board and I struggled so that I almost knocked us both off the gangplank. I did not know at

---

* John Tyler was born in 1790 and fathered his last child, Lyon Gardiner Tyler, Sr., at the age of sixty-three. That son fathered two children, Lyon Gardiner Tyler, Jr., at the age of seventy-one and Harrison Ruffin Tyler at the age of seventy-five.

the time, but I learned later that it was the President whose life I almost consigned to the water."[243]

Despite the tragedy of the *Princeton*, the story has one happy ending. The trauma of the tragedy caused Julia Gardiner to have a change of heart. In reflecting back on the moment later in life, she recalled, "After I lost my father, I felt differently towards the President. He seemed to fill the place and to be more agreeable in every way than any younger man ever was or could be."[244] Whether it was true love or a manifestation of what Carl Jung called the "Electra Complex," John Tyler was pleased with the outcome and cared little about the motivations. He seized the moment, and on April 20 sent a message to Julia's mother, Juliana, to once again ask for her daughter's hand in marriage. He had written her a condolence letter on March 1, expressing his sorrow and informing the widow that her husband's remains had been moved from the ship to the executive mansion, where they lay protected alongside the secretary of state, secretary of the navy, minister to Belgium, and commodore of the Navy.[245] Given the change in circumstances and the loss of the family patriarch, the once skeptical mother and now widow offered her blessing.

The wedding was without precedent, as John Tyler's wife Letitia's death in September 1842 made him the first widower president. Two years later, on June 26, 1844, the president married Julia Gardiner at the Church of the Ascension, on Fifth Avenue in New York City, keeping their nuptials a secret until the following day.[246] The bride was stunning, described by the *New York Times* as "robed simply in white, with a gauze veil depending from a circlet of white flowers wreathed in her hair."[247] Her brother walked her down the aisle and gave her away to the president. The Right Reverend Bishop Benjamin Onderdonk—who would later be put on trial for serial groping (the 1840s version of sexual harassment)—married the couple in front of a crowd that was "not more than a dozen people," including the "brother and sister of the bride, John Tyler, Jr., and lady, two Misses Wickliffe, daughters of the Postmaster General; Mr. Postmaster Graham, and one or two others."[248]

At twenty-four, Julia became the youngest first lady in American history; a title she retained until Grover Cleveland fell in love with Frances Folsom, who was a student at Aurora College in New York. At twenty-one years old, her marriage to President Cleveland gave her the title. Tyler and his young bride would go on to have seven children, on top of the seven that Tyler already had living (his third child Anne died at birth). This grand total of fifteen was more than any other president in history. He fathered the last of the batch at the ripe age of seventy, Pearl Tyler, whose death would have been on her father's 157th birthday.

Forcing Texas

The *Princeton* explosion dealt a significant blow to Tyler's Texas agenda[249] because of the loss of Upshur and who replaced him. In a dispatch sent back to Texas on March 5, 1844, the Texas chargé revealed just how close they were to completing the treaty: "For some days previous to Mr. Upshur's death we had been engaged in discussing the terms of a treaty of annexation and had agreed on all the main points. . . . I was awaiting a reply to my last communication. . . . Had instructions arrived to authorize me to consummate it, the treaty could have been concluded in half a day. Who may be called to the State Department is yet uncertain. I fear it will not again be so well filled."[250] He recalled that just days before the accident on board the *Princeton,* he "had given to [Usphur] for examination an outline of the points which would be required to be included [in the treaty]; and he had submitted to me a similar draft, in his own handwriting embracing his views, which corresponded fully with my own in every main particular." The chargé was just awaiting a reply and what remained would take about half a day with likely Senate approval.[251]

The Texas chargé's caution about who would fill Upshur's seat proved to be prescient. While the loss of Upshur was a setback, it was the choice of his successor that nearly torpedoed the president's annexation plans. The new secretary of state, John C. Calhoun, wanted to wrap a sectional bow around annexation, lest there be any ambiguity about whether the administration was driven by the southern cause. His goal was confrontation, to hijack annexation as a southern cause that would antagonize the North and forge the southern party of his dreams.[252]

By April 12, Calhoun had a signed treaty that was ready to go to Congress. All he had to do was deliver the treaty without doing anything to disrupt the current discourse. Everything changed following a communiqué from Richard Pakenham, the British minister to the U.S., who wanted to inform the administration that while England opposed slavery and would like to see it abolished, she had no plans to direct those sentiments at either Texas or Mexico. By all accounts the message was an amiable overture by the new minister and the president took it in good faith. Calhoun, who was looking for a fight, accused his British counterpart of fomenting insurrection and plotting nefarious activities. Tyler was unaware of the content of Calhoun's letter to the minister and so he thought nothing of it when he secretly sent the treaty, along with this letter and other documents, to the Senate for consideration. Not surprisingly, Calhoun's letter—which would become known as the "Pakenham Letter"—caused outrage among abolitionists, who made sure it was leaked to the press.[253]

The Pakenham Letter could not have come at a worse time, for everybody. The presidential campaign of 1844 was heating up. Former president Martin Van Buren was the clear front-runner for the Democrats, while Henry Clay seemed to have shored up the nomination for the Whigs. Both candidates wanted to avoid the slavery issue at all costs. The last thing either needed was to have Texas annexation introduced into the campaign under the pretext of expanding slavery. Both were quick to publish letters denouncing annexation, but their attempts to navigate an increasingly complex issue created a perfect storm that would rob them both of the presidency. Clay argued that "the United States, still unable to pay off its own debt, would have to assume a Texas debt of $13 million" and suggested that annexation of Texas would "menace the existence if not certainly sow the seeds of dissolution of the Union" by provoking an almost guaranteed war with Mexico.[254] Van Buren shared this view that annexation would lead to an unwanted war with Mexico.[255]

Van Buren was the first to fall. He had enemies within the Democratic Party, who used his opposition to annexation as a way to thwart his election prospects. Instead, the Democratic Party hastily turned to James K. Polk, a relative unknown from Tennessee who had championed both the annexation of Texas and the reoccupation of Oregon.[256] Henry Clay and the Whigs were initially ecstatic. They were confident about defeating Van Buren, but they were certain about defeating Polk. This was not an unreasonable assumption to make, given that Polk was the nation's first dark horse candidate and was not of the same political stature as Clay.

As Clay and Polk went head-to-head, President Tyler still lingered in the campaign and while he had no chance of winning on a third-party ticket, his presence took votes from the Democrats. Recognizing this, the

Democrats made a move to cut a deal with Tyler. In exchange for Tyler dropping out of the race, the Democrats met each of his three demands: Immediately halt the public thrashings in the Democratic *Washington Globe,* guarantee that Democrats holding office would be retained in the Polk administration, and the immediate annexation of Texas.[257] With his demands met, the president withdrew from the race on August 20 and called on all annexation enthusiasts to throw their support behind Polk.

With the Democrats now positioning themselves as the party for annexation, Clay found himself in the difficult political position of speaking out against a policy that benefited his southern base. When this led to charges that he was pandering to northern abolitionists—the kiss of death in the South—he published a letter in Alabama's *Independent Monitor,* in which he insisted his pro-annexation stance was motivated entirely by a desire to preserve the Union. His defensive posture weakened his political position and opened him to criticism from the Democrats. This was nothing compared to what followed in a second letter. On July 27, Clay published a reversal of his position on annexation in yet another Alabama paper, in which he explained that he had "no personal objection to annexation and that the existence of slavery in Texas had nothing to do with its propriety."[258]

Clay's second letter proved fatal. The Whig Party had been working to rally the opposition to Texas annexation and get them behind Clay as the Democrats had done with the pro-annexation camp. Instead, Clay played into Democratic hands, by helping them divide the anti-annexationist camps, leaving the Whig Party without the harmony that it would need going into the election. And when the election finally came, the Democrats won a decisive victory, claiming 170 electoral votes to the Whigs' 105 and carrying eight states that had gone to the Whigs in 1840.

Following the loss in 1844, the Whigs thought long and hard about the party's future. Southern Whigs, in particular, pushed the party to move past the tariff and Texas annexation, two issues they blamed for their poor showing in 1844. With the 28th Congress set to convene from December 3, 1844, to March 3, 1845, before Polk was inaugurated, they were eager to extricate themselves of the toxic Texas issue so that it did not resurface during the next election. The lame-duck president, having failed to achieve ratification of the Texas treaty in the Senate, made no secret of his intention to annex Texas through a joint resolution of Congress, which could be achieved by a simple majority.

With a Democratic-stacked Congress, it was clear that the joint resolution would pass. However, there were still open questions about the substance of the joint resolution. Seizing the opportunity to tip annexation further in favor of the South, Milton Brown, a southern Whig congressman from Tennessee, rallied the southern Whigs to present an alternate plan. Under the terms of Brown's plan, the whole Republic of Texas would be admitted to the Union as one slave state rather than as a territory. The issue of the Mexican boundary would be handled by the United States, while Texas would keep its public lands so long as it paid off its debt. Brown also added a future clause that allowed Texas to be divided into as many as four additional states that could choose to be free or slave.

Northern Whigs and Van Buren Democrats opposed the Brown plan, insisting on a revised treaty with Texas that would admit only the settled area of the republic as a slave state and leave the status of the rest for future determination. But a bloc of southern Whig supporters for the Brown plan helped tip the balance[259] and on January 27, 1845, the House of Representatives passed a joint resolution on annexation 120 to 98. On March 1, just three days before leaving office, Tyler signed the joint resolution and after conferring with President-elect Polk, he formally invited Texas to join the Union.[260]

———

William Henry Harrison's death marked the first time in American history that presidential power abruptly transferred from one man to another. It is a testament to the American system that without precedent or clarity in the Constitution, power transferred so seamlessly and swiftly through a seminal historic moment of ambiguity. This particular transfer of power was made all the more remarkable by the extraordinary set of events that followed, including political circumstances that led to the annexation of Texas in 1844 and precipitated war with Mexico. The war, which was fought by Tyler's successor, James K. Polk, failed to win popular support from a population that supported admission of Texas, but preferred not to fight.

Once war with Mexico commenced, the question was not whether the U.S. would win, but how it would handle the spoils of victory. At the war's onset, Ralph Waldo Emerson, the philosopher and father of transcendentalism, warned somewhat prophetically, "The United States will conquer Mexico, but it will be as the man swallows the arsenic, which brings him down in turn. Mexico will poison us."[261]

Zachary Taylor was the hero of the Mexican War, elected as the second Whig president. He opposed the Compromise of 1850, but died just over a year into office.

Millard Fillmore fired the entire Taylor cabinet and worked with Congress to break the deadlock over slavery in the new territories and temporarily avert civil war.

CHAPTER TWO

Over My Dead Body

T he Battle of Monterrey was among the bloodiest of the Mexican-American War. The belligerents fought to the point of hand-to-hand combat through the streets.[1] Led by General Zachary Taylor, the Americans squeezed out a narrow victory, but gained little ground. Taylor, who was more concerned with the well-being of his troops than the larger war, recognized the exhaustion on both sides and negotiated an eight-week cease-fire with his defeated enemy. President James K. Polk was apoplectic and vowed to undo Taylor's unilateral accommodation of Mexico.

The victory at Monterrey was meant to be the precursor to a war-ending assault on Mexico City,[2] for which the president and the Democratic Party would enjoy the political benefits of victory. After conferring with his advisors, Polk reversed Taylor's cease-fire and found a way to mastermind his great victory with bells and whistles and punish his rogue general at the same time. Believing that this would be the final battle of the war, Polk, who had pledged a single term in office,[3] wanted a loyal Democrat to reap the benefits of military victory and triumph in the presidential election of 1848 as his anointed successor. He chose Winfield Scott, a decorated general with a hunger and savvy for politics, to lead the invasion and equipped him with an additional ten thousand veterans and regulars whom he commandeered from Taylor. Reduced to five thousand volunteers who lacked the experience and discipline that he expected from his troops as a professional soldier,[4] Taylor was stripped further of his dignity and relegated to defend the small town of Buena Vista.

While Polk played musical chairs with American troops and politics with his generals, the Mexicans saw an opportunity in Taylor's weak position and planned a secret attack on Buena Vista. Despite its marginal geographic significance, the Mexicans needed a victory to boost morale for the bigger fight to defend Mexico City. Leading the charge was General Antonio López de Santa Anna, who on February 23, 1847, stormed Taylor's position with twenty thousand well-equipped troops. It should have been a decisive victory for Mexico. Instead, the outnumbered Taylor achieved a miracle that day—although a number of soldiers died, including Henry Clay's son James—and led his five thousand volunteers to turn back the experienced Mexican fighters.[5]

Taylor's victory at Buena Vista may not have ended the Mexican-American War, but tales of the sixty-two-year-old general defying unthinkable odds transformed him into a nationwide celebrity. Polk's plan failed. Instead of punishing Taylor and elevating Scott, his political interference fostered a public perception that one biographer described as "Taylor as David being sent unnecessarily to face the Goliath Santa Anna." This story of valor and beating the odds only made the stories of heroism that much greater.[6]

As Taylor was transformed, soldiers and colleagues came out of the woodwork to share extraordinary—and often hyperbolized—stories of his bravery and humility. In one widely circulated anecdote from a steamboat in Port Isabel, Texas, Taylor is said to have offered his stateroom to sick and wounded soldiers while he slept on a mattress in the hallway. When the ship's servants attempted to locate the general for dinner, a fireman on board the ship insisted that he had seen "a clever old fellow asleep there under the sail in front of the fire!"[7] Americans fell in love with the general and his appeal grew into a sort of "Taylormania," with one New Yorker reporting how pictures of him were on every ice cart, butcher's stall, fish stand, cigar box, and carriage throughout the city, along with his nickname "Rough and Ready."[8] Taylormania catapulted him into a suprapartisan symbol, making him ripe for political exploitation.

Meanwhile, the Democrats and Whigs muddled through their respective identity crises. Each struggled to develop a narrative around the war with Mexico that could unite their sectional factions. The Whigs opposed the war with Mexico as a folly caused by the ex-Whig Tyler's annexation of Texas, but this strong position against the war alienated its southern faction. The Democrats sought to unify under the aspiration of "manifest destiny"—that America should stretch from coast to coast. But this strategy, too, got caught in a cobweb of sectional politics with many northerners resenting the slaveholding president's attempt to expand the peculiar institution, as slavery was known, under the auspices of patriotism. But as difficult as it was to navigate the politics of the war, managing victory proved to be a far greater challenge as the country entered a presidential election year.[9]

The Spoils of Victory

Eighteen forty-eight began with spectacular promise. The discovery of gold in January led droves of Americans to head out west in search of instant wealth.[10] On February 2, the war with Mexico officially ended,[11] which unloaded a massive financial burden stifling the economy. Waves of European revolutions caused significant capital flight to the U.S., which helped further stimulate the economic recovery.

While the economy boomed, the country readied itself for a political changing of the guard. The great titans of the political system—Henry Clay, John Calhoun, and Daniel Webster—still maintained enormous political influence, but their old age meant the curtain was closing on their final act. Within four years they would all be dead. A new crop of young and dynamic politicians like Abraham Lincoln, Jefferson Davis, and Stephen Douglas emerged to share the stage and prepare to take the baton. They brought energy, charisma, and for better or worse a new style of leadership to a changing political context and a lot of new territory.

The Treaty of Guadalupe Hidalgo—ratified in March by the United States and in May by Spain—set the terms for peace with Mexico. For the United States, the spoils of victory were prodigious, including the acquisition of present-day California; most of present-day New Mexico, Arizona, Nevada, Utah; and parts of present-day Colorado, Wyoming, and Texas. This massive landmass—known as the Mexican Cession—marked the largest single annexation since the Louisiana Purchase[12] and grew the United States from 1,753,588 square miles to 2,944,337 square miles[13]— almost a 68 percent territorial growth that extended America from coast to coast.[14]

Despite the territorial gains, these spoils of victory carried the seeds for disunion.[15] Without the slavery issue, Americans probably would have celebrated this expansion. Instead, the question of how to deal with slavery in the new territories meant that old wounds—patched up by temporary fixes like the Missouri Compromise—were reopened. The thesis of previous compromises stipulated that America would have to maintain a balance of free and slave states in order to ensure against disunion. Now with the addition of such vast territory the country found itself overstretched and beginning to tear at the seams.

There was no easy fix. Mexico abolished slavery in 1829 through the Guerrero Decree, which meant slavery had been banned under Mexican law in each of the acquired territories for nearly two decades. Even so, none of the new territories were conducive to slavery—New Mexico and Utah had very few people and California was already a free territory—so the balance would inevitably flip. For many in the South, these prospects spelled not just the end of slavery as an institution, but the entire region's marginalization. For northerners, the opportunity to achieve greater political influence was all too appealing. As sectional tensions grew, statesmen from all factions were reminded of Thomas Jefferson's ominous warning from twenty-eight years earlier. In reacting to the Missouri Compromise, he wrote, "We have the wolf by the ear, and we can neither hold him, nor safely let him go."[16] Now, faced with the same wolf, but bigger and feistier, the country would have to elect a leader to guide and navigate through perhaps the greatest inflection point in American history. The two major political parties, Democrats and Whigs, were split across sectional lines, and without a path to balancing free and slave states something would have to give.

President Polk, nearing the end of his administration, was in no position to play this role. As a staunch supporter of slavery, it's possible he would have made a last-ditch effort to push slavery into the new territories, but illness caused by toxins in the White House prevented him from seeking a second term (he would die three months after leaving office). With no incumbent in the 1848 presidential election, an open field of Whig and Democratic candidates battled it out over the single issue of slavery in the new territories. The Whigs believed the election was theirs for the taking, but only if they pivoted away from establishment figures like Henry Clay—who in April declared his candidacy for the fourth time in his career—and found a way to avoid agitating either sectional faction of the party.[17] This meant they needed a candidate who had name recognition, but whose politics were too unknown to be divisive. Recalling their success eight years earlier in electing William Henry Harrison, the party revisited its strategy of turning to a military hero[18] who could be easily elected and molded later. But even on the heels of war with Mexico, there were slim pickings. Whether they could convince the right military hero to pursue the presidency, let alone as a Whig, remained an open question.

Wooing a General

All eyes were on Zachary Taylor, who fit the bill. As a military leader, he was a giant and as he had not yet become a political figure, his views were unknown. Taylor was a child of the frontier without a political bone in his body. Despite being the son of an old aristocratic family,[19] he didn't enjoy the pleasantries of the aristocratic lifestyle. His parents preferred exploration to ostentation, and as a result he spent his youth on the frontier, where the threat of Indian warfare was constant.[20] As a boy, his house was often barricaded and the guns readied in case of an attack in the middle of the night.[21] He would later recall an incident where a group of Indians murdered and scalped his classmates moments after he and his brothers separated from them just a hundred yards away.[22] The rough frontier life nurtured young Taylor's lust for adventure and at times he deliberately sought reckless valor. At the age of seventeen, he swam across the Ohio River, from the Kentucky to the Indiana shore, ignoring the freezing temperature and floating ice.[23] Why? "Just to prove that he could do it."[24] His formal education was limited and most accounts of his early writing skills describe him as semiliterate.[25] Inspired by his older brother, he joined the Army, where he was first commissioned by Thomas Jefferson on May 3, 1808.

Taylor had an odd physical presence, at least relative to many of his contemporaries. He was short and stocky, five feet eight inches with an oversized head, slightly stooped shoulders, and legs that were too short for his body.[26] He hesitated when speaking, which sounded like a slight stutter.[27] His social anxiety and discomfort led to several physical quirks, such as closing one eye when speaking.[28] He was rough around the edges, described by Daniel Webster as "a swearing, whiskey-drinking, fighting frontier colonel."[29]

These attributes, flattering and unflattering, are part of what made him so loved. He was admiringly called "Old Rough and Ready," while his fancier rival Winfield Scott was disparagingly referred to as "Old Fuss and

Feathers." Taylor's modesty was legendary. A Virginia officer observed that "he was perfectly unaffected by his brilliant successes" and described him as "plain and unassuming in his kind manners mild and affable in his disposition and kind and courteous in his demeanour."[30] Part of his modesty stemmed from a dislike of formality.[31] He put no effort into his appearance and found discomfort in wearing uniforms. The spotlight irked him, as did fame. When Congress authorized a special medal in his honor, the commissioned artist couldn't find an existing portrait and had to travel to Mexico to paint him in person.[32]

Taylor initially scoffed at the idea of running for president, telling one Whig politician who had proposed the idea, "Stop your nonsense and drink your whiskey!"[33] He thought little of politics and politicians and had never voted in an election, either national or local. But whether Taylor wanted the office or not made little difference. The Whigs needed a war hero to win and he was their best, if not only, option.

While Taylor was indifferent toward politics, he was forthcoming in his hatred of President Polk,[34] which it seems the Whigs openly exploited to draft him as a candidate. But despite their best efforts, Taylor was still unwilling to affiliate himself with any party. Despite being a southern slaveholder, he saw himself first as an American. He understood that the slavery question threatened to tear the country apart, writing to Jefferson Davis, "The intemperate zeal of the fanatics of the North, and the intemperate zeal of a few politicians of the South [would] no longer admit of a proper and calm discussion, neither in the pulpit or congress, in the newspapers or in the primary assemblies of the people."[35]

Throughout the winter of 1848, the Whigs were still trying to get Taylor to abandon his politically naive aspiration to be a candidate transcending parties. His reluctance to run as a Whig was endlessly frustrating to his champions, particularly John Crittenden, the political kingmaker who had destroyed his longtime friendship with Henry Clay to back Taylor. By April 1848, the Whig machinery grew increasingly anxious. Taylor wasn't budging and time was running out. If he didn't declare himself a Whig, the convention would be left with no choice but to nominate Clay, who was almost guaranteed to lose in a general election. In a desperate ploy to knock some partisan sense into the stubborn general, a delegation of Whigs set sail on April 22, traveling up the Mississippi River from New Orleans to Taylor's hometown of Cypress Grove, Mississippi.[36]

Taylor agreed to hear them out and engaged in niceties, even meeting the men at the dock and inviting them to spend the night at his plantation. After some corralling, Taylor agreed to sign a letter stating, "I am a Whig but not an ultra-Whig. If elected I would not be the mere president of a party" and will only exercise veto power in "cases of clear violation of the Constitution."[37]

His message was filled with caveats; hardly the forward-leaning proclamation the Whigs had hoped for. But they had what they needed. Taylor's most important credential was electability, not Whig zealotry. As the owner of nearly three hundred slaves, he was sure to have appeal with the South, but his valor in the war against Mexico also made him compelling in the North, even among those who had opposed the war. He had also opposed the annexation of Texas and had advocated fair treatment of Indians and honoring treaty rights, which made him appealing to northern Whigs.[38]

Nomination and Victory

On June 7, the Whig delegates gathered in Philadelphia and nominated Taylor on the fourth ballot. For the second time in history the Whigs selected a war hero and political enigma as their nominee for president. Recalling Harrison's election and death in office, they were eager to ensure that history did not repeat itself. Taylor remained an elusive figure, which meant the party needed a good northerner with solid Whig credentials—a proponent of the "American System"*—to join him on the ticket.[39] But they also needed someone who could satisfy Henry Clay's disappointed supporters.[40]

The Whigs chose Millard Fillmore, a poor farmer turned legislator from upstate New York, to round out the ticket. He was a mediocre choice at best, but there was a dearth of options. In contrast to Taylor, Fillmore came from an impecunious background. He lacked access to basic education, similar to Taylor, but unlike "Old Zack," he worked tirelessly to build

---

* On Feburary 2, 3, and 6, Henry Clay delivered a speech in the Senate in which he defended what he called the "American System." This program, which came to define the Whig agenda, included a tariff, national bank, and internal improvements. (See U.S. Senate Historical Society: https://www.senate.gov/artandhistory/history/common/generic/Speeches_ClayAmericanSystem.htm.)

on the few years of formal schooling he had as a boy. He had a diction-
ary on him at all times, and when some neighbors organized a lending
library, he read all the books.[41] As a young man, Fillmore was "strikingly
handsome, tall and dignified and always dressed meticulously in the latest fashion."[42] But underneath this physical facade, Fillmore carried himself like an understudy in life, going to enormous lengths to conceal his
meager background.[43] He was neither nostalgic nor reflective about his
humble upbringing. One biographer describes him as a "parvenu who
seemed always worried that someone might discover he did not belong
in proper society. He changed churches as he became more successful and
moved to bigger and better houses. Outward appearances truly mattered
to him."[44] He was insecure about his own accomplishments, so much so
that in 1855 he turned down an honorary doctorate from Oxford, saying,
"I have not the advantage of a classical education and no man should, in
my judgment, accept a degree he cannot read." In explaining this decision,
he acknowledged a fear that "they would probably ask, who's Fillmore?
What's he done? Where did he come from? And then my name would, I
fear, give them an excellent opportunity to make jokes at my expense."[45]
Twenty-two years earlier, former president Andrew Jackson—another
poorly educated president—was ridiculed when he accepted an honorary degree from Harvard, although it is not clear if Fillmore had this as a
frame of reference.

These insecurities fueled Fillmore's ambition. He rose quickly within
the legal profession, securing early admission to the bar at twenty-three
years old. Soon after, he became politically active and gravitated toward
fringe groups that nurtured his propensity for conspiracy theories and
ethnic disparagement, which is part of why he entered politics as an anti-
Mason in the 1820s.[46] His fraternizing with such groups made him hateful of outsiders—Catholics, immigrants, abolitionists, and fugitive slaves
who questioned what he perceived to be their inferior birth.[47] He evolved
politically, tabling his xenophobic views, and ultimately won four terms
in Congress.[48]

For Fillmore, all politics was local and his ambitions were modest, as
evidenced by the fact that he was among a small group of men who actually wanted the vice presidency. During the election of 1844, he made an
unsuccessful attempt to join Henry Clay on the Whig ticket, but was dis-

appointed when the party chose someone else.[49] Fillmore had no illusions about what the vice presidency was; in fact, he was well aware of what it was not. But the presidency didn't interest him. He believed that the vice presidency would provide him with a platform to advance his home state's interests and, more important, position him to hand out patronage posts to friends in New York. This inside track could offer a huge advantage relative to his powerful rivals in Tammany Hall—New York's Democratic machine—which would allow him to serve out his term as vice president and return to New York as a political hero.

No vice president in history had sought the position, let alone actively campaigned for it. Fillmore correctly assumed the Whigs would have a hard time finding a northerner whose political views were acceptable to both abolitionists and proponents of slavery. He had always been careful when discussing slavery, which he declared "an evil"—not surprising for a northerner—but qualified this view with a suggestion that the federal government should not make determinations about where it does or does not exist.[50] Thus by default, a man who had never been elected to state-wide office, served in the Senate, or been appointed to the presidential cabinet,[51] found a reasonably unobstructed path to the vice presidential nomination.

With Fillmore rounding out the ticket, the only thing left to do was notify Taylor that he had won the Whig nomination for president. James Turner Morehead, the chairman of the Whig Party, excitedly sent formal word via telegraph to Memphis, where a side-wheeler coincidentally named *General Taylor* carried the message with flags flying, signal guns firing, and her crew cheering each passing vessel.[52] The letter arrived at the Baton Rouge post office on June 18,[53] but by June 28, Taylor had not replied. Morehead sent a second letter, but that, too, went unanswered.[54] After days turned into weeks, the Whigs grew anxious and some feared embarrassment. It was not out of the realm of possibility that Taylor— who never really wanted the nomination and who reluctantly declared himself a Whig—might decline to accept it. But Taylor *was* inclined. As it turns out, he was not ignoring the convention, but having grown tired of being saddled with postage fees, he ordered his local post office to hold his mail.[55]

Taylor eventually accepted the nomination and embarked on a presidential campaign that lacked all the hallmarks of the previous two campaigns, except for the fact that it skirted the issue of slavery altogether. With the exception of the Free Soilers, who used their third-party platform to argue against slavery in the new territories,[56] the other parties were quiet and noncommittal on the most important issue facing the country. The Whig strategy was reminiscent of the 1840 campaign, except without the gimmicks: Avoid any substantive issue, remind the country of Taylor's heroism, and say nothing. Part of this was to sidestep the issues that were dividing the country and part of it was because the party really did not know what Taylor believed and thus might say.[57] Taylor was more than happy to accommodate this strategy since he didn't care much for campaigns anyway. He did not participate in his own campaign and showed almost no emotion or interest in the outcome, other than exacting political revenge on President Polk.[58] It is uncertain whether he bothered to vote in the election.[59]

Election Day finally came on November 7, 1848, when for the first time Americans went to the polls on the same day[60] and the results were carried by telegraph.[61] Nearly three million Americans from thirty states (half slave and half free) voted in the election.[62] This was an unimpressive showing, as it meant just over 13 percent of the total population of 22 million participated, which paled in comparison to the 82 percent voter turnout the last time a Whig general ran for president.[63] Taylor received 47 percent of the vote, squeezing out a victory over Lewis Cass, the former secretary of war and Democratic nominee, by just thirty-six electoral votes and 138,000 popular votes. Despite Taylor being a slaveholder, the majority of his electoral votes came from northern states.[64]

There was little time for celebration. Sectional tensions were mounting and the future looked grim. Northerners believed the slave states were overreaching and dangling the prospects of disunion as leverage. Southerners feared a northern conspiracy to marginalize them.[65] In the middle was a newly elected president with no track record, no political experience, and no public pronouncements of his position on any major issue. Both sections thought they had a read on the new president and both would prove wrong. Southerners assumed that because he was from the Deep South and owned more than three hundred slaves, he would have a personal incentive to defend the institution.[66] Northerners had made the same assumptions, which probably caused them some anxiety. His deci-

sion to choose four of the seven cabinet secretaries from slave states reinforced what both sections believed to be true.[67] But while Taylor's pedigree
should have lent itself toward a more southern bias, he had spent most
of his life as a professional soldier and saw the country through the lens
of what was best for the Union. He was neither a sectionalist, nor a pro-
slavery zealot. He was a proud Unionist.

"Five Gaping Wounds"

Taylor inherited a divided Congress. On one end of the political spectrum,
there were advocates of the Wilmot Proviso, a controversial amendment
proposed in the House that would restrict slavery in the new territories. While this faction was comprised of some abolitionists, there were
others—including David Wilmot (who proposed the amendment)—who
cared little for the welfare of slaves, but wanted the new territories kept as
free soil for white labor.[68] On the other end of the political spectrum were
those such as John Calhoun, who represented a hard-line southern faction
threatening disunion.

While stalwarts on both sides planted flags on opposite ends of the
spectrum, neither had a sizable enough bloc to implement their vision.
With neither section able to dominate, there was an opportunity to find
middle ground and avert disunion, which would almost certainly lead to
civil war. But there was little time to waste as already the tensions around
slavery in the new territories were manifesting themselves in several
contexts—"five gaping wounds," as Henry Clay later described, that required immediate attention from the president and Congress. The first
was what to do with California, which desperately needed a civilian government. The Gold Rush had led to a population explosion and the failure
of so many wealth seekers to find gold had contributed to a general state of
lawlessness,[69] which was beyond the Army's ability to manage. Residents
demanded statehood, but the fact that most of the population came from
northern states meant that southerners saw California's admission to the
Union as a threat to the balance of power in the U.S. Senate.[70]

The second issue had to do with New Mexico and its border with
Texas. As with California, there were the same debates about slavery and
whether New Mexico should stay a territory or become a state. Given that
New Mexico was largely unsettled except for a handful of villages, some

scattered Indian pueblos, and Mexican settlements around Santa Fe and Tucson, slavery was not viable. But unlike California, the borders of New Mexico were less defined. Texas laid claim to a substantial part of eastern New Mexico, including Santa Fe, which was in part a historic claim and in part a way to extend Texas's strict slavery laws that forbade emancipated slaves—known as "freedmen"—in the state.[71] More than a light political claim, Texas was ready to enforce its position in New Mexico by military force if necessary.[72]

A third issue had to do with the Mormon State of Deseret, also known as the Utah Territory. The territory was only lightly populated, which as with New Mexico made it unlikely that slavery could thrive there. But left open was the possibility of statehood, which if achieved would put another free state in the North's column.

The fourth and fifth contexts both had to do with slave laws. The Fugitive Slave Act of 1793—upheld by *Prigg v. Pennsylvania* (1842)—permitted slave masters to track down their fugitive slaves and, after receiving a certificate of removal, take them home.[73] But enforcement of the law had been relatively weak. Frustrated by the lack of cooperation from northern states, the South demanded revisions that would force compliance. Northerners in turn insisted on an abolition of the slave trade in Washington, D.C., which at the time was the largest slave market in North America[74] and carried the nickname "the Congo of America."[75] The area around the Capitol was a particularly active cesspool for such activities, where it was not uncommon for traders to march their chained and shackled slaves just steps from Congress. And when those same slave traders ran out of space to house their human goods, they could find solace in the fact that any Washington jail could be rented on the cheap.[76] Adding to this shameful narrative, Civil War scholar Adam Goodheart writes:

> Enslaved cab drivers greeted newly arrived travelers at the city's railway station and drove them to hotels, such as Gadsby's and Willard's, that were staffed largely by slaves. In local barbershops, it was almost exclusively black men—many of them slaves—who shaved the whiskers of lowly and mighty Washingtonians alike. . . . Enslaved body servants attended their masters on the floor of the Senate, in the Supreme Court chamber—and sometimes even in the White House. . . . Black men and women [were] frequently ad-

vertised for sale in the newspapers, and occasionally even sent to the auction block just a few hundred yards from the White House.[77]

It was in the context of these contentious sectional tensions that Taylor began to form his government. In doing so, he kept a very small and unorthodox circle around him. First among those who could claim closeness to the president was Jefferson Davis, who in addition to having been married to Taylor's eldest daughter, Sarah, was a Democrat. The relationship was complex, with Taylor initially opposing his daughter's relationship with Davis, insisting, "No daughter of his would ever marry an army officer."[78] During their romance, the animosity between soon-to-be father- and son-in-law grew to such epic proportions that the two almost faced off in a duel. But when Sarah fell ill and died in 1835 (the same year they were married), Taylor and Davis found peace with each other and became close friends. By the time Taylor won the presidency, Davis and his new wife, Varina, had become such important fixtures in the president-elect's life that the future traitor to America enjoyed greater access to and confidence of the aloof president than any other figure of the time.[79]

As for the Whigs, Taylor didn't trust the established figures, particularly Henry Clay and Daniel Webster.[80] He preferred outsiders and thought little of politicians, especially those who made it a lifelong trade. They didn't like him either. The party establishment spent most of the pre-inauguration period complaining about Taylor. Daniel Webster found it "strange that there should be nobody here [in Washington] by this time possessing General Taylor's confidence. Many things require attention before the 3rd of March. . . . I fear that neither he nor those about him take a proper view of the state of things, and of what the future requires to be attended to now."[81] Clay also complained about his exclusion, noting that he "had no proof of any desire" on the part of the president "to confer or consult with [him] on any subject."[82] As a result, the new president formed one of the weakest cabinets in American history, without a single position occupied by a national figure from either party.[83]

James Polk's term and the 30th Congress officially ended at noon on March 4, 1849,[84] which fell on a Sunday. Taylor refused to take the oath on the Sabbath[85] and insisted on pushing the inauguration back one day, which created some confusion about who was president. Historians have debated who filled the power vacuum, given that both Polk and his vice president, George Dallas, were no longer in office. Recalling the near death of president Tyler on board the USS *Princeton,* without a vice president the next in line was the president pro tempore of the Senate, who in this case was David Rice Atchison, a forty-two-year-old, pro-slavery Democrat from Missouri. That Sunday, Atchison assumed the role (who wouldn't want to grab the presidency, even if for just a day), although it is not clear what that entailed and how seriously he took the assertion. In his final resting place in Plattsburg, Missouri, his gravestone reads: "David Rice Atchison President of the United States One Day." Atchison would later joke that he had led "the honestest administration this country ever had,"[86] although he later denied he had ever laid claim to the presidency during an interview with the *Plattsburg Lever* in 1872.[87]

Inauguration day was chilly and gray with strong gusts of wind.[88] Polk and Taylor shared what must have been an awkward carriage ride down Pennsylvania Avenue and while the two had exchanged pleasantries at dinner the previous week, they had mutual disrespect for each other. The city was packed with Taylor fans and it must have been particularly painful for the outgoing president to watch as the enthusiastic hysteria required the police to work twice as hard to hold all the Taylor fans back from their hero. Taylor hardly relished in the moment, simply nodding, smiling, and waving his hat from time to time; such modesty only made the throngs of supporters love him more.[89]

That evening, Vice President Fillmore readied himself for his first opportunity to build a bond with the new president. There were three inaugural balls and Taylor and Fillmore rode through a blizzard to attend each. They began the evening at Carusi's Saloon at 11th and C Streets, for the military ball. They continued on to the Washington Assembly Rooms in the Jackson Hall on Pennsylvania Avenue for a gathering of prominent Democrats. Finally, at about 11:45 p.m. they arrived at the main ball, which took place at City Hall. The main ball was organized by a hodgepodge of 230 sponsors including Captain Robert E. Lee. It was a festive occasion with the band playing "Hail Columbia" and the crowd of almost five thousand attendees erupting each time the new president stood and made himself visible.[90] By all accounts everyone, including Taylor, enjoyed the festivities, although Fillmore felt no closer to the president after the evening. Abraham Lincoln, the young congressman from Illinois, stayed until 4:00 a.m. and couldn't find his top hat so left without it.[91]

Taylor Has a Plan

Taylor's agenda was almost completely consumed by the Mexican Cession and what to do about it. Southerners were soon to be disappointed, as he seemed to advocate a more northern position. His plan to save the Union rested on quick admission of California and New Mexico as free states. Not surprisingly, it was attacked from all directions. It was dismissed by many as completely impractical, particularly as it failed to acknowledge Texas's claim to Santa Fe and other portions of New Mexico.[92] His plan also ignored the Fugitive Slave Law and abolition of the slave trade in the District of Columbia. Whether intentional or not, his proposal was predictably incendiary. Adding to this was the fact that the State of Deseret— home to the Mormons—had already petitioned for admission to the Union.[93] Southerners were irate over the prospect of three new free states entering the Union, not to mention that such a proposal came from one of their own.

Taylor's plan did not reflect a change of heart about slavery. He still owned slaves (including the fifteen he brought to the White House and forced to sleep in the attic),[94] he still bought property that included slaves, and he at no point declared it a moral evil. But as a Unionist, he looked for the most pragmatic way to balance sectional differences. Given that California, New Mexico, and Deseret were all naturally inclined toward being free states, Taylor believed that his plan would allow the South to save face[95] and avoid a lengthy and contentious congressional debate on slavery[96] that it would lose, at least in the territories. He did not view his plan as selling out the South; instead, he saw it as helping them salvage what was already a precarious position.[97]

Eighteen forty-nine ended worse than it started. The president's plan was a dead end, yet he refused to get out of the way for compromise. His stubbornness made the task for Congress more difficult, as it now needed to arrive at a compromise proposal sufficient to override a presidential veto. Even without this high bar, the 31st Congress was too chaotic and dysfunctional to achieve even the most modest milestone.[98] The Democrats had a slight majority over the Whigs, but loyalties were sectional more than partisan. Congress was so divided by party and faction that it took them three weeks to elect a speaker of the house. In the words of one South Carolina representative, the House was "not a Hall" but "a cavern—a mammoth cave, in which men might speak in all parts, and be understood in none."[99]

Taylor's administration entered 1850 deadlocked with Congress, where most legislators viewed his plan as impractical at best, dangerous at worst. So long as he insisted on immediate admission of California and New Mexico, no progress would be made. The absence of presidential leadership created a power vacuum and a proliferation of alternative bills—none of which would prove viable. On January 16, in an attempt to offer an alternative to the president's plan, Senators Thomas Hart Benton of Missouri and Henry S. Foote of Mississippi introduced conflicting legislation for dealing with Texas and New Mexico: Benton focused on dividing Texas into two equal-sized states—one slave and one free—in exchange for $15 million and maintaining the territorial integrity of New Mexico; Foote proposed validating Texas claims to New Mexico and keeping California's territorial status.[100] But the details of the bills were not as important as the fact that neither seemed likely to pass. Instead their contradictory nature fueled greater divisiveness as partisans and sectionalists aligned with one camp or the other.

Henry Clay, who had reemerged from retirement when Kentucky's state legislature* elected him to a seat in the Senate,[101] was shocked by the change in political climate. A lot had happened in eight years. New blood had cycled in, and while the great triumvirate was reunited, all were now old men. In writing to a friend, he observed that he was forced to "listen to the grating and doleful sounds of dissolution of the Union, treason, and war" and observed that "there is a very uncomfortable state of things here both for the Whig party, and I fear for the Country . . . the feeling for disunion, among some intemperate Southern politicians, is stronger than I supposed it could be."[102] Despite Clay's skepticism, he managed to use the leadership void to resurrect himself. On January 21, he took his carriage to Daniel Webster's house and banged on his door without warning at

---

* Prior to the Seventeenth Amendment, ratified in April 1913, United States senators were selected by their state's legislatures.

7:00 p.m. The two men sat together for an hour discussing the substance of what a compromise could look like. It was during the course of this conversation that Webster really understood Clay's mortality as the pace of the conversation, which was by all accounts a productive one, seemed to drain his old rival. Nonetheless, Webster left the conversation convinced of Clay's eagerness for one last act before his own expiration.[103]

On Tuesday, January 29, Clay finally got his encore and read a series of resolutions intended to break the deadlock[104] between parties, sections, and competing branches of government. Despite his feeble health, he stood before the Senate, and addressing the president of the Senate offered what he believed to be an all-encompassing collection of proposed bills that would once and for all break the impasse between free and slave states.[105] As recorded in the *Congressional Globe,* Clay's plan "would admit California as a state without any congressional action on slavery, and New Mexico and Deseret (Utah) would be given territorial status on the same bias." As for Texas, it "would relinquish part of its claim to New Mexico in exchange for federal assumption of the Texas public debt." A bone would be thrown to northerners by abolishing the slave trade in the District of Columbia, but with a carve-out to placate the South, whereby slavery would be allowed in the nation's capital "as long as it existed in Maryland or until Maryland and the District would be willing to accept a fully compensated emancipation." The last of Clay's proposals proved to be the most controversial and called for Congress to enact a new and effective fugitive slave law and formally absolve Congress of any jurisdiction over the domestic slave trade.[106]

Congress debated Clay's plan from February 11 until March 12 with more than a dozen speeches in the Senate and another twenty-two speeches delivered in the House. These included memorable speeches from each of the era's political giants. A cadaverous[107] and walking-dead version of John Calhoun, barely able to stand due to his failing health, called for a "constitutional amendment guaranteeing equilibrium"[108] of free and slave states and threatened disunion should the South be forced to lose her honor. Daniel Webster politically immolated himself on the Senate floor with a three-hour speech pandering to compromise and throwing the abolitionists under the bus by expressing a willingness to accept a revised fugitive slave law. William Seward, the influential senator from New York, who everyone knew enjoyed a special relationship with

the president, admonished the suggestion of compromise, and in denouncing the Fugitive Slave Law observed that there is "no authority for
the position that climate[109] prevents slavery anywhere" and went further
to declare that "there is a higher law than the Constitution."[110] Seward's
speech sparked an uproar from both sides—particularly as many thought
he spoke for the president—leaving Taylor fuming.[111] But after he bought
the president a silver currycomb for his favorite horse—Old Whitey—all
was forgiven.[112]

Despite an even split of northern and southern speeches, fewer than
a third advocated compromise.[113] Amidst all of this, President Taylor was
conspicuously silent and had become bitter that his own plan had not
been taken seriously. He resented Clay's crusade for compromise and believed that Clay was mounting a coup against him to reclaim his title as the
leader of the Whig Party. The president's notorious temper kicked in and
it became clear that regardless of the substance, any compromise carrying
Clay's name would meet a firm veto from the chief magistrate.[114]

By March 16, Clay felt the prospects of compromise slipping away.[115]
Grandstanding on both sides only tightened the resolve in both parties
and the president showed no sign of budging on his position. Amidst this
deadlock, John Calhoun died.[116] He spent his final hours frantically trying
to thwart what he believed to be a plan to destroy the South. As his body
gave out, he used his last ounce of mental cognizance to draft a plan for a
divided Union on a few scraps of paper. His plan, which he had previewed
during his March 4 speech, proposed a constitutional amendment calling for the United States to be led by co-presidents—one from the North
and one from the South—and requiring all laws to bear both their signatures.[117] While few, including the hard-line southerners, embraced Calhoun's plan, it offered a frightening premonition of what was to come.

Congress Turns Violent

Recognizing that Congress had to act on how to handle both the new territories and the slavery questions, the Senate formed a special Committee
of Thirteen comprised of six Democrats and six Whigs to be elected[118] by
secret ballot. They were split equally from free states and slave states and
a thirteenth member was to be selected by the twelve to ensure that the
odd number would force them to compromise.[119] They chose Henry Clay,

giving him a lifeline and calling him back for a second encore, where he would use all of his remaining energy to break the deadlock.

The committee needed to act fast as tempers in Congress were reaching a boiling point. The same day as their election, April 17, a routine debate over slavery[120] became so heated that two prominent senators nearly fought to the death. The two combatants, Henry Foote of Mississippi and Thomas Hart Benton of Missouri, loathed each other. Their feud was more than a decade old, replete with character assassinations and physical threats. Earlier that year, Foote had referred to Benton as a "Napoleon of parliamentary strife," while Benton responded by asking if he could "take a cudgel to him."[121] Given the violent tendencies of the 31st Congress, these threats were not to be taken lightly, particularly when they came from Benton, whose claim to fame was that he once engaged Andrew Jackson in a sword-and-pistol brawl that left "Old Hickory" severely wounded.[122]

Whenever Foote was involved in a heated exchange there was always potential for violent escalation. He was both a political force and liability. At forty-six years old, he was in his political prime. It would be easy to infer, as one biographer has, that he was "talkative" and "pugnacious" with a habit of threatening his adversaries.[123] He earned the nickname "Hangman Foote" when he threatened to personally hang another senator if he stepped foot in Mississippi.[124] He was volatile and ready to challenge anyone who stood in his way with a fistfight or a duel, if necessary.[125] During four duels, two of which were against the same opponent, he had been shot three times.[126] He didn't discriminate by party or even his own state, once raising fists against his fellow Mississippi senator Jefferson Davis and brawling with another senator to the point where the two wrestled and rolled down the Senate aisle.[127]

On this particular day, while the insults may have been par for the course, the stakes were higher than ever. After a heated exchange, Benton had heard enough from Foote, jumped from his seat,[128] tossed his chair aside,[129] and charged forward. Foote, likely believing that Benton was armed and dangerous—perhaps because he had challenged him to a duel several days prior—spotted Benton rushing toward him. Terrified of a physical thrashing, he sprang toward the vice president's[130] dais and drew a five-chambered revolver[131] with his right hand and cocked it with his left hand while walking down the main aisle of seats in the Senate chamber.[132]

Several senators tried to prevent the confrontation,[133] but found it near impossible to control the situation. Vice President Fillmore banged his gavel furiously in hope to call the chamber to order, but he had lost control. Senator Foote stamped the floor in a sort of temper tantrum,[134] waving his drawn pistol as multiple senators attempted to restrain him.[135] Benton, who was unarmed, threw open his coat, lunged toward the pistol-wielding senator, and shouted: "I have no pistols! Let him fire: Stand out of the way! Let the assassin fire![136] I scorn to go armed. Only cowards go armed."[137] The Senate chamber was shocked and on edge[138] as the chaos that ensued began to subside. At that moment, it appeared as if one senator might commit murder right there on the floor. Foote quickly realized the implications of what he had done and could offer a mediocre excuse at best, insisting that he drew his gun in self-defense. But Benton, eager to remind everyone who was armed, quipped back, "Nothing of the kind, sir. It is a false imputation. I carry nothing of the kind, and no assassin has a right to draw a pistol on me."[139]

Fillmore quickly accommodated a motion to adjourn.[140] He had miraculously managed to restore order to the chamber—although several senators were to thank for that outcome. Daniel S. Dickinson, the New York senator who would eventually lead the conservative Hunker faction of the Democratic Party, testified that he noticed Foote standing nearly in front of his seat, with the pistol in his hand, the muzzle pointing obliquely toward the floor. The mild-mannered New Yorker stepped from [his] seat, took hold of the barrel of the pistol near the muzzle, and said, "General give this to me," after which the infuriated Foote "turned his eye on me and released it to [him]."[141] With the pistol safely out of Foote's hands, Dickinson uncocked it, and locked it in his own desk. A sigh of relief could be felt throughout the Senate chamber and in an attempt to help everyone move past the incident, Dickinson attempted to shift the focus, asking, "Mr. President, what is the question before the Senate?"[142]

Fearing more violent disturbances, the Committee of Thirteen got to work. After nearly a month of deliberations, they reached their conclusion, which came in the form of an Omnibus Bill, which, the prominent Henry Clay biographer Robert Remini writes,

linked together as one measure the admission of California as a free state, establishment of territorial governments for New Mexico and Utah without the right to legislate on slavery, and adjustment of the boundary of Texas with compensation for relinquishing all claim to any part of New Mexico. The bill also called for a fugitive slave law with two amendments, one requiring slaveholders to produce documentation for their claim of loss and the other providing trial by jury if the alleged fugitive so desired in the state from which he or she had fled. Finally the report recommended the abolition of the slave trade in the District of Columbia.[143]

When the committee unveiled the bill on May 8, the president made it clear he would do everything possible to defeat it. He opposed the bill on substance, but his hatred of Henry Clay enhanced this view.[144] Thus, the president stuck dogmatically to his plan, and in a chapter of Whig history disturbingly reminiscent of the John Tyler years, Taylor found himself isolated within his own party. He lacked sectional support from southerners, who felt he had abandoned their cause, northerners, who still resented the fact that he was a slaveholder, and the pro-compromise bloc from both parties who felt he was the primary impediment to compromise.[145] The completely isolated Taylor became a sad tale of a president, who was most respected as a general and person, but who almost nobody had confidence in as a political leader. Some, like Georgia congressman (and later the Confederacy's first secretary of state) Robert Toombs, believed the president well-intentioned but poorly advised, describing his cabinet as having "brought the Whig party to the brink of ruin," and observing Taylor as "honest and well meaning" but in "very bad hands."[146] Charles S. Morehead, a Whig representative from Kentucky, said, "I have never been able to converse one minute with the President upon politics without his changing the subject."[147] And by May 1850, Webster was openly saying, "The administration is doomed, & the Whig party doomed with it."[148] For Clay, the Taylor nightmare was starting to feel like John Tyler all over again. He complained: "I have never before seen such an Administration. There is very little co-operation or concord between the two ends of the avenue. There is not, I believe, a prominent Whig in either House that has any confidential intercourse with the Executive."[149]

With his prized Omnibus Bill in hand, Clay decided he was done pandering to Taylor and got ready himself for war with the administration. On May 21, he famously proclaimed, "The country . . . was threatened by five gaping wounds, but the president's plan would heal only one of them while leaving the other four to bleed more profusely than ever."[150] Over the coming weeks, Clay's attacks against the president grew in both their frequency and ferocity,[151] culminating in his assertion that the administration "seem[s] utterly regardless of public feeling and opinion, and blindly rushing on their own ruin, if not the ruin of their Country."[152]

Taylor had heard enough. Against advice from his closest friends and confidants, he began to fight back[153] through the administration's media arms, of which *The Republic* was the best known.[154] As Taylor held tightly to his position, the consequences to the Whig Party of having successfully run a completely unknown political quantity became all too clear. The general had led many to believe he would play the role of an aloof executive and allow Congress to pass the laws while he deferentially signed whatever came his way. But instead of a bystander president, Congress found a formidable adversary in President Taylor, who proved to be as stubborn as he was strong-minded.[155] Having shattered their expectations of what was supposed to be high times for their legislative agenda, President Taylor found himself with only a few allies left and his fellow southerners now represented some of his greatest adversaries, some calling for a June convention in Nashville to consider secession[156] and others hinting at impeachment.

As the legislative and executive branches engaged in political warfare, events in Texas and New Mexico threatened to play out with or without a legislative outcome. On May 25, 1850, when delegates from New Mexico created a new state constitution that made slavery illegal,[157] it sparked rumors that President Taylor had used a secret presidential emissary to urge its citizens to seek statehood.[158] Peter H. Bell, the fiery pro-slavery governor of Texas who had been elected on the heels of a campaign promise to fight New Mexico, accused Taylor of trampling over his state's rights and threatening its stability.[159] Some in the Senate accused the president of ordering troops into Santa Fe and went so far as to pass a resolution to investigate.[160] While Taylor insisted that he did not issue such an order, he must have liked the idea of it, since he openly threatened to send troops into New Mexico—declaring that he would lead a regiment himself—should any force from Texas seek to trample on her territory.[161] When Secretary of War George W. Crawford told President Taylor that he would refuse to sign any order that curbed Texas's ability to exert influence over

New Mexico, the commander in chief brushed his protest aside and said he would sign it himself.[162]

The combination of the president's blocking the Omnibus Bill and the prospects of the president sending troops into New Mexico was the last straw, even for those southerners in Congress who had once supported him.[163] On July 3, 1850, Robert Toombs went to scold "Old Zack," bringing along several other southern Whigs as reinforcement, including Alexander Stephens, the southern zealot from Georgia who would eventually become vice president of the Confederate States. The delegation cautioned Taylor that his encouragement of both California and New Mexico statehood, not to mention his adversarial tone toward Texas, could drive southern Whigs out of the party.[164] As White House historian Robert Seale writes, some in the group went as far as declaring "that if California were admitted as a free state, the southern states would band together and send their militias to take New Mexico and declare it a slave territory."[165]

Taylor had spent his professional life fighting for preservation of the Union and did not take such threats lightly. Having confronted the most able-bodied enemies in battle, he was never one to back down in the face of a threat. The mere suggestion that he should sent him into frenzy. He stood from his chair, irate with blood boiling through his face,[166] and proclaimed that "if it becomes necessary . . . I will take command of the Army myself!"[167] The congressmen expected a debate. After all, Taylor was infamously stubborn. But his response was unexpected and was sufficiently explosive to spark a hasty exit for the startled members of Congress. As a professional soldier, Taylor loathed disloyalty to the chain of command and viewed even the insinuation of betrayal to the Union as the ultimate act of treason. Still fuming like a general whose own men had just committed a mutiny, the president chased them down the stairs and threatened to "hang them as high as I hung spies in Mexico, and I will put down any treasonable movement with the whole power of the government, if I have to put myself at the head of the army to do it."[168] Three days later, Stephens published an open letter in the *National Intelligencer,* in which he called for impeachment proceedings against the president.[169]

Taylor was predisposed to oppose the Omnibus Bill, but the shameless attempt to bully him into backing down—coupled with Texas's attempt to use force against New Mexico to ensure the spread of slavery—meant his pride was now wrapped up in fighting it. The vote would be close and the possibility of the vice president having to break a tie was not out of the realm of possibility. For his part, Fillmore had shown little interest in national issues and instead focused on how to leverage his position to help his home state of New York, and curry favor with Senators William Seward and Thurlow Weed, who in addition to being trusted presidential advisors were also the co-emperors of the state.[170] But that dream never became a reality. Instead, the two New York power brokers left him without any ability to get his friends appointed to even the lowliest of positions.[171] Part of this was political. Taylor's inner circle wanted to thwart any northern challenge to his renomination in 1852 while at the same time creating an opening for Seward to succeed him in 1856.[172]

By November 1849, Fillmore had reached the height of his frustration. In what must have seemed like a degrading form of high-level whining, he went to see President Taylor and expressed his frustration that the administration's appointments had diminished his influence in New York. During the ninety-minute[173] interview, Fillmore reminded the president that he "had been a loyal supporter, but he felt badly mistreated." Fillmore asked rather shamefully if in the future he would be "treated as a friend or foe?" Somewhat unsatisfactorily, the president offered an ambiguous assurance that he "would be given greater consideration in the future."[174] These assurances, however, were mere lip service as the president remained aloof and the rift between Fillmore and his colleagues from New York grew wider.

Shut out of the administration and wounded by his lack of access to patronage, the vice president no longer felt any loyalty toward his boss. Fueled by a sense of bitterness, Fillmore sent a note to Taylor in July in which he warned that should the Omnibus Bill reach a tie in the Senate, he "might" break with the administration and vote in favor.[175] Several months prior, this would have infuriated Taylor, as he abhorred disloyalty; but he had bigger issues to worry about. A major scandal—known as the Galphin Affair*—had erupted involving three members of his cabinet, which threatened to cast a stain of corruption on the entire administration, destroy any leverage the president had in fighting the Omnibus Bill, and even result in impeachment.

---

* The Galphin Affair refers to a long-standing estate settlement that made Secretary of War George Crawford a wealthy man. The scandal eventually forced his resignation.

The whole Galphin Affair was a mess. It didn't matter that it was complicated and hard to follow, something about an Indian trader from Ireland and claims related to his estate in Georgia. The scandal gave Taylor's enemies an opening and they piled on. Democrats and Whigs alike used the incident as an opportunity to win cheap political points and further isolate the president.[176] On July 6 the House of Representatives censured the president by a vote of 91 to 88 and newspapers from both parties called for his impeachment.[177] It seemed inevitable that they would eventually wear the president down, but unexpected events soon changed everything.

Here We Go Again

July 4, 1850, was a blistering hot day even for the already miserable summer heat that D.C. had come to expect. Following the busy morning schedule, the president scarfed down several green apples[178] in an effort to cool off. He then went by carriage[179] in the early afternoon to the day's most anticipated event, which was a dedication ceremony at the site of the future Washington Monument.[180] There he would watch the laying of its cornerstone[181] and the depositing of dust from the tomb of Thaddeus Kosciuszko,[182] a Polish emigrant who became an American Revolution hero and bequeathed his American possessions and assets to fund the education of former slaves.

The ceremony lasted three hours with the heat pounding the president's exposed skin.[183] Taylor returned to the executive mansion badly dehydrated, and this time binge-ate entire bowls of raw cherries, vegetables, and iced milk[184] to try to regain his strength. Such raw foods should not have been consumed under any circumstances, particularly given the terrible sanitary conditions of the nation's capital and the fact that Washington was deemed a high risk for Asiatic cholera.[185] Within hours, he fell ill with symptoms that resembled an acute case of gastroenteritis.[186] At first, it didn't seem alarming,[187] but that evening the president's health took such a turn for the worse that family members summoned Dr. Robert C. Wood from Baltimore. Dr. Thomas Miller, the controversial doctor who ten years prior was accused of bleeding General Harrison to death, eventually joined the mix as well.[188]

By morning, despite an uncomfortable night's[189] sleep, the president appeared to rally. He was still physically weak, but well enough to sign the Clayton-Bulwer Treaty, which designated the future Panama Canal Zone an area of cooperation between the U.S. and England. He also mustered enough strength to accept an invitation to the New York State Fair at Syracuse[190] and to write a letter thanking a Bostonian for two "delicious salmon" which "arrived most opportunely."[191]

But despite the president's apparent recovery, his condition worsened by late afternoon, at which point someone at the White House called yet another doctor, this time an Army surgeon named Dr. Alexander S. Wotherspoon.[192] The practice of utilizing a military physician was relatively new, with President Polk being the first commander in chief to take advantage of the perk.[193] By the time Wotherspoon arrived, Taylor started having bouts of diarrhea, some of it bloody.[194] The physician diagnosed the president's illness as *cholera morbus,* which at the time covered a range of intestinal ailments ranging from diarrhea to dysentery but not related to Asiatic cholera,[195] which was everyone's primary concern. Reflecting the amateurish medical practices of the time, the president's physician undertook a series of reckless procedures, including slicing open a vein and bleeding the president.[196] He also prescribed calomel (a mercuric compound[197]) and opium,[198] which created the appearance of improvement and allowed the doctor to head home for the evening. That same evening, the White House, no longer able to mask the reality of the president's condition, issued a bulletin announcing that the president was gravely ill. It didn't take long for the rumor mill to spin as all of Washington wondered whether a second Whig general turned president would die in office.[199]

As Taylor dozed in and out of sleep—high on opium and still in some degree of discomfort—there was a greater threat to his life than illness. Medical practices of the 1850s were mediocre at best and doctors were belligerently experimental in how they cared for the ailing president. They lacked familiarity with the microbes that cause Salmonella and other foodborne illnesses,[200] which would eventually contribute to infection. In Taylor's case, what caused contamination by Salmonella or some similar microbe is not known with any degree of certainty. As Ross Anderson writes in *Food Safety News,* "if it wasn't in the cherries, then perhaps the water used to wash them. Or the unpasteurized milk. Or the green apples. Or the previous day's lunch. Whatever the source, it probably was aggravated by the hot weather, by Washington's open, fly-infested sewers."[201]

By Sunday, July 7, the reality of the president's condition began to sink in and he confessed to doctors, "In two days I shall be a dead man."[202] The next day, he began deliriously reflecting in the face of death: "I did not expect to encounter what has come to me in this office," he said. "God knows I have tried to do my honest duty. But I have made mistakes, my motives have been misconstrued, and my feelings have been outraged."[203] With the president on his deathbed, the White House struggled to contain the news.[204] That same day, the White House issued a second bulletin to the public: "The President is laboring under a bilious remittent fever, following an attack of serious *cholera morbus*; and is considered by his physicians seriously ill."[205]

It was left to Daniel Webster[206] to deliver the news to his colleagues in the Senate. He arrived just after noon and found his colleague Andrew Pickens Butler busy on the Senate floor lambasting the Taylor White House and defending slavery. Amidst Butler's emotional tirade, Webster frantically waved down the speaker of the house and raised his hand to speak: "I have a sorrowful message to deliver to the senate," he interjected. "A great misfortune threatens this nation, the President of the United States is dying, and may not survive the day."[207]

The president awoke uncomfortably in his bedroom and "was conscious although very weak." He informed the doctor on hand, "You have made a good fight, but you cannot make a stand."[208] By 2:00 p.m. it was clear that Taylor was on a downward spiral without any possibility of recovery.[209] Someone[210] on hand inquired how long Taylor could last. The doctor's answer was honest and grim: "I hope for many years, but I fear not for many hours."[211] In one last attempt to save the president's life, the doctors tried a number of additional faulty methods, but the bleeding and blisters induced by the doctors proved as fruitless as the previous calomel and opium remedies.[212]

By the late evening, a small group had assembled around the president, including his family, the physicians, and Jefferson Davis, who was Zachary Taylor's closest friend. Anticipating Taylor's imminent death, the cabinet and Vice President Fillmore were in another room. Just after ten o'clock that night Taylor raised himself and spoke. "The storm in passing had swept away the trunk[213] . . . I am about to die," he said. "I expect the summons very soon. I have tried to discharge my duties faithfully; I regret nothing, but I am sorry that I am about to leave my friends." As his wife,

Margaret, knelt beside the bed he tried to speak to her, but couldn't muster the strength.[214] He died at 10:35 that evening.[215]

As Taylor took his last breath, the cabinet, which had gathered anxiously in the anteroom since earlier that day, quickly drafted a note informing Fillmore of Taylor's death and addressed him as "President of the United States."[216] It is a testament to the Tyler precedent that they did this without hesitation. Fillmore, who for the past several days had expected the president's death, immediately drafted a message to the cabinet:

> I have no language to express the emotions of my heart. The shock is so sudden and unexpected that I am overwhelmed with grief. I shall avail myself of the earlier moment to communicate this sad intelligence to Congress, and shall appoint a time and place for taking the oath of office prescribed to the President of the United States. You are requested to be present and witness the ceremony.[217]

That Saturday, two days after taking office, Fillmore received an anonymous letter from a concerned citizen suggesting foul play in Taylor's death. Back then, presidents typically opened and read all of their own mail. The writer declared "a most solemn duty owing to my country to acquaint you with the facts which I know for certain, that Zachary Taylor . . . died an unnatural death by poison administered to him by a secular Coadjutor of the Jesuits."[218] The verbal assailant was undoubtedly taking a jab at William Seward, who as governor of New York had cozied up to the New York Catholic leadership. That same day, Fillmore received a second letter, this time from "a rustica ofellus," which pleaded with him to be more cautious than normal, asking: "How did the Union know what Gen'l T. ate at dinner? How easy was it to get into the Prest's House while Prest. was listening to Foote's foolish invidious speech, and poison his food?"[219]

The letters were taken seriously but yielded no credible theories worth investigating further, at least at the time. But according to an August 29, 1881, article in the *New York Times* entitled "Assassination of the Presidents," suspicions that Taylor had been poisoned resurfaced five years later, shortly after Abraham Lincoln's murder. John Armor Bingham, who had been one of a handful of lawyers tasked with prosecuting the Lincoln assassination conspirators and the primary author of the Fourteenth Amendment, took it upon himself to probe the president's death. The article accuses Jefferson Davis of having concocted a plot* to poison Taylor.[220]

But the most thorough of investigations was conducted 144 years after the alleged assassination, when a Florida author named Clara Rising made a claim that Taylor was poisoned with arsenic. Rising had a theory that the president had been murdered in response to his push to bring California into the Union as a free state. After fruitlessly searching for original Taylor hair follicles to test, she convinced the president's descendants to disentomb their ancestor. On June 17, 1991, Taylor's body was exhumed from its elegant mausoleum at the National Cemetery in Louisville.[221] According to reports in the *New York Times* and *Los Angeles Times,* expert doctors were called in from across the country, where "hair, fingernails and bone scrapings from Taylor's body were analyzed for arsenic, which [all the] doctors [agreed] would still be detectable in the samples."[222] Dr. Victor A. McKusick, a medical geneticist at Johns Hopkins University involved in the spectacle, said that it should be "a very simple matter for a coroner's laboratory to determine if any arsenic is in the tissues."[223] Despite the public attention and cost of the exhumation, there were no new findings. Dr. George Nichols, the Kentucky medical examiner, concluded that "President Zachary Taylor was not poisoned by arsenic,"[224] thus burying any suspicion or speculation.

The Compromise of 1850

Millard Fillmore's first major action as president was to clean house. Taylor's cabinet had been among the weakest in history—Whig outliers with little stature—and now it was scandal-ridden. But performance of the cabinet had little to do with Fillmore's decision, which was deeply personal. He resented Taylor's inner circle for shutting him out for the past sixteen months and cutting off his access to patronage. He wanted them all gone. Following a precedent set when Harrison died in office, the members of

---

* Joseph Yannielli, an enterprising doctoral student at Yale University who manages the Yale Slavery and Abolition Portal, conducted what appears to be thorough research into this claim. In a November 22, 2013, post entitled "Assassination of Zachary Taylor," Yannielli "could find no substantial information about his investigation into a conspiracy to murder Zachary Taylor."

the cabinet tendered their resignations, but they were surprised when Fillmore accepted all of them in what many assumed was an act of political revenge. Adding insult, the new president then requested that each stay on for a month until he could appoint their successors.[225] Rather than reject his request altogether, they found it more insulting to say they would agree to stay on, but just for one week. Thus, the government was without cabinet secretaries or a vice president for several months. There was also no president pro tempore from July 9 to 11 and the speaker of the house was too young to be in the line of succession.[226] Of all the accidental presidents throughout history, Fillmore remains the only one to immediately sack his predecessor's entire cabinet—although several, including John Tyler, whose cabinet tried to defy him, Calvin Coolidge, whose cabinet stank with corruption, and Lyndon Johnson, whose cabinet misled him on Vietnam, should have taken this same decisive action.

The president's brash decision met the harsh reality that finding capable men willing to serve him was no easy task. In seeking advisors, he focused his attention on finding men who possessed what he called a "national outlook,"[227] meaning they were capable of rising above sectionalism. But this high standard proved tough to meet and he was without a secretary of war until mid-August and without a secretary of interior until September.[228] The crises facing the nation didn't pause as Fillmore governed without department heads, nor did his decision to embrace compromise.

The new president's policy shift left a string of political casualties. The first were William Seward and Thurlow Weed, who, while not part of Taylor's administration, had wielded massive influence, particularly around patronage. In recognition of the influence he was about to lose, Seward lamented, "Providence has at last led the man of hesitation and double opinions, to the crisis, where decision and singleness are indispensable."[229] Then, there were the Free Soilers and antislavery Whigs who ironically were worse off with a northerner who favored compromise than they were with a southern slaveholder who had no interest in discussing a revised fugitive slave law until California and New Mexico were admitted as free states. The final political blow was to Jefferson Davis, who did not enjoy the intimate relationship with Fillmore that he had with Taylor. Without an executive to contain him, Davis's sectionalism grew.

In contrast, President Taylor's death meant that Henry Clay and his

Committee of Thirteen had lost a formidable adversary,[230] not to mention the raison d'être for the Omnibus Bill. In the weeks following, Clay remarked that the general's passing "will favor the passage of the Compromise bill"[231] and described his "relations to the new Chief ... [as] intimate and confidential."[232] After sixteen months on the sidelines, Clay had been resurrected, once again brought into the inner circle of power and elevated to an informal role as White House liaison to Congress.[233] Passing the Omnibus Bill would still require some finessing—including restoring the principle of popular sovereignty in the territories.[234] Clay, intoxicated by his return to center stage, on July 22 delivered the final speech of his life, speaking for over four hours[235] appealing to "reason, unselfishness, human tolerance, understanding, and, finally, a sense of destiny."[236] He had every reason to believe that the bill would pass.

As Clay charged forward, he was blind to one of the bill's greatest vulnerabilities. The Omnibus Bill was a package created to avoid presidential veto. In many respects, the Omnibus united northerners and southerners who had grown frustrated with Taylor, and the president's rabid opposition to the bill meant that its proponents could appeal to anti-Taylorism. But that obstacle was removed and there was no longer a need for an omnibus bill. Breaking up the Omnibus into separate bills would give senators more flexibility and increase the chances of passage.[237]

The bill's adversaries understood this and launched an assault. On July 31, Jefferson Davis delivered an incendiary speech against the Omnibus Bill. The speech ignited a secret batch of senators who had come out of hiding to oppose the bill. They attacked it with amendments, and by the time they were done[238] all that remained was a provision for a territorial government in Utah to remain without any ban on slavery, which was either designed to placate Clay and his cohorts or insult them, depending on one's interpretation of history. It didn't matter, Clay's grand finale—his brilliantly crafted Omnibus Bill—had become nothing more than a footnote in history; or in the New York Tribune founder Horace Greeley's words, "smashed—wheels, axles and body—nothing left but a single plank termed Utah."[239]

Clay, who had given seventy speeches over six months,[240] was exhausted and in poor health. He lacked either the momentum or the energy to charter a post-Omnibus path. On August 1, he conceded defeat, reluctantly declaring, "I was willing to take the measures united. I am willing now to see them pass separate and distinct."[241] He then took a long overdue vacation—probably more for health than escape—and when he returned in late August he found that the Illinois senator Stephen Douglas had picked up the pieces of the Omnibus Bill and nearly jammed them all through as separate bills. In a private letter to two Illinois friends, Douglas explained his critique of Clay's approach: "By combining the measures into one Bill the Committee united the opponents of each measure instead of securing the friends of each." Douglas took a piecemeal approach, beginning by combining the Texas boundary-debt and New Mexico territory measures into what became known as the "little omnibus," whereby Texas would accept a $10 million payment in exchange for dropping its claim to New Mexico.[242] Then came California entering the Union as a free state, followed by a revised fugitive slave law and a bill to abolish the slave trade in the District of Columbia.

Just as Douglas began to move on his plan and jam these bills through the Senate, Fillmore, still without a cabinet, faced his first great test. Ironically, the test was meant for Zachary Taylor, whom the overzealous Texas governor Peter Bell had written just days before his death. His letter called for the United States to recognize the Texas claims to New Mexico, including Santa Fe, and demanded the president renounce the U.S. Army's active defense of the New Mexico Territory.[243] On August 6, nearly one week after the collapse of the Omnibus, Fillmore shared the communication with Congress and asked them to take action. In his message, Fillmore informed Congress that "it is the duty of the President either to call out the militia or to employ the military and naval force for the United States or to do both in his judgment the exigency for the occasion shall so require. . . . If Texas militia, therefore, march into any one of the other States or into any territory of the United States, there to execute or enforce any law of Texas, they become at that moment trespassers."[244] Based on this view, he pledged to send 750 additional troops to the region,[245] in what may have been his only action as president congruous with his predecessor.

The debate over each of the bills on the Senate floor was as heated as ever, although the finest speeches came from the far flank of the southern bloc. Jefferson Davis declared that "for the first time . . . we are about permanently to destroy the balance of power between the sections." He cautioned that should this happen, it "may lead us to the point at which aggression will assume such a form as will require the minority to decide whether they will sink below the conditions to which they were born, or maintain it by forcible resistance."[246] Despite these ominous—nearly apocalyptic—words, California statehood passed the Senate on August 13 by a sixteen-vote margin. On August 15, the New Mexico bill made it through the Senate with a seventeen-vote margin.[247]

The following week, Fillmore sent a private letter to a friend, dated August 20, 1850, in which he expressed

strong hopes that the several bills which have passed the Senate, may pass the House and that harmony may again be restored to our beloved, but distracted country. This is the height of my ambition. I ask no prolongation of my present term. I occupy the position, by the suffrage of my fellow citizens and the inscrutable will of Heaven. I never sought it. I do not seek its prolongation. But my only desire is to discharge my duty. To act for the good of the whole country; to know nothing but the United States; "One and indivisible," and their prosperity and harmony. Let my friends aid me in accomplishing this, and I ask no more. They may divide the accruing honors among themselves.[248]

A revised fugitive slave law passed the Senate on August 26, although the total vote breakdown is unknown since it was taken by verbal "yays" and "nays."[249] By September 9, President Fillmore was ready to put his pen to work and sign bills on the Texas boundary with New Mexico, California statehood, and Utah Territory.[250] But he couldn't bring himself to sign the revised fugitive slave law. He did not plan to veto it; after all, the bill was just about the only victory the South could claim,[251] but the substance of the bill weighed on his conscience. Fillmore's delay was in part fueled by his struggle with the reality that in signing the bill, he would have a constitutional obligation to enforce it. To begin with, there were more than 150,000 blacks living in the North, most of whom were not fugitive slaves. There were some fugitives in the North, but not in large numbers as southern slave owners had claimed. And, among the fugitive slaves living in the North, most had been there for over a decade,[252] as opposed to yet another faulty suggestion that the North was swarming with recent escapees. There was another problem with the law in that its enforcement also meant fining federal marshals $1,000 if they failed to "use all proper means to diligently" implement the law. State militias as well as the United States Army were required to provide support if called upon.[253] And finally, the incentives outlined in the bill were all wrong. As observed by Paul Finkelman, a biographer of Millard Fillmore, in instances where a judge ruled against the claimant, thus setting the alleged slave free, the judge was entitled to a five-dollar fee. If the judge ruled for the master, he got a ten-dollar fee.[254]

Despite what Fillmore believed a bad bill, he was terrified of southern secession. So while he hesitated on the Fugitive Slave Law, he did nothing to intervene or alter it.[255] The president signed the bill on September 18 and then a few days later tried to balance the equation by signing the bill banning the slave trade in Washington.[256] In the case of the fugitive slave bill, Fillmore's presidency would be consumed with enforcing a bill he felt necessary, but did not personally support. When many years later an autograph seeker asked him to share his opinion on the Fugitive Slave Law, Fillmore wrote,

> Permit me to speak frankly. . . . I am and ever have been opposed to slavery and nothing but a conviction of Constitutional obligation could have induced me to give my sanction to a law for the reduction of fugitive slaves. I knew that when I signed it I signed my political death warrant, and by its execution arranged against myself the most fanatical hostility . . . but that man is not worthy of public confidence, who hesitates to perform his official duty, regardless of all consequences to himself.[257]

The passing of the Compromise of 1850—albeit as a cluster of bills instead of an Omnibus—resulted in massive celebrations throughout the country. Some politicians truly believed the tensions had been resolved. More seasoned politicians were in denial. Daniel Webster, who had joined the cabinet as secretary of state, proclaimed, "I can now sleep at nights. We have gone thro' the most important crisis, which has occurred since the foundation of the Government; & what ever party may prevail, hereafter, the Union stands firm. Faction, Disunion, & the love of mischief are put under, at least, for the present, & I hope for a long time."[258] Henry Clay expressed his relief that "the fact is no longer doubtful that the fires are extinguished and extinguishing daily in the furnaces of the country."[259]

In the nation's capital, celebration ensued. The Marines offered a hundred-gun salute in honor of Utah and California,[260] while the Marine Band paraded in both directions on Pennsylvania Avenue playing "The Star-Spangled Banner," "Yankee Doodle," and "Hail, Columbia."[261] The hotels were decorated with elegant lights,[262] while fireworks lit the night sky.[263] Foote, Cass, Speaker of the House Howell Cobb, Douglas, Houston, Texas senator Thomas Jefferson Rusk, Dickinson, Kentucky congressman Linn Boyd, Webster, and others were serenaded in turn by huge crowds for their roles in averting crisis.[264] They had fun, a little too much fun, according to one next-day account by a naval surgeon in Washington: "This morg. Mr. Foote has diarrhoa from 'fruit' he ate—Douglas has a headache from 'cold' &c. No one is willing to attribute his illness to drinking or frolicking—yet only last evg. all declared it was 'a night on which it was the duty of every patriot to get drunk.' I have never before known so much excitement upon the passage of any law."[265]

===

Zachary Taylor stubbornly fought for his position, even if it meant a conflagration that could lead to civil war. Despite being a southerner, he was prepared to blockade major ports in the South if the southerners subverted the laws. If that didn't work, he would go a step further and send troops into New Mexico to repel an attack from Texas.[266] Had he survived, he would have fought vehemently to oppose the Compromise of 1850 and it is hard to imagine he would not have vetoed at least some portion of it, whether packaged as an omnibus bill or pushed as individual pieces of legislation, particularly the Fugitive Slave Act.[267] Fillmore fought for compromise, but took no principled position on any of its provisions. Never expecting to be president, he was thrust into battle without a plan. After firing his cabinet, he was left without advisors just as he began his administration. He relied on Clay, Douglas, and others to orchestrate a compromise that would stem the threat of secession and even war. He took a backseat to their leadership and would have likely signed almost anything that passed both chambers of Congress.

The real casualty of the Compromise of 1850 was the Whig Party, which would never again occupy the White House, although Abraham Lincoln was a former Whig. Fillmore, who had never sought, nor desired, the presidency, found himself as the only viable candidate to run on a

Whig platform in 1852. No Whig could win the presidency without the support of the southern Whigs, and Fillmore, having supported the revised Fugitive Slave Act, had a southern credential to go with the largely pro-northern compromise. But Fillmore didn't want the nomination, despite having gotten the majority of delegates. He tried, instead, to push his delegates toward Daniel Webster, but they refused. With nowhere else to go, the delegates cast their ballots in favor of Winfield Scott, who secured the nomination for the Whig Party's final appearance in a national election.[268] Thus Scott became the Whig nominee in 1852, who with William Seward's endorsement was guaranteed to lose all support from the southern Whigs. The party was dead and Franklin Pierce—an unremarkable, pro-slavery Democrat—easily won the election in 1852. On January 6, just two months before taking office, Pierce's eleven-year-old son, Benjamin, was killed in a train accident. Thus, Fillmore's presidency began and ended with the White House draped in black mourning cloth. Pierce never recovered from this loss and neither did his wife, who would tragically be referred to as a White House ghost. He was a melancholy president, a sporadically functional alcoholic, who in his one high-profile decision signed the Kansas-Nebraska Act in 1854, which had the effect of repealing the Missouri Compromise, and pushing the country closer to civil war.[269]

That same year, a group of frustrated antislavery Whigs, Free Soilers, and other antislavery political types joined forces to establish the Republican Party. They put up John C. Frémont, senator from California, as their first presidential nominee, and William Dayton, ex-Whig senator from New Jersey, to join him on the ticket in 1856. The Republican duo put up a respectable fight, carrying eleven states—all from the North or Midwest—and 33 percent of the popular vote, but ultimately lost to James Buchanan, a Pennsylvania Democrat with an impressive pedigree that included secretary of state, ambassador to the U.K. and Russia, U.S. senator, and member of the House of Representatives. Despite his extraordinary reputation and experienced résumé, Buchanan struggled to deal with the fault lines that were breaking the country apart and became the eighth president in a row to serve one term or less. It would take another twenty-eight years for a Democrat to win the White House.

By 1860, the Democrats broke across sectional lines and the party split. A rival spinoff called the Southern Democrats organized a convention and nominated John Breckinridge for president. The Republicans nominated

Abraham Lincoln, who despite carrying only 40 percent of the popular vote won election. Even without the split in the Democratic Party, Lincoln probably would have had enough concentrated electoral votes in the North to win, but the breakdown of votes across sectional lines and the low percentage of the popular vote meant that the new president lacked a strong national mandate. Seven states had seceded from the Union and formed the Confederacy by the time Lincoln took the oath of office on March 4, 1861. On April 12, Confederate troops fired on Fort Sumter and the Civil War began.

Abraham Lincoln *expected to lose his bid for reelection in 1864. He wanted Andrew Johnson as his vice president, a war Democrat from a border state and the only southern senator who had remained loyal to the Union.*

Andrew Johnson *was a slave owner and a racist, but he loved the Union. So long as the Confederacy remained intact, he would push for civil rights and harsh punishment of traitors. When the Civil War ended, he helped the South reconstitute and would prove to be the biggest catastrophe of the eight accidental presidents.*

CHAPTER THREE

Lincoln's Choice

A
fter three years of civil war, it seemed entirely possible that there would be no presidential election in 1864. War was at a stalemate and the cloud of uncertainty meant a real chance that the presidential victor would preside over a defeated nation. Eleven states and more than 9.1 million people—including more than 3.5 million slaves—remained behind enemy lines in the Confederate States of America.[1] The Confederate Army had scored a few decisive victories just six months before the election, including the Battle of Cold Harbor, where thousands of Union troops were lost in less than thirty minutes.[2] So uncertain were these times that there were serious conversations about postponing or suspending elections during the crisis. However, President Lincoln insisted and two days after emerging victorious, he responded to a serenade by reflecting on the matter, "We cannot have free government without elections; and if the rebellion would force us to forgo, or postpone a national election, it might fairly claim to have already conquered and ruined us."[3]

As the tide of the war shifted dramatically to the North's victory, it became increasingly clear that November's election would determine who would be responsible for winning the peace. Such a vital moment in American history should have belonged to Abraham Lincoln. Instead, John Wilkes Booth's bullet gave it to Andrew Johnson. The tailor from Tennessee may have had similar upbringing to his deified predecessor—poor with little access to education—but the contrast between the two men could not have been greater. Abraham Lincoln was a northern abolitionist, while Johnson was an unabashed racist who owned at least eight slaves[4] (the last president to do so), which he wouldn't free until more than seven months after the Emancipation Proclamation. Lincoln engineered landmark legislation with the Thirteenth Amendment abolishing slavery, while Johnson opposed almost all civil rights legislation—the Freedmen's Bureau Bill, the Civil Rights Act of 1866, and the Fourteenth Amendment forbidding states from restricting the rights of citizens—and with the exception of slavery, resurrected just about every vestige of the political and economic system that would hold blacks back for more than a century. On his watch, the defeated southern states would enact the Black Codes as the precursor to the Jim Crow laws and elect much of the ex-Confederate leadership, albeit under a Union flag and accompanied by a lackluster loyalty oath. He had more vetoes overridden than any president in history,[5] failed to generate momentum in either party for a run at the presidency in 1868, and distinguished himself as the first president to be impeached—although the law he violated was later deemed unconstitutional.

Given what we know today, it seems irresponsible that Lincoln would have placed such a misguided man a heartbeat from the presidency. Unlike presidents who assumed they would never die, Lincoln was all too aware of his own mortality. He thought about and dreamed of death, including an eerie premonition that he had been murdered just a few days before his assassination.[6] Lincoln's choice, as baffling as it may seem in hindsight, was viewed by his contemporaries as a stroke of political genius. Those contemporaries were seduced by a very different Andrew Johnson, who, transformed by the context of disunion, temporarily shed the southern baggage that would come to influence his approach to Reconstruction. This short-term choice and long-term miscalculation would have devastating consequences.

The Outsider

Abraham Lincoln's election in 1860 sparked a wave of defections to the Confederacy. As Andrew Johnson's southern Senate colleagues committed treason one after another, the freshman senator from Tennessee made a declaration of loyalty that sent shock waves throughout the North and South. Northerners had underestimated Johnson's patriotism and southerners had overestimated his sectionalism. Despite having earned his place in the privileged class, Johnson preferred to stay true to his roots. Rather than trying to emulate the southern aristocracy, he preferred to displace it with more hardworking men such as himself.

This mentality put Johnson at odds with his aristocratic colleagues in Congress. His opposition to an appropriations bill for West Point Academy, for example, drew the ire of Jefferson Davis, who, with a tone that was as patronizing as it was disparaging, asked the chamber, "Can a blacksmith or a tailor construct the bastioned field-works opposite Matamoras? Can any but a trained man do this?" By attacking his class, Johnson believed the Mississippi senator had challenged his honor. In a fuming response mixed with pride in his station, Johnson wasted no time responding, "I am a mechanic [laborer] . . . and when a blow is struck on that class I will resent it. I know we have an illegitimate, swaggering, bastard, scrub aristocracy who assume to know a great deal, but who, when the flowing veil of pretension is torn off from it, is seen to possess neither talents nor information on which one can rear a useful super-structure."[7] At the time, Jefferson Davis could not have imagined that the man he so obstreperously belittled on the Senate floor would one day preside over the death of the Confederacy, reconstruction of the South, and his personal fate.

Johnson owed his success to the Union and would never abandon her. His loyalty never waned; it strengthened as the Civil War persisted. His bold stance as the sole southern loyalist in the Senate was extraordinary. He was exalted as a political hero and earned both the affection and admiration of President Lincoln, who never forgot Johnson's loyalty. He admired his bravery; one might even say he was in awe of the position Johnson took. Despite losing his state when Tennessee seceded, Johnson refused to give up his Senate seat.[8] He inspired Congressman Horace Maynard to follow his example and do the same with his seat in the House of Representatives. Johnson became Lincoln's only friend in the South, and his flamboyant defense of the Union made him one of the embattled president's most important assets. "Show me the man who fires on our flag and I will show you a traitor," Johnson declared in a March 1861 speech.[9] He was already on Lincoln's radar, but that speech offered the faithful Unionist from Tennessee a special place in the president's heart.

Johnson's stance transformed him into a national curiosity overnight. As the sole southern senator to remain loyal to the Union, he became a traitorous demon in the South and grew to mythical proportions in the North. His extemporaneous nature, flamboyant loyalty, propensity to speak his mind, and colorful oratory added to the mystique. Northerners were in awe, while southerners viewed him as a greater enemy than

Lincoln. Johnson's polarization only deepened his resolve. He became the greatest champion of the Union cause and took his place among the radicals who advocated for harsh punishment of traitors and civil rights for blacks.

Lincoln understood the celebrity around Johnson and his tactical value. Johnson became his prop, a political jack-in-the-box that he could parade around the Union. Johnson was a brilliant stumper, perhaps one of the best in the country. His speeches became famous with one *New York Times* reporter describing how "he cut and slashed and tore big wounds, and left something behind to fester and be remembered. His phraseology may be uncouth but his views are easily understood, and he talks strong thoughts and carefully culled facts."[10] The biographer Howard Means describes how "he could lay out a proposition and craft rebuttals and rejoinders while he caught his breath. He had a warehouse of allusions, enough demagoguery to stir the juices, the salt of bitterness to keep things interesting, a healthy disrespect for authority if it ran counter to his own instincts and beliefs, and the stamina to stay at it all day and night if need be."[11]

Johnson was willing to perform just about any task and assume any position, as long as it helped the Union. When Lincoln called on him in 1862 to give up one of the safest seats in the Senate, move to the enemy's country, and assume the role of military governor of Tennessee, he didn't hesitate.[12] The outcome of the war remained uncertain and Johnson would have to accept the position as military governor knowing the threat it posed to his safety. He assumed the risk, defended Nashville, emancipated the slaves, and presided over Tennessee's transition to civilian government and return to the Union.

The biographer Robert Winston put it best:

> As Lincoln contemplated Andrew Johnson during these years of war and persecution he was no doubt amazed and awestruck. How could a human being endure what he endured? Of the public men of Tennessee if not of the South he stood alone. Defying the Secessionists, he had gone into their midst and dared them to do their worst. . . . Alone at the president's request the Greeneville tailor had dared all, suffered all, sacrificed all, for country. A seat in the Senate, he resigned; the chances of capture and certain death, if captured, he underwent. His estate, including eight slaves, was

confiscated and sold; from his wife and children he was separated; disease and death invaded his household.[13]

Had Johnson's career stopped here, he may have been remembered as one of the more extraordinary Americans in history. Throughout the Civil War he became a champion for abolition, civil rights, and the harshest punishment of Confederate leadership. Many mistook him for a Radical Republican. But these positions had nothing to do with a change of heart—he was as racist as ever—but he was such a bleeding-heart Unionist that so long as the country remained at war, he would do anything to break the back of the Confederacy. Abolition, civil rights, and harsh punishment of traitors would certainly achieve this goal and as such sustained his endorsement into his early presidency. When the Civil War ended, Johnson recalibrated. The assassination of Abraham Lincoln had brought a very different man to the helm of power and history would pay a heavy price.

Choosing Johnson

Abraham Lincoln's reelection in 1864 seemed unlikely. At least that's how things looked in the summer of 1863. No president had been reelected since Andrew Jackson more than thirty years before, and Lincoln had more cards stacked against him than any of the fruitless incumbents who had been sent to their political graveyards. He lacked a good military story as the Union was far from being able to claim the upper hand in the war. Small victories for the North were canceled out by similar wins for the South. Radical elements within the Republican Party—led by Congressman Thaddeus Stevens and Senators Charles Sumner and John Frémont—feared Lincoln was positively inclined to show mercy at the end of the war and exploited the lack of military progress as an opportunity to call for his political head. Thurlow Weed, the all-powerful party boss from New York, declared that four years of death and destruction had left northerners tired of fighting and "wild for peace." Weed and other luminaries of the time feared the worst of the war was yet to come and they didn't want to take any chances. In speaking with his good friend and secretary of state William Seward, he made it abundantly clear that he thought Lincoln's reelection was "an impossibility."[14] Henry Jarvis Raymond, who at the time served as chairman of the Republican National Committee, urged Lincoln to make a move for peace,[15] or fear losing the election.

Lincoln understood that he needed a miracle to win. He and his advisors fretted over how to appeal to a broader constituency, especially with the Radical Republican movement gaining steam. Their solution was to establish the National Union Party, which they formed in May 1864 as a way to bring in Democrats[16] who supported the war—or "War Democrats" as they became known.[17] Lincoln and his advisors knew they needed a compelling face, and the incumbent vice president, Hannibal Hamlin, did not fit the bill.[18] Hamlin had added little electoral value to the ticket in 1860.[19] His ideological move toward the Radical Republicans made him potentially toxic for Lincoln.[20] More important, it offered a convenient excuse to drop him from the ticket.[21]

Historians have debated Lincoln's involvement in the twin intrigues of dropping Hamlin from the ticket and choosing his replacement. The evidence suggests that Lincoln set the wheels in motion in early 1864 by dispatching Simon Cameron, the former secretary of war turned Republican senator from Pennsylvania, on a secret mission to Fort Monroe to take the temperature of a popular Union general and War Democrat named Ben Butler. Butler was a strange-looking figure, described as "corpulent, partially bald, and afflicted with a drooping eyelid that gave him the appearance of being cross-eyed." Appearance aside, there are several reasons why Lincoln thought Butler an attractive running mate. He had quite the pedigree, mainly that he was a War Democrat, who had himself served with valor in New Orleans and elsewhere. His charisma and political savvy made him a fan favorite among his colleagues, who were more than willing to overlook widespread rumors of corruption and shady business dealings.[22]

Cameron and Butler were old friends[23] and the former wasted little time getting to the point of his visit. "The President, as you know, intends to be a candidate for re-election," he began.

> As his friends indicate that Mr. Hamlin is no longer to be a candidate for Vice-President, and as he is from New England, the President thinks that his place should be filled by someone from that section; and aside from reasons of personal friendship which would make it pleasant to have you with him, he believes that

being the first prominent Democrat who volunteered for the war, your candidature would add strength to the ticket, especially with the War Democrats, and he hopes that you will allow your friends to co-operate with his to place you in that position.[24]

But Butler had no appetite for the vice presidency. General Ulysses Grant had just entrusted him with important responsibilities in the coming military campaign around Richmond, an opportunity far more appealing than a powerless office.[25] He gave Cameron an answer that must have shocked the president in its hubris:

> Please say to Mr. Lincoln . . . I would not quit the field to be vice-president, even with himself as President, unless he will give me bond with sureties, in the full sum of his four years' salary, that he will die or resign within three months after his inauguration. Ask him what he thinks I have done to deserve the punishment, at forty-six years of age, of being made to sit as presiding officer over the Senate, to listen for four years to debates more or less stupid, in which I can take no part or say a word, nor even be allowed a vote upon any subject which concerns the welfare of the country, except when my enemies might think my vote would injure me in the estimation of the people, and therefore, by some parliamentary trick, make a tie on such question, so I should be compelled to vote; and then at the end of four years (As nowadays no Vice-President is ever elected President) . . . not to be permitted to go on with my profession.[26]

Lincoln accepted Butler's decision and shifted his attention elsewhere. We know that shortly thereafter momentum shifted toward Andrew Johnson, but how exactly that happened and the president's involvement is debated among Lincoln scholars. Was Lincoln pressured to choose Johnson? Did he need, and get, the Border States? Who would he have chosen if he'd had his druthers? Did William Seward have any say in the decision?

Lincoln was not driving the decision or the effort, but he didn't need to. All he needed to do was subtly give a nod. And it appears he did this, setting in motion a chain of events that landed Andrew Johnson on the ticket. Years later in an interview with *Galaxy Magazine*, Gideon Welles, who served as Lincoln's secretary of the navy, recalled how the late president "felt the delicacy of his position, and was therefore careful to avoid the expression of any opinion; but it was known to those who enjoyed his confidence that he appreciated the honesty, integrity, and self-sacrificing patriotism of Andrew Johnson, of Tennessee."[27]

Welles was not alone in this understanding. After Simon Cameron returned from the Butler visit empty-handed, he insists that Lincoln expressed his preference for Johnson as a second option. Alexander McClure, the Pennsylvania newspaper editor who had been instrumental in helping Lincoln get the Republican nomination in 1860,[28] swore at the time and as late as the 1890s that it was the president who had "engineered the coup"[29] over Hamlin. He claimed that, just before the Baltimore convention, the president urged him to round up a number of contemporaries to work for the selection of Johnson.[30] Over the years, several of those contemporaries would corroborate McClure's story. Abram Dittenhoefer, a twenty-something South Carolinian abolitionist and New York political operative for the Republican Party,[31] claimed to have met with Lincoln ten days before the convention and insists that the president made his intention known, writing, "I had known from the President's own lips, at my last interview, that he desired the selection of Andrew Johnson."[32] Ward Lamon, who in addition to being both a Washington, D.C., marshal and Lincoln bodyguard, was among a small circle who could claim an intimate relationship with the president; and he, too, alleged to have been aware of the Johnson plan. Lamon's assertion goes a step further, later claiming to have traveled to the convention with a letter documenting Lincoln's positive inclination toward Johnson and strict instructions to only disclose its contents if absolutely necessary.[33] Also claiming to be in the loop were Jim Lane,[34] the quirky general turned Republican senator from Kansas, and Leonard Swett, a fellow lawyer from Illinois who had been part of the cabal that won Lincoln the nomination in 1860. The circle of those supposedly in the know extended even further to William Stoddard, a former aide who had become a U.S. marshal in Arkansas, and to Solomon Pettis, a Pennsylvanian jurist with a first-class legal mind and snazzy appointment as judge in the Colorado Territory.[35] Pettis would later claim that he called on the president en route to the Baltimore convention, where Lincoln expressed his preference for Johnson.[36]

It was easy to coalesce around Johnson, mainly because nobody else matched his qualities. He was a War Democrat from Tennessee—there weren't many of those lingering around, and no others with his credentials.[37] He had the distinction of being a real-time civilian war hero who had creditably invested in the average man, most notably laborers. He was also popular among working-class voters, particularly Irish Catholics, who appreciated his long-standing denunciation of religious prejudice[38] while governor of Tennessee.[39] All of these groups, particularly when combined with the yeoman Democrats—small-town craftsmen and farmers[40]—formed a very powerful political base that would be desirable for any presidential hopeful.[41] It also helped that he wanted to be vice president. In fact, after championing the Homestead Act* in the Senate, he had hoped to land the Democratic vice presidential nomination in 1852.[42]

For the Lincoln campaign, Johnson on the ticket could also be useful abroad. The Union remained concerned about England and France losing confidence, or worse, lending direct or indirect support to the Confederacy. Johnson would signal an important message to England and France that the Confederacy was fractured, and thus any aid efforts would be a poor investment that would likely leave them on the wrong side of history.[43]

Lincoln's Hidden Hand

Choosing Johnson and making him the vice presidential nominee were two distinct tasks, especially as President Lincoln wished to conceal his hand. Balancing the ticket was one of several pieces in a larger reelection strategy. Lincoln had to figure out how to contain the radical wing of the Republican Party, which was eyeing its own convention and presidential nominee. In response, the Lincoln machine aimed to attract War Democrats by rebranding the Republican Party as the National Union Party. The new "party" was unceremoniously established on May 21, 1864, and gathered for a nominating convention on June 7.

---

* The Homestead Act of 1862 provided 160 acres of publicly owned land to any settler willing to move west, provided they had never taken up arms against the Union and were able to pay a small processing fee. Under the law, ownership would be transferred after a five-year period of continued habitation. May 20, 1862 (Homestead Act), Public Law 37-64 (12 STAT 392), in General Records of the United States Government, 1778–2006 (Series: Enrolled Acts and Resolutions of Congress, 1789–2011), https://catalog.archives.gov/id/299815.

As the new National Union Party prepared for its first convention, the Radical Republicans made the first move. Convening in Cleveland on May 31, they gathered 156[44] "malcontents,"[45] radicals, abolitionists, frustrated office seekers, and Copperheads,[46] * who believed Lincoln was responsible for the slow progress of the war.[47] But while this crew of anti-Lincolnists feared the president could not win the war, they were more concerned about how he would prosecute the peace. Radical Republicans thought Lincoln would adopt a lenient posture toward the Confederates and wanted to marginalize the president's role in architecting Reconstruction. It was Congress, they argued, not the president, who should run point on Reconstruction. More substantively, the Radical Republicans believed the presidency should be limited to a single term,[48] called for a constitutional amendment abolishing slavery (although Lincoln also favored this), and advocated for the seizure of Confederate properties for redistribution to loyal Union soldiers.[49]

The Radical Republicans nominated John Frémont,[50] the California senator who had been the Republicans' debut candidate eight years earlier, for president, and John Cochrane, a decorated Civil War general, for vice president. While their effort proved fruitless in obstructing Lincoln's nomination, it was certainly going to hinder his efforts to win the general election. At the National Union Party convention in Baltimore, Lincoln was unanimously renominated on the first ballot, making him the only incumbent to be renominated since Martin Van Buren won the Democratic nomination in 1840.[51] With Lincoln's nomination shored up, all attention shifted toward the second spot on the ticket, which the president still refused to publicly press.

The evidence suggests that privately Lincoln was anything but indifferent. His subterfuge of neutrality was nonsense, but this was not known to those closest to him.[52] Instead he looked to several principal agents outside his inner circle—many from Pennsylvania, for some reason—to subversively and quietly push the convention toward Johnson.[53] If Lincoln wished to conceal his plan from those closest to him, he succeeded. Several delegates and emissaries attempted to secure Lincoln's preference during the convention, but the president wouldn't budge and instead insisted on his neutrality.[54] Noah Brooks, the gifted journalist who made a name for

---

* Copperhead was the disparaging name given by Republicans to antiwar Democrats.

himself by getting Lincoln to open up, visited the president on the eve of the Baltimore convention and failed to secure his preference. Eager to give Brooks something so he wouldn't go away empty-handed, Lincoln offered an elusive statement of "hope that the convention would declare in favor of the constitutional amendment abolishing slavery." He also requested that Brooks keep him apprised of all "the odd bits of gossip" that someone with his savvy might discover.[55]

His own advisors were in the dark. Nobody spent more time with the president than his two young aides, John Nicolay and John Hay, and both were in the dark. Confused delegates, led by Burton Cook, chairman of the Illinois delegation, assumed Hamlin would be renominated[56] and upon learning otherwise turned to Nicolay. Nicolay had no idea, which illustrates the brilliance of Lincoln's plan. If he was clueless, then surely the president must truly have no opinion on the matter? After enough pestering,[57] Nicolay wired Hay to ascertain Lincoln's preference, only to receive word back that the president wished "not to interfere in the nomination even by a confidential suggestion"[58] and that the "Convention must judge for itself."[59]

When it came time for the vote, Simon Cameron moved for Lincoln's and Hamlin's renomination and called for a swift vote by applause rather than balloting.[60] It was an incongruous move by someone who had been surreptitiously read into the Johnson nomination intrigue. Fortunately for the political conspirators, Cameron's motion triggered a verbal avalanche of "No, no!" leading to a kind of political pandemonium.[61] It is conceivable that both Cameron's nomination of Hamlin and the subsequent challenges were staged. This would not have been beyond the scope of what was already plotted. What's clear is that Hamlin lacked robust backing.

Following the Hamlin rebuff, New York made the next move, with Lyman Tremain, a respected jurist and average politician, putting forth Daniel Dickinson's name.[62] This was as much a move for Dickinson as it was an affront to Seward, who unbeknownst to Tremain was working behind the scenes to push for Johnson. William Brownlow of Tennessee[63] was ready with a short speech speculating that Johnson might be the guy. "We have a man down there whom it has been my good luck and bad fortune to fight untiringly and perseveringly for the last twenty-five years," he told the crowd, and paused for a moment of suspense, before proudly revealing that man to be "Andrew Johnson." Shortly after, Cyrus Allen, a delegate from Indiana who in 1860 had tried to thwart Lincoln's nomination at the Republican convention,[64] jumped in to nominate Johnson, who was immediately seconded by William Stone of Iowa, and endorsed with a short speech from Horace Maynard of Tennessee.[65] The bookending of Johnson's nomination with two supportive delegates from his home state—in this case Maynard and William Brownlow—was in and of itself an endorsement of Johnson. After all, there had been much debate about whether states that had seceded from the Union should be allowed to seat delegates and vote.[66]

Johnson won the nomination after just a few ballots.[67] Lincoln would have been pleased, except he seemed to be last to hear the news. A telegram was delivered to the White House on June 8, but the message had been sent to his office while he ate in another room.[68] He never saw the telegram or encountered the messenger, so after lunch he went over to the War Department to await word. The telegraph clerk handed him a telegram with the news that Andrew Johnson received the vice presidential nomination, assuming that the president was already aware of his own good fortune. Somewhat shocked, Lincoln proclaimed, "What! Do they nominate a Vice-President before they do a President?" Is that not putting "the cart before the horse?"[69] The poor operator—in what must have been a prized interaction with the president—somewhat skittishly replied that he had transmitted news of Lincoln's nomination several hours earlier while the president was having lunch. "It is all right," replied Lincoln. "I shall probably find it on my return."[70]

Johnson shared Lincoln's view of the seceded states, which was that they never legally left the Union. In formally accepting the vice presidential nomination on July 2, 1864, he observed that "by taking a nominee from one of the rebellious states, the Union party declared its belief that the rebellious states are still in the Union, that their loyal citizens are still citizens of the United States."[71] But he was also cautious to remind Democrats and Republicans alike that "minor considerations and questions of administrative policy should give way to the higher duty *of first preserving Government*, and then there will be time enough to wrangle over the men and measures pertaining to its administration. This is not the hour for strife and division among ourselves."[72] In this regard, he would prove to be a unifying figure, at least temporarily.

Hamlin handled the slight with dignity and respect. He praised the

Tennessean for "his long and varied experience in the counsels of his country" and acknowledged that "his intellectual abilities and heroic patriotism" make him "eminently fit to discharge the duties of President, should he in the providence of God be called to do so." Of particular note was his recognition of Johnson's sacrifice. "With us loyalty costs nothing. Not to be so was simply infamous," he acknowledged. "But to men who lived in the midst of treason and rebellion, and who literally took their lives in their hands, for adhering to their country's flag, there was indeed much merit. Such was the position of Andrew Johnson, faithful he stood among the faithless."[73] This was not gratuitous flattery; he understood that loyalty cost Andrew Johnson everything.[74] Hamlin would not learn until September 1889 that Lincoln had himself made the choice of Andrew Johnson in 1864. "Undoubtedly Lincoln was alarmed about his reelection and had changed his position," Hamlin would write to Judge Pettis, who as a congressman had been part of the scheme. "I was really sorry to be disabused."[75]

Johnson deserved Hamlin's praise. He had been a marked man since he became a loyalist to the North and traitor to the South. So real were the threats that for much of the early 1860s Johnson rarely spoke without placing a revolver on the lectern. He survived multiple assassination plots, in some cases personally fighting off the attackers. It is only by several strokes of luck that he lived long enough to assume his role as vice president.

Assassins nearly killed him in April 1861. During a stop in Lynchburg, Virginia, on his way south to Tennessee, a vicious pack of rabble-rousers boarded his train,[76] during which time three political malcontents led by William Hardwicke felt "the impulse of the moment" and "attempted to pull [Johnson's] nose."[77] Had the Tennessee senator not pulled a pistol on them, effectively dispersing the crowd,[78] they would have likely gone for his life and not just his nose. It was not until October 3, 1864, however, that Johnson would fully appreciate just how serious the incident at Lynchburg had been. In a letter from William Ballagh, who had been one of two men to help rescue him (the second man was called "Kinnier"), Johnson—then military governor of Tennessee—learned that the perpetrators ended up "sho[o]t[ing] Mr. Button, the editor of the Virginian, and regretted very much they did not" have the opportunity to also shoot Johnson.[79]

The Lynchburg incident wasn't the only close call. In other instances,

Johnson lucked out by avoiding the scene of the potential assassination. On June 7, 1861, another group of attackers plotted to kill him as he traveled to Knoxville by train.[80] Fortunately for Johnson, he was tipped off and traveled to Greeneville instead by horse-drawn carriage. In April 1862, in another instance of skirting an assassination plot, Johnson avoided rebel forces that had seized Greeneville and in the process taken control of his house. The rebels arrived with an ominous Confederate decree that gave them broad search-and-seizure powers, which they used to terrify his wife, Eliza, and their youngest son, Andrew "Frank" Johnson, and subsequently order them to leave town within thirty-six hours.[81] Had Johnson gone back to challenge them he would have been a dead man. Keenly aware of this, he would charge that the Confederates "went to my home while my wife was sick; my child, eight years old, consumed with consumption. They turned her and the child into the streets, converted my house, built with my hands, into a hospital and barracks. My servants [presumably his slaves] they confiscated."[82]

"Atlanta Is Ours"

Lincoln expected to lose the election, even with Johnson on the ticket. He wasn't alone in this. The Confederate leadership didn't think he would win either. Jefferson Davis, sure of Lincoln's political demise at the ballot box, felt assured that after Lincoln's defeat the North would be ready to compromise.[83]

Lincoln's poise during this period of political and military uncertainty hid how much he cared about reelection. In public, he could not show himself to be a political animal, but behind closed doors he was obsessed with victory, constantly plotting and fretting over every electoral detail.[84] "You think I don't know I am going to be beaten, but I do, and unless some great change takes place, beaten badly," he confided in another trusted Republican.[85] Lincoln's persistence was not about vanity. He carried a tremendous burden on his shoulders of what would happen should he lose.

In anticipating his loss, on August 23, Lincoln insisted that each member of his cabinet sign a blind memorandum without reading its contents, most likely to avoid a leak. The memo read: "This morning, as for some days past, it seems exceedingly probable that this Administration will not be re-elected. Then it will be my duty to so co-operate with the President elect, as to save the Union between the election and the inauguration; as he will have secured his election on such ground that he cannot possibly save it afterwards."[86]

Neither Lincoln nor Johnson did much canvassing. Back then it was unorthodox for candidates to directly take to the campaign trail, let alone during a war. The election of 1864 would be no exception. Lincoln was busy presiding over the war, and for his part, Johnson was still consumed with his position as military governor in Tennessee. He had his work cut out for him and desperately wanted to see a civilian government elected before he took office as vice president.

Johnson's correspondence with Lincoln during the campaign reflected this reality with almost none of it having to do with politics. Instead the two men were all business, focusing their correspondence on appointments,[87] requests to commute sentences,[88] and battle updates on the Tennessee front. By fall, things began to change and the reelection committee pleaded with Johnson to take the stump in the Midwest. He was less than enthusiastic about the idea, but the campaign persisted in its requests. In a letter from James Bingham, chair of the campaign, sent September 16, 1864, he writes, "There is a great battle to be fought there, and soon too.... If you would go to Indiana immediately, and make one of your strong speeches, have it reported, and sent to the Committee here without delay, *they would have it printed and spread broad cast all over the country.*"[89]

Johnson eventually acquiesced and made the trip in October 1864. To one crowd, he addressed the civil rights issue by asking, "If we are white men, and white men of principle and humanity, ought we not be disposed to give the black man a chance?"[90] But despite the campaign's grand plan for wide circulation of Johnson's Indiana speech, there is no record that it was either printed or disseminated.[91]

With the exception of his quasi-compulsory stumping in Indiana, Johnson seems to have spent almost no time thinking about either the campaign or the vice presidency. In reading through his correspondences during the campaign period, the breadth of issues he had to address was daunting. Some, like protection of loyalists from Confederate troops and bandits, were quite serious. He also had an emancipated black population that demanded his attention. In one illuminating appeal to the governor, a concerned citizen begs him to intervene on behalf of freedmen, who were being dangerously exploited by railroad contractors. "The negrous," he wrote, "are totally neglected in a Medicinal point of view, having noone to lok to no medicins at hand, they dye by dozens from shere neglect. . . . I hav known the Negrous to go for days and [e]ven a week without having any rations issued to them."[92]

While the candidates stayed relatively quiet, their supporters were vocal. The summer of 1864 was dominated by interparty fighting between supporters of Lincoln and Johnson on the Union ticket and Frémont and Cochran on the Radical Republican ticket. This was good news for Democrats, who spent the summer exploiting fissures within the Republican Party.[93] Believing they were now running against a fracturing opponent, the Democrats descended on Chicago in late August to nominate General George McClellan. Like the Radical Republicans, they saw the war as a failure, but they also wanted to cut their losses and achieve an immediate end to hostilities[94] through a negotiated peace that would restore the Union.[95] McClellan, in accepting the nomination, suggested that peace could be had before a restoration of the Union, which alienated mainstream Democrats, including many of the troops who would likely cast absentee ballots[96] for the general. His comments came to be viewed by many would-be supporters as treasonous,[97] proving disastrous for the party. Both flanks of the Republican Party—Unionists and Radical Republicans—rejoiced in what one Lincoln campaigner described as the "Chicago abortion,"[98] while beleaguered Democrats prayed for a miracle.

The Democrats were only part of the problem for the Lincoln and Johnson ticket. Radical Republicans had continued to gain momentum throughout the summer. Everything changed on September 3, when General William T. Sherman telegrammed Washington with the news that "Atlanta is ours, and fairly won." Within a day, public opinion about the success of the war dramatically transformed. Within weeks, Lincoln and Johnson's likely victory was all but guaranteed by General Philip Sheridan's subsequent September and October victories in the Shenandoah Valley.[99] Within a month, Radical Republicans lost their raison d'être and Frémont withdrew from the race. One by one, whether they wanted to or not, the Radicals fell in line and took the stump for the Union Party ticket.[100] As Election Day approached, Lincoln's focus shifted from military tactics to setting the terms of peace. It was clear that both the election and the war would be won and, more important, that he would have four more years to focus on the postwar order.

A Drunken Impression

On Election Day, Lincoln and Johnson won a landslide victory, taking every state except for New Jersey, Delaware, and Kentucky.[101] While votes from Johnson's home state of Tennessee would not be counted, he appealed to Democrats throughout the Union, which helped the ticket win by 400,000 votes.[102] Given how fractured the nation was and the fact that Lincoln ran with a Democrat, there is probably no other vice presidential nominee in history whose addition to the ticket did more to tip the balance than Andrew Johnson. The election was a proper annihilation of the Democratic Party, with the Union Party winning thirty-seven seats in Congress and twelve gubernatorial races, which left the Democrats with just a single governor in the North, Joel Parker in New Jersey.[103] The party also flipped a number of state legislatures, which would choose the next round of senators.[104] Lincoln had the mandate he needed to win the peace and set the terms for Reconstruction.

While Lincoln continued as president, Johnson spent most of his time as vice-president-elect frantically finishing the job in Tennessee. On January 13, he presided over a convention of five hundred delegates from all over the state and achieved a unanimous vote to ratify the abolition of slavery in Tennessee.[105] In addressing the convention the following day, he applauded the delegates: "You sounded the death-knell of negro aristocracy and performed the funeral obsequies of that thing called slavery. You have opened the grave and let the carcass down."[106] The voters still had to endorse the ordinance in a vote scheduled for February 22, but Johnson was confident the strict citizenship oath he imposed on the population would all but guarantee ratification.

Lincoln was thrilled to hear the news and telegraphed Johnson immediately. While grateful for Johnson's hard work on abolition, the president pressed him to come to Washington and share suggestions on who was to replace him as military governor.[107] There is no evidence that Johnson responded to this invitation. He had his own plans, wishing to be replaced by an elected, rather than an appointed, governor and two weeks later issued a proclamation setting the election date[108] for March 4, 1865—the same day as the presidential inauguration.

As inauguration day loomed, Johnson became increasingly anxious about the timing of Tennessee's transition to civilian rule. Just as he had predicted, the voters of Tennessee ratified the abolition ordinance, which meant the state was now ready to come back into the Union. Thrilled by the fulfillment of his own prophecy, Johnson wired Lincoln with good news: "Thank God the tyrant's rod has been broken."[109] After more than two years working to exorcise the rebellious spirit from Tennessee and turn her back to the Union, Johnson wished for nothing more than to be there to personally oversee the transition to a civil government.[110] The only thing standing in his way was the inauguration.

Johnson had been so consumed with Tennessee that he had little time to think about the office he was about to take. As a result, he thought nothing of it when asking Lincoln if he could skip the inauguration. Coincidentally, Johnson had also developed a terrible and persistent fever, which also gave him a legitimate excuse of illness. Johnson understood how missing the inauguration might be perceived, but hoped that he could rely on precedent to convince Lincoln that it didn't matter. He enlisted his friend John Forney to research precedents for vice presidents arriving later than inauguration day.[111] Forney, eager to oblige, sent an inquiry to William Hickey, chief clerk to the secretary of the Senate, to inquire about Johnson taking the oath in Tennessee. To Johnson's satisfaction, the clerk sent back a list of six vice presidents and one president who took post-inauguration oaths. On January 27, 1865, Forney sent a memorandum to Johnson, in which he cited these precedents but cautioned him that "all our friends will be greatly disappointed if you are not in Washington at a very early day. Not alone your own interests but the interests of the country demand your presence. You are in fact the representative of the Democratic element without which neither Abraham Lincoln nor yourself could have been chosen." He predicted "the great Union Party will be a failure, and the Democratic Party will [be] reorganized, either under bad or good auspices" should Johnson choose not to attend.[112]

Despite Forney's caution, Johnson was determined to skip the inauguration and conveyed such to Lincoln, using the precedents cited in Forney's research. In a letter to Lincoln, sent on January 17, 1865, Johnson relayed the schedule for the transition and expressed his preference to remain "where I am until that time, and then hand it all over to the people in their representative character." He concluded with a petulant acknowledgment that he "would rather have the pleasure and honor of turning over the State . . . to the people . . . than be Vice President of the United States."[113]

Johnson misjudged the uniqueness of the situation. Upon receiving the note, Lincoln described any absence as "unsafe" and insisted the vice-president-elect arrive in Washington by inauguration day.[114] With the country still engulfed in civil war, Lincoln needed his southern Democrat present to show a unified face domestically and internationally. Gideon Welles would later recall that Lincoln felt the absence of the vice president "would . . . have an unfortunate influence and construction abroad."[115]

Johnson had two other reasons to be reluctant to attend the inauguration, although neither would sway Lincoln. Physical safety—not the political "safety" that Lincoln highlighted—was always a concern and Johnson understood the risks associated with travel to Washington. Health was the other reason. Johnson's illness was not manufactured or exaggerated. He really was sick, probably with typhoid fever. In the weeks leading up to the inauguration, he had been scheduled to deliver a speech about southern Reconstruction to the American Union Commission, but had to pull out of the event due to illness.[116]

The thought of making a long journey when he really should have been in bed was of deep concern to the vice-president-elect. Nonetheless, he began his journey by railway[117] on February 25 and arrived on March 1. He was joined by his personal physician, General A. C. Gillem, James Fowler, Colonel W. A. Browning, and other close friends.[118] By the time he arrived, recently emancipated blacks had poured into the streets in unprecedented numbers, leading some observers to describe Washington as "the capital of a black nation."[119] For anybody present, it was clear that change was in the air, and for the first time in history black Americans had reason to be optimistic that slavery's days were numbered. The crowds expected imminent news of the Confederacy's collapse and the rejoicing throngs of people wore their best outfits to celebrate in style.[120] So great was the anticipation that the city's taverns and hotels had far exceeded capacity. A bed could not be found in the entire city, yet people kept pouring into town, some resorting to leaning against a wall instead.[121]

Eager to rest after his long journey, Johnson stayed at the Kirkwood House, which was a centrally located hotel at the corner of Tenth Street and Pennsylvania Avenue.[122] Johnson's illness persisted and he was sicker than when he had left Nashville. He foolishly attended a party hosted by

John Forney on the eve of the inauguration. Showing even worse judgment, he consumed several glasses of whiskey[123] that night and either because of the whiskey or the illness found himself in a compromised state the next morning.[124]

Inauguration day, March 4, 1865, was a miserable day. The previous evening's thunderstorm wreaked havoc on the city, which transformed the dirt streets into rivers of mud, horse manure, and trash from the throngs of people who had come to town with nowhere to go.[125] The few carriages willing to brave the weather were challenged by Washington's dilapidated streets and the storm was sufficiently hazardous that women were advised not to brave the vicious conditions.[126] The thunderstorms continued well into the morning, and long after they subsided, dark clouds lingered seemingly close to the ground, creating an ominous portrait in the sky. Despite all of this, there must have been at least twice as many people in attendance relative to Lincoln's first inauguration.[127] The scene was nothing short of extraordinary. "Great crowds of men and women streamed around the Capitol building in most wretched plight," observed the journalist and Lincoln pal Noah Brooks. "The mud in the city of Washington on that day certainly excelled all the other varieties I have ever seen before or since, and the greatest test of feminine heroism—the spoiling of their clothes—redounded amply to the credit of the women who were so bedraggled and drenched on that memorable day."[128] And for the first time ever, there was a photograph taken of the presidential inauguration.[129] That photograph captured Lincoln's future assassin in a shockingly proximate position. "What an excellent chance I had, if I wished, to kill the president on Inauguration day!" Booth bragged to his actor-friend Samuel Knapp Chester. "I was on the stand, as close to him nearly as I am to you."[130]

The day was about to get worse, even as the weather got better. As was the tradition, the vice president's inauguration was to take place first. Andrew Johnson made his way to Hannibal Hamlin's office in the late morning, where he found the outgoing vice president and his son Charles waiting patiently for their pre-inauguration meeting. Johnson may have been dressed in a dignified manner—a new black frock coat, silk vest, and doeskin pants[131]—but his face could hardly conceal the nasty hangover. As the three men engaged in what one could only assume was an awkward conversation, Johnson acknowledged, "I am not fit to be here, and ought not to have left my home, as I was slowly recovering from an attack of typhoid fever. . . . I am now very weak and enervated and today require all the strength I can get, and I wish for some spirits.[132] Can you give me some good brandy?"[133] Hamlin, a committed teetotaler who in one of his first acts as vice president called for a liquor ban in the Senate chambers,[134] did not have any spirits on hand, but graciously sent for some.[135] While it is unlikely that Hamlin, who was still sour over being tossed off the ticket, deliberately aimed to get Johnson drunk, he certainly didn't stop him.

Forney, who had gotten the vice-president-elect drunk the night before, was called upon to fetch some French brandy and described himself as "amazed and aghast" after watching Johnson guzzle down the entire bottle as if he was on the verge of dehydration and had just been handed some water.[136] After knocking back the first glass, he had another just before it was time to head to the ceremony. The small group collectively nudged the vice-president-elect toward the door and all made their way to the Senate chamber. At some point along the way, Johnson thought it a good idea to have one last drink and ran back to down a third glass.[137]

What happened next was a disaster. A red-faced[138] Andrew Johnson—sick with typhoid and three brandy glasses deep—entered the Senate chamber around noon, arm in arm with Hamlin, moments away from the most disgraceful and humiliating start to a vice presidency in American history. He ambled to his seat on the dais with the presiding officer,[139] while Hamlin introduced the vice-president-elect—whom he didn't much like—in a short 250-word[140] speech. After expressing his gratitude to his colleagues for their kindness during his tenure as vice president, Hamlin suppressed whatever bitterness he felt about having been tossed off the ticket and asked: "Is the Vice-President Elect now ready to subscribe the oath of office?"[141] The combination of Hamlin's introduction and Johnson's speech was supposed to be a matter of minutes;[142] instead it turned into a twenty-minute spectacle.

Andrew Johnson sauntered to the podium, where he began to speak extemporaneously[143] in what seemed like an endless diatribe fueled by drunken bitterness toward everyone. The unusually high temperature in the Senate chamber certainly did little to counter the effects of alcohol flowing to his brain.[144] Fortunately for Johnson, the combination of slurred speech and rustling in the visitors' gallery made it almost impossible to understand what he was saying.[145]

At perhaps the most important moment in his career, Johnson was overcome with hubris, condescendingly admonishing all who sat before him as not having earned their place through the same hard work that allowed him to ascend. His speech was absurd, declaring that all who stood before him owed their positions to the people. He then turned to publicly shame each member of Lincoln's cabinet: "I will say to you, Mr. Secretary Seward, and to you, Mr. Secretary Stanton, and to you, Mr. Secretary . . ." At this point Johnson embarrassingly forgot the name of the secretary of the navy, paused his speech, and whispered to Forney, "Who is the Secretary of the Navy?" After being told the name, he continued his harangue, "and to you, Mr. Secretary Welles, I would say, you all derive your power from the people,[146] whose creatures you are!"[147]

Hamlin had seen enough and after seventeen excruciating minutes pulled on Johnson's coattails as both a nudge and gesture for him to stop.[148] Johnson eventually took a moment to pause—presumably to breathe in between tirades—at which point Hamlin hastily administered the oath.[149] Predictably, the oath of office, too, was a disaster. Johnson slapped his hand on the Bible, forcefully held the book up, and proclaimed in the sloppiest of voices, "I kiss this Book in the face of my nation of the United States."[150] And kiss the book he did. According to Benjamin Butler, the Massachusetts senator who would later lead the impeachment effort against Johnson, he "slobbered the Holy book with a drunken kiss."[151]

The spectacle wasn't yet finished. Following the vice presidential oath, it had been tradition for the new vice president to swear in the new senators. Johnson tried to fulfill this duty, but by this time had become so disoriented that he handed the responsibility over to Forney,[152] muttering to the surprised Senate clerk, "Here, you swear them in. You know it better than I do."[153]

The crowd was aghast, particularly as very few of them knew that Johnson had been sick or how much alcohol he had consumed. Beginning with the cabinet, Attorney General James Speed "sat with his eyes closed," turned to his right, and whispered to Gideon Welles, "All this is in wretched bad taste. That man is certainly deranged." Welles, still recovering from Johnson forgetting his name, conveyed his displeasure to Secretary of War Edwin Stanton, whispering, "That man is either drunk or crazy." Stanton, who himself "appeared to be a petrified man," agreed "there is evidently something wrong." Postmaster General William Dennison "was red and white by turns." On the other hand, Secretary of State

William Seward "was as bland and serene as a summer day,"[154] later coming to Johnson's aid by suggesting that his behavior was triggered by what must have been overwhelming "emotion on returning and revisiting the Senate."[155]

The Supreme Court remained stoic—as they are supposed to be—except for Justice Samuel Nelson, whose "lower jaw . . . dropped clean down in blank horror" until a glare from Chief Justice Salmon Chase forced him to "close up his mouth."[156] Henry Wilson, a friendly Union senator from Massachusetts who would later become vice president under Grant, sat with his face flushed. Charles Sumner covered his face with his hands and lowered his head to his desk.[157] In writing to his wife, Zachariah Chandler, the Republican senator from Michigan, declared that he "was never so mortified in [his] life" and that had he "been able to find a hole" he "would have dropped through it out of sight."[158]

Lincoln, like everyone else, was visibly displeased. He closed his eyes and painstakingly averted his eyes from the humiliating spectacle.[159] Senator John Henderson of Missouri, a close friend of Lincoln's and coauthor of the Thirteenth Amendment, observed that the president, awaiting his own inauguration, sat with his "head dropped in the deepest humiliation," not so much for himself, but on behalf of a man who appeared to be destroying a life's reputation in less than twenty minutes.[160] After recovering from the initial shock of the moment, he bent over and whispered to Henderson, also acting as a marshal for the inauguration, "Do not let Johnson speak outside."[161]

As the inaugural party moved from the Senate chamber to the steps of the Capitol's east portico,[162] it was as if the dark clouds that greeted Andrew Johnson dissipated just in time to inaugurate Abraham Lincoln. The president, with his inebriated vice president by his side, looked for any opportunity to ease the discomfort he had just witnessed. He noticed Frederick Douglass, the famous former slave whom Lincoln called a friend, standing in the crowd next to Mrs. Thomas Dorsey, the wife of another well-known ex-slave. Douglass had been a frequent visitor to the White House and Lincoln proudly pointed him out to Johnson. What happened next is subject to interpretation. As Douglass would later recall in his autobiography, "The first expression which came to [Johnson's] face, and which I think was the true index of his heart, was one of bitter contempt and aversion. Seeing that I observed him, he tried to assume a more-friendly appearance; but it was too late; it was useless to close the door when all within had been seen. His first glance was the frown of the man, the second was the bland and sickly smile of the demagogue." He would describe this exchange of looks as one of those "moments in the lives of most men, when the doors of their souls are open, and unconsciously to themselves, their true characters may be ready by the observant eye." Douglass had drawn his conclusion. Turning to Mrs. Dorsey, he said, "Whatever Andrew Johnson may be, he certainly is no friend of our race."[163]

Perhaps this was the real Andrew Johnson's unveiling, showing himself as a former master unable to conceal his disdain for the former slave.[164] It is also possible that Johnson was just drunk, his surroundings spinning, his nausea kicking in, and his mind not entirely present. Anyone who has ever had too much to drink can imagine how a drunken glance could be mistaken as hateful and angry if the recipient was predisposed to judgment and unaware of the intoxication. Regardless of whether the look was real or just sloppy, that moment was seared in Douglass's mind. "No stronger contrast could well be present between two men than between President Lincoln and vice-president Johnson on this day," he observed. "Mr. Lincoln was like one who was treading the hard and thorny path of duty and self-denial; Mr. Johnson was like one just from a drunken debauch. The face of the one was full of manly humility, although at the topmost height of power and pride, the other was full of pomp and swaggering vanity."[165]

Douglass wasn't the only critic. The press was unforgiving, particularly the Democratic papers that in another context might have been more conciliatory toward Johnson. His speech could be compared to the "spewings of a drunken boor," wrote the *New York World*, which also accused the vice president of defiling the Senate chamber.[166] The *New York Herald* described the speech as "remarkable for its incoherence which brought a blush to the cheek of every senator and official of the government."[167] A columnist for the London *Times* wrote that should anything happen to President Lincoln and Johnson become president, the country would "sink to a lower depth of degradation than was ever reached by any nation since the Roman Emperor made his horse a consul."[168] The pile-on continued with the *Cincinnati Gazette* referring to Johnson as a "national insult and disgrace" and calling him out for his "idiotic babble" in which he "boasted himself as a specimen of the working of American institutions." The paper went further and called for Johnson's resignation at once, presciently noting the nation "cannot afford to keep open the risk of such an alternative in case of the death or disability of the President."[169] The *Philadelphia Age* joined in criticizing Johnson, but took the position that forcing either an apology or resignation "would cast him back among that very lowest class of plebeians from which he boasted, with such untimely and indecorous glee, he had risen."[170]

Most of the pro-Johnson papers tried to downplay rather than deny what had happened. Some simply omitted mention of it, arguing that it wasn't dignified to publish. But *Spirit of the Times*, which was run by a New Yorker named George Wilkes, offered perhaps the most outlandish explanation, suggesting that "Johnson, just before his inauguration drank some liquor, but not enough to have any effect upon him. . . . Poison had been secretly introduced into the liquor, for the purpose of killing him and this was what affected him so strangely."[171]

By the time the vice president sobered up, he seemed to have almost no recollection of what had happened. He began to read the papers, which offered varying accounts, and not surprisingly he was eager to get his hands on what exactly he had said during the drunken tirade. He went straight to the source and reached out to Richard Sutton, the official Senate reporter. In a letter to Sutton, dated March 9, 1865, Johnson describes himself as unwell, "having been confined to my room for some days past." He noted that the *Congressional Globe* had not yet published his remarks and acknowledged that there had been "some criticism." In what must have been a humiliating request, Johnson concluded the letter by asking him "to preserve the original notes . . . retain them in your possession, and . . . bring me an accurate copy of your report of what I said on that occasion."[172] Sutton responded the next day with a promise to "furnish you with the copy as you desire & pay my respects in person. I have the notes and will retain them as you suggest."[173] What Johnson got in return was a copy of his speech, which had been revised and cleansed into a sedate six-minute transcript that could be published.[174]

While many in the press called for Johnson's resignation, there were some in the legislature who wanted to take him down even more forcefully. Charles Sumner called for prompt impeachment. Impeaching him, however, proved difficult with the House not in session. As a recourse,

Sumner assembled a caucus of agreeable Republicans and drafted a resolution that would demand Johnson's resignation. Despite some sympathetic ears in the Senate, most of his colleagues didn't care enough about the vice presidency and Sumner's motion was easily defeated.[175] The press stoked the fire of shame and propagated with exaggerated stories of Johnson being moments away from removal. Even *The Sun,* a Democratic paper positively inclined toward Johnson, admitted, "It still remains to be decided" whether the vice president "has survived the period of his usefulness, or whether his removal . . . may not be necessary to the honor and dignity of our country."[176] Of course, none of these rumors materialized, and by the end the Senate settled for a resolution that banned whiskey in the restaurants of Washington,[177] although it is unclear whether it ever went into action.

While Johnson would never recover from his mistake, Lincoln tried to redeem him. This included rebuffing attempts by his advisors to agitate on the issue of the new vice president's behavior. When Treasury Secretary Hugh McCulloch tried to discuss Johnson's debauchery, the president dismissively responded, "Oh, well don't you bother about Andy Johnson's drinking, he made a bad slip the other day, but I have known Andy a great many years, and he aint no drunkard."[178] When another advisor asked Lincoln what he planned to do about Johnson, the president once again came to his defense: "It has been a severe lesson for Andy, but I do not think he will do it again."[179] During a March 6 interview, Lincoln went a step further by stating, "No man has a right to judge Andy Johnson in any respect who has not suffered as much and done as much for the nation."[180] And Lincoln meant it. In speaking to Johnson shortly after the debacle, the president consoled his number two, reminding him: "The great heart of the American people is too generous to sacrifice a man for one fault." This must have been a tremendous relief to Johnson, who was quick to respond, "Mr. President, it shall be the last."[181]

No vice president in history entered office with a greater cloud of shame hanging over his head than Andrew Johnson. Given these circumstances, it is amazing that he showed his face at all in the coming weeks. But just two days after the inauguration—and free from his hangover—the disgraced vice president made a brief appearance at the Capitol before skipping town to hole up until the special session of Congress ended on March 11.[182] While in seclusion, Johnson appears to have had only one correspondence with Lincoln, in which he asks the president to meet with two Tennesseans on his behalf.[183]

Johnson's return to Washington in March coincided with news that Union troops had taken the Confederate capital at Richmond. Johnson viewed the fall of Richmond as an opportunity to articulate his position on traitors. "It is not the men in the field who are the greatest traitors," he explained. "It is the men who have encouraged them to imperil their lives, while they themselves have remained at home expending their means and exerting all their power to overthrow the government." Those men—the "evil-doers" as he called them—deserved an entirely different fate. With regards to these men, Johnson declared, "I would arrest them; I would try them; I would convict them, and I would hang them." But "death," he felt, "is too easy a punishment . . . treason must be made odious and traitors must be punished and impoverished, their social power broken . . . they must be made to feel the penalty of their crime."[184] As this was Johnson's last speech to be reported in the press before Lincoln's assassination,[185] many would later view it as perhaps the best indication of how Johnson would approach the losing parties in the Civil War.

On April 4, 1865, President Lincoln made his historic visit to Richmond and invited Andrew Johnson. Johnson must have been relieved to receive the invitation, as it was a public reinforcement of the president's conciliatory tone vis-à-vis his inaugural debacle. While Lincoln basked in the glory of the defeated Confederacy—even sitting in Jefferson Davis's office chair—Johnson was stunned by the city's desolation. Wherever he looked, the once vibrant city had been reduced to rubble. The torched fields were arid and the remaining livestock now roamed the deserted city like emaciated hyenas in search of food. It was a horrid scene. As a southerner, this experience likely had a significant impact on the vice president, who had a voracious appetite to extend the harshest punishments the law would allow.[186] Instead, he returned from Richmond with a degree of empathy and shock in how much southerners had suffered already.

Johnson would give one final speech as vice president, although it was not reported in the press. In a speech in front of the Patent Office, he reiterated his belief that treason should be punished in the harshest terms. When a reporter urged there be no hanging, Johnson quipped back, "A very good way to disfranchise them is to break their necks!"[187] In this same speech, Johnson also expressed his desire to enfranchise "negroes" who were "very intelligent" or fought for the Union,[188] yet another data point that would later be used in anticipation of Johnson's Reconstruction policies.

As Lincoln contemplated what to do next, skeptical Radical Republicans began reacting to fears that the president would not go far enough in punishing traitors and enfranchising blacks. In contrast, the disgraced vice president seemed to be the greatest champion of both causes, but on the heels of his drunken display nobody took him seriously as a man of influence even with Lincoln's support. As we know from history, both assumptions would prove incorrect.

Andrew Johnson would see Abraham Lincoln one final time, making a visit to the White House on Good Friday, April 14, 1865. In their brief meeting, Johnson pleaded with Lincoln to take a hard line on traitors and resist any inclination toward leniency.[189] The vice president's plea fell on deaf ears and Lincoln quickly moved on to other business and his social plans for the evening, which involved a trip to Ford's Theatre with his wife, Mary.

Assassination and Transition

As President and Mrs. Lincoln headed to Ford's Theatre, the first lady would later say of her husband, "I never saw him so supremely cheerful—his manner was even playful." So surprised was she by his jubilant mood that she remarked, "Dear Husband, you almost startle me by your great cheerfulness." "And well I may feel so, Mary," Lincoln replied. "I consider this day, the war, has come to a close. . . . We must both, be more cheerful in the future—between the war & the loss of our darling Willie*—we have both, been very miserable."[190]

What happened next is widely known history. Booth shot Lincoln in the head, jumped off the balcony onto the stage, yelled *"sic semper tyranus,"* Latin for "thus always to tyrants," and fled the scene. That same evening Booth's co-conspirator, Lewis Powell, invaded William Seward's home and stabbed him repeatedly while he lay in bed. As part of the massive conspiracy, Booth and his co-conspirators also planned to kill Andrew Johnson.

---

* William "Willie" Wallace Lincoln, the third son of Abraham and Mary Todd Lincoln, died of typhoid fever on February 20, 1862. He was eleven years old.

Earlier that day, Booth ventured to the Kirkwood House, where Andrew Johnson lived in an unguarded room (suite 68), since there was no vice presidential residence at the time and he had not purchased a home.[191] Booth wasn't interested in seeing Johnson, but he did want to inquire about his whereabouts. He asked the front desk clerk for a piece of paper and scribbled a cryptic note to be left for Johnson: "Don't wish to disturb you. Are you at home? J. Wilkes Booth."[192]

The stage had been set. Another of Booth's co-conspirators, George Atzerodt, checked into the Kirkwood House that morning, where he paid for room 126—one floor above Johnson's suite—in all cash.[193] After he panicked and told Booth he didn't want to go through with the plan, the actor threatened him, suggesting that if he tried to weasel his way out of the plan, Booth would make sure he ended up dead.[194] The next day, several items were found in Atzerodt's room that would suggest he had every intention of carrying out the plan: a loaded revolver stuffed below the pillow, along with three boxes of Colt cartridges; a large-bladed Bowie knife hidden under the sheets; and a bankbook indicating a $455 deposit with Ontario Bank of Canada by a Mr. J. Wilkes Booth.[195] Despite the intent, Atzerodt got drunk at a nearby bar instead of murdering the vice president.

Booth's master plan nearly made Lafayette Sabine Foster, the president pro tempore of the Senate, the first "Acting President of the United States." Foster, sixty years old, had quite the pedigree, Ivy League educated with a father who fought in the American Revolution and lineage that could be traced back to the Pilgrims. Like Lincoln he began his career as a devoted Whig, practiced law, and eventually became a Republican. He was also no friend of the Radical Republicans, and felt only the most able and intelligent blacks should be enfranchised.[196]

His tenure as president pro tempore was as long as Lincoln's second term—roughly six weeks. As we recall from the death of William Henry Harrison, the Presidential Succession Act of 1792 was vague about whether the vice president was "president" or "acting president." Ironically, the act was crystal-clear about what happens if both the president and the vice president die in office. According to the law, the president pro tempore—in this case Foster—becomes the "Acting President." The secretary of state, William Seward, would have then been required to organize a special election to be held on the first election day following Lincoln's and Johnson's deaths, which would have been November 7, 1865, followed by the convening of the Electoral College that December. The winner of that special election would then be sworn in on March 4, 1866. Had the assassination attempt on Seward resulted in his death, the duty to organize the special election would have fallen to the assistant secretary of state, which at the time was the position equivalent to today's deputy secretary of state (the number two job). The assistant secretary of state was Frederick Seward, the son of the secretary of state, who was also nearly assassinated that same night defending his father. After Lewis Powell broke into the Seward home, the younger Seward confronted the assassin at the top of the stairs and tried to prevent him from entering his father's bedroom. In response, Powell fired his gun at Frederick's head, but after the gun malfunctioned, he resorted to bludgeoning his skull with the weapon instead. Badly injured after a direct hit, Frederick fell to the floor, where he lay immobile.[197]

Johnson went to sleep on April 14, 1865, having no idea that the man who was supposed to kill him was drinking his sorrows away just down the block. At around 10:00 p.m., Leonard Farwell, the prominent former Wisconsin governor and now examiner at the Patent Office, who had also been at Ford's Theatre that evening, began frantically pounding on the door of Johnson's room, screaming, "Governor Johnson, if you are in the room, I must see you!" Johnson rolled out of bed, turned on the lamp next to his bed, quickly made himself presentable, lit a candle lamp, pulled on his trousers, and came to the door. "Farwell? Is that you?" he asked. "Yes. Let me in!"[198] For a brief moment, Johnson must have been very confused as to why someone from the Patent Office was hysterical and barging into his room in the middle of the night. After slamming the door shut and locking it, Farwell caught his breath and explained that he had been at Ford's Theatre and that President Lincoln had been shot![199] He also relayed the news that Seward had been stabbed and that the vice president's life was almost certainly in danger. Johnson ordered Farwell to find out the condition of both men, and when he returned two hours later, the news was grim. Seward was in critical condition and Lincoln was dying.[200]

Lincoln lay on his deathbed at the Petersen House across the street from the theater with no chance of survival. Everyone knew it. But the physicians wouldn't sit idle and instead made one last effort to save the president. In an act of desperation more than scientific intuition, they stripped off Lincoln's clothes, spread mustard plasters on the front of his body, and covered him with heated blankets.[201] But these attempts were useless and while the president lay dying, nobody with constitutional authority was running the country.

The official communication to Vice President Johnson, written that evening, reveals certainty about the president's fate. In referring to his death, the first sentence of the letter initially read "this [evening]," rather than "last," and ended with "the hour of," leaving the time of death to be filled in by another hand.[202] Both adjustments to the letter appear to have been in Edwin Stanton's hand, which is also important as he jumped the constitutional queue—in a move that is more familiar to us today as an "Al Haig moment" of declaring one is in charge without the constitutional authority—and unofficially placed himself in charge of the country while Lincoln was incapacitated.

Nobody seemed to question Stanton's temporary assertion of authority, not even the vice president. Johnson, Farwell, and an Army major named James O'Beirne[203] made their way from Kirkwood House to the Petersen House, where Johnson encountered the cabinet for the first time since his drunken inaugural.[204] He remained for about thirty minutes, which must have been painfully discomforting,[205] but stood mostly off to the side, until Charles Sumner politely asked him to leave, explaining that his being there agitated Mrs. Lincoln.[206] It seemed not to sink in with anyone in the room that Andrew Johnson was about to become president, not even Johnson, who acknowledged Sumner's request and quietly left. Should Johnson have been in charge at this time? Was that his constitutional obligation? In the context of 1865, it really wasn't clear. Given there was no chance of Lincoln's recovery, it would seem that Johnson should have taken the oath right then and there. By doing so, the powers of the presidency would be vested in him.

Many years later, Johnson would recall the gravity of the situation that lay before him. "It was evident from the first that Booth's shot would prove fatal," he remembered. "I walked the floor all night long, feeling a responsibility greater than I had ever felt before more than one hundred times I said to myself: What course must I pursue, so that the calm and correct historian will say one hundred years from now, 'He pursued the right course'? I knew that I would have to contend against the mad passions of some and self-aggrandizement of others."[207]

Failed Expectations

Abraham Lincoln took his last breath at 7:22 a.m. on April 15, 1865. James Speed and Hugh McCulloch, the attorney general and secretary of the treasury respectively, bolted to Kirkwood House, where they brought Andrew Johnson the official news—signed by every member of the cabinet except the critically injured Seward. "By the death of President Lincoln, the office of President has devolved under the Constitution upon you," the note read. "The emergency of the Government demands that you should immediately qualify, according to the requirements of the Constitution, and enter upon the duties of President of the United States."[208]

At Johnson's request, Chief Justice Salmon Chase administered the oath of office in the parlor room of Kirkwood House around 11:00 a.m. that same day. The room was dark with the shades drawn and a small gas chandelier illuminating the ceremony,[209] which was a small affair, no more than twelve men,[210] including the secretary of the treasury, attorney general, senators from Vermont, New Hampshire, Nevada, Minnesota, and Illinois, and Lincoln's trusted advisor Francis Preston Blair, Sr., and his son Montgomery, whom Lincoln had appointed postmaster general.[211] For all those present (perhaps even Johnson), the moment must have felt particularly uncomfortable given the drunken display from the previous month. McCulloch would later recall, it felt "not entirely relieved of apprehensions" tying back to Johnson's "unfortunate" drunken display from inauguration day, but "hopeful he would prove to be a popular and judicious President."[212] But Johnson's sobriety this time around took the elephant out of the room and he eloquently took the oath. He then respectfully touched his lips to the book at the twenty-first verse of the eleventh chapter of Ezekiel,[213] after which Chief Justice Chase shook his hand and proclaimed, "You are President. May God support, guide and bless you in your administration."[214]

Earlier that day, Johnson realized that he might have to give a small speech and appears to have asked the chief justice to write the initial draft. The chief justice obliged and penned a humble statement, fewer than two hundred words, acknowledging the tragedy that had befallen the nation.[215] Ignoring the chief justice's draft, Johnson went in a completely different direction. He never mentioned Lincoln by name and glossed over the nation's tragedy, simply saying he was "overwhelmed by the announcement of the sad event which so recently occurred."[216] He would later face criticism for this omission and for mentioning himself on eight occasions.[217] As the small audience listened, the real question, however, was whether he would reveal any of his policy inclinations. Johnson was deliberately vague, saying, "As to an indication of any policy which may be pursued by me in the administration of the Government, I have to say, that that must be left for development as the administration progresses. . . . The course which I have taken in the past, in connection with this rebellion, must be regarded as a guarantee of the future."[218] The following day, Chase reminded Johnson what had happened with previous successor presidents and offered words of caution. "John Tyler addressed a *long* exposition to the American People on taking the place of Harrison," he told the new president. "I hope your adm[inistration] will resemble his in nothing except in the fact that you also succeed a President universally beloved & lamented."[219]

Immediately following the ceremony Johnson convened the cabinet and asked each member to stay on.[220] The following morning, Easter Sunday, he convened the cabinet a second time. After arriving thirty minutes late to the meeting, the president was surprised to find the secretary of war not there. Stanton arrived an hour late to the meeting, reflecting a disregard for the president that foreshadowed a political crisis between the two men.[221]

Johnson had every inconvenience imaginable, beginning with three months of homelessness. At the request of Robert Todd Lincoln[222]—the late president's son—Johnson allowed Mary Todd Lincoln to remain in the White House until June 9.[223] Sam Hooper, a republican congressman from Massachusetts and successful businessman, had an extra home at the corner of Fifteenth and H Streets and let Johnson take residence.[224] "My mother and myself are aware of the great inconvenience to which you are subjected by the transaction of business in your present quarters,"[225] Robert Todd would write President Johnson on April 25, "but my mother is so prostrated that I must beg your indulgence. Mother tells me that she cannot possibly be ready to leave here for two and a half weeks."[226]

Mary Todd's refusal to leave the White House meant the mansion was left unsupervised, which was a problem since she let the public come and go as they pleased. Tourists came from all over the country to capitalize on the onetime opportunity to loot the White House. The steward, Thomas

Stackpole, was helpless against a daily routine, which went from morning to evening each day of Mary's stay.[227] The East Room, which had been the temporary resting place for President Lincoln, remained outfitted for the funeral throughout the month of April. When all the other artifacts had been taken, writes the White House historian William Seale, "visitors walked up and down the bleachers and picked the mourning vestments to pieces; crepe, silk rosettes, wilted flowers—whatever could be slipped into a coat or reticule—were fair game."[228] Pieces of the mourning cloth are still found at auctions to this day. The looting became such an embarrassment that Benjamin Brown French, the Commissioner of Public Buildings, had to step in to have "the room restored." But despite his best efforts, "the souvenir hunting continued." When Stackpole finally "took inventory in May," he was shocked to find "no lamps, vases, or other small movables remained."[229] When Mary Todd Lincoln vacated the White House, Johnson refused to move in until "the inventory was a matter of record," lest he be accused of complicity in the missing property or on the hook to pay for it.[230]

Mrs. Lincoln never got over her hostility toward Johnson and she harbored permanent suspicions that he had somehow been involved in her husband's death. "My own intense misery, has been augmented by the same thought—that that miserable inebriate Johnson, had cognizance of my husband's death," she wrote. "Why, was that card of Booth's, found in his box[?]. . . . I have been deeply impressed, with the harrowing thought, that he had an understanding with the conspirators & they, knew their man. . . . As sure, as you & I live, Johnson, had some hand, in all this."[231]

While Mrs. Lincoln's theory was paranoid, she was not alone in her suspicion. Beverley Tucker, the prominent southerner who had once enjoyed the confidence of President Tyler, made similar accusations. After learning that his name was on a list of southerners who would not be granted amnesty, he fled to Canada and sought revenge by issuing an "Address to the People of the United States." He accused Johnson of having "a strong motive to plot the assassination with Booth," but Confederates could have had no reason to want to remove the generous-hearted Lincoln in order to make Johnson president. "Where," asked Tucker, "is the record of *his* humanity, magnanimity and mercy?"[232] As farcical as the rumors seemed, they gained enough traction—particularly within Radical Republican circles—that in January 1867, the House Judiciary Committee allowed testimony on the matter. They found nothing.[233]

Johnson also had to contend with a debilitating illness in May 1865 that nearly claimed his life in his first month as president. Due to his own ascension to the presidency, the vice presidency was vacant and there was still no constitutional mechanism for filling it. Had Johnson died, many constitutional scholars of the day surmised that Lafayette Sabine Foster, who served as president pro tempore of the Senate, would have become an "acting" president until a special presidential election could be scheduled. At the time, Foster was traveling out west, where in addition to his duties as acting vice president and president pro tempore, he was also part of a special committee that had been tasked with assessing the well-being of the Indian tribes, particularly with regard to their treatment by the civil and military authorities of the United States.[234] While preparing to depart from Taos, New Mexico, to Denver, Colorado, a messenger intercepted the group and delivered several telegrams—one from Secretary of State Seward and the other from Secretary of War Stanton—both informing him of Johnson's illness and pressing for his "immediate return to Washington." Foster continued on to Denver, where more telegrams awaited him, this time notifying him of President Johnson's road to recovery, but suggesting he stay in close proximity to a telegraph until the president was restored to health.[235]

All of this had to be an annoying distraction for Johnson, who had enormous issues to deal with. The Civil War would be over within weeks. Lincoln had left no blueprint for Reconstruction, and the new president found himself left to answer two of the biggest questions in American history: How should the Confederate States be treated and what terms would be required to bring them back into the Union? What fate awaited blacks in a post-slavery America and what status would they enjoy? His rhetoric over the previous four years—harsh treatment toward traitors and civil rights for blacks—created certain expectations for how the new president would answer both of these questions. Johnson also had a tactical decision to make regarding Reconstruction. Congress was not in session and he needed to make a determination about whether to move ahead on his own, or call a special session to consider the postwar plan.[236]

Loyalists and rebels alike understood both the significance of the moment and the power that had devolved to Andrew Johnson. Jefferson Davis's reaction was telling. Following the Confederate leader's capture in Macon, Georgia, he was shocked to learn that authorities believed he was connected to the Lincoln assassination conspiracy and that there had been a $100,000 reward posted for his arrest.[237] In his defense, he suggested that his accusers ask Andrew Johnson if he would vouch for Davis's innocence: "He (Johnson), at least, knew that I preferred Lincoln to himself."[238] Lincoln's assassination, he would say, "could not be regarded otherwise than as a great misfortune to the South. [Lincoln] had power over the Northern people, and was without personal malignity toward the people of the South. . . . His successor was without power in the North, and [was] the embodiment of malignity toward the Southern people, perhaps the more so because he had betrayed and deserted them in the hour of their need."[239] On May 4, 1865, Horace H. Lurton, a lawyer and future associate justice on the Supreme Court, wrote a letter to his friend stating, "We anticipate nothing but the most uncompromising hostility from Johnson— we regret Lincoln's death very much as removing one tyrant to give place to a more unprincipaled [sic] one."[240]

But while southerners were dismayed and feared the new president, Radical Republicans—most notably Thaddeus Stevens, Salmon Chase, and Charles Sumner—rejoiced in what they perceived to be one of their own ascending to the presidency. Their policy prescriptions were clear: Full pledge of loyalty from the seceded states, swift justice (prison or hanging) for the most senior figures in the Confederate government, and long-awaited civil and political rights for blacks, which, while obsequiously articulated in terms of moral imperative, was really more about their desire to secure a greater swath of the southern vote for the Republican Party.[241]

Radical Republicans, believing they had a friend in Johnson, smothered the new president. The Committee on the Conduct of the War— dominated by the Radicals—paid him a visit to convey their enthusiasm that the Lincoln chapter of the Republican Party—filled with policy disagreements and perceived obstacles to their agenda—was over. Led by Senator Benjamin Wade from Ohio, they expressed goodwill toward Johnson and his presidency and declared an end to their feud with the administration.[242] Charles Sumner twice called on the president in the early weeks in a display of optimistic brownnosing.

Johnson did nothing to disavow these Radical power brokers of their belief that he was one of them. In an April 21 speech to a visiting Indiana delegation, he insisted "[traitors] must not only be punished, but their social power must be destroyed. If not, they will still maintain an ascendency, and may again become numerous and powerful," adding, "After making treason odious, every Union man and the Government should be remunerated out of the pockets of those who have inflicted this great suffering upon the country."[243] Radical Republicans must have been thrilled to read the transcript of these remarks, especially since this was a clear instance of the new president going on the record to endorse the confiscation of rebel property and subsequent redistribution to Unionists.[244]

In an address to loyal southerners on April 24, Johnson gave the Radical Republicans more reassurance. He noted that "pardoning power should be exercised with caution," and that while "clemency and mercy" should be offered "to the thousands of our countrymen" who "have been deceived or driven into this infernal rebellion," Johnson was adamant about harsh punishment for the leaders and instigators of the crisis.[245] And when, four days later, the internal revenue commissioner, Joseph Lewis, brought almost four hundred fervent Pennsylvanians residing in Washington[246] over to see the president, he offered the same message.[247] The consistency is important as it demonstrated Johnson's view at the time, which was not that of a man pandering to his southern supporters.

Radical Republicans weren't the only political faction to rejoice over Johnson's ascension to power. For northern Democrats, the elevation of Johnson to the presidency gave them hopes of having a politically kindred spirit and ally in the White House. After all, Johnson had been a Democrat and the possibility that one of their own now held the keys to the executive mansion led to an avalanche of party members throwing their unwavering support to the new president.[248]

There was even optimism from many in the black community. Despite Frederick Douglass's inaugural encounter with Johnson, the latter's statements throughout the Civil War had suggested amenability toward the plight of the freedmen. Just a few days into his presidency, Johnson received a letter from John Mercer Langston, who, in addition to being president of the National Equal Rights League, would become the first black congressman in Virginia's history. His letter requested that the president ensure "complete emancipation, and . . . full equality before American law." He acknowledged that the president's "past history . . . gives us full assurance that in your hands our cause shall receive no detriment, and that our liberty and rights will be fully protected and sustained."[249]

The group terrified of a Johnson presidency were the soon to be defeated southern aristocrats, whose fate lay in the hands of someone they knew had spent a lifetime resenting them. It would not take long for them to realize their fears were misplaced and that whether he realized it or not, Johnson had become one of them.

The Real Andrew Johnson

The Civil War officially ended on May 9, 1865, while Congress remained in recess. Johnson, who two months earlier had politically immolated himself, was now in charge of winning the peace, which meant getting Reconstruction right. Lincoln had held a strong belief that Reconstruction policy should be dictated by the president, not by Congress. Johnson shared this view and rather than call a special session, he went ahead with his own policy.

Johnson had a prodigious task ahead of him. Both sides had paid a vicious price over the four years. In the North, the war cost the federal government a hefty $3 billion and that didn't include the cost to states, cities, and towns. The additional financial burdens of a $2.8 billion national debt, rampant inflation, and the world's highest tax rate exacerbated an already grim economic situation. As if this wasn't bad enough, the North also had to deal with the fact that a significant portion of its population had been mobilized for war, nearly three million soldiers and sailors. The casualties were daunting—110,000 combat deaths, 250,000 disease-related deaths, and more than 275,000 wounded. Entire families and communities had been wiped out as they deployed to the same battalions and died on the same battlefields.[250]

The situation in the South was worse. Of the more than 20 percent of white southern men who fought in the war, 240,000 died on the battlefield, while another 260,000 had either been severely wounded or died from disease. The Confederacy saw $2.3 billion evaporate into the war effort, and upon defeat found its infrastructure destroyed, its population impoverished and starving, large swaths of the soldiers crippled, and an entire region psychologically traumatized by what they had seen and experienced. Added to this was the addition of nearly four million emancipated slaves.[251]

In his first postwar act, Johnson issued an executive order, which empowered the existing and loyal state government in Virginia to oversee the state's readmission to the Union. On May 29, he unveiled the first elements of his Reconstruction plan, which included two proclamations, the first of which guaranteed a full pardon and amnesty—along with the return of property—to all but fourteen categories of disloyalists, so long as they were willing to take a loyalty oath.[252] Those disloyal citizens assigned to one of the exempted categories were not permanently cast away, however; they could appeal directly to the president with a special application.[253]

The second proclamation dealt with North Carolina, but was to serve as the model for how to treat the former Confederate states. Johnson used his presidential prerogative to appoint a provisional governor, William Woods Holden, the Raleigh-based *North Carolina Standard* editor[254] who had supported secession. Under Johnson's direction, Holden was instructed to call a convention to reverse any of the 1861 laws associated with North Carolina's secession, ratify the Thirteenth Amendment prohibiting slavery, forgive the state's war debts in full,[255] and establish a new state government capable of reintegrating back into the Union.[256] As for who could participate in the election of delegates to the convention, Johnson took a hard line. Whereas some in his cabinet advocated extending suffrage to "all loyal citizens," Johnson restricted enfranchisement to those men who had both been eligible to vote in 1861 and who had taken the loyalty oath.[257]

Noticeably absent from the North Carolina proclamation was mention of suffrage for blacks. This was the first red flag that Johnson's earlier articulations about civil rights may not have reflected his views. Several members of Johnson's cabinet—particularly Stanton—had urged the president to include black suffrage out of the gate. But Johnson wouldn't budge. Now that the war was over, he no longer needed to champion the concept. The omission of black suffrage in these early proclamations foreshadowed the sentiments that Andrew Johnson had all along, but that had been put aside for the sake of winning the war. Now the war was over and it was time for the real Andrew Johnson to assert himself.

Despite the disappointment by radicals over the exclusion of black suffrage, most were willing to give Johnson the benefit of the doubt, particularly as he had been forward-leaning on the issue throughout the war. It was early, and these initial moves were perceived to be mere experiments, as opposed to doctrine. That summer Johnson enjoyed a grace period, where public opinion was high and the patriotism that had made him so attractive to Lincoln was back on display for all to see.[258] This had less to do with Johnson and more to do with an identity crisis in the Republican Party now that the war was over and desperation on the part of the Democrats to claim the president as one of their own.

By the fall everything had changed and the real Andrew Johnson made himself known. When Congress came back into session in December 1865, the stage was set for a showdown. The questions were clear: Would he favor presidential-driven Reconstruction, or allow Congress to take the lead? Johnson's unwillingness to call a special session of Congress indicated he would try to hold the reins tight. Would he stay true to his rhetoric and hang the ex-Confederate leadership and how far down the chain would he go? Most predicted yes and pretty far down the chain. Would the southern states return to their prewar status and all the rights that came with it? Would they even preserve the right to be states? Probably. Johnson had been clear and consistent in his view that secession was illegal and thus the former Confederate states had never left the Union. It was, however, harder to predict how exclusionary he would be in who could vote or hold public office. How much freedom would emancipated slaves really enjoy? Would this include the vote, equal education, equal treatment in a court of law, and the right to hold public office? In what would prove to be the biggest miscalculation, most—particularly the Radical Republicans—believed that Johnson shared their views. Was the North entitled to reparations?[259] Given that Johnson had talked about confiscating southern property, the assumption here was also that the North would profit.

In the backdrop of all of this was the presidential election of 1868, which while still more than three years away featured prominently in everyone's thinking about Reconstruction. The Radical Republicans had a plan for victory, which included a two-pronged strategy: black suffrage as a path to increasing the Republican voter base; and disfranchising the Confederate leaders, who quite conveniently registered as Democrats.[260] Johnson also had a plan. Politically, he sat at a crossroads between Democrats and Republicans and he believed that he could form a new political union free of radicals from both parties, most notably the Radical Republicans, and attracting the bulk of conservatives and moderates from both sections and parties. To do this, he would use his high office to sing a different tune by opposing civil rights and calling for sectional reconciliation.[261] Both were consistent with his view that the seceded states had no legal authority to leave the Union, meaning his aim was to hasten reintegration, not retard it with extra requirements and obstacles. Since he saw no legal requirement for black suffrage, he determined this was better left for the states to decide after committing to the Union.[262] Thus restoration of the Union became a presidential prerogative at the expense of everything else, including civil rights. What happened next is one of the great missed opportunities in American history.

Civil Rights Squandered

History has been unfair to Johnson as a loyalist, but it has been justifiably critical of him for squandering the postwar Reconstruction and peace. His honeymoon period didn't last long. His first few months were occupied by the apprehension of Booth and his co-conspirators, Lincoln's funeral, and the formal conclusion of the war. He bought time by waiting until after the summer to begin articulating policy, which created sufficient ambiguity for just about every political faction to claim him as its own.

Johnson's policy shifts surprised almost everyone. It may have seemed as if he had a change of heart, but in reality the only thing that changed was context. Previously, secession and Civil War were the immediate concern and Johnson was willing not only to put his own biases aside, but also contradict his own beliefs for the sake of crushing the Confederacy and winning the war. But he was a racist, from his youth to his death. "Negroes have shown less capacity for government than any other race of people," he said in an 1867 address. "No independent government of any form has ever been successful in their hands. On the contrary, wherever they have been left to their own devices, they have shown a constant tendency to relapse into barbarism."[263] So long as the Civil War raged, Johnson tactically embraced civil rights because it would hurt the Confederacy. When the war ended, he had no strategic reason to embrace a platform he fundamentally rejected. His new focus of restoring the Union offered the perfect opportunity to delegate the fate of blacks to the states. Realizing that Johnson was more like-minded than radical, the southern states seized this opening and sought to regain as much of their losses as possible.

The consequences for civil rights were devastating. Beginning in November, Mississippi and South Carolina began enforcing what became known as the "Black Codes," which were the precursor to the Jim Crow laws. The rest of the southern states quickly followed and Johnson showed little interest in intervening. The greater his apathy, the more they pushed. Within a year, the old aristocracy had managed to re-create a bondage that, while not slavery, would hold blacks back for more than a century.

In South Carolina, any black man seeking employment other than as a farmer or a servant first had to obtain a special court permit and cover a hefty annual tax that could run as high as $100.[264] In Mississippi, any blacks who were vagrants or who committed a long list of offenses could be hired out to whites should they fail to pay a stipulated fine.[265] The state defined "vagrant" loosely as any black man who could not provide documentation of home ownership and employment to the white mayor of his city.[266] In one of the more extreme measures, North Carolina passed a law that effectively returned orphaned children to a life of slavery. Even in instances where a child's grandparents or other relatives were alive and desired guardianship, the state mandated that they be returned to the former masters of their families, where treatment was often brutal and worker compensation was not enforced.[267] Kentucky required all contracts to be validated by a white citizen, which guaranteed their legal control over the black population.[268] Other absurd laws included one provision where if a black employee left a white employer without permission, he or she was subject to arrest and a heavy fine. Designed to effectively circumvent the Thirteenth Amendment, the law stated that if that employee was unable to pay the fine, he would be forced to pay in free labor.[269]

Johnson didn't have to take an obstructionist position on civil rights. The defeated South was reluctantly prepared to face and even accept harsh punishment and drastic change. But in order to understand his actions, we need to understand Andrew Johnson. Much of Johnson's personal and professional ambition was fueled by a desire to join the aristocratic class so that he could one day destroy it. Part of joining the aristocratic class meant he needed the notch on his belt of owning slaves. But unlike actual aristocrats with vast plantations, Johnson didn't really need slaves. In his brilliantly researched book *Andrew Johnson and the Negro*, the biographer David Bowen describes how

Johnson acquired the necessary element for membership in the "master class" in 1842, with the purchase of a Negro girl called

"Dolly." Not long after, he bought her half-brother, Sam, who according to contemporary accounts became Johnson's favorite slave.[270] Sam became a trouble-maker about town and even demanded money from Mrs. Johnson at one point. Johnson let him get away with anything, so much so that his daughter—Martha Patterson said that "Sam did not belong to her father but her father belonged to Sam."[271]

By 1860, Sam had become such a nuisance to Johnson's family that his son Charles pleaded with his father in 1860 to get rid of him.[272] For Johnson, Bowen notes, "the servants were procured for what might be best described as cosmetic purposes"—a racist 1850s version of an accessory or a handbag—"since they were clearly not an essential part of the family's economic support."[273] In his life, Johnson came to own as many as eight slaves and held on to them through the early part of the Civil War.[274] His slaves became a source of pride, and he explained on one occasion that he "made them by the industry" of his own hands and boasted to his colleagues, "What I own cost me more labor and toil than some who own thousands, and got them because they were the sons of moneyed people."[275] This was vintage Johnson, always comparing his self-made ascension with the inherited success of the southern aristocratic class.

In the lead-up to and after Johnson's nomination as vice president, there appears to have been no scrutiny over the fact that he was a slave owner, even by the Radical Republicans. This may have been a result of Johnson's flamboyant "abolitionism" during both his time as military governor in Tennessee and the 1864 campaign. In one example, on October 24, a late-night procession of freedmen descended on the steps of the Tennessee capitol and in a sea of emotional fervor called for their military governor.[276]

Johnson emerged like a colonial governor greeting his subjugated people. After explaining that "for certain reasons, which seemed wise to the President, the benefits of that [Emancipation] Proclamation did not extend to you or to your native state," he proudly announced. "I, Andrew Johnson, do hereby proclaim your freedom, full, broad and unconditional, to every man in Tennessee."[277] Naturally, the crowd was ecstatic to hear these words and what was to come. "Negro equality, indeed!" he shouted as loudly as he could. "Looking at this vast crowd of colored people ... I am almost induced to wish that, as in the days of old, a Moses might arise who should lead them safely to their promised land of freedom and happiness." At that point, a man in the crowd screamed, "You are our Moses," which was followed by several others repeating the same sentiment. Perhaps feeling a religious epiphany, Johnson accepted the role and responded, "Well, then . . . humble and unworthy as I am, if no other better shall be found I will indeed be your Moses, and lead you through the Red Sea of war and bondage, to a fairer future of liberty and peace."[278]

Unfortunately, for this crowd and others, Johnson was more a Pharaoh than a Moses. It is easy to understand how so many people failed to see this. Both Lincoln and Johnson forcefully advocated for the eradication of slavery throughout the Civil War. What many failed to realize is the radical differences in their thinking and motivations. Slavery weighed on Lincoln's conscience. He was haunted by its cruelty and reviled the institution. Johnson had no moral objection to slavery. As a slave owner, he never exhibited any guilt either during or after emancipation; instead, his abolitionist fervor was reserved for the southern aristocrats, who represented a class of man he had spent a lifetime resenting. It was never about the plight of men, women, and children who had been held in bondage, nor was there ever any hint of moral obligation.[279] But Johnson did want to win the war and he viewed breaking the institution of slavery as a way to destroy the Confederacy and reunify the country.[280] In speaking about emancipation in the midst of the 1864 campaign, Johnson insisted that it was not "Mr. Lincoln's" proclamation that freed the slaves; "it was the proclamation of Fort Sumter."[281]

As a postwar president, Johnson's views were not tempered by larger objectives. Once unconstrained, he could hardly restrain himself. Perhaps no moment is more revealing than Andrew Johnson's second encounter with Frederick Douglass. On February 7, 1866, Douglass brought a group of fellow freedmen, civil rights activists, and black leaders to the White House to brief President Johnson on the matters discussed at the recent Afro-American convention that had gathered in Washington.[282] His last trip to the White House was for an inaugural ball where Lincoln had to personally intervene to ensure Douglass was allowed into the party. "Until that interview," Douglass notes in his autobiography, "the country was not fully aware of the intentions and policy of President Johnson on the subject of reconstruction, especially in respect of the newly emancipated class of the South."[283]

The meeting could not have gone worse. Johnson allowed the delegation's chair, George Downing, along with Douglass, to make a few opening remarks. Douglass reminded the president that Lincoln had entrusted blacks to fight for the Union and expressed hope that "his successor . . . will favorably regard the placing in our hands the ball with which to save ourselves."[284] Johnson took offense to what he perceived as a lecture from ex-slaves and, according to Douglass, spent the next forty-five minutes offering "what seemed a set speech, and refused to listen to any reply on our part."[285]

"I have owned slaves and bought slaves, but I never sold one," Johnson said defensively. "So far as my connection with slaves has gone, I have been their slave instead of their being mine. Some have even followed me here, while others are occupying and enjoying my property with my consent. For the colored race my means, my time, my all has been periled." Following this tirade of out-of-touch self-pity, Johnson snapped at Douglass, "I do not like to be arraigned by some who can get up handsomely-rounded periods and deal in rhetoric, and talk about the abstract ideas of liberty, who never periled life, liberty, or property."[286]

Douglass attempted to interrupt Johnson several times, but the president continued his diatribe. Instead of acknowledging the plight of the freedmen, Johnson insisted that they had risen from bondage to freedmen as a result of the Civil War. The majority of whites living in the South, he argued, were "forced into the rebellion" and had lost everything.[287] Instead of addressing any of the delegation's concerns, Johnson offered a flippant observation that it would all naturally play out. Douglass offered a final caution to Johnson that such positions would lead him to "enfranchise your enemies and disfranchise your friends."[288]

As the meeting ended and the delegation stood to leave the room, Douglass made a comment that seemed to draw the ire of the president. "The President sends us to the people, and we go to the people," he said, not expecting Johnson to overhear. A somewhat agitated Johnson quickly sniped back, "Yes, sir; I have great faith in the people. I believe they will do what is right."[289] What he said in private was a different story altogether. Recalling the exchange to a *New York World* reporter,[290] a presidential aide who had been in the meeting recalled President Johnson's description of the "darky delegation."[291] Johnson was apparently in a tirade, saying to his confidants, "Those d[amne]d sons of b[itche]s thought they had me in a trap! I know that d[amne]d Douglass; he's just like any nigger, and he would sooner cut a White man's throat as not."[292]

Following the meeting, the delegation regrouped. They reached out to a few congressional friends within the Radical Republican faction and expressed a concern that Johnson would not go along with black suffrage. They gathered again that evening and concluded that Johnson's prepared remarks were most likely designed for easy distribution to the press. Eager to beat him to the punch, they determined that its most famous member—Frederick Douglass—should draft a reply to be published at the same time.[293] We take issue with "your attempt to found a policy opposed to our enfranchisement," Douglass's letter read; particularly "upon the alleged ground of an existing hostility on the part of the former slaves toward the poor white people of the South."[294] He also criticized the president for leaving the door open on colonization*—the movement to "return" freedmen to Africa—and inadequately giving black people the means to protect themselves.

Johnson took a similar view to the Radical Republicans that the Confederate leadership should be harshly punished. As a southerner, it was hard for him to see the physical devastation of the South. Railroads were in shambles, huge swaths of cotton fields had been burned, public buildings were left ramshackle, the colleges and universities would have to be completely rebuilt, the banks had either been forced to close their doors or were on the verge of collapse, business of all kinds had come to a standstill, many of the sprawling plantations were deserted, and much of the land had become overgrown due to lack of care. With an entire generation of husbands and fathers killed on the battlefield, homelessness and white vagrancy reached unprecedented numbers, and with the Confederacy destroyed and the states still not reintegrated, there was no government vehicle to care for them.[295] The South had suffered, but Johnson had to make a choice about how many of her people to punish. Should the old

---

* Founded in 1816, the American Colonization Society claimed James Monroe, Daniel Webster, and Andrew Jackson as founding members.

guard be allowed to return to government, the result would be devastating for civil rights.

It is ironic that Johnson spent his entire life hating southern aristocracy and now they came crawling to him by the thousands, hat in hand, begging for amnesty.[296] In the summer of 1865, Johnson granted close to 5,300 pardons just in Virginia, Alabama, and North Carolina. His willingness to pardon large numbers of southerners from the fourteen exempted categories in his first amnesty proclamation came as a surprise to many. The pardons continued into the fall and with each wave came a greater willingness to offer amnesty. As time passed by and the qualifications for amnesty broadened, the public call for harsh punishment began to evaporate. By October, even the Confederate vice president, Alexander Stephens, who had just been released from his stint at Fort Warren prison in Boston Harbor, found a presidential pardon waiting for him.[297] He would eventually commute Jefferson Davis's sentence and pardon Robert E. Lee in 1868.

The pardons of the Confederate establishment were significant for a couple of reasons. First, they contradicted just about everything that Johnson had said about the Confederate leadership throughout the Civil War. Instead of hanging them, he offered pardons. Second, these men enjoyed enormous popularity and power in the South, even after the war ended. Not surprisingly, many of them ran for national office and won, including Alexander Stephens, who just four months after receiving his pardon was elected to the Senate from Georgia. Third, Johnson's willingness to pardon the southern aristocracy meant he also was willing to return their property, something he had spoken against during the war.

All the states complied with Johnson's insistence that they adopt the Thirteenth Amendment, repeal secession ordinances, and abolish war debts,[298] so from his perspective their integration back into the Union should have been swift and seamless. But his attempt to resurrect the South's old guard at their most vulnerable moment was met with great hostility by radicals in Congress. Johnson expected this. But the benefit of the pardons and land return to the Democrats led moderate Republicans to also oppose seating southern officials. He didn't expect that.[299]

What played out over the next few years was an exhausting and dramatic legislative battle between the president and Congress. Johnson tried to oppose multiple Freedmen's Bureau bills and lost. He then opposed multiple civil rights bills and lost again. He expressed his subtle—and at times not so subtle—disapproval of the Fourteenth Amendment, which passed anyway. Congress curtailed his presidential power with two Military Reconstruction Acts, both of which Johnson vetoed, and both of which Congress overrode. And the Tenure of Office Act, which Johnson vetoed and Congress overrode, prevented the president from firing any Senate-confirmed cabinet members.

The culmination of this battle between branches was the president's impeachment. Radical Republicans had long sought an opportunity to impeach the president, but his firing of Edwin Stanton from the War Department—a clear violation of the Tenure of Office Act—was the smoking gun they needed, although Johnson's defense team argued this was not a violation of such legislation. Johnson narrowly escaped being booted out of office by a single vote in the Senate, which would have provided the constitutionally mandated two-thirds for a conviction. Had he been convicted and removed from office, the presidency would have passed to the president pro tempore, since there was no vice president.

Having anticipated an impeachment trial and a likely conviction, Radical Republicans secured enough votes to install one of their own into the line of succession, Benjamin Wade, as president pro tempore of the Senate on March 4, 1867.[300] It was rumored that during the trial, Radicals attempted to secure additional votes for conviction by drafting a short list of cabinet appointees that Wade would draw on in the event that Johnson was removed from office. Even Seward was allegedly told he could keep his job as secretary of state if he jumped ship and abandoned the president. But the Radicals underestimated Seward's loyalty. "I'll see you damned first," he told them. "The impeachment of the president is the impeachment of his cabinet."[301]

Had Wade become president it likely would have had a significant influence on policy. He had been a staunch abolitionist. "I will never recognize the right of one man to hold his fellow man a slave," he once remarked. "I loathe and abhor the cursed system."[302] When the president and Mrs. Lincoln invited him to a White House gala, he was appalled and sent the invitation back with his agitations scribbled on the side: "Are the President and Mrs. Lincoln aware that there is a civil war? If they are not, Mr. and Mrs. Wade are, and for that reason decline to participate in feasting and dancing."[303] There were many who were concerned about the possibility of Wade's ascension. James Garfield, a conservative Republican congressman from Ohio who would later become president and die in office, panicked at the idea of "a man of violent passions, extreme opinions, and narrow views; a man who has never studied or thought carefully of any subject except slavery, a grossly profane, coarse nature who is surrounded by the worst and most violent elements in the Republican party."[304]

Johnson declined to attend the impeachment trial. When his treasury secretary suggested he follow the proceedings, he shot back: "I am tired of hearing allusions to impeachment. God Almighty knows I will not turn aside from my public duties to attend to these contemptible assaults which are got up to embarrass the Administration!"[305] The question of whether a president could govern while being on trial was a hot topic at the time. Johnson clearly thought he could, a precedent that would prove important when Bill Clinton went on trial more than 130 years later. Charles Sumner and the Radicals thought differently and tried, unsuccessfully, to make the argument that while the president was on trial he was legally disabled. But even Johnson's detractors in Congress thought the conflation of impeachment with disability was a bridge too far.[306]

There were several other issues with presidential succession that arose at this time. First, there was a conflict of interest in having elected officials—particularly Benjamin Wade, who was the president pro tempore of the Senate and part of the Radical machination to remove Johnson[307]—be part of the line of succession when he was part of the very impeachment process that could make him president. After his acquittal, Johnson pushed for a constitutional amendment that would place cabinet officers immediately after the vice president in the line of succession. As Johnson was politically dead from the trial, his proposal generated little momentum. It did, however, become the basis for the Presidential Succession Act of 1886.[308] Second, should a presidential vacancy occur while Congress is in recess—assuming there is no vice president—there could arise a situation where there is neither a president pro tempore of the Senate, nor a speaker of the house to act as president.[309]

———

Andrew Johnson spent his final months in office in disgrace. He squandered a historic opportunity with Reconstruction and sold out the freedmen. He was vanquished by Congress, who overrode fifteen of his twenty-nine vetoes, which was the most in history.[310] And eventually he was impeached, narrowly escaping conviction by one vote. This is the Andrew Johnson that history remembers and that successive generations resented so greatly. Countless books on Abraham Lincoln gloss over Johnson's good years, and skip right to his disastrous presidency. To do so is a disservice to Abraham Lincoln, who should be vindicated for choosing a man as his running mate who in 1864 was a political prize, a patriot, and at least appeared to be a champion for civil rights.

Toward the end of his administration Johnson still held out hope that the Democrats would nominate him for the 1868 presidential election.[311] But it appeared that like another accidental president who came before him, Johnson was a president without a party. When it came time for nomination, delegates at the convention felt he had drifted too far from the party and left it with too many blemishes. He had joined a Republican ticket, which was the political equivalent of bedding the enemy. His cozy appeal to moderates had irked the party's base. And as president he showed limited party favoritism when it came to political patronage.[312] Even if there were some Democrats who wanted to nominate Johnson, these were unforgivable sins. Instead, the party stuck Horatio Seymour from New York with the nomination only to see him decimated by Ulysses S. Grant.

Grant and Johnson loathed each other, a feud that began in the second half of Johnson's presidency, but intensified during the lame-duck period. Johnson believed Grant to be a runaway Radical and political novice who would be easily manipulated by Congress, while Grant rebuked Johnson as a malevolent, vengeful, and impetuous man without principles.[313] To be fair to both of them, these assessments were fairly spot-on. In a rather sophomoric move, Grant refused to allow his children to attend a birthday celebration for Johnson's five grandchildren at the White House.[314] Their feud became even more petty when just a few months later, the general-turned-president-elect refused to attend Johnson's 1869 New Year's Day reception. To add insult to injury, he sent three staff members to represent him, including an Indian named Ely S. Parker.[315]

As plans for the inauguration were under way, Grant made it clear that he would not share a carriage with the outgoing president during the inaugural parade, leaving the honorary marshals scrambling for an alternative, which ended up being two presidential carriages. Johnson, however, rejected this plan and chose to skip the inauguration altogether.[316] This wasn't unprecedented. John Adams had left the capital before dawn to avoid Thomas Jefferson's inaugural and his son, John Quincy Adams, refused to appear with Andrew Jackson. When Grant's entourage passed by the White House en route to the inauguration, they were told that the president was preoccupied with the affairs of state and would not be able to attend.[317] Johnson was holed up in the cabinet room signing some final bills while conversing with friends.[318]

Johnson attempted a life after the presidency. He ran for the Senate in 1869, but narrowly lost when the Tennessee state legislature voted. It was a humiliating defeat and his first since 1837.[319] He would try again in 1872, this time for the House of Representatives, but finished a demeaning third in the voting. Finally, on January 26, 1875, the Tennessee state legislature elected the sixty-two-year-old Andrew Johnson to the Senate on the fifty-fourth ballot, by just a single vote.[320] That March, Vice President Henry Wilson, who seven years earlier had voted to remove Johnson from office, now stood before the ex-president to administer his Senate oath of office.[321] Andrew Johnson died five months later.

James Garfield won the Republican nomination for president without running. He was universally loved and promised to take on the spoils system. He was assassinated just four months into office.

Chester Arthur was a product of the spoils system and represented the worst of machine politics. The nation was horrified by the idea of his rise to the presidency, but he was impacted by Garfield's death and managed to have a respectable presidency.

CHAPTER FOUR

Prince Arthur

On August 10, 1881, President James A. Garfield lay dying, shot the previous month by a deranged office seeker. He survived the initial assassination attempt, but the severity of his wounds and incompetence of the doctors meant that his life hung in limbo. His condition oscillated between what some days seemed like full recovery and others looked like certain death. That Wednesday—twenty-nine days after the shooting—was one of the president's best days. His physician allowed him to sign a document, his only official act during the eighty-day period between being shot and dying.

The document, which had been prepared by the State Department, concerned a minor extradition matter over a Missouri fugitive named Gaiten Derohan.[1] Derohan had escaped from Missouri State Penitentiary in the winter of 1881. The "notorious swindler and bogus priest, with a score of aliases" had been imprisoned for forgery less than a year earlier. He wasn't dangerous or infamous like Billy the Kid, who had also escaped around the same time from a prison in New Mexico, but as a practiced con artist and forger he was smarter than the average fugitive. He sought refuge in Halifax, Canada. Once there, as reported by the press, "the [Halifax] authorities refused to give him up, on the ground that forgery, the crime of which he was convicted, is not an offense for which a prisoner is subject to extradition." The Missouri prison warden, J. R. Willis,[2] sent his son to Halifax as a state agent tasked with returning Derohan to the United States.[3]

Derohan's case was not unusual. Prison escapes were fairly common in the 1880s. Wardens and prison guards had free rein and there was little if any effort to regulate their behavior. Prisoners were stripped naked and forced to wear bags of heavy bricks. Iron cages were used to trap inmates' heads and some prison guards suspended their felons by the ankles and lashed them with leather straps. The Missouri State Penitentiary was among the worst and had gained a reputation for its escapees terrorizing the cities and towns nearby.*

The unique context of an ailing president needing to prove he could perform presidential duties elevated this otherwise inconsequential case to unusual importance. While the document was never seen by the public, news reports at the time describe how Dr. Willard Bliss, Garfield's lead physician, verbally presented the extradition case to the president and urged him to sign it. The weak and dying president said, "I guess so." Having been bedridden for over a month, he asked for pen and ink so he could practice a few attempts to make sure he was up to the task. As reported in the press, after signing his name on a blank piece of paper, "the extradition warrant was laid before him and, notwithstanding the awkwardness of his position, his signature was affixed very credibly. The president fully understood the nature of the document asking for a repetition of the name when the contents were read to him."[4] "Gaiten Derohan, Gaiten Derohan," Dr. Bliss repeated.

War with the Machine

By 1880, most Americans had tired of politics, and more specifically of New York politicians. One of the most powerful political figures in America—William "Boss" Tweed—was exposed for stealing as much as $45 million from New York taxpayers.[5] Tweed's downfall in 1871 elevated New York senator Roscoe Conkling, a close friend of president Ulysses S. Grant, whose exploitation of the spoils system enabled him to build an unrivaled political machine. Conkling's relationship with Grant meant he and the president dealt out patronage to their friends and allies.

Conkling and Grant were chief executive and chairman of this machine. Chester A. Arthur, a relatively unknown lawyer from New York, known more for his socializing and political mingling than his experience, was their chief operating officer. Like Conkling, Arthur was a grand

---

* The problem of escapees persisted into modern times. James Earl Ray escaped from the prison in 1967, where he was serving a twenty-year sentence for armed robbery, and then murdered Martin Luther King, Jr., a year later. See "Missouri State Penitentiary: History," https://www.missouripentours.com/history.

figure, standing six feet two inches with a large body and relatively small head. He was "symmetrically built," according to one colleague, with "a head adorned with silken, wavy hair, always carefully combed." His signature muttonchops—or "whiskers" as some referred to them—gave him an aristocratic aura that was complemented by his "blue, kindly eyes, straight nose, [and] ruddy cheeks."[6] In December 1871, President Grant appointed Arthur as collector of the United States Custom House in New York, which in addition to yielding the highest government salary—grossing more than $50,000 per year and exceeding the president's annual salary—came with thousands of patronage posts to be handed out to political allies of the New York machine. Arthur served an unprecedented two terms and earned the goodwill and loyalty of thousands of men.

By 1876, Grant's status as a general and war hero may have remained intact, but he left office in political disgrace. So widespread was the corruption and abhorrent the scandals that Grant thought it best to do some paid speeches abroad, and let time heal and resurrect his reputation. The succeeding administration under Rutherford Hayes fared only marginally better. He had lost the popular vote and the Electoral College results were disputed, which led a special congressional commission to cut a bipartisan deal that gave Hayes and the Republicans the White House in exchange for an end to Reconstruction.[7] Hayes did restore a sense of dignity to the White House but his obsession with a meritocratic system, not to mention temperance, irked New York party bosses, particularly when he purged the United States Custom House for "corruption within its ranks." His support for civil service reform was noble, but he lacked the mandate to be an effective champion.

Hayes had pledged not to seek a second term, which allowed the party bosses to bide their time until the 1880 election. They anticipated the residue from the Grant administration would have evaporated and created an open pathway for their triumphant return. Grant was still the most famous man in America, even if he was largely seen as a corrupt and failed politician. The party bosses were convinced that he could be returned to the White House for an unprecedented third term. This was a naive miscalculation by out-of-touch machine politicians. Voter tolerance for Republican Party bosses continued to decline. The Democrats, who had not won the presidency since James Buchanan in 1856, were gaining ground. The closeness of the 1876 election had less to do with Hayes's weakness, which was the conclusion of Republican Party bosses, and more to do with real change. By 1877, the Republicans had lost the House of Representatives and their grip on state governments was loosening. It seemed that New England was the only fertile ground for the GOP.[8] With the 1880 election on the horizon, the Republican Party needed a messaging refresh. Its Unionist ideology had become tired and extraneous in the post–Civil War era and voters were far less avid for civil rights than they had been about abolition.[9]

Republicans faced a choice between its two factions—"Stalwarts," who sought to return Ulysses Grant to the White House and sustain the spoils system—and "Half-Breeds," who supported the Maine senator James Blaine and civil service reform. Most understood that the Republican Party was at a crossroads. The presidential election of 1880 was about the future of the party.

The excitement was evident in the crowds throughout the city of Chicago, which was the site of the Republican National Convention. They were at it all day, drinking in local taverns, singing and dancing, and offering themselves as good-paying customers for the influx of prostitutes that had inundated the city.[10] Grant took an early lead, but the subsequent ballots seesawed between him and Blaine and Treasury Secretary John Sherman a distant third. By the thirty-fifth ballot the candidates were deadlocked, leaving the Wisconsin delegation to throw their support to James Garfield, who wasn't even running. He was horrified by such an unexpected outcome. Garfield's presence at the convention was as Sherman's campaign chief. "I challenge the correctness of the announcement," he protested. "The announcement contains votes for me. No man has the right without the consent of the person voted for to announce that person's name and vote for him in this Convention."[11] Garfield's humility did little to halt momentum and on the thirty-sixth ballot it was over. An *Inter-Ocean* reporter on the scene described the surprise nominee as "pale as death" and noticed that he "seemed to be half-unconsciously to receive [*sic*] the congratulations of his friends."[12]

The Grant crowd was furious. Roscoe Conkling was enraged; he and his machine now looked as if their exile might last at least another four years. Conkling had nothing personal against Garfield, but he viewed him as a lightweight. Four years earlier, Democrats had shocked Republicans by winning the popular vote for the first time in nearly a quarter century.

This time around, they planned to run General Winfield Hancock, the hero of Gettysburg who had presided over the execution of four Lincoln assassination conspirators. The Democrats, having lost the last six presidential elections, were now better organized and ready to capitalize on the Republican infighting.

Angry Stalwarts questioned how an unknown like Garfield could defeat such a vigorous candidate. The Stalwarts would prove myopic in their understanding of how formidable a candidate Garfield would prove to be. He was a physical and intellectual presence. George Alfred Towsend—the famous Civil War correspondent who wrote under the pseudonym "Gath"—described him as a "ruddy, brown-bearded man" with a captivating "military face" and piercing "blue eyes" that fit nicely on top of his "erect figure and shoulders." His 225-pound frame, "large back and thighs, and broad chest" gave the impression of a man "evidently bred in the country on a farm."[13] More impressive than his physical presence was Garfield's intellectual rigor and simple beginnings. He was the last president born in a log cabin and rose to become the first in his family to go to college. He proved such a gifted student that he was made an assistant professor during his sophomore year. By twenty-six he became the college president. He was a voracious reader, boasting a personal library of three thousand books,[14] and drawing comparisons to John Quincy Adams.[15]

Garfield hadn't desired the presidency, but once nominated he planned to win. This required unifying the party. The Stalwarts would never be happy about him on the top of the ticket, but he might be able to appease them with one of their own as his running mate. Unfortunately, he was not the only one with this idea and the process of courting a vice president reflected the lack of party unity. From Garfield's perspective, Levi P. Morton, a wealthy New York banker turned congressman, was the safest Stalwart choice. The two had developed a trusting relationship in Congress and Morton was extremely popular in his district.[16] Garfield sent Ohio governor Charles Foster to track Morton down on the convention floor and extend the offer.[17] This plan was naive, since neither Morton, nor any Republican who hoped for a future, would accept the offer without first consulting the party's boss. Conkling had already made his position widely known, lamenting that to run with Garfield would be taken as a personal affront and ominously explaining to his friend and U.S. Attorney Stewart L. Woodford, "I hope no sincere friend of mine will accept it."[18]

Meanwhile, William Dennison, the former postmaster general and defector from the Andrew Johnson administration, took it upon himself as chairman of the Ohio delegation to find Roscoe Conkling on the convention floor and deputize the New York delegation—meaning Conkling—as the vice presidential kingmaker.[19] The problem, however, was that nobody bothered to tell the nominee,[20] who learned by accident in a hotel suite after Dennison boasted that he had just struck the deal of the century.

As if things couldn't get more complicated, there was also Chester Arthur, who unbeknownst to Garfield or the Ohio delegation had already been offered the vice presidential nomination. Learning of the Ohio delegation's open offer, he had expressed interest to his good friend and New York police commissioner Stephen French. French, intrigued by the idea as well as the opportunity to do a favor for New York's second-most-powerful man, relayed Arthur's interest to Tom Murphy, who as a former chief of the United States Custom House himself had a natural affinity for his fellow New Yorker.[21] The two men raced by carriage to the Grand Pacific Hotel, where they lined up New York delegates to vote for Arthur.[22]

Like Morton, Arthur understood Roscoe Conkling all too well and wanted the big man to hear it from him first. But the mini–party boss had a difficult time finding the big party boss, who had left the convention floor to go blow off steam. Eventually Arthur found him stewing in a quiet room, pacing back and forth, silently fuming over Grant's defeat.[23] "I have been hunting everywhere for you, Senator," he said with a mixture of relief and excitement. Conkling simply replied, "Well, sir," as if to suggest he'd deliberately sought solitude at this moment and didn't want to be bothered. Arthur understood Conkling's moods better than anyone and knew that this was a bad time to broach the subject of the vice presidency. He was also cognizant that the matter was time-sensitive. "The Ohio men have offered me the Vice Presidency," Arthur announced. "Well, sir, you should drop it as you would a red-hot shoe from the forge," the senator responded. "I sought you to consult, not—" Conkling didn't let Arthur finish. Despite their closeness, the senator was uninterested in hearing any explanation that would justify such insubordination to the Stalwart master. "What is there to consult about?" he snapped back. "This trickster of Mentor, [Ohio—Garfield's birthplace] will be defeated before the country."

Arthur tried to appeal to Conkling's good senses. "There is something else to be said," he told him. Conkling asked, "What, sir, you think of accepting?" And in that same wounded whimper from earlier in the conversation, Arthur looked Conkling in the eye and said, "The office of vice president is a greater honor than I ever dreamed of attaining. A barren nomination would be a great honor. In a calmer moment you will look at this differently." Shocked by Arthur's audacity, Conkling could think of nothing else to say, but issued a threat, warning that "if you wish for my favor and my respect you will contemptuously decline it." "Senator Conkling," Arthur said, "I shall accept the nomination and I shall carry with me the majority of the delegation," he told him. Conkling stormed out of the room.[24] The formidable Roscoe Conkling had suffered his second defeat of the day, this time from his own mentee.

Whereas most men cowered in the face of threats from Roscoe Conkling, Arthur had a unique ability to withstand them. The two were close. They traveled together, often shared hotel suites, were constantly by each other's side, and there had never been any daylight between them. This was not a real falling-out. Conkling was just in one of his moods and Arthur believed that once he calmed down, the benefits of having a Stalwart on the ticket would become clear.

The Ohio delegation was shocked and some appalled by the idea that Chester Arthur had been offered the nomination. He was a Conkling lackey who had lost his only public sector job as part of the previously mentioned anti-corruption purge. He was a machine politician, mixed up in the scandals of the Grant administration, and there was great concern that he would taint the ticket.[25] The New York delegation rejected all of these criticisms, particularly Tom Murphy, who threatened, "Gentlemen, if that is what you have to say, New York doesn't want the Vice Presidency."[26] It was not difficult to read between the lines. The Stalwart message was clear: Accept Arthur on the ticket, or New York will sit on the sidelines come November. The Ohio delegation caved but nobody bothered to tell Garfield, who was still out there fishing for a vice president. Arthur's nomination moved forward on a single ballot.

For Garfield it was painful to have Arthur on the ticket. Garfield's humility had appeal and empowered him to forge a real connection with the American people. Arthur was a man so vain that he moved his birth year back to appear younger.[27] Garfield had served in combat and led troops into battle. Arthur served honorably in the Civil War as a quartermaster at the rank of brigadier general and was the one who encouraged colleagues to refer to him as "general."[28] Garfield was elected to nine terms in Congress. Chester Arthur had never run for or been elected to office. Garfield was serious and focused on work. Arthur preferred the art of the dinner party. Garfield loathed politics, Arthur couldn't get enough of politics. Garfield was a scholar, Arthur was more about showing off his ability to recite great works of literature.[29]

Despite his faults, Arthur had some redeeming qualities, most notably his commitment to abolition. Like Garfield, he was an advocate of civil rights, but whereas Garfield's claim to fame was hiding a runaway slave as a boy, Arthur had advanced the cause in the courtroom. As a young lawyer, he worked to fight for the rights of black men to ride New York streetcars in 1854[30] and was the attorney for the people in the Lemmon Slave Case, which in 1857 went to the New York Court of Appeals.[31]

To those who knew Arthur best, his rise was unexpected. Unlike Garfield, Arthur came from means, but in his younger years he lacked ambition. Everything changed when he met Ellen Lewis Herndon in 1856 and married her three years later. "Nell," as he affectionately called her, wanted wealth, fame, power, and connections. Chester's position as a lawyer was not enough to give her what she wanted. He yearned to please her and when Civil War broke out he saw an opportunity for advancement. After landing a job as engineer-in-chief for the quartermaster general in New York he built "a well-organized system of labor and accountability," for which his successor, General S. V. Talcott,[32] offered praise. Arthur lacked only one thing: money.

Using his military connections, Arthur quickly rose within the ranks of the New York Republican political machine. It didn't take long for Arthur to get his big break. William Tweed, who was New York's powerful Democratic boss, fell from power amidst scandal in 1871. The fall of "Boss Tweed" rattled Tammany Hall—New York's influential Democratic political machine—and created an opening for Republicans in New York. Luckily for Arthur, this political moment coincided with his appointment as collector of the New York Custom House, which gave him control over 75 percent of the nation's customs receipts.[33]

This taint of corruption was not something Garfield had wanted or invited onto the ticket, and as such the pairing was awkward. When the convention adjourned, the odd couple linked up at the Grand Pacific Hotel and made their way to the main ballroom, where they stood next to each other for several hours shaking hands with supporters and presumably having to

endure never-ending job requests. The experience must have been unpleasant for both, but probably more so for Arthur, whose right hand became so
inflamed that a ring he had worn for years had to be filed off.[34]

Garfield's supporters were disgusted by the idea of Arthur added to the
ticket, comforted only by the fact that the position was deemed irrelevant
and powerless. John Sherman, the Ohioan whom Garfield initially endorsed
for president, wrote privately in letters to friends that Arthur's nomination
was "a ridiculous burlesque," deriding the New Yorker for having "never
held an office except the one he was removed from" and suggesting that his
nomination was a "blunder" that brought "all the odiom of machine politics" to the ticket. He wrote, "The only reason for his nomination was that
he was discharged from an office that he was unfit to fill."[35] Even the sitting
president, Rutherford Hayes, took shots at Arthur. "Gen[eral] Garfield's
nomination at Chicago was the best that was possible," he acknowledged,
but "the sop thrown to Conkling in the nomination of Arthur, only serves
to emphasis [sic] the completeness of his defeat. He was so crushed that it
was from sheer sympathy that this bone was thrown to him."[36]

Arthur's addition to the ticket didn't guarantee Stalwart support,
which meant that if Garfield wanted the presidency, he had his work cut
out for him. It wasn't even clear if Arthur would support his own ticket
unless Stalwart demands could be met. To unite the party, Garfield had
to convince Roscoe Conkling to at a minimum remain neutral. The task
proved harder than expected, particularly as Stalwart leadership knew
they could make Garfield work for it.

There was almost no disagreement on substantive matters, but this
was not a campaign about the issues. The difference between the Republican nominee and the Stalwarts was over patronage, not policy. The party
had an easy time uniting around its platform, which focused on touting
their role in freeing four million people, pensions for veterans, internal
improvements of seacoasts and harbors, rejection of polygamy, opposition to restrictions on Chinese immigration, a tariff to protect American
labor, and the distribution of more land grants to behemoth corporations,
particularly railroads.[37]

Eventually the factions resolved their issues and united around the
ticket. It was easy to forget that Arthur was running for vice president. But
he had a gift for playing politics in the weeds and he seemed to enjoy it.
When it came to fundraising, he knew every trick in the book. As a former

collector of the New York Custom House, he had no qualms about hitting up New York's twenty thousand[38] government employees[39] and thousands of federal employees[40] for "voluntary contributions."[41] He kept meticulous accounts, which included $40,446 worth of payments that were ambiguously labeled as "campaign purposes," which every political insider understood as code for "floating" votes, either through purchase or importing extra voters.[42]

Arthur's scheming may have made the difference. When voters went to the polls on November 2, the Garfield-Arthur ticket won by just 1,898[43] votes—less than one-tenth of one percent of the ten million ballots cast and the narrowest margin in history.[44] Garfield and Hancock each won nineteen states—Garfield the entire North and Midwest, Hancock the entire South, and divided in the West.[45]

Garfield's victory should have marked a turning point in American politics. He was to be a different kind of president from the compromise choice of Hayes and the machine politicians such as Grant. Never in history had a man brought as much humility to the office as James Garfield. During such a politically fractious time, he managed to mean something to almost everyone. He gave hope to America's poor through his own success. Black Americans and abolitionists knew him to be a friend of their cause before, during, and after the Civil War. He connected with immigrants in the East and West who saw a parallel with his own life story. Garfield's parents had lived their struggle. He had seen not just the deprivation, but also the discrimination that came with it.

As president, Garfield was determined to unshackle the office from the trappings of the spoils system and would not allow himself to be beholden to any party boss or constituency. Having won the nomination by accident and against his will, he truly owed nobody any favors. His humility, personal story, and gifted oratory skills meant that he was what the *Washington Post* editorial board later described as a "forceful and widely respected advocate for what he believed in, [someone who] inspired trust among many and felt strongly on the great issue of his day—the future of newly emancipated Americans."[46] But victory sent Garfield into a deep state of melancholy. He had battled depression his whole life, but this was something different. "There is a tone of sadness running through this triumph which I can hardly explain,"[47] he confided to his diary shortly after the election. He knew the pain and agony that awaited him with the swarms of entitled, crazy, and even carnivorous office seekers. These were the same tactless men who had worn down so many of his predecessors to total exhaustion. "My God!" he scribbled in his diary after one particularly overwhelming day. "What is there in this place that a man should ever want to get into it?"[48] He would lament that "these people would take my very brain, flesh and blood if they could."[49]

The office seekers were a nuisance, but they didn't stand in the way of policy. The Stalwarts, however, were a completely different story. In addition to having some of the most domineering personalities in politics, they had one of their most skilled operatives ensconced in the administration as vice president. Within hours of Garfield's victory, the Stalwarts sought to cash in on what they thought the president-elect had promised them during the campaign. But Garfield had no intention of letting the Stalwarts boss him around; instead, he aimed to create an administration that represented all factions of the Republican Party equally. As the political melee commenced, he braced himself for difficult times. He faced vicious opposition from both outside and inside his administration, the latter coming from his vice-president-elect. Arthur was the implementer of mischief in Conkling's war against Garfield. At stake was the future of New York's Republican machine. This was less about pride and ego and more about the fact that Conkling and crew would be deprived of the White House for another four years, effectively drying up their patronage pipeline.

Conkling, Arthur, and Grant were relentless in their badgering of Garfield, who they believed had gone back on a promise to appoint a Stalwart to the Treasury Department.[50] Absent such an appointment, the vice-president-elect was committed to thwarting any effort by Garfield to form a cabinet. The first showdown between the two was over Garfield's secret appointment of Levi Morton, who after declining the vice presidential nomination crossed his mentors and accepted an appointment as secretary of the navy. Garfield swore him to secrecy, but it was no use; Conkling and Arthur found out and dispatched their lackeys to enter Morton's bedroom at night, force him out of bed, and drag him through the snowy streets to face the wrath of Arthur, who "denounced" him as "ruinous to the Republican Party of New York."[51] Garfield wrote in his diary, "Morton broke down on my hands under the pressure of his NY friends, who called him out of bed at four this morning."[52] Next came the Iowa senator William Allison, who took his name out of the running to lead the Interior Department.[53]

Arthur's plan left the president-elect frazzled. There were plenty of Stalwarts interested in cabinet posts, but few who could withstand intimidation from Conkling and Arthur. Garfield knew he could not form a government without forming a cabinet that reflected all factions. He had tried working directly with the Stalwarts, which failed. He attempted secret appointments, but Conkling and Arthur seemed to have eyes and ears everywhere. In one such instance, the exasperated president-elect was hunched over his desk trying to put the finishing touches on his inaugural address,[54] when the two men barged in unannounced to berate[55] him over a secret appointment of postmaster general.[56]

In addition to the fights over cabinet formation, Arthur threatened to taint the administration before it even started. First, there was his inappropriate electioneering for an open Senate seat in New York.[57] Second, Arthur couldn't resist the urge to flaunt some of the shadier practices used to win the presidential election. His most reckless showboating came on February 11 during a dinner hosted at New York's famous Delmonico's restaurant. It was a splendid affair, put on by some of the most well-regarded members of the Union League Club[58] to honor Stephen W. Dorsey, the former Arkansas senator and secretary of the Republican National Committee. Throughout the evening, several prominent Republicans, including Ulysses Grant, spoke. Eventually Arthur rose and, perhaps because he was among friends or loose-lipped from the wine, offered the most reckless toast of his career. Most people knew votes had been bought, particularly in the Midwest, but nobody thought the vice-president-elect would admit it. "I don't think we had better go into the minute secrets of the campaign . . . because I see the reporters are present," he told the two hundred guests, among them J. P. Morgan, John Jacob Astor,[59] and several members of the press. "You cannot tell what they may make of it, because the inauguration has not yet taken place . . . if I should get to going about the secrets of the campaign, there is no saying what I might say to make trouble between now and the 4th of March."[60] Everyone understood that he was talking about corrupt money. Unable to constrain himself, Arthur recounted the manner in which Indiana, which had been a Democratic state, managed to flip Republican. Baiting the boastful vice-president-elect, several dinner guests shouted, "Soap!" the not so secret code for vote buying.[61] To this, Arthur simply replied, "If it were not for the reporters I would tell you the truth, because I know you are intimate friends and devoted adherents to the Republican Party."[62] The press had a field day. Garfield was mortified by the suggestion that their narrow margin of victory had been bought. The dinner was "a curious affair, whose whole significance I do not yet understand," he wrote not long after hearing what had happened.[63]

The president-elect found Arthur impossible to marginalize given his role within the Stalwarts. This burden was quite literally making him sick. He began to develop severe headaches and was unable to sleep. He had nightmares about Arthur, abruptly awakening in the middle of the night with a cold sweat. He'd slept alone in a strange bed that night, visiting a friend in Cleveland. He'd had a strange dream: In it he, Arthur, and an aide had been riding on a canal boat during the night. A heavy rain had come and, in the dream, Garfield had jumped off onto dry land. He'd turned back to look and saw the boat sinking with "General Arthur lying on a couch very pale, apparently very ill." Garfield started to jump into the water to save Arthur, but the aide stopped him, saying, "He cannot be saved, and you will perish if you attempt it." As the story goes, they were stranded in a dangerous place, completely naked, and left to weather a brutal storm in the middle of the night. To Garfield, the whole situation felt like an obfuscation of his new reality. "For the first time in a dream, I knew I was the President-elect," he recalled. In the next chapter of this nocturnal narrative, they meandered in search of clothes and eventually found a house where, as he described it, "an old negro woman took me into her arms and nursed me as though I were a sick child."[64]

Insubordination

Over an inch of snow had fallen the night before inauguration day.[65] It was a bleak, uncomfortable, stormy morning, threatening to blemish the elaborate parade that had been planned for that afternoon. The unforgiving gray sky impeded any chance of sunlight and the heavy precipitation had left the flags so drenched and heavy that they barely moved in the wind.[66] But by late morning, the clouds shifted and the storm subsided.[67]

Just after noon an exhausted Garfield stepped to the podium to take the oath of office and deliver his remarks. He had struggled with the crafting of his speech, drawing on previous inaugurals in hope this would catalyze a clear vision for his own.[68] He didn't finish writing his remarks until 2:30 a.m. and arose just a few hours later.[69] The speech was largely unmemorable. He gave a much desired nod to civil service reform, pledging to instruct "Congress to fix the tenure of the minor offices of the several Executive Departments and prescribe the grounds upon which removals shall be made during the terms for which incumbents have been appointed."[70] He noted that the "elevation of the negro race from slavery to the full rights of citizenship is the most important political change we have known since the adoption of the Constitution of 1787" and challenged southern assumptions that to enfranchise blacks in practice would make most cities ungovernable. "The danger which arises from ignorance in the voter cannot be denied," he said, suggesting instead that "removing the illiteracy" and pursuing a path toward "universal education" is the only way forward.[71]

Unfortunately for Garfield, none of these positions seemed to matter as he began his presidency where he left off, trying to unite the party. The Stalwarts, co-led by his own vice president, were irrepressible. In an effort to accommodate them, Garfield had agreed to appoint a batch of Conkling cronies, a pledge he honored just two days later by sending five nominations to the Senate for confirmation and appointing two of the Conkling cronies for local postmaster positions. He also appointed Levi Morton as minister to France, which seemed to be an adequate consolation prize for not getting Treasury.[72] In exchange, the Stalwarts offered détente.

The agreement was fragile and neither party could have expected it to last long. The fact that it didn't last a full day is a testament to how difficult it was to bury the hostility. What happened next looked like a showdown over patronage, but was a systematic effort by the vice president to sabotage his own administration in the name of faction loyalty. On Monday, March 21, the Senate was slated to review the latest list of presidential nominations, including those that Garfield had agreed on with Conkling. Nobody, especially the Stalwarts, expected any surprises. Instead, they got a bombshell. A clerk interjected with Arthur at his chair and delivered an official message from the White House. Arthur read the note and saw William Robertson's name listed for collector of the New York Custom House, grew agitated, and ordered a clerk to bring the paper over to Conkling.[73] Robertson was the president pro tempore of the New York Senate and during the 1880 convention; he had led a faction of the Republican Party to abandon Grant for Blaine, a move that deadlocked the vote and paved the way for Garfield's dark-horse nomination.[74] Neither Arthur nor Conkling liked him; but more important, neither had been consulted, which from their perspective was a serious infraction. It was tantamount to a declaration of political war. If it was a war Garfield wanted, it was a war he would get.

Having fired the first shot, the president put on his political armor and prepared for battle. The Stalwarts, readying themselves for political war, mobilized in the downstairs of the building where Arthur and Conkling shared an apartment. They concocted a proposal whereby Robertson would become New York City's district attorney instead of collector,[75] a prestigious position but without massive patronage. Blaine and Robertson both objected to the Stalwarts' proposal, but Garfield, who was eager to find a middle ground, responded favorably and set a meeting at the White House that afternoon.

At this point the Stalwarts could have claimed political victory, but Conkling chose to play one too many games. Like a rancorous man-baby, he declared, "I am no place-hunter, and I won't go."[76] While loyal to their master, the Stalwart elites had grown tired of Conkling's antics, particularly in this instance where there was a favorable deal on the table. Arthur and the rest of the pack left him behind and arrived more than two hours later for their meeting with the president. They tried to downplay Conkling's absence, but Garfield was familiar with Conkling's snubs. "I must remember that I am president of the United States," he reminded them. "I owe something to the dignity of my office and to my own self-respect." He was visibly angry and in addition to expressing his displeasure, he made it clear that the previous deal was now off the table. "You may say to this senator that now, rather than withdraw Robertson's nomination, I will suffer myself to be dragged by wild horses."[77]

Garfield believed Conkling had made a tactical error and felt emboldened. At this point, any further agitation from Conkling was unhelpful. Sensing the Stalwarts spiraling out of control, Arthur took the reins and on Saturday, April 2, convened another strategy meeting, this time at his home on Lexington Avenue in Manhattan. Aware that there was no longer a deal on the table, the Stalwarts focused on devising a strategy that would block Robertson's nomination.[78] It was agreed that the vice president would make an appeal on behalf of the entire party. If Robertson's nomination went forward and was confirmed by the Senate, it would "inevitably defeat the party in New York," he told Garfield during an April 14 interview at the White House. The president found it ironic that anyone from the Stalwart camp would attempt to speak on behalf of a party they had divided. "Yes, if the leaders determine it shall," he replied, insinuating the fate of the party rested in Stalwart hands. "Summed up in a word, Mr. Conkling asks me to withdraw Robertson to keep the other leaders of the party from destroying themselves."[79] Garfield was proud of himself for standing his ground. "Of course I deprecate war," he wrote a reporter friend[80] that evening. "But if [war] is brought to my door the bringer will find me at home."[81] Arthur next tried blackmail,[82] then threats, and eventually crafty use of senatorial rules to prevent Robertson's nomination. None worked.

Conkling described the president's actions as "perfidy without parallel."[83] He and Arthur decided to hit the president hard by enlisting friendly journalists and pro-Stalwart editors to attack the administration. Thomas B. Connery, the editor of the *New York Herald,* was a Stalwart sycophant ripe for seduction. Knowing this, Arthur invited him to meet with Conkling in Washington for what must have been cast as the story of the year.[84] He arrived within a day or two and upon walking into the house shared by Conkling and Arthur simply asked, "What's all the mystery about?" Eager for the opportunity to deliver a sucker punch against Garfield, Arthur explained that the president "has not been square, nor honorable nor truthful with Conkling. . . . It is a hard thing to say of a president of the United States but it is, unfortunately, only the truth. Garfield—spurred by Blaine, by whom he is too easily led—has broken every pledge made to us; not only that, but he seems to have wished to do it in a most offensive way."[85] This should have read like inside baseball and been a nonstory, but Connery was ready to write whatever the two men wanted.

The story broke on Wednesday, May 11, headlined "The Wriggler" and referred to Garfield as the "angry boy" and a "small and pitiable figure."[86] Conkling was so thrilled by the exposé, which exposed absolutely nothing, that he purchased and organized a bulk order to be sent to Washington by train from New York City.[87] But the story had little impact, as it became clear the president would have enough votes to get Robertson's nomination approved. Conkling was about to receive the knockout punch. But then the unthinkable happened. On the morning of May 16, a nervous Chester Arthur banged the ivory and gold gavel that had been given him as a gift by his New York friends,[88] and read resignations from Senators

Conkling and Thomas Platt. The resignations were meant to save face, but they could not prevent Robertson's nomination. Both assumed they would be quickly reelected by the state legislature. The strategy was ill-conceived and looked more like political self-immolation.[89]

By resigning, Conkling and Platt had weakened themselves, the vice president, and the Stalwart faction.[90] The resignations had handed a majority to the Democrats, but the session expired without the election of a president pro tempore. Arthur as the presiding officer used rules and procedures to prevent the election of Delaware's Thomas F. Bayard or any other Democrat to this position who had not stood firm against Robertson's confirmation. As president of the Senate, Arthur refused to vacate the chair, thus preventing election of a president pro tempore. The session expired and left a gaping hole in the line of succession.[91]

In contrast, Garfield was "pleased,"[92] but we can infer from his subsequent actions that he went from emboldened to unshackled as he received the greatest political gift of his young administration.[93] Their resignations were "a very weak attempt at heroic[s]," he observed in his diary. "If I do not make a mistake, it will be received with guffaws of laughter. They appeal to a legislature which they think is already secured. Even in this they may fail."[94] Two days later, the Senate, now without the president's two biggest adversaries, confirmed Robertson's nomination in twenty-five minutes without debate or a roll call. "This leaves Conkling's attitude ridiculous,"[95] Garfield wrote in his journal.

On May 22, a desperate Stalwart leadership once again gathered at Arthur's home on Lexington Avenue. Having lost the New York Custom House, they devised a plan to descend on Albany and return Conkling and Platt to the Senate.[96] They arrived in Albany on May 24, for what they believed would be a seamless process. Instead, the New York state legislature dragged the process out for several months.[97] Smelling blood in the water, Conkling's many adversaries pounced on the chance to eat him alive. The president was not one to gloat and instead watched his demise from afar.[98]

With Conkling on a one-way trip to political irrelevance, the press turned its attention to the vice president and heir apparent to the Stalwart throne. None of it was favorable. The *New York Tribune* speculated: "If General Arthur does not desire four years of public contempt he would do well to desist from the business in which he is now engaged before his inexcusable indiscretion becomes a national scandal. . . . The moral of his performances is that we must not expect to change a man's nature by electing him to the Vice-presidency."[99] Next came the *New York Times*, which observed, "Active politicians, uncompromising partisans, have held before now the office of the Vice President of the United States, but no holder of that office has ever made it so plainly subordinate to his self-interest as a politician and his narrowness as a partisan."[100] William Hudson, a reporter for the *Brooklyn Eagle*, said the vice president "lobbied like any political henchman" and described him as Conkling's flunky in Albany, meaning his responsibilities included paying bar tabs and organizing carriage transfers, while the real men negotiated and played politics.[101]

As the special election approached, the Stalwarts lost more credibility when Thomas Platt tried to sneak a mistress into the Delavan House in Albany. When a lobby hand spotted a young woman visiting the ex-senator's hotel suite, he alerted some known enemies of Platt and Conkling, who subsequently congregated around room 113. Eager to catch Platt in the act, one of them had the brilliant idea to grab a ladder and see what was happening on the other side of the window. There they found the senatorial candidate literally with his pants down. A note that read, "We will give you ten minutes to get out of that room. Yours, etc., The Half-Breeds," was then slipped under the door.[102] Platt's political career was over. The next day, July 1, he dropped out of the race, leaving Conkling isolated.

With Conkling hanging on by a thread and the future of the Stalwart faction resting on his now slim chances of reelection, Arthur convinced him they needed to take some time to recuperate and clear their minds. That evening, they bolted out of Albany by steamboat and took the long overnight journey back to New York City. It must have been a particularly unpleasant trip.

In Washington, the mood was very different. For Garfield, it meant that he could finally start his presidency. He had issued a few special messages, one on April 6 relating to the "capitulations of the Ottoman Empire"[103] and the other on May 20, dealing with the "case of Michael P. Boyton,"[104] an American citizen who had been arrested and imprisoned by the authorities in Great Britain. He had also made good on his promise to appoint several freedmen to important government positions, most notably John Mercer Langston, who became minister to Haiti, former senator Blanche Bruce, who was given a role as registrar of the treasury, and Frederick Douglass, who as the country's most famous ex-slave received an appointment as Washington, D.C., recorder of deeds.[105] Now, everything was different. Platt and Conkling were out of the Senate. His insubordinate vice president had become a disgraced pariah and would soon become irrelevant. And on a personal note, his wife, Lucretia, had nearly died from malaria and was now expected to make a full recovery.[106] The timing could not have been better as the president planned to take his first extended vacation since assuming office.

Presidential Limbo

President Garfield would have had his moment had it not been for a thirty-nine-year-old madman named Charles Guiteau. A struggling lawyer and writer from Freeport, Illinois, Guiteau had had a life defined by one rejection after the next. After believing divine intervention was responsible for his surviving a ship collision on Long Island Sound, he had thrown himself into the 1880 presidential election for Garfield, whom he would later claim credit for electing. He had canvassed for Garfield and even on one occasion was mentioned in the newspaper as a supporter of the Republican nominee, but most who encountered him saw that there was something off. He stalked James Blaine, who found him a pestering annoyance, and managed at one point to get an audience with Garfield. No one would have anything to do with him, with the exception of Chester Arthur, who out of pity indulged him only slightly more than the others.

Guiteau expected to be rewarded for his hard work and awaited a coveted appointment. No job offer came and he concluded that it was the sitting president who stood in his way. Vice President Arthur, on the other hand, had been more tolerant of him and Guiteau believed the two had struck a special bond. He awoke one morning with what he thought a brilliant idea. He would make Chester Arthur president by killing Garfield. This, he believed, would ingratiate him with Arthur, who would reward him with the lucrative post of consul general in Paris.

For a man who had just decided to commit murder, Guiteau was shockingly matter-of-fact about the whole thing. He had nothing personal against Garfield, but a change had to be made. After convincing a sympathetic relative to lend him $15, he wandered over to John O'Meara's gun shop on the corner of 15th and F Streets in Washington to check out murder weapons. He splurged for an extra dollar on the .44 caliber 5-shooter English Bulldog, mainly because of its ornate ivory handle, which he thought would look better in a museum after he performed the deed.[107] He got his shoes shined and visited the local jail the Saturday before assassination day to make sure the accommodations suited his needs. Unclear as to the purpose of his visit, the deputy warden found him strange and told him to return on Monday.[108]

As the president prepared for vacation, the assassin stalked him on three occasions. In the first instance, he had both the president and Mrs. Garfield in sight as they walked by the train, but later confessed that "[Mrs. Garfield] looked so thin and clung so tenderly to the President's arm"[109] that he couldn't bring himself to perform the task. Shortly after, the aspiring assassin trailed the president to Vermont Avenue, where he intended to kill him while he attended church. From a window outside the church, he had a perfect shot at the president's pew, but chose to abort his mission.[110] The next opportunity presented itself the evening of July 1, when Garfield planned to visit the home of Secretary of State Blaine. His future assassin stood waiting in Lafayette Park, just in front of the White House, and followed him to Blaine's house. He fancied the idea of killing the president in the same place where William Seward was nearly murdered sixteen years earlier. Standing in a nearby alley, he caught a glimpse of Mrs. Blaine in the window, which caused him once again to change his mind.[111] "I was several yards behind him," he recalled several months later following his arrest. "It was a splendid chance. . . . I walked along on the opposite side of the street from him. . . . The pistol was in my hand and in my pocket."[112]

The president was exposed. Absent periods of war, there were no provisions for presidential protection, and at the time there was no real advocate to change that. While other world leaders had been assassinated, their deaths were attributed to the exotic problems of faraway lands. Memories of failed assassinations faded fast and Lincoln's death was largely dismissed as an anomaly of war. As Candice Millard explains in *Destiny of the Republic*, "Americans reasoned that, because they had the power to choose their own head of state, there was little cause for angry rebellion. As a result, presidents were expected not only to be personally available to the public, but to live much like them."[113]

Garfield rejected a proposal for uniformed guards to be stationed at the executive mansion on the grounds that such protection might be required for European monarchs, but surely America was a completely different place. "Assassination can no more be guarded against than death by lightning," he wrote to John Sherman, and it is therefore "not best to worry about either."[114] He had taken this same attitude during the campaign. When one of his supporters raced by carriage from Cleveland to Mentor to alert Garfield of a plot on his life, he flippantly responded, "Well, if assassination is to play its part in the campaign, and I must be the sacrifice, perhaps it is best. I think I am ready."[115]

July 2, 1881, was the beginning of James Garfield's first vacation as president. He had finished all of his business the previous evening, which included appointing twenty-five foreign ministers and consuls, dismissing a railroad commissioner and a register of wills, and naming James Blaine's son Walker as third assistant secretary of state.[116] After a family breakfast, Garfield sent his family to the Washington depot of the Baltimore and Potomac Railroad, where he would soon follow with James Blaine. At 9:00 a.m., he bid farewell to his young aide Joseph Stanley-Brown, saying, "You have had your outing and now I am going to have mine. Keep watch on things and use the telegraph as freely as you deem necessary."[117]

That same morning, Charles Guiteau began his day walking along the bank of the Potomac River, where he used sticks sunk in the mud for target practice.[118] Once he felt sufficiently confident in his marksmanship, he wanted to make sure he looked the part for his anticipated arrest. This meant getting his boots shined to a perfect, glossy black. Finally, he needed his getaway car, so he found some poor cabbie, promised him an extra $2, and convinced him to wait until he was done so that he could flee to the Congressional Cemetery.[119]

Garfield arrived at the depot with Blaine around 9:20 a.m.[120] In a departure from his usual frugality, he sported a brand-new, light gray summer suit,[121] which was a rare extravagance reserved for this particularly exciting occasion. As they descended from the carriage, walking with their arms locked together, word spread of the president's arrival. Most of the presidential party—Secretary of War Robert Todd Lincoln, Secretary of the Navy William H. Hunt, Postmaster General Thomas L. James, Secretary of the Treasury William Windom, and all of their wives—had already arrived and were in the designated car arranged for them.[122]

Guiteau knew that this would be his last chance to murder the president. As the president came into sight, he fired two shots and yelled, "I did it and will go to jail for it. I am a Stalwart, and Arthur will be President!"[123]

The first shot grazed the president's arm and the second hit him right in the back.[124] "My God! What is this?" a stunned Garfield exclaimed as he fell to the floor. Blaine recognized the assassin as the office seeker who had routinely badgered him for an appointment to France. He ran after him before realizing there was nobody by the president's side. Mrs. Sarah E. V. White, who had responsibility for tending to the women's waiting room, raced to the president's side and knelt beside him to soothingly place his head in her lap.[125]

Two of Garfield's sons, Harry—better known as "Hal"—and James, had been nearby and, after hearing screams and shouts that the president had been shot, rushed to their father's side. The first doctor on the scene was Smith Townsend, who was the health officer for the District of Columbia. By the time he arrived, fifteen minutes after the shooting, the president was already dizzy, light-headed, and vomiting.[126] He was moved to an upstairs office where the physicians[127]—which included Charles Burleigh Purvis, the first black doctor to treat a president of the United States[128]—got to work trying to stabilize the wounded president. Despite the pain he was suffering, the always empathetic Garfield thought only of his wife, who herself had just recovered from a prolonged illness that had nearly claimed her life. He motioned his secretary (a Williams graduate just like him and old Army friend), Colonel Almon F. Rockwell, to his side and dictated a message for him to send to Mrs. Garfield: "Mrs. Garfield, The President wishes me to say to you from him that he has been seriously hurt—how seriously he cannot yet say. He is himself and hopes you will come to him soon. He sends his love to you. A. F. Rockwell."[129]

Robert Todd Lincoln, who was part of the presidential entourage, bellowed to an aide to track down Dr. Willard Bliss, who had made a name for himself while running a large Army hospital during the Civil War. He had also been Garfield's longtime doctor and was familiar with his medical history. Bliss arrived fifteen minutes later,[130] after which Lincoln withdrew into isolation as memories of his father's death came back to haunt him.[131] "How many hours of sorrow I have passed in this town!" he was overheard muttering to himself (little did he know that just twenty years later he would bear witness to a third presidential assassination).[132] Bliss and the hodgepodge of physicians collectively determined that the president needed to be moved to the executive mansion as quickly as possible.[133] An ambulance was summoned and the president transported. Upon arrival, the president remained both conscious and in good spirits, even putting on a bit of a show for the concerned crowds that had gathered. As the doctors transported him on a stretcher, he lifted his right hand, curled his neck up just high enough to make his face visible, and with a cheerful grin performed a perfect military salute.[134]

Guiteau's motives were not yet understood and the possibility of conspiracy could not be ruled out. The lessons from 1865 led the secretary of war to call on soldiers quartered in the barracks of the Washington Arsenal to mobilize around the White House and executive grounds. This relieved the Metropolitan Police, who were able to focus on containing the growing crowds that had taken to the streets.[135] However, it did not take long to determine that the assassin acted alone. Shortly after his arrest, the police discovered two letters. The first was addressed "To the White House" and explained how "the President's tragic death was a sad necessity, but it will unite the Republican Party and save the Republic." He declared himself "a Stalwart of Stalwarts" and boasted that he had been "with General Grant and the rest of our men, in New York, during the canvass." He offered a disclaimer that he "had no ill-will toward the President" but "his death was a political necessity."[136]

The second letter was addressed to Vice President Arthur, in which Guiteau took credit for the "assassination" and notified Arthur of his ascension to the presidency. The letter then went on to advise him on cabinet appointments, insisting that the new secretary of state must be "Coulsburg,"[137] while Levi P. Morton would be appropriate for secretary of the treasury, Emory A. Storrs for attorney general, and John A. Logan for secretary of war. For some reason, Guiteau felt strongly that the postmaster general, Thomas L. James, retain his position, and in the humble opinion of the assassin, shake-ups at the Departments of the Navy and Interior were optional.[138]

A third letter, addressed to General William T. Sherman, was found with a street vendor nearby. In this, Guiteau declared, "I have shot the president. I shot him several times, as I wished him to go as easily as possible. . . . I am going to jail. Please order out your troops, and take possession of the jail at once."[139]

While the letters dispelled any myth of conspiracy, they served as an indictment of the spoils system. They would come to shape public opinion, spark a movement, and turn the population against some of the most powerful machine politicians of the era. Vice President Arthur, who was called out by name and linked to the assassin—whether he knew him or not—would become the punching bag for a population that yearned for both answers and retribution.

The vice president was unreachable, which was cause for some concern. Arthur and Roscoe Conkling had left Albany the previous evening and were making their way down the Hudson River back to New York City.[140] As they got closer to shore, several men shouted, "The President's been shot! The President's been shot!" But Arthur could not decipher the sounds and the fog was too heavy to see them clearly. The boat lingered in the distance for another hour, after which the fog let up enough for their boat to navigate its way to shore.[141]

As Arthur and Conkling stepped onto the dock, a messenger handed the vice president a telegram. Several reporters, who knew more than the vice president did, had congregated on the dock to watch the reactions of Garfield's two biggest enemies. But reporters didn't get their gotcha moment;[142] instead, Arthur was in shock. He was horrified by the idea of potentially having to take Garfield's job. The vice presidency had been the pinnacle of what he wanted in life, all the prestige and none of the work. His responsibilities were nonexistent and he was in a position to advocate for New York patronage from the top of the federal government. When he accepted the vice presidency, he believed he had signed up for four years of dinner parties, entertaining, and handing out jobs to his friends in New York.[143] Dumbfounded and perhaps in a state of shock, Arthur turned to Conkling, who took control of the situation and hailed a carriage that raced the two men to the Fifth Avenue Hotel.[144] Unlike Arthur, who was stricken, Conkling went into full strategy mode to figure out what Garfield's death would mean for the Stalwarts.

The crowds greeted Conkling and Arthur with fierce displeasure. Arthur, however, was still in the dark on the various ways that Guiteau had implicated him in the assassination. A young hotel clerk confronted them both with the reality of just how hated they both were at this precise moment. He urged them to take care as the people were out for blood and there had been "warnings that should Garfield die, Arthur, Conkling and [Thomas Platt] should pay the penalty."[145] This was not an isolated threat. Conkling's and Arthur's lives were both in danger and immediate security measures had to be taken.

At a time when there was no presidential protection,[146] there was certainly no protocol for protecting the vice president. But in recognizing the immediacy of threat, New York police commissioner Stephen French shadowed both men and stationed a couple of uniformed officers at the hotel's main entrance to be accompanied by a detective in the lobby. As an extra precaution, there were also several undercover detectives dressed like hotel guests who blended with the crowd in the hallway outside their hotel suite.[147] But none of this seemed to deter the threats, which continued. That day, the proprietors of the hotel had received a card, written in a scrawling hand, which read: "*Gens:* We will hang Conkling and Co. at nine P.M. sharpe. THE COMMITTEE."[148] It was in Garfield's home state of Ohio where the most obstreperous crowds roared the loudest, openly broadcasting their intention to "shoulder their muskets and go to Washington to prevent the inauguration of Arthur."[149] The Ohio police took the threats seriously and prepared for the worst. Officers geared up and mobilized across the state as they braced themselves for potentially violent confrontations in the streets.[150]

Conkling showed little emotion, which only increased the animosity toward him. But Arthur's reaction was different. When a group of reporters approached him, he could only think to ask them, "What is the latest report?" To most reporters present, it was clear that Arthur felt deep sorrow over what had happened. He was told, "The latest dispatch says that Dr. Bliss does not think the wound will prove fatal."[151] He was visibly relieved.

While Arthur scrambled about the Fifth Avenue Hotel, Secretary of State Blaine was sending him repeated dispatches to his home on Lexington Avenue, which he only discovered that afternoon. Among them was a 1:00 p.m. telegraph stating, "The President's symptoms are not regarded as unfavorable, but no definite assurance can be given until after the probing of the wound at three o'clock."[152] Arthur was not eager to go to Washington, lest it create the appearance that he was hungry for the presidency. He decided to wait things out at home. At 9:30 p.m. another telegram arrived from Blaine, this time conveying "the judgment of Cabinet that you should come to Washington tonight by midnight train."[153] The seriousness of the president's condition was reinforced by a subsequent telegram from the postmaster general describing the president as "no better" and expressing "fear" that he is "sinking."[154]

Arthur caught the last ferry of the day from the Desbrosses Street pier across the Hudson River and made his way to the Jersey City railroad station at around 10:30 p.m. He was joined by a small entourage that included Senator Conkling, who in an interesting irony was now carrying Arthur's luggage,[155] Senator John P. Jones, who offered to put the men up in his Washington townhouse, and detective Frank Cosgrove from the New York Police Department, who was armed with a pistol locked and loaded on the inside of his coat for Arthur's protection.[156]

The midnight train arrived in Washington at 7:00 a.m.[157] on Sunday, July 3. They arrived without ceremony, finding no greeting party at the station, and made their way outside without anyone noticing. After hailing a curbside carriage taxi, they finally reached Jones's large granite[158] townhouse at 3 Independence Avenue, just across the street from the Capitol.[159]

While Conkling was thinking about politics, Arthur could think only of the president. At first, he didn't remember Guiteau, but eventually recalled that he had been in his Fifth Avenue Hotel suite "at least ten and possibly as often as twenty times" throughout the campaign. He remembered having spoken with him "once or twice in answer to his requests to be employed in the campaign as a speaker" and, of course, "returning the ordinary salutations of the day."[160] These interactions, along with Guiteau's letters—particularly the one discovered in his apartment addressed to "President Arthur"[161]—caused him great angst that the ailing president might suspect he had something to do with the assassination. It didn't help that he had taken some time to reply to Blaine's telegrams or that he had initially forgotten about meeting Guiteau. Arthur needed to set the record straight and was persistent in trying to see the president.[162]

But the doctors carefully guarded access to the president. Arthur's multiple requests were denied without explanation,[163] which had to have struck a nerve with him. He refused to take no for an answer as he became ever more consumed with seeing the president. He sought the help of Attorney General Wayne MacVeagh, visiting his office:[164] "I was so nervous and depressed last night. . . . I was so late receiving the news of his injuries and feared the President might misinterpret my silence," Arthur told MacVeagh. "It is my earnest desire to see the President. Is there no possibility of seeing him?"[165] But there was little MacVeagh could do as he, too, had been prevented from seeing the president.

Arthur realized that if he wanted to see the president, he could no longer arrange an interview by proxy. He decided to go to the White House and make a personal appeal. This approach was no more successful, as the doctors still wouldn't let him visit. Only "attendants and persons whose presence was necessary,"[166] they told him, with no exceptions. Dr. Bliss, the physician in charge, determined early on that Garfield's best hope for survival lay in "being kept perfectly quiet." He caved to nobody, not even the president, who on multiple occasions asked to hold cabinet meetings and discuss the affairs of state.[167]

Arthur was forced to settle for a brief condolence call with Mrs. Garfield. She hated him, but any awkwardness was put aside by his genuine grief. He was so overcome with emotion that he completely broke down, "unable to conceal his emotion," tears pouring down his face, his eyes transformed into puddles of water, and his usually confident voice muffled by a shortness of breath that prevented him from being able to speak.[168] He expressed his desire to wait with her by the president's bedside, but this was not something Mrs. Garfield or anyone else seemed to want.[169] Senator Benjamin Harrison, who was in the private secretary's office as Arthur came out, appears to be one of the few who actually saw Arthur immediately after his meeting with the first lady. He took note of the vice president's distraught look and a few years later recalled, "He showed deep feeling and seemed to be overcome with the calamity."[170]

Before leaving the White House, Arthur was shepherded to an anteroom[171] where the cabinet and a handful of foreign dignitaries[172] were assembled. The situation turned awkward when he hesitated at the room's entryway, awaiting an invitation to enter. To his surprise and chagrin, there was not a single salutation. They gave him an inimical glare as he stood in the doorway unsure what to do next. Arthur was flummoxed and ready to bolt, but fortunately one of the men had been too engrossed in conversation to join in the initial standoff. Perhaps recognizing the need to defuse a painfully uncomfortable situation, he approached the vice president with an air of affability and gestured him into the room.[173] Arthur broke the ice, saying, "I pray to God that the President will recover. . . . God knows I do not want the place I was never elected to."[174] The apology worked and they all sat to discuss logistics, agreeing that the president's condition remained too uncertain for the vice president to leave. July 13 was set as the date through which Arthur ought to stay in town, during which members of the cabinet would visit him to give updates and to show the public that political factionalism had been put aside.[175] During that time, Arthur refused to leave his house, turned down any requests for interviews, and tried to steer clear of Conkling.

Arthur's inability to see the president—and perhaps the guilt he felt— was enough to bring him into a deep state of melancholy. But the worst was yet to come. It was one thing to experience his own guilt, but another to be publicly accused directly or indirectly of murder. "General Arthur has been untrue to his better self," wrote the *New York Times*. "Grossly slanderous as it would be to impute any suggestion of homicidal intent. . . . The man to whom the criminal act of Guiteau ought to bring the gravest reflections is the man who has apparently most to gain from its fatal issue."[176] Some papers went further, most notably Henry Watterson and his *Louisville Courier Journal*, which wrote: "Mrs. [Mary Surratt of the Lincoln murder conspiracy] was hanged on less circumstantial evidence than occurs to the mind as to Roscoe Conkling and Chester A. Arthur . . . we should not be eager to assume the innocence of a body of political wretches."[177]

Not surprisingly, the evening of July 3 was a restless night for the vice president. When a reporter called him the next day to obtain a reaction to press speculation that he had a relationship with the president's assassin, Arthur snapped back: "No one deplores the calamity more than Senator Conkling and myself. These reports are so baseless and so unfounded that I cannot believe they will be credited. If it were possible for me to be with the President I would not only offer him my sympathy, I would ask that I might remain by his bedside. All personal considerations and political views must be merged in the national sorrow. I am an American among millions of Americans grieving for their wounded chief."[178]

Things were about to get worse for Arthur, particularly as Guiteau was not a sufficient scapegoat for a grief-stricken public. Lincoln's assassination, however tragic, could be understood as a tragedy of war. The murder of Czar Alexander II in Russia five months earlier was perceived to have been political murder. But the shooting of Garfield was to many Americans perplexing. "The deed was done in the most peaceful and prosperous moment that this country has known for a half century and the shot was fired absolutely at a man without personal enemies, and a president whom even his political opponents respect,"[179] observed one contemporary biographer.

The American people were dismayed by the idea of Chester Arthur as president and the press knew it. He was barely known and what little people knew of him they didn't much like. Garfield was universally trusted and respected, a man of great moral rectitude, intelligence, and depth. Arthur was shallow, elitist, lazy, and uninspiring. Whereas Garfield was a self-made man who rose from abject poverty to the nation's highest office, Arthur was a product of the spoils system. Garfield had achieved the GOP nomination without even putting his name forward, while Arthur was imposed on the ticket in what was disparaged as placating the party's most unscrupulous constituents.[180] Garfield had spent his time as president advocating for a better and more equal America, while Arthur spent his entire tenure as vice president plotting with Garfield's chief opponents.[181] And now the man who assassinated President Garfield claimed to do so on behalf of Chester Arthur, whom he had met with on several occasions. No sooner had newsboys shared the tragic news of Garfield's shooting throughout the country than rumors began circulating that Chester Arthur was the man responsible. He more or less had to go into hiding for two months for fear of what a mob might do to him.[182]

Almost everyone, certainly the Stalwarts, assumed that should Garfield die, Arthur would hand the keys of government to Roscoe Conkling. They anticipated a reinvigoration of the spoils system and an immediate halt to any progress made toward civil service reform. E. L. Godkin of *The Nation* wrote, "It is out of this mess of filth that Mr. Arthur will go to the Presidential chair in case of the President's death."[183] *Harper's Weekly* found the prospect of an Arthur presidency abhorrent, and noted that future nominating conventions would place a higher premium on the vice presidential nomination.[184]

Luminaries reacted with the same horror. "Chet Arthur President of the United States! Good God!" cried out one Republican.[185] John Sherman, writing to Hayes, predicted "strong anticipations of evil to come" if Garfield should succumb to his wounds.[186] On the day of the assassination, former president Hayes wrote: "Arthur for President! Conkling the power behind the throne, superior to the throne! ... [a] national calamity whose consequences we cannot now confidently conjecture. . . . This is the result of placating bosses."[187] Even Jefferson Davis had something to say. Now living in a cabin on a southern patron's plantation, he shared his thoughts with his friend Findley S. Collins. In a letter dated July 5, 1881, he wrote, "I am thankful the assassin was not a Southern man, but will say I regret that an American crime, black enough in itself, has a deeper dye from the mercenary motive which seems to have prompted it. I sincerely trust the President may recover, and that the startling event will arouse the people to the consideration of a remedy for the demoralization which a wild hunt after office is creating."[188]

There was a feeding frenzy over Arthur and calls for his head, both literally and figuratively. Some even used the occasion to resurface a campaign rumor that Arthur was not a U.S. citizen and thus could not serve as president. It was true that according to a naturalization document, his father, William Arthur, did not become a U.S. citizen until August 1843,[189] nearly fourteen years after Arthur was born; but this did not make Chester a foreigner. The rumor, stoked by a New York attorney named Arthur P. Hinman during his investigation in August 1880, tried to prove that Arthur was born in either Ireland or Canada.[190] As hatred toward the vice president grew, so, too, did rumors spread about his anxiety. In one rumor, Arthur had allegedly poisoned himself out of grief.[191] And, in one even more extraordinary anecdote, two inmates in a New York prison brawled over the prospects of an Arthur presidency, leading one of them to kill the other with an ax.[192]

Animosity toward Arthur intensified or lessened depending on Garfield's condition, which the general public was updated on through public bulletins posted outside the White House. Garfield tried to stay engaged while recovering. Staff would read him the headlines each morning, of which several papers made the case that Arthur and Conkling were responsible. Even though Garfield strongly disliked both his vice president and Roscoe Conkling, he never gave credence to the absurd rumors. In response to one particularly damning accusation, he fervently shook his head, declaring in no uncertain terms, "I do not believe that."[193]

Arthur Is President

During Garfield's eighty-day period of disability there were matters that needed the president's attention: The country's foreign affairs had become a mess, there was a Supreme Court vacancy[194] that needed filling, and the prosecution of postal charlatans implicated in the Star Route Scandal*

---

* On March 3, 1845, Congress passed legislation allowing private contractors to take over the postal service in the more remote parts of the U.S., particularly the territories out west. These were called Star Routes and they were highly lucrative four-year contracts. The system was ripe

grew more difficult with each passing day, threatening the credibility of his administration.[195] The uncertainty about the president's survival and the long period of waiting hurt the country's economy. The stock market became completely unreliable with prices dropping suddenly; then surging, only to drop again. But despite these fluctuations, the stock market's trajectory was downward and would continue on that trajectory for another year. The country's economic situation grew worse when in September (just days before Garfield died) a terrible drought ravaged crops across the country and spoiled corn, cotton, wheat, and pork production.[196] All of this was exacerbated by the fact that the 46th Congress recessed on March 3, 1881, and other than the brief special session Garfield had called that same month, it was not set to reconvene until December 5. Today, the notion of a nine-month recess seems hard to imagine, but as Ruth Silva explains in *Presidential Succession,* "Before adoption of the Twentieth Amendment an old Congress expired on March 3 of the odd numbered years and a new Congress did not convene until the following December unless called into special session. This meant that for nine months out of every twenty-four there likely would be no statutory successor."[197]

Despite these pressing needs and issues, the government froze, its chief executive sidelined first by an assassin's attack and then by the malpractice of his doctors, whose rejection of new theories about sanitation led them to stick dirty fingers in the president's wounds as they searched for the bullet.[198] Three presidents had died in office, but none had hung on longer than a few weeks. Such an extended disability was unprecedented and proved to be both a trying moment for the Constitution and a moment for precedent. The Constitution did not address prolonged presidential disabilities. At the time of drafting, the framers added a vague clause toward the tail end of the Constitutional Convention, in which they stated the following: "[I]n case of [the president's] removal as aforesaid, death, absence, resignation or inability to discharge the powers and duties of his office, the vice-president shall exercise those powers and duties until another President be chosen, or until the inability of the President be re-

---

for exploitation and during the Ulysses Grant administration, corruption was rampant around the bidding process, including bribes in exchange for contracts, padded reimbursements, and delinquency on the postal delivery part of the arrangement. ("Star Routes," U.S. Postal Service, usps.com.)

moved."[199] The subsequent Presidential Succession Act of 1792 did little
to clarify this ambiguity and the inadequately documented deliberations
do not capture any of the arguments—if any at all—that were debated at
the time the law was passed.[200]

During the first two months, Garfield was physically weak and at times
a bit delirious, but for the most part he was mentally alert. The day after
signing the extradition treaty for Gaiten Derohan, a "decidedly better"[201]
Garfield managed to write a full letter to his mother. "Don't be disturbed
by conflicting reports about my condition. It is true I am still weak and on
my back, but I am gaining every day and need only time and patience to
bring me through."[202] That same day, he asked for "full information concerning the recent rainfall at his home near Mentor, Ohio,"[203] and was able
not only to scarf down some strawberries courtesy of Archdeacon and
Co., but also to instruct his secretary to ask them to send raspberries.[204]

Garfield relapsed physically and mentally and despite the ups and
downs would never recover.[205] With nobody in charge of the government,
his lieutenants struggled with what to do. The first point of confusion had
to do with the role of the cabinet. In the immediate aftermath, Garfield's
cabinet tried to assert control, with its senior member, James Blaine, flirting
with a role as presidential regent. The press beat back this approach, collectively arguing that cabinet members were not elected officials. The *New
York Times* and the *New York Herald* objected to the cabinet leading the government without a president, although some of this was motivated by their
mistrust of Secretary of State Blaine.[206] Blaine, who himself had presidential
aspirations, was by no means taking advantage of the situation, but his view
of himself as presidential material made the role feel almost natural.

As for the vice president, there was discussion as to whether he could
temporarily assume the presidential duties but Arthur had no intention
of accepting the presidency, temporary or permanent, so long as Garfield
lived. He had been openly hostile toward the president, directly undermined him both in government formation and in his administration, and
the public blamed him for the assassination. He wasn't looking to add
usurper to the list of grievances.

Unclear how long Garfield's disability would last, the cabinet was
growing restless. Having exhausted a number of options, they regrouped
and devised a plan with three potential courses of action. The first was a
do-nothing strategy. Since Congress was on a long recess and nothing of

great significance was taking place, they could avoid any constitutional crisis by simply riding out Garfield's recovery. There was a risk, however, that should an emergency arise requiring the president's attention, there would be no mechanism to act on it. The second plan focused on "delegation" rather than the "devolution" of executive power. Given the debate about whether a vice president's ascendance meant presidential abdication, "delegation" was presented as a middle option that "would allow Garfield to recover his powers if and when his disability ceased." As part of this particular proposal, the president could "delegate executive power to a cabinet member and authorize him to sign the name 'James A. Garfield.'" But this option had no plan for getting around the president's doctors. Finally, they suggested Congress pass an act providing for the "temporary discharge of presidential duties during the president's inability,"[207] but Congress was out of session with little appetite to reconvene.

Ultimately, the cabinet rolled the dice and went with the first option. The risks never materialized, because Garfield eventually died. This option also yielded the cabinet enormous amounts of power, each member running his respective department with complete autonomy and without accountability. This trend did not go unnoticed. "The government is practically without a head, and is conducted by the Cabinet—a body unknown to the Constitution," wrote the *Times* on August 11, 1881. "We almost might say that the secretary of state, instead of the vice-president's 'acting as president.' This certainly was not contemplated by the constitution."[208]

President Garfield died at 10:20 p.m. on September 19, 1881. His death marked the second assassination of a president and the fourth time that one had died in office. The official bulletin of the autopsy cited "secondary hemorrhage from one of the mesenteric arteries adjoining the track of the ball"[209] as the cause of death. The country mourned the loss, but unlike previous deaths, Garfield's had been drawn out over the course of eighty days. By the time he died, the country was ready for it.[210]

To almost everyone's surprise, Chester Arthur took Garfield's death harder than anyone. At around midnight on September 20, Arthur heard a knock on the door while he was with friends in the second-floor study of his New York townhouse. His servant, Aleck Powell, opened the door not realizing that his boss had trailed behind him. "The President is dead," a reporter from *The Sun* told him. Arthur looked stunned. "Oh, no, it cannot be true," he said. "It cannot be. I have heard nothing."[211] But the reporter insisted, informing him "the dispatch has just been received at the office." Arthur's face quivered, his eyes watered, and he fell into a state of shock. "I hope—my God, I do hope it is a mistake," he told the reporter. Overwhelmed with emotion, he went back upstairs to the library, where his friends awaited news. "They say he is dead," he shared in utter disbelief. "A dispatch has been received at the *Sun* office."[212]

Arthur needed a moment to digest the news and the terrifying realization that he would become the twenty-first president. He didn't want the job, describing it to a friend as "the most frightful responsibility,"[213] and was worn down by vicious attacks from the press that he expected to get worse now that Garfield was dead.[214] He fled the study to the privacy of his own room, where he had a near breakdown. His sobs and shrieks could be heard in all parts of his townhouse. Reporters, eager to catch the first moments for the new president, descended on the steps of 123 Lexington Avenue, but were turned away by the butler. "He is sitting alone in his room sobbing like a child, with his head on his desk and his face buried in his hands," Powell told them as they scribbled on their notepads. "I dare not disturb him."[215]

Arthur had always been an emotional creature, but since his wife died in January 1880, he had become particularly fragile about death. Nell was the love of his life and during their years of courtship he would frequently gush over her in long love letters. You are "my darling, dearer to me than all the world beside," he wrote her in a birthday note dated 1857. "[This morning] my heart was full to overflowing with love. . . . I feel the pulses of your love answering mine."[216] She hated being left alone, yet he often left her there while engaging in machine politics. When illness struck her, he was off electioneering in Albany—mainly trying to get his friend the speakership—and couldn't make it back in time to say goodbye. Transportation on Sundays was far from plentiful and as a result he had to take a milk train that chugged south at a painfully slow pace. He finally reached Manhattan late in the evening and hurried home to find Nell intoxicated with morphine, after which she never regained consciousness.[217] Arthur never forgave himself for arriving too late and was forever pained by the harsh reality that she died alone. Thus much of Arthur's immediate grief over Garfield's death was fueled by the burden of never having had the opportunity to speak to him and set the record straight.

The childlike sobbing over Garfield's death was largely the result of having to come to grips with the responsibility that now fell on his shoulders. He reemerged when the news formally arrived from New Jersey, via a telegram signed by the entire cabinet. Remembering his delayed response when Garfield was shot, Arthur was quick to reply, sending the following telegram: "I have your telegram, and the intelligence fills me with profound sorrow. Express to Mrs. Garfield my profound sympathy. C. A. Arthur."[218] His mind turned to succession and his first priority was to take the oath of office. He dispatched his friends to find a judge, sending two carriages, one with two lawyers, Elihu Root and Dr. Pierre C. Van Wyck, and the other with Police Commissioner Stephen B. French and District Attorney Daniel G. Rollins.[219] The first group had located Judge John R. Brady of the New York Supreme Court and delivered him just before 2:00 a.m. Around 2:15 the second group returned with Charles Donohue, also of the State Supreme Court. Both men were Democrats.[220] Arthur had also sent for his son Alan, who was studying at Columbia and rushed downtown to make it just in time for the ceremony.

Judge Brady swore Arthur in on September 20, 1881, at 2:15 a.m.,[221] reading off a scrap of paper in which the oath was hastily written.[222] The quick ceremony took place in the front parlor[223] area of Arthur's Lexington Avenue townhouse. The new president spent his first night restless with an additional burden of his own creation. During his tenure as vice president, in one of his many political moves, he refused to vacate his Senate seat so that he could block attempts to select a president pro tempore. There was also no speaker of the house since Congress was on recess until December. Now as president, this meant that he had no successor.[224] His opponents resurrected rumors of his "Canadian birth" so as to try to argue his ineligibility for ascension to the presidency.[225] If something should happen to him, the absence of a chief executive meant that there would also be no individual with the legal authority to call a special session of the Congress.[226] He planned to take this action upon his arrival back to Washington, but what if he didn't make it there alive? The restless new president decided to write a decree summoning the United States Senate into immediate special session, for the sole purpose of electing a president pro tempore.[227] He sealed the letter in an envelope, addressed it to "the president," and sent it to the White House first thing in the morning, just in case he was killed en route to Washington.[228] But as soon as he would prove able to call the special session from Washington, the letter would be returned to him.[229] Arthur, of course, survived the trip and three weeks later called a special session of the Senate, which chose Thomas F. Bayard as president pro tempore and Arthur's successor.[230]

From New York City, Arthur joined the funeral procession in the small coastal town of Elberon, New Jersey, where Garfield had arrived by train to spend his final moments resting in a beach cottage. Several weeks prior, volunteers had worked around the clock to lay 3,200 feet of new track so that the dying president could be brought directly to his hotel room by train car.[231] At one point the train stalled going up a hill and those same volunteers pushed it to its destination. Arthur held his first cabinet meeting in Elberon and then joined the group including Blaine and Grant, who had both come to pay their respects, in a special train car.[232]

It's noteworthy that Arthur, who worried about his life even at that moment, still refused presidential protection, which he had accepted as vice president. But Arthur lived a nocturnal existence and enjoyed his independence. He liked the late-night walks with friends through the overgrown trails that weaved through the National Mall. The old hands of the White House—Thomas Pendel, the doorman who had worked through two presidential assassinations, among others—found the new president's resistance negligent and reckless. They had seen all types of volatile personalities visit the White House on a daily basis and witnessed firsthand the growing number of threats. In one instance, "a very ugly customer" brought a loaded pistol onto the executive grounds and was actually apprehended by Pendel and a few colleagues inside the White House.[233]

Upon his arrival in Washington, Arthur was advised to repeat the oath. His previous oath had been administered by a New York state official and without any federal record, which some legal minds thought could present a legitimacy problem down the line.[234] This time it would be less hasty, taking place at noon in the Capitol on September 22 with roughly forty esteemed figures[235] that included ex-presidents Grant and Hayes, two associate justices of the Supreme Court,[236] and a collection of senators, members of Congress, and several cabinet secretaries.[237] Morrison R. Waite, the chief justice of the Supreme Court, was also on hand to ensure documentation of the "inauguration," which was memorialized in the official Supreme Court records.[238]

After taking his second oath in two days, Arthur gave a brief inaugural address and once again convened the cabinet. Following the precedent set by previous accidental presidents, he asked each to stay on at least until Congress reconvened in December. They also concurred with the decision to call a special session of the Senate for October 10, 1881,[239] which closed the loop on the succession crisis.

Despite the adversarial role he had played toward his predecessor, Arthur enjoyed a honeymoon period as president. Public opinion had shifted and it seemed that citizens and the press alike were ready to give him the benefit of the doubt as president. This was due in large part to what by all accounts was his admirable and respectful behavior during the period in which Garfield lay mortally wounded. The *New York Times,* which had been critical of Arthur, observed that if Garfield's "legal successor has not disarmed criticism, he has at least done nothing to sharpen it."[240] Charles Foster, the Republican governor from Ohio, predicted, "The people and the politicians will find that Vice President Arthur and President Arthur are different men."[241] They were right. When faced with several cabinet vacancies, Arthur rose to the occasion and though some of the men were Stalwarts, they each added some meaningful policy value.[242] He did eventually try to offer Conkling a seat on the Supreme Court— and he did catch some flak for it—but this would not have been a power-behind-the-throne kind of position and the New York Stalwart preferred to wallow in self-pity anyway.[243] Not surprisingly, the die-hard Stalwarts were disappointed. John O'Brien, one of Arthur's old machine buddies, acknowledged, "he isn't Chet Arthur anymore, he's the president."[244]

Arthur had an easy time prolonging the honeymoon period, mainly because he did little to disrupt anything of consequence. He was basically a socialite in the White House and when it came to governing, he wasn't much interested. For any other president, this would have tainted him out of the gate. For Arthur, the country was so relieved by his unwillingness to cave to the Stalwarts that his policy apathy went largely unremarked. He cared much more about maximizing his lifestyle in the White House, starting with the most superficial aspects—the renovations. "I will not live in a house like this," he protested to Colonel Rockwell,[245] and refused to move in until a robust renovation project had been planned and executed. To be fair, the place needed it. The mourning drapes from Garfield's funeral had been drenched by the constant rainfall, which sent streaks of black dye down the walls of the executive mansion.[246] Arthur personally oversaw the renovations and left no detail uncovered and no outdated item behind. He noted all items that had overstayed their welcome, clearing out twenty-four wagonloads of furniture[247] and artifacts dating back to the first Adams administration and instructing staff to sell them at public auction.[248] Among the items were Nellie Grant's—Ulysses Grant's third child—birdcage and a pair of Abraham Lincoln's trousers.[249] For an extra-special finish, he hired Charles Lewis Tiffany, the famous jeweler and founder of Tiffany & Co., to build the interior glass for the revamped mansion. The two knew each other through their membership in the exclusive Century Club and had struck a bond. He also installed wood-burning fireplaces in all the rooms and commissioned the White House's very first elevator.[250] Because he outsourced or ignored most official business, Arthur busied himself with visiting the construction site as a favorite after-dinner activity, where much to the chagrin of the workers he meticulously inspected every feature and offered plenty of unsolicited feedback.[251] And when he was not on site, he was busy barking orders from afar. In the end, the renovations cost a fortune, far exceeding the allocated budget and making it the most ambitious White House renovation since its reconstruction after the War of 1812.[252]

Arthur's vanity hardly subsided after moving into the White House, particularly as it provided a distraction from responsibility. As president, he fabricated his own coat of arms[253] and had a special presidential carriage custom made. And when both were completed, he unveiled them with all the bells and whistles one might expect of a reigning king. Wrote the *New York Times,*

> It is no exaggeration to say that it is the finest which has ever appeared in the streets of the capital. The carriage, from the New York Broome Street Brewsters, is a landau of novel design, painted a dark, mellow green, relieved with enough picking out in red to show the outline without being conspicuous. The trimmings are of Morocco and cloth, the cushions and doors being faced with heavy lace. . . . The inside of the carriage is Labrador otter, beautifully lined with dark green and having the monogram CA.A. worked in silk.[254]

Arthur's obsession with fine tailoring rivaled his interest in renovations and fancy carriages. He was famous for his love of fine brands and he was said to try on twenty pairs of trousers before deciding which to wear. He dressed formally, not so much because of the office he held, but because he had refined taste. His friend and colleague Thomas Platt described him as "veritable chesterfield"[255] and John Wise labeled him as "a very prince of hospitality."[256] He had previously gone to great lengths to upgrade his wardrobe so that he could look fresh in his new role as vice president. One Arthur confidant observed that he purchased six brand-new suits, several pairs of pants, a dress coat, and had two other coats altered and two others pressed at Clarence Brooks & Co. alone, running up a bill of $726.75—roughly $18,000 in today's dollars—that he paid in cash.[257]

Both before and during his presidency, Arthur loved his indulgences. He turned the White House into an almost daily dinner party and rarely went to bed before 2:00 a.m.[258] He could drink more than anyone, but in a life-of-the-party kind of way. One of his contemporaries, who had seen him in action on multiple occasions, described his "power of digestion" and noted his ability to "carry a great deal of wine and liquor without any manifest effect other than great vivacity of speech."[259] His physique, however, was a different story. So indulgent was he at the dinner table that his weight often surged, at times reaching well over 225 pounds.

As president, he cared more about parties than running the country, hosting as many as fifty state dinners[260] during his presidency, the first of which was held for General and Mrs. Grant in March 1882. His lavish parties at the White House were an almost daily occurrence, where the upper echelons of Washington society ate food cooked by an imported French chef and doled out by an abundance of servants wearing customized uniforms personally selected by the president.[261] Upon discovering that the table in the state dining room only seated thirty-five to forty, he grew anxious and experimented with different table configurations until he found that an "I" shape was the best way to increase capacity.[262] Not surprisingly, his ostentatious presidency drew criticism, like that which described him as "a novel species of president."[263] Some were less flattering, like that of former president Hayes, who disparaged his behavior as nothing more than a debauchery of "liquor, snobbery, and rosé."[264]

As his vanity and indulgences would suggest, Arthur really didn't work very hard. He longed for his days as vice president, which afforded him status without responsibility. Now as president, everything would change. He had to go to the office, manage real responsibilities, and perform a number of tasks that he was neither programmed for nor interested in doing. He was probably lazier than any other man to serve the office, rarely arriving in the office before 10:00 a.m. and even then almost never working either a full day or week. He took Sundays and Mondays off and considered an hour or two of receiving people on other occasions as a full day of work.[265]

Arthur was a procrastinator, who in the words of one White House clerk "never did today what he could put off until tomorrow."[266] He seemed "oppressed with either duties or the inversion of his natural hours"[267] and hated working where he lived. He loathed decision making and found the simplest tasks annoying, once taking an entire month to copy a letter of condolence prepared in the State Department for transmission to a European court.[268] His staff became so embarrassed by his lack of work that they created what was called a "property basket," filled with official-looking documents, which he was known to carry into his office on his way to delayed appointments to create an appearance of industry although the contents were never disturbed.[269]

A Respectable Presidency

On August 27, 1881, then vice president Arthur had received the first of several dozen letters from a mysterious pen pal named Julia Sand.* While unsolicited letters were not uncommon, her two-page letter seemed overly familiar and critical, yet spot-on in its analysis. She reminded him that "the day [Garfield] was shot, the thought rose in a thousand minds that you might be the instigator of the foul act." She asked, "Is not that a humiliation which cuts deeper than any bullet can pierce?" She described him as "rich" and "powerful," but without support, noting that "all over the land not a prayer was uttered in your behalf, not a tear shed . . . the great American people was glad to be rid of you," meaning they would have preferred to not have him as president. Expecting Garfield to die, she expressed a "faith" in Arthur's "better nature" and urged him to silence the critics with "reform." She asked him to prove that he can be the "firmest companion" for civil service reform and cautioned him to lead by example and not to "remove any man from office unnecessarily."[270] In future letters, she begged him to stay out of the affairs of New York State and to

---

* I owe a debt of gratitude to Candice Millard, who first discovered the Sand letters, wrote about them in her book, and encouraged me to go through them in the Library of Congress.

remain "passive." "Stay in Washington," she told him. Remain "absorbed in national affairs, not showing by the movement of an eyelash that you take an interest in what is going on"[271] in your home state.

Sand's gift with words and the intimacy of her writing elevated her importance. In reality, she was a thirty-one-year-old invalid who lived with her family on East Seventy-fourth Street in Manhattan. By her own admission, she had "not been in society for years" and "rarely go[t] out of the house." She suffered from loss of hearing and spinal impairment, which made mobility difficult. Politics was her indulgence and she became a harmless stalker who obsessively read about the president's movements and paid close attention to every mention of him in the press. Like a vigorous researcher, she triangulated each article for truths about his intentions and did not shy away from questioning him and challenging his actions. She described herself as a "detective" whose very nature is "cold, questioning, and skeptical."[272] Her letters were candid to the point of being mean, digging into what must have been Arthur's greatest insecurities and trepidations. She was the nineteenth-century equivalent of today's Internet trolls.

Sand focused mostly on politics, but she often went on side tangents about his health and well-being, once inquiring about why his "pictures vary about 100lbs in weight."[273] She described Arthur as "Henry V" and referred to herself as his "little dwarf," as if to suggest she was his able advisor or court jester. In truth, she was more like a minder. It seemed that every action, rumor, and feud caught her attention and made its way back to him through her long, inquisitive, and at times accusatory letters.

With a self-appointed written conscience following his every move, Arthur managed to defy expectations and have a respectful presidency. He did not sever ties with the Stalwarts; quite the contrary, as he frequently welcomed them to lavish banquets[274] at the White House and lavish entertainments. But as Sand advised, he neither dished out patronage to them, nor did he fire those men like Robertson whom he had fought so viciously against. Adhering to more of her wisdom, he resisted the urge to meddle in New York politics and most notably stayed on the sidelines for Alonzo Cornell's gubernatorial reelection campaign in the fall of 1881. Having been demonized over Garfield's assassination, he understood the importance of optics. When New York's state convention gathered, he made the decision to leave for Washington, lest it look as if he had his hand in state politics.[275]

As president, his policy agenda was not ambitious, but when Congress ran afoul of his convictions, he proved willing to use his office and the veto power to influence the outcome. One such example related to a bill introduced by Senator John F. Miller that called for a twenty-year exclusion of Chinese laborers as well as a permanent ban on citizenship for Chinese residents. Despite the bill's popularity on both sides of the aisle,[276] Arthur vetoed it based on the fact that it infringed upon preexisting treaty arrangements between the Chinese emperor and the U.S. government; but truth be told, he found the bill abhorrently racist and xenophobic. Californians were furious and took to the streets to burn him in effigy. Arthur wasn't religious like his father and it came at the expense of their relationship. However, he admired his father's religion-inspired opposition to slavery and generally found himself empathetic to the plight of those on the other end of discriminatory practices. He knew that Congress had the votes to override his veto,[277] but it was good enough for him to send the message. Congress got the message, indeed, and revised the bill to shrink the exclusion period from twenty years to ten.[278]

When it came to those issues most important to his predecessor—civil rights and civil service reform—President Arthur rose to the occasion, at least sort of. Of the two, civil rights advocacy was the more natural fit. Arthur could have done more, but he took important steps particularly in supporting blacks not only in the South, where their well-being was conveniently tied to making Republican gains below the Mason-Dixon line.[279] As president, he personally donated money to an all-black church, showed up in person to present diplomas to graduates of a black high school in Washington, and invited the choir from Fisk University to perform at the White House, a performance that brought the president to tears. He also made several noteworthy appointments of blacks to public office, including P. B. S. Pinchback, the newspaper owner and former acting governor of Louisiana, who became surveyor of the port of New Orleans; H. C. C. Astwood, Pinchback's associate editor, who became assistant United States commissioner general; Mifflin W. Gibbs, who was made receiver of monies at Little Rock, Arkansas; and former senator Blanche K. Bruce, who was named consul to Trinidad. He called for education for blacks in each of his three annual messages to Congress and he came out forcefully against the Supreme Court's 1883 decision to declare the Civil Rights Act of 1875 unconstitutional,[280] going so far as to state he would back any legislation that would reduce the impact of that ruling.[281]

All of this was quite natural, but when it came to civil service reform, Chester Arthur was an unlikely advocate. He owed his entire career to the spoils system and had been one of its most active practitioners. But President and Vice President Arthur were very different. The combination of a deranged office seeker making him president, the subsequent animosity he felt from the American people, and the decimation of Republicans in the 1882 elections were enough to force a change of mind.

There was also Julia Sand, whose letters persisted in their urging of civil service reform. She called out the detectives who surrounded him and observed this danger to be a symptom of the "absolute need for political reform."[282] Her letters taunted him, suggesting that perhaps he was too much of a coward to push for reform. Sand reminded Arthur that like Cardinal Thomas Wolsey, the infamous almoner to Henry VIII, he had a habit of using his "great ability for small ends" and begged him not to slide backward. She knew him to be capable of shepherding reform, but questioned his courage and strength to act on it. "Are you content to sit, like a snake-charmer, and let loathesome serpents coil about you, priding yourself on it that not one of them dares sting you?" she asked. "I would rather think of you like St. George in shining armor striking death to the heart of the dragon."[283]

Arthur understood that a nudge from him would go a long way in creating momentum for reform and at a minimum demonstrate that he would not stand in its way. He took his first action in July 1882, announcing that government employees had no obligation to give to campaigns and their decision to participate or abstain would have no impact on job security.[284] This was a big deal as Arthur himself had been among the senior party bosses who most frequently shook down public officials for campaign contributions. Both parties were shocked and while neither knew how far he would go with his support, they understood that at a minimum he would not obstruct this legal protection for government employees. In response, champions of civil service reform doubled down. Those on the fence tipped in its favor. And its greatest detractors struggled to mount an effective opposition. The result was the Pendleton Act, which the president signed into law on January 16, 1883, just a month and a half before leaving office. The act created the Civil Service Commission, which was quick to praise the president for his "constant, firm, and friendly support"[285] in abolishing the spoils system, at least in name. In practice, the president could still determine which jobs would be based on political affiliation, but the symbolic neck of the spoils system had been broken.

It is hard to gauge Sand's influence, but it was not without consequence. As early as November 1881, she began suggesting they meet. She thought he would never come and at times became agitated over his lack of response to her requests. But to her surprise, on the evening of August 20, 1882, an elaborately decorated carriage appeared out of nowhere and parked at the entrance of the Seventy-fourth Street residence owned by Miss Sand's brother, and out stepped the president.[286] They discussed music and he consumed some delightful claret in a sherry glass. He stayed for about an hour in what she would later describe as a "very stiff visit." In a letter to Arthur written four days later, she became defensive and agitated about their meeting, accusing him of using her to get to her mother and sisters.[287] She seemed nonplussed that he had not come by the house in the morning when she was alone and noted that this led to accusations that she had used her family to protect her from a presidential scolding. Most hurtful to her, however, was his "inexorable 'no' at parting when" she asked if he "had forgiven some of the harsh things" she had said.[288] Arthur never visited again and she never received any correspondence. Over the next year, the tone of her notes became more incoherent and volatile, some addressing him as "my very bad friend" and "my very, very, bad friend."[289]

Arthur may be best remembered for civil service reform, but where he really deserves credit is for being proactive around national defense. This was in large part because of the nostalgia he felt over his time served as quartermaster in the Army. But he genuinely cared about the issue. Not since a previous accidental president, John Tyler, had a peacetime president pushed such an ambitious naval plan. During the fifteen years since the Civil War, America's once world-class naval position had declined to the point of leaving the country dangerously exposed, not to mention it was a global embarrassment.[290] America's dire naval situation was described in a report submitted to the president on November 7, 1881, by a Garfield-appointed Naval Advisory Board,[291] which revealed a capacity better fit for the Revolutionary War. The report found that the Navy lacked "a single up-to-date warship, and of its two hundred craft, not one carried a high-powered cannon . . . thirty-three of the thirty-seven United States ships of the first, second, and third rank were made entirely of wood," and the entire naval fleet was reliant in "full on sail power." The poor quality of the ships was rivaled only by the low caliber of incompetent men manning the decks. Despite almost "4,500 workers . . . employed in nine navy yards and five naval stations," they seemed "unable to repair harbor fortifications, eliminate overlapping bureaus, enforce discipline, or boost sagging morale." There were a "disproportionate number of officers" within the ranks, insubordination was rampant, and a number of officers seemed to treat the Navy's ships "as if they were private yachts."[292]

Capitalizing on some initial momentum generated by Garfield in his short time as president, Arthur wanted to make America a great commercial power, which would require a much stronger Navy. The first Naval Advisory Board recommended the construction of sixty-eight ships, which would mostly be made of steel. Congress scoffed at such an unrealistic request by responding with authorization for the construction of two new steel ships, but no new funding. Arthur played musical chairs with his secretary of the navy and appointed William Chandler to devise a more realistic plan for seven additional cruisers and four gunboats. He devoted a substantial amount of energy to this proposal in his final State of the Union address. On March 3, 1883, Congress appropriated $1,895,000 for three new armor-plated cruisers and one dispatch boat. The four ships—the *Atlanta, Boston, Chicago,* and *Dolphin,* later known as the "ABCD" ships—represented the birth of the modern-day Navy.[293]

====

During his presidency, Arthur had developed Bright's disease,* which he concealed from the public. At the time, Bright's disease was not well understood, but the burdens of the disease destroyed Arthur's body in the latter stages of his presidency. By the spring of 1883, he started to delay official business until noon.[294] One of Arthur's physicians, a cousin by marriage named Brodie Harndon, routinely checked up on him and confided to his private diary, "The president is sick in body and soul."[295]

---

* As New York physician Robert Hiensch explains, "Bright's disease is a historical term that today encompasses various kidney disorders with specific clinical criteria and etiologies." Medical historians have retroactively diagnosed Arthur with glomerulonephritis, which is an inflammatory disease of the nephrons that prevents the body from ridding itself of toxins. "Had the precise diagnosis been known back then, it probably would not have mattered since they did not have the right treatments and the outcome likely would have been the same."

The disease left him with little appetite to run in the 1884 election. He wouldn't have had much of a chance anyway. He had angered the Stalwarts by not allowing them to take control of his administration. The Half-Breeds never regained their trust in him and independents within the party questioned the authenticity of his civil service reform and remained incensed about his inability to secure convictions of the Star Route perpetrators.[296] Nonetheless, when the convention met on June 3, 1884, Arthur received a substantial portion of the delegates, but eventually lost to James Blaine, who as the Republican nominee would lose a close election to the Democratic governor Grover Cleveland. Arthur was a lame-duck president, sick with a terminal illness, and politically damned by the prospects of watching a Democratic president elected for the first time in thirty years.

There was a move in Albany to send ex-president Arthur to the Senate, just as the state legislature in Nashville had elected Andrew Johnson. But the prospect of still serving as president while pressing for an election to a subordinate position seemed beneath his dignity.[297] It didn't matter anyway. By Election Day 1884, Arthur was too sick to vote. He died two years later on November 18, 1886, at the age of fifty-six, younger than all his predecessors except James K. Polk, who died at fifty-three.[298]

Arthur's legacy is more triumphant than his political demise would suggest. In fact, by the time Chester Arthur left the White House he was politically unrecognizable to those who knew him. "No man ever entered the Presidency so profoundly and widely distrusted," the journalist Alexander McClure wrote, "and no one ever retired . . . more generally respected."[299] He didn't pander to the Stalwarts. He rejected the spoils system and signed the Pendleton Act. His use of the veto power was both judicious and principled, particularly with regard to Chinese immigration. Civil rights evolved during his tenure. And he set in motion the construction of a modern Navy that would prove useful nearly two decades later during the Spanish-American War.

Over the next sixteen years, the emergence of a post–Civil War generation and the subsequent age of imperialism created a war-hysterical restlessness that swept the nation. Grover Cleveland, the first Democrat elected president since James Buchanan, tried desperately to turn the temperature down throughout his two nonconsecutive terms in office. He opposed the construction of a canal through Nicaragua, citing the need to avoid complex alliances. When American settlers attempted to topple the Hawaiian queen Liliuokalani and annex the islands, Cleveland urged them to cease. And when Congress backed the Cuban revolutionaries against Spain, he once again urged neutrality and restraint.

Despite his best efforts, Cleveland could slow down, but not stem the tide of a nation that was hungry for war. It didn't help that his two terms were separated by Benjamin Harrison, who had risen from the U.S. Senate to narrowly unseat Cleveland in 1888. If Cleveland's hope had been to keep the U.S. out of trouble and free of entanglements, Harrison seemed committed to the pursuit of both. His imperialistic view of the world was a throwback to the manifest destiny era, but on a more global scale. What he described as commercial reciprocity looked more like interventionism and reflected a territorial expansionist view of the world, particularly in the Western Hemisphere. He nearly took the nation to war with Chile over a skirmish with some sailors, increased the U.S. presence in Haiti, went head-to-head with Italy over organized crime in the Americas, established a protectorate over Samoa, stood firm against Spain's treatment of those living in their colonies, and supported the overthrow of the Hawaiian monarchy as part of a path to annexation. He also built on Arthur's investment in the Navy and further accelerated the development of a world-class fleet that both enhanced U.S. preparedness for war and fed demands from the voyeuristic masses who hoped to see it on display and in action.

By the time William McKinley took office in 1897, it appeared as though war with someone was inevitable and Spain was the most obvious target. Tensions had already built around revolutions against Spanish rule in the Philippines and Cuba. In the case of Cuba, the U.S. took provocative measures and deployed the USS *Maine* into Havana Harbor, where it exploded on February 15. In all likelihood the explosion was an accident, but for warmongers—supported by fake news of the era—it provided the trigger that justified the war. The following month, President McKinley gave the people what they yearned for and declared war on Spain. The fighting lasted ten weeks, included both Caribbean and Pacific theaters of combat, and resulted in a decisive U.S. victory. At the war's conclusion, the U.S. came away with the Spanish colonies of Guam, Philippines, and Puerto Rico, as well as a protectorate in Cuba. For a war-hungry nation eager to grab its slice of the imperial pie, 379 lives lost was a small price to pay for what John Hay described to Theodore Roosevelt as "a splendid little war."[300]

William McKinley *was a friend of the trusts and big business and, while he didn't seek conflict with Spain, he presided over a two-front war in Cuba and the Philippines.*

The New York Republican Party bosses thought they had sidelined **Theodore Roosevelt** *by engineering his nomination as vice president. Instead, an anarchist's bullet made him president and in 1904 he became the first accidental president elected in his own right.*

CHAPTER FIVE

A Most Ambitious Man

Theodore Roosevelt was the most exciting thing to happen to the small town of Pittsfield, Massachusetts, where just a decade earlier a physicist named William Stanley, Jr., transformed an agricultural village into a bustling electrical manufacturing city. The president's visit took place on September 3, 1902, just a few months before the midterm elections, part of a thirteen-day,[1] six-state tour of New England in which he stumped for Republican candidates. It began a few weeks earlier in Connecticut, where in typical Roosevelt fashion he made history as the first sitting president to ride publicly in an electric car.[2] From there he went on to Rhode Island, New Hampshire, Vermont, Maine, and eventually back down to Massachusetts. At every stop, he unleashed an assault on the trusts,[3] spoke of income inequality, and called for a revitalization of the social order. Theodore Roosevelt always performed and the crowds loved it.

The day started as expected—the usual thousands of adoring Roosevelt fans "poured into the city from the country to see and hear the president" deliver what likely promised to be an electrifying speech at the City Park. His remarks were brief but dynamic. He called on his old friend and ex-senator Henry Dawes, who had retired to Pittsfield and now resided in a small house on Elm Street just a short drive away.[4] The two had shared a commitment to conservation—although Dawes had a more mixed record on this[5]—and with Dawes about to turn eighty-six, the president didn't want to miss the opportunity to pay his respects one last time.

After leaving the senator's home, the president's motorcade, which at that time consisted of four small carriages, was making its way down South Street at around 10:15 a.m.[6] when the two mounted troopers flanking the carriage noticed an electric trolley speeding toward them. In those days, trolley tracks ran through the middle of the streets, so it was the speed, rather than the trajectory, that caused alarm. Recognizing the immediate danger, two of the local cavalry turned their horses onto the track and both waved to the motorman to stop. Massachusetts governor Winthrop Crane—who, along with the president's personal secretary (and later secretary of state), George Cortelyou,[7] was with the president—rose to his feet and waved his arms.[8]

It was too late. The trolley struck the back left wheel[9] at high speed as a loud moan went up from the frenzied onlookers who thronged the roadside and who but a moment before were cheering the president.[10] The impact was so powerful that it smashed the back of the vehicle[11] and plowed through to the front wheel,[12] sending the carriage flying in the air. The president and his entourage were thrown more than forty feet and landed at the bottom of their carriage.[13] Roosevelt landed on his face. The crowds were aghast. Several onlookers rushed to the president's carriage, expecting him to be dead.[14]

The presidential party had been tossed and scattered all over the street and not all were accounted for. William "Big Bill" Craig, the president's favorite Secret Service man, was nowhere to be found. Craig was a forty-eight-year-old giant, whose broad frame and six foot three inch height made him difficult to miss. After a search of the accident site was made, Craig's body was found lying lifeless behind the car, his shoulders and chest crushed and the body dreadfully mangled.[15] All eight steel wheels of the trolley had passed over him, leaving behind a trail of blood and bone fragments.[16] He was pronounced dead at the scene, marking the first time in history a member of the Secret Service was killed in the line of duty.

As reported in the press, the president's driver, David J. Pratt, "struck the head of the horse immediately in front of him and rolled clear of him."[17] Pratt, however, came crashing to the ground, resulting in a fractured skull[18] leaving him unconscious. As he lay on the ground, "blood oozed from his ears,[19] his shoulder was dislocated, his ankle sprained and his face badly cut and bruised."[20] He died soon after. The carriage horses took a hard fall and were dead.[21] Some other horses raced off, but a group of men standing nearby reacted quickly enough to stop them.[22]

For a moment, Roosevelt lay on the gravel road like a corpse, perhaps in a mild state of shock. His sight was blurred, and not knowing if this was a result of his poor eyesight or a concussion, he found his spectacles in the grass nearby, remarkably intact, and determined his head was fine. Captain George A. Lung, the president's trusted physician, bolted toward him. "Are you hurt, Mr. President?" he asked. Roosevelt responded, "No, I guess not,"[23] but without the usual flair and theatrics. Governor Crane jumped to his feet and raced over to the president and then together they aided Cortelyou.[24] Crane suffered slight injuries, while Cortelyou was bruised and scratched, in addition to a cut on the head.[25]

For Lung and others, at first glance it appeared that Roosevelt had only slight bruises and a few scratches,[26] but the right side of his chin and face were swollen,[27] there was a gash on his leg, and his lip was cut and blood was flowing from the wound.[28] After brushing himself off, he charged the driver of the trolley, Euclid Madden, brandished his epic teeth, raised his fists, and appeared as if he might knock him senseless before exercising the restraint one would expect of a president. "Did you lose control of the car?" he asked. "If you did, that was one thing. If you didn't, it was a God-damned outrage!" The nervous driver replied, "You don't suppose I tried to do it, do you?" Then, forgetting he was speaking to the president, he snapped, "Well, I had the right of way anyway."[29]

The police dragged Madden off, along with his conductor, James Kelly. He was arrested and charged with manslaughter, for which he served six ·months in prison.[30] It was never discovered why the trolley came at the president's carriage with such velocity. One witness claimed that "the motorman was speeding his car in order to reach the [country] club" and simply wanted to get ahead of the presidential motorcade.[31] Others suggested that the driver was responding to the paparazzi-like urges of his passengers, who wanted to catch a glimpse of their colorful president. There was also a less credible theory of malicious intent, which, while unlikely, could not immediately be ruled out.

No sooner had Roosevelt lowered his fists from Madden's face than he saw the corpse of his favorite bodyguard. Agent Craig had been a remarkable figure, but on this day the legend of a British immigrant who had once protected Queen Victoria[32] was reduced to a blood-soaked scene. "Too bad, too bad," said Roosevelt. "Poor Craig. How my children will feel." Craig was adored by Roosevelt's kids, particularly four-year-old Quentin, with whom he shared a love for comics.[33]

Roosevelt, Cortelyou, and Crane retreated to the home of Charles R. Stevens, a prominent local figure who lived nearby.[34] Remarkably, the president resumed his schedule, traveling to Lenox, where he sent word ahead that there should be no cheering.[35] Eventually he cut short his tour and returned to his Oyster Bay home on Sagamore Hill.[36]

Theodore Roosevelt's rest and recuperation didn't last long. Three weeks later, he was back on the campaign trail, this time touring the Midwest, where he once again stumped for Republican candidates.[37] The midterms were too important to let mourning get in the way and his ambitious legislative agenda needed every congressional seat his party could retain or flip. The trip through the Midwest also came to an abrupt halt. It began in Detroit and got as far as Noblesville, when Roosevelt's neglected leg wound from the Pittsfield accident became infected and abscessed.[38] He required emergency surgery. But ever the theatrical character, Roosevelt gave one more speech at the Columbia Club[39] in Indianapolis, during which he suffered excruciating pain from his leg and was seen limping off the stage.

On September 23, the president was taken to St. Vincent's Hospital in Indianapolis.[40] Despite the pain and inconvenience, he was in good humor, joking with his doctors: "Gentlemen, you are formal! I see you have your gloves on!"[41] Using natural light coming through the windows, Dr. John H. Oliver[42] performed the surgery with assistance from two presidential physicians. They removed two ounces of pus[43] from his leg, during which the president refused anything but local anesthesia, perhaps to ensure that even the doctors were not deprived of the quintessential Theodore Roosevelt experience.[44]

Following the surgery, the doctors ordered Roosevelt, to the extent that anyone could, to stay off his leg and rest for at least ten days. His recovery took longer than expected, dragging well into the second week of October and leading him to cancel a planned trip to Princeton to visit Grover Cleveland. "It is almost impossible for me to write in my present position," he wrote the former president. "I am sincerely sorry to have to say that the doctors tell me that in all probability it will be impossible for me to go to Princeton on the 25th. The wound in my leg is healing rapidly, but I shall have to exercise great care because I have narrowly escaped serious trouble with the bone."[45]

For Roosevelt, who was always in motion, being grounded had to have been utterly claustrophobic. He spent that period in a wheelchair.[46] His time in a wheelchair may have been brief, but the aftereffects of his injury would create discomfort for the rest of his life.[47]

Roosevelt's good fortune reduces what could have been a major moment in history to a mere anecdote. There was no question that the accident was a close call. The *Daily Chieftain* of Indiana wrote, "Narrow Escape from Death Experienced by President Roosevelt,"[48] and the *Houston Daily Post* described it as "Roosevelt's Escape" from death.[49] But what almost none of the contemporary papers noticed and what few historians discuss is that had he died, there was no vice president. The issue of a constitutional mechanism for replacing the vice president had still not been addressed and Roosevelt wouldn't have been in much of a rush to fill the vacancy anyway. None of the previous four accidental presidents had filled the vacancy.

Congress revised the presidential succession law in 1886 by removing the president pro tempore and the speaker of the house from the line of succession and replacing them with the cabinet, beginning with the secretary of state.* In this case, the secretary of state was John Hay, who would have become the acting president, and given the Republican majorities in both chambers of Congress, it is likely that a special election would not have been held, lest they risk handing the presidency to a Democrat.

The 1886 law fixed the term of the acting president for the balance of the regular unexpired term,[50] although a handful of amendments made the mechanics far more complex. For example, the acting president was required to call Congress together, and that body would decide whether it deemed a special election desirable, not to mention constitutional.[51] William McKinley had vigorously opposed the law while representing Ohio in the 49th Congress, suggesting the immediate special election option was more democratic: "I would leave that power with the people where it properly belongs. I am opposed to any step in the opposite direction."[52] As he lay dying a number of years later, the reality of Theodore Roosevelt succeeding him as president may have been on his mind.

---

* The Presidential Succession Act of 1886 was designed to address certain flaws in the existing legislation, particularly a scenario in which there is nobody to succeed a dying president.

A Force of Nature

Roosevelt lived his life as a sprint. His charisma was off the charts. He never shut up and was such a presence that he left an indelible impression on everyone he encountered. The cowboys in the West found him out of place in how he looked and talked, but quickly embraced him as a "dude." His political adversaries thought him insufferable, but understood his appeal and were often happy to ride his coattails. His professor at Harvard, so overwhelmed by Roosevelt's classroom monologues, on one occasion shouted: "See here, Roosevelt, let me talk. I'm running this course."[53]

Roosevelt had a greater lust for adventure than any president who came before or after. He truly was a Renaissance Man who excelled at everything he did or exhausted himself trying. He was a prolific writer, authoring thirty-five books and more than 150,000 letters. He was a gifted and candid orator. His memory was near photographic. He was an amateur zoologist, biologist, ornithologist, and taxidermist. He shot every kind of animal imaginable, including lion, elephant, rhinoceros, buffalo, and a grizzly bear, which he only narrowly escaped, at least according to one of his likely embellished tales.[54] He stuffed his own trophies. He brought his hobbies everywhere, including the Harvard dormitory, where he filled his room with specimens of birds and other small animals, likely to the dismay of his dorm mates.

Roosevelt was a first-rate sportsman, horseback riding, rowing, wrestling, and even boxing, until a recreational fight with an aide left him blind in his left eye. He was an avid swimmer, who was known to take a dip in the coldest temperatures. While governor in New York, the champion middleweight wrestler of America happened to be living in Albany, and Roosevelt invited him for some roughhousing three or four afternoons a week.[55] As president, he kept a "tennis cabinet."[56] "We thus swam Rock Creek in the early spring when the ice was floating thick upon it," he wrote in his autobiography. "If we swam the Potomac, we usually took off our clothes. I remember one such occasion when the French Ambassador, [Jean-Jules] Jusserand, who was a member of the Tennis Cabinet, was along, and, just as we were about to get in to swim, somebody said, 'Mr. Ambassador, Mr. Ambassador, you haven't taken off your gloves,' to which he promptly responded, 'I think I will leave them on; we might meet ladies!'"[57] That same ambassador was held hostage by President Roosevelt, who insisted that they play two sets of tennis, go for a jog, and then undertake an intense workout with a medicine ball. When Theodore Roosevelt asked his guest, "What would you like to do now?" he responded, "If it's just the same with you, Mr. President, I'd like to lie down and die."[58]

At a time when few people left the country, Roosevelt had cruised the Nile in Egypt, visited Syria and Palestine (present-day Israel), and traveled to at least eight countries in Europe, including Greece and Turkey. He and his siblings spent five months living with a German family in Dresden.[59] While living in Dresden, he often ventured into the country, where, in his autobiography, he described how he "collected specimens industriously and enlivened the household with hedgehogs and other small beasts and reptiles which persisted in escaping from partially closed bureau drawers."[60]

While the list of Roosevelt's gifts, hobbies, and accomplishments is as overwhelming as it is impressive, the roots of his ambition are far more interesting. His disregard for the impossible and the breadth of his activities were neither random nor accidental. He was meant to die young and he knew it. Born with severe asthma and health problems, "I was a sickly, delicate boy," he wrote, "suffered much from asthma, and frequently had to be taken away on trips to find a place where I could breathe."[61] Compounding his asthmatic challenge was a nervous digestive system and bad eyesight.[62] His ailments left him with no option other than homeschooling. Despite the nontraditional education he received at home, Roosevelt was accepted to Harvard. While there, he underwent a routine medical examination and was told by doctors that his heart was weak and any unnecessary exertion could kill him.[63] But Roosevelt always knew better, or at least thought he did, and confidently proclaimed that he had no intention of following the doctors' advice.[64]

"I was nervous and timid," Theodore Roosevelt wrote. "Yet from reading of the people I admired—ranging from the soldiers of Valley Forge, and Morgan's riflemen, to the heroes of my favorite stories—and from hearing of the feats performed by my Southern forefathers and kinsfolk, and from knowing my father I felt a great admiration for men who were fearless and who could hold their own in the world."[65] His father believed his son had the drive to overcome his physical weaknesses. He built a gym in their townhouse and instructed his son to transform his body.[66] Roosevelt took the guidance literally and from that moment on lived a life of such physical vigor that he left his disabilities in the dust.

Physical limitations were only one category of obstacles that Roosevelt had to overcome. He also struggled with depression. He lost his mother and his wife within hours of each other on the same day, February 14, 1884, a tragedy that exacerbated his emotional struggles. Roosevelt learned that he could outpace his depression if he stayed in motion. He ran through life and ran fast, leaving behind any emotional obstacle that might stand in the way. This meant never speaking of his first wife, Alice, and remaining somewhat distant from their only daughter. He burned the love letters and referred to their daughter, Alice, as "baby Lee" so as not to remind him of his wife with the same name.

What Roosevelt had to overcome physically and mentally to achieve a position of power is nothing short of extraordinary. He was not the first politician with broad ambitions, but what he overcame to get there makes his accomplishments that much more remarkable.

A Nuisance to the Political Machine

What we know and admire of Theodore Roosevelt today is what drove the New York party bosses mad. New York was Thomas Platt's turf, at least when it came to the Republican Party. Platt, nicknamed the "easy boss," was a ruthless political operator, but not in the way that Roscoe Conkling and William Tweed had been. When it came to politics, he played the long game.[67] He climbed back from the twin embarrassments of resigning his Senate seat and a treacherous sex scandal in 1881, eventually constructing a formidable political machine that put William L. Strong into the New York mayor's office in 1894.[68] With Albany and New York City firmly in his control, Boss Platt played the party politics like a marionette he guided from his political pulpit at the Fifth Avenue Hotel in Manhattan.

Platt was not unaware of increasingly populist sentiments calling for attention to the civil service and other reforms. He paid lip service to all of it, but like many bosses of his era, he was in no hurry to overhaul a system that worked just fine for him. By the time he clawed his way back to power, a young nuisance named Theodore Roosevelt had entrenched himself in the State Assembly and was causing trouble. At twenty-three, Roosevelt was the youngest state legislator[69] and while his arrival in Albany was initially welcomed, his zealotry for reform irked the old-timers. He was too colorful and wanted too much change. And while Platt could do little to prevent Roosevelt's presence in the Assembly, he fought the young progressive's agenda with all his might. And he was mighty, "the absolute boss of the Republican Party,"[70] who unlike so many other political bosses was not vulnerable to the same allegations of corruption since he refused to financially profit from his position.[71]

Ambition was the fuel that kept Theodore Roosevelt going. "I intended to be one of the governing class," he remarked shortly after his election to the New York State Assembly.[72] His presence in the Assembly proved seminal. He used his time to connect with the most vulnerable segments of society and saw firsthand the hardships of the urban poor, particularly laborers and new immigrants, whom he believed government had a responsibility to help.[73]

Roosevelt was not well-liked by many of his colleagues. Some of this was his personality and some of it his progressive zealotry, and he drew attention from some of the more uncouth Tammany Hall characters. One such fellow was "Big John" McManus, an ex-prizefighter and Tammany stooge[74] who did much of the dirty work as the party's designated thug. McManus had been stewing about Roosevelt one afternoon, bragging that he would find Roosevelt and toss "that damned dude" in a blanket.[75] When Roosevelt caught wind of the threat, he tracked down McManus and came at him with a threat of his own. "I hear you are going to toss me in a blanket," he scolded. "By God! If you try anything like that, I'll kick you, I'll bite you, I'll kick you in the balls, I'll do anything to you—you'd better leave me alone."[76]

It didn't take long for another, this time more violent, showdown. As one legend goes, Roosevelt had been conversing with another young Republican assemblyman named William O'Neill, when the two decided to stop into an Albany saloon for an afternoon drink. J. J. Costello, another Tammany character, took note of Roosevelt's arrival without a coat and said, "Won't Mamma's boy catch cold?" Roosevelt gave him a sock to the jaw and knocked him to the ground. When he stood back up, Theodore Roosevelt hit him again, and when he got up one more time, he hit him yet again. "Now you go over there and wash yourself. When you are in the presence of gentlemen, conduct yourself like a gentleman."[77]

Because of these encounters and his colorful responses, Roosevelt took the State Assembly by storm. "Within forty-eight hours of his committee appointment," writes the biographer Edmund Morris, "he had introduced four bills, one to purify New York's water supply, another to purify its election of alderman, a third to cancel all stocks and bonds in the city's 'sinking fund,' and a fourth to lighten the judicial burden on the Court of Appeals."[78] If his proliferation of legislation agitated party bosses, his rhetoric—referring to "the wealthy criminal class,"[79] as one such example—was infuriating.

Roosevelt was threatening to the party bosses, both because of what he proposed and because he had his finger on the zeitgeist. The country was hungry for reform. By 1893 America had descended into unprecedented economic chaos. Sloppy financing of railroads and excess construction created a bubble that eventually burst with the failure of the Reading Railroad. As chaos turned to panic, unemployment hit an all-time high—25 percent in Pennsylvania, 35 percent in New York, and 43 percent in Michigan. More than five hundred banks shut down and another fifteen thousand businesses closed their doors. Farmers were hit particularly hard, resulting in widespread food shortages and desperation, as people were willing to do just about anything for food, including prostitution.[80]

As conditions worsened, Roosevelt moved from the State Assembly to the Civil Service Commission, where he took a number of positions that would later prove on the right side of history, but politically unpopular, including women's rights.[81] But it was his appointment as police commissioner of New York that propelled him into the spotlight as a crusader for reform. He was ruthless in taking on corruption, a mandate that he believed came straight from Mayor Strong.[82] A close friendship with Jacob Riis, the social activist, photographer, and author of *How the Other Half Lives,* had been an "enlightenment and an inspiration." "I was still ignorant of the extent to which big men of great wealth played a mischievous part in our industrial and social life," he wrote in his autobiography.[83] He made note of how the police interacted with shopkeepers and merchants and how they treated newly arrived immigrants, many of whom were illiterate.[84]

The press found Roosevelt both fascinating and ridiculous. He was gimmicky—carrying a small notebook with him and recording the names of crooked cops[85]—but he got results. In his first two years as commissioner, complaints brought against officers nearly doubled from 3,757 to 6,134.[86] Later in life, he would reflect that these two years as police commissioner, particularly the late-night visits to the slums with

Riis, made him appreciate the extent of social and economic injustice in the country.[87]

It didn't take long for the Democratic Machine of Tammany Hall, including the mayor, to tire of Roosevelt, but getting rid of him was a different story altogether, given his popularity. His move to ban liquor sales on the Sabbath, however, presented an interesting opportunity—both because many of the saloonkeepers were Tammany flunkies and because German Americans were a powerful voting bloc in New York City.[88] The move was seen as highly political, a veiled attempt to thrash his partisan enemies.[89] The party bosses called for his head. Bullheaded Roosevelt scoffed at their demands and snubbed his nose at the criticism. If they wanted him out, they would have to drive him out of town.

The party bosses, however, had a different plan: do it the old-fashioned way—a suitable promotion for an ambitious man. But the timing was not right. The Democrats controlled the White House. That being said, with the 1896 presidential election looming and a Republican victory likely, Platt and his underlings salivated over the prospect of shipping Roosevelt off to a cushy job in Washington.

To Washington and Back

Grover Cleveland's second shot at the presidency—the only president to serve two nonconsecutive terms—was doomed from the start, and by 1896 the Democrats stood little chance of holding on to the White House. The nation, and certainly the Republican Party, was all about financial interests. Led by the business tycoon Mark Hanna, the party targeted the machine bosses and industrialists of the time and made William McKinley the face of the party's march toward American prosperity. The Democratic nominee, William Jennings Bryan, had only a slim chance of winning. He would lose the election by the largest margin in twenty-five years.

When a position opened up in Washington for assistant secretary of the navy, Boss Platt lobbied hard for McKinley to choose Roosevelt. He didn't even have to fake it. Roosevelt was more than qualified. He had written the definitive book about U.S. naval preparedness and had the critical acclaim to show for it.

Roosevelt's credentials aside, McKinley had misgivings. He had campaigned as an isolationist and feared Roosevelt was a hothead with a fetish for war. There was a lot of truth to this. McKinley had served valiantly as a major in the Civil War and understood the horrors. Roosevelt read, studied, dreamed, and fantasized about going to war; but he had never been given the opportunity to serve. He believed that the "triumphs of war" were greater than the "triumphs of peace"[90] and that America "need[ed] a war."[91]

McKinley was nervous about having Theodore Roosevelt in any position where he could influence military decisions. When a Roosevelt emissary lobbied him for war, McKinley responded by telling her, "I want peace and I am told that your friend Theodore—whom I know only slightly—is always getting into rows with everybody."[92] Roosevelt was part of a faction of jingoists* who believed that America needed to shift toward a more interventionist mind-set.[93]

After prodding by Roosevelt's close friend and mentor, Senator Henry Cabot Lodge, McKinley offered Roosevelt the appointment.[94] But as McKinley suspected, Roosevelt was dangerously antsy as assistant secretary of the navy. He didn't like being second in command.

His moment came at 9:40 p.m. on February 15, 1898. An explosion rocked the USS *Maine*, which was docked in Havana Harbor and was a symbol of America's growing naval prowess.[95] Two hundred sixty Americans lost their lives (several more succumbed to their injuries after the fact) and the public was outraged. Cuba was one of Spain's last colonies in the Western Hemisphere, so it is not surprising that suspicions began to swirl about a Spanish attack on America.

President McKinley urged calm and caution until the truth about what had happened was fully understood. It was not unusual for ships at the time to combust due to any number of factors and if he was going to prepare for war, he wanted there to be irrefutable doubt that this was a Spanish attack. Roosevelt found McKinley's restraint infuriating, stewing in private and agitating to just about anyone who would listen.

As McKinley proceeded cautiously on Cuba, Roosevelt looked for a path to war with Spain. On February 25, 1898, he got his moment. His boss, Navy Secretary John D. Long, took half the day off to enjoy a "me-

---

* "Jingoist" was a term lifted from British vernacular and used to describe the American war hawks of the late nineteenth and early twentieth centuries.

chanical massage," which was the 1890s version of a Sharper Image massage chair.[96] Roosevelt would have several uninterrupted hours as acting secretary of the navy. Long was not unaware of Roosevelt's hyperactivity and left strict instructions for him to avoid taking "any step affecting the policy of the administration without consulting the President or me."[97]

It may seem ridiculous to issue such a stern caution for a half-day reprieve, but these were not ordinary times and Roosevelt was no ordinary deputy. War with Spain lingered over Cuba and tensions were rising over another Spanish colony, in the Philippines. Any escalation or miscalculation on either side could push the tension over the edge. Roosevelt had been agitating for war in the Philippines, Cuba, or really anywhere that Spain had colonies. He believed that "Spain attempted to govern her colonies on archaic principles which rendered her control of them incompatible with the advance of humanity and intolerable to the conscience of mankind . . . unspeakable horror, degradation, and misery."[98] Furthermore, he didn't view war as a horror; instead, he romanticized it, yearned for America to engage in combat, and he himself desired the chance to throw on a uniform and volunteer for the front lines. He resented what he perceived to be McKinley's "unwilling[ness] to prepare for war" and blamed the president's caution on the "many honest but misguided men [who] believed that the preparation itself tended to bring on the war." He confessed that he was so incensed by this thinking, whether real or perceived, that "whenever I was left as Acting Secretary I did everything in my power to put us in readiness."[99]

Roosevelt adhered to Long's instructions for about five minutes before agitating. He instructed Commodore George Dewey, who commanded the Asiatic Squadron out of Hong Kong, to keep the ships packed with coal and on standby to attack Spain's Philippines fleet at full capacity for a decisive victory in the event of a declaration of war.[100] Roosevelt and the war hawks saw Spain as a threat that needed to be removed, and as with Cuba in the Western Hemisphere, they tried to argue that the Philippines was a Spanish colony that could threaten America's Pacific shores. They said what they knew would appeal to Americans, which in this case was a moral imperative to aid the Filipino people in their quest for independence. In the words of one biographer, "[Long] should have known better. Like a mischievous child, Roosevelt churned out an orgy of orders while the adult was out of the room. Among other things, he asked the House Naval Affairs Committee to authorize the enlistment of 'an unlimited number of seamen,' and had guns sent from Washington to the Brooklyn Navy Yard to be mounted on cruisers."[101]

The secretary was dismayed. "The very devil seemed to possess him yesterday afternoon," Long confided to his diary. "He has gone about things like a bull in a china shop. . . . It shows how the best fellow in the world, and one with splendid capacities, is worse than useless if he lacks a cool head and careful direction."[102] But his headaches didn't stop there. Roosevelt looked for opportunities to accelerate preparations for war. On Saturday night, March 26, 1898, he gave a fiery pro-war speech at Washington's Gridiron Club. "We will have this war of freedom," he told the crowd, after which he turned to Mark Hanna and said that anyone who wanted to stand in the way of popular opinion was "welcome to experiment."[103]

The American press and people agreed with Roosevelt and by April, with the aid of some fake news and the catchy rallying cry of "Remember the Maine, to hell with Spain," the Spanish-American War had begun in both the Philippines and Cuba. For many, the Cuba front was an adventure not to be missed. Private citizens lined up to volunteer. Roosevelt was no exception to this and a prestigious job in the administration certainly was not going to deprive him of finally getting onto the battlefield.

Roosevelt resigned his post in the Naval Department and rounded up the First United States Volunteer Cavalry, better known as the "Rough Riders." His boss thought he had "lost his head. . . . He means well, but it is one of those cases of aberration—desertion—vain-glory; of which he is entirely unaware."[104] Long was not alone in these sentiments, nor was he wrong.

His time in Cuba is well-documented, but what's most important is Theodore Roosevelt got his romantic moment. He was reckless, even suicidal in how he approached battle. The result was extraordinary valor, noted in the many Medal of Honor endorsements he received.* "In moving to the assault of San Juan Hill, Colonel Roosevelt was most conspicu-

---

* Despite many glowing endorsements, Theodore Roosevelt did not receive the medal of honor until January 16, 2001, when outgoing President Bill Clinton awarded him the honor posthumously for his gallantry on San Juan Hill during the Spanish-American War.

ously brave, gallant and indifferent to his own safety," wrote one endorser. "He, in the open, led his regiment; no officer could have set a more striking example to his men or displayed greater intrepidity." Another described how he "killed one of the enemy with his own hand" and yet another described "his absolute fearlessness and gallant leading."[105]

Roosevelt returned from Cuba the most famous man in America. He wasn't the only hero of the war with Spain, but his personality made him impossible to resist. This created an interesting dilemma for Platt and the New York Republican machine. Scandal was rocking the governor's mansion, with its Republican inhabitant, Frank S. Black, accused of squandering over a million dollars in "improper expenditures" on an Erie Canal expansion project.[106] If Black couldn't prove his innocence, Platt would need to find a viable Republican quickly, or risk his party losing the gubernatorial seat. He looked for anyone but Roosevelt,[107] but as the clock wound down, so too did his options.

Roosevelt understood his popularity and knew that he could win, regardless of party affiliation. He spent months flirting with independent movements within the Republican Party, before choosing the latter. "The leaders were in a chastened mood and ready to nominate any candidate with whom they thought there was a chance of winning," he recalled. "I was the only possibility."[108]

TR knew he could obtain the Republican nomination in his sleep, but he didn't take election for granted. He was willing to work for it. During the campaign, he made as many as two dozen whistle-stops in a single day, and during one week in late October, he gave 102 speeches.[109] He was a celebrity, who wowed the crowds with his candor and lofty rhetoric. "He called a spade a spade, a crook a crook,"[110] recalled Boss Platt, which gave the appearance of authenticity at a time when the public was tired of machine politics.

Roosevelt crushed his opponent and sailed to victory. Once there, he did what he always did, which was push for reform. He attacked Platt for his mishandling of the civil service, describing the system as being in a state of "utter confusion," and called for a harmonized civil service code for the entire state of New York.[111] He was incredibly productive, wrote the biographer Paul Grondahl, "signing into law more strict licensing regulations for textile factories; increasing the power and scope of factory inspections and prosecuting safety violations; and regulating the hours of drug clerks and state workers to an eight-hour shift. He had made significant headway in fighting to stiffen labor laws and closing loopholes for employers' liability." Finally, he "championed the franchise tax bill," which would prove most provocative of all.[112]

The franchise tax matter was the divergence that proved a breaking point between Roosevelt and Platt.[113] Platt owed his political livelihood to big business and a franchise tax would hurt the street railway companies, gas and electric lighting companies, and other public service corporations.[114] For Roosevelt, the issue "was a matter of plain decency and honesty that these companies should pay a tax on their franchises, inasmuch as they did nothing that could be considered as service rendered the public in lieu of a tax."[115] Platt felt Roosevelt's position to be "altruistic" and wrote the governor, "When the subject of your nomination was under consideration, there was one matter that gave me real anxiety. . . . It was *not* the matter of your independence. . . . The thing that did bother me was this: I had heard from a good many sources that you were a little loose on the relations of capital and labor, on trusts and combinations."[116] Things got messier even after the law was signed; when the businesses "turned round and refused to pay the taxes," Roosevelt insisted instead that "the law was unconstitutional."[117]

For Platt and his cronies, the moment was reminiscent of Roosevelt's days as police commissioner. Only at this moment, he was better known, possessed more power, and constituted a far greater threat to the machine. Roosevelt understood how to utilize the power of his celebrity and had learned to masterfully leverage the press to build his "bully pulpit." He managed to get the newspapers to write about everything, often in the precise way he desired. For the first time, Roosevelt became a topic of conversation for president. New York had done well in the past, with governors or former governors having made a competitive showing in five of the seven presidential elections since the Civil War.[118]

It didn't take long for Platt and others to conspire. In what seemed like a Groundhog Day[119] moment, they planned to get him out of New York, only this time it was not obvious where to park him. Then on November 22, 1899, Platt got his moment with an unexpected opening in the vice presidency.

Political Exile

Vice President Garret Hobart died on November 21, 1899. Even with four vice presidents having ascended to the presidency, few took seriously the significance of who would succeed the late vice president. Never mind that one out of every three of the last twelve elected presidents had died in office. Instead, the papers focused on curiosities and meaningless trivia. "A queer coincidence of the death of Vice President Hobart," wrote the *Wheeling Daily Intelligencer,* "is found in the fact that of the six vice presidents who have died in office four of them died within a few days of the same day of the month in the year of their deaths, the death of Mr. Hobart being the 21st of November, 1899; that of Mr. Wilson, the 22nd of November, 1875; that of Elbridge Gerry, November 23, 1814, and that of Hendricks, November 25, 1885." The other two—Clinton and King—both died in April.[120]

The fact that Hobart had battled illness for most of his vice presidency should have provided adequate time for the McKinley administration to plan a contingency. Vice President Hobart's heart troubles were initially concealed from the public. Rumors began swirling during his trip to Long Branch in the summer of 1898, but neither his physicians nor his family would admit he was seriously ill.[121] The following summer his condition grew so severe that few expected his return to public life. He was sent to Paterson, New Jersey, to recuperate.

Hobart had been an unlikely choice for vice president, having never served as a governor or a national legislator.[122] But he was from New Jersey—which in 1896 would prove an important battleground state—and had played a key role in some significant Republican victories there.[123] All of that was good enough. It's astonishing in today's world to accept such apathy, particularly as McKinley was fifty-four years old when he took office, eight years older than the average life expectancy.[124]

While McKinley and Hobart barely knew each other prior to the election, they would develop a close personal friendship. The president even looked to his vice president for help with his personal finances.[125] McKinley wasn't likely to find such a kindred spirit in any new vice president and probably gave the position little thought. He would have likely left it vacant had the 1900 election not forced him to choose a running mate. The initial idea was to grab a friend from the Senate or cabinet, extending the offer first to Senator William B. Allison of Iowa and then to Elihu Root, a respected jurist from New York who would later serve as secretary of state and secretary of war. When both men declined,[126] McKinley opted to leave the decision open and let the convention decide.[127]

McKinley had not considered Roosevelt, nor did he spend time contemplating additional choices. This apathy was the gift that Platt had been waiting for. On February 10, he summoned Roosevelt to Manhattan for a two-hour meeting that also included New York Republican Party chairman Benjamin Odell. They agreed to keep the substance of the meeting a secret, but when Governor Roosevelt was asked if they had discussed the vice presidency,[128] he couldn't resist the temptation to go on the record. Should any inquiring press minds want to know, he would seek the renomination as governor of New York.[129] Platt played into this charade by planting endless stories in the press describing Roosevelt as perfect for the job. The combination of Platt's intrigue, the press's desire for a story, and Roosevelt's indicating he would seek reelection meant that the momentum driving him into the vice presidency seemed unstoppable. McKinley also needed help in the West—Roosevelt was known as a popular writer and had lived out on the frontier—and a counterbalance to William Jennings Bryan's populist appeal.

Roosevelt liked the attention. He both desired and believed he would be able to win another term as governor, but that calculus soon changed, even if he never admitted it. Platt wanted Roosevelt out of New York and as his reelection prospects seemed increasingly difficult, the vice presidency, however dissatisfying, was looking like his only political opportunity. The more this reality settled in, the more promiscuous he was with messaging his disinterest in the position, perhaps to avoid any perception that this was his only option. Roosevelt's remonstrations repeated with such frequency and were so unsolicited that rumors swirled of an ulterior motive.[130] Lending credence to this theory was Roosevelt's bizarre trip to Washington in May 1900, when he called on the president to decline a nonexistent offer to join the ticket. Secretary of State John Hay found Roosevelt's visit amusing. "Teddy has been here have you heard of it?" he wrote a friend. "It was more fun than a goat. He came down with a somber resolution thrown on his strenuous brow to let McKinley and Hanna know once and for all that he would not be Vice-President, and he found to his stupefaction that nobody in Washington . . . had ever dreamed of such a thing."[131]

As late as April, Platt was still uncertain if Roosevelt was putting on a show, or if he would turn down a nomination. He decided to force the governor's hand by making him one of New York's four delegates-at-large to the Republican National Convention.[132] The move was not subtle. Platt reasoned that if Roosevelt wanted the vice presidency, he would agree to serve as a delegate. Roosevelt's close friend Senator Henry Cabot Lodge saw Platt's move as a trap and cautioned Roosevelt to avoid the convention unless he actually wanted the nomination.[133] Roosevelt ignored Lodge's advice and accepted Platt's offer. Roosevelt's decision to attend the convention was confusing. He continued to insist he had no interest in the vice presidency and answered inquiries with explanations that made no sense. "It would be impossible for me not to go to the National Convention," he told one supporter. "It seems to me that I can help the party more by running for Governor of New York State than by being a candidate for the Vice-Presidency, and we simply have got to make the people at Washington and elsewhere understand it."[134] Once at the convention, Roosevelt did little to maintain a low profile. He arrived late, in dramatic fashion, and wore a broad-brimmed black felt hat instead of the straw hats that all the other delegates wore to fit the summertime fashion.[135] He should have been aware that his "acceptance hat," as it became known, would draw attention. But then again, he had also chosen to make himself known in the various hotel lobbies, weaving through the crowds of delegates and mingling with the party's power brokers.[136]

As the vote loomed, there remained one final obstacle to Platt's plan. Mark Hanna, the big business McKinley operative, hated Roosevelt and in an era when nobody really thought about presidential succession, he seemed conscious of what it would mean to have Roosevelt a heartbeat away from the presidency. It's not that Platt disagreed, but priorities were local. "I want to get rid of the bastard," he exclaimed. "I don't want him raising hell in my state any longer. I want to bury him."[137] But Hanna didn't want him either. "Each took a position opposite to that of the other," Roosevelt wrote many years later, "but each at that time cordially sympathized with the other's feelings about me—it was the manifestations and not the feelings that differed."[138]

More than Platt's scheming or Hanna's acquiescence, however, was the fact that Roosevelt needed the vice presidency as a political lifeline. This didn't mean he was excited about the position, or that he was blind to the risks associated with taking what most perceived as political exile. Vice presidents did not have a good track record of winning the presidency, Martin Van Buren standing alone as the only vice president to win the presidency since 1800.[139] Roosevelt knew this and recognized that his name being floated for vice president was not an endorsement. "For a young man there is not much to do [as vice president]," he wrote the Massachusetts senator Henry Cabot Lodge. "It hardly seems to me as good as being Governor of this state. . . . If I am vice-president I am 'planted' for four years."[140] He felt the vice presidency was a place where he "could do nothing," observing himself to be "a comparatively young man" who "like[s] to work" and who would "not like to be a figurehead."[141]

Despite these reservations, Roosevelt had been successful because he took risks. Ambition drove him to routinely take jobs he didn't really want or that didn't match the aspirations he had for himself. In each instance, whether on the Civil Service Commission or as police commissioner, he took relatively low-level jobs and elevated both himself and the position. Just forty years old, he had a long life ahead of him. If he was perceived as having the position forced upon him, perhaps the vice presidency could prove to be a worthwhile gamble? He would bide his time and make a serious run at the presidency in 1904.

The convention opened in Philadelphia's Exposition Hall on June 19. The outcome was entirely predictable. "Being unable to stem the tide of the demand of delegates," wrote the *San Francisco Call*, "the popular governor of New York will be chosen . . . today to take second place on the ticket. . . . Governor Roosevelt will evidently be nominated in spite of himself and in spite of the administration."[142] The papers got it right. Roosevelt was nominated on the first ballot, which would have been unanimous had it not been for his sole dissenting vote against himself. He accepted the outcome, publicly describing himself as "touched" and the office "worthy of the ambition of any man in the United States."[143] In private, he told his friends he "now expected to be a dignified nonentity for four years."[144] He said nothing disparaging, however, about what would come after those four years.

Platt gloated from afar, basking in the glory of what he saw as a political coup for New York's Republican machine.[145] But despite these victory laps and Roosevelt's humility brags, the McKinley-Roosevelt ticket still had an election to win. Most agreed that victory would be easily achieved. McKinley could have nominated a corpse and still won the election. Bryan's "free silver" threat had failed in 1896 and was irrelevant by 1900.[146] Eighteen ninety-nine had also been a very strong year. So good, in fact, that the New York Times declared it "will stand marked in our national history as a period of unprecedented commercial and financial prosperity."[147] The country was flourishing and an explosion of technological innovation, the proliferation of new consumer goods, and the birth of modern advertising campaigns were largely responsible. The prosperity was felt throughout much of the country, particularly in the Midwest; growing demand throughout the country led to soaring prices for corn, pork, wheat, beef, and cotton. Whereas the previous decade had seen farmers struggle to get by, their newfound fortunes allowed them to purchase such extravagances as bicycles, lace curtains, and pianos.[148]

Americans wanted to talk about imperialism and McKinley had a good story to tell. America had taken control of Cuba, put down the Boxer Rebellion in China, colonized the Philippines, and annexed Hawaii.[149] His administration proved to be far more interventionist than was anticipated and even the anti-imperialist bloc had a hard time refuting the virtues of an expansionist foreign policy.[150] The campaign capitalized on the direct connection between interventions abroad and economic benefits at home, adopting slogans like "Four more years of the full dinner pail" and "prosperity at home, and prestige abroad."[151] William Jennings Bryan launched a Democratic campaign that was stuck in 1896, when he had lost with a stronger hand to play. Four years later, Americans liked imperialism, trusts were not yet seen as the villainous creatures they would become, and the economy was growing. The fact that this could be attributed in large part to a spike in the world's gold supply[152] was also a devastating blow to Bryan's free silver platform.

On top of all this, McKinley had a top-notch surrogate who was a force of nature. Roosevelt traversed the country, wowing crowds, telling stories, promoting McKinley's policies, and shaking as many hands as possible. By the time the campaign ended, the New York Times estimated that he traveled 21,209 miles, which according to other sources included visits to hundreds of towns and cities, where he spoke to more than three million people.[153] Even Platt had to acknowledge that "Roosevelt broke all records as a campaigner. He traveled more miles, visited more states, spoke in more towns, made more speeches and addressed a larger number of people than any man who ever went on the American stump."[154]

The campaign "increased [Roosevelt's] prestige, power and popularity one hundred fold." Platt recalled the governor's powerful rebuttals to Bryan and observed that he "vanquished the Democratic Presidential candidate off every field. He answered all of Bryan's questions. Bryan could answer none of his."[155] In a humbling lesson of careful what you wish for, even Platt would later accept that his plan had failed. Ultimately he conceded that "instead of 'shelving' Roosevelt, I must plead guilty to the charge of 'kicking him upstairs.'"[156]

The campaign proved a Theodore Roosevelt commercial. He was a showman, which played well to the large crowds. On one campaign stop in Iowa, he engaged the crowd with such over-the-top enthusiasm that someone in the crowd asked: "Has he been drinking?" "Oh, no," someone else replied, "he needs no whiskey to make him feel that way—he intoxicates himself by his own enthusiasm."[157]

When the campaign ended and the excitement of canvassing subsided, the realities of his political exile began to sink in. Roosevelt hated being vice president. He had far too much time on his hands and not nearly enough power. The position is but a "functionless official," he wrote, "who possesses so little real power" that, regrettably, "his political weight . . . is almost nil."[158] He found the office an "irksome, wearisome place," declaring he "would rather a great deal be anything, say a professor of history, than vice-president."[159] Over time, his view that the office was nothing more than a ceremonial position led him to believe that it "ought to be abolished."[160]

The greater his boredom, the more Theodore Roosevelt grew nostalgic for his past moments of influence. "I have really much less influence with the President now that I am Vice-President than I had even when I was governor," he wrote a friend.[161] Over time, he grew fatalistic, concluding his political death warrant had already been issued: "It is very unlikely that I shall be able to go on in politics after my term as Vice-President is over, and when I have gone out of public life I shall be able to do very much less in trying to steer straight young fellows of the right type, who ought to take an interest in politics."[162]

While Roosevelt wallowed, Mark Hanna remained suspicious. So long as Roosevelt was next in line for the presidency, he would never fall back on complacency. While he eventually voted for Roosevelt as vice president, doing so was deeply painful. He advised McKinley, "Your duty to the country is to live four years from next March." Hanna found Roosevelt insubordinate and resented the way in which he had pushed the U.S. toward war over Cuba. Hanna tried to sound the alarm bells a few months earlier and was overheard saying, "Don't any of you realize that there's only one life between that madman and the Presidency?"[163] But it wasn't just the notion of Roosevelt being a heartbeat away from the presidency that concerned Hanna. Roosevelt was beginning to lay the groundwork for a 1904 run,[164] or at least that's what Hanna perceived to be true. Roosevelt had already remarked that he expected to get "fearfully tired in the future" and that he "should like a more active position."[165]

"The President Is Shot!"

On September 4, 1901, President McKinley arrived at the Pan-American Exposition in Buffalo, New York, which even by World's Fair standards was an extraordinary event. More than eight million visitors came from all over the world to experience the latest and greatest technology and to shake hands with President McKinley, who in an unprecedented step had agreed to meet the crowd. The receiving line made his security detail nervous and they urged him to reconsider the public meeting. When security arguments failed to dissuade him, they attempted to play to his political instincts, warning that his participation in a public event would leave thousands of supporters disappointed if they didn't get a handshake. But McKinley wouldn't budge, suggesting only, "They'll know I tried, anyhow."[166]

The next day, McKinley moved forward with the receiving line at the Temple of Music, a majestic dome structure designed by the famous German-born architect August Esenwein. He was in good spirits, shaking hands when an anarchist named Leon Czolgosz extended his handkerchief-covered hand, revealed a hidden .32 caliber Iver Johnson revolver, and fired two shots. The first bullet ricocheted off a button on the president's suit and the second penetrated his skin through his abdomen.[167] Nearby, James Parker, a six foot four inch man who had been laid off as a restaurant worker at the exposition, was also waiting in line and lunged toward Czolgosz, striking him right in the neck with one hand and trying to grab the revolver with his other.[168] According to an eyewitness, the force of Parker's fist knocked Czolgosz onto the floor, after which the Polish anarchist made one last attempt to "discharge the revolver," only to find that it had already been "knocked from his hand by" the same Secret Service agent.[169] Others soon piled on, momentarily ignoring that the president had collapsed and was on the ground. Despite being badly wounded, the president mustered up the strength to say, "Don't let them hurt him."[170]

It took eighteen minutes for medics to retrieve the wounded president and take him by electric ambulance, invented just a few years earlier, to the Exposition Hospital.[171] When they arrived, doctors and surgeons were nowhere to be found, leaving them with no choice but to rely on a handful of interns and nurses who were on month-long rotations for the duration of the fair. There was one highly capable surgeon in the area, Dr. Roswell Park, who specialized in gunshot wounds. He was in Niagara Falls removing a malignant neck tumor from another patient. Efforts were made to summon Dr. Park, including someone interrupting his operation: "Doctor, you are wanted at once in Buffalo." Park rebuffed the intrusion: "Don't you see that I can't leave this case even if it were the president of the United States?" "Doctor," the medical gatecrasher told him, "it is for the President of the United States."[172]

The fruitless scramble for an appropriate specialist meant that McKinley's fate was left in the hands of several doctors who could be summoned from nearby locations, but lacked the expertise needed to save his life. Initially it appeared as though they would be up to the task, but it may have been circumstances that would seal the president's fate. The hospital conditions were less than adequate, particularly the lack of light. The surgeons—already operating outside of their field of expertise—had the added challenge of McKinley's weight, which required them to navigate a three-inch layer of abdominal fat to access the abdominal cavity. They were almost entirely dependent on natural light for the operation,[173] including relying on one medical assistant using a mirror to reflect sunlight onto the wound so the surgeon could see what he was doing.[174] One of the surgeons likened the experience to operating at "the darkened end of a big hole."[175]

Much of the initial surgery focused on trying to find the bullet,[176] but having learned the lessons from President Garfield twenty years earlier, the doctors adhered to proper sanitation practices. It's a tragedy that on display at the exposition was a primitive X-ray machine, which could have helped locate the bullet, but doctors feared it would bother the patient and not be that helpful anyway.[177] As with most new technology, the scientific community had yet to embrace the novel tool and they certainly lacked an appetite to experiment on such an important patient.

It took twenty-three minutes for news of the shooting to reach the White House, where the telegraph room—adorned with various maps of the United States and the rest of the world—was busy with its operators. The first to receive the news was Major Benjamin Montgomery, who saw the telegraph "snap out a few words" around 4:30 p.m. He quickly retrieved the message, which was from the chief operator at Western Union in Buffalo and conveyed that the president had been shot by an American anarchist. The news "flew like wildfire through the White House," recalled Colonel William Crook, who had protected every president since Lincoln and was at the time stationed at the White House. He was in the War Room when he heard someone scream, "The president is shot!" The reality of the situation quickly sank in, leaving Crook to mutter to himself, "Good God! First Lincoln—then Garfield—and now McKinley!"[178]

McKinley was moved to the home of John G. Milburn, a successful Buffalo lawyer who also served as the Exposition's president. Given concerns that the assassination may have been a conspiracy, a decision was made to deploy local police around the house and rope off the streets for a block in each direction. All vehicles were prohibited. As an extra precaution, a detachment of soldiers from the Fourteenth U.S. Infantry was dispatched to expand the security coverage.[179] Not since the Civil War had such extraordinary measures been taken to protect the president. There were legitimate reasons for concern. The previous year, writes the historian Paul Grondahl, "authorities had uncovered a plot to assassinate the president. Investigators tracked down a group of anarchists in Paterson, New Jersey, who had already been linked to the murders of two statesmen in Europe as part of a scheme to kill six leaders from around the world. The anarchists had placed President McKinley fifth on their hit list."[180] Anarchists had also unleashed a flurry of assassinations in London, Rome, Barcelona, and France, where on June 24, 1894, the president was stabbed to death.[181]

McKinley's assassin, however, was a different kind of anarchist. A Polish immigrant, Czolgosz was raised in an optimistic and warm household with dreams of making it in America. Instead, he fell on tough times after the 1893 financial crisis and like so many disaffected young people turned to anarchy. He was easily influenced, finding himself drawn to the teachings of anarchists like Anton Zwolinski, Albert Parsons, and Emma Goldman. "I don't believe in the Republican form of government," he told investigators after his apprehension, and "I don't believe we should have any rulers. It is right to kill them." He made no attempt to defend his actions. "I am an anarchist. . . . I fully understood what I was doing when I shot the President. . . . I done my duty. I don't believe in one man having so much service, and another man should have none."[182]

Theodore Roosevelt received the news as he was preparing to give a speech in Burlington, Vermont.[183] The lieutenant governor and others around him were of the strong belief that he should not seem overly eager and ought to avoid Buffalo and head straight to Washington or Sagamore Hill until more was known about the president's condition.[184] Chester Arthur had set a precedent for this after President Garfield was shot and Roosevelt's advisors thought it best to stick with that plan, particularly as it had been received favorably. Instead, Roosevelt raced to Buffalo. "I am so inexpressibly grieved, shocked and horrified that I can say nothing," he told reporters,[185] but he was optimistic that the president would make a speedy recovery. So reassured was he that on September 10 he was able to leave Buffalo and join his family for an outdoors vacation in the Adirondacks at the base of Mount Marcy—also known as Tahawus—which is New York's highest peak.[186] Knowing he would remain vice president meant that he would not be needed and could disappear into one of the most remote parts of the country. There he could be alone with his family, nature, and his thoughts.

By the time McKinley took a turn for the worse, Roosevelt was near the top of the mountain. There are various accounts of Tahawus Club guides speed-climbing the mountain and dramatically handing Roosevelt the telegram that would change his destiny: "The President appears to be dying and members of the cabinet in Buffalo think you should lose no time coming."[187]

Roosevelt wasted no time rushing back. While he lusted after the presidency, this is not how he wanted to attain it. Arthur had been terrified by the prospect, Roosevelt was not. Hoping to make it to Buffalo while McKinley was alive, Roosevelt mounted his horse and in a journey as dramatic as it was real, he bolted through the rain, "chang[ing] horses two or three times."[188] At one point, amidst rainfall, he stopped his horse in an overwhelming moment of rage toward the president's assassin and shouted, "If it had been I who had been shot, he wouldn't have got away so easily. . . . I'd have guzzled him first."[189] At another point in the journey, he took a rest "to let the horses blow," but revealing his true motivation for stopping, he adjusted his tie and patted his suit to free it of wrinkles, and justified the tidying up by explaining there might be some "notables" waiting at the station.[190]

Roosevelt did not make it back in time. McKinley took his last breath at 2:15 a.m. on September 14.[191] He arrived at the North Creek train station in upstate New York at 5:22 a.m. after a grueling journey that began Friday night and ran through the early hours of Saturday morning, where he covered the final forty or fifty miles by train.[192] Upon arrival, he boarded a private train that would take him on to Terrace Station in Buffalo.[193] His trusted aide, William Loeb, Jr., stood waiting on the platform with a telegram from Secretary of State John Hay, which read: "The president died at two-fifteen this morning."[194] Theodore Roosevelt was now the twenty-sixth president of the United States.

Today, we live in a world in which every moment is accounted for. But on September 14, 1901, the sense of urgency was treated differently. For three hours and seven minutes, Roosevelt was unaware that he was president. Arriving in Buffalo around 1:30 p.m., he was met by an elaborate Secret Service detail and Elihu Root, the senior cabinet member present in Buffalo, who oversaw Roosevelt's impromptu inauguration.[195] Despite having lived through the Garfield assassination and Arthur's ascension, Root had not committed the procedural precedents to memory. Twenty years was a long time and it's doubtful he expected ever to find himself in the same position. To figure it out, Root dispatched an aide to the Buffalo Public Library and instructed him to cull through periodicals about Chester Arthur's inauguration and take note of procedures and precedents.[196]

Roosevelt, understanding the gravity of the moment, gave a polite bow, cleared his throat, and said, "I shall take the oath at once" . . . "And in this hour of deep and terrible national bereavement I wish to state that it shall be my aim to continue absolutely unbroken the policy of President McKinley for the peace, the prosperity, and the honor of our beloved country."[197] If one counts this as an inaugural address, it was the shortest in history.

Roosevelt understood that the country was in mourning, but he had no intention of looking backward. Instead he reflected on the moment coolly, writing to Senator Lodge, "It is a dreadful thing to come into the Presidency this way; but it would be a far worse thing to be morbid about it. Here is the task and I have got to do it to the best of my ability; and that is all there is about it."[198]

Roosevelt had little time to contemplate what to do about the cabinet. He knew the McKinley men disliked him. But he was also aware, as he later wrote, that the three previous accidental presidents had pursued "a reversal of party policy, and a nearly immediate and nearly complete change in the personnel of the higher offices, especially the Cabinet. I had never felt that this was wise from any standpoint."[199] If he had resolved to keep the cabinet intact, he would need to make sure they stayed in line. All it would take was a little intrigue and a rumor or two to keep them on their toes.

Roosevelt wasted little time and used the quiet and somber mood of the memorial service to shore up the cabinet. Most of the McKinley men fell into line, except Mark Hanna, who on the train back to Washington was stewing with rage. "I told William McKinley it was a mistake to nominate that wild man," he told one of the distinguished gentlemen sitting near him. "I asked him if he realized what would happen if he should die. Now look, that damned cowboy is President of the United States!"[200] Herman H. Kohlsaat, the *Chicago Times-Herald* publisher, who had also been a McKinley confidant, was sufficiently concerned about Hanna's rage that he thought it best for both men to give Roosevelt a heads-up. He urged the new president to treat Hanna with care, cautioning that he wielded the power and influence to thwart Roosevelt's entire legislative agenda during the coming session of Congress. Never one to fear rival power, Roosevelt responded expressionlessly and rhetorically, "What can I do?"[201]

The train arrived at Washington's Sixth Street Station at 8:38 p.m.[202] Conscious of the moment's significance, the ever theatrical Theodore Roosevelt did not disappoint. He was the last to step off the train and waited an extra fifteen minutes as suspense built. Finally, just before 9:00 p.m. he came down the steps, jaw set sternly, and walked over to the cabinet, which had partially surrounded his car. Roosevelt first approached John Hay, extended his hand, and whispered into his ear in rather dramatic fashion, "Stay." He then repeated the same ritual with Secretary of the Treasury Lyman Gage. At that moment, McKinley's coffin arrived on the shoulders of soldiers and sailors. As the crowd made room for them, the scene was completely silent except for the somber sound of taps being played as the coffin was placed into the hearse. A loud crackle filled the silence, along with a bright flash from a window across the street. It sounded like a gunshot, which had everyone on edge given Czolgosz was hardly the only anarchist. Roosevelt flinched as he became uncharacteristically startled, leading the five Secret Service agents already surrounding him to be on the highest alert,[203] which he didn't like because it compromised his Rough Rider, cowboy image. Quickly realizing it was not a gunshot, the president asked, "What was that?" to which his brother-in-law, Commander William S. Cowles, replied, "A photographer." Having restored his tough-guy demeanor, Roosevelt said, "Something should be done with that fellow."[204]

McKinley's death changed the way the nation thought about presidential protection, a paradigm shift accelerated by Roosevelt's desire to mix with the people. Prior to his ascension, the Secret Service had supported this function on an ad hoc basis, but it was not their mandate. Traditionally, the view had been held that the president should be accessible to the public. Following two presidential assassinations and growing threats, circumstances called for a recalibration of that thinking. How to implement change was a different story altogether. When in 1891, Congress passed new legislation forbidding any government agency from hiring private detectives, it forced the executive branch to look for in-house remedies. A decision was made to begin borrowing officers from the Secret Service— at the time an anti-counterfeiting unit within the Treasury Department— when there was a heightened need for presidential protection. The first such incident occurred in 1895, after authorities had it on good evidence that there was a plot to kidnap and demand ransom for President Grover Cleveland's children.[205] Over time, this precedent extended more broadly to presidential travel and very public events, including the Pan-American Exposition where McKinley was shot.

Ironically, it was during the McKinley administration that some of the most dramatic changes to presidential protection occurred, but these were untested protocols. New rules forbade White House ushers from carrying firearms,[206] for example, which left both the executive mansion and the president dangerously exposed. The Spanish-American War once again forced the government to reexamine how to protect the president. Absent the right legislation, the wartime effort was improvisational, comprised of a scrappy coalition of policemen, ushers, and Secret Service agents who had been detailed to the White House during the war.[207]

By the time Roosevelt took office, the country had returned to a period of peace and the Secret Service agents went back to catching counterfeiters, making lists of known or suspected anarchists, and detaining as many of them as they could find.[208] Still, the impact of McKinley's assassination meant that Roosevelt was better protected with more agents than any previous peacetime president.[209] He hated the idea of having to be "protected," but understood the necessity and just a few weeks into his presidency agreed to ask Congress to supplement both the Secret Service and the Washington police with more resources.[210] While Congress considered the new appropriation, the details of his protection were also fleshed out, including a decision to include a minimum of two plainclothed Secret Service agents to be permanently on duty outside the president's office.[211] In addition to these agents, Metropolitan Police would be stationed throughout the White House grounds and at each entrance, while an additional detail of equestrian agents were dispatched for all of Roosevelt's movements.[212] The Secret Service also needed to be professionalized. McKinley's Secret Service detail was comprised of personal friends, including his chief bodyguard, who was an acquaintance from Ohio, not a trained and experienced agent. The new and improved Secret Service would also need to be given some degree of authority over the president, since McKinley had on three separate occasions overruled requests to cancel what advisors* correctly saw as a foolishly risky public reception in Buffalo.[213]

Despite tacit cooperation, Roosevelt never grew comfortable with protection and found subversive ways to fight it throughout his presidency. He had fought off a grizzly bear, big game in Africa, personally apprehended outlaws in the West, competed as a boxer, and rode head-on into gunfire on the island of Cuba. He did all of that without any protection. But despite his macho huffing and puffing about protection, this was one battle that Roosevelt could not win. Even when he successfully reduced the number of guards to a few, we know from the letters of his second wife,

---

* Secretary Cortelyou had been chief among the advisors in raising objections.

Edith, that she would subvert this by furtively adding agents to secretly guard her husband.[214] Well aware of his wife's heavy hand, the president would at times identify these agents and send them home with strict instructions to avoid his wife.[215]

A Man with a Mandate

Theodore Roosevelt wasted no time signaling his intentions as president. First, he courted Booker T. Washington, the former slave who received the only written correspondence from Roosevelt's first day as president. "I must see you as soon as possible," he wrote. "I want to talk over the question of possible future appointments in the south exactly on the lines of our last conversation together."[216] Washington had some misgivings about such a meeting, but believed he had a duty to accept the president's invitation. He came north the last week of September to discuss the matters Roosevelt had alluded to in his letter.

Several weeks later and much to the surprise of Washington, he received another message from the president, this time inviting him to dine at the White House,[217] a privilege never before offered to a black American,[218] let alone a former slave. The dinner took place on October 16, 1901, setting off a flurry of coverage in the press and an unexpected backlash for Roosevelt. While the reaction rattled the new president and provoked a rare Rooseveltian moment of second-guessing—he told his friend Albion W. Tourgée that he "felt ashamed" over his hesitation—the overture was necessary.[219] The South was struggling. Sustained economic depression had made life difficult for white farmers, who responded with disfranchisement tactics against blacks that had been alarmingly effective, most notably by reducing southern black turnout in general elections from 85 percent at the height of Reconstruction to single digits.[220] McKinley hadn't helped. After southern and northern whites fought together in the Spanish-American War, he visited Atlanta, where he told the state legislature, "In the spirit of fraternity we should share with you in the care of graves of the Confederate soldiers."[221] These comments had eroded any support he had with a southern black constituency and gave him nothing in return from white voters. Roosevelt had no interest in making the same mistake.

The details of Roosevelt and Washington's discussion mattered less than the symbolism. The dinner conveyed a powerful message: Roosevelt would not pander to white supremacists of the South and through Washington he would take a pragmatic and far more conservative approach to his relations with southern blacks.[222] The two never dined again.

Roosevelt understood the public's fascination with both the late president's assassin and the growing tide of anarchism he represented. Czolgosz had been convicted on September 24, and was scheduled for death by the electric chair on October 29. Roosevelt capitalized on the public interest by mounting an assault on anarchy. He insisted that anarchism "is no more an expression of 'social discontent' than wife-beating or pick-pocketing." Its advocates, he said, have "perverted instincts" and prefer "confusion and chaos to the most beneficent form of social order."[223] His crusade against anarchy was not cosmetic. He was highly strategic and crafty in how he admonished the movement. By choosing to focus on many of the social issues that bred discontent, he was building a mandate to pursue a progressive agenda in the name of national security. He understood these issues well from his time in New York, but no president since Lincoln had advocated for such radical social justice measures. This was not a coincidence. Without an immediate threat to the country's national security, the country wasn't ready for such change. But Roosevelt understood that the national psyche, that same thinking that made the Spanish-American War wildly popular, could secure progressivism in a way that readied the country for change.

Roosevelt quickly left McKinley in the dust, something none of the previous accidental presidents had been able to achieve. He had already demonstrated little interest in continuing McKinley's policies and reserved demeanor. He had imagined his presidency far more than Tyler, Fillmore, Johnson, or Arthur and had played it out many times in his own head. He jumped at the chance to unshackle the presidency from the rich industrialists and establish himself as the agent of populism.[224] He was a champion for the urban middle class and shared its belief that corporations were corrupting politics, overpricing goods, and selling unsafe merchandise, as well as maintaining unsafe working conditions. His vision for America sounded more like that of the defeated Bryan than it did McKinley. He was not afraid to attack corporate corruption, upheld the Sherman Anti-Trust Act, and as the biographer I. E. Cadenhead writes in *Theodore Roosevelt: The Paradox of Progressivism,* he "placed his primary emphasis on the problem of trusts and the conviction in the minds of many Americans that these trusts were detrimental to the general welfare. He made it clear that he did not believe the laws and customs of the past were sufficient."[225]

On foreign affairs, Roosevelt and McKinley shared similar policies, although they subscribed to different mentalities. McKinley was a reluctant imperialist who felt dragged into imperialist ventures, while Roosevelt actively pursued them. With his own corollary to the Monroe Doctrine of American isolationism, Roosevelt declared that "in the Western Hemisphere, the adherence of the United States to the Monroe Doctrine may force the United States, however reluctantly, in flagrant cases of such wrongdoing or impotence, to the exercise of an international police power."[226]

On November 8, 1904, Roosevelt won reelection in an overwhelming landslide that shocked him to the point of uncharacteristic humility. "I am stunned," he told his son Kermit, "by the overwhelming victory we have won."[227] He recognized the symbolic importance of his victory, gleefully explaining to his wife: "I am no longer a political accident."[228] It was the first time in history that a man ascending to the presidency had subsequently won the office in his own right; and Roosevelt achieved the most decisive victory since Andrew Jackson clobbered Henry Clay in the 1832 presidential election.[229]

The victory represented a glorious triumph for a man who believed he was destined to be president. The campaign itself had been uneventful, particularly as Roosevelt followed the unspoken rule that incumbents shouldn't take to the campaign trail.[230] He was also enormously popular and even opponents within his own party would not dare challenge him—as they did previous accidental presidents. His humility may have been false, but he played it perfectly, agonizing over the prospects of defeat and constantly worrying that he had fallen out of public favor.[231]

The people loved him and he knew it. He was now at the height of power, with a gigantic mandate, and a full agenda to implement. But caught in the moment, he made the greatest political mistake of his life. Following his victory, he spoke to adoring crowds, and without properly thinking through the implications of his words declared, "Under no circumstances will I be a candidate for or accept another nomination."[232] Once the glory dust settled, he quickly realized he had made a concession he could not retract. He would later attempt to justify his actions, saying he felt obligated to correct a misperception among his supporters that his first term was incomplete and therefore didn't count against the two-term precedent.

His explanation that "the power of the President can be effectively used to secure a re-nomination"[233] represented the best retroactive argument he could make. But it's doubtful he believed it at the time and even he had to know that this was classic Roosevelt revisionism. Elevated by the moment, he went for a hasty crowd-pleaser and in exchange for the fifteen-minute bump he threw away his future.

As late as 1911, Roosevelt was still attempting to justify his decision. "I did not wish simply and specifically to say that I would not be a candidate for the nomination in 1908," he wrote, "because if I had specified the year when I would not be a candidate, it would have been widely accepted as meaning that I intended to be a candidate some other year; and I had no such intention."[234] But this was absurd, as he clearly did have such intention and not only would he run again in 1912, but after losing he harbored hopes of running again in 1916 and then again in 1920.

It's noteworthy that amidst this fumble, he did offer one caveat, which, while not helpful to him, would conveniently serve his fifth cousin Franklin several decades later. "If, for instance, a tremendous crisis occurred at the end of the second term of a man like Lincoln, as such a crisis occurred at the end of his first term," he offered as an example, "it would be a veritable calamity if the American people were forbidden to continue to use the services of the one man whom they knew, and did not merely guess, could carry them through the crisis."[235]

This political misstep, however disappointing to him, did not temper his excitement over the inauguration. "Tomorrow," he cried on inauguration eve, "I shall come into my office in my own right. Then watch out for me!"[236] A victory in his own right would unleash him, or so he believed; but most historians would argue this happened the moment he took the first oath of office. The symbolism was important to him. At his earned inauguration, he wore a ring, sent to him by John Hay the previous evening and that contained small pieces of Abraham Lincoln's hair.[237] His presidency was no longer an accident.

To be fair to Roosevelt, this wasn't entirely about ego. His election marked an endorsement of his agenda and formalized the widespread support he knew he had. Reelection completed the Republican Party's shift from conservative economic interest to social reform, established modern American foreign policy, and cemented his legacy as the first man to inherit the presidency and then win it in his own right. Had McKinley survived, progressivism may have taken decades to gain steam. The early 1900s would likely have seen income inequality grow. Powerful, white, Anglo-Saxon, Protestant men may have continued to go unchallenged as the leaders of big business and government. Upton Sinclair's depiction of abysmal factory conditions may have still made for good literature, but would have received little attention from the federal government. And despite the success of the Industrial Revolution, many Americans, including the massive influx of immigrants from the late 1800s and early 1900s, would have struggled to survive.

Roosevelt's elevation to the presidency countered the argument that he was too progressive to get the Republican nomination. Once in office, he was able to change the party platform, win on his progressive agenda in 1904, and set in motion a political successor to extend the progressive era beyond his administration. His vice president, Charles Fairbanks, had been a logical choice for the 1904 ticket since he appealed to conservatives and the Midwest, but as vice president, he actively subverted Roosevelt's progressive agenda and thus drew the ire of the president. As the 1908 presidential election approached, Roosevelt returned the snub and rather than supporting his own vice president, he chose his friend William Howard Taft as his successor, and guided him to victory. He expected Taft to continue his agenda, focusing on trust busting and furthering the economic development of Latin American countries.

———

Roosevelt's four years out of the White House watered down his progressive movement and his anointed successor had proven a disappointment. Eager to reignite the movement, he sought a return to politics in 1912; but his retirement had created a vacuum that shifted power back to the party bosses and the financial powers that backed them. At the convention in Baltimore, they denied the former president the nomination and instead gave it to Taft. A confident Roosevelt, certain that his popularity would sustain even if he was loathed by the party bosses, created the Progressive Party—better known as the Bull Moose Party—and ran for a third term.

That run was nearly cut short. On October 14, 1912, while giving a speech in Milwaukee, Wisconsin, John F. Schrank, an immigrant from Bavaria who believed McKinley's ghost had asked him to kill Roosevelt, fired shots at the progressive candidate. The bullet hit the former president's glasses case, penetrated a fifty-page speech, and eventually lodged itself in his chest. Drawing on his expertise as an amateur taxidermist, Roosevelt examined his wound and determined he would likely survive. He then proceeded to share with the crowd that he had been shot and declared that he would give the one-hour speech anyway. At the speech's conclusion, he was taken to a local hospital. Taft and Woodrow Wilson, who was the Democratic nominee for president, both suspended their campaigns as Roosevelt recovered, and within a few days the campaign was back in full swing.

It is ironic that the bullet of an assassin brought him to the presidency in 1901 and nearly ended his attempt to return to the presidency in 1912. But while Roosevelt survived the assassination attempt, the campaign proved politically disastrous for him. Two progressives—one a Republican, the other a Bull Moose—with only subtle differences between them led to confusion within the Republican Party and split the vote. On Election Day in 1912, Roosevelt easily defeated Taft, but he faced a formidable Democratic candidate in Woodrow Wilson, who proved to be just about the only candidate more progressive than he. Roosevelt wanted to regulate the trusts, Wilson pledged to dissolve them.

The schism in the Republican Party deprived both men of victory and allowed Wilson to win the presidency. Thus, by returning to politics, he had saved the progressive movement from Taft, but he had handed the baton to another party to champion the cause. Roosevelt would come to regret this decision, finding both himself and his movement displaced by a man with what he believed to be naive idealism.

Wilson would serve two terms in office and by the time the Republicans recaptured the White House, Roosevelt's party was unrecognizable. He lived long enough to make another run with his Progressive Party in 1916—but Taft and other conservative Republicans ensured that as Roosevelt aged, so too did his movement. He never lived to see Warren Harding capture the White House in 1920 and it is probably better that he didn't.

Harding's pro-business administration proved to be a corrupt throwback to the Grant administration. He surrounded himself with men far worse than Mark Hanna and ushered in a laissez-faire era of business that prevailed through two more Republican presidents until another Roosevelt came in to reignite the progressive flame.

Warren Harding *was elected on a promise to "return to normalcy." His administration was ridden with scandals and controversy. The office wore him down and the strain of scandal became too much to handle. He died in office on August 2, 1923.*

Calvin Coolidge *distanced himself from Harding's scandals and, despite his image as "Silent Cal," took advantage of broadcast radio to reach the American people.*

CHAPTER SIX

Averting Scandal

Double Suicide

Jess Smith blew his brains out on May 30, 1923. The suicide was the second to rock Warren Harding's administration in just ten weeks. The twin suicides—the other being a top official from the Veterans Bureau named Charles Cramer—sent the press and gossip machines into a frenzy of suspicion.[1] President Harding, who earlier that year had learned of massive corruption within his cabinet, was deeply disturbed by Smith's death, and with good reason. He knew a hurricane of scandal was fast approaching and he was sitting right in its direct line.

Smith's suicide was particularly troubling to Harding, because of both Smith's unofficial role in the administration and his centrality to a web of scandal that Harding had deliberately ignored and personally benefited from for three years. Smith could have brought down the entire administration, but in truth, he was far too loyal to do so. However, in death, particularly one so mysterious and high-profile, Smith might have proven to be a dangerous link between the president and the illicit happenings around town. It all depended on what kind of trail he left behind and what his ex-wife and close friend, Roxy Stimson, was willing to share. "She knows enough to hang us all," remarked one close presidential advisor. President Harding had no way of knowing.

Smith had been an omnipresent figure in Washington and was a memorable-looking fellow for all the wrong reasons. He was tall and pigeon-toed,[2] and his skin was a florid complexion.[3] He had puffy cheeks, a double chin and a big, amorphous nose, and little ears that flanked his oversized head. He wore "round, owlish spectacles"[4] and had a thick black mustache that drooped over his upper lip. These cartoonish features made him look like the caricature of a political gangster and he liked it that way.

Smith also dressed and acted the part, deliberately playing into this persona. He wore a gray hat that was the hallmark of a high-class thug. The way in which he wore it, always at a slight tilt forward and to the side, suggested a mixture of friendliness and "don't mess with me." He loved clothes, a combination of his feminine side and an earlier career in the clothing business. It was all about a good combination that matched, he used to tell friends, and he had no scruples about making his whole outfit "a symphony in gray and lavender."[5] Underneath all of this was an uncomfortable drawstring belt, which Smith was forced to wear after his late-stage diabetes prevented an incision from his appendicitis operation from healing.[6] He wore flashy jewelry, partial to diamond rings, but made no secret of the fact that his favorite ring was one set with two large rubies and a number of small diamonds.[7] Such gems told the world, Look at me, I'm important.

He was colorfully loudmouthed, which made him a presence. "Smith was basically naive, extremely friendly and gregarious," wrote one Harding-era biographer. He was known for his trademark greeting, which was a sly "Whaddayaknow?" followed by a hum of his favorite tune, "My God, How the Money Rolls In."[8] He was a talker and what some might call a sprayer, so much so that his detractors liked to snipe, "Here comes Jess. Get your umbrella."[9]

Smith had come a long way since running a small business in the small town of Washington Court House, Ohio. Lacking a father figure in his life, he struck political gold when Harry Daugherty, a prominent local and future attorney general, took an interest in him.[10] Daugherty was a heck of a wagon for Smith to hitch his ride to. The elder Ohioan could claim partial credit for winning Harding the White House in 1920. Thus, when Daugherty became attorney general, Jess Smith, that awkward and sad little boy from Ohio, found himself transformed into one of the most influential men in Washington.

Well aware of his good fortune and insecure about it, Smith bragged about his influence to anyone who would listen—especially after a few drinks. He boasted of his membership in the elite Metropolitan Club, described how he had been listed in the Social Register, and swanked about powerful men coming to him with favors and senators calling him "Mister."[11] He had no official job, but he didn't need one. Now that Harry

Daugherty was running the Justice Department, Smith had his own office on the sixth floor right next to the attorney general. Remarkably, he was never on the government payroll. His "work" was not of the type that Daugherty would want on the books.[12]

Smith understood that his power almost entirely derived from his relationship with the attorney general and, therefore, indirectly with the president.[13] Daugherty and Smith had an unusual bond, some speculating with reasonable likelihood that their friendship was more than platonic. "They lived together," Smith's ex-wife (and still close friend), Roxy, recalled. "They were intimate friends, and Jess adored him. . . . He lived for him, he loved him."[14] In addition to the suite they shared at the Wardman Park Hotel[15]—and before that a rented house at 1509 H Street—Daugherty became rather dependent on Smith, recalling many years later, "It became absolutely necessary to take Jess Smith with me wherever I went."[16] And when they traveled, they would either share a hotel suite or stay in two adjoining rooms. Smith was everything to Harry, serving as his valet, private secretary, gofer, bookkeeper, and roommate.[17]

Smith's intimate relationship with Daugherty placed him smack in the middle of President Harding's most trusted inner circle. As the attorney general's guy, he became the chief fixer for the Ohio Gang, a group of Harding cronies who descended on Washington and built a criminal enterprise on the president's good name. They were mostly political hangers-on, and like Smith most did not hold official office; instead, they peddled their authority in that underground gray area where the public sector meets the private sector.[18] They occupied a little house on H Street, which was owned by Edward "Ned" McLean, the powerful owner of the *Washington Post*, whose holdings also extended to banks and energy companies.[19] Like Smith, he had a special status at the Justice Department, where he enjoyed an appointment as a "special agent" and carried his own badge and secret code number.[20] Together, they spent $50,000 a year to retain[21] the discreet location, which the Gang used as a secret underground headquarters to pursue a wide range of criminal enterprises.

There was booze that arrived in suitcases,[22] gambling, stashes of cash buried in the backyard, bribery, fight fixing, smuggling, extortion, and, of course, women—lots and lots of women.[23] In fact, there were so many women coming in and out that the house became known as the "love nest."[24] It was not unusual for Harding himself to sneak away from the

White House and indulge in the debauchery behind these safe walls.[25] One of the more outlandish stories involved a group of New York chorus girls who were in town for a local performance and subsequently invited to dine with the president and his band of degenerates. As was typically the case, the party got a bit rambunctious and by 3:00 a.m., the crowd was jubilantly wasted. At its height, some guests proposed transforming the dinner table into a stage for the girls to dance upon. The excited men started throwing plates, glasses, and bottles,[26] one of which struck a girl on the head and knocked her out cold. She died several days later, a tragedy that was covered up by two central figures with roles in both the Justice Department and the Ohio Gang—Attorney General Harry Daugherty and Bureau of Investigation* chief William "Billy" Burns.[27]

For Harding, the Ohio Gang was all fun and games, allowing him to comfortably pop in and out of the escapades. As a man who was never comfortable in presidential shoes, he found it refreshing to be with this group of old buddies who didn't think of him as the president. To them, he was just "Warren." He had no trouble looking the other way on the many illegalities.[28] But the same was not true for the other men, particularly Daugherty, who were focused on far more than just a good time. For them, it was a fast-growth underground business. They were getting fantastically rich off their proximity to power and jeopardizing the very administration that had given them this opportunity. The key to Daugherty's riches was Jess Smith, who from his office at the Justice Department and the little house on H Street ran point on all the illegal operations. He ran an account, known as "Jess Smith Extra No. 3," which served as a secret political account that they could both access.[29]

The magnitude of the corruption was astounding and the hubris of running it out of the attorney general's office was reckless. This was the age of prohibition† and it was right there, next door to the attorney general, that Smith used his neighboring office to sell permits—in some cases for $20,000 a pop—to shady characters eager to help the government unload confiscated liquor from its warehouses.[30] Smith also used this same

---

* The Bureau of Investigation was the predecessor organization to the FBI.

† Ratified on January 16, 1919, the Eighteenth Amendment prohibited the "manufacture, sale, or transportation of intoxicating liquors" within the United States and its territories. It was repealed by the Twenty-First Amendment, passed on December 5, 1933.

office to sell immunity to notorious bootleggers, with some paying more than $250,000.[31] The attorney general and Smith also kept a ticker-tape machine in the Justice Department so that they could game the market and leverage whatever inside information they had to inform their personal stock purchases.[32]

Smith's exploitation of government resources to commit his mischief was both shameless and deliberate. In addition to the office he occupied and the badge he possessed, Smith also played a semiofficial administrative role for the attorney general, including handling his official mail, tasking Justice Department secretaries, and conducting his business using the attorney general's stationery. He roamed freely throughout the department, had access to all the files, and carried a badge and credentials for the Bureau of Investigation. Always conscious of his own standing, he was promiscuous in his name-dropping, frequently talking up his relationship with "Harry" and referring to his friend "Warren."[33]

Eventually the wall of secrecy became too porous and Smith too toxic to have around the president. Harding wanted him shunted from the inner circle, removed from any presidential travel manifest, and exiled back to Ohio.[34] He instructed Daugherty to relay the news to Smith and to ensure that he was pushed out of town.

"[Jess] received [the news] as a prisoner receives a death sentence,"[35] Daugherty recalled, leaving an utterly crushed man. Smith begged his attorney general friend to plead with the president. Daugherty, recognizing this was a fool's errand, stymied the effort.[36] All that Smith had worked for was falling apart. He tried to put up a facade, but as he made the rounds about town, fellow partygoers observed that he looked like a defeated man. At one of the many events, a concerned acquaintance inquired into his melancholy state and received his candid admission back, "It's all up with me. They're going to get me."[37]

Banished by Harding, Smith returned to Ohio, where his ex-wife, Roxy, encountered a very different man from the one she knew. Smith, who usually bombarded her with his stories of being a Washington bigwig, seemed quite different. He wasn't showing her a money belt stuffed with $75,000 cash, name-dropping, or regaling her with stories from the many parties he attended. Instead, he was now seeking her assistance in destroying documents, bank records, and canceled checks.[38] He also made another peculiar request, handing her a portfolio of stocks to sell and opening a blind account for her at the brokerage firm Ungerleider & Co., which was used by the president and attorney general[39] for their most discreet transactions. He made cryptic comments expressing concern for his safety.

Smith returned to Washington for a few days to prepare himself for a life in political exile. Perhaps to soften the blow, Daugherty invited Smith for a weekend getaway outside Washington, but this excursion resulted instead in a falling-out. This fight was the straw that broke the camel's back, and in all likelihood it was that moment on May 27 that Smith decided to take his own life (if it was in fact a suicide). He was known to be terrified of guns[40]—always declining invitations for recreational shootings with other members of the Ohio Gang. He walked into a hardware store, bought the firearm, and told the clerk it was for the attorney general.[41]

Daugherty was concerned and asked Warren Martin, one of his special assistants,[42] to keep an eye on Smith until he returned to Ohio.[43] It was no use. At 6:30 a.m. the next morning, Martin heard a loud bang and found Smith wearing his pajamas and lying dead with his head in a trash can and his hand still gripping the .32 caliber revolver. Blood oozed from his right temple, where the bullet entered, before penetrating through his skull and ultimately lodging in the doorframe.[44]

Martin called Billy Burns, who lived on the floor below[45] at the same hotel. Burns took charge, and when the Metropolitan Police responded to investigate, the gun had gone mysteriously missing.[46] The "misplaced" gun was not the only oddity. Smith was right-handed, yet the bullet had entered his left temple and exited the right side of the skull. There was also no trace of gunpowder deposits on either hand and no autopsy allowed.[47]

Burns quickly notified the White House, where Joel Boone, a trusted White House physician, shared the news with the president and Mrs. Harding. Daugherty had been staying with them at the White House, but knowing how devastated he would be by the news, the president chose to wait until after breakfast.[48] What followed was a day of sadness that carried through dinner. It was a somber dinner, with both the president and Daugherty distraught. Few words were spoken and eyes pointed downward at the food. Other dinner guests joined in silence without attempting to lighten things.[49] After dinner, the group adjourned to a private screening room upstairs, where they could be together in the silence of a motion picture.[50]

Mourning aside, Harding and Daugherty were concerned about what

Smith might have left behind. It didn't help that the rumor mill showed no signs of letting up, including gossip that someone had killed Smith to keep him quiet. Alice Longworth, the rambunctious firstborn daughter to Theodore Roosevelt and famed Harding critic, offered her analysis that he had died of "Harding of the arteries."[51] But there was no smoking gun. Smith had destroyed everything before killing himself, burned all correspondence, and eliminated any trace of evidence of Harry Daugherty's personal affairs.[52]

Daugherty and Harding would both get over Smith's death and for the time being the rumors lacked sufficient evidence to maintain their momentum. Harding was as popular as ever because the public didn't know what was happening inside the administration. He fretted and constantly looked over his shoulder as if he understood the inevitability of it unraveling.[53] This stress would grow over time and eventually take such an emotional and physical toll that it would kill him before the end of his first term in office. His vice president, Calvin Coolidge, found himself an accidental president left to pick up the pieces with less than a year to run for election as president in his own right.

"Return to Normalcy"

The 1920 presidential election offered an opportunity for America to reset. World War I had occurred and the Senate's veto of Woodrow Wilson's international adventures with the League of Nations reflected the overall mood. The cost of war in dollars and lives left America with a significant burden at home. President Wilson, who had suffered a debilitating stroke in October 1919, could barely function, leaving the executive branch paralyzed.[54] Not since James Garfield lay bedridden for three months had the government been held hostage by a president's extended illness. But differently from 1881—when the country was at peace and Congress was in extended recess—there were an infinite number of urgent matters that needed Wilson's attention.

To paraphrase several biographers of the times, there was a lot going on: Common economic woes—runaway inflation, business failures, mortgage foreclosures, and reduction in wages[55]—were part of the problem. But trends in urbanization and immigration were also having a profound impact on the country's economy. For the first time in history, more

Americans resided in urban areas, most in cities along the East Coast and in the Midwest.[56] The economy struggled to keep pace with such rapid trends, which led to a high cost of living and widespread unemployment.[57] Such economic hardship manifested itself in discontent within the labor force and record numbers of strikes, more than 3,600 in 1919 alone.[58]

These economic pressures, along with perceived threats from abroad, fueled social unrest throughout the country. Patriotic unity from the war had all but disappeared and was quickly replaced by many of the same political, social, and economic tensions[59] that characterized the prewar era. Groups like the Ku Klux Klan (KKK), the American Legion, and the Industrial Workers of the World (IWW) exploited these fissures to strengthen their respective movements. Other groups looked outward and played to fears that Russia's recent Bolshevik revolution was so contagious that it could spread to America. Fear was ever present in the air.

Outside the U.S., a number of foreign policy issues lingered. There was the question of how the U.S. ought to interact with the League of Nations, and what to do about postwar disarmament; and there was political unrest in the Western Hemisphere.[60] Finally, there remained the small detail that the United States and Germany were technically still at war.

As these issues festered and America geared up for a presidential election, nobody knew what to do about the sitting president's incapacity. First lady Edith Galt stood like a phalanx in front of anyone who tried to bother him with affairs of state. She screened every visitor, intercepted every document, and shielded the public from his condition. Despite her efforts, there were multiple attempts to break through this force field, including one widely disseminated report suggesting that Wilson was unable "to discharge the powers and duties" of president and under the disability clause of the Constitution ought to be replaced by Vice President Thomas Marshall. The report gained so much steam that the Senate anointed two of its own, Albert Fall from New Mexico and Gilbert Hitchcock from Nebraska, to visit the president and assess his mental capacity. Those optimistic that their visit would yield damning evidence found themselves painfully disappointed. Fall and Gilbert, nicknamed the "Smelling Committee," concluded that the old man was weakened, but not incapacitated. He laughed and joked with them and proved able to follow every aspect of the conversation.[61]

Wilson may not have been sick enough to warrant removal from office, but his insistence on hanging on despite a clearly incapacitated condition and a country in chaos all but guaranteed a Republican victory in 1920.[62] The question was which Republican? Theodore Roosevelt's death the previous year created an open field with no clear front-runner.[63] As the Republican convention approached, there were dozens of names tossed around, most notably former Army chief of staff Leonard Wood, Illinois governor Frank O. Lowden, and California senator Hiram Johnson,[64] but none who inspired a wave of support.

Warren Harding had thrown his hat in the ring, but he was not a serious contender. *Literary Digest*, which at the time had among the most authoritative polls, put Harding a distant sixth behind the three leaders— Wood, Lowden, and Johnson—as well as Herbert Hoover, who was running the American Relief Agency charged with feeding Europe, and Charles Evans Hughes, who was a former associate justice on the Supreme Court.[65] Harding's odds were even worse in a *Wall Street Journal* poll, which put his chances at eight to one. Poking fun at the unlikeliness of Harding's nomination, the humorist Ring Lardner gave him odds as high as two hundred to one.[66]

There was nothing wrong with Harding. His career was perfectly respectable—Ohio state senator, publisher of the *Marion Star* newspaper, lieutenant governor, and one-term U.S. senator—but he didn't stand out either. While in the Senate, he made it his business to do nothing. During his rather unremarkable time in the U.S. Senate, he introduced 134 bills, of which 122 were exclusively focused on Ohio,[67] 86 were pension bills, 17 were bailouts for Ohio financial and commercial institutions,[68] and the rest covered a range of mundane issues like the "celebration of the landing of the Pilgrims,"[69] "encouraging the teaching of Spanish," "authorizing the loan of Army tents to relieve the postwar housing shortage," enhancing protection for "furbearing animals in Alaska," conferring unused "rifles to the sons of veterans,"[70] and "investigating influenza."[71] It didn't matter. Nineteen twenty was the year when those who had been more active legislators found those same actions disqualifying them with some group of unhappy delegates. As the various front-runners fell one by one, Harding was enough in the mix to ride the many rounds of balloting even if he had no expectation of winning.

It helped that he looked the part of a president. He was a handsome man, his features so dashing that some attributed his election to the mere fact that he "looked like a president." He was tall, standing just over six feet in height, and had a bulky frame that carried 210 pounds. His high fore-head, heavy square jaw, and sympathetic, calm gray eyes made him seem inviting.[72] It didn't hurt, either, that he was from the electorally important state of Ohio, had no real enemies, and most important, was what one bi-ographer described as the "available man."[73] The convention knew it and so did he. "I feel like a man who goes in on a pair of eights and comes out with aces full,"[74] he told a friend just after his victory. He wasn't alone in this view. "There ain't any first-raters this year," observed the Connecti-cut senator and powerful convention delegate Frank B. Brandegee: "We've got a lot of second-raters and Warren Harding is the best of the second-raters."[75]

To balance the ticket, the convention chose Calvin Coolidge, who was probably best described as a third-rater. He had risen to prominence ear-lier that year when he stood firm against organized labor during the Bos-ton Police Strike.[76] This made Coolidge palatable, but in all likelihood he owed the nomination to a single fan, Mr. Wallace McClamant of Oregon, who after reading Coolidge's book, *Have Faith in Massachusetts*—perhaps its only reader—decided to interrupt the nomination speech for Irvine Lenroot of Wisconsin and thus change the course of history.[77]

Harding and Coolidge campaigned on a "return to normalcy," which was basically the 1920s version of what the forty-fifth president, Donald Trump, later branded "make America great again." In a throwback to the McKinley era, Harding spent most of the campaign on his porch, speak-ing to more than 600,000 people who had traveled to Marion[78] to hear him speak. The rest of the campaign was spent fighting off scandals, first rumors of his affairs and indiscretions and then a rumor that suggested Harding had black ancestry. The women were a problem, but a far greater concern for the campaign was how to prove that Harding wasn't part black. William E. Chancellor from the College of Wooster collected a batch of notarized affidavits asserting that Harding's great-grandparents were both black, that his grandfather was a black man who married a white woman, and his father was a mulatto man who married a white woman.[79] In addition to politically opposing Harding, it appears that Chancellor was swayed by vengeful rumors that had been started by Harding's father-in-law, Amos King, after the two engaged in a business dispute. As Harry Daugherty recalled, the eleventh-hour attack saw an "attempt to circulate" the supposed evidence in "suburban trains running into Chicago," which "resulted in fist fights that cleared each coach promptly of the intruders."[80]

The slander didn't matter, as the election wasn't even close. The Harding-Coolidge ticket won a landslide victory with more than 60 percent[81] of the vote, which at the time was a historic margin.[82] In this sweeping victory, which came on Harding's fifty-fifth birthday and included the first time in history a wife voted for her husband as president,[83] he carried thirty-seven of the forty-eight states and collected 404 electoral votes to James Cox's 127. Harding's big win was shared with Republicans, who won the House and made meaningful gains in the Senate.[84]

"He Was Just a Slob"

Alice Roosevelt Longworth had it right when she said, "Harding was not a bad man. He was just a slob."[85] Whether he knew it or not, his administration had been a ticking time bomb since the moment he won the presidency. He kept bad company, a group of friends and hangers-on who ran amok on the Harding name. Sometimes he knew, sometimes he didn't; sometimes he was a participant and other times guilty only by association. "It was rather shocking to see the way Harding disregarded the Constitution he was sworn to uphold,"[86] wrote Alice Roosevelt, and she wasn't wrong.

While Harding struggled, his friends and close associates took extraordinary measures in exploiting their proximity. Whether he realized it or not, the aggregate of all his mini-debaucheries helped set a tone for running fast and loose. To understand what this looked like, one need not journey further than the president's rectangular poker table, where twice a week he gathered his poker cabinet at the north end of the White House library.[87] To be at that table was to be in the innermost circle and to be excluded meant utter irrelevance.

The poker cabinet consisted of some of the usual suspects—Attorney General Harry Daugherty and his henchman Jess Smith; Interior Secretary Albert Fall; Secretary of War John Weeks; New Jersey senator Joseph Frelinghuysen; Harding's personal secretary, George Christian, Jr.; his physician, Charles Sawyer; *Washington Post* owner Ned McLean and his marketing guy, Albert Lasker.[88] Other regulars included mint director Ed Scobey, Comptroller of the Currency Dick Crissinger, Veterans Bu-

reau chief Charlie Forbes, and head of the Alien Property Bureau Thomas
Miller. It's not a coincidence that some of the biggest scandals of the administration involved the very men around this table.

Harding was addicted to both the game and the associated gambling.
He was compulsive, placing repeated bets and side bets, and when he ran
out of money, he bet his dishes, jewelry, and other valuables.[89] The president's gross disregard for prohibition laws was one of the worst-kept secrets in Washington. He kept a rolling bar next to the poker table and
when the game finished, he was known to enjoy an evening scotch while
winding down with the crew. If the night grew long, he would follow it
with a refreshing ale. When hosting reporters, he was only slightly more
discreet, once telling the journalist and author Mark Sullivan he "felt that
since the national prohibition was in effect, they ought not to drink in
the ordinary rooms of the White House, nor offer drinks to their friends
but that in their bedroom they might properly follow their personal standards."[90] But he frequently violated this rule as well. In the summer of
1922, at the height of the mining and railroad strikes, Harding called on
Bert "B.M." Jewell, who was president of the railway employees department of the American Federation of Labor, to determine whether a peaceful resolution to the labor dispute could be achieved. According to Jewell,
Harding had downed several shots of whiskey from a bottle on his desk
and was so drunk that he couldn't speak.[91]

Those who partook in the escapades enjoyed a chance to skirt the law
and kick back some stiff ones. But to those who stumbled upon it accidentally, the scene could be quite shocking. "No rumor could have exceeded
the reality," Alice Roosevelt Longworth said, having tagged along with the
Ohio congressman—also son-in-law to the late Theodore Roosevelt—
Nicholas Longworth to a poker game in the White House. "The study
was filled with cronies . . . the air heavy with tobacco smoke, trays with
bottles containing every imaginable brand of whisky stood about, cards
and poker chips ready at hand—a general atmosphere of waistcoat unbut-
toned, feet on the desk and spitoons alongside."[92]

Nowhere was Harding more reckless than with his many women.
While he was neither the first philanderer, nor the most prolific, his affairs
are certainly the most documented of any president throughout history,
including with an alleged German spy during World War I.[93] But of all
the affairs, it was a relationship with Nan Britton, whom he initially met

as a smitten twelve-year-old while he was running the *Marion Star* (but
didn't date until he was in the Senate), who posed the greatest threat to
his presidency.[94] The affair, which is detailed in her explosive memoir, *The
President's Daughter,* began when she was still in school and resulted in
a love child, which was born while Harding was running for president.
Their romance continued throughout his presidency, including trysts in
hat closets, payoffs, and a conspiracy of deceit.

As sexually adventurous as this must have been for Harding and his
young mistress, the burdens of the presidency eventually left him with little appetite for such indulgences. By the summer of 1922, Florence Harding's health began to deteriorate, which exacerbated the president's sense
of angst. One of her kidneys had failed and doctors (as well as the president) assumed she would die. At the president's direction, Mrs. Harding's
condition was made public and an outpouring of love from around the
country could be felt from coast to coast,[95] which some around the president wanted to seize as a political opportunity. Her physical demise coincided with the height of the coal and rail strikes, which put the president
in the difficult position of having to figure out how to divide his time.[96]
The news of the first lady's declining health effectively knocked the strikes
off the front pages of newspapers throughout the country and somewhat
awkwardly turned her physical condition into a political asset.[97]

To outsiders, everything seemed fine, but to intimates of the president
it was obvious that something was wrong; and it wasn't the first lady's
health. Nan Britton's final visit in January 1923 coincided with the beginning of Harding's troubles within his administration. He had grown tired,
overwhelmed, and regardless of the lack of love that existed between him
and Florence, he felt obligated to take care of her. During their visit, Nan
was hysterical in the Oval Office and unlike previous visits when he consoled her meltdowns with promises, this time he just shushed her, saying,
"Darling, they can hear out there in the hall." Wondering what happened
to the Warren she knew, she suggested they go into the anteroom for a
sexual adventure, only to be turned down again. "Can't do it, dearie," he
said. "I've got to keep going—why, right now I am the cynosure of the
whole world—the President of the United States, with a sick wife."[98]

Nan could tell that something was wrong. While she was disappointed
in the visit, she had "a feeling that he was not telling me the whole of
his troubles. . . . The haggard face, the bent figure, the white head!"[99] He

seemed more worried than normal and sounded almost desperate in his desire to maintain the veil of secrecy. "Nan, darling, you must help me," he told her. "Our secret must not come out. Why, I would rather die than disappoint my party."[100] That was the last time they ever spoke.

Death and Demise

The more Harding dug into the interworkings of the Ohio Gang the more he discovered, and the more he found, the greater his burden. By the spring of 1923, he could barely hold it together. It seemed he was excommunicating people left and right and covering the tracks wherever possible, first at the Veterans Bureau, then at the Navy and Interior Departments. Adding to these woes was the fact that his party had been decimated in the midterm elections, the previous summer had seen a contagion of labor strikes, his relationship with Congress was growing increasingly contentious, and Florence's health was not getting any better.[101] All the while, he felt he was constantly looking over his shoulder to make sure none of the salacious details from his affairs—personal or political—became public.

Despite all of this, Harding was determined to take a long-awaited and historic trip to Alaska, where he would embark on a "voyage of understanding" to kick off his reelection campaign, advocate for the United States to join the World Court,[102] and make history as the first sitting president to visit both Alaska and Canada.[103] But while the president desperately wanted to take this trip, he harbored the secret that he was almost certainly dying.[104] The trip was a mistake, not on substance—although perhaps a bit long—but because Harding was not taking care of himself. The journey was a massive undertaking that would begin on June 20, last two months, and take him and his sixty-five-person entourage[105] fifteen thousand miles, which would be the second-most number of miles traveled by a sitting president, after William Howard Taft.[106] The cross-country journey went from Washington, D.C., to St. Louis, Kansas City, Denver, Salt Lake City, Helena, Spokane, Portland, and Tacoma. Once they reached Washington state, the presidential party was to board the USS *Henderson* and journey to Alaska,[107] after which they would visit Vancouver. From there, the presidential party would make its way down the Pacific Coast and cut through the Panama Canal before returning back to Washington, D.C.

As the trip approached, some close to Harding pleaded with him not to go. James E. Watson, a Republican senator from Illinois, predicted it would kill him and Dr. Sawyer cautioned that the itinerary was far too grueling for a man of his health.[108] Mrs. Harding became increasingly concerned about her husband's health, and having just made a full recovery herself from a near fatal illness, she wasn't going to take any chances. She read Colonel Edmund Starling, the head of the president's Secret Service detail, the riot act: "I want you to promise me something. Whenever we stop, I want the doctors, General [Charles E.] Sawyer and Captain [Joel T.] Boone as close to the President's room as possible. If they can be put in the adjoining suite, I would appreciate it. At any rate, I want to be informed of the room number in each place."[109] The first lady also brought along Ruth Powderly, the nurse who had tended to Woodrow Wilson,[110] whom she insisted also be on hand at all times.

In truth, Sawyer and Boone were probably more concerned about the first lady's health than the president's. Sawyer went so far as to arrange for a coffin to be placed on the presidential train just in case she died along the way.[111] But by the time they reached the Midwest, Dr. Sawyer became deeply concerned about the president, feeling he made too many speeches and spent too much time in the heat. Harding was badly dehydrated and his lips were blistered by the sun, requiring ice compresses to try to heal them.[112] The remedy didn't work and by the time he reached Kansas City, the wear had become apparent.

Political drama seemed to follow the president at every stage of the trip. In Kansas City, Emma Fall, wife of the soon to be disgraced secretary of interior, boarded the president's train for a private interview. Harding never spoke of this meeting, but a witness observed that the body language suggested that Emma must have "told him something that was a wallop on the jaw," such as the intimate details of how her husband had used sales from the Teapot Dome oilfields to spruce up their Three Rivers Ranch.[113] Both the disturbing news and sunburn followed Harding to his next stop in Hutchinson, where William Allen White, the progressive hometown newspaper editor, noticed that "his lips were swollen and blue, his eyes puffed, and his hands seemed stiff when I shook hands with him."[114] It was in this conversation that Harding famously said, "My God, this is a hell of a job! I have no trouble with my enemies. I can take care of my enemies all right. But my damn friends, my God-damn friends, White, they're the ones that keep me walking the floor nights!"[115]

The presidential party eventually reached the West Coast and as it traveled north from Tacoma,[116] Washington, Harding invited Herbert Hoover to join him in his stateroom for a post-lunch chat. In a somewhat cryptic conversation, the president asked the commerce secretary and future president, "If you knew of a great scandal in our administration, would you for the good of the country and the party expose it publicly or would you bury it?"[117] Hoover was quick to reply, "Publish it and at least get credit for integrity on your side." Clearly grappling with this himself, Harding said that it might be "politically dangerous," but when Hoover asked for "more particulars," the president was no less vague, saying "that he had received some rumors of irregularities, centering around Smith, in connection with cases in the Department of Justice." The president gave him "no information about what Smith had been up to" and when Hoover probed further about Daugherty's involvement, the president "abruptly dried up."[118]

Alaska offered a temporary reprieve. Harding seemed to have recaptured some of his stamina as the first couple visited Metlakatla, where Florence was surprised and impressed by the Native Alaskan musicians who performed in their bare feet. They also visited the gravesite of a well-known Anglican missionary named Father William Duncan.[119] The president and first lady visited Ketchikan, where they received tribal gifts of gold and ivory jewelry, after which the president laid the cornerstone of the local Masonic Temple.[120] Governor Scott C. Bone hosted the first couple at his mansion and the Hardings took a train from Willow to Wasilla and then traveled from Fairbanks to Sitka.

The euphoria didn't last long. The drama back home literally caught up to the president as they made their way back down the Alaska coast.[121] A naval[122] seaplane[123] landed alongside the *Henderson* and a messenger boarded the presidential ship with an encoded message that he delivered to the president. The message, which arrived directly from Washington,[124] must have been sufficiently urgent and sensitive—radio and telegram ruled out as too risky[125]—to warrant a procedure and set of protocols usually reserved for wartime.

To this day, nobody knows whom the message was from or what it said. Harding destroyed it. Gaston Means, one of the few Ohio Gang men who was sleazier than Jess Smith, suspected it revealed the misdoings of Smith and Daugherty,[126] but Means had his own motivations for propagating this theory. What happened next, however, is not refuted. "After reading it," recalled an aide on board the ship, "[Harding] suffered something like a collapse."[127] He recovered fairly quickly, but spent the day in a state of shock from whatever he had read. He never regained his composure and his preoccupation with the contents of the message led him to hastily ask anyone who would listen what a president was to do when his friends misled him.[128]

This was the beginning of the end. The president's emotional and physical conditions worsened as the *Henderson* moved south to Vancouver. By the time he arrived in Canada, Harding was a mere shadow of himself, with one of his porters observing the president to be "beyond being merely fatigued. He is an entirely exhausted man, and the rest he requires is not that of a day or two or three."[129] On July 26, he joined F. W. Peters, the general superintendent of the Canadian Pacific Railway, and D. A. McDonald, the chief justice of the British Columbia Court of Appeal,[130] for a round of golf at the Shaughnessy Golf Club in Vancouver, but he was too sick to finish. After playing just six holes, he ventured over to the seventeenth to play the last two so as to create the appearance of good health.[131]

His return to Seattle was delayed due to fog[132] and then when the weather permitted entry into Washington's Puget Sound, the USS *Henderson*, which was escorted by two destroyer divisions and a squadron of U.S. Navy planes,[133] struck the *Zeilin*,[134] which was one of the destroyers. The result was a terrible crash, in which the *Henderson* incurred some minor damage, but was back up and running again in just thirty minutes. The *Zeilin* had to be pulled ashore to avoid sinking[135] and the president retreated to his stateroom, where his valet found him facedown on the bed. Harding lay there motionless and refused to look up when asking his valet what happened. When told of the accident, he spoke in a muffled voice, his head still buried in his hands like a man on the verge of ruin: "I hope the boat sinks."[136]

At some point, Harding collected himself and managed to disembark the *Henderson* and deliver a speech at the University of Washington stadium to no fewer than sixty thousand people. There was much anticipation among the crowd to see their president and hear his tales from Alaska. But he struggled through the speech, stammering on several occasions, slurring his words, and referring to Alaska as "Nebraska." His hands shook and at the midpoint he began swaying in delirium, and dropped his manuscript.[137] By good fortune, Herbert Hoover was sitting nearby and quickly gathered the speech to help the president recover.[138]

Harding somehow managed to get through the speech, but his health would suffer greatly. After a night of "acute indigestion," Dr. Sawyer made the controversial diagnosis that the president's illness had been caused by bad crabmeat.[139] Instead of taking care of himself, the president became restless and chose to play cards into the odd hours of the night. Clearly in a downward spiral, the emotionally and physically ailing president turned to drinking, on one occasion asking one of the traveling correspondents for a bottle of whiskey.[140]

The president was in a bad enough state that his handlers decided to have him skip Portland[141] and go straight to San Francisco to get some rest. The train arrived at 8:00 a.m. on Sunday, July 29, and after a night's rest Harding woke up feeling a bit better. He insisted on dressing himself, refused a wheelchair, and against the advice of his doctors walked to the car and continued on to the Palace Hotel,[142] where he was put in room 8064.[143] By a somewhat eerie coincidence, Daugherty was in town on other business, but for some reason made no attempt to see Harding.[144]

By the evening, his health had once again deteriorated, a trend that continued for the next few days until he had stabilized and concluded he was "out of the woods."[145] This was not wishful thinking. He was tired, but he really did feel better and the doctors appeared to agree. The August 1 bulletins conveyed this perceived improvement to the public.[146] That evening, in an effort to lift the president's spirits, Mrs. Harding read him a *Saturday Evening Post* article entitled "A Calm View of a Calm Man," which was a flattering profile of the president,[147] along with a cartoon depicting him at his desk hard at work while his adversaries—represented as mini-figurines—run amok around him. "I think that as an American, as President, and as a human being," Samuel Blythe's article read, "the Hon. Warren G. Harding hasn't had and isn't having fair treatment from all this gang of knockers, maligners, self-seeking politicians, disappointed applicants for his favor, theorists and fanatics and fools who want to reform the world in half an hour."[148] "That's good," Harding told his wife. "Go on, read some more."[149] It was as if all the arguing, infidelity, and tension had disappeared and the two were genuinely brought together by this moment. It was a fitting end that allowed them to part in peace.

Moments later Harding died. Mrs. Harding burst out of the room hysterical and calling for help. Stephen Early, an Associated Press reporter, happened to be just outside the room and overheard. The Secret Service quickly arrived on the scene and attempted to seal off the entire floor in order to prevent news leaks.[150] It was too late. The official cause of death was cerebral apoplexy, which is better understood today as a stroke. But since Mrs. Harding wouldn't allow an autopsy, the final diagnosis was up for debate.[151] It didn't take long for rumors of foul play to surface, most notably a theory that Harding had been poisoned. At the time it seemed at least plausible, particularly as there were many things that didn't quite add up. Why did Mrs. Harding so aggressively refuse an autopsy even when the doctors pleaded with her? Knowing there was strong disagreement, why did all the president's doctors—Boone, Wilbur, Charles M. Cooper, Sawyer, and Hubert Work—agree to sign a death certificate attributing death to the same illness? Why had Dr. Sawyer insisted that Harding fell ill due to bad crabmeat? All the others who ate the same crab were perfectly fine. And why did he not back away from this theory? Rumors that Florence Harding was responsible for poisoning her husband gained steam when Sawyer dropped dead about a year later, under similar circumstances, and while Mrs. Harding was visiting.[152] These rumors were later aided by the exposure of multiple sex scandals that gave sensationalists a motive they could assign to Mrs. Harding.

Vice President Coolidge was asleep at his father's home in Plymouth, Vermont, when the news arrived. Harding's aides had been desperately trying to find a way to get in touch with him, but he was not easy to find. They couldn't message him directly since the "farmer's line" at his 250-year-old house lacked the technical infrastructure to receive long-distance calls[153] and upon news that Harding was recovering a few days before he died, most of the reporters who had gathered in Plymouth had already departed. As a recourse, they sent a message to Bridgewater, the nearest telegraph station in town. Upon receiving the message, the telegraph office then tried to call Miss Florence Cilley, who had the closest known telephone line in her store across the road from the Coolidge home. Unfortunately, she slept right through the ring.[154] At this point, the Bridgewater telegrapher, Winfred A. Perkins, decided to take matters into his own hands and locate Coolidge's staff, who were staying in a nearby town. He managed to wake up Coolidge's driver, his personal stenographer,[155] and a local reporter,[156] who all jumped into a car as they raced the ten miles to the southern end of the Green Mountains.[157]

They carried a message, which arrived around 10:30 p.m.[158] on August 2, 1923, and read: "The President died instantly and without warning and while conversing with members of his family at 7:30 p.m. His physicians report that death was apparently due to some brain embolism, probably an apoplexy."[159] As he approached the home, the young stenographer—presumably feeling the sense of urgency—shouted, "President Harding is dead and I have a telegram for the vice-president." Colonel John Coolidge, the vice president's father, poked his head out of a bedroom window.[160] He bolted up the stairs yelling "Calvin! Calvin!"[161] and barged into his son's room to wake him up.[162] Calvin recalled how his father's voice "trembled," noting that "the only times I have ever observed that before were when death had visited our family, I knew something of the gravest nature had occurred."[163] He and his wife, Grace, took a moment to pray before heading down the stairs to figure out what to do next.[164]

In the telegram, the attorney general, along with other members of the cabinet, insisted that the vice president take the oath of office. But Coolidge wasn't sure and believed that his vice presidential oath had been adequate.[165] But others took a different view and as word of his hesitation spread hordes of key figures—including Congressman Porter Dale of Vermont's 2nd District, who lived close by[166]—showed up one by one to reinforce Daugherty's view that Coolidge must take the oath of office. Still not convinced, Coolidge brought Dale and several reporters across the street to Miss Cilley's store, where he spoke to Charles Evans Hughes over the phone for another opinion. "[The oath] should be taken before a notary," the secretary of state told him. "Father is a notary," Coolidge told him, to which Hughes responded, "That's fine."[167]

When Coolidge informed his father that he would like him to administer the oath, the colonel quickly dashed upstairs to shave and wash up for the extemporized ceremony.[168] One of those gathered at the house had located a copy of the Constitution in the home library, found the language for the oath of office, and quickly typed it up.[169] _____

There, at 2:47 a.m. on August 3, 1923, Colonel John Coolidge, aided by the light of a kerosene lamp,[170] swore his son in as the thirtieth president of the United States. It was a special moment, as Calvin remembered his father's devotion and felt particularly moved by having his father be the first to recognize him as the new president.[171] While sitting for a portrait many years later, a quiet yet confident Coolidge explained to the painter, Charles Hopkinson, that upon learning that he was to become president, "I thought I could swing it."[172]

Coolidge was only the third president to take the oath of office outside the nation's capital.* Similar to the case of Chester Arthur, this caused some controversy around the validity of the oath due to a belief by some that a state officer was not qualified to administer federal oaths.[173] To address any controversy, Coolidge took a second oath, which was secretly administered by Justice Adolph A. Hoehling at the New Willard Hotel in Washington two weeks later.[174] The second oath represented a funny game of theatrics whereby the attorney general swore the judge to secrecy for fear that the less dramatic hotel swearing-in would overshadow what had become a popular tale around a father swearing in the son in a simple Vermont house.[175]

The Scandals Break

Despite Harding's terrible state of mind, he died enormously popular and while there had been rumors of scandal, none of them had yet implicated him.[176] His pro-business posture fit the times, he reversed a period of economic hardship and ushered in an era of prosperity, and he brought the war with Germany to an official close. Even his cabinet, which would soon be lambasted for its corruption across multiple departments and agencies, received lavish praise for having Andrew Mellon, who some claimed was "the greatest [secretary of the treasury] since Alexander Hamilton" and a commerce secretary, Herbert Hoover, who managed trade efficiently.[177] To be fair, these were the two shining stars in the administration. Even so, the outpouring for the late president was described by the *New York Times* "to be the most remarkable demonstration in American history of affection, respect, and reverence for the dead."[178] This was not a man in disgrace.

The Coolidges graciously allowed Florence Harding to remain at the White House for an extra week while they stayed nearby at the Willard

---

* George Washington took the oath of office in New York, which at the time served as the nation's capital. John Adams took his oath of office in Philadelphia, which served as a temporary capital until the development of Washington, D.C., was completed.

Hotel.[179] It seems that Mrs. Harding spent most of her extra time burning and destroying documents,[180] presumably to protect her husband's legacy. White House staff observed that despite the blistering August heat, she had built a fire in the Treaty Room, which seemed to burn for most of her extended stay. George Christian, Harding's personal secretary and aide, pleaded with her not to burn all of his papers, but all he could do was grab whatever papers he could from the Oval Office and instruct anyone on hand to package and hide them in the pantry on the ground floor.[181]

For seven straight days, the White House chimneys spewed black smoke, which literally contained the ashes of scandal that would eventually land on the new president's lawn. It's difficult to imagine Coolidge was blind to the hazards that awaited him, but Harding's scandals were not his indiscretions and thus he showed no immediate concern. To the extent he did worry, it was entirely plausible that the scandals would die with Harding. He would have had good reason to believe this, particularly given the two men were complete opposites: Harding was a "slob" and Coolidge was a good Puritan with few vices, who didn't really drink, gamble, or cheat on his wife. His frugal lifestyle meant that he kept things simple and understated. "I know very well what it means to awake in the night and realize that the rent is coming due," he once remarked, "wondering where the money is coming from."[182] He didn't buy things he didn't need, choosing to share a party line instead of owning his own telephone, and he saw no reason to buy a car.[183] It was tough to criticize his character, as there were not many targets. He did have a penchant for silly jokes that could be interpreted as mean, but it is doubtful that he meant any ill. According to chief usher Irwin "Ike" Hoover, some of his favorite pranks involved "ringing the White House doorbell and then hiding behind the curtains, or pressing the buzzer to announce his impending arrival at the White House, only to head out the door for a stroll as staffers scurried around to prepare for him."[184]

He was studious, having read for history, Latin, and Greek,[185] and his work ethic afforded him the opportunity to be the first in his family to go to college.[186] At Amherst, he developed an eloquence in both his speech and debate. He entered a career in public service in 1898, spending most of his career in local politics. He joined the city council of Northampton, where he was eventually elected its mayor. He sought and won election to both the Massachusetts House of Representatives and later the State Senate, where in 1913 he became its president. His meteoric rise continued; within two years he was elected lieutenant governor, and by 1919 he was the governor of Massachusetts. As a politician, he understood the mood of the country and the demand for progressive reforms,[187] which he supported knowing that this would put him on the right side of history.

Coolidge seemed a nonentity. *The Nation* described him as a "midget statesman"[188] and Alice Longworth popularized an observation from her doctor that Coolidge "look[ed] as if he had been weaned on a pickle."[189] Upon learning that Harding died, a number of senators responded with disbelief—Henry Cabot Lodge bellowed, "My God! That means Coolidge is president!" Peter Norbeck of South Dakota said Coolidge could "no more run this big machine at Washington than could a paralytic." And Harold Ickes, the Chicago Republican who would later play a major role in Franklin Roosevelt's New Deal, disparagingly observed, "If this country has reached the state where Coolidge is the right sort of a person for president, then any office boy is qualified to be chief executive."[190]

Their descriptions were not without merit. Coolidge had done little to make his mark. As a public servant, he wasn't hardworking, nor was he particularly memorable. Both before and during the presidency he was known to sleep nearly eleven hours, including a regular nap in the afternoon.[191] While in the State Senate, he worked short hours and was a bit of a loner, choosing to spend his lunch hour eating in solitude at a corner table in the Senate dining room, facing the wall.[192] He seemed equally nameless and faceless as vice president, when he frequently went unnoticed at public events. When the baseball American and National Leagues printed complimentary baseball passes, they got his middle initial wrong.[193] He was completely absent from a popular 1921 book about the power brokers of Washington, in which Harding, Wilson, Lodge, and others were all featured at length. Coolidge was used to going unnoticed, but when the Willard was evacuated after a fire, he suffered a now infamous embarrassment. As the vice president attempted to return to his hotel suite, a marshal stopped him, at which point he insisted, "I'm the vice president." It seemed all was well and Coolidge had effectively pulled rank, until the marshal asked, "What are you vice president of?" A visibly annoyed Coolidge answered, "I am the vice president of the United States," a response that led the marshal to order him, "Come right down. . . . I thought you were vice president of the hotel."[194] And when as vice president he signed with a speaker's agency to bring in some extra income, even the discounted rate was not enough incentive for any clients to take a bite.[195]

It's true that Coolidge was virtually unknown as vice president, but he was not the political pariah he would later (and conveniently) claim to have been during the Harding administration. He enjoyed Harding's confidence, with the president-elect telling him that he should expect "to play a full part in the coming administration."[196] He did not wish for Coolidge to be "a mere substitute in waiting," and instead, he hoped for "reestablishing coordination between the executive office and the senate."[197] He meant it, too, seeking his advice on both appointments and policies.[198] Harding had invited him to join the cabinet, where he sat at the end of the table during its meetings on Tuesdays and Fridays.[199] "I am quite aware that there is no constitutional or statutory provision for such participation," Harding wrote, "but cabinet councils are wholly of an advisory nature in any event, and I am sure your presence and your suggestions will be welcome to the members of the Cabinet and I know they will be gratefully received by me."[200] Coolidge himself acknowledged that being part of the cabinet prepared him for the presidency and trained him to "think his way through some of the great principles of the American government and American civilization."[201] As a formality, President Harding always let him say a few words at the end of each cabinet meeting, but they were rarely memorable.[202] His participation in the meetings and active involvement in the administration also meant he understood the Harding men, their strengths, weaknesses, trustworthiness, and presumably who was crooked.

It was only a matter of weeks before Coolidge suspected that trouble was brewing. Myopia was not an option and navigating Harding's indiscretions would require a strategy. With just a year left of an inherited term, the new president was in a race against the election clock. He needed Harding's positive legacy to sustain long enough so he could capitalize on it to win the presidency in his own right. He didn't have the confidence or charisma of Theodore Roosevelt, so any action carried unnecessary risk. Thus, he neither articulated a legislative agenda, nor did he speak before Congress until December 6, 1923, a full 129 days after taking the oath of office.[203] If Americans expected something earth-shattering, they certainly didn't get it. "Whatever his [Harding's] policies were," he told Congress, "are my policies."[204] In essence, this meant he would attempt to slash the

$22.3 billion national debt, advocate for U.S. membership in the World Court, and further tighten immigration controls.[205]

This initial do-nothing strategy wasn't working. The scandals were boiling closer to the surface and while Coolidge played for time, he also needed to get ready to create some distance from his predecessor. This would require a delicate maneuver as he had to get elected first. Until Coolidge, no president had ascended to the office toward the tail end of his predecessor's term. As such, he would be saddled with whatever Harding had given him and would not have enough time to distinguish himself in his own right. But trouble was brewing and Coolidge knew it. The scandals were about to break and there were a lot of them. This was not just a bad seed here and there. Three years of crooked department heads and presidential negligence (and even involvement) meant that Coolidge would either need to delay the maelstrom or find a way to distance himself.

The scandals were not just Coolidge's problem, the Republican Party had also gotten itself mixed up in the milieu. The party had fallen over a million dollars in debt following the 1920 presidential election and the men ready to make the necessary contributions were deemed too connected to oil and other crooked dealings for the party to accept them without scandal. But without any other good options, Republican chairman Will Hays, in what was effectively a money-laundering scheme, accepted contributions in the form of Liberty Bonds, which he then sold to wealthy Republicans for cash.[206] Should this come out prior to the election, the Republicans would almost certainly take a hit at the ballot box.

By the time the election season started, hints of scandal had trickled out, particularly related to corruption at the Veterans Bureau and related to Teapot Dome. This certainly created headaches, but the scandals had not yet grown into something beyond Coolidge's control. This was important, because while he was not actively involved in the corruption, the Democrats could easily argue that his presence and subsequent silence in the Harding administration made him unfit for office. This would have been a fair accusation, particularly as then vice president Coolidge held that disagreement should yield silence, not opposition. He told his close political friend and trusted advisor Frank Stearns, "My conception of my position is that I am vice president. I am a member of the administration. So long as I am in that position it is my duty to uphold the policies and actions of the administration one hundred percent up to the point where I cannot conscientiously agree with them. When I cannot conscientiously agree with them it is my duty to keep silent."[207] And keep silent he did.

It took just three months from the time of Harding's funeral for the scandals to break. The first to explode was the Veterans Bureau, which during Harding's time had wielded an enormous amount of influence with a $500 million budget[208] and thirty thousand jobs to dish out. Its previous secretary, Charles Forbes, had become chums with the president after he seduced his sister, Carolyn Votaw.[209] Forbes used his high-profile lover to get close to prominent businessmen, whom he could subsequently offer an extra edge in bidding on his department's highly lucrative contracts for veterans hospitals. In instances where the bidding was competitive, he offered to unseal existing bids, so they would know what was needed in order to win. In addition to cheating the bidding process, Forbes routinely worked with companies to hike up the bid so that he could receive a nice kickback.[210] He also made a practice of selling off the massive surplus of wartime supplies at a lucrative profit,[211] including $70,000 worth of floor wax and floor cleaner, which was enough to last a hundred years.[212]

Forbes had been living the high life, enjoying power, getting rich, and having sex with the president's sister. But love has a funny way of turning things, particularly when adultery turns bad. Carolyn had grown tired of Forbes's infidelities and, predisposed to find something damning about him, found enough to corroborate the rumors with her powerful brother.[213] The president's entire inner circle, including his trusted attorney general—himself involved in a laundry list of crooked activities—urged the president to toss his crooked Veterans chief.[214] But even after learning that Forbes had swindled over $200 million,[215] Harding chose to cover up what had happened. Forbes got off easy, particularly given the president's unwillingness to either distance himself from the crimes, or call for a congressional investigation into wrongdoing at the Veterans Bureau.[216] Terrified of the embarrassment this could mean for the administration, Harding quietly asked Forbes to resign and then shipped him off to Europe so as not to attract attention.[217] The plan was not entirely successful, however, as details began to trickle out, which resulted in a Senate investigation of Forbes on March 2, 1923.[218] But like all things, the cover-up is sometimes as bad as the crime and Harding must have been deeply concerned that the Senate would learn he had pushed the scandal under the rug. The Senate spent six months gathering facts[219] and finished just at the time that Harding died. Three months later, Forbes returned from Europe to stand trial.[220] He was convicted and sentenced to a $10,000 fine and two years in prison.[221]

The Forbes scandal was a hiccup, but not an insurmountable challenge for Coolidge. Harding had done enough and justice had been served, so the president could tell a story of accountability and move on, so long as it remained an isolated incident. Unfortunately, it didn't. The next shoe to drop was Teapot Dome, which until Watergate would be considered the greatest political scandal in U.S. history. The scandal centered around three oilfields that in 1909 had been legally allocated to the United States Navy—a safeguard against possible shortage of oil in time of emergency. They were Naval Reserve No.1, at Elk Hills, California; No. 2, at Buena Vista, California; and No. 3, at Teapot Dome, Wyoming.[222] As the oil lay dormant underground, there became concerns that adjacent wells would either advertently or inadvertently siphon off the oil. Congress addressed these concerns by giving the secretary of the navy discretion over how best to conserve and utilize the oilfields.[223]

Harding's interior secretary, Albert Fall, had his own plan. Rather than receive competing bids for the leases of the reserves, he would sole-source the leases under a national security justification.[224] He would then lease the three reserves to three separate friends with terms that were disproportionately favorable to the oil companies.[225] The punch line of Fall's scheme was that by making the oil companies richer, he would earn kickbacks in the form of no-interest loans, Liberty Bonds, livestock, and cash that would make him a very rich man. Fall would then retire from government and use the money to build out his Three Rivers Ranch in New Mexico. This would include adding 9,500 acres of land through two separate transactions, a home renovation, the purchase and installation of a new hydroelectric plant, paying off his back taxes, and what must have been a massive landscaping project.[226] All he had to do was get the president to transfer the three reserves from the Department of the Navy to the Department of the Interior.

It turns out that this was a pretty easy task. Through his exploitation of the president's friendship and his own art of persuasion, Fall convinced the president to become an unknowing accomplice in his scheme. On May

11, 1921, he drafted a memo to Harding formally seeking his approval for the transfer of the naval reserves to the Interior Department.[227] He faced no opposition from Navy Secretary Edwin Denby, who was primarily focused on preventing drainage and ensuring readiness of the reserves for national defense purposes.[228] With his cabinet seemingly in agreement, Harding, in one of his first acts as president, authorized the transfer through his May 31 issuing of executive order No. 3474.[229] With the executive order in place, Fall spent the following year orchestrating the leases as planned, which he consummated at Teapot Dome on April 7, 1922, and at Elk Hills on December 11 that same year. On January 2, 1923,[230] less than one month after the Elk Hills deal, Fall had completed his mission and retired a wealthy man.[231]

It didn't take long for rumors to circulate about Fall's activities and while they plagued Harding's administration, they never rose to the level of incriminating the president. Given that he wasn't directly implicated, Harding replicated his response to Charlie Forbes and gave no credence to the rumors. It's quite remarkable that even after the Charlie Forbes betrayal and concern from his most trusted advisors, Harding didn't further scrutinize the rumors over Fall's indiscretions. This abdication was a critical mistake, as it led Fall to take one additional step that would directly implicate Harding. On June 7, 1922, Fall came to see the president and confidently offered his seventy-five-page—appendixes and all—report dealing with the oil leases.[232] Harding should have read the report. Instead, trusting Fall, he just sent it along to the Senate, unknowingly implicating himself in a cover letter: "[The new naval plan] was submitted to me prior to the adoption thereof, and the policy decided upon and the subsequent acts have at all times had my entire approval."[233] President Harding had immolated himself, committing to pen and paper his complicity in the Teapot Dome scandal.

Had Fall's fortune not so visibly improved, it is more than possible that his indiscretions would have gone unnoticed. But the oil industry—that is, those companies who were not offered an opportunity to compete for reserves that totaled more than $100 million—was looking for any opportunity to cry foul play and Fall's ostentatiousness was a suspicious thread worth pulling. The *Wall Street Journal* took notice and on April 14, 1922, broke the first explosive story about the oil tycoon Harry Sinclair, Mammoth Oil, and the Teapot Dome lease.[234] The story did not yet capture the public interest, but Congress took notice and on April 15, Wyoming Democratic senator John Kendrick introduced the first resolution calling for an investigation into Teapot Dome.[235] Few members of Congress thought the investigation would go anywhere. Recognizing this, the Senate appointed Thomas J. Walsh, the junior senator from Montana, to see the investigation through. The long recess, summer, and Harding's death delayed the committee kicking off its work, which didn't start until October 1923. After Harding died, it became clear that everyone had underestimated Walsh.

President Coolidge, who had heard the whisperings while serving as vice president, quickly understood the implications of Teapot Dome, but didn't realize in the initial months of his presidency that the scandal went all the way up to his predecessor. He just knew he had some shady characters in the cabinet and some housecleaning was in order. The former interior secretary was damaged goods and it was becoming increasingly clear that both the navy secretary and the attorney general were equally complicit. He would deal with these individuals, but he needed to simultaneously ensure that any further investigation remained bipartisan so as not to taint him or the Republican Party going into the election. Fortunately, the Walsh Commission's own investigation into the oil deals revealed wrongdoing by both parties, making it hard for a Democrat-led investigation to follow. Coolidge pounced on this fact and quickly announced the establishment of a bipartisan commission on January 28, 1924, adding that he would not "determine criminal guilt or render judgment in civil cases."[236] This was important, as any hint of defensiveness would have made the Republican Party a target. Unfortunately, he misfired with his initial choice of prosecutors to lead the commission—a Republican lawyer from Pennsylvania named Owen Roberts and former Democratic senator from Ohio Atlee Pomerene—who were found to be mixed up in some shady and complex transactions as well as money-laundering schemes.[237] But while these controversies aroused unhelpful Senate opposition,[238] the bipartisan commission did in fact reveal the most damning evidence, including connecting the cash and Liberty Bond exchanges with the selling of the leases. In all, Fall pocketed at least $400,000 and the committee had him nailed.[239]

The bipartisan commission was a stroke of political genius. It implicated both Democrats and Republicans and achieved the more important goal of playing for time as the various trials dragged out long enough to avoid impact on the election. That June, the commission called for the prosecution of Fall and his cronies,[240] but most convictions and subsequent sentencing occurred after the election.[241] At that point, the public had largely lost interest and moved on. Albert Fall was less fortunate, as he earned the distinction of being the first cabinet secretary in U.S. history to serve prison time.[242]

The third major scandal to break had the furthest sweeping implications for Harding's legacy and was potentially the most threatening to Coolidge's elections prospects. To tell the previously relayed story of Jess Smith is to reveal the essence of the attorney general as the refinery of corruption in the administration. Harry Daugherty was a shady, crooked individual who abused his office as attorney general repeatedly and unabashedly for personal gain. He personally ran a bootlegging operation in which his henchmen—mainly Jess Smith and the rest of the Ohio Gang—accepted hundreds of thousands of dollars from bootleggers in exchange for immunity, which was not always granted.[243] Bootlegging wasn't the only black-market enterprise that yielded bribe money for Daugherty and his cronies. Gaston Means, another Jess Smith type—he wrote a scathing book called *The Strange Death of President Harding*—used to rent two adjacent rooms at the Vanderbilt Hotel in New York and put a large glass fishbowl in the middle of one room and watch through the peephole of another room while the bribe money arrived in crisp bundles of one-hundred-dollar bills.[244] And as if this was not enough, they also ran a racket of film-smuggling operations, the most famous of which was the exploitation of the famed July 2, 1921, prizefight between Jack Dempsey and Georges Carpentier, dubbed the "fight of the century."[245]

Harry Daugherty also ran the Justice Department as a ruthless tyrant and drew the ire of many enemies. As attorney general, he obstructed justice, most notably during the Teapot Dome investigations.[246] When on February 20, 1924, the Montana senator Burton Wheeler introduced a resolution specifically calling for an investigation of the attorney general, Daugherty responded—or at least the FBI chief did on his behalf—by harassing him both publicly and privately. As Wheeler pursued the investigation, witnesses were physically intimidated, had their rooms ransacked and their documents stolen, all with the goal of preventing them from testifying. When that failed to halt Wheeler, Daugherty manufactured bribery charges against him in his home state of Montana.[247]

Daugherty appears to have gotten away with just about all of this. Where he ultimately ran afoul was in his dealings with the Alien Property Custodian, which he manipulated to facilitate the illegal acquisition of foreign companies by American enterprises. In what became a damningly well-documented example, he targeted the American Metal Company, a German-owned firm that had been confiscated during the war and was worth more than $6.5 million. The Daugherty corruption machine arranged its illegal transfer to an American-based firm and shaved off $441,000, which they dispersed among themselves with cash payments and Liberty Bonds through a shady buddy of Jess Smith named John T. King. This time, however, Daugherty got caught red-handed. He escaped prosecution, mainly because Jess Smith had killed himself and King also died mysteriously. But Coolidge had had enough.[248]

Harding may have been blinded by loyalty, but Coolidge knew exactly who Daugherty was and wanted him out. At the same time, he needed support in the Senate over his actions related to Teapot Dome and in particular needed the help of William Borah, the progressive senator from Idaho. Despite being a Republican, Borah had been no fan of Warren Harding and while he was more positively inclined toward Coolidge, their relationship soured when the new president made what the senator believed to be a false promise to open trade with the post-revolutionary government in Russia. Now needing him to navigate the Teapot Dome scandal through the 1924 presidential election, Coolidge sought to make amends by offering Borah a front-row seat to watch Daugherty get canned.

When the president summoned the attorney general to the White House Daugherty may have expected the worst, but he was flabbergasted to find Borah, who was one of his chief critics, hanging out in the president's office for the meeting. Daugherty was shocked and in a moment of heightened emotions, he awkwardly sniped at his enemy, sarcastically suggesting not to "let my presence embarrass you." Borah, empowered by watching Daugherty against the ropes, told him, "I think I should be the least embarrassed person here." The two then engaged in a shouting match, while Coolidge smoked a cigar. Once it became clear that the purpose of the meeting was to ask for Daugherty's resignation, the attorney general knew his time had come. He tendered his letter of resignation on March 28, 1924.[249]

What followed was a purge of the Justice Department, beginning with the Investigation Bureau chief William Burns, who was replaced by his lesser-known deputy, J. Edgar Hoover.[250] In this sense, Coolidge had elevated a man who would take all of the teachings and lessons learned from the Daugherty era and apply them to a forty-eight-year reign that spanned nine presidents and saw a transition of the bureau to what we now know as the Federal Bureau of Investigation.

Daugherty eventually got his day in court, maybe not literally, but at least figuratively. In an ironic twist, it was Jess Smith's ex-wife, Roxy, bitter and vengeful over Jess's suicide, that ultimately did him in. She blew the whistle on the entire Ohio Gang, and having been Jess's confidant even after their divorce, her testimony was credible.[251] As mentioned, Daugherty had been forced from office, but not before refusing to testify, saying that he did not want to implicate the late president. By doing this, he had effectively protected himself and seeded an idea that everyone would soon latch on to: Blame Harding.

By mid-1924, Coolidge was forced to confront the undeniable truth behind many of the accusations, particularly the suggestion that senior members of the cabinet had been deeply involved. This was a dilemma for the new president, who in addition to having been at least nominally part of the cabinet had retained these same Harding advisors. So much had unfolded in just his first few months as president and now with the 1924 presidential election fast approaching, Coolidge knew he had to distance himself from his predecessor. Harding had been good to him, but the scandals occurred on his watch, and it was much easier for a dead man's head to roll.

With Harding unable to defend himself and those responsible for the many scandals hardly eager to out themselves, Coolidge didn't wait long to throw his dead predecessor under the bus. It was a good strategy. The president was the first to publicly absolve himself of responsibility, making a statement on January 26, 1924, that while he was vice president he had never heard the oil leases discussed at any cabinet meeting. On January 31, Hughes made a similar statement and on that same day, Hoover added further confirmation. The next day, Secretary Weeks mimicked that same recollection, which was enough to put the issue to rest.[252]

The Coolidge plan worked. Not only did he get a free pass on the scandals, but the more the press and some politicians attempted to connect him and his administration to the past, the more unpopular such opponents became. Perhaps the greatest victim was John W. Davis, the Democratic nominee for president in 1924, who foolishly misread the public and tried to capitalize on the Harding scandals.[253] He paid a heavy political price. Harding may have been a scandal-ridden president and his administration may have even been a failed one, but the vote to put America first was real and there was little public appetite to get bogged down in who did what and when.

Coolidge didn't have to lift a finger to win the 1924 presidential election with the largest popular vote[254] in Republican history. It was fortunate, too, as the unexpected death of his son left him too emotionally distraught to campaign.[255] But as William Allen White observed, "In a fat and happy world, Coolidge is the man of the hour. Why tempt fate by opposing him."[256] His ascension to the presidency in 1923 fulfilled the country's desire for a return to normalcy, making for an easy case to the American people that they should "Keep It Cool with Coolidge" and vote for a continuation of prosperity.

The Coolidge Facade

In many respects, Coolidge represented a return to normalcy far more than his predecessor. He was even more hands-off than Harding and while he may have been saddled with his predecessor's scandals, the public was more interested in enjoying the prosperity that he had also inherited. If he could effectively distance himself from the scandals and associate himself with the prosperity, Coolidge rode the Roaring Twenties right through the 1924 election. He had good reason to be confident. Politically, drama over the League of Nations had evaporated and there seemed to be no demand to revive the conversation. Radicalism in all forms—labor, communism, and the KKK—had lost much of its steam and the American people were not much interested in political metadata. So long as the country prospered, Coolidge could play the role of its caretaker.[257]

And prosper it did. Unemployment was at its lowest and economic growth was at its highest-ever-recorded numbers in the twentieth century. This was the era of manufacturing, in which cars and radios were rolling off assembly lines and giving Americans unprecedented access to information and mobility. To put this in perspective, the 1920 presidential election returns were the first to be broadcast by radio. Just eight months later, the previously mentioned prizefight between Dempsey and Carpentier was broadcast to nearly 75,000 auditoriums, theaters, country clubs, ships, and homes across eighty different points throughout the country.[258]

Major brands like Edison, Ford, and Firestone were fast making America the innovation and entertainment capital of the world. They were also improving not just the overall economy but individual lifestyles with real per capita income rising from $522 to $716.[259] This was also the era of fads and fashion, sports and entertainment. Americans relished watching Babe Ruth attain new heights in home-run blasting. New foods and snacks like Eskimo pies had become popular American favorites. And, a proliferation of new publications and tabloids kept everybody informed.[260]

Coolidge was hardly the electrifying figure to represent these exciting times, but that is precisely why his quiet image worked. America neither wanted, nor did it need, a figurehead. This was an incredible era that spoke for itself. Americans wanted government to stay out of the way and Coolidge responded to that demand by cultivating an image as "Silent Cal," which is about all that has survived of his legacy. There are more anecdotes about his silence than there are memories of his policies. Journalists relished the opportunity to try to get him talking, with one trying his luck by demanding an exclusive interview. The president, however, agreed and answered every question with "no comment."[261] Coolidge loved to toy with reporters, such as when a pool peppered him with questions during the 1924 campaign: "Have you any statement on the campaign?" asked one. "No," replied Coolidge. "Can you tell us something about the world situation?" "No." Then, as the disappointed reporters started to leave, Coolidge said solemnly: "Now, remember—don't quote me."[262] And in one anecdote that has become the hallmark of the Silent Cal image, one partygoer at the White House, well aware of the president's reputation, approached him saying, "I made a bet today that I could get more than two words out of you." To her dismay, President Coolidge replied: "You lose."[263]

Despite the tales, the image of Silent Cal was a facade, something he played into for his own strategic purposes. Coolidge took a truth—his quieter, good Puritan personality—and cultivated its exaggeration to play into the notion that a man so silent couldn't possibly have had a seat at the table, or been involved in any misdoings of the previous administration. He played it perfectly, saying things like "they can't hang you for what you don't say"[264] and "If you don't say anything you can't be called on to repeat it."[265] But in truth, he was highly vocal; he just didn't bother with the extemporaneous musings at events and with big crowds. Instead, he harnessed the power of broadcast radio—newly ubiquitous and in the homes of average Americans—delivering carefully crafted narratives[266] that were eloquent and humble, so much so that of more than twenty-two speeches, in which he spoke 52,094 words, he only once used the word "I."[267]

Coolidge's frequent engagement with the press offers further evidence of the facade. During his presidency, he participated in 520 presidential press conferences and entertained more interviews with reporters than any of his predecessors.[268] He understood that the press could be your enemy or your friend and at a time when access was everything, he could use the press to cultivate an image of innocence and steer the reporting toward a narrative that had Harding and a few cronies largely acting alone.

Where the image did match reality was in the president's work ethic. When Coolidge consulted his good friend former president Taft, he advised, "Do nothing . . . Your wisest course is to be quiet for a while."[269] This role was natural for the new president, who took Taft's advice literally and made it his business to do as little as possible. This guidance resonated since Coolidge didn't like to work long hours and the country's prosperity meant he could steer it on autopilot. The pro-business mentality that got him and Harding elected in the first place seemed to be working just fine, so he saw no reason to tinker with the status quo. "Coolidge had no cabinet of any kind," recalled chief White House usher Ike Hoover, "he went [at] it alone in all things." He never gathered a group to brainstorm or think through policy options. Instead, he was completely hands-off and let his principals and advisors make most of the policy decisions. He had a simple "rule of action," as he described it, which was "never do . . . anything that someone else can do for you."[270] On one occasion, a White House staff member woke him from a nap for something he perceived to be urgent. A groggy Coolidge squinted his eyes, gave an agitated smirk, and said: "Is the country still here?" That same staffer recalled, "Coolidge used to argue that it was in the national interest for him to take long afternoon naps because he couldn't be initiating anything while asleep."[271]

If the Coolidge presidency seemed uneventful, it's because it was.

He vetoed the soldiers bonus and bickered a bit with Congress, but by and large he sat back and let the good times roll. The country, intoxicated with the perks of prosperity, mortgaged its future at every level as it marched blindly toward the greatest economic catastrophe in history. The Model A, first unveiled on December 2, 1927, was just the beginning of an automobile explosion that would transform transportation. Broadcast radio, which had been popularized by President Coolidge, now reached one-third of American homes.[272] It was an era of electronics, and indulgences—refrigerators, cosmetics, telephones, cigarettes,[273] and gadgetry of all kinds—were flying off the shelves of every major store.

Americans had greater capacity than ever before to purchase, which only made the demand for these goods skyrocket. Frederick Allen, a scholar of the Roaring Twenties, observed, "Between 1922 and 1927, the purchasing power of American wages increased at the rate of more than two percent annually. And during the three years between 1924 and 1927 alone there was a leap from 75 to 283 in the number of Americans who paid taxes on incomes of more than a million dollars a year."[274] Interest rates dropped. Both inflation and unemployment went down. And President Coolidge managed to reduce the national debt by 25 percent, while holding the federal budget flat at around $3.3 billion.[275] This was the prosperity that people hoped a "return to normalcy" would produce.

Meanwhile, the late president lay six feet underground and was saddled with the growing reputational damage that came with each new revelation. When it came time to dedicate his memorial on July 4, 1927, President Coolidge was "too busy," lest he risk any association with his radioactive predecessor. Nan Britton's publication of *The President's Daughter* dealt the dead president a devastating blow as she detailed their torrid affair in 440 pages of salacious anecdotes of sex and scandal.[276] Successive biographies and autobiographies followed, each deepening the narrative of Harding's failure. In many respects, Warren Harding became a lightning rod for the Republican Party. All that was bad was attributed to the late president, while all that was good and prosperous could be associated with Republican policies.

Harding was undoubtedly flawed and a failure of a president, but his death was exploited in the most Machiavellian terms by the very political opportunists he had elevated. Harding was corrupt, but so were many others in the Republican Party. His tragic death probably saved the party from implosion by giving it a fall guy. Had he survived, it all would have exploded just as he was gearing up for reelection, and unlike Coolidge he would have had no way to escape. There were simply too many scandals involving too many cronies and public servants, and had he not died it is unlikely he would have finished his term in office.

The 68th Congress, while still Republican, was not as friendly as the previous legislature, particularly given the results from the midterm elections. While maintaining a slight control of Congress, the Republicans had lost seventy-seven seats in the House and another six in the Senate. It's hard to know if a Republican-controlled Congress would have gone so far as to impeach a president from its own party, but it may have faced enough political pressure to do so. Given Harding's health and mental state, it seems more likely that he would have resigned, either of his own volition or under pressure from his own party. And had he not been removed or resigned, it seems likely that the Republican Convention would have been messy and scandal-ridden, making it more difficult for Harding or any other nominee to win against a viable Democrat.

=====

It was tempting for Coolidge to consider a run in 1928, and at the time the country was so prosperous that he probably could have won. But following the precedent set by Theodore Roosevelt, a debate ensued about whether an accidental president could serve out his predecessor's term and then win election twice in his own right. This was a new debate, as Roosevelt had hastily announced he would not seek reelection upon winning the election in 1904. The third-term argument, made by a number of papers, including the *New York Times*, ultimately won out and Coolidge agreed to retire in 1928.[277]

The 1920s was the Republican era, a period in which the prosperity was so great that it overshadowed the man in the White House. The party cared little if the president was Calvin Coolidge or Herbert Hoover, so long as he was Republican and the party could build on its political endowment. Little did they know that this political endowment was resting on a far shakier foundation than they realized. The approach was nearsighted and as Henry "H.L." Mencken, a well-known satirical journalist of the time, observed, "[Coolidge's] chief feat during five years and seven months in office was to sleep more than any other President—to sleep more and say less. . . . While he yawned and stretched the United States went slam-bang down the hill—and he lived just long enough to see it fetch up with a horrible bump at the bottom."[278]

Harding, Coolidge, and Hoover had all been architects of the policy that put American business first. Each bears responsibility for rebuffing demands to regulate the financial sector and for permitting rampant stock market speculation.[279] Both the financial sector and the stock market were in dire need of regulation and we know in hindsight that the trickle-down effect of booming economic times had created a bubble that was ready to burst. The success of the economy was in fact widening income inequality and further depressing the persisting agricultural crises. In truth, it all could have come crashing down during any one of the three presidents' administrations. But by a stroke of bad luck and opting into a continuation of the same policies, Herbert Hoover was left holding the bag and to navigate the impossible.

Hoover's election in 1928 was seen as a vote for prosperity, and by all accounts he had the right pedigree to continue the momentum. As a star member of both the Harding and Coolidge cabinets, where he served as commerce secretary, Hoover distinguished himself as both a savvy and competent executive. He had overseen the Food Administration during World War I, served as a member of the Supreme Economic Council, and headed the American Relief Administration in the postwar era, where he earned a reputation as the man who fed Europe. Capitalizing on this reputation, he promised that the era of universal prosperity was within sight and went with a catchy slogan: "A chicken in every pot . . . vote for Hoover." With the country's economy continuing to boom and a nasty anti-Catholic campaign targeted at the Democratic nominee, Al Smith, Hoover had an easy time winning in a massive landslide that even flipped some of the southern Democratic states.

The celebration was short-lived. Less than a year after taking office, calamity hit. As the market crashed in October 1929, so too did the Republican era of good and plenty. The Roaring Twenties came to a disastrous end. Hoover's principle of "rugged individualism"—the notion that the government should keep its hands out of the economy—made his administration seem negligent and vulnerable to criticisms that he had missed all the warning signs. He scrambled to deal with the aftermath of the market crash and launched both a public works program and a series of measures designed to protect labor and subsidize agriculture. But it was too little, too late and while some of what he put in place proved helpful in laying the foundation of the New Deal, the voters saw no material improvement when he ran for reelection in 1932.

An already impossible victory was made that much harder by Hoover's formidable opponent, the young Franklin D. Roosevelt, who had his own impressive pedigree, said all the right things, and carried a famous last name. He promised to use the machinery and resources of the federal government to balance the budget, put Americans back to work, care for the elderly, and reinvigorate American agriculture. "I pledge you, I pledge myself, to a new deal for the American people," the charismatic Democrat declared in his acceptance speech. "This is more than a political campaign; it is a call to arms." With lofty rhetoric and promises galore, FDR won a sweeping victory, capturing 472 electoral votes to Hoover's 59 and winning 42 states. His victory marked the beginning of a twenty-year Democratic run in the White House, during which time America recovered from the Great Depression, went to war against Nazi Germany and Imperial Japan, emerged victorious, redesigned a new world order, and entered into a new and colder war with a different kind of adversary. That seminal journey in American history, however, almost had a very different beginning.

By 1944, **FDR** was a dying man. Knowing the vice president would likely become president, the Democratic Party bosses schemed to get Henry Wallace off the ticket.

Harry Truman was a parochial politician from Missouri, who only reluctantly accepted being added to the 1944 presidential ticket.

CHAPTER SEVEN

"That Damn Mule!"

Near Miss and the Twentieth Amendment

The friendship between Vincent Astor and Franklin Roosevelt marked one of the great relationships between political power and American business. They had little in common beyond wealth and sprawling estates in the Hudson Valley. Astor was awkward and crass, often making jokes at other people's expense. Roosevelt was a modest and well-mannered gentleman whose charisma was off the charts. Astor's hands were deep in the financial sector and he had a penchant for extravagant homes, yachts, and race cars. He was also a Republican. Roosevelt was a staunch Democrat and progressive, keen to fight the banks and power structure.[1]

Their relationship ushered in a new age of government and private sector interaction. During the First World War, Roosevelt, as assistant secretary of the navy, tapped his billionaire friend to contribute millions to the Liberty Loan, lend his Hudson Valley estate to the government for hospital use, and deploy his personal yacht to fight in combat.[2]

When FDR was stricken with polio in 1921, Vincent was among the few close enough to understand the full extent of his handicap. His late father, John Jacob Astor IV, had built the first indoor heated pool in their Rhinebeck estate and Roosevelt traveled from Hyde Park to use the pool for leg therapy. FDR's wife, Eleanor, enjoyed the basement shooting range, where she could enjoy the sport without facing scrutiny that it was unladylike.

When Roosevelt reentered public life after a seven-year political hiatus, Astor stood ready to offer his support. In 1928, he helped back FDR for governor of New York and in 1932, he once again bet on the right horse with Roosevelt's presidential victory. He promised to elevate the economy and end the Depression. His victory gave people hope and ushered in an era of optimism.

When the U.S. entered World War II, Vincent stood ready to leverage his vast resources. As director of Chase National Bank, he provided FDR with privileged banking information, while his employees at Western Union Telegraph Co. snooped on American correspondence for national security. He was pivotal in securing secret military equipment, conducting counterespionage operations that apprehended over thirty Nazi secret agents, and illegally accessing diplomatic correspondence. Astor donated his mega-yacht and agreed to be secretly dispatched to the Pacific as a personal spymaster for the president. Roosevelt also leveraged his childhood friend's position to avoid America's Neutrality Laws and skirt congressional oversight by using the cover of business as a vehicle for moving resources around the world. Vincent truly was the president's billionaire.

This was a chapter that almost ended before it began. To celebrate FDR's presidential win, Astor put together a last hurrah for his friend a few weeks before the inauguration. It was the 1933 version of what we call "boys' trips," with Roosevelt, Astor, and some old Harvard and political friends[3] taking off from New York for eleven days of fishing[4] and drinking on the high seas. They traveled on board the *Nourmahal,* which was Astor's 264-foot nautical palace that he had commissioned partly with profits from his highly lucrative investment in the original MGM film of *Ben-Hur.*[5] The ship was a stark contrast to the progressive movement that Roosevelt would champion. It was over the top, with eleven staterooms, a library, a dining room for eighteen, a special operating room in case of emergencies, and cabins for all the officers of the forty-two-man crew.

After the exhausting campaign, the excursion offered an endowment of relaxation for the president-elect that left him "jovial, tanned, [and] . . . fit in every way." It was "a marvelous rest—lots of air and sun," Franklin wrote his mother. "I shall be full of health and vigor—the last holiday for many months."[6] The *Nourmahal* arrived in Miami around 7:00 p.m.[7] on February 15, signaling that Roosevelt was back to work. The governor of Florida, the mayor of Miami, and a number of local politicos boarded to greet the president-elect. Roosevelt schmoozed and joked around like a political pro. The reporters who had come on board lobbed soft questions his way, hoping to get an anecdote or two, and Roosevelt certainly didn't disappoint.[8]

FDR and his yachting buddies grabbed a quick bite and then it was off to Bay Front Park to say a few words to the American Legion Convention.[9] The president took the front vehicle in the three-car motorcade, a green Buick convertible that included Secret Service agent Gus Gennerich, press aide Marvin H. McIntyre, and Miami mayor R. B. Gauthier.[10] In the second car were Vincent Astor, Kermit Roosevelt, the second son of Theodore Roosevelt, and Raymond Moley, the Columbia professor who had become one of Roosevelt's top advisors on the campaign.

As the motorcade made its way, Moley told his companions, "This kind of thing scares me to death. The possibility of presidential assassination is very great. How can the Secret Service possibly protect any man with the crowds pressing in on each side of the roadway so closely?" Part of what triggered his concern were the magnesium flashbulbs, standard for those days, which made a popping noise somewhat similar to a low-powered pistol.[11]

When the motorcade arrived, Roosevelt lifted himself onto the back of the open car[12] so the crowds could see him, took a small portable microphone,[13] and delivered brief remarks. The speech was so quick[14] that a desperate sound crew begged him to repeat his remarks so they could pick them up for broadcast radio. Roosevelt wasn't in the mood to stick around and neither was the Secret Service. George Brodnax, the lead agent on the scene, instructed the driver to go, but just as they started moving, Roosevelt spotted a familiar face, Chicago mayor Anton Cermak, who had been a political opponent until the final ballot of the 1932 Democratic National Convention. Eager to extend a friendly hand, he told the driver to stop. FDR called the mayor over, fastened himself to the backseat,[15] and as Cermak stepped onto the running board, the two shook hands.[16]

At this moment, Cermak handed Roosevelt a telegram as a series of loud cracks came from the crowd. Giuseppe Zangara, a bitter Italian immigrant, drew his nickel-plated .32 caliber double-action revolver[17] and from thirty-five feet away[18] took aim at Roosevelt[19] and fired off five shots in fifteen seconds. The shots hit several people but missed the president-elect's head by less than two feet.[20] A remarkably calm Roosevelt, perhaps recalling his cousin Teddy's resolve when victim of an assassination attempt—waved to show he was unhurt. He seemed unaware that anyone had been injured.[21]

The scene was chaotic. "Those fifteen seconds of terror," recalled one eyewitness, "saw mayor Cermak crumple almost at my feet with a bullet in his right lung, and Mrs. Joseph Gill, wife of the president of the Florida Power & Light Co., fall with a bullet in her abdomen." Margaret Kruis, a dancer from New Jersey, was also hit and fell to the ground beside Mayor Cermak. Several others were wounded, including Russell Caldwell, a Coral Gables architect, and William Sinnott, a New York detective on vacation, who were both shot in the head.[22]

As for Zangara, he was far enough away that the Secret Service had to push through the crowd to get to him. Vincent Astor recalled seeing one of the agents punch a spectator in the nose,[23] presumably because he obstructed their path. The UPI reported that detectives and Secret Service tackled Zangara with the still hot gun in his hand.[24] The crowd, ready to play judge and executioner, swarmed their villain with a fiery rage. Calls of "lynch him" could be heard throughout as the officers on hand ushered him away from the angry mob and onto the trunk rack of the car.[25]

As Roosevelt's boating buddies tried to understand what had happened, there was a loud smash on the back of their car. Police officers were hitting the vehicle. They are "trying to smash the back of our car," Moley yelled. Kermit asked why they would do that.[26] Astor recalled, "It was extraordinary because you don't expect to see police begin clambering all over the back of an official car in an official parade."[27]

Despite all this, the wealthy tagalongs had no reason to believe the president had been in danger, or that anybody had been shot. Part of the confusion may have been caused by the fact that Roosevelt's car took several minutes to start moving. Despite repeated Secret Service orders to the driver, FDR refused to let the car move. He countermanded Brodnax's order for the driver to speed away. Astor saw Cermak attempting to pass between the two cars and noticed a large spot of reddish-brown color spread on his shirt. He appeared to stagger until the president's car was thrown open and he was pulled inside.[28] When the mayor had been placed in the backseat[29] Roosevelt allowed the car to move.

As Roosevelt's car sped toward the hospital, he tried to keep Cermak calm and conscious. Despite the fact that a madman had just tried to kill him, he seemed unaffected. Nothing in his later reflections suggests otherwise. He recalled, "I put my left arm around him and my hand on his pulse, but I couldn't find any pulse.... I held him all the way to the hospital and his pulse constantly improved.... I talked to mayor Cermak nearly all the way. I said, 'Tony, keep quiet—don't move. It won't hurt you if you keep quiet.'"[30]

At Jackson Memorial, Roosevelt remained poised. He wheeled his way through the hospital corridors to Mayor Cermak. "You look fine," he told him with a smile. "I hope you will be back on your feet soon—certainly in time for the inauguration."[31] Cermak mustered enough strength to say, "I am glad it was me instead of you, [but] I wish you would be careful. The country needs you. You should not take any chances with the country in the frame of mind it is."[32]

Despite having narrowly skirted death, Roosevelt was remarkably stoic about the day's events. When he returned to the *Nourmahal* that evening, his friends were shocked. The group stayed awake until 2:30 a.m. and the president's friend and temporary physician on the fishing trip, Dr. Leslie Heiter,[33] drew medical pictures to help him understand the extent of Cermak's injuries. During the chaos, Heiter had been accidentally left behind by the motorcade. In a letter to his father the following day, he recounted how upon hearing that there had been a shooting, he rushed to the scene of the crime, only to be stopped by the police. Unable to reach the park, he ventured to the "county jail . . . to see what hospital the wounded had been taken to—and while there waiting telephone communication in they dump the would be assassin [Giuseppe Zangara] kerplunk on the floor."[34] The group was emotional about the day's events and as Moley recalled, "All of us were prepared, sympathetically, understandingly, for any reaction that might come from him." But as they sipped drinks on Vincent's yacht, "there was nothing—not so much as the twitching of a muscle. . . . Roosevelt was simply himself."[35]

This was Roosevelt's personality. He had succumbed to polio, resurrected a political career, and was now elected president of the United States. He took a pragmatic approach to life's obstacles and didn't dwell on them. Much like his cousin Theodore, he was always in forward motion, although instead of outpacing life's challenges, he simply chose to deny their existence. This was part of the power of FDR.

What FDR didn't realize, however, is how lucky he was to escape the gunshots unharmed. When interviewed about the incident many years later, Vincent Astor rattled off the list of fortunate mishaps, including Zangara's inaccurate shooting, observing that he "shot five times and also hit five people, which you couldn't have avoided doing because there was a great press of people." He speculated that perhaps it was the "very small pistol," or the "very short cartridges which had very little penetration," or the fact that "he was also a very short, small man," or that the "crowd was much bigger than had been expected," or the fact that he "stood on a somewhat shaky camp stool."[36] All of these were reasonable theories, but the more likely reason FDR survived was because of the heroism of a physician's wife named Lillian Cross and Thomas Armour, a local Miami contractor.[37]

Like so many others, Lillian Cross had come to the park that day to catch a glimpse of Franklin Roosevelt. She was an unassuming woman, petite, weighing just one hundred pounds, and easily lost in the crowd. As she remembered, "I stood on one of the benches [so I could see], and this man stood up with me. The bench nearly folded up. . . . I glanced up at him and saw he had a pistol. He began shooting toward Mr. Roosevelt. . . . My mind grasped the situation in a flash. I said to myself, 'He's going to kill the president!'"[38]

Zangara's gun, Mrs. Cross said, "was pointed over my right shoulder, directly in line with the president."[39] She quickly transferred her handbag to her left hand and threw her full one hundred pounds against the armed maniac.[40] Without hesitation, Cross recalled, she "grabbed his arm and pushed it with all my strength into the air, and called for help." Zangara put up a fight, but fortunately he wasn't much bigger than Mrs. Cross or he probably would have knocked her off the bench. "The shots made a terrific noise in my ear," she said. "He kept shooting and trying to force my arm down, but I wouldn't let go. I couldn't have held much longer." As she struggled to restrain the shooter, Mr. Armour, who was standing nearby, came to her aid immediately and "also grabbed [the assassin's] arm." Soon a group of men joined the fray, piled on, and "were choking him."[41] Mrs. Cross, who believed there was no "doubt that if his aim hadn't been spoiled, he would have hit Mr. Roosevelt"[42] was rightfully recognized by police as the woman who saved the next president[43] and the country.

It didn't take long for Zangara to be tried and sentenced to twenty years in prison for four counts of attempted murder—one for each of his victims. The clearly disgruntled would-be assassin was defiant in his response: "Don't be stingy, give me more—give me 100 years!"[44] He eventually got a punishment far worse. Mayor Cermak succumbed to his wounds on March 6, after which Zangara was tried for murder and sentenced to die in the electric chair. Justice was swift. On March 20, 1933, he was electrocuted at the state prison at Raiford, Florida. No less defiant the second time around, he yelled, "Keep hands off. I not afraid to sit in chair I do it myself." Clearly frustrated that there were no photographers to capture his moment of infamy, he uttered some final aggrieved words: "You no take my picture? You lousy bums. . . . Push the button, push the button!"[45]

The assassination attempt on President-elect Roosevelt seemed to come and go and history has shown a remarkably light interest in what transpired that day. A mayor was dead, a handful of others were injured, and a crowd of people terrified. Within two weeks, Roosevelt took the oath of office. Within five weeks, the would-be assassin was tried and electrocuted. And, as we know, FDR would serve more than twelve years in office, preside over the New Deal, fight a world war on multiple fronts, and go on to achieve legendary status as one of the greatest presidents of all time.

But the significance of the Miami incident is far too important to be lost. What if Roosevelt's speech was longer than a few minutes? The Twentieth Amendment—specifying that in the absence of a president-elect, the vice-president-elect fills the vacuum and assumes the role upon inauguration day—had been ratified on January 23, just weeks before the shooting, although it wouldn't take effect until October 15.[46] The amendment was not conceived to address presidential succession. Its purpose was to adjust the lame-duck sessions of Congress by moving the inauguration date from March 4 to January 20 and the start and end date for congressional terms from March 4 to January 3.[47] Over the years, newly elected members of Congress—as well as those holding on to their seats—had grown irritated by "the actions of defeated or retiring officials during the period after an election and before the inauguration of their replacements."[48] This was compounded by the historic fact that "three Presidents—Thomas Jefferson, John Quincy Adams, and Rutherford B. Hayes—had been elected by the vote of . . . [a] lame-duck House,* not the incoming House elected at the same time that they ran for President."[49]

---

* Congress has intervened in three presidential elections—1800, 1824, and 1876. Each was unique. In 1800, Thomas Jefferson and Aaron Burr tied under the original system, where the president and vice president were determined by the first and second vote getters. This was solved by the Twelfth Amendment, which called for electors to cast two votes—one for the president and one for the vice president. In 1824, neither John Quincy Adams nor Andrew Jackson achieved the required 131 electoral votes required to win the presidency. Following the Constitution, along with a new provision in the Twelfth Amendment, the House of Representatives deliberated on the top three vote getters (the third was Treasury Secretary William Crawford), and selected John Quincy Adams as president. In 1876, Samuel Tilden won both the popular vote and electoral college, but Republicans challenged results in three states. Congress intervened to

The Twentieth Amendment was crystal clear about succession, particularly as the electors in the Electoral College had already cast their votes on January 9 and Congress had tabulated the final votes on February 8. But given the October take-effect date, it is unclear what would have happened. In all likelihood, the ratification of the amendment would have led the electors to do in effect what the Twentieth Amendment stipulated and would have made Vice-President-elect John Nance Garner[50] the president on March 4, 1933. Garner was a self-made man, born in a log cabin during the Grant administration (it had been fifty-two years since America had a president born in a log cabin). From these humble beginnings, he rose to become a prominent lawyer, judge, and member of Congress from Texas, where he served fourteen terms and was eventually elected speaker in 1931.[51] Historians such as Alan Brinkley have argued that had he ascended to the presidency, "the New Deal, the move toward internationalism—these would never have happened. It would have changed the history of the world in the 20th century."[52]

The Dying President

Roosevelt was a sick and dying man when he ran for a fourth term in 1944. He must have had some sense of this as early as the winter of 1943 and it is difficult to imagine he didn't grasp the realities of his health by that fall. His first two terms were grueling and the third had driven him into the ground. Following Pearl Harbor, FDR's days grew longer, his travel more frequent, and his stress compounded. His days were consumed with navigating the war and trying to imagine the postwar order. These tasks took him further and wider than any other president in history. He had replaced John Garner for his third term with Henry Wallace, a move that caused anxiety among some of the party elite. They saw him as a far-left ideologue with a distorted worldview and feared he would hand the reins of Democratic power to the ultra-liberal labor movement.[53] Influential southern Democratic leaders opposed Wallace. They shared the belief that

---

negotiate a compromise that gave Rutherford Hayes the presidency in exchange for an end to Reconstruction. In each case, the new Congress was elected on the same day as the unresolved presidential election, but wouldn't be sworn in until March 4. This meant that the three congressional interventions to choose a president were conducted by a lame-duck Congress. (Source: https://history.house.gov/Institution/Origins-Development/Electoral-College/)

Wallace had been imposed upon them, but their greater concern was that he was pulling Roosevelt further left on civil rights.[54] Now he was about to embark on a presidential campaign! It was to be the last chapter in a long story of medical deception that had begun many years earlier with the onset of polio.

The president's health was up and down throughout 1943. It could have easily been attributed to stress and fatigue. It wasn't until he traveled to the Middle East in November—first to Cairo for a meeting with Winston Churchill and Chiang Kai-shek,[55] and then to Tehran for a meeting with Churchill and Joseph Stalin—that it was clear that something was wrong. The Tehran Conference proved the turning point for Roosevelt's health and many of those around him knew it.[56]

Roosevelt had been courting a meeting with Stalin since the U.S. entered the war in 1941. After some back-and-forth with Churchill about two of Stalin's most pressing issues—securing a British commitment to help drive the Nazis out of France and delivering wartime materials through the Arctic to the Soviet Union[57]—Roosevelt wrote Stalin on April 11, 1942, to request a bilateral meeting, but the response was evasive.[58] He tried again on December 2, 1942, this time suggesting that Churchill join and the three "meet secretly in some secure place in Africa."[59] Again, Stalin's response was lukewarm and on December 8, Roosevelt wrote, "I am deeply disappointed you feel you cannot get away for a conference in January [1943] . . . I want to suggest that we set a tentative date for meeting in North Africa about March first."[60] His eagerness may have led Stalin to prolong the courtship. Roosevelt continued trying and eventually Stalin agreed to meet. But he would travel no further than Iran.[61]

As the presidential party made its way to Iran, his underqualified and overly empowered physician, Ross McIntire, pleaded with the president to make part of the trip by train. When Roosevelt refused, he emphasized that the flight should stay at sub-wartime protocol elevation. "Nothing over seven thousand, five hundred—and that's tops," McIntire instructed the president's son Elliott, who somewhat hesitantly agreed to talk to the pilot.[62]

During three meetings at Tehran, the three leaders—or "Big Three" as they became known—committed to Operation Overlord. The Soviet Union would open an eastern front against Nazi Germany.[63] The implications were profound as it set in motion the movement of troops that would ultimately define the postwar order. Some more conservative historians, most notably Robert Nisbet, have gone as far as to argue that what Munich was to World War II, Tehran (and later Yalta) was to the Cold War.[64] Proponents of this theory observe that Tehran was the start of the Cold War and that Stalin entered with a blank piece of paper and left with a strategy for Soviet domination of the postwar world. Other historians, such as John Lewis Gaddis, have argued that unlike the prewar meeting in Munich, which catalyzed a series of escalating events, the post–World War II divisions of Europe were inevitable. Roosevelt and Churchill disagreed strongly over Soviet intentions. That rift was supposed to remain private, but it began to reveal itself in front of Stalin. First, when threatened with assassination rumors, Roosevelt chose to stay with Stalin instead of Churchill.[65] Second, he made a series of jokes at Churchill's expense, presumably to score a cheap laugh from Stalin. He called him "cranky" and talked about how he "woke up on the wrong side of the bed." He gave the prime minister a hard time over his "Britishness," teased him about John Bull, and taunted him enough to turn him red and scowling.[66]

While Tehran was significant in terms of the agreements reached, it marked a watershed moment, where Roosevelt's declining health was on full display for both Churchill and Stalin. Harry Hopkins, the former commerce secretary and trusted presidential advisor, described the president as "inept," Churchill told a member of his delegation, although the degree to which his mood and temperament skewed this recollection is hotly debated among historians. "He was asked a lot of questions and gave the wrong answers."[67] Amidst discussions about access to the Baltic Sea, the president seemed to be hit abruptly with flulike symptoms. "He turned green and sweaty," observed his interpreter Charles Bohlen, who said that they "were all caught by surprise." Hopkins took the handles of the president's wheelchair and brought him to his room to be examined by Dr. McIntire.[68]

What McIntire found left him again concerned about the elevation of the flights. Given the flight path was dangerously close to enemy-occupied territory, military aides recommended flying above the clouds; McIntire overruled them and ordered the plane not to exceed an altitude of eight thousand feet.[69] They flew from Tehran to Cairo, where the U.S. ambassador described being "dumbfounded" by FDR's fragile appearance.[70] One friend said that he thought Tehran was "the turning point of . . . [Roosevelt's] physical career" and others observed that "a definite physical change was obvious to everyone."[71] Samuel I. Rosenman, one of his most trusted advisors, recalled how the "President developed some sort of bronchial affliction in Tehran" that really marked the beginning of his physical demise.[72] Whatever stomach issues he suffered in Tehran repeated themselves several more times in early 1944 during a trip to South Carolina, where he stayed on the estate of the businessman Bernard M. Baruch.[73] According to medical historians, the illness was cholecystitis, which is a condition caused by inflammation of the gallbladder.[74]

By 1944, FDR's health went from bad to worse. Grace Tully, who spent more time with the president than anyone, recalled the "latter years" when she "observed the signs of cumulative weariness, the dark circles that never quite faded from under his eyes, the more pronounced shake in his hand as he lit his cigarette, the easy slump that developed in his shoulders as he sat at a desk that was always covered with work."[75] The pattern of fatigue did not cease. It started with FDR "occasionally nodding over his mail or dozing a moment during dictation . . . [but] as it began to occur with increasing frequency I became seriously alarmed. It was evident that the grind was becoming too severe for him; the next step might well be a real breakdown in his health or a dangerous decrease in the soundness and force of his judgment."[76]

On March 27, after a thorough examination of the president, Dr. Howard Bruenn found his high-profile "patient breathless and slightly cyanotic." It was clear that the "heart [was] dangerously enlarged at the left ventricle [the main chamber of the heart] . . . [and] his blood pressure [was an alarming] 186/108 (high)."[77] There was also a concern that any shift in his emotional state or physical appearance could lead to a sudden spike in his blood pressure.[78] These physical signs, he explained, justified the diagnosis of "reduced lung capacity, high blood pressure [and] acute bronchitis."[79] So serious were these diagnoses that according to Bruenn, "it seemed apparent that some degree of congestive heart failure was present." As part of his summary, the young cardiologist advised FDR's medical ensemble to immediately adopt a strict diet, have him take digitalis for his failing heart, and subject him to no less than one week of bed rest. McIntire, likely threatened by Bruenn's recommendations, rejected all of them due to "exigencies and demands on the president."[80]

Historians have argued that FDR was in denial and this is likely true. It seems more likely that he was in denial about his timeline, not his illness. The war was almost over. The postwar world would need the right guiding hand. And Roosevelt believed he was essential for both. He believed he could persevere. It's not quite denial, but rather charging forward through a systematic distortion aimed at generating strength. It's a well-practiced art.

Roosevelt's decision to run for a fourth term was driven by his desire to finish what he started. But everyone around him should have seen or experienced some hint that he was dying. While his perseverance is to be admired, it was a failure in leadership. It made it impossible to prepare for the inevitable. It is possible that the legacy of Woodrow Wilson was a driving factor behind this. Before his debilitating illness, Wilson had suffered small strokes and was often sick. FDR had been a member of Wilson's war cabinet. He had watched how illness had prevented him from realizing his dream of a postwar order, although Patricia O'Toole, a Woodrow Wilson scholar and author of *The Moralist*, argues that his folly was moral dogmatism when he should have been making the case against Soviet aggression.[81] Roosevelt had remarked: "As we came in sight of the portico, we saw the president in a wheelchair, his left shoulder covered with a shawl which concealed his left arm, which was paralyzed, and the governor said to me, 'the President is a very sick man.' . . . Wilson looked up and in a very low, weak voice said, 'Thank you for coming.' . . . His utter weakness was startling."[82]

Where this gets interesting in an eerie foreshadowing, is the fact that despite being in the mix, Roosevelt did not realize just how debilitating Wilson's stroke had been; nor did he see the machinery that concealed this from the public. But along with the rest of the country, he would learn the truth behind that final year.

All this does not explain the lack of attention to a successor. It would seem that for a man in his precarious physical condition, at least part of this perseverance strategy would include considerable planning for a successor. His conversations with Stalin at Tehran and the ambiguity he left for the Soviet leader to interpret indicates that he didn't view Tehran as a final meeting, but rather an initial conversation. That is not a strategy fit for a dying man. We know that he idolized and studied the experience of his cousin Theodore, whose choice of his friend William Howard Taft as a successor left him disappointed and frustrated. But even with that lesson in mind, Roosevelt seems to have been oddly apathetic about whom he ran with.

Anyone but Wallace

FDR waited until the last minute to announce for a fourth term. His third had been unprecedented. More important, he needed the campaign to be as short as possible, lest his stamina give out. The Democratic leadership didn't wait for an announcement. They knew he would run and worked to engineer a campaign that would obscure the president's failing health as early as 1943. Using the war as a pretext, Frank Walker, the party's chairman, told the press he would "seek an agreement with the Republicans" to ensure the election "be confined to the shortest possible period so as not to disturb the war program."[83] Harrison E. Spangler, the chairman of the Republican Party, responded with a counterproposal: "If you can and will give the people of this country satisfactory and positive assurance that Mr. Roosevelt does not have any ambition for, and will not under any circumstances accept, a nomination for a fourth term, then we will welcome proposal for a short campaign during wartime.... If you find you cannot give us such assurance, we must assume that you are already nominating Mr. Roosevelt and we have nothing to discuss."[84] With both party chairmen flatly rejecting each other's proposals, a war of words ensued in the press, which dragged out well into 1944.

Some in the Democratic Party feared Roosevelt's run for a fourth term. Chief among them was Edwin W. Pauley, the party's secretary and acting treasurer. Pauley admired Roosevelt and didn't seek to cause him harm, but he didn't believe Roosevelt would survive a fourth term. He hated Henry Wallace and believed that the sitting vice president "was not a fit man to be President of the United States."[85] Pauley therefore determined "that [he] could make no greater individual contribution to the Nation's good than to do everything in [his] power to protect it from Wallace during the war and postwar period."[86]

Pauley wasn't alone in this view. Edward Flynn, who became Chicago boss following Cermak's death in Miami, came to the same conclusion, both about the president's condition and Henry Wallace. He was alarmed by Roosevelt's appearance during a White House meeting a few weeks before the campaign began. As he sat with the president, he noticed him clutching a table or chair to prevent his hands from trembling.[87] At that moment, it dawned on Flynn that the next vice president would become president. He committed himself to getting Vice President Henry Wallace off the ticket.[88]

While Flynn and Pauley represented the party elite, some of Roosevelt's advisors shared their concerns and were mounting a movement to confront the president directly about not running. The problem was that nobody wanted to have the conversation. James Farley, the outspoken former postmaster general and Democratic National Committee heavyweight who challenged Roosevelt for the nomination (he captured a single vote), wrote in his diary, "Anyone with a grain of common sense would surely realize from the appearance of the president that he is not a well man and there is not a chance in the world for him to carry on for four more years and face the problems that a President will have before him; he just can't survive another term."[89] But Farley also lacked the courage to do anything about it. None of the physicians spoke to the president directly, either, even though there was some conversation about the issue. Finally, Undersecretary of State Edward R. Stettinius tapped Tommy "the Cork" Corcoran, the Rhode Island lawyer who became one of FDR's most trusted advisors, to convince the president not to run. Unfortunately, "the Cork" got cold feet.[90] In the end, only one Roosevelt advisor expressed concern to the president (and first lady) and it didn't end well for him. Benjamin Cohen, who had been a principal architect of the Lend-Lease policy—the idea that foreign assistance could be provided to the Allied Power without compensation— harmed his relationship with the president by suggesting he not seek a fourth term, although this had nothing to do with the president's health.[91]

Eleanor Roosevelt also had an opinion. The usually outspoken first lady also opposed a fourth term, so much so that the two of them couldn't even talk about it. Part of this, by her own admission, had to do with the fact that she was "very conscious of age and the short time in which I have to live as I like," which really meant she was tired of the White House life.[92] But she knew he would do what he wanted. "I wouldn't discuss it with him," she said, "because I hated the idea and he knew I hated it. Either he felt he ought to serve a fourth term and wanted it or he didn't. That was up to the man himself to decide and no one else."[93] She, too, remained largely silent.

On July 10, 1944, FDR finally acknowledged his intention to run. "If the Convention should carry this out, and nominate me for the presidency, I shall accept," he wrote to Robert Hannegan, chair of the Democratic National Committee. "If the people elect me, I will serve."[94] He intended to finish what he started and once he made up his mind, colleagues, family, and the party got on board. There was no doubt he would sail easily to renomination, but for the first time in history it was the vice presidential nomination that garnered the attention.

Roosevelt couldn't campaign in 1944 with his usual vigor. He had neither the energy nor the bandwidth. While the extent of his poor health was not widely known, it was obvious to many Americans that he was tired and worn. FDR knew this and didn't bother trying to disabuse the public. Instead, he avoided it altogether. Citing the demands of the war, Roosevelt pulled a Lincoln and made it clear that he would not campaign during wartime. He also declared that neither he nor Eleanor would attend the convention.

In addition to minimizing campaign activities,[95] Roosevelt avoided being photographed as much as possible. It was becoming increasingly difficult to conceal his ghostlike appearance. He occasionally made exceptions and they were always regrettable, such as an unfortunate photograph snapped while he delivered his acceptance speech via radio. Roosevelt's guard was down that day and he had had a seizure earlier that morning.[96] The photographer, George Skadding, meant no harm, but in selecting a negative that would capture the president talking, he inadvertently selected a damning cadaverous image of the president with his mouth wide open.[97]

By running an aloof campaign, Roosevelt could dodge the health questions and run as the wartime incumbent. In doing so, he lost some leverage in choosing a vice president, at least publicly. This did not, as some historians have suggested, mean that Roosevelt ceded the choice. Instead, he once again drew from Lincoln's electoral playbook and chose his own stealth operation.

FDR still had leverage over the bosses and he had to be careful not to lose it. The party had taken a beating in the 1942 midterm elections and by early 1944 it was clear that Roosevelt was their best play, whether healthy or unhealthy. "It is quite obvious," wrote The Star, "that as long as the President remains a potential candidate, no other Democrat will get anywhere as a possible nominee for the presidency. This for the simple reason that no other Democrat would have a chance of being nominated against the

President with all the political power he wields."[98] Roosevelt understood this power and he intended to use it. But he had to be smart about how he did this, particularly given the party bosses—Robert Hannegan, Edward Flynn, Frank Hague, and Edward Kelly—would push hard to have Wallace dropped from the ticket. They had never supported Wallace and believed, rightfully or wrongly, that FDR had imposed him on them. This was compounded by the fact that the president was politically weakened and, as evidenced by the barrage of unsolicited letters and telegrams sent to party leadership, there was enough dissent to fracture the party.[99] Should this happen, Roosevelt would likely lose the election.[100]

The anti-Wallace bloc of party bosses felt they had a good hand. Their position was bolstered, or at least so they thought, by a seemingly endless flow of letters from Democratic unions, local organizations, and concerned party members from across the country. These letters served as evidence that the tide had shifted from Wallace. Some of these concerned Democrats shared their own polling numbers with Hannegan, which in the case of one central New York state party leader had Wallace trailing behind Harry Truman, Stettinius, Senate Majority Leader Alben Barkley, and even a Republican candidate on a split ticket.[101] Some local party leaders accused Wallace of being susceptible to "pressure groups" and of "creating class distinctions."[102] Some just expressed their feedback in broad superlatives, suggesting that "the majority of the people here do not want Wallace. They just don't like him."[103] The letters with the most influence were those from local party leaders who reinforced a narrative that "the nomination of [Henry] Wallace w[ould] cost the party at least 1 [million] votes."[104]

Roosevelt liked Wallace and would have preferred to keep him on the ticket, a sentiment that his assistant Grace Tully heard him articulate "so many times."[105] It didn't hurt Wallace's cause that Eleanor was strongly in his corner.[106] But the times had changed and this was not 1940 when FDR could bully the party's leadership into accepting the incumbent vice president. The context was very different and he would have to be far more manipulative to get his way. Roosevelt was, as Tully remembers, "more engrossed in the war than in a political issue, and he had less energy to dissipate on multiple problems."[107] This didn't mean he was ready to throw Wallace under the bus, at least not initially, it just meant he wouldn't help him win, although he would not have been upset with that outcome.

Despite his inclination toward Wallace, Roosevelt lacked the energy for a fight. He understood that the party was "already split enough between North and South" and that waging a public battle to keep his vice president would "split the party wide open." Losing would "prolong the war and knock into a cocked hat all the plans" that he and others had been orchestrating for the postwar period.[108] Losing over an internal political war would have been an unforced error and the party was too fragile and the stakes were too high to take such a risk.

What the president did in private was a different matter. Roosevelt didn't actually care whom he ran with, so long as he won and that there was no perception that he had been steamrolled by his own party. He needed to project strength to influence Congress in his postwar ambitions and any perception that a successor had been imposed upon him would weaken that hand. FDR kept up the act, creating a facade of apathy and disinterest all the while manipulating the outcome. It drove the bosses mad and, more important, clipped their wings, which is exactly what he wanted.

Throughout the early summer, Roosevelt engaged in a political charade, in which he declared himself noncommittal, but sent mixed messages to everyone, including Wallace and especially James "Jim" Byrnes, the director of the Office of War Mobilization, who hoped to become vice president. He even did a political dance with Wendell Willkie, who had just lost the Republican primary. As Doris Kearns Goodwin writes, "Roosevelt's dream was to join hands with Willkie in the creation of a new liberal party that would combine the liberal elements of the Democratic Party, minus the reactionary elements in the South, with the liberal elements of the Republican Party."[109]

The president enjoyed casually throwing new and seemingly random names into the mix. It offered a reminder that he was both unpredictable and in charge. He was neither confused nor out of touch, understanding full well that there were never more than three serious contenders—Henry Wallace, Jim Byrnes, and Harry Truman.[110] It's plausible that Roosevelt also believed he could win with any one of the three. But he had issues with each, so he could play his games with some element of authenticity. Wallace would bring him too many headaches within the Democratic Party and could lead to a split that would hand Republicans the presidency. He had nothing against Truman, except maybe his age; but he also wasn't about to appear pressured into embracing a distant acquaintance. "I hardly know Truman," Roosevelt told one of his advisors. "He has been over here a few times, but made no particular impression on me."[111] As for Byrnes, he was a southerner who had left the Catholic Church, which presented problems with both Catholic and northern black voters. Furthermore, he was pushy and manipulative, often threatening to resign to try to get his way.[112]

Of the three, Truman had the fewest strikes against him. Labor leaders liked him, northerners and southerners found him palatable, the industrialists found him supportive,[113] and as Ed Flynn pointed out to Roosevelt, he "had never made any racial remarks."[114] He had very few enemies, was from a border state, and was described by *Time* magazine as "the Upper House's most outstanding senator," something that would undoubtedly help FDR as he sought Senate approval for the United Nations.[115] He practiced frugality, played ball with the New Deal, and when he opposed Roosevelt's policies—such as his packing of the Supreme Court or even wartime spending—he did so quietly.[116]

Truman understood his attractiveness to the party bosses, but that didn't mean he wanted the job. He knew the bosses didn't speak for the president and there were three strikes against him that he assumed would be unpalatable to FDR. The first was his close association with one of the most corrupt political bosses in modern American politics, Thomas J. Pendergast, which he assumed would taint the ticket. The second had to do with his days running the Senate's war committee, which while not criticizing the president directly had heavily scrutinized a number of the war agencies. The third potentially disqualifying factor, at least from Truman's anxious perspective, was that he had opposed Roosevelt's running for a third term.[117]

While Truman was busy disqualifying himself, it became increasingly clear that momentum was building in his direction. This terrified him and led to his obsession with some of the unknown skeletons that could prove embarrassing to him, his family, and the president. First, he had a propensity to put family members on the government payroll, beginning with his wife, Bess, in 1941, who by 1944 was the highest-paid official in his office. On September 1, 1943, he added his sister, Mary Jane, although he put her on a more modest salary.[118] Second, his father-in-law had committed suicide, which was not known publicly and Truman feared that his nomination would result in this revelation. Finally, the Trumans didn't like the Roosevelts. They found Eleanor to be a publicity hound and they abhorred the divorces of the Roosevelt children.[119] While they were not conspicuous about their feelings, they had done enough badmouthing over the years that it seemed inevitable some of it would get back to the president or end up in the press.

If Truman hoped to avoid being a serious contender for vice president, Roosevelt's decision to send Henry Wallace on a long trip abroad proved unhelpful to his cause. In late May, the vice president began his two-month sojourn to the far-flung corners of Russia, which some interpreted as the president clearing the field for Truman. The trip was a fact-finding mission to Siberia and China, which was lengthy but meant to get him back to Washington a week and a half before the Democratic National Convention.[120] The timing, not to mention the symbolism of Siberia as the corner of earth, was certainly curious and associates of Wallace cautioned that this prolonged absence would hurt his chances of renomination.[121] The president offered no political annotation to explain the logic behind Wallace's mission. The Soviets paraded him about and made good use of him for propaganda purposes. They took him to an active gold-mining center called Magadan, which the vice president marveled at and praised as "a combination TVA and Hudson's Bay Company."[122]

There is some evidence that while Wallace was out of the country, Truman became increasingly concerned about the mounting public pressure to make him vice president. "They are plotting against your dad," he wrote his daughter, Margaret, on July 9. "Every columnist prognosticator is trying to make him VP against his will. It is funny how some people would give a fortune to be as close as I am to it and I don't want it."[123]

Wallace returned to the U.S. at 9:30 a.m. on Monday, July 10, and by all accounts still believed he was the president's top choice. He soon learned that the president had zeroed in on Truman and enlisted Samuel Rosenman, FDR's White House counsel and speechwriter credited with coining the phrase "New Deal," to break the news.[124] But when Rosenman insisted on a meeting with the vice president, he received a telegram saying, "Believe should see president before meeting you."[125] Rosenman ignored the message and forced a meeting with Wallace. According to recollections in Icke's diary, they discussed the vice presidency and Rosenman explained that while the president wanted him, he "either did not think [he] could win in the convention nor help him win in the fall."[126] The president, he explained, had instructed him to offer the ambassadorship to China, which he thought would "fit him well."[127]

Deputizing the delivery of bad news backfired as Wallace was armed with valuable information and able to advocate for himself. He met with the president that same day around 4:30 p.m., regaling him with stories of the trip and presenting him with some Outer Mongolian stamps for his collection. The conversation turned to politics and after some back-and-forth FDR did nothing to reinforce Rosenman's message. Instead he seemed to make it clear to Wallace that he wanted him on the ticket. This is not Wallace's manufactured hearsay. The president actually offered to formally state that if he "were a delegate to the convention [he] would vote for Henry Wallace,"[128] which was later memorialized in a letter. Wallace believed he had the president's support locked down, even offering some token humility, telling the president, "If you can find anyone who will add more strength to the ticket than I, by all means take him."[129]

When the two met for lunch the following day, it was more of the same. Wallace came prepared, furnishing FDR with a list of 290 first-ballot convention votes—nearly 50 percent of the 589 votes required—pledged by delegates ready to support his renomination as vice president.[130] He also brought the latest Gallup numbers, showing 65 percent of registered Democrats favored his candidacy for vice president, while Alben Barkley had 17 percent, Texas congressman Sam Rayburn garnered 5 percent, Byrnes had 3 percent, and Truman had a measly 2 percent of those polled.[131] If Wallace is to be believed, the president put his arm around him and said, "I hope it's the same team again, Henry."[132]

The party bosses were watching two months of hard work evaporate. The combination of Wallace's access and close friendship with the president seemed to be yielding a reversal of Truman's momentum. They'd decided to mount an offensive. Led by Pauley and the president's appointments secretary Major General Edwin M. "Pa" Watson, the leadership unleashed a blitzkrieg of anti-Wallace sentiments into the Oval Office. They controlled the schedule and ensured that nobody walked through those doors unless he was anti-Wallace.[133] As those guests entered, Pauley was careful to remind them, "You are not nominating a vice president of the United States, but a president."[134]

For presidential visitors, that reality struck a real chord, particularly given the country's obvious inflection point. Roosevelt's declining health was an evaporating secret both inside and outside the White House. The rumor mill weighed on Robert Hannegan in particular, who was inundated with letters from concerned party members about the president's health. "No man—not even the President of the United States of America, has a LEASE on LIFE," wrote C. T. Ray, a concerned Democrat in the mix of party politics.[135] Other anxious Democrats, such as Sam Hepburn, who was a concerned party member, urged Hannegan not to choose the vice presidency "on the basis of political expediency alone, but in sober realization of the fact that the man elected to be vice president on the Democratic ticket next November has a better than ordinary likelihood of being President before four years have passed." He observed, "Mr. Roosevelt's vitality appears it may not be adequate to four more years of the sort of strain that he had had to bear. Therefore—whoever is chosen Vice President—should this time, more than ever before, be of true Presidential caliber."[136]

The persistent complaints against Wallace were working and the anti-Wallace brigade just needed to deliver the final blow. On July 11, Ed Flynn convened a high-powered dinner[137] at the White House to force the president's hand. The stakes were high enough that they conducted a rehearsal.[138] Their choreography was clear: Strategically run through various names, exhaust the options, and casually arrive at Truman.[139] Sam Rayburn, they argued, was well-regarded, but would have been unable to get the support of his state's delegation since he was seen as too valuable a figure in Congress (validated by the fact that he later served seventeen years as Speaker of the House); while Alben Barkley, a good Democrat from Kentucky, was compelling, but too old.[140] They then moved to Jim Byrnes, who had a problem with Catholics and blacks.

Having checked the box of seeming objective, the leaders steered the conversation toward Wallace. Roosevelt must have seen through their plan because he responded to their barrage of criticism somewhat oddly, first suggesting John G. Winant, the ambassador to London and former governor of New Hampshire.[141] Then he offered William O. Douglas, a highly capable Supreme Court justice, but not a name that had been widely considered at any point in the process. Imagine the surprise when Roosevelt went from a mere suggestion to doubling down on Douglas. He had "the following of the Liberal Left Wing of the American people, the same kind of people who Wallace had," he told the group, further explaining "that he had practical experience in the backwoods of the Northwest as a logger; that he looked and acted on occasion like a boy scout; and would have, in his opinion, appeal at the polls and besides, played an interesting game of poker."[142] The poker clause of his argument made it seem almost as if Roosevelt was toying with them.

The reaction was dead silence[143] followed by a somewhat awkward transition, which if nothing else revealed their hand. With nowhere else to go, they shifted to the grand finale, a conversation about Harry S* Truman. To their surprise, Roosevelt raised no objection, which might suggest he was messing with them all along. He did, however, ask about Truman's age, which surprisingly nobody seemed to know. Eager for an answer, he dispatched his son-in-law and presidential aide John Boettiger to track down a *Congressional Directory* and resolve the matter.[144] Truman was sixty, just two years younger than FDR, which was surprising given their drastically different appearances.

What happened next is subject to varying accounts,[145] although most agree that FDR recognized that the party bosses preferred Truman, leading him to give some kind of nod—verbal and written. As described by Robert Ferrell in *Choosing Truman*, by this phase of the dinner, Roosevelt got the message. He turned to Hannegan and said, "Bob, I think you and everyone else want Truman!" Then, responding to his own observation, the president put his hand on Hannegan's knee and said, "If that's the case, it's Truman." Roosevelt had said similar things in the past, but his actions suggested that this time it was real. He began assigning tasks of who would break the news to some of the other vice presidential hopefuls. Walker was assigned to tell Byrnes, Hannegan would break the news to Wallace, Pauley would talk to Rayburn, and several others were sent to share the news with lesser contenders.[146]

David McCullough's seminal book on Harry Truman does not mention a dinner exchange of this nature, instead suggesting, "Roosevelt had not said yet whether he himself wanted Truman." Pauley recognized that this wasn't going to change so long as the full group remained, and he suggested they retire for the evening. But the savviest of the bosses knew the game was not yet over and reconvened downstairs. FDR was more than capable of crowd pleasing and changing his mind. Walker, who had been instrumental in orchestrating the dinner, grabbed Hannegan outside and told him they'd better get a decision from FDR in writing. Using the

---

* Harry Truman had no middle name, just an initial "S," which was a reference to his two grandfathers, Solomon Young and Anderson Shipp Truman.

pretext of a forgotten jacket—a legitimate excuse, as he had taken Pauley's coat—Hannegan went back up to the living quarters to find FDR and insist that he memorialize a commitment in writing.[147]

While scholars differ on whether there was a conclusive side conversation at dinner, most agree with some version of Hannegan running back upstairs to get the note. But what that note actually said is a different story altogether. In McCullough's version, the president scribbled a note on scrap paper in pencil,[148] writing, "Bob, I think Truman is the right man, FDR."[149] This is also the note that Truman claims to have seen, "written on a piece of scratch paper about two inches by eight and it had only one name mentioned in it and that was mine,"[150] although it has never been found.[151] But Ferrell's narrative differs in its claim that Pauley had also come back in search of his jacket when he overheard Roosevelt telling Hannegan, "I know this makes you boys happy, and you are the ones I am counting on to win this election. But I still think Douglas would have the greater public appeal."[152]

On July 13, Roosevelt had a long afternoon session with Hannegan to talk strategy for the convention, which was less than a week away. That evening, FDR traveled from Washington to Hyde Park before beginning a longer journey that would take him to California and then to Hawaii, where he would sit with General Douglas MacArthur and Admiral Chester Nimitz to devise a plan to win the war in the Pacific.[153] The trip lasted twenty-nine days and took the president more than ten thousand miles,[154] which was grueling for a man in his condition. The journey was supposed to serve both functional and political purposes, which in the case of the latter was to demonstrate his stamina.

As Roosevelt embarked on this journey, his biggest problem remained that Jim Byrnes was not getting the hint and so long as he stayed in contention, Truman would continue to resist.[155] On Friday, July 14, Byrnes made a pushy phone call to FDR at Hyde Park[156] in which he exclaimed, "Hannegan and Frank Walker stated today that . . . from your statements they concluded you did prefer Wallace but did prefer Truman first and Douglas second, and that either would be preferable to me . . ."[157]

The president did not like being put on the spot and when Byrnes did this, he simply defused the situation with more misinformation. "Jimmy, that is all wrong. That is not what I told them. It is what they told me. When we all went over the list I did not say I preferred anybody or that anybody would cost me votes, but they all agreed that Truman would cost fewer votes than anybody and probably Douglas second. This was the agreement they reached and I had nothing to do with it. . . ."[158] The president then reinforced the need to be "damned careful of language." Somewhat defensively, he explained, "They asked if I would object to Truman and Douglas and I said no. That is different from using the word 'prefer.' That is not expressing a preference because you know I told you I would have no preference."[159]

What Roosevelt did next is fascinating and represents the worst of his political mischievousness. He urged Byrnes to run, reminded him of their close relationship,[160] and then disparaged the competition, saying "I hardly know Truman. Douglas is a poker partner. He is good in a poker game and tells good stories."[161] Byrnes took detailed notes from the call and was quick to make use of them. His first target was Hannegan. Hannegan, who had only known FDR for a few months, was baffled by what seemed to be a complete contradiction. Unsure what to make of the president's comments, all he could say was, "Well, I can't call the president a liar."[162] He also tracked down Harry Hopkins to give the readout.[163]

Believing he had the president's support locked down, Byrnes sought to secure Truman's endorsement. He had seen a newswire earlier that day suggesting that Truman wasn't running and thought the best way to ensure that was to give him a call and secure his support. "Harry . . . the president has given me the go sign for the Vice Presidency and I am calling up to ask if you will nominate me," he said.[164] Truman had no idea he was being manipulated and agreed, recalling, "I told him that I would be glad to do it if the President wanted him for a running mate."[165] It was one thing to stay out of the race when his name was being floated, but it was another to be the party's only viable choice and to bow out. The issue was that nobody had convinced Truman. Truman would later learn of Byrnes's manipulation and describe him as a "slick conniver," but in the moment he was both happy and honored to be the nominator.[166]

Meanwhile, President Roosevelt was still proving a disruptive force in the process. In addition to his mixed messages to Byrnes, he maintained some semblance of support for Wallace. "I have been associated with Henry Wallace during the past four years as Vice President, for eight years earlier while he was secretary of Agriculture, and well before that," Roosevelt wrote in a letter to Senator Samuel D. Jackson of Indiana, who was slated to chair the Democratic convention. "I like him and I respect him, and he is my personal friend. For these reasons I would personally vote for his renomination if I were a delegate to the convention. At the same time, I do not wish to appear in any way as dictating to the convention."[167]

The advisors and bosses were confused as were the candidates and noncandidates. Someone needed to have a candid conversation with FDR and figure out if he was going to stick to his July 11 pledge to Truman,[168] or if something had changed. Furthermore, while the general public may have been blind to FDR's health and were victims of his great deception, those around FDR understood how precarious his health was at this point. They may have been experiencing their own denial of sorts, but they knew enough to fear a Wallace presidency.

On July 15, Hannegan stepped up and went to see FDR. As recalled by Grace Tully, "En route [to the West Coast and the Commander-in-Chief's trip to Hawaii and Alaska] we stopped, by request, in Chicago for Hannegan to board the Presidential train for a further discussion of political strategy."[169] The forty-five-minute meeting started at 3:00 p.m.[170] and took place in the president's car, also known as the Ferdinand Magellan.[171]

Following their meeting, Hannegan came away with a note from FDR, on official White House stationery and sandwiched between the pages of his copy of National Geographic,[172] which as it exists today says, "Dear Bob, You have written me about Harry Truman and Bill Douglas. I should, of course, be very glad to run with either of them and believe that either of them would be a real strength to the ticket. Always sincerely, Franklin Roosevelt."[173] But according to Grace Tully, the president's diligent secretary who neither fabricated nor exaggerated, the original version of the letter had Bill Douglas's name first. As she recalls, Hannegan approached her with a request, saying, "Grace, the President wants you to retype this letter and to switch these names so it will read 'Harry Truman and Bill Douglas'!" From his perspective, the note wasn't ideal, but it mentioned Truman's name and if they could just switch the order it would be a more powerful signal. Tully recalled having her assistant, Dorothy Brady, retype the letter with the names reversed.[174]

Hannegan was frustrated that the president was making it harder for them to engineer a Truman nomination.[175] Hannegan had nothing against Byrnes, but so long as Byrnes stayed in contention, Truman would stay out; and so long as Truman stayed out, Wallace would likely win.

Perhaps this is what FDR wanted. Hannegan, along with others in FDR's inner circle, understood all too well that the boss was a master political manipulator. It is also conceivable that FDR wanted to drag the process out as long as possible, keeping the leaders preoccupied and asserting his power over them.

Everything FDR did was deliberate, particularly in politics. The leaders admired him, but they didn't trust him. They viewed him as "warm-hearted in everything but politics and there he was cold-blooded."[176] They learned to countermand this side of the president by making his promises as official as possible, which in this case meant getting a commitment for Truman on White House stationery.[177] Hannegan failed to get a letter—although he still had the Truman-Douglas (or just Truman) letter—leaving him to settle for FDR's commitment to stay neutral throughout the convention.[178] This meant nothing, as the president had broken countless verbal promises.

Truman was still not willing to step into the race. He was fully behind Byrnes and had committed to nominating him at the convention. With Truman out and Byrnes in, along with Roosevelt's subtle insinuations, it is not surprising that the press believed that the president wanted Wallace and that he would be nominated. This is almost certainly what Truman believed, or at least hoped.

The July 15–16 confusion and Hannegan's failure to resolve the issue caused a panic within the party leadership. On Monday, July 17, Flynn, Hannegan, and Walker huddled at the Blackstone Hotel to come up with an intervention plan. They knew that above all, Roosevelt cared about winning, which was probably the only card they had left to play. That evening, around 6:45 p.m., they placed a call to the president's train and one by one got on the phone to reinforce the same message: Byrnes was a political liability.[179] He would cost the president hundreds of thousands of black votes in his home state, alienate the labor vote, and turn off Catholics who resented his conversion out of their faith.[180] He would split the party, create political chaos, and should this happen, Roosevelt had a decent chance of losing. One would say it. Then another would reinforce it. Yet another would repeat it. And they did this round robin until finally the president broke.

Until this point, much of the evidence suggests that Roosevelt's games were giving Wallace the upper hand. The Monday night phone call changed everything. The prospect of losing, coupled with his declining appetite for drama, was enough for FDR to agree to help engineer Byrnes out of contention. It was decided that Leo T. Crowley, who ran the Foreign Economic Administration, would inform Byrnes that the president didn't want him and that the president would reinforce that message with a phone call the following morning. Hannegan would inform Truman.

Hannegan went to see Truman after the call with the president—probably around 7:30 p.m.[181] Truman's recollection of that conversation offers an incredible picture of a man who even after being told he was the choice by the powers that be still intended to resist the position. Truman was well aware of others being given the same offer, so was skeptical of this second-hand information. [182]

When Hannegan pushed further, Truman snapped rather uncharacteristically, "Tell him [FDR] to go to hell. I'm for Byrnes." Hannegan made another go at it, but Truman cut him off and said in no uncertain terms, "Bob, look here I don't want to be Vice-President. I bet I can go down on the street and stop the first ten men I see and that they can't tell me the names of the last ten vice presidents of the United States. I bet you can't tell me who was McKinley's vice president." He was right, Hannegan couldn't think of Theodore Roosevelt's name, even though he became president.[183] This was not the first time Truman had thought about this. "Do you know . . . what happened to most Vice-Presidents who succeeded to the Presidency?" he had asked a St. Louis Post-Dispatch reporter. "Usually they were ridiculed in office, had their hearts broken, lost any vestige of respect they had had before. I don't want that to happen to me."[184] Earlier that year, he told Harry G. Waltner, who was director of the Unemployment Compensation Commission of Missouri, "the Vice President simply presides over the Senate and sits around hoping for a funeral. It is a very high office which consists entirely of honor and I don't have any ambition to hold an office like that."[185]

Hannegan's conversation with Truman and Crowley's conversation with Byrnes all happened less than an hour from the time the call with FDR concluded. Following these communications, Truman—clearly not as defiant as his words to Hannegan would suggest—called on Byrnes to confirm that he had lost FDR's support.[186] This conversation would seem to indicate that Truman's main preoccupation at this stage was whether he was in fact the choice, or whether he was just one of several people being told the same thing. "I freely admit that I was disappointed and I felt hurt by President Roosevelt's action," Byrnes recalled, but "I had assured him

[Truman] of this [information] on Monday night (July 17) when he called to tell me in view of the President expressing a preference for him (Truman), he felt he should be a candidate and asked that I release him."[187] The July 17 phone call between Byrnes and Truman is the earliest evidence that Truman believed he would be the vice presidential nominee. [188]

In all likelihood, this is the moment when Truman must have realized he had lost control of the situation. At some point around the opening of the convention, he called Tom L. Evans, who was his closest personal friend in Kansas City and would always tell it to him straight. "Are you my friend?" Truman asked, to which Evans replied, "I hope so, why?" Truman pleaded with him, "If you are, I need you up here [at the Convention] to help keep me from being Vice President."[189] Evans made the trip to Chicago, the site of the convention, and along with John Snyder, who was another close Truman friend, tried to dissuade delegates from drafting Truman.[190]

The convention opened on Wednesday, July 19, and Byrnes withdrew from the race that morning. The next day Roosevelt was nominated and seconded by Wallace. In the backdrop of this, competing factions engaged in a war of letters with Hannegan distributing copies of the Truman-Douglas letter, while Senator Samuel Jackson, who was also the convention chair, was busy showing the other FDR letter praising Wallace.[191]

What happened next nearly changed the course of history. As described by Robert Ferrell, while the political bosses made their maneuvers and showed their respective letters, they missed a massive intrigue that was taking place on the convention floor.[192] In a surprise move reminiscent of Sparta and the Trojan Horse, Wallace supporters had secretly flooded the convention floor, where they mixed discreetly and unemotionally among the crowd. The release of the Jackson letter the previous day had given them the green light and top cover they needed, which indicates that someone very high up was the ultimate approver of the plan, perhaps Wallace himself.[193]

There is no doubt that Wallace wanted the nomination. In a very awkward moment, Pauley and Hannegan had phoned Roosevelt's train to give the president the update on their plan to stop a Wallace nomination. Wallace, along with his campaign manager, was standing right next to them and heard the conversation. Realizing they had been caught red-handed, Pauley said to the vice president, "Well, at least you've heard it play-by-play."[194] Wallace, knowing the political tsunami that was about to hit his opponents, was calm and collected. He tapped on his briefcase and said, "This is my campaign speech. This is the one that will do it."[195]

Wallace's comment was an understatement. As Pauley recalls, the vice president went onstage and delivered what was, in his opinion, "the most inspiring talk he had ever given."[196] The crowd agreed. The combination of an awe-inspiring speech with the political equivalent of the hidden baseball trick was an utterly brilliant move that should have handed Wallace the nomination and subsequently the presidency. "We want Wallace," they yelled from every corner of the convention hall. And miraculously signs and posters adorned with "Roosevelt-Wallace" sprang up almost in unison. The seemingly organic momentum for Wallace overpowered the far less organized movement for Truman and almost took on a festive feel. Even the convention organist, Al Melgard, caught the fever—although it is certainly conceivable that someone greased him—and joined the movement as he played the Iowa state song—a tribute to Wallace's home state—and the crowd sang along, "Iowa, Iowa, that's where the corn grows!"[197]

Pauley later described the scene as "a strange mixture of actual Communists, would-be Communists, do-gooders and other hypertension personalities who had jumped on his [Wallace's] bandwagon."[198] Wallace's opponents needed to do something and do it fast, or their worst nightmare would come true. Senator Jackson, a staunch Wallace supporter, stood onstage ready to support Wallace's nomination, which had someone motioned—as Senator Claude Pepper of Florida tried to do—would have almost certainly gone through.

The bosses moved quickly to stop the stampede. Pauley, who was overseeing the convention, grabbed his deputy, a fellow from Chevy Chase, Maryland, named Neale Roach, and ordered him to "stop that organ!" But this was not easily achieved as the organist's telephone rang with a light, not a bell.[199] "Tell me how? He won't answer the phone," he frantically asked. Pauley told him to "get an ax." He must have been serious because Roach sent his assistant, a young man named Bryne Austin, "with instructions to get a fire ax and stop that organ any way he could,"[200] presumably by chopping the wires.

At that point, Hannegan had the quick thinking to open the convention hall doors under the pretext of creating more ventilation. For context, it was a brutally hot day—some claimed over 120 degrees inside the convention hall—which had created great discomfort and even caused a few people to collapse.[201] Hannegan's real motivation, however, was to overcrowd the convention hall so they would have a reason to call for an immediate adjournment. The plan worked, as Mayor Kelly swiftly proclaimed a fire hazard, which had the virtue of being true since the thirty thousand attendees far exceeded the twenty-thousand-person capacity,[202] and Hannegan pressured Senator Jackson to recognize Pittsburgh mayor David Lawrence, who much to the senator's surprise moved for adjournment until 11:30 a.m. the next day.[203] Jackson, feeling the ominous pressure from Hannegan and others, called for a vote on the motion and despite resounding cries of "No, No" and "We want Wallace," he declared the ayes had it.[204] It was a close call. According to Kelly, the president phoned that night, asking, "What the hell's going on there? Are you letting this thing get out of hand?"[205]

The party bosses now had a different problem on their hands. They had gotten FDR to go along with ousting Wallace and replacing him with Truman. But now the crowd seemed to want Wallace and Truman remained noncommittal.

That afternoon, Hannegan summoned Truman to the Blackstone Hotel. In their conversation, it was clear he had been rattled by the push for Wallace and seemed reluctant to commit. Truman recalled a "crowded room" filled with "every damn political boss in the country" all saying to him that he had to take the job.[206]

When he told them he didn't want it,[207] Hannegan placed a call to FDR to settle the matter once and for all. As Truman recalled:

> I sat on one of the twin beds, and Hannegan with the phone, sat on the other. Whenever Roosevelt used the telephone he always talked in such a strong voice that it was necessary for the listener to hold the receiver away from his ear to avoid begin deafened, so I found it possible to hear both ends of the conversation. "Bob," Roosevelt said, "have you got that fellow lined up yet?" "No," Bob replied. "He is the contrariest Missouri mule I've ever dealt with." "Well, you tell him," I heard the President say, "if he wants to break up the Democratic party in the middle of a war, that's his responsibility." I was completely stunned. I sat for a minute or two and then got up and began walking around the room. . . . "Well," I said finally, "if that is

the situation, I'll have to say yes, but why the hell didn't he tell me in the first place?"[208]

The convention reconvened on Friday, July 21, with the party bosses more in control. This time, they relied on ushers and local law enforcement to deny entry to Wallace supporters by demanding they present "the right kind of tickets."[209] Voting commenced and the initial tally saw Truman trailing Wallace 319½ votes to 429½,[210] with neither capturing the 589-vote majority. Wallace's lead was short-lived. After some delegate manipulation and smart tactics, Truman won the nomination on the second ballot. The party bosses could take a deep breath. Henry Wallace would not become president.

=====

Roosevelt probably had a preference for Wallace and we know he eventually came around to Truman, but in all likelihood he didn't actually care whom he ran with as long as he won the election. After all, he didn't plan to work with them anyway. His primary concern and what drove his motivations and political manipulations was a desire to make sure none of the party bosses could claim to have imposed a candidate on him. This is likely why he threw random names like Douglas and William C. Bullitt, America's first ambassador to the Soviet Union, into the mix. It's why he lied and schemed and it is also why even the most savvy of the party elite couldn't make sense of why he was doing it. They were all looking at his behavior through the lens of candidates and trying to attribute his actions to a real preference.

What FDR really wanted was to keep everyone as confused as possible for as long as possible. Had he believed that the stated liabilities of either Wallace or Byrnes were credible, it is doubtful that he would have played such games. But as evidenced by the fact that Wallace almost got the nomination and by all accounts should have, it seems that as late as the convention Roosevelt still cared more about his posture with the bosses than whom he ran with. He must have believed he could win regardless of whom he was paired with. He must have known he was physically weak. He could certainly feel the physical strain. He must have also known that they thought he was weak and he was determined to prove them wrong. His agenda depended on it.

August 18, 1944, **President Roosevelt** *hosts Harry Truman for lunch on the White House lawn. After the inauguration, Vice President Truman only had two meetings with the president.*

April 12, 1945, **Harry Truman** *takes the oath of office upon the death of Franklin Roosevelt. He has not yet been briefed on the Manhattan Project, nor has he been given any readout from Yalta.*

CHAPTER EIGHT

"Give 'em Hell Harry!"

End of an Era

Everyone knew Harry Truman would be president, even Franklin Roosevelt. It wasn't discussed, nor was it acknowledged by the president, who made no effort to get to know the man who would almost certainly succeed him.[1] On August 18, they sat for lunch underneath a magnolia tree[2] that had been planted by Andrew Jackson on the White House lawn. It was a perfectly staged lunch for photographers, with a delicious platter of roast sardines on toast, peas, beans, tomatoes, and an asparagus salad. Describing the meeting to his daughter, Margaret, Truman sounded awestruck by the moment, almost marveling over the aura of the presidential setting.[3] But this wasn't the case.

As Margaret remembered, he didn't dare tell the truth. There was little chemistry between the two. Truman, wearing a red and white striped tie, smiled for the cameras, while Roosevelt, wearing a black bow tie, seemed stoic and ghostlike. Their conversation was barely substantive, mostly focusing on campaign tactics. "He told me," Truman remembered, "that because he was so busy in the war effort I would have to do the campaigning for both of us, and we mapped out our program."[4] This seemed a little strange, but he could also tell that something was wrong. It was during this lunch that Truman noticed Roosevelt's hand shaking while he struggled to pour cream into his coffee.[5] Only later did Truman realize that "I was in reality doing so"—meaning campaigning—"as much on my own behalf as in that of Roosevelt's."[6]

Roosevelt and Truman won convincingly in November. For FDR, victory meant he could carry on for one final push. For Truman, it meant he became a president in waiting with one small caveat: He wasn't yet the vice president. Roosevelt still had to live long enough for the electors to cast their votes, a joint session of Congress had to count those votes, and an inauguration had to take place. If Roosevelt died during the three-month interlude, a real possibility, Wallace would become president. That much was certain. The question then would become who takes the oath of office on inauguration day? These questions are not an exercise in historic counterfactuals. Shortly after the election, Roosevelt took off for Warm Springs, where he stayed largely out of the public eye and in recovery mode until his return to Washington on December 19.[7] The president may have returned rested, but his appearance wasn't deceiving anyone. He was dying.

Had FDR died before inauguration day, there are two dates that matter: December 18, when the electors cast their votes, and January 6, when those votes are tabulated by a joint session of Congress.[8] If FDR died after the electors officially cast their votes, the script was pretty clear. Under the Presidential Succession Act of 1886, Vice President Wallace would ascend to the presidency for the duration of FDR's term. As for what would happen at the end of the term, the Yale constitutional lawyer Akhil Amar explains that in such a scenario, "Section 3 of the Twentieth Amendment in effect says, 'act as if a dead man can be sworn in, and one nanosecond after this fictional swearing in the Vice President will become President under Article II.'"[9] Thus on inauguration day, Vice-President-elect Truman would have taken the oath of office as president for a full term.[10] If the electors had not yet cast their ballots, Amar explains, "we would need to know whom the electors in fact voted for when they met. If they voted for Truman for president it's easy: Truman's the man on January 20. If the electors instead voted for the then-dead FDR and for Truman merely as VP," they would have had to rely on what he calls the "Horace Greeley precedent."[11]

Back in 1872, the Democrats had reluctantly nominated Horace Greeley for president* as a way to hold the anti-Grant faction together. He was also nominated by the Liberal Republican Party. On Election Day, Gree-

---

* Some disaffected Democrats, mostly southerners who were unhappy with Greeley as the nominee, scrambled to build a new faction called the "Straight-Out Democratic Party." They convened in Louisville, but failed to gain traction after their nominee, Charles O'Conner, did not accept the nomination.

ley's showing was poor and he ended up mustering a mere 66 electoral votes to Grant's 286. Three weeks after the presidential election Greeley died. As the Electoral College had not yet met to officially cast their votes, the electors—presumably under some kind of party pressure—decided to divide his 66 votes among the other candidates, including those running for vice president.[12] Had FDR suffered the same fate, his votes would have likely been redistributed to other Democrats, which meant that if party leaders wanted a different Democrat, they would have had a mechanism to change the outcome.

Roosevelt barely made it to inauguration day. He was likely aware of the fate that awaited him, but reminded his son James, "I don't dare shake the faith of the people that's why I ran again. . . . The People elected me their leader and I can't quit in the middle of the war."[13] But it was his father's appearance more than his instructions that gave James the most concern. "The first moment I saw Father I realized something was terribly wrong. He looked awful . . . [and] sick, his color was bad, he looked terribly tired and I noted that he was short of breath." By his own recollection, he saw his father only twice during the entire election season, the second time being inauguration day. "Each time, I realized with awful irrevocable certainty that we were going to lose him."[14] He confronted the president's physician, Admiral Ross McIntire, who, so accustomed to spin, made no exception for the president's eldest son.[15] James wasn't convinced, recalling, "Regardless of what the doctor said, I knew in my heart that his days were numbered."[16] He raised his concern with his father, who also shrugged it off. "A few days in Warm Springs will fix me right up," he told his son.[17]

The inauguration speech must have been tragic to watch, particularly for those who for twelve years had been moved by Roosevelt's inspiring oratory skills. Standing with his leg braces for the first time since August 1944[18]—a challenge given how much weight he had lost—it was clear that the president struggled through the speech, which was five minutes long, the shortest official[19] inaugural since George Washington's second.[20] It covered peace and friendship and included a long quote from his old schoolmaster Dr. Endicott Peabody. James, who was standing behind his father, noticed immediately that something was wrong. A spasm spread from the president's heart, causing his entire body to tremble and making it appear as though he might lose his balance, his speech, or both.[21]

Those in attendance were shocked,[22] most notably Edith Galt, the widow of Woodrow Wilson, who told Secretary of Labor Frances Perkins, "He looks exactly as my husband did when he went into his decline." Perkins, recognizing the gravity of such a statement coming from such a credible source, nervously interjected, "Don't say that to another soul. He has a great and terrible job to do, and he's got to do it even if it kills him."[23]

It's not surprising that FDR looked for ways to avoid the post-inaugural festivities. He lacked the stamina required to entertain the crowd—nearly two thousand people and the largest luncheon of his presidency—and asked Eleanor to handle the receiving line so he could rest in the Green Room with his son James. In addition to the fatigue, he began to experience unbearable pain and spasms in his chest. He was desperate for a remedy and turned to his son, saying, "Jimmy, I can't take this unless you get me a stiff drink. You'd better make it straight."[24] As Roosevelt threw back a whiskey, he told James[25] that he would be a trustee of his estate and executor of his will. He provided him with detailed funeral instructions and asked him to wear the Roosevelt family ring.[26] James later wrote, "That conversation clearly indicates that he was thinking of death. . . . Now that I look back, I realize why he insisted mother go to the trouble of having all thirteen of his grandchildren at that inauguration."[27]

Hazardous Apathy

The Big Three met at Yalta from February 4 to 11, 1945. Roosevelt had ceded far more to Stalin in Tehran than he did at Yalta,[28] but the latter conference almost certainly encouraged the Soviet leader to put into effect what he believed he had already been given. It didn't help that Roosevelt's poor health was on display, that he had left most of the Soviet experts—George Kennan, Loy Henderson, and William Bullitt, to name a few—at home, and largely ignored insights and recommendations coming from the State Department and Ambassador W. Averell Harriman in Moscow.[29]

At Yalta, Roosevelt indicated to Stalin a willingness to withdraw all American troops from Europe not much more than two years after the German surrender. He also raised the fate of Hong Kong and expressed his hope that they could address it at a later stage. Roosevelt sought Stalin's commitment to enter the war in the Pacific, for which he was willing to make very generous concessions related to territory, particularly at China's expense.[30] The British delegation to Yalta feared Roosevelt was too trusting of Stalin, particularly with regards to sharing some of the most sensitive military secrets.[31] The British prime minister expressed his displeasure with some aspects of Roosevelt's judgment at Yalta. "[I was] shocked at Yalta too when the President in a casual manner spoke of revealing the secret [bomb] to Stalin on the grounds that de Gaulle, if he heard of it, would certainly double-cross us with Russia."[32] Given the implications of the bomb to both the war and eventually postwar contexts, an agreement between the two transatlantic allies prohibited any unilateral sharing of information about the atomic bomb.[33] But there was also a concern that Roosevelt was blind to Russia's territorial ambitions. "Of one thing I am certain, Stalin is not an imperialist,"[34] he was recorded as saying in the diary of Alan F. Brooke,[35] chief of the Imperial General Staff. Whether Roosevelt actually trusted Stalin or viewed accommodation as the easiest path to a decisive Allied victory, Roosevelt's comments—both to Stalin and in private—continued to cause alarm.[36]

Despite the precarious situation and the significance of Yalta negotiations, nobody thought of looping Harry Truman into the details. This would later prove problematic when it became clear he had inherited a mess for his own meeting of the Big Three at Potsdam. He was in Washington, unaware of what he was missing and seemingly unconcerned. Truman's wife, Bess, insisted that her husband had been kept in the dark and at no point was he informed.[37] And FDR paid no more attention to Truman as vice president than he had during the campaign.

"In my eighty-two days as Vice-President," Truman recalled, "only a few Cabinet meetings were held, for the President was abroad the greater part of the time or at Warm Springs."[38] When Roosevelt was in town, which was not "more than thirty days,"[39] he preferred to do things without his vice president. The one exception to this, at least in theory, pertained to domestic issues, for which Roosevelt was slightly more willing to include his vice president. He knew of Truman's reputation with the Senate and invited him to the Monday meetings of the "Big Four," which included himself, the speaker of the house, the majority leader of the house, and the majority leader of the Senate. But given Roosevelt's frequent absence, the group barely met.[40]

The cabinet meetings, for which Truman was in attendance, were convened very infrequently, and as he later told Jonathan Daniels—an aide he eventually inherited from FDR—"Roosevelt never discussed anything important at his Cabinet meetings. Cabinet members, if they had anything to discuss, tried to see him privately after the meetings."[41]

Roosevelt must have believed he could power through, win the war, and achieve a successful vote on the charter of the United Nations. He didn't want Truman lingering in the shadows, as it reminded him, and presumably others, of his mortality. When I asked Henry Kissinger if he thought Roosevelt's ignoring his vice president was due to denial about his health, he explained almost certainly, adding that "as a general proposition, until very recently, vice presidents have always been excluded because it is unsettling to have someone around you whose happiest moment will be when you drop dead."[42] Truman, who was only two years younger but looked far more vigorous, made the mental exercise of denial harder. Reinforcing this is the fact that Roosevelt's neglect of Truman doesn't calibrate with how he interacted with his previous two vice presidents, particularly Wallace. FDR sent Wallace all around the world, conferred with him, and respected his international perspective. They met frequently, enjoyed a personal relationship, and the president sought his advice.

Some of the culpability rests with Truman. In later years, he saddled FDR with the blame, writing, "I was handicapped by lack of knowledge of both foreign and domestic affairs—due principally to Mr. Roosevelt's inability to pass on responsibility."[43] Biographers have also let Truman off the hook for the same reason. But this is an unacceptable excuse. Had he tried and failed that would have been a different story. Truman knew the boss was terribly ill and by his own admission he understood the very real possibility that he could be president. He chose to do nothing in preparation.

Even if Roosevelt shut him out, Truman could have sought opportunities to get informed on the war and foreign policy. He could have requested intelligence reports, engaged the State Department, which Roosevelt had largely ignored, or attempted to carve out a role for himself in anticipation of the postwar plans. Instead, he allowed himself to slide into the same role that so many of his predecessors accepted (ironically, Wallace being an exception)—vice president without portfolio, left with no option other than bouncing around town as a Washington socialite. The difference, however, was that Truman seemed to enjoy it. "My father loved parties and people," Margaret Truman recalled, "and he cheerfully accepted more invitations than any other vice president in recent memory."[44]

There was also the issue of the Map Room, which Roosevelt frequented for the latest briefing at least twice a day.[45] When in town, Roosevelt "preferred to go to the Map Room alone to be 'briefed'"[46] and without access, it was hard for Truman to participate. The Map Room was small—a converted ladies' powder room[47]—and access was heavily restricted. As William M. Rigdon and James Derieux write in *The White House Sailor,* "Only six persons had sufficient security clearance to enter. . . . None of the President's Secret Service bodyguards was allowed to enter the room; therefore, the responsibility for pushing the presidential wheelchair went to the watch officer. At one point early in the war, Ensign Ed Carson became so nervous at his solemn responsibility that he banged the President of the United States into a desk. As a result of this episode, regular wheelchair practice was scheduled, at which the Officers of the Day would take turns pushing each other around the room in a spare wheelchair."[48]

With FDR gone for a lengthy trip to Yalta and the Middle East, Truman could have requested access. What's odd is that the vice president understood the importance of the Map Room. He knew that to understand the war you had to be inside.

Ruth Silva, one of the premier scholars on presidential succession, writes, "Franklin D. Roosevelt is said to have once told Senator Harley Kilgore of West Virginia that he wished the Vice President could be given authority to act for a President who is out of the country. He said that this would give a President an opportunity for a vacation. As the Constitution stands, he thought, a President must keep up with daily work even though he is vacationing on the high seas."[49]

If Truman by his own admission understood that the president was sick and that he might be president, how do we explain such apathy? It was irresponsible and shortsighted. It is also perplexing. One possible explanation is that Truman was undoubtedly influenced by his distaste for the president. After one of their rare meetings, he complained to a friend, "He does all the talking . . . he talks about what he wants to talk about, and he never talks about anything you want to talk about, so there isn't much you can do." He thought Roosevelt conniving and described him to colleagues in the Senate as a "liar."[50]

A possibility that seems most plausible is that Truman may have been experiencing his own form of denial. He was overwhelmed by the prospect of having to replace the great Franklin Roosevelt, and may have found it easier to convince himself that he would power through.

Truman understood the gravity of the situation. He may have been deluding himself, but he knew. He saw it firsthand, first during the campaign and then again at the inauguration. He was concerned about FDR's health, but wasn't quite sure what to do. "The very thought that something was happening to him left me troubled and worried," he wrote in his memoirs. "This was all the more difficult for me because I could not share such feelings with anyone, not even with the members of my family."[51]

What he saw on the campaign and inauguration day was reinforced by rumors, some more credible than others. Just one month after inauguration day Truman thought Roosevelt had died. For a brief moment he felt what it was like to imagine himself as president. In his autobiography, he recalls, "February 20, 1945, while I was presiding over the Senate, a rumor that the President was dead swept through the corridors and across the floor. I left my place at once and headed for the office of Les Biffle, Secretary of the Senate. As I entered, I said to Biffle, 'I hear the President is dead. What will we do? Let's find out what happened.'"[52]

Truman recounts this moment with such an absence of emotion that even after he left office, it is still possible to feel the apathy. His anecdote lacks any mention about a state of shock, how it felt to realize that he was president, or any sense of agony. The way he recounts the false alarm is equally unemotional, simply writing, "Biffle called the White House and was informed that it was Major General Edwin M.—'Pa' Watson, the appointment secretary to the President—who was dead."[53] He had died on board the *Quincy*, just two days after the presidential party left Algiers.[54]

This scare seems to have had little impact on Truman, who by all accounts (including his own) went back to his day-to-day socializing. This seems hard to explain. It is, of course, possible that the rumor came and went faster than Truman could process the news. Despite his wife's recollection, Truman by his own admission was aware of the writing on the wall. An original draft of his memoirs included an opening paragraph, later deleted, that read, "Long before it was whispered in Washington circles, I already sensed that Franklin Delano Roosevelt was mortally wounded."[55]

Those whispers began on inauguration day and only grew louder as the Yalta Conference came and went.

Roosevelt addressed a joint session of Congress on March 1, 1945. To those in the know, it was immediately clear why he had even asked whether he should do this. For the first time in his 159 months as president, FDR allowed the curtain to be opened slightly for all to peer inside. "I hope that you will pardon me for this unusual posture of sitting down during the presentation of what I want to say," he told the joint session in his first public acknowledgment of his disability, "but I know that you will realize that it makes it a lot easier for me not to have to carry about ten pounds of steel around on the bottom of my legs."[56] But it was not so much his paralysis that was on display that day; it was his ghastly appearance and shaky performance. "He adlibbed considerably during the presentation," recalled Grace Tully, and "there were increasingly open references to the 'shocking' appearance of the President and the indications that he was seriously failing in health."[57] He experienced excruciating pain, which some historians have attributed to "temporary cerebral aphasia and labial difficulties."[58]

Vice President Truman witnessed the alarming performance. Like Tully and others, Truman had already been "shocked by his appearance," noting specifically that "his eyes were sunken. His magnificent smile was missing from his careworn face. He seemed a spent man."[59] His frailty during the speech—both in how he looked and how he performed—deepened the president's image as a sick man. "Not even my father could bring himself to comment favorably on the President's Yalta speech," Margaret Truman recalled. "He had to resort to sarcasm."[60] When Truman inquired about the president's health, he replied, "As soon as I can, I will go to Warm Springs for a rest. I can be in trim again if I can stay there for two or three weeks."[61]

The next several weeks were painful for the president. Despite the risk, doctors discontinued digitalis in the hope that he would regain his appetite.[62] They also instructed him to take lengthy naps. Harry Easley, a Truman friend and Missouri influencer, recalled Truman telling him "that the last time he saw him [FDR] that he had the pallor of death on his face and he knew . . . that he would be President before the term was out."[63] From this conversation, Easley believed that "he [Truman] knew that he was going to be the president of the United States."[64]

None of Truman's letters to family, friends, or colleagues reveal the slightest hint that he was thinking about the possibility of becoming president.[65] After the fact, he was only slightly more reflective. "I had done a lot of thinking about it at the Chicago convention," he wrote. "I recall wondering whether President Roosevelt himself had had any inkling of his own condition. The only indication I had ever had ... [was] just before I set out on my campaign trip for the vice-presidency in the fall of 1944. He asked me how I was going to travel, and I told him I intended to cover the country by airplane. 'Don't do that, please,' he told me. 'Go by train. It is necessary that you take care of yourself.'"[66] Roosevelt left for Warm Springs on March 29, 1945, and Harry Truman never saw him again.[67]

Truman's myopia in the last two weeks of FDR's life is baffling. As late as April 6, 1945, just six days before FDR's death, Truman was still making light of his political irrelevance. In a letter to Hugh F. Williamson, prosecuting attorney of Fulton, Missouri, he refers to himself as a "political eunuch" and reminds him that he wants to be included in key Missouri happenings.[68]

Meanwhile, the fate of the world was being hashed out by a dying man. Truman was nowhere near those conversations. Just as was the case during Yalta and immediately after, during those final weeks he received no briefings, readouts, or intelligence reports. He made no inquiries, sought out no meetings, and took no proactive steps to better understand the situation he was about to inherit. He ignored every warning sign, data point, and rumor.

Even if part of Truman's reluctance stemmed from a fear that he would be seen as waiting for FDR to die, he still could have made note of some of the ways in which the president was telegraphing his postwar intentions. From FDR's rhetoric and actions, it could be surmised that he remained skeptical of Churchill and obsequious and accommodating of Stalin. He believed that America had to find a way to work with the Soviets, so much so that he often replaced facts and negative trends with an optimistic spin. "I would minimize the general Soviet problem as much as possible," he wrote in his final message to Churchill on April 12, "because these problems in one form or another seem to arise every day and most of them straighten out."[69] That same day he wrote to Stalin, thanking him for his "frank explanation of the Soviet point of view on the Berne incident* which it now appears has faded into the past without having accomplished any useful purpose."[70]

"You Are the One in Trouble"

Thursday, April 12, felt like any other day for the vice president. In the late afternoon, he had gone to visit Speaker of the House Sam Rayburn, who had invited him over for a few glasses of bourbon and branch water. Truman had an agenda, which as he recalled was to "get an agreement . . . on certain legislation and to discuss the domestic and world situation generally." When he arrived, White House press secretary Steve Early had already left a message for him to call the White House.[71]

"Jesus Christ and General Jackson," he muttered loudly enough to be heard by Lewis Deschler, the iconic House parliamentarian who would continue serving until 1974. If we go by Truman's account, which does not include such an exclamation, he assumed that at worst he would be berated by FDR and at best he had to venture over there for something nonsensical. Truman phoned the White House as requested and was told in what he described as "a strained voice" to "please come right over and come in through the main Pennsylvania Avenue entrance." The latter part of this request seemed strange, but Truman didn't think this had anything to do with the president's health.[72]

The president had been in agony since 1:00 p.m.[73] and died at 3:35 p.m.[74] According to Truman's recollection, he did not arrive at the White House until 5:25 p.m. This means for at least two hours, the new president—who *was* reachable—had no idea he was president. In peacetime this might not have been a big deal, but the events were playing out by the minute, including the war's fiercest battle in Okinawa. That same day, around the same time as the tragedy, the Japanese launched one of its most organized attacks against the American front.

---

* Refers to secret negotiations in the spring of 1944 among the United States, Great Britain, and Nazi Germany. The negotiations, which occurred in Switzerland, focused primarily on the Nazi surrender in northern Italy. When Stalin learned about these negotiations, he scolded Roosevelt and accused him of secretly pursuing a separate peace with Germany.

Furthermore, it was wartime and the new president arrived to the White House alone in a black mercury sedan without bodyguards. As he recalled, "The Secret Service had assigned three men to work in shifts when I became Vice-President . . . reinforced, as a routine practice, during the time President Roosevelt was away on his trip to Yalta and again when he went to Warm Springs."[75] But that afternoon, while running through the basement of the Capitol to get to Sam Rayburn's office, Truman had lost them.[76]

When he arrived at the White House Truman was unaware of the news awaiting him. Upon entering the front gate, he recalled being "immediately taken in the elevator to the second floor and ushered into Mrs. Roosevelt's study," where the first lady stood waiting with John and Anna Roosevelt Boettiger and Steve Early. As Truman entered, Eleanor approached him and tenderly put her arm on his shoulder. "Harry," she said quietly, "the President is dead."[77] "Is there anything I can do for you?" Truman asked, to which she responded, "Is there anything *we* can do for *you*? For you are the one in trouble now."[78]

Americans were stunned, particularly those in the armed services. In an interview for this book, George H. W. Bush, then a twenty-year-old lieutenant junior grade in the Navy, recalled his shock at the news,

> "Bar[bara] and I were living in Lewiston, Maine. I had already been shot down, and was back in training. I remember that day. I went home early to tell Bar. We were stunned. We had never voted for him. We were too young. But he had been our President almost our whole life. And he was our Commander in Chief in War. And no one had heard of Harry Truman. Who was he? My parents were not Roosevelt people, but we all mourned his death."[79]

Henry Kissinger recalled being a twenty-two-year-old military intelligence sergeant deployed to Osterode, Germany. He heard the news just as his division had reached the Elbe and the Russians were either already on the other side or expected to be there. "You have to remember that for me, Roosevelt was an extremely symbolic figure," he told me. "When I was in Germany under the Nazis all I knew about America was Roosevelt. Why I knew that? As a kid in Germany . . . he was to me a symbol of freedom. And so I had that universal view of him."[80]

That Friday, on his first day as president, Truman told reporters, "I felt as though the moon and the stars and all the planets fell on me last night when I got the news. I have the most terribly responsible job any man ever had."[81] He wasn't wrong. He lacked the subject matter expertise to fight the war and had at best a novice's understanding of what it would take to win the peace. Like Lincoln dying before Reconstruction, FDR left a blank piece of paper for the postwar order. Lincoln had an excuse for not preparing Johnson. He was in good health. For FDR and Truman there was no excuse. The country was left vulnerable by their mutual apathy, but as former president George H. W. Bush told me, "It turned out, Truman did a fine job. Thank heavens. We all assumed we were training for the invasion of Japan. I always felt Harry saved our lives [by dropping atomic bombs on Hiroshima and Nagasaki]." It was a political miracle.

Truman inherited a greater burden and with less preparation than any accidental president. The war in Europe persisted and while the Germans were on the defensive and victory seemed likely, it was unclear what that would look like and at what price. Hitler was still alive and commanding the Nazis from his bunker.[82] Roosevelt's relationship with Churchill had been complex and the two had not seen eye-to-eye on Russia. Stalin appeared to be reneging on every promise he had made at Yalta and was proving unpredictable at best, villainous at worst. There was also the Pacific theater, which raged on. War with Japan was still a fierce fight and the U.S. was faced with the grim prospect of having to move over one million men from the European theater for an invasion of Japan in November. A ferocious battle for Okinawa had already commenced.[83] Bureaucratic battles between the Army and Navy were undermining the war effort. The new president had to grapple with how to make use of a new weapon capable of unleashing unimaginable destruction.

Truman had the twin burdens of having to play rapid catch-up and follow one of the greatest figures in American history. He ascended to the presidency knowing he had impossible shoes to fill. He knew the country would have a hard time moving on from FDR, so much that he was reluctant to change anything at the White House apart from items on the desk.[84]

The magnitude sobered the new president. "I was beginning to realize," he would later write, "how little the Founding Fathers had been able to anticipate the preparations necessary for a man to become President so suddenly." Truman rose to the occasion, but the immediate moment was rattling. "A vice-president cannot equip himself to become President merely by virtue of being second in rank," he wrote. "Ideally, he should be equipped of the presidency at the time he is elected as Vice-President. The voters . . . should select him as a spare Chief Executive. As such he should be kept fully informed of all the major business transacted by the President."[85]

Truman had "spent a great deal of time reading the history of past-administrations" and even had a personal connection to a previous accidental president. By a strange coincidence, "John Tyler's brother was the father of [his] great-grandmother, and the whole Tyler family is mixed up with both sides of [his] family."[86] Despite the fact that Tyler was a distant and roundabout relative, that connection stuck with Truman. In his memoirs he wrote, "I could now appreciate how Tyler had felt on finding himself suddenly catapulted into the nation's highest office."[87]

For a man who thought little of succession while vice president, Truman seemed remarkably attuned to succession vulnerabilities during his earliest moments as president. While the line of succession was clear, he held a strong belief that the next in line should be someone who had been a "candidate for elective office" and that "any man who stepped into the presidency should have held at least some office to which he had been elected by vote of the people."[88] Without a vice president, the next in line was Secretary of State Edward R. Stettinius, Jr., an able secretary of state, but not one who fit the bill.

President Truman wanted to replace Stettinius as soon as possible and he had his eye on Jim Byrnes. Byrnes, as assistant to the president, was fully read into the war, Yalta, and could help get Truman up to speed. More important, he had also been a seven-time congressman from South Carolina's 2nd District and twice elected a U.S. senator from the same state, meaning he is someone who had previously been elected to a national office.[89] Within hours of taking the presidential oath, Truman sent a plane to fetch Byrnes from South Carolina for a 2:30 p.m. appointment the next day.[90] Byrnes was told that Truman wanted "his firsthand account of what had gone on at Yalta, and all the information he had of the meetings between Roosevelt, Churchill, and Stalin," but he also wanted to talk to him about becoming secretary of state.[91] He got the job three months later, an appointment that Truman would eventually come to regret.*

Truman was faced with some daunting decisions, some on a level never before confronted by a seasoned president, let alone an accidental one. Most were tough, but expected, with the notable exception of the atomic bomb. It would take the new president weeks to get properly briefed on the details of the Manhattan Project, which was the secret research and development project that produced the world's first nuclear weapons.

The long process of briefing the president began at his first cabinet meeting, held at 7:09 p.m. on April 12, 1945, just moments after he took the oath of office. All members were present except for the postmaster general, who was sick. Truman invited each member of the cabinet to retain his post and told press secretary Early that he could let the press know he intended to stick with the April 25 date for the San Francisco conference on the United Nations.[92] He made it clear that it was his "intention . . . to continue both the foreign and the domestic policies of the Roosevelt administration." But he also "made it clear" that he "would be President in [his] own right and that [he] would assume full responsibility for such decisions as had to be made."[93]

After a short cabinet meeting, everyone left except for Secretary of War Stimson, who lingered.[94] That impromptu briefing would be the first in an accelerated effort to read Truman into the atomic bomb. While Stimson should be acknowledged for understanding the importance of briefing the president at the earliest possible time, he failed to offer enough detail to bring home the reality. "He asked to speak to me about a most urgent matter," Truman recalled, and "told me that he wanted me to know about an immense project that was under way—a project looking to the development of a new explosive of almost unbelievable destructive power." But Stimson left it there, telling the new president "that was all he felt free to say at the time." The secretary of war's statement left Truman "puzzled" and without "details."[95] Truman was president and should have asked for more.

---

* Truman believed Byrnes was running foreign policy without authorization and always suspected that had Dean Acheson, the undersecretary of state at the time, been at Potsdam, the outcome would have been different.

The fact is that there was nothing that Stimson actually told him that he had not already been familiar with from his time in the Senate. The details of the Manhattan Project were highly classified, but the notion that "something unusually important was brewing in our war plants" was not a secret. During his days in the Senate, Truman's committee had dispatched investigators out to some of the plants as part of an examination into wartime spending. Such scrutiny had prompted a visit from Stimson, who urged him to back off, saying, "Senator, I can't tell you what it is, but it is the greatest project in the history of the world. It is most top secret. Many of the people who are actually engaged in the work have no idea what it is, and we who do would appreciate your not going into those plants."[96] Truman wasn't about to meddle with the war effort and told the secretary he'd take his word for it and "order the investigations into those plants called off."[97]

Recalling this conversation, the president may not have given much weight to Stimson's short briefing. But the next day, when Jim Byrnes came by, the details of this special project became clearer. We are "perfecting an explosive great enough to destroy the whole world," he told Truman. That was quite a superlative, but still, Truman didn't fully understand what he was talking about. Later that day, "Vannevar Bush, head of the office of scientific research and development, came to the White House" and gave the president the "scientist's version of the atomic bomb."[98] Truman, who was with Admiral William Leahy at the time, found his chief of staff dismissive of the project, suggesting, "That is the biggest fool thing we have ever done. . . . The bomb will never go off and I speak as an expert in explosives."[99]

Over the next several weeks, the briefs about the Manhattan Project became more frequent and more detailed.[100] Stimson recommended that Truman establish an advisory committee comprised of scientists and experts to advise him on use of the weapon. But because there had not yet been a successful test, the bomb did not dominate Truman's thinking.

All of this changed on July 16, when the first atomic test was successfully conducted at Alamogordo, New Mexico, just after Truman left for the Potsdam Conference with Stalin and Churchill.[101] "Stimson flew to Potsdam the next day to see me," Truman remembered, "and brought with him the full details of the test. I received him at once and called in Secretary of State Byrnes, Admiral Leahy, General George Marshall, General

Henry Arnold, and Admiral Ernest King." It was too early to understand the implications and as Truman recalled, "we were not ready to make use of this weapon against the Japanese." In his memoirs, Truman wrote that the plan was to stay the course "with the existing military plans for the invasion of the Japanese home islands."[102]

Truman's diary reveals a different and more telling narrative. His mind appears to have already been made up shortly after confirmation of the Alamogordo test, which is not surprising given he had a full understanding of what an invasion would entail. "We have discovered the most terrible bomb in the history of the world," he confided to his diary in a July 26 entry. "This weapon is to be used against Japan between now and August 10th. I have told the Sec. of War, Mr. Stimson, to use it so that military objectives and soldiers and sailors are the target and not women and children."[103] That same entry reveals not just the intent, but also the thinking behind the target. "Even if the Japs are savages, ruthless, merciless and fanatic, we as the leader of the world for the common welfare cannot drop this terrible bomb on the old capital [Kyoto] or the new [Tokyo] . . . The target will be a purely military one and we will issue a warning statement asking the Japs to surrender and save lives."[104]

Truman was face-to-face with Stalin, aware that he possessed the deadliest weapon the world had ever seen. To use that as leverage, he would have to make sure Stalin knew about it. It's likely that Roosevelt would have done the same, particularly as he had already debated it with Churchill at an early stage. At the time, Churchill's opposition was based on the fact that the weapon had not yet been proved and that Roosevelt seemed too comfortable sharing it.

At Potsdam, however, the context was very different. Shortly after the Alamogordo test, Truman had received two telegrams, both of which he shared with the British prime minister over lunch. When Truman suggested that the time had come to inform Stalin, Churchill concurred with his assessment, but stressed that he should not be given any of "the particulars." The two discussed the best way to share the information— verbally or in writing—and ultimately, agreed that Truman would find the right opportunity either during or after one of the meetings with Stalin.[105]

On July 24, Truman "casually mentioned to Stalin that [the U.S.] had a new weapon of unusual destructive force." Stalin's reaction was rather mute. He said "he was glad to hear it and hoped we would make 'good use of it against the Japanese.'"[106] A number of historians have speculated about the Soviet premier's lack of surprise and some have surmised that Julius and Ethel Rosenberg, the notorious Soviet spies who were eventually caught and executed at Sing Sing prison in 1953, had snatched information about the Manhattan Project and that Stalin was scripted for the moment when he was formally told.

It wasn't until Truman left Potsdam that more concrete atomic bomb deliberations began, first in England and then on board the USS *Augusta* as it made its way westward. The war had been bloody, but the Pacific front had been particularly so. The Japanese strategy attempted to draw the Allied Powers into brutal and protracted warfare on their home islands, which they hoped would leave them with no choice but to negotiate for peace.[107]

Coming battles promised to be long and bloody. Iwo Jima was the first of these, where the surprise introduction of organized kamikaze units resulted in the only Pacific battle where the American casualties exceeded that of the Japanese, an estimated 26,000 (more than 6,000 deaths) and 21,000 (mostly deaths) respectively.[108] The total casualties at Okinawa was even worse. The battle played out over three months and was the bloodiest campaign in U.S. military history, seeing close to three times the number of casualties as Iwo Jima (35 percent of the deployment),[109] including the commanding lieutenant general Simon Bolivar Buckner, Jr., whose chest had been pierced by a Japanese shell fragment. Also killed at Okinawa was Ernie Pyle, an award-winning war correspondent for the Scripps-Howard newspaper group, who was hit by a sniper's bullet.[110]

With the costly victories in Iwo Jima and Okinawa, Truman assembled a joint committee of senior Army and Navy officers to plan the end of the war. The plan was codenamed "Downfall"[111] and it included a two-phased effort for the invasion of Japan. The first phase, scheduled for November 1, 1945, was code-named "Operation Olympic" and called for 650,000 ground troops to invade the island of Kyushu.[112] The second phase, targeted for March 1, 1946, "Operation Coronet," would draw on thirty-six divisions and 1.5 million combat soldiers to take mainland Japan.[113]

Invasion or the bomb? Supreme Allied Commander Douglas MacArthur, Army Chief of Staff George Marshall, and Chief of Naval Operations Ernest King had already ruled out the other options: aerial bombing and a naval blockade.[114] Former president Herbert Hoover resurfaced to offer unsolicited advice. The U.S., he believed, had to give up on its demand for Japan's unconditional surrender[115] in order to avoid one million casualties. While Truman was alarmed by the potential casualty numbers Hoover cited, he had no interest in entertaining the former president's suggestion.[116] He needed more information before he was prepared to make his decision.

On June 17, 1945, President Truman tasked Chief of Staff Admiral William D. Leahy to present a further analysis on what it would take to invade Japan both in terms of time and American casualties.[117] The numbers were worse than expected. The Japanese had predicted correctly that Kyushu would be the initial target—not far-fetched given the island's geography—and began moving into their defensive positions.[118] Without the element of surprise, the U.S. could expect heavy casualties.

Invasion had additional problems. First, as was evidenced at both Iwo Jima and Okinawa, not to mention many other battles, there was an assumption that Japanese culture would mandate its soldiers fight to the last death. If Tokyo was captured and Emperor Hirohito surrendered, there was a high probability that resisting armed forces would drag the U.S. into multiple Okinawa-size battles both on the mainland and on surrounding islands.[119] Landing troops on the mainland would also prove difficult since the beaches had been strategically sprinkled with land mines.[120] There were also 168,500 prisoners of war, including 15,000 Americans, who in the event of an invasion would almost certainly be executed.[121] Many of the veteran units had also been broken up, which meant that the invasion ran the risk of lacking coherence. The Russians were a shaky ally in the Pacific and the Japanese had either guessed correctly or gained valuable intelligence about American naval movements during the October 1944 Battle of Leyte Gulf.[122]

Truman approved the invasion on July 24, 1945, and ordered Supreme Allied Commander General Douglas MacArthur to proceed.[123] Two days later, the Allies issued the Potsdam Proclamation, signed by Harry Truman, Winston Churchill, and Chiang Kai-Shek, which gave Japan the choice of "unconditional surrender of all the Japanese armed forces" or face "prompt and utter destruction."[124]

The Japanese did not heed the warning,[125] sparking subsequent conversations among Truman and his advisors about what to do next. It took less than two weeks for Truman to give the order. On August 6, 1945, the first bomb was dropped on Hiroshima. Truman received the news on board the *Augusta* coming back from Potsdam.[126] The Army minister urged the army to continue fighting as a way of demonstrating the minimal impact of the attack on Hiroshima.[127] Truman addressed the nation and consulted his top military brass. Despite having only one additional atomic bomb, a consensus was reached to drop the second, thinking the Japanese would believe America had a stockpile of atomic bombs that could be deployed on more cities. Recognizing that they could need more bombs, Leslie Groves, who directed the Manhattan Project, was told to keep the sites on standby and as he later recalled, "Our entire organization both at Los Alamos and on Tinian was maintained in a state of complete readiness to prepare additional bombs in case the peace talks should break down."[128] On August 9, the second atomic bomb was dropped on Nagasaki, the same day that Truman arrived back in the U.S. Earlier that day, the Soviets broke their neutrality and invaded Manchuria. Japan announced surrender on August 15, making it official with the signatures of Japanese general Yoshijiro Umezu and foreign minister Mamora Shigemitsu on September 2. The war was over, but winning the peace would prove far more complicated.

All of this took place in the first four months of Truman's presidency. Given how little he knew as vice president, it's extraordinary that he approached the situation with such resolve. In fact, so confident was he in the decision that he gave the order and went to bed. "The final decision of where and when to use the atomic bomb was up to me," he wrote. While a number of people attempted to influence the decision, Truman asserts that he was unwavering, "regard[ing] the bomb as a military weapon and never ha[ving] any doubt that it should be used." He had entrusted the recommendation to a committee of advisors and key scientists, including Robert Oppenheimer, Arthur Compton, E. O. Lawrence, and Enrico Fermi. "It was their recommendation," he wrote after leaving office, "that the bomb be used against the enemy as soon as it could be done. They recommended further that it should be used without specific warning and against a target that would clearly show its devastating strength." When he consulted with Churchill on its use, he concurred with the advice of the committee and reinforced the view that it "might aid the end of the war."[129]

There is reason to believe that Roosevelt would have made the same decision. He would have wanted to prevent the massive casualties associated with an invasion of Japan. He said as much to his son James, who attempted to prepare his father for the possibility that he might be one of the many Americans killed in a ground invasion of Japan. This was an alarming prospect, to which FDR responded with confidence, "There will be no invasion of Japan. We will have something that will end our war with Japan before any invasion takes place." When James asked for details, his father said, "I am sorry; even though you are my son, I cannot tell you. Only those who need to know, know about it. But it is there, it is something that we can use and will use if we have to, something we certainly will use before you or any of our sons die in an invasion of Japan."[130]

A Decisive Cold Warrior

Harry Truman's rise to the presidency is an unlikely story. The fact that he became one of the two most successful accidental presidents is even more remarkable given the shortness of his vice presidency and the weight of what he inherited. He had been a machine politician from Missouri whom everybody underrated, including himself. But part of what made Truman successful is that he was remarkably decisive, both about his policies and his choice of advisors. His ability to make monumental decisions during his first year in office showed tremendous confidence and continued throughout his presidency. His quick decisions about whom he should listen to were equally impressive.

Unlike Roosevelt, who thought he could handle Stalin, Truman made the decision to proceed with caution and skepticism. He viewed the Soviet premier as an adversary, with whom he had to partner in formulating the postwar order. To be fair to Roosevelt, the dynamic with the Soviet Union was fluid and while he had been positively inclined toward Stalin, the circumstances and context were already changing rapidly in the weeks leading up to his death. Whether FDR would have changed his views on the Soviet Union had he survived is an open question and there is not sufficient evidence to do more than speculate. Would repeated Soviet delinquency on promises from Tehran, Yalta, and eventually Potsdam have led him to adopt the adversarial mind-set of Harry Truman? Truman was more willing to listen to the voices of advisors around him, the insights from the State Department, and the analysis of the mission in Moscow.

There are two contradictory views related to the FDR-Stalin relationship. The first is the view that Roosevelt thought he could handle Stalin and that the origins of his atheism were incorrectly cited as part of what drove his hostility toward the West. It was Stalin's suspicions of the West that caused his opposition. Another point of view holds that Roosevelt was maneuvering Stalin. The latter interpretation suggests that FDR had no choice except to show goodwill so that if necessary he could turn on him. Kissinger's view is that it is a "combination of the two," believing that "he was genuinely—I don't want to say taken in by Stalin—but he followed the line . . . that the personal relationship between leaders is crucial."[131] There is at least a hint of this from about the time of his death, when he drafted a tough message to Stalin that he was beginning to revise. FDR's daughter Anna claimed that on March 23, 1945, less than three weeks before his death, her father told her, "Averell is right. We can't do business with Stalin. He has broken every one of the promises he made at Yalta."[132] If FDR was indeed turning and had his health held up, he might have proven an implacable adversary.[133]

Once president, Truman wasted no time trying to understand what Roosevelt had been working on. "I spent the first day as president d[oing] more reading than I ever thought I could,"[134] he wrote. In addition to tapping Byrnes for all he knew about Yalta, Truman enlisted Harry Hopkins for "more firsthand information about the heads of state with whom I would have to deal, particularly Stalin." Knowing Hopkins was a close Roosevelt confidant and was looking to retire, Truman made a special ask: "I hope you don't mind my calling you in at this time, but I need to know everything you can tell me about our relations with Russia—all that you know about Stalin and Churchill and the conferences at Cairo, Casablanca, Tehran, and Yalta." Hopkins, who knew very little about where the new president stood, told him, "I'm confident that you will continue to carry out the policies of Franklin Roosevelt," before adding that "Stalin is a forthright, rough, tough Russian. He is a Russian partisan through and through, thinking always first of Russia. But he can be talked to frankly."[135]

Truman was left to make sense of competing interests and contradictory advice; he never allowed himself held hostage to the views of others. Unlike Lyndon Johnson, who would later be swayed by the influence of

Kennedy's advisors on Vietnam, Truman developed an independent view. Various individuals, departments, and agencies must have thought themselves able to shape Truman's view and they certainly tried. The State Department, for example, thought Roosevelt had a blind spot on Stalin and much like some of Kennedy's advisors would do with LBJ, they sought to shape the novice's views, albeit with better intentions. In its first memo to the new president, the State Department wrote of the Soviet Union: "Since the Yalta Conference the Soviet Government has taken a firm and uncompromising position on nearly every major question that has arisen in our relations,"[136] a message that insinuated the impossibility of trusting the Soviet Union with any agreement.

There was also Eleanor Roosevelt, who through a frequent and lengthy correspondence with President Truman believed she was dutifully representing her husband. The former first lady enlisted herself as Truman's pen pal, volunteering for the role of personal muse and offering unsolicited advice on just about every issue imaginable. Often invoking the name of Franklin, and without regard for the burdens the new president shouldered, she was relentless in both her advice and criticism. Her opinions were strong, and she mastered the art of subtly reminding him of her late husband. The letters are significant because her status meant that Truman had to respond to each letter, often at greater length than hers. His responses, which were often in defense of his policies, offer remarkable insight into how he thought about Russia, the Cold War, and the various characters involved.

Eleanor had done the same with FDR but she took far greater liberties with Truman, particularly on foreign policy. She wrote him concerning the quandaries of every group imaginable. She wrote about the plight of displaced persons, the unemployed, the Secret Service, refugees in Shanghai, conscientious objectors seeking amnesty, the poor conditions of U.S. Army troops stationed in Germany, orphans, Jewish stowaways on Ellis Island, civil servants subjected to loyalty oaths, and the crimes against Japanese Americans in the West,[137] which provoked Truman to write, "This disgraceful conduct [toward American-Japanese] almost makes you believe that a lot of our Americans have a streak of Nazi in them."[138] And when she wrote to him about an incident involving American Zionists who had illegally attempted to take a boat filled with Jews to Palestine (three refugees refused to disembark in protest against being stopped),[139]

Truman's response was that the incident was a "most embarrassing one." He went on to express his fear that "the Jews are like all under dogs—when they get on top they are just as intolerant and as cruel as the people were to them when they were underneath."[140]

Eleanor recommended candidates for jobs in the administration, particularly Democratic women. She saw it her duty to bring to the president's attention turf wars, bureaucratic drama, and inefficiencies in departments and agencies. She told him about an emissary in Germany mixing with the wrong labor groups, complained of embassy staff and the ambassador in Moscow, commented on Secretary of State Jim Byrne's inadequacy, tried to torpedo Clinton Anderson as Robert Hannegan's replacement as DNC chair,[141] and stepped in the middle of a feud between the president and Harold Ickes, to which the president had to write a long letter defending himself and his actions to the former first lady.[142]

Mrs. Roosevelt offered advice on policies ranging from containing communism, the economic recovery of Europe, and tensions between Greece and Turkey, to the situation in China, Israel-Palestinian issues, and U.S. policy toward Africa.[143] On one occasion she wrote to suggest that Truman consider making her home at Hyde Park the headquarters of the United Nations.[144] But nowhere were her letters more dogmatic than with regard to Russia, where she gave the appearance of representing her husband's views. She viewed Churchill as overly suspicious of the Russians (including during Clement Attlee's tenure as prime minister) and, much as did Franklin, an unaccommodating obstacle in what she believed should be a more robust effort to win over Stalin. "He [Churchill] is suspicious of the Russians and they know it," she wrote in one of her first letters. "If you will remember, he said some pretty rough things about them years ago and they do not forget."[145] She reminded Truman that "any lasting peace will have to have the three great powers behind it" and offered advice on how to manipulate Churchill to make him easier to work with. "If you talk to him about books," she advised, "and let him quote to you from his marvelous memory everything on earth from Barbara Fritchie to the Nonsense Rhymes and Greek tragedy, you will find him easier to deal with on political subjects. He is a gentleman to whom the personal element means a great deal."[146]

"Mr. Churchill," she went on, "does not have the same kind of sense of humor that the Russians have." The Russians are "more like us" in that "they enjoy a practical joke, rough-housing and play and they will joke about things which Mr. Churchill thinks are sacred." The prime minister's problem, she explained, is that "he takes them dead seriously and argues about them when what he ought to do is to laugh." She believed it was essential for Truman to understand this, noting "that was where Franklin usually won out because if you know where to laugh and when to look upon things as too absurd to take seriously, the other person is ashamed to carry through even if he was serious about it." [147]

Of course, Truman had a much harder time with Stalin than he did with Churchill. They started off on the wrong foot, disagreeing early about the future of Poland. Stalin had made movements toward the "conclusion of a Soviet-Polish treaty of mutual assistance" and installed a Soviet-friendly provisional government in Lublin. Furthermore, he refused to recognize the more democratic, Western-friendly, Polish government-in-exile. These provocative steps were a direct snub at the agreements reached in Yalta,[148] although FDR had given Stalin enough wiggle room, including a personal note saying, "The United States will never lend its support in any way to any provisional government in Poland that would be inimical to your interests."[149] Truman was "disturbed" and "directed the state department to register a protest in Moscow."[150]

Vyacheslav Molotov, Stalin's protégé and foreign minister, paid a visit to Washington on his way to San Francisco for the inaugural meeting of the United Nations. His meeting with the president did not go well. Truman gave him a message demanding a democratic government in Poland and asked him to immediately transmit it to Stalin.[151] Molotov was irate. "I have never been talked to like that in my life," he said. The president told him, "Carry out your agreements and you won't get talked to like that."[152]

The Russians were used to FDR's finesse and artful wording of even the toughest messages. That wasn't Truman's way. Stalin was furious and unrelenting in his April 24 response. It was, as Truman described, "one of the most revealing and disquieting messages to reach me during my first days in the White House." Stalin demanded a government in Poland "friendly toward the Soviet Union" and insisted that this was "demanded by the blood of the Soviet people abundantly shed on the fields of Poland in the name of liberation of Poland."[153]

Hoping to reverse course, Truman sent Hopkins to meet with Stalin in early May. Hopkins was able to secure a meeting of the Big Three at

Potsdam and confirm that the Russians would enter the war against the Japanese. That was the good news. But Stalin was also very upset about the Lend-Lease policy, citing it as "an example of the cooling-off attitude of America toward the Soviets" and warned "that if the refusal to continue Lend-Lease was intended as pressure on the Russians in order to soften them up it was a fundamental mistake."[154] Stalin, as Truman would learn from archived correspondence over Poland, Italy, Yugoslavia, and Germany, was paranoid about secret Anglo-American bilateral arrangements that left the Russians out.[155]

It was around this time that Eleanor accelerated the number of Russia-related letters to President Truman. The tone of her letters reveals a condescending belief that she knew best because she understood what FDR wanted. On most issues, she spoke for herself, but when it came to Stalin and Churchill, Russia and the U.K., she believed she was speaking for Franklin. She offered her views on Russian attitudes and even sent Truman a six-point program for peace. This continued for months, even years. She believed that Truman underestimated the importance of demonstrating American integrity. "One can only be successfully firm," she wrote, "if the people one is firm with particularly the Russians, have complete confidence in one's integrity." She questioned whether "our attitude on questions like Spain and the Argentine and even in Germany itself, has been conducive to creating a feeling that we would always keep our word and that we would always talk things out absolutely sincerely before we took action." This was Eleanor sounding like vintage FDR, casting aside the double standard from Moscow, holding to a belief that the Russians needed to be handled with care.[156]

By 1946–47, her tone grew more adversarial, suggesting a belief that Truman's policies were advocating a departure from her husband. She felt his policy toward Spain, Argentina, and Germany[157] was a complete pivot, to which Truman replied, "I am truly sorry that you are not pleased with the attitude of the United States. . . . Naturally we expected to have difficulty with the Russians, French and British but none of the difficulties are insurmountable and I have every reason to believe that most of them will work out in a satisfactory manner."[158] In a later letter, Eleanor informed the president that she was "very much disturbed by the whole Greek-Turkish situation"—referring to escalating tensions between the two countries, the prospect of Greece falling to communism, and Soviet demands for navigation rights to the Turkish Straits—and suggested that his advisors were shortsighted. She called out Admiral Leahy as an isolationist, described Averell Harriman as weak, and pegged Undersecretary of State Dean Acheson and U.S. Ambassador to Britain Lewis Douglas as "sympathetic to the British point of view."[159]

The letters continued but Truman's responses changed. He was exasperated and done explaining himself. Truman was not FDR, and he didn't need to be. He had proven an able wartime president, capable of making big decisions. It was now up to him to prove his worth in the postwar era, something that Roosevelt had thought about, but never had the chance to do. He took a major step in this direction when the British government announced that effective March 31, 1947, it would discontinue its military and economic aide to the Greek government in its civil war against the Communist Party. Truman feared that if this assistance gap was not immediately filled, communism would find it far easier to gain traction in Europe. On March 12, 1947, he appealed to a joint session of Congress to call on America to fill the void in both Greece and Turkey, where the British had also discontinued their aide. His speech became known as the "Truman Doctrine," setting the precedent that it would be "the policy of the United States to support free peoples who are resisting attempted subjugation by armed minorities or by outside pressures."[160]

While it is impossible to know how FDR would have handled this same situation, Truman lacked the patience and accommodating spirit that characterized FDR's approach to the Russians and their indiscretions. Eleanor may have been channeling her late husband in her expression of angst over the Greece and Turkey situations, but she lacked the facts that he surely would have had as president. Had FDR been challenged this many times, over and over again by the Russians, he would have almost certainly altered his position. "To what seems to me nearly the limit," Truman wrote Eleanor in defense of his policies, "we have made concessions to Russia that she might trust and not fear us."

His list was lengthy, including: agreement at Tehran to support Tito's Partisans in Yugoslavia; agreement at Yalta to give the Kuril Islands and southern Sakhalin to Russia, to recognize the independence of Outer Mongolia and Soviet interests in Dalian, Port Arthur, and the Chinese Eastern Railway; also at Yalta, agreement on the Curzon line as the western border of the Soviet Union, and the admission of Byelorussia and Ukraine to the United Nations; at Potsdam, agreement to the annexation by Russia of the northern portion of east Prussia, to the recognition of Soviet claims for preferential reparations from western Germany, to the necessity for modification of the provisions of the Montreux Convention. In the peace treaty negotiations Truman noted "we have made concessions particularly in regard to reparations from Italy and in our efforts to meet the Yugoslav and Soviet point of view on boundaries and administration of Venezia Giulia and Trieste."[161]

The president also lamented that in addition to these concessions, the U.S. had done an enormous amount to relieve Russia, including $250 million in Lend-Lease support, military and technological information, $250 million of United Nations Relief and Rehabilitation Administration aid, and another $250 million in thirty-year credit goods.[162] He reminded Mrs. Roosevelt that the U.S. had only lodged protests "against . . . violation of democratic procedures pledged at the Yalta conference, in Poland, Rumania, Bulgaria, and Yugoslavia," all of which were unsuccessful.[163]

It's in the context of this lengthy correction of the facts—which Truman acknowledges in a postscript as taking a long time to put together—that we begin to see the state that led him to the Truman Doctrine:

> Let us think, therefore, of Greek and Turkish aid against the background of these positive measures. The results of our efforts thus far disappoint and dishearten many in this and other countries. . . .
> So it seems to me . . . that we must take our stand at this strategic point in a determined effort not to let the advance of communism continue to overtake countries who choose to maintain a free way of life, who have requested our aid, and who do not wish to submit to subjugation by an armed minority or by outside pressure.[164]

It's quite possible that Roosevelt's patience would have worn thin with Stalin, but still, it seems unlikely that he would have responded with the same aggressive posture as the Truman Doctrine or on such an accelerated timeline.

═══

By the end of Truman's first term, he could point to a long list of accomplishments. He had ended World War II, launched the Marshall Plan to rebuild Europe, succeeded where Woodrow Wilson had failed in establishing the United Nations, recognized the state of Israel, and authorized the Berlin airlift. This wasn't a bad record for a politico from Missouri with no experience in foreign affairs who had the impossible task of following FDR. Still, he entered the 1948 presidential election with dipping popularity and divisions within his own party. His decision to desegregate the military through Executive Order 9981 infuriated the segregationist flank of the Democratic Party, which under the leadership of Senator Strom Thurmond of South Carolina broke away and formed the States' Rights Democratic Party, better known as the Dixiecrats. The split within the party made the path to victory far more difficult, a reality that was reflected in the polls.

Truman didn't expect to win in 1948. "I've got to face the situation from a national and an international standpoint and not from a partisan political one," he wrote his sister, Mary Jane, one year before the election. "It is more important to save the world from totalitarianism than to be President another four years."[165] He had reason to believe his election prospects were bleak. He was an accidental president. The Democrats had been in control of the White House since 1933, his party was divided, and many of his social policies had agitated a fractured nation. Polling showed that the Republican ticket of Thomas Dewey and Earl Warren would likely win and the *Chicago Tribune* even printed the now infamous headline "Dewey Defeats Truman," which the president-elect proudly held up on election night. But Truman's cold warrior approach toward the Soviet Union resonated with Americans at precisely the moment that the Red Scare was sweeping the nation. Congress had advised both Truman and Acheson that if the administration wanted their support, they would need to communicate the communist threat to the American people. Having been through the freedom zealotry with Woodrow Wilson, many in Congress had little appetite to repeat the same folly with Truman. In the lead-up to the establishment of the United Nations, he made sure to work closely with both parties—notably the republican senator Arthur Vandenberg and the democratic senator Tom Connally—to avoid the same mistakes that Wilson made with the League of Nations. When it came time for the election, to the surprise of many, including himself, he won a convincing victory and became the third accidental president to win the presidency in his own right.

If Truman's first term focused on ending wars and building the post-war order, his second term was defined by new wars, cold wars, and more red scares at home. During his first term, he issued Executive Order 9835, which established loyalty boards to test the "loyalty" of all government employees. He would regret this decision, acknowledging in his memoirs that exonerated employees faced eternal damnation as long as the case files remained accessible. While he sought to remedy an intrusive process that he had set in motion, it proved difficult, as Wisconsin senator Joseph McCarthy and the other red-scare-mongers used the president's loyalty program as a precursor for an invasive purge that accelerated during Truman's second term.[166]

The era of McCarthyism coincided with increased communist expansionism. The red threat was heightened by the Soviet detonation of an atomic bomb and the trial and conviction of Julius and Ethel Rosenberg, as well as Alger Hiss, who had all been convicted for espionage. In late 1949, Mao Zedong took over mainland China, proclaimed the communist People's Republic, and drove the Western-friendly, albeit totally corrupt, government of Chiang Kai-shek off the mainland to Taiwan. Truman kept the U.S. neutral and agreed to nonintervention. That posture of neutrality proved short-lived. The following year, Kim Il-sung invaded South Korea. The North Korean leader had been backed by both the Soviets and Mao's new People's Republic. Truman found himself with yet another big decision to make. Having just concluded one war, would he now initiate another?

Despite the magnitude of these decisions, Truman proved no less decisive than he had been during his first term. Rather than ask for a formal declaration of war from Congress, he simply put them on notice and commenced a war that would last more than three years, claim 1.2 million lives (36,914 American), and result in a stalemate at the 38th parallel that remains today. Fearing that Korea was the next domino to fall—even though the "Domino Theory" had not yet been coined—Truman dispatched the Navy's Seventh Fleet to the Taiwan Strait as part of a larger containment strategy.

"Mr. Truman's War," as it became known, represented an early test for the nascent United Nations, which, because the Soviets boycotted the Security Council over its refusal to seat Mao's government, adopted U.N. Resolution 84. The resolution, which called for North Korean withdrawal from South Korea, was a big diplomatic win for President Truman in this early Cold War battle. The war itself, however, was messy, first with the U.S. unable to enforce a naval blockade and later with an overzealous General Douglas MacArthur defying the president's orders and wanting to take his military adventures beyond the Korean Peninsula into China.

The Korean War damaged Truman's popularity. His actions left him with an approval rating hovering around 22 percent by the end of his second term, which is one of the lowest of any president in history. But public opinion polls from 1952 should not obscure the fact that what Truman achieved was extraordinary. The steep learning curve had made Truman his own man faster than any other accidental president in history. When Roosevelt died, the Missourian had no choice but to buckle down and learn fast. There was perhaps no man less prepared for the challenges that awaited him than Harry Truman, yet he proved to be only one of two success stories—the other being Theodore Roosevelt—among the eight accidental presidents.

John F. Kennedy was the youngest man elected president. He said the right things on civil rights, but was not prepared to act. He escalated America's involvement in Vietnam just before his assassination on November 22, 1963.

Lyndon Johnson gave up the most powerful position in the Senate to become vice president, where he found himself ostracized by the Kennedy men, whom he disparagingly nicknamed "the Harvards." He achieved landmark legislation on civil rights, but plunged the U.S. deep into war in Vietnam.

CHAPTER NINE

The Last Time

Head-Snapping Transition

John F. Kennedy's path to reelection was not going to be easy. He may have charmed many Americans with his oratory skills, good looks, and youth, but that would not be enough. With heightened tensions at home and abroad, he had a weak track record on both fronts. Soaring rhetoric was one thing, but when it came to policy, he had floundered. From the Bay of Pigs fiasco to his window dressing on civil rights, his presidency lacked any significant accomplishment. As he geared up for reelection, he knew that winning would require a fight. He had only narrowly won the presidency in 1960.[1] Now the country was more divided on civil rights, tensions with the Soviet Union had brought the world to the brink of nuclear war, and the Democratic Party was plagued by competing factions.

He'd have to work for a win, which meant campaigning in the South. The strategy was for Lyndon Johnson to wrangle some support since Kennedy had only narrowly won Texas in 1960. On the swing through Texas the president would be joined by the vice president and John B. Connally, the governor. John and Jackie Kennedy arrived on November 21, 1963, stopping in San Antonio and then Houston before heading on to Dallas the following day, where he would give a luncheon speech at the Trade Mart for the Dallas Citizens Council, Dallas Assembly, and the Graduate Research Center of the Southwest. The president's aides were uncomfortable. The Texas crowds were unfriendly and rowdy. "If anybody really wanted to shoot the president of the United States," Kennedy told his aide Kenneth O'Donnell on the morning of November 22, "it was not a very difficult job—all one had to do was get a high building someday with a telescopic rifle, and there was nothing anybody could do to defend against such an attempt."[2] That same morning, he made a joke to his wife: "We're heading into nut country today. . . . You know, last night would have been a hell of a night to assassinate a President."[3] President Kennedy was shot at 12:30 p.m. (CST) on November 22 as his open limousine made its way through Dealey Plaza. He was pronounced dead thirty minutes later. The entire country watched it on television.

Americans weren't the only ones shocked. The Soviet Union viewed the transition with confusion and wild speculation. According to a top-secret report from FBI director J. Edgar Hoover to the White House,[4] the Soviets believed Kennedy's assassination was a "well-organized conspiracy on the part of the 'ultraright' in the United States to effect a 'coup.'" According to the report, the Soviets "seemed convinced that the assassination was not the deed of one man, but that it arose out of a carefully planned campaign in which several people played a part. They felt that those elements interested in utilizing the assassination and playing on anticommunist sentiments in the United States would then utilize this act to stop negotiations with the Soviet Union, attack Cuba and thereafter spread the war." The "Soviet officials were fearful that without leadership some irresponsible general in the United States might launch a missile at the Soviet Union."[5]

Kennedy's assassination created an intelligence challenge for the Committee for State Security, better known as the KGB, whose station chief in New York, Colonel Boris Ivanov, convened his local spies on November 25 to inform them that "President Kennedy's death had posed a problem for the KGB." One FBI source indicated that the "KGB was in possession of data purporting to indicate President Johnson was responsible for the assassination." Ivanov "emphasized that it was of extreme importance to the Soviet Government to determine precisely what kind of man the new president Lyndon Johnson would be." He issued instructions to all of its agents to immediately obtain all data available concerning Johnson, "including his background, his past working experience and record in Congress, his present attitude toward the Soviet Union, and particularly all information which might have bearing upon the future foreign policy line he would follow." At the direction of Moscow, they began collecting "information concerning President Lyndon B. Johnson's character, background, personal friends, family, and from which quarters he derives his support in his positions as President of the United States." According to one FBI source cited in the documents, the KGB claimed to be in possession of data purporting to indicate President Johnson was responsible for the assassination of President Kennedy.[6]

Kennedy and Johnson could not have looked more different: Kennedy was young and handsome with an elevating voice, while Johnson was older and haggard with a rougher-sounding tone; Kennedy was graceful and elegant, Johnson was uncouth and used foul language; Kennedy was Harvard, a Pulitzer Prize–winning author and decorated war hero, Johnson was an intellectual outsider with a questionable military award for his service during World War II.[7]

The superficial differences may have favored Kennedy in the popularity contest, but Johnson had the superior skill and more impressive political background: Johnson had served in Congress since 1937 and held the Senate's highest leadership positions, Kennedy never served in the leadership; Johnson had a legislative track record and a mastery of rules and tactics, Kennedy rarely showed up to vote and had no significant legislative achievement; Johnson had real relationships in Congress and an ability to unite the Democratic Party and work across the aisle, Kennedy was aloof and polarizing even within his own party.

Both viewed their careers through the lens of politics. Johnson, in particular, had a one-track mind. He thought only of politics. He had risen to the highest ranks of the Senate after barely making it there. He was about to narrowly win a Senate seat in 1941, only to have the ballot boxes stuffed at the last minute. Rather than contest the election, he waited seven years to make a run at it, once again barely winning. This time, *his* camp also stuffed the boxes and did so much more effectively than his opponent.[8] He was disparagingly given the name "Landslide Lyndon," and would never fully escape the scarlet letter of rigging his way to the Senate. But it didn't matter.[9]

When Johnson gave up the most powerful position in the Senate to serve as vice president, he knew that this was political castration. Had it been entirely up to John Kennedy, Johnson may have fared better within the administration. But others were incensed by Johnson having scrutinized Kennedy's Catholicism and exploited his life-threatening illnesses—describing him as a "little scrawny fellow with rickets"[10]—during the Democratic primaries. His brother Robert Kennedy held a grudge that he brought with him to the Democratic convention in Los Angeles in 1960. He loathed the very idea of him, especially on the ticket. As JFK shuttled between Johnson's suite and his own, trying to convince the Senate majority leader to be his

vice president, Bobby did everything possible to prevent the consummation of that political union.[11] Frustrated by the uncertainty this was causing,
Johnson eventually called John Kennedy and insisted on confirmation that
he would be on the ticket. JFK gave him this assurance, but Johnson never
forgot that Robert Kennedy had put him in that awkward position.[12]

The feud between LBJ and RFK grew worse throughout the Kennedy
presidency and continued on through Johnson's presidency. Joseph A.
Califano, who served as Johnson's top domestic policy advisor, writes that
"LBJ saw Robert Kennedy as ruthless, ambitious, positioning himself as
the heir apparent, feeding on any available discontent among the dismayed
and baffled citizens who thought the country was coming apart at the
seams, and horrified that Johnson was sitting in his brother's chair."[13] Robert Kennedy was relentless in his hatred of Johnson, who as vice president
lacked any real constituency inside the administration. The tension wore
him down, and to those who knew Vice President Johnson it was painful
to see him as a broken man. Henry Kissinger remembered, "He was being
treated with great aloofness" and he could see Johnson trying to exercise
"restraint" when he was "clearly agitated."[14] This proved too difficult a task
and throughout Kennedy's presidency (and even into his own), LBJ let his
frustration get the better of him, at times exploding either at RFK or about
him to others. According to Eric Goldman, who served as a special consultant to LBJ from 1963 until 1966, "Robert Kennedy commanded more attention and consumed more energy and raw emotion than any other single
concern of state that the new President confronted after Dallas."[15]

Given the power Johnson wielded as Senate majority leader, it is hard to
believe he could have made such a significant miscalculation by taking the
vice presidency, although statistically there was a 20 percent chance of the
president dying in office. But he believed that "power is where power goes,"[16]
and as Doris Kearns Goodwin writes, "Johnson believed he could carry his
powers with him. Give him time, and he would make the vice-presidency
powerful." Furthermore, he still harbored presidential ambitions and the
"vice-presidency was a way of shedding his regional image once and for all."[17]

When President Kennedy dispatched Johnson to Vietnam in May
1961, Robert Kennedy sent their brother-in-law, Steve Smith, as a minder.
From the president's perspective, there was a substantive purpose to this
trip. Kennedy had sent a letter to the South Vietnamese president the previous month that had gone unanswered. He hoped Johnson could force a

response to collaborate "in a series of joint, mutually supporting actions in the military, political, economic and other fields in the struggle against Communist aggression."[18]

When Johnson met with President Ngo Dinh Diem, he explained that the "letter represents President's thoughts on what might be done about situation in Viet-Nam and offers basis for what US role might be in cooperation with GVN [Government of Vietnam]."[19] Diem responded point by point and agreed to respond with a letter and a joint communiqué. Johnson urged Diem to include "his views on additional assistance which he feels Viet-Nam will really need to stem Communist tide in this country" and he suggested he make "reference to [the] possible one hundred thousand increase in armed forces (over 20 thousand increase already agreed to) and measures of economic and social aid."[20]

Johnson did his job and by all accounts he did it well. But despite his effort, his trip became an international joke. Some of this was of his own making and some could be linked to his detractors. He knew how to mix with political crowds in the United States. To the Asians, he was a fish out of water. As the motorcade made its way through Saigon, he repeatedly forced the driver to stop, so that he could give South Vietnamese children free passes to the U.S. Senate. He seemed tone-deaf to the fact that they lacked any understanding of what the U.S. Senate was, let alone the economic means to ever travel outside of their country. He compared Diem to Winston Churchill, asked photographers to capture him chasing a herd of cattle around one of the suburbs, and subjected foreign reporters to watching him get naked, dry off, and change his clothes after a hot shower.[21] In Karachi, Pakistan, he encountered a camel driver named Bashir Ahmed, whom he invited to come visit him in America. Ahmed took Johnson up on the offer.

The NBC reporter Tom Brokaw shared a conversation with Smith, in which the latter recalled that Johnson had a whole huddle of girlfriends— "babes," Smith called them—around him in the evenings. At the end of the trip, LBJ summoned Smith to his hotel suite, where, surrounded by a bunch of women and with a huge drink in his hand, he told Steve, "You go tell your brother-in-law that I behaved just fine over here."[22]

These are the stories that dominated Johnson's tenure as vice president. It was a missed opportunity for the Kennedy administration, who might have deployed him to advance their legislation. But the Kennedys showed no interest. Instead, "once he got into office," former vice president Dick Cheney observed, "the thing you remember about Johnson is going to [Pakistan] and bringing back some camel driver. . . . This guy is one of the greatest legislative geniuses we ever had in the White House. They didn't use him. That's another reason why it is a bad job to be vice president."[23]

Johnson's power evaporated with each day he served as vice president and with no future as president of the United States. He was almost certainly going to be dropped from the ticket in 1964, although not because of Robert Kennedy's animosity toward him. He was at the heart of a Senate investigation that was about to destroy him.

At the center of this scandal was Bobby Baker from Pickens, South Carolina, who had risen from a Democratic page to become secretary and trusted advisor to Johnson when he was Senate majority leader. In this role, Baker enjoyed an "incredible mingling of high office, high influence, and high living" as he worked diligently for Johnson in "marshaling votes, handling campaign funds," and playing the role of a fixer. According to *Life* magazine, he was a messenger, a pleader of causes, a fundraiser, source of intelligence, and became so indispensable to Johnson that he earned the nickname "Lyndon's boy."[24]

There was nothing wrong with having such a trusted confidant, except for the fact that a lot of what Baker did was illegal and implicated his former boss, the vice president. It was a vending machine company that he had established in 1962 that was the initial source of scandal. In an explosive cover story on November 8, 1963, *Life* revealed the "Bobby Baker bombshell," reporting how the super-aide was forced to resign after finding himself engulfed in a $300,000 lawsuit that credibly accused him of exerting his influence to stack defense plants with vending machines from his own company.[25]

The lawsuit resulted in a barrage of scrutiny. Baker had purchased and moved his family to a $124,500 home a few steps from LBJ's residence in Washington. He had bought a $28,000 townhouse for Carole Tyler, who was his stunning blond secretary. He frequented the Quorum Club, where lobbyists and legislators went to mingle and exchange influence for money and sexual favors. Mixed up in all of this was a German call girl named Elly Rometsch, the wife of an airman posted to the West German military mission in Washington[26] who knew both Baker and Tyler. Finally, he had taken a 50 percent stake in the Carousel Motel and Nightclub in Ocean

City, Maryland, where on July 22, 1962, he brought in buses of celebrities and glamorous women for the grand opening.[27]

Life asked the question, "How had a simple, hardworking majority secretary, earning $19,612 a year, struck it so rich in so short a time?" The underlining question was how Baker could strike it rich without implicating Lyndon Johnson. The Senate Rules Committee, chaired by Democrat of North Carolina B. Everett Jordan, suggested that the Baker affair "is a reflection on something in the Senate."[28]

Had Kennedy not been shot and the corruption investigation gone forward, Johnson would have almost certainly been gone because they had enough evidence to bring him down, he had no advocates within the administration, and it would have been hard for him to stay on the ticket. He later claimed, in one of the now available LBJ tapes, that it was "pretty definite" that Robert Kennedy was behind the Bobby Baker breadcrumbs.[29] At the time, CBS was tracking the Bobby Baker case very closely and they may have even had the dossier, but after Kennedy's assassination they either moved on or made a deliberate decision to drop the story. Even without knowing the details of what they had or didn't have, there should be little doubt that LBJ's unexpected ascension to the presidency essentially exonerated him from his role in the Baker misdoings. Given the stakes, this was tantamount to LBJ getting the equivalent of a pardon because of the mood of the country and his ascension to the presidency.[30]

More important, however, is the fact that had either CBS or Time Life published the story the following week as planned, Johnson would have almost certainly been forced to resign. Following the Presidential Succession Act of 1947, signed into law by Harry Truman, the order of succession was vice president, followed by speaker of the house. With Johnson's ascension to the presidency, the vice presidency remained vacant until the election of 1964 catapulted Hubert Humphrey into the role on January 20, 1965. Therefore, had the dossier been published and the investigation continued, the next in line would have been John W. McCormack, a Democrat from Boston who had assumed the speakership following the death of Sam Rayburn.

In today's world of social media, it would be impossible to keep such information a secret. In 1963 the country had just gone through such a head-snapping transition that nobody including the media had the stomach for a presidential scandal. With Kennedy's assassination, you had a "cool, elegant, Ivy League, attractive family from Massachusetts with their distinctive style and all the people it attracted," recalled Brokaw, and then, "suddenly we do a 180 and we get the outsized Texan with his not much of a feel for language, including when he stepped off the plane at Andrews [Air Force Base]."[31]

Johnson handled the transition in a strategic manner. He understood the importance of showing unity with the Kennedy team. He understood the importance of having Jackie Kennedy in the picture while he took the oath of office on the plane two hours and eight minutes after JFK's assassination. He approached his early days with humility and deference to his predecessor. In an effort to compensate for oratory skills that he knew to be inferior to those of his predecessor, he choreographed the gestures and tone of his early speeches, particularly during his first address to Congress. All of this was masterly theatrics. He worked the phones, drank with old colleagues, and did what he did best, which was playing the politics.

Civil Rights

The election of John F. Kennedy felt like a euphoric moment for black America. African Americans heard Kennedy pay lip service to civil rights and they believed he was serious. "The Kennedys had not just said segregation was illegal, they said it was immoral," Jesse Jackson recalled. "It was the first time I ever heard a prominent white politician say that segregation was an abomination. That was a big deal."[32] Many in the black community were ready to put all of their hopes and faith in Kennedy.

It didn't take long for civil rights leaders to begin questioning how serious the Kennedys were about effecting change. They had heard JFK say the right things, but when tested, he proved unwilling to act. Nowhere was this more obvious than on September 15, 1963, when members of the Ku Klux Klan rigged Birmingham's 16th Street Baptist Church with dynamite and killed four young girls, injuring many others.[33] The next day, President Kennedy said, "If these cruel and tragic events can only awaken that city and state—if they can only awaken this entire nation to a realization of the folly of racial injustice and hatred and violence, then it is not too late for all concerned to unite in steps toward peaceful progress before more lives are lost." Former secretary of state Condoleezza Rice, who grew up in Birmingham and remembers that day well, describes how there were some skeptics who thought Kennedy was prepared to talk about civil rights, but it was unclear if he could actually do anything. His reaction to the bombing proved to be "great words," but the assassination precluded this from happening.[34]

The Kennedy courtship of black America was an extraordinary deception. The black community had put their hopes in the Kennedys not unaware of the emptiness of Kennedy's promises, which would not be fully appreciated until long after his death. Instead, JFK's assassination terrified black America. In addition to the same sorrow and fear felt throughout the country, there was an even more daunting reality that they were now stuck with Lyndon Johnson. For Jesse Jackson, Kennedy's death was a critical inflection point in the civil rights movement. He remembers walking across campus at North Carolina A&T and hearing it on the radio. "I couldn't believe it," he remembered. "Presidents didn't get killed. Lincoln had been killed, but that was so long ago. I felt like there were two assassinations, Kennedy and civil rights. I would eventually realize that I was wrong."[35]

When Kennedy died, standing in his place was Lyndon Johnson, who was a southerner who used the "N" word with advisors and friends and who as President Barack Obama later pointed out opposed every piece of civil rights legislation during his first twenty years in Congress and "once call[ed] the push for federal legislation a farce and a sham."[36] Johnson mixed with a segregationist crowd and as we learned from the release of declassified documents from the Kennedy assassination, he may have been a "member of the [Ku Klux] Klan in Texas during the early days of his political career,"[37] although if true, this was probably driven by political opportunism. As Senate majority leader, Johnson in 1957 told President Dwight Eisenhower he would not introduce the civil rights bill in its current form, as it would fracture the Democratic Party. A version of the bill was eventually introduced and it did pass, but Johnson made sure to slice and dice it to such an extent that he could tell his segregationist colleagues in the South—many of whom he would need when he made his 1960 run for the presidency—that the bill had no teeth and they need not worry. At the same time, he felt the bill gave him the credential to tell civil rights leaders that he was trying and show northerners that he was more than just a southerner.

Kennedy was more cautious on civil rights than Johnson proved to be. Henry Kissinger, who knew Jack Kennedy and found him "extremely charming," observed that he lacked the decisiveness of his brother Robert, or Johnson.[38] Robert was seen by some as the stronger-willed brother, but when it came to civil rights, he was, as Tom Brokaw observed, "a kind of hard-ass younger brother and very unsentimental about civil rights."[39] Robert Kennedy acknowledged this in *His Own Words*, when reflecting on his circumvention of Harris Wofford, who President Kennedy had appointed as special assistant for civil rights. "I didn't want to have someone in the Civil Rights Division who was dealing not from fact but was dealing from emotion and who wasn't going to give what was in the best interest of President Kennedy . . . but advice which the particular individual felt was in the interest of a Negro or a group of Negroes or a group of those who were interested in civil rights," he wrote.[40] He would later make what Tom Brokaw described as "one of the greatest transitions of any national politician" and become a staunch defender of civil rights, but he had reservations about getting too much in Dr. King's embrace with the 1964 election coming up.[41] While this was a political decision, it may have been reinforced by another more personal factor. We know from declassified JFK files that there may have been some credence to rumors that RFK had made a deal with FBI chief J. Edgar Hoover to target Dr. King in exchange for burying some damaging information about the president,[42] which may have included his affair with Marilyn Monroe.

As president, Lyndon Johnson made such an extraordinary transition that even today many people are baffled. Getting the 1964, 1965, and 1968 Civil Rights Acts passed was something that only he could do. There are theories about Johnson's transition, including his biographer Robert Caro's suggestion that growing up an underdog, Johnson came to identify with the civil rights movement. Johnson's transition was likely driven by political pragmatism. This was not unlike Andrew Johnson's transition one hundred years earlier, only this time around the president was on the right side of history.

In that sense, his transition was a strategic move by a pragmatic politician who understood the changing mood of the country. As colleagues witnessed his shift, they concluded that one of two things had happened: Either he had had a personal transformation, or the pragmatism of the moment had awakened him to the reality that the country was about to explode and unless he did something to stop it, the consequences would be on his watch.[43]

It's also likely that President Johnson believed only he could do it. He had the relationships, the understanding of Congress, and legislative savvy. Over the years Johnson had accumulated a prodigious amount of political capital and held a strong belief that if you do the first favor for your colleague, they are indebted to you for life. As Senate majority leader and minority whip, Johnson had taken care of a lot of legislators and he expected them to rally behind him. With civil rights, he chose to cash in his chips. The job was still tough—he had to rely on Everett Dirksen, Senate minority leader from Illinois, to get the bill passed, for example—but as he gamed it out, he could see a path forward.[44]

Second, and more superficially, LBJ had the right pedigree, a white southerner from Texas who had been a segregationist.[45] George H. W. Bush told me the reason why only Johnson could have passed civil rights in the 1960s: "You had a southern president calling his former Senate colleagues in the South, and in that wonderful Texas drawl of his, telling them to do the right thing," he said. "JFK's Boston twang would not have had the same effect. LBJ knew how to push."[46]

Third, Johnson was tough, even ruthless in deal making. He was willing to take on the southern establishment, work the phones, threaten, cajole, extort, whatever he needed to do. James Gaither, who had been a staff assistant for legislative affairs in Johnson's White House and a frequent note taker in meetings, described a recurring process that was relayed to me by Condoleezza Rice:

The way [Jim] tells it is every week the legislative director would say you don't have the votes Mr. President. Next week, you still don't have the votes Mr. President. Finally, Johnson walked in one day and said, "Son, I've got the votes. Everett Dirksen is going to vote for this thing and don't you ask why." You know, that was Johnson. He was tough with the Congress. He would threaten people. I don't think of that as Kennedy's strength, certainly, not with the southern Democrats.[47]

A fourth reason for his success on civil rights is that, unlike Kennedy, he needed the Civil Rights Acts to prove he could make the impossible happen and show that he "wasn't the bumpkin from Texas that everyone—the antithesis in some ways of John F. Kennedy—thought him to be," as Condoleezza Rice puts it. That meant he was going to push harder and achieve more than anybody believed could be done.[48]

Finally, Johnson understood how to find the balance between the aspirations and needs of the civil rights community and segregationists. "[Kennedy] would go to Harlem and kiss a black baby because that's what good liberals did," recalled Jesse Jackson. "But Johnson launched his campaign in Appalachia, where the poor, racist white people were. He understood that you needed to bring them along."[49]

Johnson worked with the civil rights leaders, but he had strong opinions of his own and he didn't necessary listen to them. When he expressed willingness to put a black man on the Supreme Court, the leadership wanted William Hastie, who had been governor of the U.S. Virgin Islands before sitting on the U.S. Court of Appeals for the Third Circuit. Hastie had gone to Amherst and Harvard, he was fair-skinned, and he spoke well. Johnson said, "If I'm going to appoint a nigger I'm going to get one that has a record of helping poor black people." He chose Thurgood Marshall, who was a descendant of slaves, had gone to Howard University for law school, which was a historically black college, and grew up in a modest background.[50]

If these were the qualities that uniquely positioned Johnson to lead on civil rights, it was the 1964 presidential election that gave him the political opportunity to make his first big legislative bet with the Civil Rights Act of 1964. It was a bold move that paid off, and on the evening of July 2, 1964, he signed it into law. Recalling the founding fathers and their call for each generation to fight for, renew, and enlarge the meaning of freedom, Johnson told the nation that "now our generation of Americans has been called on to continue the unending search for justice within our own borders." This act of legislation, he said, will make it so "those who are equal before God" can "now also be equal in the polling booths, in the classrooms, in the factories, and in hotels, restaurants, movie theaters, and other places that provide service to the public."[51] Upon accepting his party's nomination on August 27, he said, "I ask the American people for a mandate—not to preside over a finished program—not just to keep things going, I ask the American people for a mandate to begin."[52]

Despite the fact that Johnson had taken on such a polarizing issue, his legislative success emboldened him as he sailed to a landslide victory in the 1964 presidential election, the greatest validation of his political career. This enabled him to throw his weight around on Capitol Hill, something that would be required to get additional legislation passed. He cautioned Senators Al Gore of Tennessee, William Fulbright of Arkansas, and Robert Byrd of West Virginia that if you can't vote for civil rights legislation and you can't support it, don't get on the floor and start speaking against it. Neither Gore nor Byrd heeded his advice.[53]

The sequencing of the legislation was important. Johnson knew that starting with voting rights would risk the entire project, but if he could build pre-election momentum, win in 1964 in his own right, he could go for the big push. This is what he did and it required patience from civil rights leaders. But they saw from the 1964 act that Johnson was dead serious about this agenda. Passing the law was one thing, but implementing it was another and Johnson was ready to do this.

For many in the black community, the 1964 Civil Rights Act was *the* seminal moment when they realized the president was serious. They had seen his support for the 1957 bill for what it was, a token piece of legislation that paid lip service to civil rights, but had no real teeth. But the 1964 act was a big deal and risky for Johnson. Kennedy's shadow lingered over him and this was a gamble for a man who hadn't yet been elected in his own right. The fact that he had to fight so hard made it meaningful.

If Johnson was prepared to go further than the 1964 Civil Rights Act, the Selma-to-Montgomery marches of 1965 pushed him over the edge. The incidents leading up to the marches—the bombing of a church in Birmingham and the city's Sheriff Bull Connor allowing beatings on the street—all of this had an effect on President Johnson. When Alabama police attacked nonviolent activists marching on the Edmund Pettus Bridge on March 7, he knew things had reached a breaking point.

On March 15, Johnson addressed a joint session of Congress and pleaded with legislators to introduce and pass the voting rights bill. It was a dramatic speech and an extraordinary plea by a president of the United States. He was staring calamity in the face. This was tantamount to the Civil War and Appomattox,[54] he told Congress, and cautioned that time was running out.

As the president nudged Congress, he escalated his rhetoric. His June 4, 1965, commencement address at Howard University was a powerful defense of civil rights. "It is not enough just to open the gates of opportunity," he told the students. "All our citizens must have the ability to walk through those gates. . . . This is the next and the more profound stage of the battle for civil rights. We seek not just freedom but opportunity. We seek not just legal equity but human ability, not just equality as a right and a theory but equality as a fact and equality as a result."[55] For Jesse Jackson, this speech marked a turning point. "I'd never heard anyone so comprehensively describe the civil rights situation," he said, "and at that point it was clear that Johnson would deliver.[56]

Within two months, Congress passed the Voting Rights Act, and in his second term Johnson signed into law the Fair Housing Act, which together with the 1964 legislation changed the country forever. The three pieces of legislation addressed a number of gaps in the Thirteenth, Fourteenth, and Fifteenth[*] Amendments, which Congress had proven unwilling and unable to enforce. Whether Johnson was driven by concern for his legacy or change of heart is irrelevant. He was a creature of the Senate and was used to strong-arming southerners. He looked at the Civil Rights Act and Voting Rights Act and saw them both as something he could accomplish. He knew how to get there because he knew the Senate. The tradecraft was familiar and involved morally blackmailing legislators, exploiting his detailed knowledge of congressional rules and procedures, and cutting deals. This was his comfort zone and he was uniquely positioned to deliver. But foreign policy was a different matter altogether.

The Slippery Slope

LBJ was not the first president to inherit prodigious foreign policy challenges from a larger-than-life figure. Harry Truman had written the playbook on this and in the face of almost universally low expectations, he rose to the occasion. He had impossible shoes to fill, but he had the right team around him. George Marshall, who served as secretary of state and later secretary of defense, and Dean Acheson, a top official at the state department who succeeded Marshall as secretary of state—to name a few—had been Roosevelt men, who despite knowing that Truman would eventually become president had hardly given him any thought. They had almost nothing in common with the new president. These men were mostly

---

[*] Ratified on March 30, 1870, the Fifteenth Amendment stated that the "right of citizens of the United States to vote shall not be denied or abridged by the United States or by any state on account of race, color, or previous condition of servitude." (Library of Congress)

wealthy and Waspy, Ivy League Europeanists, while Truman was a paro-chial party boss with an "I'm from Missouri and aw shucks" attitude that at times could seem provincial. He was hardly known outside his local party circles, had a national profile on par with that of Calvin Coolidge before he was president, and his views of the world were largely unknown. He never had presidential aspirations and the vice presidency was an un-expected elevation.

FDR was revered by his advisors and they preferred to think of him as immortal, rather than acknowledge the reality that he was dying. When he died eleven weeks into his fourth term, this group of loyal Europeanists sought to carry out Roosevelt's vision with Truman as their like-minded new chief executive. These were men who wanted to save Europe, which required Truman to be successful. The new president knew very little about foreign policy, but he was a patriot and shared their vision. This alignment meant that he trusted their advice and listened to them, while they put faith in his ability to learn fast and lead. They didn't waste time questioning whether he could sit with Stalin, manage Churchill, or make the big deci-sions. They helped him do it, which is part of why he proved so decisive. When they advised him to leave the postwar future of Japan to General Douglas MacArthur, he adhered. When they urged him to focus his at-tention on Europe, he followed their advice. When they explained that the atomic bomb could save more than a million American lives, he trusted their motives. He made some of his biggest decisions in just the first nine months, which reinforced trust and confidence. In this sense, Truman was lucky, since they guided him well and were all in it for the long haul.

Truman was dealt an undeniably good hand on foreign policy, but he should still be credited for his cabinet savvy. He found Edward Stettinius unimaginative as secretary of state and lacking in fresh ideas, but under-stood that he was cooperative and should be kept on the team, but moved to New York, where he could make a good first United Nations ambas-sador. When Henry Stimson retired as secretary of war, Truman replaced him with Robert P. Patterson, a federal judge and FDR's undersecretary of war, who was more than up to the job and left an indelible mark on the U.S. military, including the desegregation of the armed forces. This astute-ness is made all the more impressive when considering his willingness to toss out several members of the cabinet—and staunch Roosevelt men—whom he thought ill fitted for his administration on the domestic front.

Henry Morgenthau, the secretary of the treasury and first Jewish cabinet official, was pushed out before the war even ended when he threatened to resign if Truman didn't bring him to Potsdam. Truman thought him a "block head, nut" and "wonder[ed] why FDR kept him around." By late June 1945, he solicited resignations from Attorney General Francis Biddle, Labor Secretary Frances Perkins, Secretary of Agriculture Claude Wickard, and Postmaster General Frank Walker. By the fall of 1946, Truman had rid himself of two thorns in his side: Secretary of Commerce Henry Wallace and Secretary of the Interior Harold Ickes, whom he viewed as completely disloyal, describing the latter as willing to cut his throat for "his high minded ideas of a headline."[57]

Lyndon Johnson inherited a very different hand and his fatal flaw was not recognizing this. Truman's approach wouldn't work with Kennedy's particular cabal of advisors and the Vietnam War context. Had he known how poorly they would advise him, he may have reconsidered keeping them. The vice presidency was a low point for him, a protracted reminder that his rambunctious personality and southern ways didn't fit with the Kennedy crowd. When he did opine on foreign policy as vice president, he appeared churlish, such as during a private briefing that CIA director John A. McCone had provided him on the Cuban Missile Crisis at the president's request. During the briefing, which McCone recorded in a memorandum of conversation, Johnson foolishly suggested that the U.S. conduct "an unannounced [air] strike [on Cuba] rather than the agreed plan [of a naval blockade]."[58] When he became president, the personality differences with Kennedy's advisors would not have been an issue if the men he inherited wanted the same thing, or if there had been no animosity between them. But Johnson was surrounded by people who were hostile and still wrapped up in his predecessor. They didn't want him to succeed and some were deeply resentful.

Nobody harbored these sentiments more than Robert Kennedy and as nasty as their feud became, his animosity could be pegged to resentment that Johnson was sitting in his brother's chair, rather than intellectual disparity. But Arthur Schlesinger, the famed presidential historian and special assistant to President Kennedy, absolutely loathed Johnson and this was more damning because he was seen as the intellectual among the intellectuals. The animosity dated back several years, when Johnson was Senate majority leader and the Harvard historian had written an article criticizing his strategy for the 1958 midterm elections. The article drew Johnson's ire and resulted in a volatile exchange of letters. Following Kennedy's assassination, LBJ tried to convince Schlesinger to stay on. It was particularly damning when he resigned less than two months after Johnson became president so that he could write the definitive history of the JFK administration.[59] Written from Schlesinger's vantage point, Johnson could likely assume that he would feature as a loathsome character in this narrative and that the comparison between the administrations would be less than flattering.

The love affair between New England intellectuals and Kennedy baffled Johnson, who saw himself as a master of the Senate. "It was the goddamndest thing," he later told Doris Kearns Goodwin. "Here was a young whippersnapper, malaria-ridden and yallah, sickly, sickly. He never said a word of importance in the Senate and never did a thing . . . somehow, with his books and his Pulitzer Prizes, he managed to create the image of himself as a shining intellectual, a youthful leader who could change the face of the country."[60]

Beyond Schlesinger and Robert Kennedy, the Kennedy men who stayed on and actually showed up for work were intimidating. This was particularly the case in areas where his time in the Senate had proven unhelpful, mostly foreign policy. He had a basic insecurity when he came up against men like Robert McNamara and McGeorge and William Bundy. At times this led him to brash actions like repeatedly threatening to fire them and creating a culture of fear, whereby various secretaries and generals were reluctant to share bad news. This kind of schizophrenic behavior deepened tensions within his own staff.

When taken out of a familiar social environment, Johnson struggled to assert himself in meaningful ways on foreign policy, particularly when it came to high-brow elites talking about world affairs. In the rare instances when he did, he stayed in his legislative comfort zone. These matters were often trivial, such as a foreign aid bill calling for provisions to finance the sale of surplus wheat to the Soviet Union,[61] but they offered him an opportunity to strut his stuff. When it came to the most serious foreign policy matters, he was out of his league and isolated by men who by the end of his administration knew Vietnam was lost and were already trying to extricate themselves by landing cushy jobs outside government. McGeorge Bundy was busy setting up a gig running the Ford Foundation, while McNamara eventually positioned himself for the World Bank. Johnson didn't have that option. He was buffeted by Vietnam and knew that whatever the outcome, he would be stuck with it. Like a compulsive gambler trying for one more hand, Johnson placed bet on top of bet in a desperate attempt to turn things around.

LBJ was blinded by a mixture of admiration and intimidation from these men he called "the Harvards," who mocked him behind his back. He felt superior to them in political craft, but also felt he needed their ideas and content.[62] He didn't necessarily like them, and throughout his presidency he found them overbearing, dogmatic, and patronizing in different ways. But he felt that while he understood the politics, foreign policy was their world. He was impressed by Secretary of State Dean Rusk, a fellow southerner, who had gone to Oxford on a Rhodes Scholarship and run the prestigious Rockefeller Foundation. Johnson was equally impressed by National Security Advisor McGeorge Bundy, whose family had basically founded Harvard and who at thirty-four years old had become the youngest dean of faculty in the university's history. Secretary of Defense Robert McNamara was the biggest brainiac of the group. He had gone to Harvard Business School and taught there as a professor, later becoming president of the Ford Motor Company. Upon meeting him, LBJ was so wowed by his brilliance that he recalled almost being able to hear the "computers clicking away"[63] in his brain. The biographer Robert Dallek likens Johnson's initial "admiration for and trust in McNamara as almost worshipful,"[64] and Doris Kearns Goodwin recounts a 1974 interview with White House press secretary George Reedy in which he claimed LBJ copied McNamara's restaurant orders for weeks in some kind of venerative attempt to emulate the upper class.[65] Kissinger recalled LBJ summoning him to the White House on one occasion to ask how he could win over the Harvard intellectuals. Johnson was surprised when he explained that it couldn't be done. "You can build alliances with them," he proffered, but told him that there were fundamental cultural differences that couldn't be reconciled.[66]

None of these men respected President Johnson and he knew it. The constant affronts combined with his insecurity fueled his growing paranoia. As pressure on his presidency mounted, he began to see elite intellectual conspiracies all around him. He lashed out at the press, insisting the New York Times was "out to destroy him." He claimed Senator William Fulbright and others on the Hill were only giving him a hard time about

Vietnam because he didn't go to Harvard. When he saw his national security advisor on television standing with five professors, he threatened to fire him based on the fact that he hadn't been consulted. In May 1965, LBJ made his speechwriter Richard Goodwin—author of the president's famous "we shall overcome" speech in response to the violence in Selma that March—take any reference to nuclear disarmament out of a commemoration speech for the U.N. charter after he learned that RFK had referenced nonproliferation a few days before. His outbursts became so frequent and so toxic that Goodwin secretly consulted a psychiatrist, who indirectly diagnosed the president with paranoid disintegration.[67]

The truth is, they saw him as an unrefined, vulgar man who pissed in sinks, displayed his manhood, and took meetings from the toilet. In many cases, these men intellectually bullied LBJ, even if it was at times subtle and unspoken. McGeorge Bundy, for example, was a proliferator of memos to the president that read like a professor lecturing a mediocre student. They were as condescending as they were patronizing and drew the ire of Averell Harriman, the U.S. ambassador to Moscow, who told LBJ it is "vital for you to make clear that Bundy speaks as your assistant and not as the President."[68]

These men outsmarted LBJ, which exacerbated a preexisting complex about his intellectual inferiority. He knew they were better informed than he was, although several of them later would attempt to self-servingly revise this history and boast of Johnson's foreign policy experience in the Senate and as vice president. Johnson was already an impulsive figure and while he knew he couldn't play at the intellectual level of a Harvard graduate, he assumed that they couldn't be as decisive and wheel and deal at the level of a man who had been master of the Senate. Sam Rayburn shared this view and wrote to then vice president Johnson acknowledging that Kennedy's advisors "may be every bit as intelligent as you say but I'd feel a whole lot better about them if just one of them had run for sheriff once."[69] Johnson knew how to be a sheriff and this was the one card he felt he could play. It led to hasty decisions, particularly in Vietnam, where he reacted brashly to the information he was fed.

Johnson's other flaw was in approaching war like a legislator, constantly looking for the compromise course and failing to realize that wartime enemies will never conform. He looked for a compromise that was never there and as the former national security advisor and Vietnam scholar H. R. McMaster told me, "what Johnson wanted to do always overwhelmed what he needed to do in terms of the decision, and so with McNamara and others he really made it clear that he didn't want to entertain the full range of options. He wanted options that allowed him to escape the big decision that could alienate key constituencies and that would get in the way of reelection and civil rights legislation."[70]

It is easy to look back on history and ask why LBJ retained the Kennedy men, particularly when there was a historic precedent with Millard Fillmore sacking most of his predecessor's cabinet. But much like with Lincoln's choice of Johnson for vice president, the context of the moment makes critique more difficult. If we look at the other unexpected transitions of the twentieth century, FDR was old and tired when he died, Harding's death happened at a time when all anyone cared about was roaring with the twenties, and McKinley was replaced by a more youthful and vibrant Theodore Roosevelt. In the case of Kennedy, he was the youngest president ever elected, charismatic with a beautiful family, and then shot to death on live television, only to be followed by a similar fate for his accused assassin. The nation was wrapped up in his assassination and politically it would have been very difficult to deviate from any path other than perceived continuity of his legacy. It's also not clear whom Johnson would have brought in since he didn't really have his own foreign policy people. Presumably some would have been from his time in the Senate, which would have only added confusion into the mix.

Instead, LBJ tried to prove that he, too, could surround himself with intellectuals. He tasked a group of his own loyalists to figure it out. That informal search committee included George Reedy, a member of his 1960 campaign team whom LBJ appointed press secretary in March 1964; Bill Moyers, a top advisor who had been spokesperson for the Peace Corps and succeeded Reedy in July 1965; Abe Fortas, a talented lawyer he eventually placed on the Supreme Court in August 1965; Horace "Buzz" Busby,[71] a fellow Texan who served as deputy national security advisor; and Richard Nelson, who had served as a top aide to Johnson during his vice presidential years. After some deliberation, they recommended the president hire Nelson's former Princeton professor Eric Goldman, which is not surprising given Goldman's high opinion of his former student. Goldman later described Nelson as a "sharp-minded, energetic young man with an offbeat sense of humor and a full quotient of his generation's puzzlement about what to do with their lives."[72] Johnson, who had neither heard of nor met him, took their advice and, as Goldman remembers it, told him, "I badly need help—I badly need it. And I especially need the help of the best minds in the country."[73] Unable to resist his political urges, Johnson insisted that they should not be drawn from New England since he hoped this effort would counterbalance the Harvards, whom Goldman recalled him describing as "overbred smart alecks who live in Georgetown and think in Harvard."[74]

Goldman was handicapped from the start with a part-time role that was ambiguously defined. It didn't help that the press kept asking if he was the new Arthur Schlesinger, who was in such a league of his own that not even Johnson would dare draw such a comparison. Goldman got to work building Johnson's brain trust and unlike Kennedy, who brought the intellectuals into the administration, Johnson wanted an external brain trust that he could rely on for a range of policy issues, including international affairs. The real motivation, however, was to avoid feeling sub-Kennedy. Goldman fulfilled the task, convening meetings with the likes of John Kenneth Galbraith, Richard Hofstadter, Clinton Rossiter, Margaret Mead, and David Riesman,[75] but the group produced very few useful ideas and at times some of them were too busy to show up.

Despite LBJ's attempts to bolster his standing with outside intellectuals, he was stuck with the Harvards because he refused to extricate himself. "Without them I would have lost my link to John Kennedy," Doris Kearns Goodwin recorded Johnson as saying, and "without that I would have had absolutely no chance of gaining the support of the media or the Easterners or the intellectuals. And without that support I would have had absolutely no chance of governing the country."[76] He should have gotten rid of the Kennedy crowd, who perhaps in pursuit of their own agendas—or out of fear for how he would react to the truth—gave him misguided information about Vietnam. Lyndon Johnson lacked the courage he exhibited on civil rights, which is part of why he kept them. He was determined to be a great domestic president and foreign policy crises were an unfortunate reality that he had to address. At first this meant resisting further escalation and holding out for a peaceful settlement. But soon, fearing he would be the one to lose Vietnam, he escalated and then escalated further. The first U.S. Marines landed in Da Nang on March 8, 1965, a significant escalation from the advisors who had previously been deployed. By the end of the year there were 189,000 troops in Vietnam and two years later that number exceeded 500,000.

Johnson continued the escalation in Vietnam though he knew it was a mistake. He was trapped by Kennedy's legacy. Trapped by politics. Trapped by his advisors. Trapped by his own demons. Both Eisenhower and Kennedy had pledged to defend Vietnam from communism and each had taken the escalatory steps necessary to do so. If Johnson didn't do the same, how would he explain that he lost it? "Everything I knew about history," he later reflected in an interview with Doris Kearns Goodwin, "told me that if I got out of Vietnam and let Ho Chi Minh run through the streets of Saigon, I'd be doing exactly what they did before World War II. I'd be giving a big fat reward to aggression."[77]

In retrospect, this fear seems misguided. But for Johnson's generation this was a credible fear. Memories of Munich endured. He had lived through the failure of appeasement. He remembered how many had criticized Roosevelt for his delay in entering the war. Why did it take Pearl Harbor to drive the U.S. into the war? Johnson saw Vietnam as bigger than Ho Chi Minh. It was about the threat of communism, Soviet progress, and the big red arrow taking over the map. It was the Domino Theory.[78]

The prospect of losing Vietnam terrified him. He was overwhelmed by the contradiction, a war we couldn't win and a war we couldn't afford to lose. "If I don't go in now and they show later I should have gone then they will be all over me in Congress," he remarked. "They won't be talking about my civil rights bill, or education, or beautification. No sir. They'll be pushing Vietnam up my ass every time. Vietnam, Vietnam, Vietnam."[79]

It's also crucial to remember that the Kennedy team—McNamara, the two Bundy brothers, Walt Rostow, etc.—didn't really begin exiting the White House until 1966. Kennedy may have listened to different advisors or drawn alternative conclusions, but he would have received similar advice and information. Henry Kissinger, who by his admission was an outside consultant who "fleeted in and out," described Johnson as a president who "did everything that his advisors recommended grumbling. He escalated. He negotiated. So, the combination of escalation and over-eagerness to negotiate tended to frustrate each other and always gave the Vietnamese a feeling that if they hold on another year, we would collapse before they do. And they were right."[80] In this sense, Johnson felt a sense of impotent frustration and trapped by the Kennedy entourage, who compared him to his predecessor. By May 1964, he was well aware of how far he had gone down the rabbit hole. During a May 27 call with McGeorge Bundy to discuss a proposed mission to North Vietnam to be headed by the Canadian diplomat Blair Seaborn, Johnson lamented,

> I just stayed awake last night thinking of this thing, the more I think of it, I don't know what in the hell . . . it looks to me like we're gettin' into another Korea. It worries the hell out of me. . . . I don't think we can fight them 10,000 miles away from home and ever get anywhere in that area. I don't think it's worth fightin' for and I don't think we can get out. And it's just the biggest damned mess I ever saw. . . . What the hell is Vietnam worth to me? . . . What is it worth to this country?"[81]

He refused to pull the cord on Vietnam and as a result, Johnson's blunder has cast a dark shadow over his presidency, but Kennedy was as capable of plunging the U.S. into war in Southeast Asia. Both were foreign policy novices. Both were cold warriors who believed in the Domino Theory that if one country falls to communism, others will fall as well. The guardians of Kennedy's reputation, most notably Arthur Schlesinger, created a myth of withdrawal around 1963. They argue that he would not have put 500,000 troops into Vietnam. He is right that it was not in his nature to, especially when he understood the political ramifications of losing Vietnam in an election year. Robert McNamara famously recalled an October 2, 1963, meeting in which President Kennedy approved a recommendation to withdraw 1,000 men by December 31, although some historians have speculated that the reductions in 1963 were part of a troop rotation home and were meant to put pressure on South Vietnam to reform.[82]

Despite these assertions and recollections, Kennedy had accelerated the deployment of Americans into Vietnam. Before his death, he had already increased the number of American military advisors from around seven hundred to more than sixteen thousand, which far exceeded the cap on advisors established by the 1954 Geneva Accord.* He also grew the foreign aid package from $223 million to $471 million.

---

* Multiple secondary sources note the 1954 Geneva Accords allowed for a total of 685 U.S. military advisors in South Vietnam. The Pentagon Papers refer to the 685-man advisor team in

Another factor to consider is the South Vietnamese coup and subsequent assassination of its president, Ngo Dinh Diem, which the Kennedy administration backed just three weeks before JFK was killed. If Kennedy favored disengagement, why did he not do more to stop the Diem coup? In fact, by not making any decision on the fate of President Diem, Henry Cabot Lodge, who at the time served as ambassador to South Vietnam and was a harsh critic of Diem, found himself with a free hand to encourage the coup.

Kennedy didn't live long enough to experience the disastrous effects of Diem's assassination. But as Kissinger says, the circumstances could have pushed Kennedy to a point of no return. "It is even conceivable," he speculated, the "odd mixture [of] people who put [the troops into Vietnam] like McNamara and Bundy didn't actually want to win. They would have liked to win the war, but they thought there was a measured way that you could get to negotiations."[83]

Following the Diem coup, the Kennedy administration drafted planning documents for a strategy that would get all U.S. military personnel out of Vietnam by the end of 1965, unless there were "justified" exceptions. But we should be cautious in placing too much emphasis on these documents, particularly as the impact of the Diem coup had not yet played out. Having seen many presidential planning documents in both Bush administrations, Condoleezza Rice urges restraint in drawing conclusions from the November 20 documents.

"I wouldn't put one penny on John F. Kennedy's planning documents," she told me.

People write these planning documents, but then conditions change and they respond to the conditions. Kennedy took on the idea that the French and British withdrawal from Indochina was a threat to the United States in a way that Eisenhower never did, but

---

Saigon as the "complement"—meaning it was completely staffed—before going on to discuss the deployment of further advisors. The Geneva Accords consists of ten documents, and the limited advisor language doesn't appear in the final summary. Even with the cap, there were no signatories to the accords, and the U.S. didn't consider itself bound by them. Kenneth L. Sterner, "President Kennedy and the Escalation of the Vietnam War" (2015). History Capstone Research Papers: http://digitalcommons.cedarville.edu/history_capstones/1.

it's unclear whether it was Johnson's hubris or Kennedy's sanity that dictated policy in Vietnam.[84]

Had Kennedy survived, he may have tried to find some kind of negotiated settlement, but much as Truman found with Mao, he would not have found a willing party in Ho Chi Minh.

Vietnam was a very different context from the Cuban Missile Crisis, and what Kennedy failed to appreciate is that Ho Chi Minh and the Vietcong wanted total victory. It is impossible to know at what point down the path of escalation he would have realized this, or whether he would have escalated to push Ho Chi Minh to the bargaining table. But this, too, would have failed and we can certainly speculate that Kennedy would have been left with no choice but to escalate further.

Kennedy's advisors held on to this view well into the Johnson administration, which offers a counterfactual window into how they might have advised him had he not been assassinated. As H. R. McMaster explained, "The Bundy brothers approached the war, [also] John McNaughten, they approached this problem set based on the reasonable-man theory of English common law and the assumption that Ho Chi Minh would respond like the Englishman in common law. They didn't consider culture, context, or brain power toward developing a political strategy for the war."[85] His advisors underestimated the regenerative capacity of the Vietcong. What's worse, some of them argued for the antithesis of a wartime strategy, meaning they called for deliberate ambiguity over the wartime objectives. In their view, Johnson shouldn't be criticized for failing to achieve an objective that was not understood. Taking this narrative a step further, John McNaughton, who served as assistant secretary of defense and was a close advisor to Robert McNamara, argued in what became known as the "Good Doctor Memo" that the U.S. didn't have to achieve an objective, it just had to get bloodied and appear as a good doctor who tried to help the patient, even if the patient dies.[86]

Johnson is held responsible for the scale of Vietnam, but the escalation of troops was dictated by the "slippery slope" problem where we find ourselves in a situation without an endpoint. It was Kennedy who started down that path. If we look at the Diem coup, Kennedy would have faced the same dilemma as Johnson. The assassination of Diem committed the U.S. to Vietnam and that was his doing. "What were you supposed to do? Assassinate Diem, then put in a government that was never going to work, and then leave?" Rice asks. "I just think this was the inexorable pull of trying to find a place where Vietnam was stable and I think they both would have done it."[87]

Another factor that makes it difficult to contrast Kennedy and Johnson is the 1964 presidential election. The election politicized Vietnam in a way that made escalation easier to sell to the American people. Senator Barry Goldwater, who was the Republican nominee for president, accused the Democrats of being weak on communism in what was effectively a dare for Johnson to double down on Vietnam. This was not an outlandish position. Big strategic thinkers, Cold War experts, and policymakers of all stripes believed they were attempting to contain an inexorable communist movement led by the Soviet Union. Both Kennedy's and Johnson's mistakes have to be evaluated in the context of the mid-1960s. Kennedy can be criticized for starting the U.S. down the slope, but in his defense the Soviets had just threatened the United States with nuclear weapons ninety miles away in Cuba. The miscalculation, however, was taking the concept of containment, which had proven successful in Europe, and assuming it could be applied to the Asian context.

Some of the blame also rests with the 88th Congress. Democrats were in control of both the Senate and House. The Gulf of Tonkin Resolution, which passed on August 7, 1964, and gave Johnson a blank check to fight the war in Vietnam, is impossible to evaluate without considering the upcoming election. It's plausible that the Gulf of Tonkin Resolution was seen as a political weapon against conservative accusations that the Democrats were not serious about fighting communism.

As with civil rights, Johnson's landslide victory in 1964 gave him a mandate on Vietnam. But while he used that mandate to make the right decisions on civil rights, he floundered on Vietnam. By the end of the war, 58,220 American soldiers had lost their lives and more than 250,000 South Vietnamese had been killed. Herein lies one of the greatest foreign policy challenges faced by all presidents. Rice explains that "when you are in that situation, there are all the sunk costs and all the credibility issues policy-makers have to navigate." The legacy of Vietnam came up when the administration was in trouble in 2006 and 2007 in Iraq.[88] So as the memories of Munich were fresh for Johnson, the images of Vietnam lived on in the White House more than half a century later and still do.

It was Nixon who came into office promising to end the war in Vietnam, although at a horrific cost to some of its neighbors. Nixon had inherited a terrible hand with Vietnam and had no illusions about where he was. He decided that it was in the long-range interest of the United States to not be perceived as selling out an ally. In the early weeks and months of Nixon's administration, Kissinger was still trying to prove himself to the new president and by his own admission, "I wasn't established enough to fight the whole environment he had [around him]." When the process of Vietnamization started, he wrote Nixon a memorandum in which he said Vietnam will become like "salted peanuts. The more you eat, the more you want. And there will be no end to it." He outlined three options for how the administration could handle the deteriorating situation. The first was to just quit, which wasn't a real option. Beyond that they had two real options. The first was to slow the process, and the second, which was Kissinger's preference, was to "present an overall plan to the outer limit of what we could accept and if they rejected it to go all out. In other words, to do in 1969 what we finally did in 1972. The counter-argument against it was that we hadn't lined up the Soviet Union yet . . . We didn't even have a way of talking to China." As it turns out, Nixon was freaked out by the second option and feared that the peace movements throughout various cities—which Nixon had an unhealthy obsession over—would burn down buildings and cars in protest.[89]

The war had taken a bad turn by the time Nixon assumed the presidency; it was now all about how we get out. But during the ramp-up period, as Tom Brokaw recalls, "there were a lot of people who drank the Vietnam Kool-Aid who should have known better."[90]

═══

The tragedy for Johnson is that Vietnam overshadows his domestic achievements. The loss for the country is that had Vietnam not gone south, LBJ may have had another four years in office to continue advancing civil rights. Had this happened, he would have died just two days after leaving office in 1969. Most presidents go into office hoping to do great things. Sometimes circumstances or missteps make them do things that are not great, that are foolish or disastrous. We cannot diminish what Johnson did on the domestic side. He was a president who thought big about trying to change America. And some of it worked and some of it didn't. The part that worked left an indelible mark on the country that would be felt for decades to come.

January 30, 1835—the first assassination attempt on the president of the United States. A mentally ill painter named **Richard Lawrence** fired at Andrew Jackson, but the gun malfunctioned and the president beat him with his cane.

Richard Pavlick filled his Buick with explosives and planned to blow himself up and president-elect Kennedy. After seeing Jackie Kennedy standing in the doorway, he stuffed his pants with those same explosives and followed Kennedy to church.

On November 1, 1950, **Oscar Collazo** and **Griselio Torresola** stormed the Blair House and in the name of Puerto Rican nationalism attempted to kill President Truman. Torresola was shot and killed, while Collazo survived. Truman was upstairs and was unharmed, but the assassins killed a White House police officer named Leslie Coffelt.

John Hinckley, Jr., shot Ronald Reagan on March 30, 1981. Hinckley had become obsessed with Jodie Foster and believed that killing the president was the only way to get her attention. He was found not guilty by reason of insanity. Despite the seriousness of Reagan's injuries, the Twenty-fifth Amendment was not exercised.

CHAPTER TEN

Close Calls

O ctober 28, 2015, was a relatively inauspicious day. America was smack in the middle of presidential primaries and Dr. Ben Carson was the front-runner in the third Republican primary debate. The Saudi-led war in Yemen raged on and air strikes had just a few days earlier accidentally targeted and hit a Doctors Without Borders hospital. Israeli Defense Forces shot and killed two suspected Palestinian militants. The U.S. renewed its commitment to fight the Islamic State on the ground. For the twenty-fourth year in a row, the United Nations General Assembly passed resolutions condemning the U.S. embargo against Cuba. And the Kansas City Royals defeated the New York Mets in the fourteenth inning of the longest World Series game in American history. That day also marked the longest period in American history without losing a president in office—18,967 days to be precise—replacing the period between George Washington's first inauguration in 1789 and William Henry Harrison's death in 1841.

The fact that only eight presidents died in office is nothing short of a miracle. There were nineteen additional illnesses, assassination attempts, and accidents that could be deemed close calls. Serious illness alone could have accounted for as many as eight additional deaths, including the country's very first close call. In June 1813, James Madison fell seriously ill for three weeks, putting his life in jeopardy and leaving him unable to perform the duties of president.[1] As word spread and the president recovered in his Montpelier home, both houses of Congress engaged in lively discussions about the possibility of Madison's death and Vice President Elbridge Gerry's succession to the presidency.[2] On July 2, however, a letter from first lady Dolley Madison exaggerating the president's recovery put a halt to the discussions. Her bet paid off and by July 7, President Madison was able to engage in substantive matters, a week later he met with a Senate committee, and by October he was back to his old routine in the nation's capital. The only consequence from the three-week blackout period seems to have been Albert Gallatin's lingering appointment to be a member of the diplomatic delegation to the upcoming peace conference in Russia.[3]

Madison was not the only president to nearly die from illness while in office. James Polk died three months after his successor's inauguration, just narrowly escaping death in office. As previously mentioned, Andrew Johnson suffered a serious enough illness in May 1865 that the president pro tempore was put on notice.[4] Beginning in 1882, Chester Arthur battled a severe case of Bright's disease that weakened him during his final two years as president and killed him a few years after leaving office. In 1893, Grover Cleveland underwent a life-threatening surgery to remove a tumor in his mouth, which doctors secretly conducted on a yacht in choppy water and without notifying his vice president.[5] As discussed at length, FDR was more or less a dying man by the time he ran for a fourth term and Dwight Eisenhower suffered three medical emergencies from 1955 to 1956, including a heart attack. During his first episode in September 1955, he directed the cabinet to manage the affairs of state in his absence. The second incident in June 1956 led his cabinet to oppose a proposal related to the Aswan Dam that Eisenhower actually supported. And by the time he fell sick for a third time, he decided to draft a letter to his vice president Richard Nixon, outlining procedures to be followed if such a disability should occur.[6]

Of all the illnesses, however, Woodrow Wilson's deserves the most attention. In September 1919, Woodrow Wilson suffered a series of debilitating strokes that should have led to his resignation. For over a month, the president was so sick that he received no visitors and his wife, Edith Galt, and physician, Dr. Cary Grayson, essentially took over the affairs of state. Wilson had lost the ability to move significant portions of his face, and to obscure the handicap, he grew a mustache and beard for the first time in his life.[7] Wilson understood the seriousness of his own illness and told his physician, "My personal pride must not be allowed to stand in the way of my duty to the country. If I am only half efficient, I should turn the office over to the vice president. If it is going to take much time for me to recover my health and strength, the country cannot afford to wait for me."

When he asked Grayson for his opinion, however, the manipulative doctor convinced him that he would be fine.[8]

In addition to the eight near deaths by illness, there were an additional nine assassination attempts that could be considered close calls. The first credible attempt on a president's life occurred on January 30, 1835, when a mentally unstable man named Richard Lawrence attempted to kill Andrew Jackson. Following the funeral of a congressman,[9] Lawrence, a British painter, who believed he was King Richard III of England, stalked Jackson to the east portico of the Capitol, where he attempted to fire two shots. The humidity in the air caused the gun to malfunction twice, a stroke of good luck that scientists later put at having odds of 1 in 125,000.[10] Jackson quickly realized he was unscathed and proceeded to beat the assailant with his cane. Lawrence was apprehended, tried, and found not guilty by reason of insanity. He was committed to a mental institution in Washington, D.C., where he died in 1861. John Tyler, then a senator from Virginia, was present, but off to the side, as he felt unwell. He recalled hearing an explosion and then watching "the old General sprung at him like a tiger . . . and manifested as much fearlessness as one could possibly have done." When Tyler visited the White House the following day, he teased the president, "Why, Mr. President, when I looked at you yesterday while springing on that man with your cane, I could have taken you for a young man of twenty-five." Another future president, Millard Fillmore, "wrote to his law partner, 'the city is all in commotion at the outrageous attempt to assassinate the president.'"[11] Despite this close call, no subsequent discussions took place to explore what would have happened if the guns fired successfully.

More alarming is the fact that Jackson remained under threat throughout his presidency. Just one year later, Jackson began receiving death threats—probably the first of any president—"over his refusal to pardon two men." One letter, which read, "You damned old scoundrel . . . I will cut your throat while you are sleeping" and suggested that the president would be "burnt at the stake in Washington," was written by an actor named Junius Brutus Booth. Twenty-nine years later, his son John would be the first to assassinate a U.S. president.[12]

At the time of the assassination attempt, Martin Van Buren was Jackson's vice president. As Van Buren succeeded Jackson as president anyway, there is little need to speculate about his policy preferences. But there was not yet a Tyler precedent and therefore we can't be certain that Van Buren would have asserted himself as president in the way that John Tyler did. Had he taken the humble approach of an "Acting President," it would have set in motion a chain of events that would have impacted at least eight presidential transitions.

Recalling the plot to kill Andrew Johnson and the assassination attempt on Franklin Roosevelt as president-elect, the next serious incident occurred during the latter's third term. In 1943, Roosevelt once again came close to assassination when a thirty-eight-year-old named Walter Harold Best had decided to kill FDR and stalked him with a .38 caliber revolver. He had learned the president's movements and had at least three opportunities—November 6, 10, and 11—to take a shot at his open limousine while it shuttled the president between engagements.[13] Documentation from the FDR Library and captured in Mel Ayton's *Hunting the President* shows that the reconnaissance paid off as Best had multiple opportunities to take his shot: On November 6, the president's motorcade took him to Camp David, where he spent the night; on November 10, he traveled from the White House to National Airport to greet Cordell Hull, his secretary of state who had just returned from a trip abroad, coming back to the White House that afternoon; and on November 11, he laid a wreath at Arlington National Cemetery, returning later that morning and leaving again that evening for Quantico, where he boarded the USS *Potomac* for what was to be a lengthy journey to the Cairo and Tehran Conferences.[14] Best never fired his shot and was arrested on November 13. As was the case with FDR's illness the following year, a successful assassination would have made Henry Wallace president.

On November 1, 1950, two Puerto Rican nationalists, Oscar Collazo and Griselio Torresola, stormed Blair House—where the president resided while the White House underwent badly needed renovations—and made an attempt on Harry Truman's life, killing one Secret Service agent and injuring two others.[15] Truman poked his head out the upstairs window to see what was going on, at which point one of the guards yelled, "Get back!" He got dressed and went downstairs to see the commotion. The Secret Service chief said to him, "Mr. President, don't you know that when there's an Air Raid Alarm you don't run out and look up, you go for cover."[16] Truman, who had been taking a nap at the time, observed, "If they had waited about 10 minutes Mrs. Truman and I would have been walking down the front steps of Blair House and there's no telling what might have happened."[17] Had Truman been killed, Alben Barkley, who was seventy-six at the time and the oldest vice president in history, would have ascended to the presidency and completed Truman's term.

The next failed attempt was Richard Pavlick's plot to kill John F. Kennedy as president-elect. Pavlick, who was a disgruntled postal worker turned suicide bomber, was incensed by the Kennedy family. Throughout the 1960 presidential election, it was not uncommon for him to rant (with profanities and all) about Catholics or about how Joe Kennedy was trying to buy political influence for his family.[18] Kennedy's victory in 1960 pushed Pavlick over the edge and he decided to kill the president-elect.

Pavlick donated his land to the Spaulding Youth Center in Belmont, New Hampshire, and purchased ten sticks of dynamite, along with four large cans of gasoline, some detonators, and blasting caps. He threw it all in his 1950 green Buick and skipped town.[19] He spent the next month stalking Kennedy across the country, first at his family compound in Hyannis Port, where the Secret Service later discovered he had come within ten to twenty feet of Kennedy.[20] Wherever he went, he collected intelligence. He photographed the homes, made note of the security arrangements, and studied layouts of the churches that JFK attended.[21]

As he followed Kennedy from location to location, he sent ranting and ominous postcards back to his hometown post office in Belmont. Fortunately, these curious postcards caught the attention of Thomas Murphy, a thirty-four-year-old postal worker and father of six[22] who had worked with Pavlick and noticed the postmarks revealed a suspicious pattern that corresponded with the president-elect's movements.[23] Murphy might have missed the pattern had it not been for two previously suspicious activities that he managed to piece together. During one of their encounters, Pavlick made a passing reference to having gone to Hyannis Port. "[Pavlick] told me the Secret Service agents were stupid," Murphy later recalled. "At the time, I was busy and didn't pay attention. Later, I got to wondering why a man who was so opposed to Kennedy would make a trip to Hyannis Port to see him."[24] Then, just before leaving Belmont on his stalking tour, Pavlick told Murphy that he should tune in to the news as something big was going to happen.[25]

Once Murphy connected the dots, he alerted his superiors to what he had seen and on Friday, December 9, 1960, they passed the information to the Secret Service. The Secret Service took the matter seriously, particularly as they had been aware of some of the deep animosity that existed toward the Kennedys. It was in interviewing several people around Belmont that they learned Pavlick had purchased dynamite and other supplies associated with explosive devices.[26]

It's a good thing that Murphy sounded the alarm bells because Pavlick was not just some crazy person. He was hot on Kennedy's trail and had a clear intention and plan to kill him. After scouting the different locations, the aspiring assassin decided that the Kennedy estate on North Ocean Boulevard in West Palm Beach would be the perfect site for the murder. His plan was simple. Having studied Kennedy's movements, he knew that every Sunday the president-elect would get in his car and head to church. At that point, he would kill him in a suicide bomb attack by driving the dynamite-filled Buick into the side of Kennedy's vehicle, killing them both.

On December 10, he checked into a motel in the cheaper part of town, which, ironically, was very close to where Kennedy's own Secret Service detail was lodged. Then, right there in the parking lot in broad daylight, he transformed his car into a murder weapon.[27] The next day was a Sunday and Kennedy prepared to make his way to St. Edward Church for morning mass. The president-elect was not particularly religious, but knowing the discomfort many felt over his Catholicism, he understood the importance of at least being seen as active and thus made the effort to go in and out of church every Sunday.[28] That morning, Pavlick made his way to North Ocean Boulevard just before 10:00[29] and parked his car down the street. Dressed in a dark blue suit, he sat calmly in the driver's seat holding in his right hand[30] a homemade ignition switch that once flicked would detonate the ten sticks of dynamite he had rigged to the car. In case the dynamite was not enough to ensure death, he filled several cans of gasoline and strategically placed them throughout the car to amplify the explosion.[31] Had he known the president-elect's limousine was not bulletproof, he would have realized there was more than enough explosive power to penetrate the car's exterior.

He also had with him a suicide note, which was addressed to the "people of the United States" and explained that he intended to kill Kennedy because he believed he had "bought the Presidency." "It is hoped by my actions that a better country ... has resulted," the note read.[32] He had with him a second letter, which was an apology to any bystanders killed or hurt by his assassination attempt. That second note explained that had Kennedy not been elected president, he would instead have targeted Jimmy Hoffa, the president of the International Brotherhood of Teamsters union.[33]

As Pavlick stalked his prey, he caught a glimpse of Jackie Kennedy in the doorway. She had walked her husband out and brought Caroline and baby John to say goodbye. This was enough to deter the assassination, as Pavlick had no interest in killing a man in front of his wife and kids.[34] He'd simply wait another hour and "get him at the church."[35] After all, he had studied St. Edward, knew where Kennedy would sit, knew the locations of doors and the general layout. It would be a perfectly suitable location for murder.

He drove his Buick to the church and transferred some of the dynamite from his car to his pants pocket. Before leaving for the church, he reconfigured his bomb by attaching the detonator switch to a belt under the loose jacket he had on. At church, he sat quietly in the back but was behaving suspiciously enough for Secret Service agents to take note of him.[36] When Kennedy found his place in the pew, Pavlick stood up and began walking toward the president-elect. Agent Gerald Blaine, who had already spotted the strange character, took his arm by the elbow and gently pulled him back before escorting him out of the church.[37]

None of the agents followed him outside, where Pavlick waited patiently for Kennedy's exit. He stood ready with his hand in his pocket and a finger on the trigger, knowing full well that by taking the president's life he would also be taking his own. But when Kennedy came within six feet of him,[38] he failed to flip the switch, later citing the swarm of women and children.[39] Just as before, he wasn't frazzled. Kennedy was scheduled to leave town the next day and would return on the sixteenth. It was no big deal, he told himself; he'd do it the following week instead.[40]

As Pavlick got back in his car and closed the door, a still suspicious Agent Blaine made note of the registration number and notified the Palm Beach Police to run the details.[41] Despite the fact that the Secret Service had Pavlick's name and unbeknownst to them he had just aborted three assassination attempts within the span of just a few hours, the aspiring assassin remained on the loose. He continued to tail Kennedy over the next several days and witnesses later told authorities that they had seen

Pavlick's car parked on the street outside Kennedy's home on and off for several days, before and after the aborted attempt.[42] This is extraordinary given that the Secret Service was now actively tracking him. They had even delivered a warning message to local authorities to be on the lookout for a 1950 Buick with the license plate "B1606,"[43] yet it seemed to go unnoticed despite his loitering on Kennedy's street.

Pavlick was on the loose for four more days and so certain that he would fulfill the task that he never even bothered to remove the dynamite from his car. After a few days, the Secret Service discovered that Pavlick requested his mail be forwarded to the Palm Beach post office and acted quickly to position undercover agents behind the post office counter.[44] Having already let Pavlick get close to the president-elect on multiple occasions, the Secret Service wanted to avoid a scene and preferred not to panic the would-be assassin. Instead, they enlisted the help of the Palm Beach Police,[45] who on Thursday, December 15, 1960, pulled him over as he drove into Palm Beach via the Royal Poinciana Bridge.[46]

Following his arrest, Pavlick was denied legal representation and while formally charged and medically evaluated as competent, he was never put on trial.[47] Instead, he was thrown in a mental institution, where he remained until March 27, 1967. Upon his release, he returned to Belmont, where he wandered around unsupervised and threatened Murphy's family.[48]

The lack of judicial process was not a legal miscue; it was a cover-up. The Secret Service had failed to protect Kennedy, who by all accounts should have been dead. In a December 1965 interview with *Look* magazine, the retiring chief of the Secret Service, Urbanus E. Baughman, admitted, "I was appalled to discover how near Kennedy had been to death. . . . [It] ranks with the closest calls any President ever had."[49] He reiterated this in his memoir, *Secret Service Chief,* when he said, "The closeness of the call was appalling. . . . Hardly anybody realized just how near we came one bright December morning to losing our president-elect to a madman."[50]

It's not clear that Kennedy ever appreciated the seriousness of the threats against him. Instead, he complained to aides, Kenneth O'Donnell in particular, that the overbearing security was "excessive" and "making me uncomfortable. . . . Nobody is going to shoot me, so tell them to relax."[51] But they were anything but relaxed and the fact that Kennedy came so close to being murdered even before the inauguration put them on edge and on high alert.

Had Jackie not come to the door with the kids, or had there not been women and children around at the church, the history of our country might be very different. Pavlick had an unobstructed path to Kennedy in both instances and in the words of a shaken Secret Service chief, "enough dynamite to level a mountain."[52] So, despite the willingness of the outgoing chief to talk, the Secret Service had no interest in making a big deal about this. A trial would have revealed the truth and it was better to downplay the severity, even if it meant thwarting justice and eventually allowing a madman to roam free and torment the hero who had discovered his plot.

If Pavlick had been successful, the death of President-elect Kennedy would have presented a tricky constitutional challenge. The electors were scheduled to cast their ballots the Tuesday after Pavlick's arrest, which meant that technically JFK was not yet the president-elect, which also meant Lyndon Johnson was not officially the vice-president-elect.[53] Furthermore, Kennedy had been elected with a narrow margin—a virtual tie in the popular vote—so while electors would have most likely cast their ballots for Lyndon Johnson, they would not necessarily have been bound to do so. But Kennedy survived, the electors cast their ballots, and on January 20, 1961, he was inaugurated as the thirty-fifth president.

In 1975, two different women tried to kill President Gerald Ford, including one taking a shot at close to point-blank range. The first attempt, September 5, 1975, took place in Sacramento, California. President Ford had come to the state capital to keynote an annual breakfast of California's rich and powerful. The group enlisted the president as the surprise guest after Governor Jerry Brown—seen as an adversary of the elite—snubbed their invite. As crowds gathered outside the capitol waiting to catch a glimpse of the president or perhaps a handshake, a twenty-six-year-old Manson Family cult member named Lynette "Squeaky" Fromme found her way into the crowd. Hidden in a leg holster underneath her long red dress was a fully loaded M1911 that she intended to use on President Ford.

As the president appeared, she moved closer and when he stopped to work the rope line outside the capitol, she managed to fire her gun from just two feet away. At first it seemed the gun didn't go off and witnesses could hear Fromme yelling, "It didn't go off! It didn't go off!" But according to Dick Cheney, who at the time was Ford's deputy chief of staff, Secret Service agent Larry Buendorf lunged toward the assassin as she went to fire and managed to get his thumb between the hammer and the cartridge of her gun. There was a lot of confusion because the Secret Service had also tackled Ford to the ground and everyone was startled. But he hadn't been hit. When the Secret Service attempted to whisk him away, the president countermanded that order and insisted that he stay and continue with the visit. Fromme explained to law enforcement that the president's environmental policies had enraged her and that she had taken it upon herself to single-handedly save the redwood forest.[54]

Seventeen days later, Ford visited San Francisco, where the Secret Service had heightened security in response to the close call in Sacramento. "It was a particularly bad day," Cheney recalled. "The President had been out and spoken to the building trades in San Francisco, which was the same group that Reagan would later speak to in 1981 when the assassination attempt was made on him back in Washington." After he had spoken, he went back up to his room to rest. Once he was ready to leave, the plan was to take a freight elevator down to the garage and get in the motorcade. However, the president didn't realize that the freight elevator's doors opened vertically instead of horizontally and as he went to step out into the basement, the top door went up, but failed to stick and came down on the president's head. He fell to his knees in agonizing pain and the force of the elevator split his scalp open. The Secret Service took him back upstairs to get the bleeding stopped, bandaged him up, changed his clothes, and tried the exit again.[55]

The president got back in the elevator, which this time around opened correctly, and stepped downstairs to the ground floor. Then, just as he stepped outside, Sara Jane Moore took a shot at him but missed, partly because an ex-Marine named Oliver Sipple hit her arm and jostled the aim. Given that her gun fired from just forty feet away, this intervention likely saved the president's life. Moore was a radical who had already exhibited enough suspicious behavior to warrant her getting picked up the previous day by law enforcement. But there had been no indication of an assassination plot.

Had either assassination attempt been successful, the presidency would have passed to Nelson Rockefeller, who had a good relationship with Ford, but didn't get along much with his top advisors. But none of them thought much about succession before, during, or after either of the assassination attempts. As Cheney remembers, "it happened so fast you didn't have time to even think of transfer of power until it was all over with. If the president had been shot, then all of the sudden you would have been in a position where you've got to deal with that." At the time, Donald Rumsfeld was chief of staff and both he and Cheney used to alternate trips. In this instance, Cheney was manning the fort back in Washington and both assassination attempts happened so fast that they were over and done with and everyone moved on. "I really hadn't spent a lot of time" thinking about Rockefeller being a heartbeat away from the presidency, he explained. "We had been dealing with that set of issues ever since Nixon resigned and spent a lot of time [on] . . . how do you go from Nixon to Ford, not because he was shot, but because he had to resign." In that sense, the country was well prepared had either assassination attempt been successful. They had just been through it and they understood the process.[56]

It didn't take long for history's next close call. In 1980, a deranged loner named John Hinckley fell in love with Jodie Foster after seeing the movie *Taxi Driver*. After months of stalking, calling, and writing to no avail, Hinckley decided that killing the president was the key to her heart. He began following President Jimmy Carter that September, first to Dallas and then to Dayton, where he got close enough to shake the president's hand in what he viewed as a rehearsal for the main event. He traveled to Nashville on October 9, ready to kill Carter, but Reagan's success in the polls was making him lose interest in the current president. He aborted his mission and returned to the airport, where the security guards' X-ray machine discovered his guns. He was arrested, had his guns confiscated, and was fined $62.50.[57]

Reagan's victory the following month reinforced Hinckley's view that Carter was yesterday's news. If he wanted to get Jodie's attention, he would need to kill the current president. On March 29, 1981, he traveled to Washington and checked into the Park Century Hotel, which was on 18th Street, NW, two blocks west of the White House and not far from the Hilton on Connecticut Avenue where Reagan would be addressing a session of the AFL-CIO's building and construction trades department the next day.[58]

March 30 was assassination day and the first thing Hinckley did was write a letter to Jodie Foster. "There is a definite possibility that I will be killed in my attempt to get Reagan," he wrote her. "This letter is being written an hour before I leave for the Hilton Hotel. Jodie, I'm asking you to please look into your heart and at least give me the chance with this historical deed to gain your respect and love. I love you forever."[59] Making good on his promise, Hinckley fired six shots in two seconds, hitting President Reagan in the chest, injuring Secret Service agent Timothy McCarthy, Metropolitan Police officer Thomas Delahanty, and press secretary James Brady,[60] who was left partially paralyzed. Reagan was rushed to George Washington Hospital, where doctors performed a two-hour surgery to remove a .22 caliber bullet that had hit the president's seventh rib and penetrated his left lung.[61] He spent nearly two weeks in the hospital and made a full recovery.

The last of these credible assassination attempts took place in Tbilisi, Georgia, on May 10, 2005, when a Georgian terrorist named Vladimir Arutyunian tried to kill George W. Bush with a grenade that malfunctioned. The attack on President Bush reveals that even in the modern era, close calls come and go without a blip. When asked about it, neither Condoleezza Rice nor Dick Cheney had more than a brief recollection of the incident. "I remember the incident. I don't remember where I was," Cheney told me. "I don't recall any sense of crisis, or gee that was a close call. . . . The president moved on and we had all moved on. It's a little bit like that Squeaky Fromme thing." Rice had a similarly understated recollection, explaining, "I gather it was pretty serious, but I actually didn't know and I don't think the president knew until we were back in the car." More etched in her mind was the post-9/11 moment when George W. Bush threw out the first pitch at the 2001 World Series. "I was just scared and I thought, I know he is wearing a bulletproof vest, but what if someone just shoots him."[62]

But the incident in Georgia *was* serious. The RGD-5 hand grenade had been thrown at the president, high enough that the shrapnel would hit him upon explosion. But the grenade ricocheted off a girl, which slowed its trajectory as it landed just sixty-one feet from the president.[63] The grenade had also been wrapped in a red tartan handkerchief to conceal it from the detection, but unbeknownst to the assassin this kept the firing pin from deploying quickly enough. The president and everyone around him also got lucky in that the two spoons that are supposed to engage and cause a chemical reaction got stuck.[64]

Dana Perino, who served as deputy press secretary, was shocked to learn of the seriousness of this attack many years later. She was with the press corps—not the reporters in the pool traveling on Air Force One, but the rest of them—and they were situated toward the back of the crowd, roughly fifty yards away from the stage. It was a sunny day and it was her birthday. She remembered a crowd that was "enthusiastic about freedom and grateful that the USA had Georgia's back against Russian aggression." The president gave a speech about liberty and the whole thing was handled so seamlessly that Perino didn't even notice a disturbance in the crowd. She learned about it much later, just before boarding the press charter. "I heard there had been a security incident with a grenade of some sort but it did not go off," she told me. "What I recall was being told that it was some-body who was not very sophisticated with bomb-making, and that it was a dud. And after that, I don't really remember hearing anything else about it." The reporters pressed her for more information, but she didn't have any. Reflecting on the details, she said, "I am shocked to think it could've been much worse, but I understand why they would downplay it in order to prevent people from thinking that such an act could be successful."[65]

Illness and assassination attempts aside, there were two serious accidents—both already discussed at length—that came dangerously close to claiming the lives of two presidents. Ironically, both of them were acci-dental presidents who had assumed office upon their predecessor's death. The first was John Tyler, who in February 1844 nearly died in the explosion on board the USS *Princeton*. Had he died, Willie Person Mangum would have been "Acting President" and it is possible the Tyler precedent would not have stuck. The second was Theodore Roosevelt, whose 1902 carriage accident injured him and killed his bodyguard. So severe was the accident that Roosevelt was flung from the carriage, and forced into a wheelchair for several weeks. His injuries from the accident would cause him pain for the rest of his life.

Beyond the actual close calls are the threats. What began as a hand-ful of letters, visits from some ominous characters, and crazy stalkers has evolved into an unimaginable danger that each successive administration faces. Over time, those threats have extended to the entire first family. Today, administrations receive tens of thousands of threats, and in the digital era those numbers are only increasing.

The fact that tragedy only struck eight times is due to a combination of luck, advancements in modern medicine, and an evolution in Secret Service protection. Through the Garfield assassination, job seekers and citizens could just walk into the White House and meet with the president. It was seen as un-American to guard a president lest there be an air of regality around them. As for the Secret Service, it took three presidential assassinations and multiple assassination attempts for the government to properly resource presidential protection and professionalize the operation. McKinley, for example, had a security detail that was comprised of friends and loyalists, not professionals. His chief bodyguard was an acquaintance from Ohio, not a Secret Service professional,[66] which is part of why three times McKinley overruled George Cortelyou and others when they urged him to reconsider his participation in a dangerous public reception in Buffalo.[67]

Finally, in 1906, Congress passed legislation giving the Secret Service the mandate and resources to add presidential protection to its duties in addition to apprehending counterfeiters.[68] From then on out, the Secret Service would grow with each successive administration. But despite the growing protection, presidents have continued to come under attack. Kennedy's assassination was the last straw and catalyzed the most serious debate about presidential succession since the Constitutional Convention. Near misses and close calls—whether pure luck, or the good work of the Secret Service—tend to come and go pretty quickly. Unless the president actually gets shot, there has rarely been much reflection about what could have happened. The Secret Service is not particularly interested in highlighting failures, the president doesn't want to engage in his own mortality, it is awkward for the vice president to say anything at all, and after Al Haig declared that he was "in control here" following an attempt on Ronald Reagan's life, cabinet secretaries are programmed to keep their mouths shut.

The Twenty-fifth Amendment

On February 10, 1967, that debate culminated in the Twenty-fifth Amendment, which essentially formalized the Tyler precedent and added provisions for how to replace the vice president. No president has died in office since the ratification of the Twenty-fifth Amendment. But on October 10, 1973, when Vice President Spiro T. Agnew resigned in scandal for receiving illegal kickbacks, Section 2 of the amendment allowed Richard Nixon to pluck Gerald Ford from Michigan's 5th Congressional District to serve as his vice president. At the time, Nixon was focused on foreign policy. Kissinger, who was dual hatted as both secretary of state and national security advisor, explained that "Nixon's opinion of Ford's foreign policy ability was very low, but he appointed him because he thought there was no possible way anyone would ever replace him with a relative novice in foreign policy." It was Kissinger's job—at Nixon's direction—to brief Ford every three weeks, which would prove useful once Nixon resigned amidst the Watergate scandal.[69]

During the dramatic period of Nixon's resignation, Nixon called Kissinger into his office the morning the smoking-gun tape was released. "Nixon had told me in the morning I should call Ford and brief him about the status of the Middle East," he remembered, and "I called him just about the time that this tape was released and he might well have thought that this was an attempt to keep me on, but Ford was very good about it. But there were no secrets. He made it very clear that he would keep me."[70] But Ford was positively inclined toward Kissinger, who had previously invited him to speak at a defense policy seminar at Harvard.

Nixon's resignation was the culmination of the long-drawn-out Watergate investigation and move toward almost certain impeachment. By the time Nixon resigned, the country was not surprised and the manner in which he disgraced the presidency meant that most were happy to see him go. This is a vastly different scenario from when a president is killed or dies abruptly. Regardless, Gerald Ford—who was the country's first accidental vice president—subsequently became the only man in history to rise to the nation's two highest offices without having been elected to either.

Unlike previous accidental presidents, Ford had a living predecessor whose very existence proved problematic. The fact that Nixon left office amidst scandal, not death, forced Ford to make a lose-lose decision to issue a pardon. The pardon received mixed reviews, but Ford was never able to escape the critique. He was also not the seasoned politician of Richard Nixon, who had served as vice president, senator, and president for a term and a half. The two men were very different. "The problem with Nixon was, or the aspect of Nixon was, he was always wary of being rejected," Kissinger explained, "so talking to him was like a Pirandello play—you know, that play of six characters in search of an author—that what you heard was rarely the thrust of what he was after." For those around Nixon, you "had to watch the cannon shots and ask yourself—even if you are close [to the president]—what is he setting up?" He was intimidating, a bit of a bully, and had the well-earned nickname "Tricky Dick."[71]

Kissinger described Ford as a "minimalist" who never thought of becoming president. He was a guy who had a great twenty-five years in Congress, had served in the Republican leadership, was much loved by his colleagues, and at most would have had aspirations to be speaker of the house. At the time he was picked to be vice president, he had already talked about retiring and was probably headed out the door. When he took over first as vice president, he viewed it as a job he had to do and his responsibility. The president asked him to be vice president and he did it. This was not out of any sense of personal ambition, particularly as he didn't see it as a step up. If anything, he had a very low opinion of the job and described it as the worst eight months of his life.

Once Ford became president that simplistic vibe became apparent. He was a man "who had never heard of focus groups" and "what you saw was what you got," Kissinger explained. He was smart, but not an operator, and lacked Nixon's mastery of the bureaucratic system. Whereas Nixon had barked orders and forced their implementation through sheer intimidation, Ford was understated and deferential. He would ask when it was convenient to come see him and relied on the expertise of his advisors. "You could say this is usual, this needs to be done.... He would say 'yes' or 'no' and you knew he wouldn't talk about some alternative to somebody else. It was very easy." This was a welcome and needed change from the Watergate anguish, which, while starting with the June 1972 break-in at the Democratic headquarters, really intensified from March of 1973 to August of 1974 and became more emotional and complex with the constantly deteriorating authority of the president.

As Cheney remembers it, during the transition, Ford was "trying to do change and continuity at the same time." On the one hand, he wanted there to be continuity, so that the new administration could "reassure the country and the world [that] we were not deviating significantly on foreign policy and national security." On day one, he told the transition team not to mess with foreign policy, saying, "I don't want you guys screwing around with the relationship with the State Department and national security, and so forth; that's off limits. [The] transition team is to focus on domestic policy, budget, domestic council, things like that."[72]

On the other hand, he needed to "wipe the slate clean and convince the American people he had gotten rid of the crowd that had brought us Watergate." He controversially pardoned Nixon and immediately turned his attention to the appointment of a vice president. He had only seriously considered three people for the job: Donald Rumsfeld, George H. W. Bush, and Nelson Rockefeller. Rumsfeld and Bush were guys he had dealt with in Congress while serving in the Republican leadership. He liked both men and had in fact mentored them, believing that they represented the future of the party. But he looked at Rockefeller as the best known of the three, as someone who had served as assistant secretary of state back in World War II, governor of New York, and was a major national and international figure. He wanted to reassure the world out there and given he had just taken office and nobody knew him outside of the 5th District of Michigan, he felt that prominence was important. By choosing Rockefeller, he felt that he was reassuring the world that there weren't going to be any radical changes in U.S. policy.[73]

Navigating all of this was complicated and took time. His decision to pardon Nixon probably cost him the election in 1976, but his initial decision to retain the national security team revealed support for Nixon's foreign policy and an intent to stay the course. That didn't necessarily mean he thought he had the right people, and he eventually corrected this. On November 3, 1975, he did make some major changes in what became known as the "Halloween Massacre," first by announcing that Vice President Nelson Rockefeller would not be part of the 1976 Republican ticket. He took Henry Kissinger's dual hat away from him—retaining him as secretary of state but bringing in Brent Scowcroft as national security advisor. He removed Secretary of Defense James Schlesinger and CIA director William Colby, replacing them with Donald Rumsfeld and George H.W. Bush respectively. Dick Cheney, who at the time was a thirty-four-year-old aide, became the new White House chief of staff, filling the vacancy left by Rumsfeld.[74] In that sense, the transition wasn't complete until the end of 1975. Only then had Ford truly come into his own, but it was still not sufficient to win in 1976.

Ford may have kept Nixon's foreign policy team, but he didn't have his predecessor's craft or relationships to effectively carry out Nixon's policies. From Kissinger's perspective, this came at a huge cost. "We would have made much more rapid progress in the Middle East," he offered as a counterfactual. "We would have accelerated the initiatives towards China and Russia and we would have attempted in the early part of that second term a kind of restructuring of our relationship with Europe, which failed because of the bureaucratic opposition to do something." He believed that absent Watergate, Nixon had real momentum, that he had extricated us from Vietnam, approached Europe as an opening to China, and that this was just the beginning. The "Year of Europe" that Nixon and Kissinger announced sank into a morass because of European opposition, but in Kissinger's view, Nixon's commanding personality could have been the kind of muscle necessary to move things forward.[75]

By 1976, Ford once again found himself in a unique situation as he became the first sitting president to run for election without having ever run for any office outside of the 5th District of Michigan. All other accidental presidents had at least been elected as vice president. Contrast that with Nixon's 1972 electoral victory, which produced one of the most overwhelming landslides in American history. Watergate aside, it was an exceptional team of campaign operatives, but the stain of scandal from that election meant that Ford couldn't use any of them. So he had to hire a hodgepodge of campaign novices, which is how Dick Cheney gets to be the White House chief of staff overseeing all operations and how James Baker, a lawyer from Texas, ends up running the delegate operation.

In retrospect, the Nixon-to-Ford transition seemed to test just about every aspect of the relatively new Twenty-fifth Amendment, yet when Reagan was shot in 1981, there was still confusion about what to do. Reagan's bullet wound was not fatal, but it was serious. In fact, it was fairly similar to the gunshot wound that ultimately claimed James Garfield's life. The president needed to undergo immediate surgery and so the question arose as to whether he should temporarily discharge his duties to Vice President George H. W. Bush. The topic was debated among advisors without any consultation with the president or his physicians. They decided not to enact the Twenty-fifth Amendment, which, given the Cold War context as well as the fact that they didn't know the seriousness of the surgery, was irresponsible if not unconstitutional.[76] But there was a reluctance to use the Twenty-fifth Amendment, which unlike previous presidential succession acts was not simply about changing the order of succession. This particular amendment stands out because it is uniquely personal and requires the very men hired by the incumbent to make a judgment about him. The country had managed through eight deaths and several prolonged illnesses without the Twenty-fifth Amendment, so it seemed unlikely that this time would be any different, particularly as Reagan's advisors expected him to recover. Furthermore, use of the Twenty-fifth Amendment had not yet become the practice that it is today, where even the shortest period of time under general anesthesia results in the president discharging his duties to the vice president.

Ironically, the provisions of the amendment were taken more seriously in 1985, when Reagan underwent colon surgery. "I am mindful of the provisions of Section 3 of the 25th Amendment to the Constitution and of the uncertainties of its application to such brief and temporary periods of incapacity," he wrote in a letter to the president pro tempore of the Senate. "Nevertheless, consistent with my longstanding arrangement with Vice President George Bush, and not intending to set a precedent binding anyone privileged to hold the office in the future, I have determined and it is my intention and direction, that Vice President George Bush shall discharge those powers and duties in my stead commencing with the administration of anesthesia to me in this instance."[77]

Over time, the practice became more professionalized and it was determined that in an age of nuclear weapons and international terrorism, every minute should be accounted for. Nobody has understood this more than Dick Cheney, who was better prepared to understand the intricacies of succession than any other vice president in history. He had experienced close calls under Ford and studied the process under Reagan while he served in Congress. "There was a time at the height of the Cold War when—specifically during the Reagan administration—when we were concerned about . . . legitimately so, the possibility of a nuclear war with the Soviets," he recalled. "When you begin to plan for that, one of the things you are concerned about—you've got the Twenty-fifth Amendment and that's all nice and so forth and hunky-dory—but if war breaks out and you've got to deal with a situation where there are hundreds of warheads coming down on the United States and an all-out nuclear exchange with the Soviets, what the hell do you do? How does that work?"[78]

As he explains it, "One of the main things you've got to do is preserve the continuity of government, the legitimacy of governmental authority, following the line of succession through the vice president, the speaker, the president pro tempore, the cabinet, and so forth. And, you've got to have some place where you have established a legitimate government for the United States of America. All hell is breaking loose, unimaginable difficulties and problems, millions of dead, and so forth. I was part of that program and I'd been selected in part because I had been Ford's chief of staff and understood and had dealt with all those different things. We actually put together teams. I ran one of the teams. We actually practiced and went through the drill."[79]

Within moments of being sworn in as vice president, he instructed his top special assistant, counsel, and chief of staff, David Addington, to do a full and comprehensive review and make sure there were no holes in the succession process. He wanted to review everything—the statutes, the Constitution, past practices, everything about a transition, a checklist of what to do—so that if it happened tomorrow, he would be ready.

Addington spent about a month working on the review and it revealed an interesting problem in the Twenty-fifth Amendment. While the Constitution has provisions for dealing with the death or incapacity of a president, it turned out that there was no way to get rid of an incapacitated vice president. As the next in line for the presidency, Cheney was greatly concerned given his own medical history. "I guess I had had about three heart attacks by then," he said, and "when you look back at Woodrow Wilson and what happened to him . . . I could see a situation where I had a stroke, or another bad heart attack and then been alive in the office, but unable to function. There was no procedure established to deal with that situation."[80]

So to deal with this situation, Cheney came up with the concept of a letter of resignation that he would sign. It was a straight resignation letter addressed to the secretary of state, which he gave to Addington to hold. In the event that he had a stroke or a severe heart attack, Addington was instructed to bring the letter to the president, who would ultimately make the call on whether to accept it. He told the president what he had done and then the three of them kept it a secret. Fearing that he might be in a situation where he couldn't get access to the White House, Addington took the letter home and stored it in a file cabinet at his house. Then one night his house caught on fire. The first thing he did was evacuate his family, but then he went back in and got his papers, including Cheney's letter.

At the time, the exercise may have seemed paranoid or obsessive, but it proved wise given 9/11, when anything could have happened. From

Cheney's perspective, "more than three thousand people were dead, the tragedy was worse than Pearl Harbor, but it wasn't as bad as what we had practiced for." As it turned out, the only instances he had to navigate were two presidential colonoscopies—the first in 2002, which lasted two hours and fifteen minutes; and the second in 2007, which lasted two hours and five minutes. In both cases the Twenty-fifth Amendment was invoked, which was the first time in history that presidential power had been transferred temporarily.

Cheney spent the time in his office and has no recollection of any decision that came up in either case. "To some extent it is a formality," he acknowledged, "but on the other hand, you really need to do that. All the time you've got the military aide with the football, the nuclear codes." He did write a letter to his grandkids about what it was like to be president of the United States, which is a practice often enjoyed by the designated survivor. But when I pushed him on whether he would be prepared to launch a military strike—for example, in the case of a known terrorist being located and there being minimal time to act—he noted that while it would depend on the situation, for something like a post-9/11 Osama bin Laden scenario there would have been a preexisting policy that would have dictated what to do. He was always very cognizant of how George H. W. Bush avoided any perception of acting as president after Reagan was shot and the juxtaposition of Al Haig's infamous moment. So it would have to be an "extraordinary set of circumstances," he explained, but "if it was a matter of life or death. If many lives were at risk and you had minutes to act, I would have acted. But it would have to be extraordinary circumstances."[81]

Afterword

We've come a long way since John Tyler ascended to the presidency and Congress debated whether he was acting president. Today, the president can't go under general anesthesia for a colonoscopy without exercising the Twenty-fifth Amendment. There is a designated survivor for when the senior leadership of government is all in one place. We have protocols for continuity of the government. The precision of our contingency plans is extraordinary. But all of this matters very little if we don't take seriously the person elected to be a heartbeat away from the presidency.

The evolution of whom we select has not evolved. In the days of big party bosses and before nationwide primaries, the party elite could have placed anyone they wanted as vice president and statistically—at least through JFK—there was a 23 percent chance that person would have become president. And that does not even take into account the close calls. But the bosses never thought of it this way, with the exception of Theodore Roosevelt, who terrified some of McKinley's advisors, and Harry Truman, whom some Democratic Party bosses viewed as simply the best way to block Henry Wallace.

Today, the power to choose is more or less consolidated in the hands of the nominee and his or her campaign team. And while candidates have paid lip service to choosing a running mate who is ready to be president, the reality is that it is driven by politics. There is nothing wrong with selecting a vice president who can help with a constituency, win a state, or fill an expertise gap—as Joe Biden and Dick Cheney did for Barack Obama and George W. Bush on foreign policy—but these should be secondary.

This is easy for a president to understand once in office, but in the thick of a campaign, when one is against the ropes and desperate to win a primary or hold on to a particular demographic, the political moment may dictate something else. A campaign advisor comes in and explains that it doesn't matter if your running mate is ready to lead if you don't win. The choice is often made in haste—sometimes depending on what the campaign needs that particular week—and not always with the most thorough vetting process. Today, campaigns hope for a quick bounce in the polls that help with momentum, and after that simply hope they don't do something embarrassing or lose the debates. These moments of desperation lead to some disastrous choices, such as John McCain's selection of Sarah Palin as his running mate in 2008.

Disastrous choices are few, but most are unremarkable by design. The presidential nominee is not motivated to pick a star, lest they overshadow. It's this fact, more than any, that leads party nominees to select a safe choice—someone who makes sense, is apt enough that nobody will question an ability to lead, a person who will not stir any controversy in debates or on the campaign trail, and who is sufficiently boring. In the case of Theodore Roosevelt, McKinley had the fast and loose New Yorker imposed upon him by party bosses. But given this was still a time when presidential nominees didn't take to the campaign trail, McKinley could dispatch Roosevelt and make use of his energy.

When victory is achieved and it comes time to govern, the marriage of political convenience may not work. Some of this is institutional in the sense that there are very real challenges associated with giving a vice president real work to do. First, they are elected, so you can't fire them or ask for their resignation in the same way you can a cabinet secretary. Second, the vice president is a constitutional officer and can't be called on to testify before Congress. This came up during the Ford administration when for a brief period there were discussions about making the vice president dual-hatted. The proposal never went anywhere, but the idea was that Nelson Rockefeller would be vice president and secretary of state, or secretary of defense. This proved problematic because if you are a cabinet member, it is a statutory job and you have to answer to Congress on your budget, you have to be up on Capitol Hill.[1]

Where does this story leave us today? There are two issues. The first is how we select a vice president. We don't have to accept a system where running mates are chosen by the campaign. The process has changed many times throughout history and to change it again doesn't require a new law, just an alteration of party rules and acceptance of norms. At a minimum, we could demand better choices from our nominees. During the primaries, for example, multiple men and women run for president and the voters have an opportunity to judge who is fit for office and who is not. Unfortunately, the current primary dynamics lend themselves to an atmosphere of such hostility that few candidates would draw from the pool of fellow aspirants.

Political parties could mandate that all vice presidential nominees must also have been contenders for the presidential nomination, even if they drop out well before the convention. Such a requirement would ensure that any vice presidential nominee would first have to demonstrate their fitness for president by virtue of competing for the job. Perhaps this change in process would also yield better party cohesion, since candidates would have a heightened incentive to avoid tarnishing each other's reputations.

Alternatively, political parties could wrest control from the nominee's campaign and establish vice presidential search committees comprised of different factions within the party. A thoughtful process conducted independently of the campaign might avoid hasty decisions or note political choices. Parties could also choose to assign the responsibility of nominating a vice president to super-delegates, which draws on the Democrat's practice of having some number of unelected delegates who can vote for any candidate of their choosing. If this is a bridge too far, they might opt for a hybrid model, whereby a nominating committee would create the short list and the campaign make the decision.

The second issue relates to how we ensure the vice president is integrated into an administration so that should the president die in office, he or she is prepared. It's still remarkable that Harry Truman ramped up as fast as he did following FDR's death, but that is not a test worth repeating. Amendments and presidential succession acts fill gaps in how we address vacancies in office, but none provide for how we encourage readiness. Our last three vice presidents—Mike Pence, Joe Biden, and Dick Cheney—have had their own national security apparatus, received intelligence briefings, and have had a foreign policy agenda that is sanctioned by the president. This is an improvement, but it is not required by law. There is nothing to prevent a president from cutting out his vice president. A presidential readiness act could require that the vice president receive daily intelligence briefs, while also granting him the right to establish his own national security positions and consult with the president over matters of national security.

Change is unlikely. The Constitution was written so that we could not easily amend it. The framers didn't think of everything, nor did they try to. They drafted a document that would demand that we be thoughtful and deliberate as we evolve. It was only after Kennedy's assassination that we finally passed the Twenty-fifth Amendment, but when it was tested with the assassination attempt on Ronald Reagan, the cabinet wasn't ready to implement it. Before its passage, we had more than a century of experimentation with laws and precedents to see what worked.

We've been lucky in that no president has died in office since 1963 and while we hope our unprecedented period without an abrupt transition endures, it is inevitable that there will be a death in office. Rather than prepare, we seem likely to leave any future outcome to chance and luck. We can, however, take a different lesson from this story, which is that the Constitution is a living document and it's our job to fill in the gaps.

Author's Note

It would be easy to look at the timing of this book and assume it was inspired by all the impeachment talk surrounding Donald Trump. In reality, I began the book before Donald Trump announced his candidacy for president, well before any speculation about impeachment, and it is being published with a cloud of uncertainty continuing to linger. My interest in this topic started with a bag of campaign buttons I purchased at a flea market in New York and subsequently evolved into an intellectual journey that had me reading presidential biographies on the playground at school. I grew up fascinated by it all—scandal, war, the campaigns—but what really attracted my attention were the unexpected transitions. The concept of a president dying in office and what happens became a historical obsession of mine. I devoured any book I could read on the subject, collected old newspapers and memorabilia depicting the events, and annoyed anyone who would listen with long regurgitations of what happened. When I saw Oliver Stone's 1994 film about the Kennedy assassination, I did what any precocious preteen would do; I set out to solve the conspiracy myself! I made charts and graphs, practiced giving talks about the magic bullet, and I was certain that I had found a second gunman on the Grassy Knoll. I even went through my own mourning process and decorated an entire "Kennedy Room"—as it became known in my house—with *Life* magazine covers, political buttons, Kennedy posters, and photographs.

Not surprisingly, my efforts to solve the Kennedy assassination mystery proved fruitless. But the exercise at least gave me an excuse to ask all the baby boomers about where they were and what they were doing when Kennedy was shot. The responses were emotional. My mother was in seventh grade, it was eighth period and she was just leaving art class. She saw people crying in the hallways and heard a classmate say, "Kennedy has been shot!" They didn't let them out of school early because it was too complicated with the buses, but as soon as she got home, she was glued to the TV. My mother like everyone else of her generation recites this without hesitation, with intimate detail. She can't recount events without reminding me that "when the Kennedys came it was magical, like having royalty in the White House. And Jackie spoke nine languages, wore size ten shoes, and had a miscarriage while in office." She compared their arrival in Washington to "the prince and princess being born and representing a whole new hope. Eisenhower was a general and represented war. This was a different time; Jackie was a fashion icon." She couldn't remember anything else from seventh grade, but asked rhetorically, "How can I possibly remember all of that?"

It didn't take long for me to develop a fascination with the Lincoln assassination. When my grandfather took me on a trip to Washington, D.C., as a young boy, I made him take me to every landmark and spot related to the assassination, Booth's escape route, and the trial of the co-conspirators. We went to Ford's Theatre and the Petersen House, and the poor guy also had to take me to Fort McNair, where I could see the tennis courts that rest on the exact spot where the four conspirators were tried and executed. I began collecting newspapers related to the assassinations, but soon broadened my interest to presidents who died in office. I liked the phrase "Tippecanoe and Tyler Too." I felt connected to Zachary Taylor since we were both born on November 24. I gave my youngest daughter the middle name Garfield. I read everything I could about McKinley and became fascinated by the Harding scandals, and spent my youth anxiously waiting for his notorious love letters to be released in 2013.

It seems that my boyhood obsession has followed me well into adulthood, as evidenced by this book. I have also felt this romanticized desire to feel connected to these moments of history and began collecting locks of presidential hair. I acquired a lock of Lincoln's hair from the night of the assassination, and was able to purchase two long strands of William Henry Harrison's hair that had been pulled off his head while his body lay in rest in the East Room. Nobody thinks this is normal, yet when people come over they can't avert their eyes from the carefully designed shadow-boxed frames where the hair dangles on ribbons.

I will continue to collect locks of hair and more odd memorabilia, but the completion of this book marks an important personal milestone, satisfying a longtime desire to understand and tell the story of our accidental presidents.

Acknowledgments

I wrote the proposal for this book in April 2014, just a few weeks after my eldest daughter, Zelda, was born. As far back as I can remember, I had a fascination with the presidents and their transitions, so there was something about becoming a father that made me reflect back on that time. I had promised myself to detach from my day job at Google and really enjoy this new chapter of life, but I kept feeling that itch to work, not to mention I had a lot of time to read.

When Simon & Schuster agreed to publish *Accidental Presidents* on that same paternity leave, I joyously embarked on a three-year project. During that time, Zelda learned to walk and talk and eventually went to school. My second daughter, Annabel, was born, a period that coincided with writer's block while researching and writing the chapter on Chester Arthur. That bump in the road, it turns out, yielded an unexpected benefit. While my wife, Rebecca, was pregnant for the second time, we struggled to come up with a middle name. One day, when I was seated at the dining room table with a stack of first edition biographies about James Garfield, we looked at each other and thought, why not Garfield? We debated whether the fact that he had been assassinated made this a bit weird, and ultimately decided he was an exceptional man and that if it didn't work out, we could always just say we named her after our favorite cartoon character.

I truly am grateful to my wife, Rebecca, and two children, Zelda and Annabel, for sticking by me while I wrote this book. It was a lot of weekends and late nights, but they supported me every step of the way. Rebecca, in particular, was a trouper and endured many overbearing conversations about dead presidents and was incredibly gracious in allowing me the space and freedom to write this book. I also want to thank my sister, Emily, who when I told her about this project said to me that "this is the book I always thought you would write." Those words of support meant so much to me as I wondered whether such a project might be perceived as random. I also want to thank my parents, Dee and Donald, for encouraging my hobby from the time I was a small boy through the present.

I also owe a huge debt of gratitude to David Kennedy, Jack Rakove, and Walter Isaacson. These three friends are also among the most respected historians in the world. When I originally set out to write this book, I consulted each of them to ask whether they thought I could pull this off. In each conversation, I told them that if they didn't think I could do it, then I wouldn't. The opposite happened and each offered his full support and enthusiasm for the project. I came back to David nearly four years later with a draft manuscript and remember eagerly awaiting his initial review. His feedback was both encouraging and candid, pushing me to take a few extra steps to produce a better product. Walter took the next read and having his support meant the world to me.

When I finally decided to draft a proposal, my agent, Andrew Wylie, was among the most enthusiastic about the project. In addition to being a world-class literary agent, he is an incredible sounding board.

Throughout the book project, I didn't use a research assistant—preferring instead to immerse myself in my childhood hobby. But I was fortunate to have a researcher, Meaghan McLean, help me in crafting the proposal. At the time, Meaghan was a superstar senior at Georgetown and looking for a research project as she planned her post-university career.

I'd like to thank Simon & Schuster for taking a chance on this project. My incredible editor, Alice Mayhew, is as much of a historian as she is an editor and I came to cherish our conversations over lunch at Michael's. Special thanks to Jonathan Karp and Carolyn Reidy for their willingness to bet on this project, and to Stuart Roberts, and Amar Deol, who helped me push it over the finish line, even if that meant overnighting copies of proofs to Ljubljana. Thank you to Jessica Chin, copyediting manager, for overseeing the copyediting process. Elizabeth Gay, Stephen Bedford, and Kirstin Berndt form an amazing public relations, marketing, and online team who are the best in the business.

I wrote this book while working a fulltime job at Alphabet, where all of my colleagues were enormously supportive. I'd like to thank my entire Jigsaw team. In particular, I owe a debt of gratitude to Dan Keyserling, who gave me great feedback on the manuscript and drove much of the public relations campaign for the book tour. His genius and creativity were key to the success of this book. Scott Carpenter helped me secure an interview with Vice President Cheney and reviewed some of my questions for other interviews. Yasmin Green, John Sarapata, Justin Kosslyn, and Jen Minary Doris were each supportive at every step of the way. I also want to thank the leadership at Google/Alphabet for always being so supportive of my work, even when the story ends well before the dawn of modern technology. Eric Schmidt, David Drummond, Sergey Brin, Ruth Porat, Sundar Pichai, and Larry Page, are all amazing leaders at the company.

I am grateful to William Hogeland, my incredible fact checker, who went through the manuscript with a fine-tooth comb and made sure each detail was accurate and properly sourced. This book could not have gone to print without his astute pen and attention to detail.

There are several others I must thank for helping me complete this book. First, I owe the greatest debt of gratitude to the many historians whose hard work and scholarly achievement created a foundation on which I could build this book. They spent years and even decades in archives and libraries, and conducting interviews, so that later writers like me could add a small supplement to their extraordinary work. The Library of Congress has done an extraordinary job putting together archives and getting periodicals online. I owe a special thanks to Paul Sparrow, Kristen Carter, Dara Baker, and William Villano at the FDR Library. Their team helped me identify key documents and correspondence that proved invaluable throughout the book. The East Hampton library, particularly Gina Piastuck, provided some of the earliest primary source material, not to mention the opportunity to hold Julia Gardiner's braid. An early phone chat with Candice Millard spurred a lot of my enthusiasm for James Garfield and her guidance in tracking down the Julia Sand letters was extremely helpful. Several friends read chapters along the way and offered feedback, including Michiko Kakutani and Jeffrey McLean.

There are a number of people who graciously made time for interviews, which were particularly helpful for the final two chapters: George H. W. Bush, Condoleezza Rice, Thomas "Mack" McLarty, Henry Kissinger, Paul McCartney, Dick Cheney, Jesse Jackson, Tom Brokaw, Dana Perino, Akhil Amar, and Alphonso Jackson. Their firsthand accounts helped me reconstruct narratives that cannot be found in books and for that I am incredibly grateful.

Finally, I have a long list of friends who were supportive at each step of the way. Jamie Reuben and I had a casual conversation at his flat in London about how he wanted to write a book about Winston Churchill and I wanted to write a book about accidental presidents. I'm still waiting for Jamie's book about Churchill, but our conversation was the kick-start that I needed. Peter Blaustein and Jessica Borowick, who have known me since we were at Stanford together, were each so supportive along the way. My amazing graduate school roommates—Jeff McLean, Decker Walker, Dov Fox, Alex Pollen, and Trevor Thompson—were as there for me on this book as they were when I was writing *Children of Jihad* on our Oxford couch. I'd like to give a big thanks to Fareed Zakaria, who was with me as I hammered away at those final touches on the first and second passes of the manuscript. Adam Grant and Alec Ross were amazing thought partners in helping me figure out how to position the book for a mass audience.

A Note on Sources

This book is written on the heels of some of the great American historians, whose written works provided the foundation for this story. Their interviews, archival research, and corroboration of varying accounts were all done in the pre-Internet era and over the course of many years. It would have been impossible to write this book without having access to their work. I approached this project with full recognition of and admiration for what they have made possible. For facts that are drawn from another source, I use endnotes. If I rely on another's analysis or lengthy factual description, I make sure the source is mentioned in the text along with a citation.

Notes

CHAPTER ONE: FIRST TO DIE

1. The primary record on Tecumseh can be scanty and at times controversial; I've attempted to capture the prevailing narrative.
2. The Shawnee were led by the veteran Blue Jacket, and some scholars have questioned whether Tecumseh was in fact present at Fallen Timbers.
3. John Sugden, *Tecumseh: A Life* (New York: Henry Holt and Company, 1997), 256. See also Adam Jortner, *Gods of Prophetstown: The Battle of Tippecanoe and the Holy War for the American Frontier* (Oxford: Oxford University Press, 2012), 51–72.
4. Jim Poling, Sr., *Tecumseh: Shooting Star, Crouching Panther* (Toronto: Dundurn, 2009), 10–13.
5. "Voter Turnout in Presidential Elections: 1828–2012," John Woolley and Gerhard Peters, The American Presidency Project, UC Santa Barbara, http://www.presidency.ucsb.edu/data/turnout .php. By 1840, 90 percent of white men were eligible to vote. Wealthy free blacks who owned substantial property could also vote, although the process was made difficult. Blacks, women, and the bottom 10 percent of the economy were still ineligible. In 1860, 81.2 percent of eligible voters turned out, and 81.8 percent in 1876. For cited statistics, see Donald Ratcliffe, "The Right to Vote and the Rise of Democracy, 1787–1828," *Journal of the Early Republic* 33, no. 2 (2013), 219–54, https://www.jstor.org/stable/24768843.
6. *Albany Rough-Hewer*, September 3, 1840, in Gunderson, *Log-Cabin Campaign*, 129, in Paul F. Boller, Jr., *Presidential Campaigns* (Oxford: Oxford University Press, 1996), 77.
7. Robert Seager II, *And Tyler Too: A Biography of John and Julia Gardiner Tyler* (Norwalk, Conn.: Easton Press, 1989; first published 1963 by McGraw-Hill), 48–72.
8. Ibid., 134.
9. Ibid.
10. The numerical split was 29–22 (56.8 percent margin of victory).
11. Philip Abbott, *Accidental Presidents: Death, Assassination, Resignation, and Democratic Succession* (New York: Palgrave Macmillan, 2008), 28.
12. Letter from Daniel Webster to Hiram Ketchum, January 28, 1837, quoted in Sydney Nathans, *Daniel Webster*, 106, in Michael F. Holt, *The Rise and Fall of the American Whig Party: Jacksonian Politics and the Onset of the Civil War* (Oxford: Oxford University Press, June 1998), 122.
13. "U.S. Presidential Inaugurations: William Henry Harrison," January 17, 2017, Library of Congress Digital Reference Section, https://www.loc.gov/rr/program/bib/inaugurations /harrison/index.html.
14. Marty Jones, "The Thirty-One Day Presidency of William Henry Harrison," *American History*, April 6, 2016, http://www.historynet.com/the-thirty-one-day-presidency-of-william-henry -harrison.htm.

15. *National Intelligencer* (Washington, D.C.), March 5, 1841; *Madisonian* (Washington, D.C.), extra for March 4; in Oliver Perry Chitwood, *John Tyler: Champion of the Old South* (Newtown, Conn.: American Political Biography Press, 1939), 201.

16. Freeman Cleaves, *Old Tippecanoe: William Henry Harrison and His Times*, 229 and 336–37, in Seager, *And Tyler Too*, 144.

17. Jane McHugh and Philip A. Mackowiak, "What Really Killed William Henry Harrison?," *New York Times*, March 31, 2014, http://www.nytimes.com/2014/04/01/science/what-really-killed -william-henry-harrison.html.

18. Ibid.

19. "Death of Harrison," April 4, 1841, call no. PGA–Currier & Ives—Death of Harrison, April 4 A. D. 1984 (A Size) [P&P], Prints and Photographs Division, Library of Congress, http:// www.loc.gov/pictures/item/2001696143/. The photo and caption are the most comprehensive reference for those in attendance, but not all can be corroborated.

20. *Vermont Telegraph* (Brandon), April 14, 1841, 118, Chronicling America: Historic American Newspapers, Library of Congress, http://chroniclingamerica.loc.gov/lccn/sn83025661/1841 -04-14/ed-1/seq-2/. See also *New-York Tribune*, April 10, 1841, Chronicling America: Historic American Newspapers, Library of Congress, http://chroniclingamerica.loc.gov/lccn/sn83030212 /1841-04-10/ed-1/seq-4/.

21. Report of the attending physicians, Charles S. Todd and Benjamin Drake, *Sketches of the Civil and Military Services of William Henry Harrison*, revised by James H. Perkins (Cincinnati: J. A. & U. P. James, 1847), 208, in Freeman Cleaves, *Old Tippecanoe: William Henry Harrison and His Times* (Easton, Conn.: Easton Press, 1939), 342. Cleaves references the Mitten Collection, which he notes has "several bulletins scribbled by Colonel Todd conveying sick-bed news to the *National Intelligencer*."

22. Leonard Dinnerstein, "The Accession of John Tyler to the Presidency," *Virginia Magazine of History and Biography* 70, no. 4 (October 1962), 447–58, http://www.jstor.org/stable/4246893.

23. Chitwood, *John Tyler*, 202.

24. Ibid., 198.

25. Ibid., 202. See also Seager, *And Tyler Too*, 148.

26. The quoted dialogue is found in John Wise, *Recollections of Thirteen Presidents* (New York: Doubleday, Page, & Company, 1906), but it is unsourced and uncorroborated; its exactness and what we know of the narrative mode of Wise's day require a caveat that he may have made it fanciful.

27. Ibid., 13–14.

28. James D. Richardson, ed., *The Messages and Papers of the Presidents*, 11 volumes (New York: Bureau of National Literature, 1914), 4:1877–78, in Robert J. Morgan, *A Whig Embattled: The Presidency under John Tyler* (Omaha: University of Nebraska Press, 1954), 7.

29. Nathan Sargent, *Public Men and Events* (Philadelphia: Lippincott, 1875), 2:122.

30. John Tyler had eight children from his marriage to Letitia, but their third child, Anne C. Tyler, died at birth.

31. Edward P. Crapol, *John Tyler: The Accidental President* (Chapel Hill: University of North Carolina Press, 2006), 9.

32. Seager, *And Tyler Too*, 148.

33. "1834–1851: Nathaniel Beverley Tucker," Scholarship Repository, Wolf Law Library, William & Mary Law School, http://scholarship.law.wm.edu/nbtucker/.

34. Edgar Allan Poe, "A Chapter on Autography (Part I)," *Graham's Magazine*, November 1841, 224–34, https://www.eapoe.org/works/misc/autogc1.htm.

35. Crapol, *John Tyler*, 9. See also Gary May, *John Tyler* (New York: Times Books, 2008), 4.

36. *Richmond Enquirer.* (Richmond, Va.), April 6, 1841. *Chronicling America: Historic American*

Newspapers. Library of Congress, http://chroniclingamerica.loc.gov/lccn/sn84024735/1841-04-06/ed-1/seq-3/.

37. Crapol, *John Tyler*, 9.

38. Both Gary May (p. 138) and Robert Seager (p. 149) refer to Brown's Hotel, the former mentioning it as Vice President Tyler's D.C. residence and the latter noting that it was the site of the oath of office. Photograph of "Brown's Indian Queen Hotel, Washington City North side of Pennsylvania Avenue about midway between the Capitol and the President's House, a few doors east of the Centre Market / / lithog. of Endicott & Swett, No. 111, Nassau Street, N.Y."; call no. PGA–Endicott & Swett—Brown's Indian . . . (B size) [P&P], Prints and Photographs Division, Library of Congress, https://www.loc.gov/pictures/item/93506552/.

39. Tyler, Lyon Gardiner, *Letters and Times of the Tylers* (New York: Da Capo, 1970, reprint), 7:11–12, in Seager, *And Tyler Too*, 148.

40. Seager, *And Tyler Too*, 148.

41. Chitwood, *John Tyler*, 203. See also Seager, *And Tyler Too*, 149.

42. Seager, *And Tyler Too*, 148.

43. Gary May, *John Tyler*, 62. For the oath of office, see "Oath of Office Administered to President John Tyler in the Presence of the Cabinet," April 6, 1841, John Woolley and Gerhard Peters, The American Presidency Project, UC Santa Barbara, https://www.presidency.ucsb.edu/documents/oath-office-administered-president-john-tyler-the-presence-the-cabinet.

44. John D. Feerick, "Presidential Succession and Inability: Before and After the Twenty-Fifth Amendment," *Fordham L. Rev.* 79, no. 3 (2011), 907–49, http://ir.lawnet.fordham.edu/flr/vol79/iss3/8, 911.

45. Gouverneur Morris (d. 1816) of Pennsylvania was in charge of the committee to draft the final copy of the Constitution. Other men who had much to do with writing the Constitution included John Dickinson (d. 1808), Thomas Jefferson (d. 1826), John Adams (d. 1826), Thomas Paine (d. 1809), Edmund Randolph (d. 1813), James Madison (d. 1836), Roger Sherman (d. 1793), James Wilson (d. 1798), and George Wythe (d. 1806). Ironically, Madison, who was the most involved in the drafting, almost lived long enough to have helped interpret this.

46. Dinnerstein, "Accession of John Tyler to the Presidency," 447–58.

47. Ibid.

48. Feerick, "Presidential Succession and Inability," 911.

49. Max Farrand, ed., *Records of the Federal Convention* (New Haven: Yale University Press, 1913), 2:537, in Robert J. Morgan, *A Whig Embattled*, 7.

50. Norma Lois Peterson, *The Presidencies of William Henry Harrison & John Tyler* (Lawrence: University Press of Kansas, 1989), 47.

51. Ibid, 47–48.

52. Seager, *And Tyler Too*, 149. See also Robert J. Morgan, *A Whig Embattled*, 59–60; and Chitwood, *John Tyler*, 270.

53. The nation had no formal protocol for how to mourn a president who died in office. Harrison's remains would eventually be sent back to his home in Ohio, but the blistering winter prevented this from happening right away. For a detailed description of the funeral, see "William Henry Harrison Funeral," The White House Historical Association, http://www.whitehousehistory.org/presentations/presidential-funerals/presidential-funerals-william-henry-harrison.html.

54. Seager, *And Tyler Too*, 149.

55. Feerick, *From Failing Hands: The Story of Presidential Succession* (New York: Fordham University Press, 1965), 93. See also Seager, *And Tyler Too*, 149.

56. Robert J. Morgan, *A Whig Embattled*, 7. See also "Oath of Office Administered to President John Tyler."

57. Peterson, *Presidencies of William Henry Harrison & John Tyler*, 51. See also Seager, *And Tyler Too*, 149.

58. Seager, *And Tyler Too*, 149.

59. William Henry Harrison and Henry Clay had a showdown over the special session of Congress.

60. "Address Upon Assuming the Office of President of the United States," April 9, 1841, John Woolley and Gerhard Peters, The American Presidency Project, https://www.presidency.ucsb.edu/documents/address-upon-assuming-the-office-president-the-united-states.

61. James D. Richardson, ed., *Compilation of the Messages and Papers of the Presidents* (Washington, D.C.: U.S. Government Printing Office, 1897), vol. 4, part 2: *John Tyler*, 4.

62. "Special Session Message," June 1, 1841, John Woolley and Gerhard Peters, The American Presidency Project, UC Santa Barbara, https://www.presidency.ucsb.edu/documents/special-session-message-9.

63. Mark O. Hatfield, with the Senate Historical Office, "Vice Presidents of the United States: John Tyler (1841)," in Mark O. Hatfield, with the Senate Historical Office, *Vice Presidents of the United States, 1789–1993* (Washington, D.C.: U.S. Government Printing Office, 1997), 137–46, http://www.senate.gov/artandhistory/history/resources/pdf/john_tyler.pdf.

64. Ruth Silva, *Presidential Succession* (New York: Greenwood Press, 1968), 37. See also Peterson, *Presidencies of William Henry Harrison & John Tyler*, 49–50.

65. *Memoirs of John Quincy Adams: Comprising Portions of His Diary from 1795 to 1848*, ed. Charles Francis Adams (Philadelphia: Lippincott, 1876, reprint), 10:463–64, in Feerick, "Presidential Succession and Inability," 919.

66. Feerick, "Presidential Succession and Inability," 919.

67. Peterson, *Presidencies of William Henry Harrison & John Tyler*, 49–50.

68. Hatfield, with the Senate Historical Office, *Vice Presidents of the United States*, 137–46.

69. Peterson, *Presidencies of William Henry Harrison & John Tyler*, 49–50.

70. *Memoirs of John Quincy Adams*, 10:463–64, in ibid, 56.

71. Hatfield, with the Senate Historical Office, *Vice Presidents of the United States, 1789–1993*, 137–46.

72. Robert V. Remini, *Henry Clay: Statesman for the Union* (New York: Norton, 1991), 578.

73. "Manly Knowledge: Dueling Part II—Famous Duels in American History," in *The Art of Manliness*, a blog by Brett McKay, http://www.artofmanliness.com/2010/03/30/famous-duels-from-american-history/.

74. John Swansburg, "The Self-Made Man," *Slate*, September 29, 2014, http://www.slate.com/articles/news_and_politics/history/2014/09/the_self_made_man_history_of_a_myth_from_ben_franklin_to_andrew_carnegie.html. Clay allegedly coined the term "while arguing on the Senate floor for a protective tariff he believed would benefit 'enterprising self-made men, who have whatever wealth they possess by patient and diligent labor.'"

75. Holt, *Rise and Fall of the American Whig Party*, 126.

76. Ibid.

77. As cited by George R. Poage, *Henry Clay and the Whig Party* (Chapel Hill: University of North Carolina Press, 1936), 28–32.

78. William Henry Harrison to Henry Clay, March 13, 1841, in Poage, *Henry Clay*, 31, in Peterson, *Presidencies of William Henry Harrison & John Tyler*, 37.

79. Norma Lois Peterson, *Presidencies of William Henry Harrison & John Tyler*, 37. See also Remini, *Henry Clay*, 575.

80. Remini, *Henry Clay*, 575. Cleaves, *Old Tippecanoe*, 339, quotes Harrison as saying "decision" instead of "suggestions." Remini cites the original source as William Henry Harrison to Henry Clay, March 13, 1841, in Henry Clay Papers, 9:514. I've relied on Remini's version since he cites directly the original source, whereas Cleaves refers to the original source through Poage, *Henry Clay*, 30–31.

81. Sargent, *Public Men and Events*, 2:115–16.

82. Henry Clay to William Henry Harrison, March 15, 1841, in Henry Clay, *Papers*, 9:516–17, in Remini, *Henry Clay*, 576.

83. Remini, *Henry Clay*, 576.

84. Nathans, *Daniel Webster and Jacksonian Democracy*, 154–58, in Holt, *Rise and Fall of the American Whig Party*, 127. See also Poage, *Henry Clay*, 28–32; and Remini, *Henry Clay*, 576.

85. Mrs. Anne Royall, *Letters from Alabama on Various Subjects* (Washington, D.C., n.p., 1830), 550, in Chitwood, *John Tyler*, 252.

86. Tyler, *Letters and Times of the Tylers*, 1:288 and 2:248; John Tyler Papers, Library of Congress, III, 6621 and 6627, in Chitwood, *John Tyler*, 255.

87. Charles Dickens, *American Notes for General Circulation and Pictures from Italy*, Centenary Edition (New York: Charles Scribner & Sons, 1909), 148–49. See also *New York Herald*, March 12, 1842, in Chitwood, *John Tyler*, 254.

88. Holt, *Rise and Fall of the American Whig Party*, 127.

89. Glyndon G. Van Deusen, *The Life of Henry Clay* (New York: Little, Brown, 1963), 336–57.

90. Holt, *Rise and Fall of the American Whig Party*, 128.

91. Dan Monroe, *The Republican Vision of John Tyler* (College Station: Texas A&M University Press, 2003), 86. See also Chitwood, *John Tyler*, 272.

92. Tyler, *Letters and Times of the Tylers*, 2:33–34, in Remini, *Henry Clay*, 583. See also Seager, *And Tyler Too*, 154.

93. *New York Herald*, August 11, 1841, in Chitwood, *John Tyler*, 225.

94. *Cincinnati Daily Gazette*, August 18, 1841, in Chitwood, *John Tyler*, 226. See also Poage, *Henry Clay*, 70.

95. Chitwood, *John Tyler*, 226.

96. Monroe, *Republican Vision of John Tyler*, 100. See also "John Tyler veto message to the House of Representatives," August 16, 1841, in Richardson, *Compilation of the Messages and Papers of the Presidents*, vol. 3, part 2: John Tyler, 1916–1921.

97. John Tyler, "Veto Message," August 16, 1841.

98. Ibid.

99. Ibid.

100. Carl Schurz, *Life of Henry Clay*, American Statesman (Cambridge, Mass.: Riverside Press, 1887), 2:207; Thomas Hart Benton, *Thirty Years' View*, 2:328–30, in Chitwood, *John Tyler*, 228.

101. Ibid.

102. "The Coffee House Letter," in Tyler, *Letters and Times of the Tylers*, 2:112. See also Seager, *And Tyler Too*, 156–57. The letter ended with "Tonight we must and will settle matters, as quietly as possible, but they must be settled."

103. *Democratic Standard* (Georgetown, Brown County, Ohio), September 7, 1841, Chronicling America: Historic American Newspapers, Library of Congress, http://chroniclingamerica.loc .gov/lccn/sn83035312/1841-09-07/ed-1/seq-1/. The letter was printed in the *Madisonian*, August 21, 1841. See also Monroe, *Republican Vision of John Tyler*, 101; *Richmond College Historical Papers*, vols. 1–2; and *Richmond Whig*, August 27, 1841.

104. *New York Herald*, August 19 and 25, 1841, quoted in Monroe, *Republican Vision of John Tyler*, 101.

105. Seager, *And Tyler Too*, 156.

106. *New York Herald*, August 19 and 25, 1841, quoted in Monroe, *Republican Vision of John Tyler*, 101.

107. Ibid.

108. *Edgefield Advertiser* (S.C.), August 26, 1841, Chronicling America: Historic American Newspapers, Library of Congress, http://chroniclingamerica.loc.gov/lccn/sn84026897/1841-08 -26/ed-1/seq-3/.

109. *North-Carolina Standard* (Raleigh), September 15, 1841, Chronicling America: Historic American Newspapers, Library of Congress, http://chroniclingamerica.loc.gov/lccn/sn85042147 /1841-09-15/ed-1/seq-2/. This quote comes from the *Montgomery Advertiser*, which is credited as follows in the *North-Carolina Standard*: "We had overlooked a part of the report of the conduct of 'all the decency' at the President's Mansion, and are now indebted to the *Montgomery Advertiser* for the facts."

110. *Edgefield Advertiser*, August 26, 1841.

111. Ibid.

112. *North-Carolina Standard*, September 15, 1841. See also Monroe, *Republican Vision of John Tyler*, 101; and Seager, *And Tyler Too*, 156.

113. *New York Herald*, August 19 and 25, 1841, quoted in Monroe, *Republican Vision of John Tyler*, 101. See also Seager, *And Tyler Too*, 156.

114. *Madisonian*, August 19, 1841, in Chitwood, *John Tyler*, 228–29.

115. *North-Carolina Standard*, September 15, 1841.

116. Tyler, *Letters and Times of the Tylers*, 7:71–72, in Seager, *And Tyler Too*, 156.

117. Kenneth Alfers, *Law and Order in the Capital City* (Washington, D.C.: George Washington University Press, 1976).

118. *New York Herald*, September 2, 1841, in Monroe, *Republican Vision of John Tyler*, 101.

119. Monroe, *Republican Vision of John Tyler*, 105, in Edward Ayers, *Vengeance and Justice: Crime and Punishment in the 19th Century American South* (New York: Oxford University Press, 1984), 9–33.

120. Seager, *And Tyler Too*, 160.

121. Tyler, *Letters and Times of the Tylers*, 8:39–40, quoted in Seager, *And Tyler Too*, 158.

122. *National Intelligencer*, September 6, 1841, quoted in Monroe, *The Republican Vision of John Tyler*, 106.

123. Monroe, *Republican Vision of John Tyler*, 106.

124. Seager, *And Tyler Too*, 159.

125. Monroe, *Republican Vision of John Tyler*, 107.

126. John Tyler veto message to the House of Representatives, September 9, 1841, in Richardson, *Compilation of the Messages and Papers of the Presidents*, vol. 3, part 2: *John Tyler*, 1921–1925.

127. Ibid., 40.

128. *New York Herald*, September 11 and 13, 1841; *National Intelligencer*, September 10, 1841, in Monroe, *Republican Vision of John Tyler*, 107–8.

129. Ibid.

130. The *Ohio Democrat and Dover Advertiser* was launched by Charles H. Mitchener, Tuscarawas County's "Father of Democracy," and a Mr. Hill on August 1, 1839, in Canal Dover, Ohio. The Democratic paper was small, comprising only six columns, and printed with equipment purchased through a joint stock company. The next year, soon after the presidential election, the paper ceased publication due to lack of support. In May 1841, Mitchener revived the paper, partnering with Charles H. Mathews, and moved its offices to nearby New Philadelphia, the county seat. The first issue of the *Ohio Democrat* was published on June 17, 1841, with the words of Roman philosopher Cicero printed below the masthead: "Where liberty dwells, there is my Country." Because the paper supported Democratic candidates and interests in a county that was predominantly Whig, the Democrat had only four hundred subscribers at first and struggled to pay its expenses. "About The *Ohio Democrat* (Canal Dover, Ohio), 1840–1900," Chronicling America: Historic American Newspapers, Library of Congress, http:// chroniclingamerica.loc.gov/lccn/sn84028889/.

131. *Ohio Democrat*, September 16, 1841, Chronicling America: Historic American Newspapers, Library of Congress, http://chroniclingamerica.loc.gov/lccn/sn84028889/1841-09-16/ed-1/seq-3/.

132. Ibid. See also Monroe, *Republican Vision of John Tyler*, 107–8.

133. *Ohio Democrat*, September 16, 1841.

134. Ibid.

135. Ibid.

136. *New York Herald*, September 12, 1841; Willie P. Mangum to Charity A. Mangum, September 5, 1841, quoted in Monroe, *Republican Vision of John Tyler*, 108.

137. John Tyler, Jr., to Lyon G. Tyler, January 29, 1883, Tyler, *Letters and Times of the Tylers*, 7:121–22, quoted in Seager, *And Tyler Too*, 160. See also Chitwood, *John Tyler*, 273.

138. Seager, *And Tyler Too*, 160. See also Chitwood, *John Tyler*, 240–41.

139. Tyler is quoted as saying this in both Seager, *And Tyler Too*, 160–61, and Chitwood, *John Tyler*, 277; Tyler, *Letters and Times of the Tylers*, 7:81.

140. Chitwood, *John Tyler*, 277.

141. Holt, *Rise and Fall of the American Whig Party*, 137.

142. Ibid., 138.

143. Seager, *And Tyler Too*, 161.

144. John Tyler, Jr., to Lyon G. Tyler, January 29, 1883, in Tyler, *Letters and Times of the Tylers*, 2:122n, in Remini, *Henry Clay*, 598. See also Seager, *And Tyler Too*, 161.

145. *National Intelligencer*, September 16, 1841, in Chitwood, *John Tyler*, 249–50.

146. Holt, *Rise and Fall of the American Whig Party*, 137. See also Poage, *Henry Clay*, 92–106.

147. Seager, *And Tyler Too*, 162.

148. Holt, *Rise and Fall of the American Whig Party*, 137.

149. *Letters and Times of the Tylers*, 2:124–126.

150. Letter from John Tyler to Thomas A. Cooper, Washington, October 8, 1841, in Tyler, *Letters and Times of the Tylers*, 2:125–126.

151. Holt, *Rise and Fall of the American Whig Party*, 139.

152. John Calhoun to Thomas G. Clemson, December 31, 1841, in Henry Thomas Shanks, ed., *The Papers of Willie P. Mangum* (Philadelphia: Lippincott, 1875), 3:247–50, in ibid., 140.

153. Tyler's First Annual Message to Congress, December 7, 1841, in Richardson, *Compilation of the Messages and Papers of the Presidents*, vol. 4, 79.

154. Robert Rayback, *Millard Fillmore: Biography of a President* (Norwalk, Conn.: Easton Press, 1989, reprint), 127–32, in Holt, *Rise and Fall of the American Whig Party*, 146–47.

155. Seager, *And Tyler Too*, 165.

156. Louis C. Kleber, "John Tyler," *History Today*, vol. 25, no. 10 (October 1975), 699.

157. Crittenden to R. P. Letcher, June 23, 1842, in Mrs. Chapman Coleman (Ann Mary Butler Crittenden), ed., *The Life of John J. Crittenden: With Selections from His Correspondences and Speeches* (Philadelphia: Lippincott, 1873), 1:183–89, in Holt, *Rise and Fall of the American Whig Party*, 147.

158. Seager, *And Tyler Too*, 169. See also Holt, *Rise and Fall of the American Whig Party*, 147.

159. Tyler to Robert McCandlish, July 10, 1842, in Tyler, *Letters and Times of the Tylers*, 2:173, in Remini, *Henry Clay*, 606.

160. Frank H. Severance, ed., *Millard Fillmore Papers* (Buffalo: Buffalo Historical Society, 1907), 2:225, in Chitwood, *John Tyler*, 251.

161. *Niles' National Register* 66 (March to September 1844), 441, in Chitwood, *John Tyler*, 318.

162. Davis to Clay, Worcester, October 14, 1843, in Calvin Colton, ed., *Works of Henry Clay: Comprising His Life, Correspondence, and Speeches* (New York: Henry Clay Publishing Company, 1897), 5:480–81, in Holt, *Rise and Fall of the American Whig Party*, 150.

163. Holt, *Rise and Fall of the American Whig Party*, 150.

164. Ibid., 168.

165. Ibid., 170.

166. Ibid., 168.
167. Ibid., 169.
168. For discussion of this, see Remini, *Henry Clay*, 634.
169. John Tyler to Henry Curtis, September 4, October 26, November 10, 1827, John Tyler Papers, Library of Congress, in Crapol, *John Tyler*, 61.
170. Ibid.
171. Ibid, 62.
172. Ibid, 62.
173. Carl Wheeless, *Landmarks of American Presidents: A Traveler's Guide* (Madison, Wisc.: Gale Research, 1996), 109, in ibid., 36.
174. John Tyler to Samuel Gardiner, November 26, 1850, Tyler Family Papers, Swem Library, College of William & Mary, in Crapol, *John Tyler*, 74.
175. Crapol, *John Tyler*, 76.
176. Abel P. Upshur to John C. Calhoun, August 14, 1843, in *William and Mary Quarterly* 16 (October 1936), 555, in Crapol, *John Tyler*, 74.
177. House Executive Document, 25th Congress, 1st Session, no. 40, p. 6, in Chitwood, *John Tyler*, 342–43.
178. Chitwood, *John Tyler*, 344.
179. Speech by Samuel Houston, delivered in New Orleans, 1845. Referenced in Chitwood, *John Tyler*, 344.
180. Crapol, *John Tyler*, 184.
181. John Tyler Papers, Library of Congress, IC, 6901–2, in Chitwood, *John Tyler*, 345.
182. Crapol, *John Tyler*, 71.
183. Ibid.
184. Ibid., 73.
185. Ibid., 217.
186. Jones to Van Zandt, December 13, 1843, in Annual Report of the American Historical Association, 1908, II, 232–35, in Frederick Merk, *Slavery and the Annexation of Texas* (New York: Knopf, 1972), 35.
187. Upshur to Murphy, January 16, 1844, in Senate Documents, 28th Congress, 1st Session (Series 435), no. 341, 43–48, in Merk, *Slavery and the Annexation of Texas*, 36. See also Chitwood, *John Tyler*, 348.
188. Merk, *Slavery and the Annexation of Texas*, 37.
189. Ibid.
190. Van Zandt to Jones, January 20, 1844, in A.H.A. *Report*, 1908, II, 239–43, in ibid., 38.
191. Sam Houston, *The Writings of Sam Houston, 1813–1863* (Austin: University of Texas Press, 1939) 3:521–23, in ibid.
192. *Niles' National Register* 66 (March to September 1844), 230–31, in Chitwood, *John Tyler*, 349.
193. Chitwood, *John Tyler*, 349.
194. *Niles' National Register*. See also *Sunbury American and Shamokin Journal* (Sunbury, Northumberland County, Pennsylvania), March 9, 1844, Chronicling America: Historic American Newspapers, Library of Congress, http://chroniclingamerica.loc.gov/lccn/sn85054702 /1844-03-09/ed-1/seq-1/.
195. Ann Blackman, "Fatal Cruise of the Princeton," *Naval History* 19, no. 5 (October 2005), https:// www.usni.org/magazines/navalhistory/2005-10/fatal-cruise-princeton.
196. Niall Kelly, "The Forgotten Tragedy: The 1844 Explosion on the USS Princeton Shook the Presidency of John Tyler," Fredericksburg.com, September 24, 2005, http://fredericksburg.com /town_and_countymiscellaneous/the-forgotten-tragedy-the-explosion-on-the-uss-princeton -shook/article_58a55481-ebdf-56f9-b5fb-b82fd2d894b6.html.

197. Sioussat, George L., ed., "The Accident on Board the U.S.S. Princeton, February 28, 1844: A Contemporary News-Letter," *Pennsylvania History: A Journal of Mid-Atlantic Studies* 4, no. 3 (July 1937), 161–89, https://www.jstor.org/stable/27766255.

198. Peterson, *Presidencies of William Henry Harrison & John Tyler*, 202.

199. *Sunbury American and Shamokin Journal*, March 9, 1844.

200. Sioussat, "The Accident on Board the U.S.S. Princeton."

201. Crapol, *John Tyler*, 207–8.

202. Interview with Harrison Tyler, Jr.: "Life Portrait of John Tyler," C-SPAN, aired May 17, 1999, http://www.c-span.org/video/?123380-1/life-portrait-john-tyler.

203. *Sunbury American and Shamokin Journal*, March 9, 1844.

204. Ibid.

205. Ibid.

206. Sioussat, "The Accident on Board the U.S.S. Princeton."

207. Peterson, *Presidencies of William Henry Harrison & John Tyler*, 202.

208. Elizabeth Tyler Coleman, *Priscilla Cooper Tyler and the American Scene: 1816–1889* (Tuscaloosa: University of Alabama Press, 2006), 101, in Seager, *And Tyler Too*, 204.

209. Blackman, "Fatal Cruise of the Princeton."

210. E. F. Ellet, *The Court Circles of the Republic* (New York: J. D. Dennison, 1869), 355–56, in ibid.

211. *Journal of Commerce*, February 28, 1844, reprinted in *The Liberator* (Boston), March 8, 1844, in Blackman, "Fatal Cruise of the Princeton."

212. Robert Seager writes in *And Tyler Too* that Gardiner's "watch had stopped at the moment of explosion. It read 4:06; Upshur's read 4:15" (p. 205).

213. *Sunbury American and Shamokin Journal*, March 9, 1844.

214. Kerry Walters, *Explosion on the Potomac: The 1844 Calamity Aboard the USS Princeton* (Charleston, S.C.: The History Press, 2006), 71.

215. Niall Kelly, "The Forgotten Tragedy."

216. Ibid.

217. Ibid.

218. There are several discrepancies that exist around John Tyler's "personal servant" who died on the *Princeton*. First, three different names have been recorded: Armistead, Henry, and Joseph. Second, most accounts refer to him as Tyler's "personal servant" and not as his slave. But given the man's description and the fact that Tyler's personal slaves were his servants while in the White House, I have concluded such here. Third, there is some debate about his age. Most accounts put him between twenty-two and twenty-four years old. However, *Niles' National Register* has an account that puts him at fifteen years old, but the latter is less substantiated.

219. Jesse Holland, *The Invisibles: The Untold Story of African American Slaves in the White House* (Guilford, Conn.: Lyon's Press, 2016), 178.

220. *Niles' National Register*, March 9, 1844.

221. Seager, *And Tyler Too*, 205.

222. May, *John Tyler*, 108.

223. Walters, *Explosion on the Potomac*, 72.

224. *Journal of Commerce*, February 28, 1844, reprinted in *The Liberator*, March 8, 1844, in Blackman, "Fatal Cruise of the Princeton."

225. Sioussat, "The Accident on Board the U.S.S. Princeton."

226. *Madisonian*, February 28, 1844, reprinted in the *Maine Farmer* (Augusta), March 7, 1844; *The Liberator*, March 8, 1844, 3, in Blackman, "Fatal Cruise of the Princeton."

227. Peterson, *Presidencies of William Henry Harrison & John Tyler*, 203. See also *Richmond Enquirer* (Va.), March 8, 1844, Chronicling America: Historic American Newspapers, Library of Congress, http://chroniclingamerica.loc.gov/lccn/sn84024735/1844-03-08/ed-1/seq-2/.

228. Seager, *And Tyler Too*, 205.

229. Kelly, "The Forgotten Tragedy."

230. This description is brought together from several periodicals that described the scene: *Rutland Herald* (Vt.), March 14, 1844, Chronicling America: Historic American Newspapers, Library of Congress, http://chroniclingamerica.loc.gov/lccn/sn84022355/1844-03-14/ed-1/seq-3/. See also *Richmond Enquirer*, March 8, 1844.

231. *Richmond Enquirer*, March 8, 1844.

232. *Sunbury American and Shamokin Journal*, March 9, 1844.

233. Crapol, *John Tyler*, 210.

234. William Waller wed Elizabeth Tyler on January 31, 1842. Letitia Tyler, who had been extremely ill, attended the White House wedding in what was her only public appearance as First Lady. See Doug Wead, *All the Presidents' Children: Triumph and Tragedy in the Lives of America's First Families* (New York: Atria, 2003).

235. Sioussat, "The Accident on Board the U.S.S. Princeton."

236. Alfred H. Miles, "The Princeton Explosion," United States Naval Institute Proceedings, 52 (November 1926), 2225–45. See also "The Dead of the Cabinet" speech delivered at Petersburg, Virginia, April 24, 1856, in Tyler, *Letters and Times of the Tylers*, 2:384–399.

237. Ibid.

238. Ibid.

239. "Willie P. Mangum," Art & History, United States Senate, http://www.senate.gov/artandhistory/art/artifact/Painting_32_00022.htm.

240. "Life Portrait of John Tyler," C-SPAN.

241. Ibid.

242. Alexander Gardiner to S. R. Ely, New York, March 7, 1844, in Seager, *And Tyler Too*, 205.

243. Kelly, "The Forgotten Tragedy." See also Seager, *And Tyler Too*, 206.

244. Kelly, "The Forgotten Tragedy." See also Seager, *And Tyler Too*, 207.

245. Letter from John Tyler to Mrs. Julia Gardiner, condolences for the loss of her husband, March 1, 1844, East Hampton Library, New York.

246. "When New York Saw a Presidential Wedding: John Tyler's Romance with Miss Julia Gardiner Culminated in Their Marriage at the Church of the Ascension in This City Seventy-One Years Ago," *New York Times*, October 17, 1915.

247. Ibid.

248. Ibid.

249. Isaac Van Zandt to Anson Jones, February 27, 1844, in Crapol, *John Tyler*, 209.

250. Van Zandt to Jones, March 5, 1844, in A.H.A. *Report*, 1908, II, 261–62, in Merk, *Slavery and the Annexation of Texas*, 43.

251. Ibid.

252. James C. N. Paul, *Rift in the Democracy* (Philadelphia: University of Pennsylvania Press, 1951), 38–47, in Holt, *Rise and Fall of the American Whig Party*, 171.

253. Holt, *Rise and Fall of the American Whig Party*, 171.

254. Clay to Willie P. Mangum, April 14, 1844, Mangum MSS in ibid., 177.

255. Crapol, *John Tyler*, 216–17.

256. Charles Sellers, *James K. Polk: Continentalist* (Princeton: Princeton University Press, 1966), 101–3, in Holt, *Rise and Fall of the American Whig Party*, 172–73.

257. Robert Rantoul, Jr. to Nathaniel P. Banks, August 9, 1844, Banks MSS (Illinois State Historical Library) in Holt, *Rise and Fall of the American Whig Party*, 174–75.

258. Holt, *Rise and Fall of the American Whig Party*, 175.

259. *Congressional Globe*, 28th Congress, 2nd Session, 360 and 372, in ibid., 221.

260. Crapol, *John Tyler*, 220. See also Peterson, *Presidencies of William Henry Harrison & John Tyler*, 255–59.

261. Edward W. Emerson and Waldo E. Forbes, eds., *Journals of Ralph Waldo Emerson* (10 vols., Boston, 1909–1914), 7:206, in Holman Hamilton, *Prologue to Conflict: The Crisis & Compromise of 1850* (Lexington: University of Kentucky Press, 2005), 24. "Poison us" is a metaphor for the postwar divisions the war would exacerbate, particularly related to slavery and ideological differences related to expansionism.

CHAPTER TWO: OVER MY DEAD BODY

1. Elbert B. Smith, *The Presidencies of Zachary Taylor & Millard Fillmore* (Lawrence: University of Kansas Press, 1988), 36.

2. John S. D. Eisenhower, *Zachary Taylor* (New York: Times Books, 2008), 63.

3. Robert W. Merry, "The Myth of the One Term Wonder," *New York Times*, February 13, 2010, https://www.nytimes.com/2010/02/14/opinion/14merry.html. Merry argues that Polk's pledge was based on an assumption that by keeping 1848 an open field, he could rally support among his party's elite.

4. Eisenhower, *Zachary Taylor*, 63.

5. Remini, *Henry Clay: Statesman for the Union* (New York: Norton, 1991), 684.

6. Eisenhower, *Zachary Taylor*, 72.

7. Henry Montgomery, *The Life of Major General Zachary Taylor* (Buffalo, N.Y.: Derby & Hewson, 1847), 345–46. This alleged incident took place November 1847, just after his victory at the Battle of Buena Vista.

8. Hudson Strode, *Jefferson Davis: American Patriot, 1808–1861* (New York: Harcourt, Brace, 1955), 2:136, in Seale, *The President's House*, 1:273.

9. Description of both the Whig and Democratic agendas drawn from corroborating several sources, including Holt, *Rise and Fall of the American Whig Party*, 331–382; Remini, 687–707 and *Henry Clay: Statesman for the Union*; Hamilton, *Prologue to Conflict*, 8–10; and Freehling, *The Road to Disunion*, 475–479.

10. Eisenhower, *Zachary Taylor*, 102–3.

11. About thirteen thousand Americans lost their lives, and another seventeen thousand were injured: John W. Chambers II, ed, *The Oxford Companion to American Military History* (Oxford University Press, 1999), 849.

12. William A. DeGregorio, *The Complete Book of U.S. Presidents: From George Washington to Bill Clinton* (New York: Wings Books, 1993), 171.

13. Ibid.

14. Elbert B. Smith, *Presidencies of Zachary Taylor & Millard Fillmore*, 2. See also John C. Waugh, *On the Brink of Civil War: The Compromise of 1850 and How It Changed the Course of American History* (Wilmington, Del.: Scholarly Resources Books, 2003), 3–4.

15. Norman E. Tuturow, *Texas Annexation and the Mexican War: A Political Study of the Old Northwest* (Palo Alto, Calif.: Chadwick House, 1978), 212.

16. Thomas Jefferson, *The Works of Thomas Jefferson*, ed. Paul Leicester Ford (New York, Knickerbocker Press, 1905), 12:159. For discussion on the discrepancy between "ear" and "ears" see Anna Berkes, "Wolf by the Ear (Quotation)," May 31, 2007, Monticello, https://www.monticello.org/site/jefferson/wolf-ear-quotation.

17. John Seigenthaler, *James K. Polk* (New York: Times Books, 2003), 152–154. For detailed discussion on the partisan debate over slavery during the election, see Joseph G. Rayback, *Free Soil: The Election of 1848* (Lexington: University Press of Kentucky, 1970), 56–80 (debate within Democratic Party); 84–98 (debate within Whig Party).

18. Hamilton, *Prologue to Conflict*, 9.

19. Elbert B. Smith, *Presidencies of Zachary Taylor & Millard Fillmore*, 25.

20. Montgomery, *The Life of Major General Zachary Taylor*, 15.

21. Ibid., 15–16.

22. Ibid., 16.

23. Ibid.

24. Edwin P. Hoyt, *Zachary Taylor* (Chicago: Reilly & Lee, 1966), 5.

25. K. Jack Bauer, *Zachary Taylor: Soldier, Planter, Statesman of the Old Southwest* (Baton Rouge: Louisiana State University Press, 1985), 4. See also Hamilton, *Zachary Taylor*, 28–29; Dyer, *Zachary Taylor* (Baton Rouge: Louisiana State University Press, 1946), 11; Elbert B. Smith, *Presidencies of Zachary Taylor & Millard Fillmore*, 26; and Eisenhower, *Zachary Taylor*, 2.

26. Montgomery, *The Life of Major General Zachary Taylor*, 358. See also Hoyt, *Zachary Taylor*, 89. For height see DeGregorio, *Complete Book of U.S. Presidents*, 175.

27. T. N. Parmalee, "Recollections of an Old Stager," *Harper's New Monthly Magazine* 47 (1873), 588, in *Zachary Taylor*, 327.

28. Montgomery, *The Life of Major General Zachary Taylor*, 358.

29. James Morgan, *Our Presidents* (New York: Macmillan, 1935), 106, in Boller, *Presidential Anecdotes*, 103.

30. Fletcher H. Archer to Mrs. Prudence Archer, May 30, 1847, Petersburg, Virginia, newspaper clipping in possession of Severn L. Nottingham, Orange, Virginia, in Hamilton, *Zachary Taylor*, 247.

31. Elbert B. Smith, *Presidencies of Zachary Taylor & Millard Fillmore*, 25.

32. Hoyt, *Zachary Taylor*, 88.

33. James Morgan, *Our Presidents*, 106, in Boller, *Presidential Anecdotes*, 103. See also Benjamin Perley Poore, *Perley's Reminiscences of Sixty Years in the National Metropolis*, 1:345–46, in Waugh, *On the Brink of Civil War*, 33.

34. Bauer, *Zachary Taylor*, 223–24.

35. Zachary Taylor to Jefferson Davis, August 16, 1847, Taylor Papers, in Elbert B. Smith, *Presidencies of Zachary Taylor & Millard Fillmore*, 40.

36. Eisenhower, *Zachary Taylor*, 80.

37. Ibid., 81.

38. Paul Finkelman, *Millard Fillmore*, The American Presidents (New York: Times Books, 2011), 44.

39. Ibid., 45.

40. Jules Witcover, *The American Vice Presidency: From Irrelevance to Power* (Washington, D.C.: Smithsonian Books, 2014), 117. See also Feerick, *From Failing Hands*, 100.

41. Elbert B. Smith, *Presidencies of Zachary Taylor & Millard Fillmore*, 43–44. See also Witcover, *American Vice Presidency*, 114.

42. Elbert B. Smith, *Presidencies of Zachary Taylor & Millard Fillmore*, 44.

43. Ibid.

44. Finkelman, *Millard Fillmore*, 7.

45. Severance, *Millard Fillmore Papers*, 2:351–54, in Boller, *Presidential Anecdotes*, 112.

46. Finkelman, *Millard Fillmore*, 8.

47. Ibid., 11.

48. Ibid., 14.

49. Eisenhower, *Zachary Taylor*, 83.

50. Witcover, *American Vice Presidency*, 116.

51. Finkelman, *Millard Fillmore*, 21.

52. Bauer, *Zachary Taylor*, 237.

53. Eisenhower, *Zachary Taylor*, 84.

54. Bauer, *Zachary Taylor*, 238.

55. Hoyt, *Zachary Taylor*, 110. See also Bauer, *Zachary Taylor*, 238; Elbert B. Smith, *Presidencies of Zachary Taylor & Millard Fillmore*, 41; and Eisenhower, *Zachary Taylor*, 84.

56. Joel H. Silbey, *Storm over Texas: The Annexation Controversy and the Road to Civil War* (Oxford: Oxford University Press, 2005), 139.

57. Minor/Third Party Platforms, Whig Party Platform of 1848 Online by Gerhard Peters and John T. Woolley, The American Presidency Project, https://www.presidency.ucsb.edu/node /273458; see also Seale, *The President's House*, 1:280.

58. Hoyt, *Zachary Taylor*, 113.

59. Bauer, *Zachary Taylor*, 247.

60. The single day of voting was in accordance with an act passed by Congress in 1845: Boller, *Presidential Campaigns*, 86. See also Bauer, *Zachary Taylor*, 245. In this case, "Voting" refers to the popular vote except in South Carolina, where the electors were appointed by the state legislature. In Massachusetts, if the electors could not garner a majority vote in the election, the state legislature would appoint the state's electors. See Bonnie K. Goodman, "Presidential Campaigns & Elections: 1848," https://presidentialcampaignselectionsreference.wordpress.com /overviews/19th–century/1848-overview/.

61. Hoyt, *Zachary Taylor*, 113.

62. Boller, *Presidential Campaigns*, 86.

63. Bauer, *Zachary Taylor*, 245.

64. Hamilton, *Prologue to Conflict*, 14.

65. Ibid., 10.

66. Waugh, *On the Brink of Civil War*, 38. See also Arthur C. Cole, *The Whig Party in the South* (Washington, D.C.: American Historical Association, 1913), 127–28.

67. Waugh, *On the Brink of Civil War*, 38.

68. Ibid., 20.

69. Elbert B. Smith, *Presidencies of Zachary Taylor & Millard Fillmore*, 96.

70. Wendy Wolff, ed., *The Senate, 1789–1989* (Washington, D.C.: U.S. Government Printing Office, 1995), 3:325. See also Harry Searles, "Compromise of 1850," American History Central, http:// www.americanhistorycentral.com/entries/compromise-of-1850/.

71. According to Section 9 of the Texas Constitution, "All persons of color who were slaves for life previous to their emigration to Texas, and who are now held in bondage, shall remain in the like state of servitude. . . . Nor shall congress have the power to emancipate slaves; nor shall any slave holder be allowed to emancipate his or her slave without the consent of congress." See Randolph B. Campbell, "Slavery," Texas State Historical Association, https://tshaonline.org /handbook/online/articles/yps01.

72. Chris DeRose, *The Presidents' War: Six American Presidents and the Civil War That Divided Them* (Guilford, Conn.: Lyons Press, 2014), 51.

73. Finkelman, *Millard Fillmore*, 42.

74. Searles, "Compromise of 1850."

75. See speech of Honorable Horace Mann, of Massachusetts: "On Slavery and the Slave-trade in the District of Columbia," delivered in the House of Representatives of the United States, February 23, 1849. (Published by Pennsylvania Anti-Slavery Society, December 31, 1849.) In his speech, Mann noted the U.S. was lagging behind "uncivilized countries" on the slave trade and called out the Senate for being a legislative blocker to its abolition in the nation's capital. He disparagingly observed, "By Authority of Congress, the city of Washington is the Congo of America."

76. Damani Davis, "Slavery and Emancipation in the Nation's Capital: Using Federal Records to Explore the Lives of African American Ancestors," *Prologue Magazine*, 42, no. 1 (Spring 2010), https://www.archives.gov/publications/prologue/2010/spring/dcslavery.html.

77. Adam Goodheart, "A Capital Under Slavery's Shadow," *New York Times*, February 24, 2011, https://opinionator.blogs.nytimes.com/2011/02/24/a-capital-under-slaverys-shadow/.

78. Eisenhower, *Zachary Taylor*, 24.

79. Seale, *The President's House*, 1:278–79.

80. William O. Lynch, "Zachary Taylor as President," *Journal of Southern History* 4, no. 3 (1938), 282. See also Eisenhower, *Zachary Taylor*, 94.

81. Daniel Webster to R. M. Blatchford, February 4, 1849, in Daniel Webster, *The Private Correspondence of Daniel Webster*, Fletcher Webster, ed. (Boston: Little, Brown, 1857), 2:295, in Bauer, *Zachary Taylor*, 250.

82. Lynch, "Zachary Taylor as President," 284.

83. Eisenhower, *Zachary Taylor*, 94.

84. "Until the 1930s, presidential and congressional terms began at noon on March 4," "President for a Day," Art & History, United States Senate, http://www.senate.gov/artandhistory/history/minute/President_For_A_Day.htm. See also William E. Parrish, *David Rice Atchison of Missouri: Border Politician* (Columbia: University of Missouri Press, 1961).

85. Christopher Klein, "The 24-Hour President," History Channel, February 28, 2013, https://www.history.com/news/the-24-hour-president.

86. Ibid.

87. Ibid.

88. Elbert B. Smith, *Presidencies of Zachary Taylor & Millard Fillmore*, 49. According to the National Weather Service, the temperature was an estimated forty-two degrees, "cloudy with snow flurries" followed by "heavy snow [that] began during the inaugural ball." Found at: https://www.weather.gov/lwx/events_Inauguration.

89. The discomfort and bitterness are reflected in James K. Polk, *The Diary of James K. Polk: During His Presidency 1845 to 1849*, Milo Milton Quaife, ed., 4 vols. (Chicago: A.C. McClurg and Co., 1910) 4: 374–377; for Taylor fanfare see Seale, *The President's House*, 1:273.

90. "Arrangements for the Inauguration of the President Elect, on the Fifth of March, 1849," in Department of State (National Archives, Record Group 59), in Bauer, *Zachary Taylor*, 258.

91. Elbert B. Smith, *Presidencies of Zachary Taylor & Millard Fillmore*, 52.

92. Remini, *Henry Clay*, 728.

93. Hamilton, *Prologue to Conflict*, 47–48.

94. Seale, *The President's House*, 1:275–76.

95. Elbert B. Smith, *Presidencies of Zachary Taylor & Millard Fillmore*, 120.

96. Hamilton, *Prologue to Conflict*, 16.

97. Elbert B. Smith, *Presidencies of Zachary Taylor & Millard Fillmore*, 102.

98. Hamilton, *Prologue to Conflict*, 34–35.

99. *Congressional Globe*, 31st Congress, 1st Session, 1425, in ibid., 42.

100. Elbert B. Smith, *Presidencies of Zachary Taylor & Millard Fillmore*, 108.

101. When a vacancy opened for one of Kentucky's Senate seats, the state voted 92 to 45 to send Henry Clay to the Senate over Democrat Richard Johnson (See Remini, *Henry Clay*, 716).

102. Waugh, *On the Brink of Civil War*, 73.

103. Ibid., 74. See also Irving H. Bartlett, *Daniel Webster* (New York: Norton, 1978), 204–5, in Bauer, *Zachary Taylor*, 301; and Remini, *Henry Clay*, 731.

104. *Congressional Globe*, 31st Congress, 1st Session, 21:244–47, in Elbert B. Smith, *Presidencies of Zachary Taylor & Millard Fillmore*, 111.

105. Remini, *Henry Clay*, 732.

106. *Congressional Globe*, 31st Congress, 1st Session, 21:244–47, in Elbert B. Smith, *Presidencies of Zachary Taylor & Millard Fillmore*, 111. It is worth noting that while much of the focus was on a revised fugitive slave law and abolition of the slave trade in Washington, D.C., there remained the problem of an illegal slave trade throughout the 1840s and 1850s. The *Wanderer*, for example, was disguised as a luxury yacht and would sail the triangle between Africa, the United States, and the Caribbean buying and selling slaves. See Hugh Thomas, *The Slave Trade: The Story of the Atlantic Slave Trade: 1440–1870* (New York: Simon & Schuster, 1997), 766–768.

107. Waugh, *On the Brink of Civil War*, 85.

108. Ibid., 92.

109. When Seward says "climate" he means it literally in reference to weather, and in the full speech goes on to talk about the tropical climates of Africa.

110. Waugh, 113.

111. Elbert B. Smith, *Presidencies of Zachary Taylor & Millard Fillmore*, 122. See also Eisenhower, *Zachary Taylor*, 129.

112. Elbert B. Smith, *Presidencies of Zachary Taylor & Millard Fillmore*, 120.

113. *Congressional Globe*, 31st Congress, 1st Session, 444–48, in Hamilton, *Prologue to Conflict*, 88.

114. Remini, *Henry Clay*, 742.

115. Waugh, *On the Brink of Civil War*, 117–18.

116. Ibid., 128–29.

117. Elbert B. Smith, *Presidencies of Zachary Taylor & Millard Fillmore*, 117.

118. Remini, *Henry Clay*, 746.

119. Waugh, *On the Brink of Civil War*, 127.

120. Joanne B. Freeman, "When Congress Was Armed and Dangerous," *New York Times*, January 11, 2011, https://www.nytimes.com/2011/01/12/opinion/12freeman.html.

121. Waugh, *On the Brink of Civil War*, 135–36.

122. Ibid., 136.

123. Ibid., 125.

124. Ibid.

125. Ibid.

126. Ibid.

127. Ibid.

128. *Congressional Globe*, 31st Congress, 1st Session, 760–63, in Remini, *Henry Clay*, 745.

129. Waugh, *On the Brink of Civil War*, 138.

130. *Congressional Globe*, 31st Congress, 1st Session, 760–63, in Remini, *Henry Clay*, 745. See also William N. Chambers, *Old Bullion Benton: Senator from the New West: Thomas Hart Benton, 1782 to 1858* (New York: Little, Brown, 1956), 359–62; Bauer, *Zachary Taylor*, 306; and Waugh, *On the Brink of Civil War*, 138.

131. Waugh, *On the Brink of Civil War*, 138. See also Bill Kelter and Wayne Shellabarger, *Veeps: Profiles in Insignificance: The American Vice Presidential Pantheon from Adams to Cheney* (Atlanta: Top Shelf Productions, 2008), 67.

132. Testimony of Mr. Jesse B. Bright in *Reports of Committees: 30th Congress, 1st Session–48th Congress, 2nd Session*, vol. 1.

133. Testimony of Mr. Henry Dodge in *Reports of Committees: 30th Congress, 1st Session–48th Congress, 2nd Session*, vol. 1. See also *Congressional Globe*, 31st Congress, 1st Session, 760–63, in Remini, *Henry Clay*, 745.

134. Testimony of Mr. George T. Brown in *Reports of Committees: 30th Congress, 1st Session–48th Congress, 2nd Session*, vol. 1.

135. Waugh, *On the Brink of Civil War*, 138–39.

136. *Congressional Globe*, 31st Congress, 1st Session, 21:517–21, 640–42, and 708–9, in Elbert B. Smith, *Presidencies of Zachary Taylor & Millard Fillmore*, 138.

137. Waugh, *On the Brink of Civil War*, 138–39.

138. *Congressional Globe*, 31st Congress, 1st Session, 760–63, in Remini, *Henry Clay*, 745.

139. Ibid. See also Chambers, *Old Bullion Benton*, 359–62, in Hamilton, *Prologue to Conflict*, 93–94.

140. "Bitter Feelings in the Senate Chamber," Art & History, United States Senate, https://www.senate.gov/artandhistory/history/minute/Bitter_Feelings_In_the_Senate_Chamber.htm.

141. Testimony of Mr. Daniel S. Dickinson in *Reports of Committees: 30th Congress, 1st Session–48th Congress, 2nd Session*, vol. 1.

142. Waugh, *On the Brink of Civil War*, 139.

143. Remini, *Henry Clay*, 747. Remini's description is corroborated in Hamilton, *Prologue to Conflict*, 95, and Elbert B. Smith, *Presidencies of Zachary Taylor & Millard Fillmore*, 139.

144. Additional analysis on the Tyler-Clay rift in Dyer, *Zachary Taylor*, 383. See also Bauer, *Zachary Taylor*, 307–8.

145. Lynch, "Zachary Taylor as President," 286.

146. Robert Toombs to John Crittenden, Washington, April 23, 1850, John J. Crittenden Papers, 1782–1913, vol. 14, Library of Congress, in ibid., 290.

147. Charles S. Morehead to John Crittenden, Washington, March 30, 1850, in John J. Crittenden Papers, in Lynch, "Zachary Taylor as President," 290–91.

148. Daniel Webster to David A. Hall, Washington, May 18, 1850, in Daniel Webster, *Letters of Daniel Webster from Documents Owned Principally by the New Hampshire Historical Society*, C. H. Van Tyne, ed. (New York: McClure, Phillips & Co., 1902), 412–13, in Lynch, "Zachary Taylor as President," 291.

149. Henry Clay to James Harlan, March 16, 1850, in Calvin Colton, ed., *The Private Correspondence of Henry Clay* (New York: A. S. Barnes, 1856), 604, in Bauer, *Zachary Taylor*, 265. See also William J. Cooper, Jr., *The South and the Politics of Slavery, 1828–1856* (Baton Rouge: Louisiana State University Press, 1978), 275.

150. Elbert B. Smith, *Presidencies of Zachary Taylor & Millard Fillmore*, 141.

151. Remini, *Henry Clay*, 751.

152. Henry Clay to Lucretia Clay, July 6, 1850, Thomas J. Clay Papers, Library of Congress, in ibid., 752.

153. Elbert B. Smith, *Presidencies of Zachary Taylor & Millard Fillmore*, 141.

154. *The Republic* (Washington, D.C.), May 27, 1850. See also Bauer, *Zachary Taylor*, 309.

155. Hoyt, *Zachary Taylor*, 145.

156. DeRose, *Presidents' War*, 53.

157. William Campbell Binkley, "The Question of Texan Jurisdiction in New Mexico under the United States, 1848–1850," *Southwestern Historical Quarterly* 24, no. 1 (July 1920), 1–38, https://www.jstor.org/stable/30234791, in Elbert B. Smith, *Presidencies of Zachary Taylor & Millard Fillmore*, 152.

158. Ibid.

159. Ibid.

160. Ibid.

161. Ibid., 153.

162. J. F. H. Claiborne, *Life and Correspondence of John A. Quitman* (New York: Harper & Brothers, 1860), 2:32–33, in Hamilton, *Prologue to Conflict*, 106.

163. Frederick W. Seward, *Seward at Washington as Senator and Secretary of State* (New York: Derby and Miller, 1891), 141, in Bauer, *Zachary Taylor*, 311.

164. Ibid.

165. Seale, *The President's House*, 1:280–81. See also Mark Scroggins, *Hannibal: The Life of Abraham*

Lincoln's First Vice-President (New York: Rowman & Littlefield, 1994), 78–79; and Waugh, *On the Brink of Civil War*, 170.

166. Seale, *The President's House*, 1:280–81. See also Peter Marshall and David Manuel, *Sounding Forth the Trumpet: 1837–1860* (Grand Rapids, MI: Revell, 2009), 338.

167. Bauer offers a more tempered version of the same story: Taylor "warned the southerners that he would order the army to defend the New Mexico border if Texas attempted to alter it." Secretary of War George W. Crawford, who was more lawyer than military tactician, subsequently heard about his boss's threat and "insisted he would not sign such an order." Taylor explained that should he be unwilling, he would be more than happy to sign his own name if necessary (Bauer, *Zachary Taylor*, 311).

168. Scroggins, *Hannibal*, 79. See also Waugh, *On the Brink of Civil War*, 59; Seale, *The President's House*, 280–81; Boller, *Presidential Anecdotes*, 107; and Eisenhower, *Zachary Taylor*, 110.

169. Waugh, *On the Brink of Civil War*, 171.

170. Witcover, *American Vice Presidency*, 118.

171. Elbert B. Smith, *Presidencies of Zachary Taylor & Millard Fillmore*, 159–60.

172. Bauer, *Zachary Taylor*, 308.

173. William Seward to Thurlow Weed, March 24, 1849, in Thurlow Weed Papers, in Bauer, *Zachary Taylor*, 263–64.

174. Elbert B. Smith, *Presidencies of Zachary Taylor & Millard Fillmore*, 162–63. He also repeated the same request to Secretary of the Treasury William M. Meredith.

175. Severance, *Millard Fillmore Papers*, 2:321–34. The specific recollection of his conversation with president Taylor is on p. 323: "I recollect having a conversation with Gen'l Taylor, in which I said to him . . . I might be called upon to give a casting vote in the Senate on the Compromise Bill, and if I should feel it my duty to vote for it . . . I wished him to understand, that it was not out of any hostility to him or his Administration, but . . . because I deemed it for the interests of the country."

176. Elbert B. Smith, *Presidencies of Zachary Taylor & Millard Fillmore*, 128.

177. Ibid., 156–57.

178. Ibid., 156.

179. Ibid.

180. Eisenhower, *Zachary Taylor*, 132–33.

181. Ibid.

182. Willie P. Mangum to his wife, July 10, 1850, in *Papers of Willie Person Mangum*, 2:369–70, in Bauer, *Zachary Taylor*, 314.

183. Waugh, *On the Brink of Civil War*, 163. See also Elbert B. Smith, *Presidencies of Zachary Taylor & Millard Fillmore*, 156.

184. Elbert B. Smith, *Presidencies of Zachary Taylor & Millard Fillmore*, 156. See also Eisenhower, *Zachary Taylor*, 133.

185. Willie P. Mangum to his wife, July 10, 1850, in *Papers of Willie Person Mangum*, 314. See also Hamilton, *Prologue to Conflict*, 107.

186. Elbert B. Smith, *Presidencies of Zachary Taylor & Millard Fillmore*, 156.

187. Eisenhower, *Zachary Taylor*, 133.

188. Seale, *The President's House*, 1:281.

189. Bauer, *Zachary Taylor*, 315.

190. Ibid.

191. Hamilton, *Prologue to Conflict*, 107. See also Eisenhower, *Zachary Taylor*, 133; and Hamilton, *Zachary Taylor*, 389.

192. Bauer, *Zachary Taylor*, 315.

193. Edward B. MacMahon and Leonard Curry, *Medical Cover-Ups in the White House* (Washington, D.C.: Farragut Publishing Company, 1987), 9.

194. Ross Anderson, "The Bug That Poisoned the President," *Food Safety News*, February 21, 2011, https://www.foodsafetynews.com/2011/02/the-bug-that-poisoned-the-president/.

195. Bauer, *Zachary Taylor*, 315.

196. Anderson, "The Bug That Poisoned the President."

197. Eisenhower, *Zachary Taylor*, 133.

198. Bauer, *Zachary Taylor*, 315. See also Elbert B. Smith, *Presidencies of Zachary Taylor & Millard Fillmore*, 156.

199. Bauer, *Zachary Taylor*, 315.

200. Anderson, "The Bug That Poisoned the President."

201. Ibid.

202. Waugh, *On the Brink of Civil War*, 163–64. See also Bauer, *Zachary Taylor*, 315.

203. Hoyt, *Zachary Taylor*, 149–50.

204. Ibid., 150.

205. *The Republic* (Washington, D.C.), July 9, 1850, in Feerick, *From Failing Hands*, 101.

206. Waugh, *On the Brink of Civil War*, 164.

207. Hoyt, *Zachary Taylor*, 150.

208. Ibid., 151. See also Waugh, *On the Brink of Civil War*, 164; and Bauer, *Zachary Taylor*, 315.

209. Eisenhower, *Zachary Taylor*, 133–34.

210. There is a discrepancy over who said this. This may have been a colleague; historical accounts say both. Hoyt suggests it was Taylor asking the question. The reference to "someone" reflects the uncertainty.

211. Hoyt, *Zachary Taylor*, 151.

212. Elbert B. Smith, *Presidencies of Zachary Taylor & Millard Fillmore*, 157.

213. Ibid.

214. Hoyt, *Zachary Taylor*, 151. See also Eisenhower, *Zachary Taylor*, 133–34.

215. Eisenhower, *Zachary Taylor*, 134.

216. Richardson, *Messages and Papers of the Presidents*, vol. 5, p. 51, in Feerick, *From Failing Hands*, 101.

217. Communication to the Senate from Mr. Fillmore, in *Senate Journal*, 31st Congress, 1st Session, 443, July 10, 1850, in Richardson, *Messages and Papers of the Presidents*, vol. 5, part 1: *Presidents Taylor and Fillmore*, 54. See also Feerick, *From Failing Hands*, 101; and Eisenhower, *Zachary Taylor*, 134.

218. Elbert B. Smith, *Presidencies of Zachary Taylor & Millard Fillmore*, 195.

219. Ibid, 196.

220. "Assassination of Presidents," *New York Times*, August 29, 1881, https://timesmachine.nytimes.com/timesmachine/1881/08/29/98918603.html?pageNumber=8.

221. Eric Harrison, "Zachary Taylor Did Not Die of Arsenic Poisoning, Tests Indicate," *Los Angeles Times*, June 27, 1991, http://articles.latimes.com/1991-06-27/news/mn-2064_1_zachary-taylor.

222. Ibid.

223. Michel Marriott, "President Zachary Taylor's Body to Be Tested for Signs of Arsenic," *New York Times*, June 15, 1991, https://www.nytimes.com/1991/06/15/us/president-zachary-taylor-s-body-to-be-tested-for-signs-of-arsenic.html.

224. Harrison, "Zachary Taylor Did Not Die of Arsenic Poisoning, Tests Indicate."

225. Feerick, *From Failing Hands*, 102–3.

226. Ibid., 104.

227. Ibid., 103.

228. Finkelman, *Millard Fillmore*, 76–77.

229. Waugh, *On the Brink of Civil War*, 169.
230. Hamilton, *Prologue to Conflict*, 107.
231. Henry Clay to James Clay, August 6, 1850, in Colton, *Works of Henry Clay*, 4:611, in Remini, *Henry Clay*, 752.
232. Ibid.
233. Hamilton, *Prologue to Conflict*, 107–8.
234. Remini, *Henry Clay*, 753.
235. Waugh, *On the Brink of Civil War*, 174.
236. *Congressional Globe*, 31st Congress, 1st Session, 21:1380–83, in Elbert B. Smith, *Presidencies of Zachary Taylor & Millard Fillmore*, 173.
237. Remini, *Henry Clay*, 760.
238. Waugh, *On the Brink of Civil War*, 175.
239. *Congressional Globe*, 31st Congress, 1st Session, Appendix, 1482–85, in Hamilton, *Prologue to Conflict*, 111.
240. DeRose, *Presidents' War*, 54.
241. Hamilton, *Prologue to Conflict*, 133.
242. Waugh, *On the Brink of Civil War*, 181.
243. Finkelman, *Millard Fillmore*, 78.
244. Elbert B. Smith, *Presidencies of Zachary Taylor & Millard Fillmore*, 181.
245. DeRose, *Presidents' War*, 54.
246. *Congressional Globe*, 31st Congress, 1st Session, 1540–45, 1551–52, and 1554–56, in Hamilton, *Prologue to Conflict*, 139.
247. Thomas Donaldson, *The Public Domain: Its History, with Statistics* (Washington, D.C.: U.S. Government Printing Office, 1884), 453.
248. *Daily Union*, August 17, 18, 21, 24, 27, and 31, and September 3, 1850, in Elbert B. Smith, *Presidencies of Zachary Taylor & Millard Fillmore*, 186.
249. Holman Hamilton explains: "Neither the *Congressional Globe* nor the *Senate Journal* gives us a yea-and-nay breakdown of the final vote on the fugitive slave bill. What we do know is that, on August 23, only twelve senators opposed and twenty-seven assented to its engrossment for a third reading. This was tantamount to passage, which followed *viva voce* on August 26." (*Prologue to Conflict*, 141).
250. Finkelman, *Millard Fillmore*, 85.
251. Elbert B. Smith, *Presidencies of Zachary Taylor & Millard Fillmore*, 200.
252. Finkelman, *Millard Fillmore*, 104.
253. Ibid., 86.
254. Ibid., 88.
255. Finkelman, *Millard Fillmore*, 102–29.
256. Ibid., 85.
257. DeRose, *Presidents' War*, 54.
258. Waugh, *On the Brink of Civil War*, 187–88.
259. Ibid., 189.
260. Elbert B. Smith, *Presidencies of Zachary Taylor & Millard Fillmore*, 188–89.
261. Hamilton, *Prologue to Conflict*, 160.
262. Ibid.
263. Elbert B. Smith, *Presidencies of Zachary Taylor & Millard Fillmore*, 188–89.
264. Ibid. See also Hamilton, *Prologue to Conflict*, 160.
265. Jonathan M. Foltz to James Buchanan, September 8, 1850, James Buchanan Papers, Historical Society of Pennsylvania, Philadelphia, in Hamilton, *Prologue to Conflict*, 160.
266. Hoyt, *Zachary Taylor*, 153.

267. Eisenhower, *Zachary Taylor*, 140.

268. Elbert B. Smith, *Presidencies of Zachary Taylor & Millard Fillmore*, 240.

269. Historian Carl Anthony has a colorful description of the tragic incident at: "The Train Accident That Broke a President, Estranged His Wife & Killed His Son," Carl Anthony Online, May 15, 2015, http://carlanthonyonline.com/2015/05/15/the-train-accident-that-broke-a-president-estranged-his-wife-killed-his-son/.

CHAPTER THREE: LINCOLN'S CHOICE

1. U.S. Census Bureau, 1860. The total population of the Confederacy was 9,103,332, which included 3,521,110 slaves. "1860 Census: Population of the United States," United States Census Bureau, January 16, 2018, https://www.census.gov/library/publications/1864/dec/1860a.html.

2. Casualty numbers vary for the June 3 slaughter. Some sources put casualties in the low thousands, while others are as high as 7,000. Even William McFeely's acclaimed biography on Ulysses Grant omits any figures, despite a lengthy discussion of the slaughter. Due to lack of consistency, I've followed Achenbach's description with "thousands" to reflect the uncertainty: Joel Achenbach, "Grant and Lee at Cold Harbor," *Washington Post*, June 3, 2014, https://www.washingtonpost.com/news/achenblog/wp/2014/06/03/grant-and-lee-at-cold-harbor/.

3. Stephen B. Oates, "Making of the President, 1864," *New York Times*, February 15, 1998, http://movies2.nytimes.com/books/98/02/15/reviews/980215.15oatest.html.

4. Accounts of exact numbers vary: "at least half a dozen," "eight," "as many as eight."

5. Johnson vetoed twenty-nine bills, with fifteen (52 percent) being overridden by Congress, more in aggregate and as a percentage than any other president in history. See "Vetoes: Summary of Bills Vetoed, 1789–Present," United States Senate, https://www.senate.gov/reference/Legislation/Vetoes/vetoCounts.htm.

6. Ward Hill Lamon, *Recollections of Abraham Lincoln, 1847–1865* (Omaha: University of Nebraska Press, 1994). Some scholars have questioned the veracity of this source, most notably Don E. Fehrenbacher and Virginia Fehrenbacher, comp. and ed., *Recollected Words of Abraham Lincoln* (Stanford, Calif.: Stanford University Press, 1996).

7. Robert W. Winston, *Andrew Johnson: Plebeian and Patriot* (Norwalk, Conn.: Easton Press, 1987; first published 1928 by Henry Holt and Company), 50. See also Boller, *Presidential Anecdotes*, 148.

8. Myers E. Brown II, *Tennessee's Union Cavalrymen* (Mount Pleasant, S.C.: Arcadia, 2008), 9.

9. Winston, *Andrew Johnson*, 244.

10. Jeffrey K. Smith, *The Loyalist: The Life and Times of Andrew Johnson* (North Charleston, S.C.: CreateSpace, 2012), 38. See also *Nashville Union*, May 21, 1849; Leroy P. Graf, ed., *Papers of Andrew Johnson* (Knoxville: University of Tennessee Press, 1986), 1, Appendix 4:678; David W. Bowen, *Andrew Johnson and the Negro* (Knoxville: University of Tennessee Press, 1989), 35; and Albert Castel, *The Presidency of Andrew Johnson* (Lawrence: Regents Press of Kansas, 1979), 5.

11. Howard Means, *The Avenger Takes His Place: Andrew Johnson and the 45 Days That Changed the Nation* (Orlando, Fla.: Harcourt, 2006), 64.

12. Winston, *Andrew Johnson*, 243.

13. Ibid., 250–51.

14. Joel Achenbach, "The Election of 1864 and the Last Temptation of Abraham Lincoln," *Washington Post*, September 11, 2014.

15. Boller, *Presidential Campaigns*, 116.

16. Castel, *Presidency of Andrew Johnson*, 9; it was also about border state Unionists.

17. See Hans L. Trefousse, *Ben Butler: The South Called Him Beast!* (New York: Twayne Publishers, 1957), 158–60, in Hans L. Trefousse, *Andrew Johnson: A Biography* (Norwalk, Conn.: Easton Press, 1996; first published 1989 by Norton), 179. See also DeRose, *Presidents' War*, 295.

18. Witcover, *American Vice Presidency*, 150.

19. A. J. Langguth, *After Lincoln: How the North Won the Civil War and Lost the Peace* (New York: Simon & Schuster, 2014), 81.

20. Ronald C. White, Jr., *A. Lincoln: A Biography* (New York: Random House, 2009), 634.

21. Kinley J. Brauer, "Hannibal Hamlin of Maine: Lincoln's First Vice-President (review)," *Civil War History* 16, no. 2 (June 1970), 176–77, https://doi.org/10.1353/cwh.1970.0072. See also Jeffrey K. Smith, *The Loyalist*, 71, which makes a stronger argument that they feared he would alienate border state voters.

22. Trefousse, *Andrew Johnson*, 177.

23. Butler said of Cameron: "The messenger and myself had been for a very considerable time in quite warm, friendly relations, and I owed much to him, which I can never repay save with gratitude." Benjamin F. Butler, "Vice-Presidential Politics in '64," *North American Review* 141, no. 347 (October 1885), 332–33, http://www.jstor.org/stable/25118532.

24. Butler, "Vice-Presidential Politics in '64," 332.

25. Ibid.

26. Ibid., 333. See also Trefousse, *Andrew Johnson*, 177. Many years later, Butler, reflecting on this electoral courtship, maintained that he had told Cameron he would not quit the military to be vice president unless Lincoln gave him bond "that within three months after his inauguration he would die unresigned." See also Witcover, *American Vice Presidency*, 150–51.

27. Charles E. Hamlin, *The Life and Times of Hannibal Hamlin* (Cambridge: Riverside Press, 1899), 606.

28. Trefousse, *Andrew Johnson*, 177.

29. Ibid.

30. David H. Donald, *Lincoln* (New York: Simon & Schuster, 1995), 506. See also Alexander K. McClure, *Abraham Lincoln and Men of War-Times* (Philadelphia: Times Publishing Co., 1892), 115–17 and 446, in Waugh, *Reelecting Lincoln: The Battle for the 1864 Presidency* (New York: Crown, 1997), 197.

31. *New York Times*, July 10, 1891 in Trefousse, *Andrew Johnson*, 177–78.

32. Abram J. Dittenhoefer, *How We Elected Lincoln: Personal Recollections of Lincoln and Men of His Time* (New York: Harper & Brothers, 1916), 80 and 83 in Waugh, *Reelecting Lincoln*, 198.

33. McClure, *Abraham Lincoln and Men of War-Times*, 197–98. Lamon made this claim in a letter to McClure later in life.

34. John Speer, *Life of General James H. Lane* (Garden City, Kans.: John Speer, 1896), 284, in Waugh, *Reelecting Lincoln*, 197.

35. *New York Times*, July 10, 1891, in Trefousse, *Andrew Johnson*, 177–78.

36. Winston, *Andrew Johnson*, 255.

37. Feerick, *From Failing Hands*, 107–18.

38. Jeffrey K. Smith, *The Loyalist*, 71.

39. Elizabeth R. Varon, "Andrew Johnson: Campaigns and Elections," The Miller Center, University of Virginia, https://millercenter.org/president/johnson/campaigns-and-elections.

40. Ibid.

41. Howard Means, *The Avenger Takes His Place*, 82.

42. Castel, *Presidency of Andrew Johnson*, 6–7.

43. Howard Means, *The Avenger Takes His Place*, 82. See also Winston, *Andrew Johnson*, 254.

44. "The Cleveland Convention: Gen. Fremont Nominated for President. John Cochrane, of New-York, for Vice-President. One Hundred and Fifty-Six Delegates in Attendance. The Platform, Speeches, etc," *New York Times*, June 1, 1864, http://www.nytimes.com/1864/06/01/news/cleveland-convention-gen-fremont-nominated-for-president-john-cochrane-new-york.html.

45. Doris Kearns Goodwin, *Team of Rivals: The Political Genius of Abraham Lincoln* (New York: Simon & Schuster, 1987), 624.

46. Ibid.

47. Boller, *Presidential Campaigns*, 116.

48. Harold M. Dudley, "The Election of 1864," *Mississippi Valley Historical Review* 18, no. 4 (March 1932), 500–518, https://www.jstor.org/stable/1898560, in Boller, *Presidential Campaigns*, 116.

49. Resolutions of the "Radical Democracy" party platform, quoted in *New York Times*, June 1, 1864, in Goodwin, *Team of Rivals*, 624.

50. Fay Warrington Brabson, *Andrew Johnson: A Life in Pursuit of the Right Course 1808–1875* (Durham, N.C.: Seeman Printery, 1972), 113.

51. DeRose, *Presidents' War*, 295.

52. Don E. Fehrenbacher, "The Making of a Myth: Lincoln and the Vice Presidential Nomination of 1864," *Civil War History* 41, no. 4 (December 1992), 273–90.

53. Ibid.

54. John Hay telegram to John Nicolay, guidance from president Lincoln "not to interfere" with the vice presidential selection, June 6, 1864, *The Collected Works of Abraham Lincoln*, ed. Roy P. Basler (New Brunswick, N.J.: Rutgers University Press, 1953–1955), 7:377n1, in Ronald C. White, Jr., *A. Lincoln: A Biography*, 634.

55. Goodwin, *Team of Rivals*, 624–25.

56. Waugh, *Reelecting Lincoln*, 200.

57. Donald, *Lincoln*, 505.

58. Hay telegram to Nicolay, June 6, 1864, *Collected Works of Abraham Lincoln*, 7:377n1, in Ronald C. White, Jr., *A. Lincoln: A Biography*, 634.

59. Hay telegram to Nicolay, June 6, 1864, *Collected Works of Abraham Lincoln*, 7:376, in Donald, *Lincoln*, 505. See also Trefousse, *Andrew Johnson*, 177. Charles Hamlin's account of these events follows the same argument; and Waugh, *Reelecting Lincoln*, 200.

60. Waugh, *Reelecting Lincoln*, 193.

61. Noah Brooks, *Washington, D.C.: In Lincoln's Time* (Chicago: Quadrangle Books, 1971), 144, in Waugh, *Reelecting Lincoln*, 193.

62. Winston, *Andrew Johnson*, 256.

63. Brooks, *Washington, D.C.: In Lincoln's Time*, 147.

64. Gary Ecelbarger, *The Great Comeback: How Abraham Lincoln Beat the Odds to Win the 1860 Republican Nomination* (New York: Thomas Dunne Books, 2009), 220.

65. Trefousse, *Andrew Johnson*, 178–79. He doesn't cite Stone by name, instead saying "quickly seconded by an Iowa member." Noah Brooks corroborates this and cites Stone by name: see Brooks, *Washington, D.C.: In Lincoln's Time*, 147. Robert Winston says that Maynard, not Stone, seconded the nomination: see Winston, *Andrew Johnson*, 256. I have not found any corroboration of this account. For more detail, see Varon, "Andrew Johnson: Campaigns and Elections."

66. Brooks, *Washington, D.C.: In Lincoln's Time*, 143.

67. Trefousse, *Andrew Johnson*, 180.

68. Francis B. Carpenter, *The Inner Life of Abraham Lincoln: Six Months at the White House* (New York: Hurd and Houghton, 1872), 163.

69. *National Republican* (Washington, D.C), June 9, 1864, in Goodwin, *Team of Rivals*, 626.

70. Abraham Lincoln quoted in Carpenter, *Six Months in the White House with Abraham Lincoln*, 116, in Goodwin, *Team of Rivals*, 626. See also Carpenter, *Six Months in the White House with Abraham Lincoln*, 30, in Seale, *The President's House*, 1:399. It is worth noting that Noah Brooks has a slightly different account, in which he recollects that Lincoln learned of his nomination during a meeting at the War Department. While there, he met with "Major

Eckert, superintendent of the military bureau of telegraphs, who congratulated him on his nomination. . . . Mr. Lincoln . . . asked Major Eckert if he would kindly send word over to the White House when the name of the candidate for Vice-President should have been agreed upon. Lincoln, later on, was informed by Major Eckert that Johnson had been nominated." (Brooks, *Washington, D.C.: In Lincoln's Time*, 148.)

71. Trefousse, *Andrew Johnson*, 180.

72. "Acceptance of Vice-Presidential Nomination," *Nashville Times and True Union*, July 20, 1864; in Graf, *Papers of Andrew Johnson,* 7:10–11.

73. "A Speech by Vice-President Hamlin: His Opinion of Union Candidates," *New York Times*, June 17, 1864, https://www.nytimes.com/1864/06/17/archives/a-speech-by-vicepresident-hamlin-his -opinion-of-the-union.html.

74. Reported in the daily press at Bangor, Maine, June 11, 1864, in Brabson, *Andrew Johnson*, 116.

75. *St. Louis Globe-Democrat*, November 15, 1891, in Winston, *Andrew Johnson*, 255.

76. Ibid.

77. Graf, *Papers of Andrew Johnson*, 2:207n. See also Boller, *Presidential Anecdotes*, 148–49.

78. Howard Means, *The Avenger Takes His Place*, 72.

79. Letter from William C. Ballagh to Andrew Johnson, October 3, 1864, in Graf, *Papers of Andrew Johnson*, 7:206.

80. Howard Means, *The Avenger Takes His Place*, 73.

81. Ibid., 76. See also Winston, *Andrew Johnson*, 232–33.

82. Howard Means, *The Avenger Takes His Place*, 76. See also Winston, *Andrew Johnson*, 232–33.

83. George Fort Milton, *Abraham Lincoln and the Fifth Column* (Washington, D.C.: Vanguard Press, 1942), 210, in Fred Kaplan, *Lincoln: The Biography of a Writer* (New York: HarperCollins, 2008), 277.

84. Howard Means, *The Avenger Takes His Place*, 81.

85. Achenbach, "The Election of 1864 and the Last Temptation of Abraham Lincoln."

86. Abraham Lincoln, "Memorandum Concerning His Probable Failure of Re-election," August 23, 1864, in *Collected Works of Abraham Lincoln*, 7:514, in Goodwin, *Team of Rivals*, 648. See also James McPherson, *Abraham Lincoln* (Oxford: Oxford University Press, 2009), 57–58.

87. On August 15, 1864, Johnson appealed to Lincoln to reappoint General A. C. Gillem as brigadier general, insisting that the Senate's failure to confirm him must be a mistake. Johnson followed up after receiving no response on September 12, and Lincoln subsequently granted the appeal the next day. See Letter from Andrew Johnson to Abraham Lincoln, September 12, 1864, in Graf, *Papers of Andrew Johnson*, 7:157.

88. On August 17, 1864, Johnson appealed to Lincoln to commute the sentence of John S. Young, son of the former Tennessee secretary of state. Lincoln delayed the sentence the following day. (See Andrew Johnson to Abraham Lincoln, August 17, 1864, in Graf, *Papers of Andrew Johnson*, 7:99–100.) On August 19, Johnson asked Lincoln to commute the hanging sentence of Private Patrick Jones for murder. Johnson noted that because Jones was fifteen years old and drunk when he committed the murder, Lincoln should commute to a life sentence and focus hanging on the big fish. The next day, Lincoln commuted (See Abraham Lincoln to Andrew Johnson, August 19, 1864, in Graf, *Papers of Andrew Johnson*, 7:103–4). On September 6, Johnson asked Lincoln for a twenty-day extension on the execution of Robert T. Bridges, a murderer and deserter (See Graf, *Papers of Andrew Johnson*, 7:137).

89. Letter from James B. Bingham to Andrew Johnson, September 16, 1864, in Graf, *Papers of Andrew Johnson*, 7:163.

90. Brabson, *Andrew Johnson*, 116–17.

91. Graf, *Papers of Andrew Johnson*, 7:165n.

92. Letter from John W. Birdwell to Andrew Johnson, November 4, 1864, in Graf, *Papers of Andrew*

Johnson, 7:265. Johnson eventually supported the arrest of a railroad contractor for failure to pay hired contrabands, a Civil War era military term for escaped slaves (Graf, *Papers of Andrew Johnson*, 7:266n). The concerned citizen was John W. Birdwell.

93. Goodwin, *Team of Rivals*, 654.

94. Boller, *Presidential Campaigns*, 116.

95. Ibid.

96. Achenbach, "The Election of 1864 and the Last Temptation of Abraham Lincoln."

97. Ibid.

98. Letter from James B. Bingham, Presidential Campaign of 1864, September 16, 1864, in Graf, *Papers of Andrew Johnson*, 7:163.

99. James McPherson, *Abraham Lincoln*, 58.

100. Boller, *Presidential Campaigns*, 118.

101. Goodwin, *Team of Rivals*, 665–66.

102. Langguth, *After Lincoln*, 81; this was 55 percent to 45 percent.

103. Waugh, *Reelecting Lincoln*, 354.

104. William F. Zornow, *Lincoln & The Party Divided* (Norman: University of Oklahoma Press, 1954), 198, in Goodwin, *Team of Rivals*, 666.

105. Letter from Abraham Lincoln to Andrew Johnson, January 13, 1865, in Graf, *Papers of Andrew Johnson*, 7:404.

106. Graf, *Papers of Andrew Johnson*, 7:408; Tennesseans still had to vote on the ordinance on February 22, but given Johnson's strict loyalty oath, this was all but guaranteed. The hard part was the convention.

107. Invitation from Abraham Lincoln to Andrew Johnson, via telegram, January 14, 1865, in Graf, *Papers of Andrew Johnson*, 7:406.

108. Graf, *Papers of Andrew Johnson*, 7:406n. See also Lately Thomas, *The First President Johnson: The Three Lives of the Seventeenth President of the United States of America* (New York: William Morrow, 1968), in Witcover, *American Vice Presidency*, 158–59.

109. Letter from Andrew Johnson to Abraham Lincoln, in Graf, *Papers of Andrew Johnson*, 7:404. See also Winston, *Andrew Johnson*, 260–61.

110. Trefousse, *Andrew Johnson*, 186.

111. Graf, *Papers of Andrew Johnson*, 7:420–21. See also Trefousse, *Andrew Johnson*, 186–87.

112. Letter from John W. Forney to Andrew Johnson, January 27, 1865, in Graf, *Papers of Andrew Johnson*, 7:439.

113. Letter from Abraham Lincoln to Andrew Johnson, January 17, 1865, in Graf, *Papers of Andrew Johnson*, 7:420–21.

114. Letter from Abraham Lincoln to Andrew Johnson, January 24, in Graf, *Papers of Andrew Johnson*, 186–87.

115. Gideon Welles, *Diary of Gideon Welles*, ed. Howard K. Beale (New York: Norton, 1960), 2:230, in Graf, *Papers of Andrew Johnson*, 7:427n. See also Welles to Joseph S. Fowler, September 4, 1875, Welles Papers, New York Public Library.

116. Letter from Benjamin N. Martin to Andrew Johnson, February 22, 1865, in Graf, *Papers of Andrew Johnson*, 7:482. See also Howard Means, *The Avenger Takes His Place*, 88.

117. Jeffrey K. Smith, *The Loyalist*, 77.

118. Brabson, *Andrew Johnson*, 118.

119. Ibid., 119.

120. Winston, *Andrew Johnson*, 263–64.

121. *National Republican*, March 3, 1865, in Goodwin, *Team of Rivals*, 697.

122. Winston, *Andrew Johnson*, 263–64.

123. *Dispatch* (Nashville), February 9, 25, and 26, 1865, in Trefousse, *Andrew Johnson*, 188. See also

"Andrew Johnson, 16th Vice President (1865)," Art & History, United States Senate, http://www
.senate.gov/artandhistory/history/common/generic/VP_Andrew_Johnson.htm.

124. Howard Means, *The Avenger Takes His Place*, 89. See also Langguth, *After Lincoln*, 82.

125. James L. Swanson, *Manhunt: The Twelve-Day Chase for Lincoln's Killer* (New York: Harper
Perennial, 2007), 1. See also Garry Wills, "Lincoln's Greatest Speech," *The Atlantic*, September 1,
1999; also Stewart, *Impeached*, 7.

126. Swanson, *Manhunt*, 1.

127. John Nicolay to Therena Nicolay, Washington, March 5, 1865, in John G. Nicolay Papers, Series
2: General Correspondence, 1811–1943, in Erin Allen, "Here Comes the Sun: Seeing Omens
in the Weather at Abraham Lincoln's Second Inauguration," *Library of Congress Blog*, March 4,
2015, https://blogs.loc.gov/loc/2015/03/here-comes-the-sun-seeing-omens-in-the-weather-at
-abraham-lincolns-second-inauguration/.

128. Brooks, *Washington, D.C.: In Lincoln's Time*, 210.

129. Swanson, *Manhunt*, 1.

130. Ibid., 4.

131. Trefousse, *Andrew Johnson*, 188.

132. Congressman John H. Rice, *Boston Journal*, May 12, 1865, in Brabson, *Andrew Johnson*, 119. See
also Trefousse, *Andrew Johnson*, 189; and H. Draper Hunt, *Hannibal Hamlin of Maine: Lincoln's
First Vice-President* (Syracuse, N.Y.: Syracuse University Press, 1969), 195, in Witcover, *American
Vice Presidency*, 159.

133. Letter from James R. Doolittle to John B. Henderson, *Century Magazine* vol. 85 (November to
April 1912), 198, in Brabson, *Andrew Johnson*, 119; this portion was added based on Senator
Doolittle's account.

134. Stewart, *Impeached*, 8. See also Kelter and Shellabarger, *Veeps*, 84.

135. See also Langguth, *After Lincoln*, 82; and Chester Hearn, *The Impeachment of Andrew Johnson*
(Jefferson, N.C.: McFarland, 2000), 41.

136. Letter from James R. Doolittle to John B. Henderson, *Century Magazine* vol. 85 (November to
April 1912), 198, in Brabson, *Andrew Johnson*, 119; Senator Doolittle at some point joined the
group. He would corroborate this account.

137. *New York Herald*, March 5, 1865, in Trefousse, *Andrew Johnson*, 189. See also Howard Means,
The Avenger Takes His Place, 89; also Stewart, *Impeached*, 8.

138. "Andrew Johnson, 16th Vice President (1865)." See also Stewart, *Impeached*, 8.

139. Trefousse, *Andrew Johnson*, 189.

140. Hearn, *Impeachment of Andrew Johnson*, 41.

141. Shelby Foote, *The Civil War: A Narrative*, 3 vols. (New York: Vintage Books, 1974), 3:811.

142. See Brian Resnick, "This *New York Times* Reporter Was Not Impressed with Lincoln's Second
Inaugural: With Mud, Crowds, and a Drunk Vice President, Lincoln's Speech was Really the
Only Redeeming Part of the Day (Provided You Could Hear it)," *National Journal*, January 22,
2013, https://www.theatlantic.com/politics/archive/2013/01/this-new-york-times-reporter-was
-not-impressed-with-lincolns-second-inaugural/454773/.

143. Observation that Johnson gave his speech with no notes is found in Winston, *Andrew Johnson*,
264. See also Langguth, *After Lincoln*, 83.

144. Brooks, *Washington, D.C.: In Lincoln's Time*, 211.

145. Trefousse, *Andrew Johnson*, 189.

146. Ibid. See also Resnick, "This *New York Times* Reporter Was Not Impressed with Lincoln's
Second Inaugural."

147. Hearn, *Impeachment of Andrew Johnson*, 41.

148. "Andrew Johnson, 16th Vice President (1865)." See also Witcover, *American Vice Presidency*, 160.

149. Hearn, *Impeachment of Andrew Johnson*, 41.

150. Brooks, *Washington, D.C.: In Lincoln's Time*, 210–13. See also Trefousse, *Andrew Johnson*, 189–90; Ronald C. White, Jr., *Lincoln's Greatest Speech: The Second Inaugural* (New York: Simon & Schuster, 2002), 39; and Howard Means, *The Avenger Takes His Place*, 90.

151. Wills, "Lincoln's Greatest Speech."

152. "Andrew Johnson, 16th Vice President (1865)." See also Howard Means, *The Avenger Takes His Place*, 90.

153. Witcover, *American Vice Presidency*, 160. For more on the drunken inauguration spectacle, see Brooks, *Washington, D.C.: In Lincoln's Time*, 210–13, in Trefousse, *Andrew Johnson*, 189–90.

154. Brooks, *Washington, D.C.: In Lincoln's Time*, 212. See also Trefousse, *Andrew Johnson*, 189–90; Goodwin, *Team of Rivals*, 698; Ronald C. White, Jr., *Lincoln's Greatest Speech*, 38–39; and Brabson, *Andrew Johnson*, 120.

155. Goodwin, *Team of Rivals*, 698.

156. Brooks, *Washington, D.C.: In Lincoln's Time*, 212. See also Trefousse, *Andrew Johnson*, 189–90.

157. Hearn, *Impeachment of Andrew Johnson*, 41. See also "Andrew Johnson, 16th Vice President (1865)."

158. Zachariah Chandler to Mrs. Chandler, March 6, 1865, Zachariah Chandler Papers, in Trefousse, *Andrew Johnson*, 190. See also "Andrew Johnson, 16th Vice President (1865)."

159. Wills, "Lincoln's Greatest Speech." See also Goodwin, *Team of Rivals*, 698.

160. "Andrew Johnson, 16th Vice President (1865)." See also Howard Means, *The Avenger Takes His Place*, 90, who uses the "inutterable sorrow."

161. Ronald C. White, Jr., *Lincoln's Greatest Speech*, 39. See also Hearn, *Impeachment of Andrew Johnson*, 41; *National Republican*, March 4, 1865, in Brabson, *Andrew Johnson*, 120–21; and Wills, "Lincoln's Greatest Speech."

162. Wills, "Lincoln's Greatest Speech."

163. Frederick Douglass, *The Life and Times of Frederick Douglass: From 1817–1882* (London: Christian Age, 1882), 319. See also Trefousse, *Andrew Johnson*, 190; Wills, "Lincoln's Greatest Speech."

164. Wills, "Lincoln's Greatest Speech."

165. Douglass, *Life and Times*, 319.

166. *World* (New York), March 6 and 7, 1865, quoted in Trefousse, *Andrew Johnson*, 190.

167. Ronald C. White, *Lincoln's Greatest Speech*, 39.

168. Howard Means, *The Avenger Takes His Place*, 93.

169. *Cincinnati Gazette*, reprinted in *Holmes County Farmer* (Millersburg, Ohio), March 23, 1865, Chronicling America: Historic American Newspapers, Library of Congress, http://chroniclingamerica.loc.gov/lccn/sn84028822/1865-03-23/ed-1/seq-3/.

170. *Philadelphia Age*, reprinted in *Urbana Union* (Ohio), March 29, 1865, Chronicling America: Historic American Newspapers, Library of Congress, http://chroniclingamerica.loc.gov/lccn/sn85026309/1865-03-29/ed-1/seq-1/.

171. *Spirit of the Times*, reprinted in *White Cloud Kansas Chief* (Kans.), May 11, 1865, Chronicling America: Historic American Newspapers, Library of Congress, http://chroniclingamerica.loc.gov/lccn/sn82015486/1865-05-11/ed-1/seq-2/.

172. Andrew Johnson to Richard Sutton, March 9, 1865, in Graf, *Papers of Andrew Johnson*, 7:514. See also Langguth, *After Lincoln*, 85–86; and Winston, *Andrew Johnson*, 265.

173. *New York Times*, July 15, 1878, in Graf, *Papers of Andrew Johnson*, 7:515.

174. Langguth, *After Lincoln*, 86.

175. Hearn, *Impeachment of Andrew Johnson*, 42.

176. Graf, *Papers of Andrew Johnson*, 7:517n.

177. Henry Wilson, *Rise and Fall of the Slave Power in America* (Boston: J. R. Osgood, 1872), 2:478, in Winston, *Andrew Johnson*, 265.

178. Hugh McCulloch, *Men and Measures of Half a Century* (New York: Charles Scribner's Sons, 1889), 373, in Winston, *Andrew Johnson*, 266. See also Trefousse, *Andrew Johnson*, 190–91; and Hearn, *Impeachment of Andrew Johnson*, 41–42.

179. Hearn, *Impeachment of Andrew Johnson*, 41–42.

180. John Russell Young, *Men and Memories*, 2 vols. (New York: Coward-McCann, 1901), 1:49–52, in Brabson, *Andrew Johnson*, 121.

181. Ibid.

182. Langguth, *After Lincoln*, 85.

183. Letter from Andrew Johnson to Abraham Lincoln, March 8, 1865, in Graf, *Papers of Andrew Johnson*, 7:511.

184. "Remarks on the Fall of Richmond," *Morning Chronicle* (Washington, D.C.), April 4, 1865, in Graf, *Papers of Andrew Johnson*, 7:544–45.

185. Graf, *Papers of Andrew Johnson*, 7:546n.

186. Jeffrey K. Smith, in *The Loyalist*, 81, argues: "The depressing scene convinced Johnson that the civilian population in the South had suffered enough, and he concluded that all future punishments should be directed at military leaders and government officials, rather than the general populous."

187. Jim Bishop, *The Day Lincoln Was Shot* (New York: Harper, 1955), 47, in Brabson, *Andrew Johnson*, 123.

188. Ibid.

189. Edward D. Neill, *Reminiscences of the Last Years of President Lincoln's Life* (St. Paul, Minn.: Pioneer Press, 1888), 47, in Trefousse, *Andrew Johnson*, 192.

190. Mrs. Lincoln to Francis B. Carpenter, Chicago, November 15 [1865], in Justin G. Turner and Linda Levitt Turner, *Mary Todd Lincoln: Her Life and Letters* (New York: Knopf, 1972), 217–18, in Seale, *The President's House*, 1:404; see also Zachariah Atwell Mudge, *The Forest Boy: A Sketch of the Life of Abraham Lincoln, for Young People* (New York: Carlton and Lanahan, 1867), 303; also Stacy Pratt McDermott, *Mary Lincoln: Southern Girl, Northern Woman* (New York: Routledge, 2015), 115.

191. Swanson, *Manhunt*, 18–19.

192. Ibid.

193. Benjamin Perley Poore, ed., *The Conspiracy Trial for the Murder of the President, and the Attempt to Overthrow the Government by the Assassination of Its Principal Officers* (Boston: J. E. Tilton, 1865), 1:62, in Howard Means, *The Avenger Takes His Place*, 20.

194. Swanson, *Manhunt*, 29.

195. Poore, *Conspiracy Trial for the Murder of the President*, 1:62, in Howard Means, *The Avenger Takes His Place*, 20.

196. "Lafayette S. Foster: Connecticut Statesman, Jurist and Acting Vice President of the United States," Law Library Services, State of Connecticut Judicial Branch, https://www.jud.ct.gov /lawlib/history/foster.htm.

197. David Morgan, "Lincoln Assassination: The Other Murder Attempt," CBS News, May 10, 2015, https://www.cbsnews.com/news/lincoln-assassination-the-other-murder-attempt/. For constitutional implications, see "The Forgotten Man Who Almost Became President after Lincoln," *Constitution Daily*, National Constitution Center, April 15, 2018, http://blog .constitutioncenter.org/2015/04/the-forgotten-man-who-almost-became-president-after-lincoln/.

198. Castel, *Presidency of Andrew Johnson*, 1.

199. Ibid.

200. Ibid., 2. See also Feerick, *From Failing Hands*, 110–11.

201. MacMahon and Curry, *Medical Cover-Ups*, 19.

202. *Sunday Chronicle* (Washington, D.C.), April 16, 1865, in Graf, *Papers of Andrew Johnson*, 7:553n.

203. *New York Herald*, April 20, 1865, in Brabson, *Andrew Johnson*, 125.

204. Feerick, *From Failing Hands*, 111.

205. Howard Means, *The Avenger Takes His Place*, 33.

206. Castel, *Presidency of Andrew Johnson*, 2. While pressured to leave, Johnson used the excuse that he wanted to create more room for doctors. To be fair, the room *was* overcrowded. See W. Emerson Reck, A. *Lincoln: His Last 24 Hours* (Columbia: University of South Carolina Press, 1994), first published 1987 by McFarland and Company, 147.

207. W. E. McElwee, July 29, 1875, Tennessee Department of Archives, in Brabson, *Andrew Johnson*, 126.

208. Letter from the Cabinet to Andrew Johnson, in Graf, *Papers of Andrew Johnson*, 7:553. See also Howard Means, *The Avenger Takes His Place*, 33; and Richardson, *Compilation of the Messages and Papers of the Presidents*, vol. 6, 284–85, in Feerick, *From Failing Hands*, 111.

209. William Seale, *The President's House*, 1:405; see also "The New President: Inauguration of Andrew Johnson. Brief and Impressive Ceremonies. The Oath of Office Administered on Saturday by Chief Justice Chase. President Johnson's Inaugural Address," *New York Times*, April 17, 1865, https://www.nytimes.com/1865/04/17/archives/the-new-president-inauguration -of-andrew-johnson-brief-and.html; also Mildred Crow Sargent, *Andrew and Eliza Johnson* (Philadelphia: Clibris Corporation, 2009), 183–184.

210. Ibid.

211. "The New President: Inauguration of Andrew Johnson. Brief and Impressive Ceremonies. The Oath of Office Administered on Saturday by Chief-Justice Chase. President Johnson's Inaugural Address," *New York Times*, April 17, 1865. See also Howard Means, *The Avenger Takes His Place*, 33–34; and Winston, *Andrew Johnson*, 268.

212. Castel, *Presidency of Andrew Johnson*, 17.

213. Letter from Salmon P. Chase to Andrew Johnson, in Graf, *Papers of Andrew Johnson*, 7:672.

214. *Evening Star* (Washington, D.C.), April 15, 1865, in Winston, *Andrew Johnson*, 268.

215. Salmon P. Chase's draft language for Johnson's oath of office expressed sadness over the loss of the "revered and beloved President . . . fallen by the hand of an assassin," provided assurance that "The agonized grief, which seizes all hearts, fills my own," asked for "the support & favor of my countrymen," and offered a pledge "to justify the trust reposed in me by the American people," Graf, *Papers of Andrew Johnson*, 7:564n.

216. "Remarks on Assuming the Presidency," *Sunday Chronicle*, April 16, 1865, in Graf, *Papers of Andrew Johnson*, 7:554.

217. Richardson, *Messages and Papers of the Presidents*, 8:3501–4. See also Feerick, *From Failing Hands*, 111–12.

218. "Remarks on Assuming the Presidency," *Sunday Chronicle*, April 16, 1865, in Graf, *Papers of Andrew Johnson*, 7:554.

219. Letter from Salmon P. Chase to Andrew Johnson, April 16, 1865, in Graf, *Papers of Andrew Johnson*, 7:564.

220. William S. McFeely, *Grant: A Biography* (New York: Norton, 1982), 226. See also Brabson, *Andrew Johnson*, 126–27.

221. McFeely, *Grant: A Biography*, 226.

222. Graf, *Papers of Andrew Johnson*, 639.

223. Castel, *Presidency of Andrew Johnson*, 33.

224. Feerick, *From Failing Hands*, 112. See also Castel, *Presidency of Andrew Johnson*, 23.

225. Jean H. Baker, *Mary Todd Lincoln: A Biography* (New York: Norton, 2008), 249.

226. Letter from Robert Todd Lincoln to Andrew Johnson, April 24, 1865, in Graf, *Papers of Andrew Johnson*, 7:639.

227. Seale, *The President's House*, 1:410.

228. Benjamin B. French, *Inventory of the White House*, May 26, 1865, commissioner's miscellaneous correspondence in Seale, *The President's House*, 1:410–11.

229. Seale, *The President's House*, 1:410–11.

230. French, *Inventory of the White House*, in Seale, *The President's House*, 1:410–11.

231. Turner and Turner, *Mary Todd Lincoln*, 345, in William Hanchett, *The Lincoln Murder Conspiracies* (Chicago: University of Illinois Press, 1983), 83.

232. Nathaniel Beverly Tucker, "Address of Beverly Tucker, Esq., to the People of the United States, 1865," ed. James Harvey Young, ser. 5, no. 1 (Atlanta: Emory University, 1948), 15–21, in Hanchett, *Lincoln Murder Conspiracies*, 82–83.

233. *House Report 7*, 40th Congress, 1st Session (1867), 2–5, 29–32, and 458–62, in Hanchett, *Lincoln Murder Conspiracies*, 83–84.

234. W. C. H. Campbell, *Memorial Sketch of Lafayette S. Foster, LL.D.* (Boston: Franklin Press: Rand, Avery and Co., 1881), https://archive.org/details/memorialsketchof00cwhw/page/n7.

235. Ibid.

236. Feerick, *From Failing Hands*, 112.

237. Langguth, *After Lincoln*, 93. See also Jefferson Davis, *The Rise and Fall of the Confederate Government* (Thomas Yoseloff, 1958), 2:683, in Howard Means, *The Avenger Takes His Place*, 151.

238. Spoken words of Jefferson Davis to Stephen Mallory in William Abbat, "The Sad Humorist," *The Lincoln Centenary in Literature: Selections from the Principal Magazines of February and March, 1909, Together with a Few from 1907–1908*, 2 vols. (New York: William Abbat, 1909), 2:15; see also Lloyd P. Stryker, *Andrew Johnson: A Study in Courage* (New York: MacMillan, 1929), 332.

239. Jefferson Davis, *The Rise and Fall of the Confederate Government* (New York: Thomas Yoseloff, 1958), 2:683, in Howard Means, *The Avenger Takes His Place*, 151.

240. Letter from Horace H. Lurton to a friend, May 4, 1864, Horace H. Lurton Collection, box 1, folder 5, Library of Congress (Chronological Correspondence, 1864–1867).

241. Castel, *Presidency of Andrew Johnson*, 18.

242. George Fort Milton, *The Age of Hate: Andrew Johnson and the Radicals* (New York: Coward-McCann, 1930), 167–69, in Brabson, *Andrew Johnson*, 130.

243. "Speech to Indiana Delegation," *Morning Chronicle*, April 22, 1865 (speech delivered April 21), in Graf, *Papers of Andrew Johnson*, 7:612–13.

244. Graf, *Papers of Andrew Johnson*, 7:615n.

245. "Address to Loyal Southerners," *Morning Chronicle*, April 25, 1865 (speech delivered April 24), in Graf, *Papers of Andrew Johnson*, 7:630–32.

246. *National Intelligencer*, May 2, 1865, in Graf, *Papers of Andrew Johnson*, 7:655n.

247. "Remarks to Pennsylvania Citizens in Washington," *National Intelligencer*, May 2, 1865 (speech delivered April 28), in DLC–Edward McPherson Papers, vol. 44, in Graf, *Papers of Andrew Johnson*, 7:654–55.

248. Castel, *Presidency of Andrew Johnson*, 21–22.

249. *Philadelphia Press*, April 21, 1865, in V7, 585–86n; Johnson's response: "I fear that leading colored men do not understand and appreciate the fact that they have friends on the south side of the line. . . . Easy thing, indeed popular, to be an emancipationist north of the line, but a very different thing to be such south of it. South of it costs a man effort, property, and perhaps life." (Letter from Andrew Johnson to John Mercer Langston, April 18, 1865, in Graf, *Papers of Andrew Johnson*, 7:585.)

250. Castel, *Presidency of Andrew Johnson*, 11; see also Stewart, *Impeached*, 127.

251. Castel, *Presidency of Andrew Johnson*, 12–15; see also Stewart, *Impeached*, 127.

252. Ibid., 26.

253. Howard Means, *The Avenger Takes His Place*, 203.

254. Ibid., 201.

255. Ibid., 202.

256. Edward McPherson, ed., *The Political History of the United States of America During the Period of Reconstruction* (Washington, D.C.: Solomons & Chapman, 1875), 9–12, in Castel, *Presidency of Andrew Johnson*, 26. See also Brabson, *Andrew Johnson*, 135.

257. McPherson, *Political History of the United States of America*, 9–12, in Castel, *Presidency of Andrew Johnson*, 26.

258. William A. Dunning and Charles P. Bowditch, "November Meeting, 1905. A Little More Light on Andrew Johnson; Treatment of Negro Seamen at the South," *Proceedings of the Massachusetts Historical Society*, 19 (1905), 395, https://www.jstor.org/stable/25079929.

259. Howard Means, *The Avenger Takes His Place*, 166.

260. Brabson, *Andrew Johnson*, 148–49.

261. LaWanda Cox and John H. Cox, *Politics, Principle and Prejudice* (New York: Macmillan, 1969), 32–33, in Castel, *Presidency of Andrew Johnson*, 29.

262. Castel, *Presidency of Andrew Johnson*, 28.

263. Howard Means, *The Avenger Takes His Place*, 218–19.

264. Langguth, *After Lincoln*, 108–9.

265. Castel, *The Presidency of Andrew Johnson*, 47.

266. Langguth, *After Lincoln*, 109.

267. Ibid. See also Castel, *Presidency of Andrew Johnson*, 47.

268. Langguth, *After Lincoln*, 109.

269. Castel, *Presidency of Andrew Johnson*, 47.

270. Bowen, *Andrew Johnson and the Negro*, 51. See also Jeffrey K. Smith, *The Loyalist*, 27.

271. Bowen, *Andrew Johnson and the Negro*, 51.

272. Ibid., 52.

273. Ibid., 51.

274. Tennessee was exempt from the Emancipation Proclamation.

275. Bowen, *Andrew Johnson and the Negro*, 53.

276. Trefousse, *Andrew Johnson*, 183.

277. "The Moses of the Colored Men Speech," *Nashville Times and True Union*, October 25 and November 9 (speech delivered October 24), in Graf, *Papers of Andrew Johnson*, 7:251.

278. "The Moses of the Colored Men Speech," in Graf, *Papers of Andrew Johnson*, 7:252–53. See also Trefousse, *Andrew Johnson*, 183; Winston, *Andrew Johnson*, 260; and Bowen, *Andrew Johnson and the Negro*, 81.

279. Howard Means, *The Avenger Takes His Place*, 59.

280. Bowen, *Andrew Johnson and the Negro*, 88–89, has a good discussion of this.

281. "Speech Near Gallatin," *St. Louis Globe-Democrat*, July 27, 1864 (speech delivered July 19), in Graf, *Papers of Andrew Johnson*, 7:41.

282. Bowen, *Andrew Johnson and the Negro*, 1–7.

283. Douglass, *Life and Times*, 336.

284. Bowen, *Andrew Johnson and the Negro*, 3.

285. Douglass, *Life and Times*, 336.

286. *New York Tribune*, February 12, 1866, in Bowen, *Andrew Johnson and the Negro*, 3.

287. *New York Tribune*, February 12, 1866, in Bowen, *Andrew Johnson and the Negro*, 4.

288. *New York Tribune*, February 12, 1866, in Bowen, *Andrew Johnson and the Negro*, 5.

289. P. Ripley to Manton Marble, February 8, 1866, quoted in Cox and Cox, *Politics, Principle, and Prejudice*, 163, in Bowen, *Andrew Johnson and the Negro*, 6.

290. McPherson, *Political History of the United States of America*, 52–55, in Castel, *Presidency of Andrew Johnson*, 64.

291. P. Ripley to Manton Marble, February 8, 1866, quoted in Cox and Cox, *Politics, Principle, and Prejudice*, 163, in Bowen, *Andrew Johnson and the Negro*, 6.

292. Bowen, *Andrew Johnson and the Negro*, 6.

293. Douglass, *Life and Times*, 336–37.

294. Ibid., 337.

295. Winston, *Andrew Johnson*, 273–74.

296. Howard Means, *The Avenger Takes His Place*, 222–23.

297. Ibid., 224.

298. Winston, *Andrew Johnson*, 312.

299. Ibid., 313; the *New York Times* wrote: "The Republicans were against him because the Democrats were for him."

300. Langguth, *After Lincoln*, 205.

301. Ibid., 206.

302. Ibid., 200.

303. Ibid., 203.

304. George F. Edmunds, *Century Magazine* vol. 85 (November to April, 1912), 863–64, in Brabson, *Andrew Johnson*, 235.

305. Welles, *Diary of Gideon Welles*, 3:62; Brabson, *Andrew Johnson*, 184.

306. Silva, *Presidential Succession*, 99–100.

307. Ibid.

308. Richardson, *Messages and Papers of the Presidents*, vol. 6, 639–45 and 691, in Silva, *Presidential Succession*, 117.

309. Silva, *Presidential Succession*, 117. The scenario as cited refers to a vacancy in general, including by death, incapacity, or resignation.

310. "Vetoes: Summary of Bills Vetoed, 1789–Present," United States Senate.

311. Langguth, *After Lincoln*, 231.

312. Ibid.

313. Jeffrey K. Smith, *The Loyalist*, 152; see also Sargent, *Andrew and Eliza Johnson*, 26.

314. Sargent, *Andrew and Eliza Johnson*, 26–27.

315. Welles, *Diary of Gideon Welles*, March 4, 1869, 3:540–41, in McFeely, *Grant: A Biography*, 287.

316. The cabinet was divided on whether Johnson should attend the inauguration. Secretary Welles took a hardline and suggested Johnson skip the festivities. Seward and others suggested twin processions. Sargent, *Andrew and Eliza Johnson*, 528; see also Seale, *The President's House*, 1:433.

317. Langguth, *After Lincoln*, 251.

318. Seale, *The President's House*, 1:433; for a slightly different account of the events see Welles, *Diary of Gideon Welles*, March 4, 1869, 3:540–41, in McFeely, *Grant: A Biography*, 287; also David O. Stewart, *Impeached: The Trial of President Andrew Johnson and the Fight for Lincoln's Legacy* (New York: Simon & Schuster, 2009), 312; an additional account has Johnson delivering a farewell address during the inauguration ceremony. See Margaret Shaw Royall, *Andrew Johnson: Presidential Scapegoat* (New York: Exposition Press, 1958), 154, in Sargent, *Andrew and Eliza Johnson*, 528.

319. Sargent, *Andrew and Eliza Johnson*, 531–535. Johnson could have won this election, but he refused to pay $2,000 for the two votes needed to win support from the Tennessee state legislature. See Stewart, *Impeached*, 312.

320. Ibid. See also Stewart, *Impeached*, 313.

321. "Obituary: Andrew Johnson Dead," *New York Times*, August 1, 1875. Once elected to the

Senate, Johnson delivered just a single speech, which lambasted president Grant. See Stewart, *Impeached*, 313.

CHAPTER FOUR: PRINCE ARTHUR

1. The author was unable to verify this name, but Gaiten Derohan's name appears with the greatest frequency. Another article lists the forger as "Fritsch." See *Vancouver Independent* (Wash. Ter. [Wash.]), August 18, 1881, Chronicling America: Historic American Newspapers, Library of Congress, http://chroniclingamerica.loc.gov/lccn/sn87093109/1881-08-18/ed-1/seq -5/. For reference to the extradition document "prepared by the state department," see F. M. Green, *A Royal Life, or the Eventful History of James A. Garfield*, 359. See also John C. Ridpath, *The Life and Work of James A. Garfield, Twentieth President of the United States* (Cincinnati: Forshee & McMakin, 1881), 579. Ridpath describes Garfield's "attestation of a paper of extradition in the case of an escaped Canadian forger, who had several years yet to serve in prison."

2. Thirty-first General Assembly of the State of Missouri, at the Regular Session, Commencing January 5, 1881 (Jefferson City, MO: Tribune Printing Company, State Printers and Binders, 1881).

3. *Salt Lake Herald* (Utah), August 18, 1881, 2, Chronicling America: Historic American Newspapers, Library of Congress, http://chroniclingamerica.loc.gov/lccn/sn85058130/1881-08 -18/ed-1/seq-2/.

4. *Omaha Daily Bee*, August 11, 1881, Chronicling America: Historic American Newspapers, Library of Congress, http://chroniclingamerica.loc.gov/lccn/sn99021999/1881-08-11/ed-1/seq -1/.

5. Kenneth D. Ackerman, "If He Wanted a Stadium, There Would Be One," *New York Times*, March 6, 2005, https://www.nytimes.com/2005/03/06/nyregion/thecity/if-he-wanted-a-stadium-there -would-be-one.html.

6. "How Presidents Dress," 40, of the Chester A. Arthur Scrapbook, Columbia University, 1883, quoted in Thomas C. Reeves, *Gentleman Boss: The Life and Times of Chester Alan Arthur* (Newtown, Conn.: American Political Biography Press, 1975), 271.

7. For discussion of the disputed 1876 election and commission, see Peskin, *Garfield*, 407–419.

8. Justus Doenecke, *The Presidencies of James A. Garfield & Chester A. Arthur*, The American Presidency (Lawrence: University Press of Kansas, 1981), 9.

9. Doenecke, *Presidencies of James A. Garfield & Chester A. Arthur*, 9.

10. Kenneth D. Ackerman, *Dark Horse: The Surprise Election and Political Murder of President James A. Garfield* (Falls Church, Va.: Viral History Press, 2011), 19. It wasn't all debauchery. The city of Chicago had become an impressive architectural site and shining example of municipal modernity. See F. K. Ayre, *Beyond Tomorrow: The True-Life Story of America's Twenty-First President, Chester Alan Arthur* (Long Beach, CA: Amayreka Publishing), 387.

11. Eugene Davis, *Proceedings of the Republican National Convention, held at Chicago, Illinois: June 2d, 3d 4th, 5th, 7th and 8th, 1880* (Chicago: The J. B. Jeffrey Printing and Publishing House). See also William R. Balch, ed. *Garfield's Words: Suggestive Passages from the Public and Private Writings of James Abram Garfield* (Boston: Houghton, Mifflin, 1881), 473; also Ridpath, *The Life and Work of James A. Garfield*, 440; also James S. Brisbin, *The Early Life and Public Career of James A. Garfield* (Philadelphia: Hubbard Bros., 1880), 473.

12. *Chicago Inter-Ocean*, June 9, 1880, in Ackerman, *Dark Horse*, 97. Three hundred seventy-eight votes were required for the nomination. The final tally was Garfield (399), Grant (306), Blaine (42), Washburne (G), and Sherman (3). See Ridpath, *Life and Work of James A. Garfield*, 441. Upon receiving the nomination, Garfield told a reporter from the *Cleveland Herald*, "I want it

plainly understood that I have not sough this nomination, and have protested against the use of my name." See Brisbin, *The Life and Public Career of James A. Garfield.* 491.

13. Telegraph from George Alfred Townsend to the Cincinnati Enquirer, n.d., quoted in Burke Aaron Hinsdale, *The Republican Text-Book for the Campaign of 1880* (New York: D. Appleton and Company, 1880), 156.

14. Doenecke, *Presidencies of James A. Garfield & Chester A. Arthur*, 23.

15. Balch, *Garfield's Words*, 352–58.

16. George Alfred Townsend, *Life of Hon. Levi P. Morton* (Philadelphia: Hubbard Brothers, 1888), 119 (excerpt provided by the Starr Library, Rhinebeck, N.Y.).

17. David M. Jordan, *Roscoe Conkling of New York: Voice in the Senate* (Ithaca, N.Y.: Cornell University Press, 1971), 341, in Ackerman, *Dark Horse*, 107. See also Doenecke, *Presidencies of James A. Garfield & Chester A. Arthur*, 21.

18. Stewart L. Woodford interview with DeAlva Stanwood Alexander, October 4, 1908 in DeAlva Stanwood Alexander, *A Political History of the State of New York*, 3 vols. (New York: Henry Holt and Co., 1909), 3:443. See also "Levi Morton," *New York Times*, September 3, 1899.

19. Scott S. Greenberger, *The Unexpected President: The Life and Times of Chester A. Arthur* (New York: Da Capo Press, 2017), 123. See also Ayre, *Beyond Tomorrow*, 398–99; also Jordan, *Roscoe Conkling*, 341, in Ackerman, *Dark Horse*, 107. See also Peskin, *Garfield*, 480.

20. Doenecke, *Presidencies of James A. Garfield & Chester A. Arthur*, 21. See also Reeves, *Gentleman Boss*, 180–81; and Witcover, *American Vice Presidency*, 190.

21. *Cincinnati Enquirer*, August 14, 1883, in Ackerman, *Dark Horse*, 108.

22. Ibid. See also Doenecke, *Presidencies of James A. Garfield & Chester A. Arthur*, 21.

23. Candice Millard, *Destiny of the Republic: A Tale of Madness, Medicine and the Murder of a President* (New York: Anchor, 2011), 96. See also George F. Howe, *Chester A. Arthur: A Quarter-Century of Machine Politics* (Norwalk, Conn.: Easton Press, 1987; first published 1934 by Dodd, Mead), 109.

24. This perhaps unrealistically detailed exchange has been widely reported, with variations, in a variety of secondary sources. William C. Hudson, *Random Recollections of an Old Political Reporter* (New York: Cupples & Leon, 1911), 96–99. Hudson claims to have been present to witness the interaction. Given the length of this narrative and the absence of witnesses, I've noted that a number of credible secondary sources have also relied on the Hudson citation. See Peskin, *Garfield*, 480–481; Ayre, *Beyond Tomorrow*, 399–400; Howe, *Chester A. Arthur*, 109; Greenberg, *The Unexpected President*, 123–24. Millard, *Destiny of the Republic*, 96, who has a slight variation on the quote; "Garfield and Arthur," *New York Times*, June 9, 1880, in Reeves, *Gentleman Boss*, 179–80; Ackerman, *Dark Horse*, 109; Zachary Karabell, *Chester Alan Arthur*, The American Presidents (New York: Times Books, 2004), 41–42; and Doenecke, *Presidencies of James A. Garfield & Chester A. Arthur*, 21.

25. "Garfield and Arthur," *New York Times*, June 9, 1880, in Reeves, *Gentleman Boss*, 181.

26. Ackerman, *Dark Horse*, 110–11. See also Reeves, *Gentleman Boss*, 182.

27. Letter by "a resident of Saratoga" in P. C. Headley, *Public Men of Today* (Hartford, Conn.: S. S. Scranton, 1882), 50, in Reeves, *Gentleman Boss*, 5. This slight measure of duplicity caused the state of Vermont in 1954 to determine the precise birthplace from an outdated photograph and thus, place a replica of Arthur's birthplace on the wrong spot. Despite being born October 5, 1829, he corrected the record sometime between 1870 and 1880 to make himself a year younger; discussed in detail in Reeves, "The Mystery of Chester Alan Arthur's Birthplace," *Vermont History* 38, no. 3 (Summer 1970), 291–304.

28. Richard Hofstadter, *The American Political Tradition and the Men Who Made It* (New York, 1948), 173, in Boller, *Presidential Anecdotes*, 173.

29. Howe, *Chester A. Arthur*, 34.

30. The case was *Jennings v. Third Avenue Railroad Company*. Detailed discussion in Ayre, *Beyond Tomorrow*, 93–99. See also "Outrage upon Colored Persons" and "Legal Rights Vindicated," both in *Frederick Douglass' Paper*, July 8, 1854, in Reeves, *Gentleman Boss*, 16.

31. For detailed opinion of the court concerning the Lemmon Slave Case, see "The Opinion of Judge Denio" in *The New York Court of Appeals Report of the Lemmon Slave Case* (New York: Horace Greely and Co., 1861), 121–130.

32. *Annual Report of the Quartermaster General State of New York, December 31st, 1863*, New York Assembly Documents, 1864, 6:3, quoted in Reeves, *Gentleman Boss*, 30.

33. Reeves, *Gentleman Boss*, 62.

34. "Gen. Arthur at Home," *New York Times*, June 12, 1880, in Reeves, *Gentleman Boss*, 182.

35. John Sherman to Warner M. Bateman, June 9, 1880; John Sherman to James M. Hoyt, June 12, 1880, Papers of John Sherman, Library of Congress, in Reeves, *Gentleman Boss*, 183. See also Theodore E. Burton, *John Sherman, American Statesmen Series*, ed. John Torrey Morse (Boston: Houghton Mifflin and Company, 1906), 296. See also *Cincinnati Enquirer*, August 14, 1833, in Ackerman, *Dark Horse*, 113; also Millard, *Destiny of the Republic*, 96.

36. Charles R. Williams, ed., *Diary and Letters of Rutherford B. Hayes, Nineteenth President of the United States, Vol. 1: 1834–1860* (Columbus: Ohio State Archaeological and Historical Society, 1922), 278, in Reeves, *Gentleman Boss*, 184. See also Witcover, *American Vice Presidency*, 191.

37. Doenecke, *Presidencies of James A. Garfield & Chester A. Arthur*, 25.

38. Ackerman, *Dark Horse*, 160.

39. Reeves, *Gentleman Boss*, 198.

40. Ackerman, *Dark Horse*, 160.

41. Account book, "Campaign of 1880, Deposit book and checques special a/c, Closed Oct. 3, 1881," Chester Alan Arthur III Papers, Library of Congress, in Reeves, *Gentleman Boss*, 198. This was a common practice among New York Republican bosses and was practiced in the Custom House long before the 1880 campaign. See F.K. Ayre, *Beyond Tomorrow*, 303.

42. Reeves, *Gentleman Boss*, 204.

43. The official number is 1,898 (National Archives and Records Administration), but there is historical debate about this. Reeves, *Gentleman Boss*, 204 and Jordan, *Roscoe Conkling*, 306, put the number at 7,018. Doenecke, *Presidencies of James A. Garfield & Chester A. Arthur*, 29, and Peskin, *Garfield* (Kent, Ohio: Kent State University Press, 1978), 510, put the number at 7,368. Walter D. Burnham, *Presidential Ballots* (Baltimore, MD: Johns Hopkins Press, 1955), 247–57, puts it at 9,070. Peterson, *Presidencies of William Henry Harrison and John Tyler*, 49, puts it at 9,457.

44. Doenecke, *Presidencies of James A. Garfield & Chester A. Arthur*, 29. See also Ackerman, *Dark Horse*, 187; 78.4 percent of qualified voters participated.

45. Doenecke writes on page 30: "The election not only solidified the South; it showed that the GOP could win without that region and that, therefore, the fate of the southern black was incidental to Republican victory. . . . The Republicans regained control of the House by 147 to 135."

46. Editorial Board, "For the Briefest Time, President Garfield was an Inspiration," *Washington Post*, February 17, 2013, http://www.washingtonpost.com/opinions/for-the-briefest-time-president-garfield-was-an-inspiration/2013/02/17/ce9f6e6e-778b-11e2-aa12-e6cf1d31106b_story.html.

47. James Garfield, November 8, 1880, quoted in Theodore Clarke Smith, *The Life and Letters of James A. Garfield* (New Haven, Conn.: Yale University Press, 1925), 2:1048, in Millard, *Destiny of the Republic*, 73.

48. Peskin, *Garfield*, 551, in Millard, *Destiny of the Republic*, 103. See also Ackerman, *Dark Horse*, 286.

49. Peskin, *Garfield*, 551. There were roughly 500,000 applicants to about 100,000 offices. See Balch, 575.

50. James Garfield journal, November 23–28, 1880, in Howe, *Chester A. Arthur*, 125.

51. T. B. Connery, "Secret History of the Garfield-Conkling Tragedy," *Watson's Magazine* 26, no. 4, March 1913, 273. First published in *The Cosmopolitan* 23, no. 2 (June 1897), 153. Also cited in Ackerman, *Dark Horse*, 218–19.

52. Entry, March 2, 1881, Harry J. Brown and Frederick Williams, eds., *Diaries of James Garfield* (East Lansing: Michigan State University Press, 1967), 552, in Ackerman, *Dark Horse*, 219.

53. Ackerman, *Dark Horse*, 219.

54. Entry, March 3, 1881, Brown and Williams, *Diaries of James Garfield*, in Ackerman, *Dark Horse*, 220.

55. Theodore Clarke Smith, *Life and Letters of James A. Garfield*, 2:1098, in Reeves, *Gentleman Boss*, 218.

56. Ackerman, *Dark Horse*, 220.

57. "New York in the Senate," *New York Times*, January 12, 1881, in Reeves, *Gentleman Boss*, 209–10. See also Howe, *Chester A. Arthur*, 127.

58. "Indiana October Vote," *New York Times*, February 12, 1881, in Reeves, *Gentleman Boss*, 215.

59. Ibid.

60. Reeves, *Gentleman Boss*, 215. See also Howe, *Chester A. Arthur*, 129.

61. Mark Aahlgren Summers, *Party Games: Getting, Keeping, and Using Power in the Gilded Age Politics* (Chappel Hill, NC: University of North Carolina Press, 2004), 16–17. See also Gareth Davies and Julian E. Zelizer, *America at the Ballot Box: Elections and Political History* (Philadelphia: University of Pennsylvania Press, 2015), 88; also *New York Times*, February 12, 1881, in Ackerman, *Dark Horse*, 211.

62. Reeves, *Gentleman Boss*, 215.

63. James Garfield journal, February 17, 1881, James Garfield papers, in Howe, *Chester A. Arthur*, 130.

64. Entry, January 20, 1881, Brown and Williams, eds., *Diaries of James Garfield*, in Ackerman, *Dark Horse*, 212–13.

65. Reeves, *Gentleman Boss*, 220. See also Ben P. Poore, *Perley's Reminiscences of Sixty Years in the National Metropolis*, 2 vols. (Philadelphia: Hubbard Bros., 1886), 2:388–91. According to the National Weather Service it had "snowed all night until about 10:00 A.M." and the temperature was a brisk thirty-three degrees, https://www.weather.gov/lwx/events_Inauguration.

66. Balch, *Garfield's Words*, 547.

67. William M. Thayer, *From Log-Cabin to White House* (Boston: James H. Earle, 1881), 383. See also James D. McCabe, *The Life and Public Services of Gen. James A. Garfield* (Cleveland, Ohio: C.C. Wick and Co., 1881), 523.

68. Doenecke, *Presidencies of James A. Garfield & Chester A. Arthur*, 35.

69. Entry, March 4, 1881. *Diary of Lucretia Garfield*, in Ackerman, *Dark Horse*, 220–21. See also Doenecke, *Presidencies of James A. Garfield & Chester A. Arthur*, 35. According to Colonel Rockwell, "sometime after midnight . . . he re-drafted nearly three-fourths of his inaugural address." Quoted in F. M. Green, *A Royal Life, or the Eventful History of James A. Garfield* (Chicago: Central Book Concern, 1882), 346.

70. First Annual Message, December 6, 1881, in Richardson, *Compilation of the Messages and Papers of the Presidents*, vol. 8, part 2: *Chester Arthur*, 11.

71. Executive Order 2, October 19, 1881, in Richardson, *Compilation of the Messages and Papers of the Presidents*, vol. 8, part 2: *Chester Arthur*, 9.

72. Ackerman, *Dark Horse*, 255–56. See also Ridpath, *The Life and Work of James A. Garfield*, 504.

73. Ackerman, *Dark Horse*, 259. See also Poore, *Perley's Reminiscences*, 2:402, in Reeves, *Gentleman Boss*, 223; Karabell, *Chester Alan Arthur*, 55; Howe, *Chester A. Arthur*, 139; and Greenberger, *The Unexpected President*, 139.

74. Howe, *Chester A. Arthur*, 139. See also Millard, *Destiny of the Republic*, 126; and Karabell, *Chester Alan Arthur*, 55; also Ridpath, *The Life and Work of James A. Garfield*, 504.

75. James Blaine had wanted Robertson as District Attorney from the very beginning. See Peskin, 562. See also Ackerman, *Dark Horse*, 271.

76. "Secret History of the Garfield-Conkling Tragedy," *Literary Digest* 25, no. 7 (June 12, 1897), 206. See also Peskin, *Garfield*, 562–63.

77. T. B. Connery, "Secret History of the Garfield-Conkling Tragedy," *The Cosmopolitan*, 23, no. 2 (June 1897), 157, in Ackerman, *Dark Horse*, 273. See also Peskin, *Garfield*, 563.

78. Ackerman, *Dark Horse*, 280.

79. James Garfield to Whitelaw Reid, April 18, 1881, and Reid to Garfield, April 11, 1881, in Royal Cortissoz, *The Life of Whitelaw Reid* (New York: Charles Scribner's Sons, 1921), 2:63–65.

80. The reporter was Whitelaw Reid, who was editor of the *New York Tribune*.

81. Cortissoz, *Life of Whitelaw Reid*, 2:64–65, quoted in Reeves, *Gentleman Boss*, 227. See also Howe, *Chester A. Arthur*, 144.

82. Doenecke, *Presidencies of James A. Garfield & Chester A. Arthur*, 43–44.

83. Karabell, *Chester Alan Arthur*, 56.

84. T. B. Connery, "Secret History of the Garfield-Conkling Tragedy," *The Cosmopolitan*, 23, no. 2 (June 1897), 147, in Ackerman, *Dark Horse*, 294. See also Millard, *Destiny of the Republic*, 127–28.

85. "Secret History of the Garfield-Conkling Tragedy," *Literary Digest* 25, no. 7 (June 12, 1897), 206. Ackerman, *Dark Horse*, 294.

86. *New York Herald*, May 11, 1881. See also *Lancaster Daily Intelligencer* (Pa.), May 11, 1881, Chronicling America: Historic American Newspapers, Library of Congress, http://chroniclingamerica.loc.gov/lccn/sn83032300/1881-05-11/ed-1/seq-2/.

87. Ackerman, *Dark Horse*, 296.

88. Howe, *Chester A. Arthur*, 135.

89. *New York Times*, May 17, 1881, and *Congressional Record*, May 16, 1881, in Ackerman, *Dark Horse*, 301–4. See also Millard, *Destiny of the Republic*, 130; Howe, *Chester A. Arthur*, 145; Greenberger, *The Unexpected President*, 142–43; and Karabell, *Chester Alan Arthur*, 58. Conkling's letter came first, followed a few moments later by Platt's. The notes are quoted in Ridpath, *The Life and Work of James A. Garfield*, 512–513.

90. Howe, *Chester A. Arthur*, 146.

91. Ibid. See also Doenecke, *Presidencies of James A. Garfield & Chester A. Arthur*, 54.

92. Karabell, *Chester Alan Arthur*, 58.

93. Ibid.

94. James Garfield journal, May 16, 1881, James Garfield Papers, in Howe, *Chester A. Arthur*, 145–46. As president of the Senate, Arthur refused to vacate the chair, thus preventing the election of a president pro tempore.

95. Howe, *Chester A. Arthur*, 146.

96. "The New York Senators," and "An Outside View," *New York Times*, May 23, 1881, in Reeves, *Gentleman Boss*, 233. See also Howe, *Chester A. Arthur*, 147.

97. George F. Howe, *Chester A. Arthur*, 147.

98. Ackerman, *Dark Horse*, 313.

99. Witcover, *American Vice Presidency*, 192. See also editorial "A Public Scandal," *New York Tribune*, May 26, 1881, quoted in Reeves, *Gentleman Boss*, 234; Greenberger, *The Unexpected President*, 145; and Ackerman, *Dark Horse*, 321.

100. Witcover, *American Vice Presidency*, 193.

101. Delavan House bill to Arthur, June 24, 1881, in Chester Alan Arthur III Papers, Library of Congress, in Ackerman, *Dark Horse*, 321.

102. Ackerman, *Dark Horse*, 326. See also Harold F. Gosnell, *Boss Platt and His New York Machine* (Chicago: AMS Press, 1924), 28, in Reeves, *Gentleman Boss*, 236; and Witcover, *American Vice Presidency*, 192–93.

103. "Special Message," April 6, 1881, John Woolley and Gerhard Peters, The American Presidency Project, UC Santa Barbara, https://www.presidency.ucsb.edu/documents/special-message-1225.

104. "Special Message," James A. Garfield, May 20, 1881, John Woolley and Gerhard Peters, The American Presidency Project, UC Santa Barbara, https://www.presidency.ucsb.edu/documents /special-message-1239.

105. Doenecke, *Presidencies of James A. Garfield & Chester A. Arthur*, 49. See also Ackerman, *Dark Horse*, 325.

106. Millard, *Destiny of the Republic*, 130–31.

107. Statement from District Attorney Corkhill in Balch, *Garfield's Words*, 670–672. Additional detail found in Ackerman, *Dark Horse*, 314.

108. Robert Kingsbury, *The Assassination of James A. Garfield* (New York: Rosen Publishing Group, 2002), 9, in Ackerman, *Dark Horse*, 323. See also Peskin, *Garfield*, 591–92. Guiteau didn't think he would end up in prison, since he assumed the people would exonerate him once they saw the virtue of his deed.

109. E. Hilton Jackson, "The Trial of Guiteau," *Virginia Law Register* 9, no. 12 (April 1904), 1024, http://www.jstor.org/stable/1100203.

110. Ibid.

111. Ibid. See also Ackerman, *Dark Horse*, 329; also Russell H. Conwell, *The Life, Speeches, and Public Services of James A. Garfield* (Boston: B.B. Russell, 1881), 348–49.

112. *New York Herald*, October 6, 1881, and Guiteau testimony, *United States v. Charles J. Guiteau* (New York: Arno Press, 1973), 692–93, in Ackerman, *Dark Horse*, 329.

113. Millard, *Destiny of the Republic*, 105.

114. James Garfield to John Sherman, November 16, 1880; in John Sherman, *Recollections of Forty Years in the House, Senate and Cabinet: An Autobiography* (Chicago: Werner, 1895), 789, in Ackerman, *Dark Horse*, 246.

115. James Garfield quoted in Green, *A Royal Life, or the Eventful History of James A. Garfield*, 344–45. Based on the text, it appears that he made this remark to both F. M. Green and General Swaim. See also "From Mentor to Elberon," *Century Magazine* vol. 23 (January 1882), 434. Somewhat prophetically, Garfield had also said in an 1880 campaign speech, "If a man murders you without provocation, your soul bears no burden of the wrong; but all the angels of the Universe will weep for the misguided man who committed the murder." This was not the last time Garfield would be flippant about assassination. In his final conversation with his mother, Eliza B. Garfield, she said, "James, I wish you would take good care of yourself, for I am afraid somebody will shoot you." He responded, "Why, mother, who would wish to shoot me?" See Green, *A Royal Life, or the Eventful History of James A. Garfield*, 350–51.

116. Ackerman, *Dark Horse*, 328. See also John Clark Ridpath and Selden Connor, *Life and Work of James G. Blaine* (Philadelphia: Historical Publishing Company, 1893) 215.

117. Joseph Stanley-Brown, "Memorandum Concerning Joseph Stanley-Brown's Relations with General Garfield," June 24, 1924, Stanley-Brown Papers, Library of Congress, in Ackerman, *Dark Horse*, 332.

118. E. Hilton Jackson, "Trial of Guiteau," 1025.

119. Statement from District Attorney Corkhill in Balch, *Garfield's Words*, 670–71. See also Charles J. Guiteau and Henry G. Hayes, *A Complete History of the Trial of Guiteau, Assassin of President*

Garfield (Philadelphia: Hubbard Bros.), 431. See also Ackerman, *Dark Horse*, 333. The name of the driver was Augilla Barton and just before exiting the carriage, Guiteau told him, "I will be right out . . . I want you to drive very fast." See James C. Clark, *The Murder of James A. Garfield: The President's Last Days and the Trial and Execution of his Assassin.* (Jefferson, N.C.: McFarland, 1993).

120. William M. Thayer, *From Log-Cabin to White House*, 394. See also J. S. Ogilvie, *The Life and Death of James A Garfield: From the Tow Path to the White House* (Cincinnati, Ohio: Cincinnati Publishing Co., 1882), 30. James McCabe, *The Life and Public Services of James A. Garfield*, 536, cites arrival time at 9:15 a.m.

121. Seale, *The President's House*, 1:501.

122. Thayer, *From Log-Cabin to White House*, 396.

123. *New York Times*, July 3, 1881, 1, quoted in Feerick, *From Failing Hands*, 118.

124. Feerick, *From Failing Hands*, 118.

125. Balch, *Garfield's Words*, 594. See also Ackerman, *Dark Horse*, 334–35.

126. Balch, *Garfield's Words*, 631.

127. Feerick, *From Failing Hands*, 119.

128. Millard, *Destiny of the Republic*, 162.

129. Feerick, *From Failing Hands*, 119. See also Balch, *Garfield's Words*, 595.

130. MacMahon and Curry, *Medical Cover-Ups*, 22.

131. Ackerman, *Dark Horse*, 336.

132. Robert Todd Lincoln cited in Charles E. Rosenberg, *The Trial of the Assassin Guiteau: Psychiatry and Law in the Gilded Age* (Chicago and London, 1968), 4, in Peskin, *Garfield*, 597. Despite his sorrow, Lincoln remembered the conspiracy to assassinate the entire senior leadership of government in 1865, and used his authority as Secretary of War to order soldiers to stand guard at the arsenal and await orders. He also responded to a telegram from General Grant asking for clarity on conflicting news reports. See Ogilvie, *The Life and Death of James A. Garfield*, 32 and 41.

133. Feerick, *From Failing Hands*, 119.

134. Balch, *Garfield's Words*, 596–97.

135. Ibid., 597.

136. *New York Times*, July 3, 1881, 1, quoted in Feerick, *From Failing Hands*, 118. Full text of letter found at Stewart Mitchell, "The Man Who Murdered Garfield," *Proceedings of the Massachusetts Historical Society* 67, 3rd ser. (October 1941–May 1944), 452–89, https://www.jstor.org/stable /25080360. Full text also found in Balch, *Garfield's Words*, 668 and Ogilvie, *The Life and Death of James A. Garfield*, 47–48.

137. Of all of Guiteau's suggestions, Coulsburg seems too obscure to track down. It is not known whom he is referring to.

138. Feerick, *From Failing Hands*, 118–19.

139. Thayer, *From Log-Cabin to White House*, 405.

140. Millard, *Destiny of the Republic*, 193.

141. There are varying accounts as to whether Arthur heard the news before they docked. One narrative suggests he couldn't hear the substance of the shouts from shore. See Ackerman, *Dark Horse*, 339. According to the *New York Sun*, July 3, 1881, another passenger named Steward Burdett deciphered the message and relayed the news to Arthur before they docked. His response, "It can't be true. This must be some stock speculation." Found in Greenberger, *The Unexpected President*, 153.

142. Millard, *Destiny of the Republic*, 193.

143. "Garfield Shot," *Milwaukee Daily Sentinel*, July 2, 1881, in Millard, *Destiny of the Republic*, 194.

144. Millard, *Destiny of the Republic*, 193. See also "Gen. Arthur's Movements," *New York Times*,

July 3, 1881, in Reeves, *Gentleman Boss,* 238; Greenberger, *The Unexpected President,* 154; and Ackerman, *Dark Horse,* 339.

145. Thomas Collier Platt, *The Autobiography of Thomas Collier Platt,* ed. Lewis J. Lang (New York: B. W. Dodge & Company, 1910), 163, in Ackerman, *Dark Horse,* 340.

146. Absent a war, there really wasn't a mechanism to protect the president. In April 1865, Congress passed legislation for the establishment of the Secret Service, but it was among a stack of documents that awaited Lincoln's signature on the eve of his assassination. Andrew Johnson signed it on July 5, 1865, but it was established as a division within the Treasury Department and given an anti-counterfeiting, not presidential protection, mandate. By 1880, the Secret Service lost half of its budget, in part because Congress felt it had drifted too far into law enforcement. That meant a downsized budget of just $60,000 and a limited focus on counterfeiting cases. (See Millard, *Destiny of the Republic,* 104).

147. *New York Tribune,* July 3, 1881, in Ackerman, *Dark Horse,* 352. See also Ayre, *Beyond Tomorrow,* 411.

148. Thomas Platt, "Thomas Platt's Autobiography: Part 2—The Garfield-Conkling Feud," *McClure's Magazine,* vol. 35 (May to October 1910), 327.

149. *Chicago Tribune,* July 3, 1881, quoted in Ackerman, *Dark Horse,* 394. See also Millard, *Destiny of the Republic,* 239.

150. Balch, *Garfield's Words,* 597.

151. "A Nation's Sorrow," *The Daily Liberal (Iowa)* 1, no. 153, July 14, 1881. See also "Garfield Assassinated," *The Cleveland Herald,* July 2, 1881.

152. Letter from James Blaine to Chester Arthur, July 2, 1881, Chester Arthur III Papers, Library of Congress. See also John Stuart Ogilvie, *History of the Attempted Assassination of James A. Garfield* (Nabu Press, March 2012; first published 1881 by J. S. Ogilvie & Company). Blaine sent Arthur five telegrams that day, the last of which was sent at 6:45 p.m. and suggested the president is "rapidly sinking." See Ogilvie, *The Life and Death of James A. Garfield,* 65–66.

153. Telegraph from James Blaine to Chester Arthur, V.P., July 2, 1881, Box 59 (Correspondence [copies]), President Chester A. Arthur (2 folders), Chester Alan Arthur III Papers, 1853–1972, Library of Congress.

154. Thomas L. James and William H. Hunt to Arthur, July 2, 1881, in *Chicago Tribune,* July 3, 1881, in Ackerman, *Dark Horse,* 354.

155. Doenecke, *Presidencies of James A. Garfield & Chester A. Arthur,* 54. See also Ackerman, *Dark Horse,* 354.

156. Ackerman, *Dark Horse,* 354. See also Greenberger, *The Unexpected President,* 159.

157. Historians disagree on the time. Ackerman puts it at 7 a.m.; Reeves puts it at 8 a.m.

158. Reeves, *Gentleman Boss,* 242.

159. Ackerman, *Dark Horse,* 356–57. See also Reeves, *Gentleman Boss,* 242.

160. *United States v. Charles Guiteau,* 896, in Ackerman, *Dark Horse,* 189.

161. Karabell, *Chester Alan Arthur,* 61.

162. Ackerman, *Dark Horse,* 355.

163. Greenberger, *The Unexpected President,* 162. See also Ackerman, *Dark Horse,* 356–57.

164. According to Feerick, they came to Arthur.

165. *Chicago Tribune,* July 4, 1881, in Ackerman, *Dark Horse,* 357. See also James McCabe, *The Life of James A. Garfield Our Martyred President,* 755–76.

166. *New York Times,* July 4, 1881, 5, quoted in Feerick, *From Failing Hands,* 123.

167. *New York Times,* July 8, 1881, 1, in Feerick, *From Failing Hands,* 125.

168. "Gen. Arthur in Washington," *New York Times,* July 4, 1881, in Millard, *Destiny of the Republic,* 239. See also Greenberger, *The Unexpected President,* 162–63.

169. Karabell, *Chester Alan Arthur,* 62.

170. "Senator Harrison on Arthur," *New York Times*, November 19, 1886, in Reeves, *Gentleman Boss*, 242. See also Ackerman, *Dark Horse*, 358.

171. Howe, *Chester A. Arthur*, 150.

172. Feerick, *From Failing Hands*, 123.

173. Theodore Clarke Smith, *Life and Letters of James Abram Garfield*, 1179–80, in Howe, *Chester A. Arthur*, 150. See also Feerick, *From Failing Hands*, 123.

174. *Evening Star*, July 4, 1881, in Ackerman, *Dark Horse*, 358.

175. Karabell, *Chester Alan Arthur*, 63.

176. *New York Times*, July 3, 1881, in Ackerman, *Dark Horse*, 357.

177. *Courier-Journal* (Louisville, Ky.), July 3, 1881, in Greenberger, *The Unexpected President*, 161, and Ackerman, *Dark Horse*, 358–59.

178. Poore, *Perley's Reminiscences*, 427–28, in Reeves, *Gentleman Boss*, 242.

179. Thayer, *From Log-Cabin to White House*, 395.

180. Reeves, *Gentleman Boss*, 3. See also Peskin, *Garfield*, 599.

181. Ibid.

182. This is inferred from multiple cited sources indicating that he kept a low profile, spent a great deal of time at the Jones house, and feared the crowd.

183. Reeves, *Gentleman Boss*, 241 and 245. See also Doenecke, *Presidencies of James A. Garfield & Chester A. Arthur*, 53–54.

184. Karabell, *Chester Alan Arthur*, 63.

185. David C. Whitney, *The American Presidents* (Garden City, N.Y.: J. G. Ferguson Publishing Company, 1967), 180, in Boller, *Presidential Campaigns*, 144.

186. John Sherman to Rutherford Hayes, July 8, 1881, Rutherford Hayes Papers, in Howe, *Chester A. Arthur*, 151.

187. *New York Times*, July 3, 1881, in Ackerman, *Dark Horse*, 349. See also Williams, *Diary and Letters of Rutherford B. Hayes*, 23, quoted in Millard, *Destiny of the Republic*, 197; Peskin, *Garfield*, 599; and Doenecke, *Presidencies of James A. Garfield & Chester A. Arthur*, 54.

188. Letter from Jefferson Davis to Miss Beauvoir, July 5, 1881, in Balch, *Garfield's Words*, 658.

189. William Arthur naturalization document, Library of Congress, https://naturalborncitizen.files .wordpress.com/2008/12/william-arthur-naturalization.pdf.

190. Arthur Hinman, *How a British Subject Became President of the United States* (New York, 1884). See also Howe, *Chester A. Arthur*, 3.

191. Millard, *Destiny of the Republic*, 242.

192. *New York Times*, September 16, 1881, in Millard, *Destiny of the Republic*, 198.

193. Millard, *Destiny of the Republic*, 209.

194. Feerick, *From Failing Hands*, 126.

195. Howe, *Chester A. Arthur*, 153.

196. Doenecke, *Presidencies of James A. Garfield & Chester A. Arthur*, 165.

197. Silva, *Presidential Succession*, 152.

198. For the best account of Garfield's doctors and their medical malpractice, see Millard, *Destiny of the Republic*, 231–294.

199. Farrand, *Records of the Federal Convention*, 499, in Robert E. Gilbert, "Presidential Disability and the Twenty-Fifth Amendment: The Difficulties Posed By Psychological Illness," *Fordham L. Rev.* 79, no. 3 (2011), 843, http://ir.lawnet.fordham.edu/flr/vol79/iss3/5.

200. Silva, *Presidential Succession*, 83–84.

201. Telegram from A. F. Rockwell to J. J. Kirkwood, August 10, 1881, James Garfield Papers, Library of Congress, reel 120, ser. 6B, vol. 3, March 5, 1881 to July 31, 1881; vol. 4, August 1, 1881 to September 20, 1881.

202. Letter from James Garfield to his mother, August 11, 1881, James Garfield Papers, Reel 120. Library of Congress.

203. Telegram from Joseph Stanley Brown to William Babcock Hazen, August 11, 1881, reel 120, James Garfield Papers, Library of Congress.

204. Telegram from Joseph Stanley Brown to Archdeacon and Co., August 11, 1881, James Garfield Papers, reel 120, Library of Congress.

205. Silva, *Presidential Succession*, 54–55.

206. Ibid., 53.

207. Ibid., 56–57.

208. Feerick, *From Failing Hands*, 137–38.

209. First Annual Message, December 6, 1881, in Richardson, *Compilation of the Messages and Papers of the Presidents*, vol. 8, part 2: *Chester Arthur*, 24–25.

210. Karabell, *Chester Alan Arthur*, 64–65.

211. Howe, *Chester A. Arthur*, 1–2. See also Ackerman, *Dark Horse*, 377.

212. Howe, *Chester A. Arthur*, 11–12. See also Peskin, *Garfield*, 608; Ackerman, *Dark Horse*, 377.

213. Ackerman, *Dark Horse*, 378; the friend was Chauncey Depew.

214. Howe, *Chester A. Arthur*, 2.

215. "The Oath administered; Gen. Arthur Made President of the United States. The News in the City," *New York Times*, September 20, 1881. See also Doenecke, *Presidencies of James A. Garfield & Chester A. Arthur*, 54; Reeves, *Gentleman Boss*, 247; Ackerman, *Dark Horse*, 378; and Millard, *Destiny of the Republic*, 269.

216. Chester A. Arthur to fiancée Ellen "Nell" Herndon of 84 East 23rd Street, New York, August 30, 1857, Chester Alan Arthur III Papers, Library of Congress. Nell was the daughter of naval commander William Lewis Herndon.

217. Reeves, *Gentleman Boss*, 158. See also Greenberger, *The Unexpected President*, 115.

218. In response to a telegram from Attorney General MacVeagh to Chester Arthur, September 20, 1881, 12:25 a.m. The message came from the Attorney General due to the absence of both the Secretary of State and Secretary of War. For Arthur's response see *New York Times*, September 20, 1881, in Ackerman, *Dark Horse*, 378. See also Ogilvie, *The Life and Death of James A. Garfield*, 441.

219. Howe, *Chester A. Arthur*, 2.

220. "The Oath administered; Gen. Arthur Made President of the United States. The News in the City," *New York Times*, September 20, 1881.

221. Karabell, *Chester Alan Arthur*, 64.

222. Howe, *Chester A. Arthur*, 2; for summary of oath of office see Reeves, *Gentleman Boss*, 247. See also Feerick, *From Failing Hands*, 129.

223. "The Oath administered; Gen. Arthur Made President of the United States. The News in the City," *New York Times*, September 20, 1881. For detailed description of the scene see Ogilvie, *The Life and Death of James A. Garfield*, 442. "The room in which the new President took the oath of office is shelved with books. In the centre is a table, and the carpet is rich and dark. Paintings by old Italian masters, in Florentine frames, adorn the walls, and a bust of Henry Clay is in the corner, nearest one of the windows."

224. Frederic Bancroft, ed., *Speeches, Correspondence and Political Papers of Carl Schurz* (New York: G. P. Putnam's Sons, 1913), 4:147, in Reeves, *Gentleman Boss*, 241–42.

225. Feerick, *From Failing Hands*, 131.

226. Silva, *Presidential Succession*, 118.

227. Statement by George Bliss in "Giving Voice to Sorrow," *New York Times*, November 21, 1886, in Reeves, *Gentleman Boss*, 247. See also Ackerman, *Dark Horse*, 379; see *New York Times*, November 21, 1886, in Feerick, *From Failing Hands*, 130n.

228. Silva, *Presidential Succession*, 118.

229. Howe, *Chester A. Arthur*, 154–55.

230. Silva, *Presidential Succession*, 119.

231. Ridpath, *Life and Work of James A. Garfield*, 615–19.

232. Reeves, *Gentleman Boss*, 247–48. See also Feerick, *From Failing Hands*, 129; Ridpath, *Life and Work of James A. Garfield*, 653–54; Karabell, *Chester Alan Arthur*, 66–68; and Howe, *Chester A. Arthur*, 155.

233. Seale, *The President's House*, 1:526.

234. Silva, *Presidential Succession*, 27–28.

235. Howe, *Chester A. Arthur*, 155.

236. John M. Harlan and Stanley Matthews.

237. First Annual Message, December 6, 1881, in Richardson, *Compilation of the Messages and Papers of the Presidents*, vol. 8, part 2: *Chester Arthur*, 25. See also Feerick, *From Failing Hands*, 129.

238. Silva, *Presidential Succession*, 27–28.

239. Howe, *Chester A. Arthur*, 157.

240. *New York Times*, August 27, 1881, 4, quoted in Feerick, *From Failing Hands*, 128.

241. Witcover, *American Vice Presidency*, 194. See also Reeves, *Gentleman Boss*, 183.

242. Ibid., 259.

243. "The Vacant Judgeship," editorial, *New York Times*, March 14, 1882, in Reeves, *Gentleman Boss*, 261. See also Karabell, *Chester Alan Arthur*, 80.

244. Witcover, *American Vice Presidency*, 195. See also Reeves, *Gentleman Boss*, 183.

245. Thomas F. Pendel, *Thirty-Six Years in the White House* (Washington, D.C.: Neale, 1902), 125, in Seale, *The President's House*, 1:513.

246. Seale, *The President's House*, 1:511.

247. Doenecke, *Presidencies of James A. Garfield & Chester A. Arthur*, 78. See also Howe, *Chester A. Arthur*, 165–66; and Esther Singleton, *The Story of the White House* (New York: McClure, 1907), 2:179–80, in Reeves, *Gentleman Boss*, 268.

248. Singleton, *Story of the White House*, 2:179–80, in Reeves, *Gentleman Boss*, 268.

249. Doenecke, *Presidencies of James A. Garfield & Chester A. Arthur*, 78.

250. Edna M. H. Colman, *White House Gossip from Andrew Johnson to Calvin Coolidge* (New York: Doubleday, 1927), 154–55, in Howe, *Chester A. Arthur*, 165–66.

251. Henry Rood, ed., *Memories of the White House: The Home Life of Our Presidents from Lincoln to Roosevelt, Being Personal Recollections of Colonel W. H. Crook* (Boston: Little, Brown, 1911), 159–60, in Reeves, *Gentleman Boss*, 268.

252. Seale, *The President's House*, 1:518.

253. Richard Crowley, *Echoes from Niagara: Historical, Political, Personal* (Buffalo, N.Y.: C. W. Moulton, 1890), 229, in Reeves, *Gentleman Boss*, 272.

254. Karabell, *Chester Alan Arthur*, 78–79. See also Doenecke, *Presidencies of James A. Garfield & Chester A. Arthur*, 79; and Seale, *The President's House*, 526.

255. Doenecke, *Presidencies of James A. Garfield & Chester A. Arthur*, 79.

256. Howe, *Chester A. Arthur*, 176. See also Boller, *Presidential Anecdotes*, 175.

257. Ackerman, *Dark Horse*, 209–10.

258. Reeves, *Gentleman Boss*, 274.

259. Ibid., 33.

260. Ibid., 270.

261. Seale, *The President's House*, 1:528.

262. Seating charts, 1881–1885, Officer in Charge of Public Buildings, National Archives, and letters sent and miscellaneous papers, in Seale, *The President's House*, 1:528.

263. Reeves, *Gentleman Boss*, 271.

264. Ibid.
265. Ibid., 273. See also Howe, *Chester A. Arthur*, 173; and Doenecke, *Presidencies of James A. Garfield & Chester A. Arthur*, 79–80.
266. Memorandum, "Mr. C. M. Hendley's Association with President Arthur," April 22, 1925, Chester Alan Arthur III Papers, Library of Congress, quoted in Reeves, *Gentleman Boss*, 273. See also Karabell, *Chester Alan Arthur*, 93.
267. Brodie Herndon diaries, entries of May 24, 26, June 8, August 1, 1882, in Reeves, *Gentleman Boss*, 273.
268. Memorandum, "Mr. C. M. Hendley's Association with President Arthur." See also Doenecke, *Presidencies of James A. Garfield & Chester A. Arthur*, 79–80.
269. Howe, *Chester A. Arthur*, 173–74. See also Boller, *Presidential Anecdotes*, 175; and memorandum, "Mr. C. M. Hendley's Association with President Arthur," quoted in Reeves, *Gentleman Boss*, 273.
270. Julia Sand to Chester Arthur, August 27, 1881, box 59 (Julia Sand Letters), Chester Alan Arthur III Papers.
271. Julia Sand to Chester Arthur, October 5, 1881, box 59 (Julia Sand Letters), Chester Alan Arthur III Papers.
272. Julia Sand to Chester Arthur, January 7, 1882, box 59 (Julia Sand Letters), Chester Alan Arthur III Papers.
273. Julia Sand to Chester Arthur, October 5, 1881, box 59 (Julia Sand Letters), Chester Alan Arthur III Papers.
274. Doenecke, *Presidencies of James A. Garfield & Chester A. Arthur*, 76. See also Reeves, *Gentleman Boss*, 260; and H. Wayne Morgan, *From Hayes to McKinley* (Syracuse, N.Y.: Syracuse University Press, 1969).
275. Reeves, *Gentleman Boss*, 314–16.
276. Karabell, *Chester Alan Arthur*, 84.
277. Ibid., 85–86.
278. Doenecke, *Presidencies of James A. Garfield & Chester A. Arthur*, 83.
279. Reeves, *Gentleman Boss*, 312.
280. Rayford W. Logan, *The Negro in American Life and Thought: The Nadir, 1877–1901* (New York: Dial Press, 1954), in Reeves, *Gentleman Boss*, 312. See also Karabell, *Chester Alan Arthur*, 126–27; and Doenecke, *Presidencies of James A. Garfield & Chester A. Arthur*, 125.
281. Karabell, *Chester Alan Arthur*, 126–27.
282. Julia Sand to Chester Arthur, November 18, 1881, box 59 (Julia Sand Letters), Chester Alan Arthur III Papers.
283. Julia Sand to Chester Arthur, January 7, 1882, box 59 (Julia Sand Letters), Chester Alan Arthur III Papers.
284. Howe, *Chester A. Arthur*, 206.
285. Civil Service Commission, *Second Annual Report*, 55, in Howe, *Chester A. Arthur*, 217.
286. Reeves, *Gentleman Boss*, 296. See also Greenberger, *The Unexpected President*, 169. Greenberger's research reveals that Julia Sand never gave her address. The return address on one of the letters was "Theodore V. Sand, Banker, 54 Wall St. (Sand, Hamilton & Co) lives at No. 46 East 74th Street." Embossed card in Chester Alan Arthur Papers. Library of Congress. Ayre, *Beyond Tomorrow*, 427, suggests that Arthur came to believe that Julia Sand somehow knew his late wife, Nell, who he remained desperate to connect with. Ayre interprets this as the primary motivation for visiting her at home. Upon arrival, he saw boxes of letters to other people, immediately understood she was unstable, and concluded she had no connection to Nell.
287. Julia Sand to Chester Arthur, August 24, 1882, box 59 (Julia Sand Letters), Chester Alan Arthur III Papers.

288. Julia Sand to Chester Arthur, August 28, 1882, box 59 (Julia Sand Letters), Chester Alan Arthur III Papers.

289. Julia Sand to Chester Arthur, September 13, 1882, box 59 (Julia Sand Letters), Chester Alan Arthur III Papers. In addition to the "very bad friend" reference, Sand opens a May 1882 letter with, "You dear good old sinner."

290. Doenecke, *Presidencies of James A. Garfield & Chester A. Arthur*, 145.

291. Howe, *Chester A. Arthur*, 232.

292. Doenecke, *Presidencies of James A. Garfield & Chester A. Arthur*, 146.

293. Ibid., 233–34.

294. Ibid., 80.

295. Ibid., 80. See also Reeves, *Gentleman Boss*, 318.

296. Reeves, *Gentleman Boss*, 371.

297. Howe, *Chester A. Arthur*, 277–80.

298. Joe M. Richardson, "The Florida Excursion of President Chester A. Arthur," Tequesta 24, no. 1 (1964), 46.

299. Millard, *Destiny of the Republic*, 291.

300. This quote is often incorrectly attributed to Theodore Roosevelt. It was Secretary of State John Hay who made this observation, in a letter to Theodore Roosevelt dated July 27, 1898. See John A. Gable, "Credit 'Splendid Little War' to John Hay," letter to the editor, *New York Times*, July 9, 1991, https://www.nytimes.com/1991/07/09/opinion/l-credit-splendid-little-war-to-john-hay-595391.html.

CHAPTER FIVE: A MOST AMBITIOUS MAN

1. Frank W. Lovering in *Boston Journal*, August 23, 1902, in Edmund Morris, *Theodore Rex* (New York: Random House, 2001), 137.

2. "August 22: Theodore Roosevelt Becomes First President to Ride in an Automobile," Learning Network, *New York Times*, August 22, 2011, http://learning.blogs.nytimes.com/2011/08/22/aug-22-1902-theodore-roosevelt-becomes-first-president-to-ride-in-an-automobile/.

3. *Literary Digest*, September 6, 1902, in Edmund Morris, *Theodore Rex*, 140.

4. *The Call* (San Francisco), September 4, 1902, 9, Chronicling America: Historic American Newspapers, Library of Congress, http://chroniclingamerica.loc.gov/lccn/sn85066387/1902-09-04/ed-1/seq-9/.

5. Dawes had played a role in moving indigenous people and opening their land to development.

6. *Vinita Daily Chieftain* (Ind. Ter. [Okla.]), September 4, 1902, Chronicling America: Historic American Newspapers, Library of Congress, http://chroniclingamerica.loc.gov/lccn/sn93050700/1902-09-04/ed-1/seq-1/.

7. Ibid.

8. *The Call*, September 4, 1902.

9. Ibid.

10. *Houston Daily Post*, September 4, 1902, Chronicling America: Historic American Newspapers, Library of Congress, http://chroniclingamerica.loc.gov/lccn/sn86071197/1902-09-04/ed-1/seq-1/.

11. *Vinita Daily Chieftain*, September 4, 1902.

12. *The Call*, September 4, 1902.

13. Ibid.

14. *Vinita Daily Chieftain*, September 4, 1902.

15. *Houston Daily Post*, September 4, 1902.

16. Edmund Morris, *Theodore Rex*, 142.

17. *Houston Daily Post*, September 4, 1902.

18. *Vinita Daily Chieftain*, September 4, 1902.

19. Edmund Morris, *Theodore Rex*, 142.

20. *The Call*, September 4, 1902.

21. *Vinita Daily Chieftain*, September 4, 1902.

22. *The Call*, September 4, 1902.

23. George A. Lung, "Roosevelt's Narrow Escape from Death in Smash-Up," *Brooklyn Daily Eagle*, January 8, 1919, in Edmund Morris, *Theodore Rex*, 142.

24. *The Call*, September 4, 1902.

25. *Vinita Daily Chieftain*, September 4, 1902.

26. Ibid.

27. Ibid. See also *The Call*, September 4, 1902.

28. Edmund Morris, *Theodore Rex*, 143.

29. Frank W. Lovering, "Eyewitness Tells of T. R.'s Pittsfield Outrage," *Berkshire Eagle*, August 20, 1960, in Edmund Morris, *Theodore Rex*, 142.

30. *Vinita Daily Chieftain*, September 4, 1902.

31. Ibid.

32. Frank W. Lovering in *Boston Journal*, September 4, 1902, in Edmund Morris, *Theodore Rex*, 137.

33. Edmund Morris, *Theodore Rex*, 137.

34. *The Call*, September 4, 1902.

35. *Vinita Daily Chieftain*, September 4, 1902.

36. Ibid.

37. "President in Hospital," *Indianapolis Journal*, September 24, 1902, http://blog.newspapers. library.in.gov/theodore-roosevelt-hospitalized-at-st-vincents/.

38. *New Ulm Review* (Brown County, Minn.), October 1, 1902, Chronicling America: Historic American Newspapers, Library of Congress, http://chroniclingamerica.loc.gov/lccn/sn89081128 /1902-10-01/ed-1/seq-2/.

39. Stephen J. Taylor, "When Theodore Roosevelt was Hospitalized at St. Vincent's," *Hoosier State Chronicles*, September 22, 2015, http://blog.newspapers.library.in.gov/theodore-roosevelt -hospitalized-at-st-vincents/.

40. Ibid.

41. Edmund Morris, *Theodore Rex*, 148.

42. Taylor, "When Theodore Roosevelt was Hospitalized at St. Vincent's."

43. *New Ulm Review,* October 1, 1902.

44. Taylor, "When Theodore Roosevelt was Hospitalized at St. Vincent's."

45. Elting E. Morison et al., eds., *The Letters of Theodore Roosevelt* (Cambridge, Mass.: Harvard University Press, 1951), 3:346, in John R. Bumgarner, *The Health of the Presidents* (Jefferson, N.C.: McFarland, 2004), 161.

46. Henry F. Pringle, *Theodore Roosevelt: A Biography* (New York: Scribner, 1958), 269, in Bumgarner, *Health of the Presidents*, 160.

47. Rudolph Marx, *The Health of the Presidents* (New York: Putnam Books, 1960), 290, in Bumgarner, *Health of the Presidents*, 161.

48. *Vinita Daily Chieftain*, September 4, 1902.

49. *Houston Daily Post,* September 4, 1902.

50. Charles S. Hamlin, "The Presidential Succession Act of 1886," *Harvard Law Review* 18, no. 3 (January 1905), 183.

51. Ibid.

52. Ibid., 190.

53. William Roscoe Thayer, *Theodore Roosevelt: An Intimate Biography* (Boston and New York: Houghton Mifflin, 1919), 22, in Boller, *Presidential Anecdotes*, 201.

54. Theodore Roosevelt, *The Autobiography of Theodore Roosevelt* (Seven Treasures Publications, 2009; first published 1913 by Macmillan), 24–25.

55. Ibid, 27.

56. Ibid., 30.

57. Ibid.

58. Lewis Henry, *Humorous Anecdotes about Famous People* (Garden City, N.Y., 1948), 98, in Boller, 194–95.

59. Theodore Roosevelt, *Autobiography*, 17.

60. Ibid.

61. Ibid., 13.

62. John Milton Cooper, Jr., *The Warrior and the Priest: Woodrow Wilson and Theodore Roosevelt* (Cambridge, Mass.: Belknap Press of Harvard University Press, 1983), 6.

63. Hermann Hagedorn, *The Boy's Life of Theodore Roosevelt* (New York: Harper & Brothers, 1918), 63–64, in John Milton Cooper, Jr., *The Warrior and the Priest*, 14.

64. Ibid.

65. Theodore Roosevelt, *Autobiography*, 21.

66. John Wood in *The World* (New York), January 24, 1904, in Edmund Morris, *Rise of Theodore Roosevelt* (New York: Random House, 1979), 32–33.

67. Paul Grondahl, *I Rose Like a Rocket: The Political Education of Theodore Roosevelt* (New York: Free Press, 2004), 228.

68. Grondahl, *I Rose Like a Rocket*, 228.

69. Edmund Morris, *Rise of Theodore Roosevelt*, 144.

70. Theodore Roosevelt, *Autobiography*, 153.

71. Ibid.

72. Edmund Morris, *Rise of Theodore Roosevelt*, 138.

73. Grondahl, *I Rose Like a Rocket*, 382.

74. Isaac Hunt and George Spinney, verbal recollections from Hermann Hagedorn dinner at the Harvard Club, New York, September 20, 1923, no date, 50, in Edmund Morris, *Rise of Theodore Roosevelt*, 149.

75. Ibid.

76. Ibid.

77. Isaac Hunt and George Spinney. Verbal recollections from Hermann Hagedorn dinner at the Harvard Club, New York, September 20, 1923, no date, 85, in Edmund Morris, *Rise of Theodore Roosevelt*, 149.

78. Carleton Putnam, *Theodore Roosevelt. Vol. I: The Formative Years, 1858–1886* (New York: Scribner's, 1958), 258, in Edmund Morris, *Rise of Theodore Roosevelt*, 152.

79. Edmund Morris, *Rise of Theodore Roosevelt*, 177.

80. Parshall, Gerald, "The Great Panic of '93," *U.S. News & World Report*, November 2, 1992, 70.

81. Grondahl, *I Rose Like a Rocket*, 214.

82. Ibid., 215.

83. Theodore Roosevelt, *Autobiography*, 95.

84. Grondahl, *I Rose Like a Rocket*, 214.

85. Ibid., 230.

86. Jay S. Berman, "Theodore Roosevelt as Police Commissioner of New York: The Birth of Modern American Police Administration," in Natalie A. Naylor et al., eds., *Theodore Roosevelt: Many-Sided American* (Interlaken, N.Y.: Hearts of Lake Publishing, 1992), 171–83, in Grondahl, *I Rose Like a Rocket*, 223.

87. John Milton Cooper, Jr., *The Warrior and the Priest*, 37.

88. Grondahl, *I Rose Like a Rocket*, 225.

89. Ibid.

90. Pringle, *Theodore Roosevelt*, 172, in Boller, *Presidential Anecdotes*, 196.

91. Walter Millis, *The Martial Spirit: A Study of Our War with Spain* (Boston: Houghton Mifflin, 1931), 38, in Scott Miller, *The President and the Assassin: McKinley, Terror, and Empire at the Dawn of the American Century* (New York: Random House, 2011), 50.

92. Mrs. Bellamy Storer, "How Theodore Roosevelt Was Appointed Assistant Secretary of the Navy: A Hitherto Unrelated Chapter of History," *Harper's Weekly* 56, no. 2893 (July 1, 1912), 9, in Scott Miller, *President and the Assassin*, 49–50.

93. Scott Miller, *President and the Assassin*, 50.

94. Edmund Morris, *Rise of Theodore Roosevelt*, 577–78.

95. H. G. Rickover, *How the Battleship Maine Was Destroyed* (Washington, D.C.: Naval History Division, Department of the Navy, 1976), 1–3, in Scott Miller, *President and the Assassin*, 114–15. At 319 feet and capable of seventeen knots, she carried four ten-inch guns and six six-inch guns in her main battery that were designed to penetrate the armor of an enemy ship.

96. Scott Miller, *President and the Assassin*, 125.

97. Grondahl, *I Rose Like a Rocket*, 248. See also Scott Miller, *President and the Assassin*, 125.

98. Theodore Roosevelt, *Autobiography*, 116.

99. Ibid., 119.

100. Grondahl, *I Rose Like a Rocket*, 248.

101. Scott Miller, *President and the Assassin*, 125.

102. John D. Long, *Journal of John D. Long*, Margaret Long, ed. (Rindge, N.H.: Richard R. Smith Publisher, 1956), 217, in Scott Miller, *President and the Assassin*, 125.

103. Edmund Morris, *Rise of Theodore Roosevelt*, 607–8. See also Scott Miller, *President and the Assassin*, 129.

104. Edmund Morris, *Rise of Theodore Roosevelt*, 640. See also Scott Miller, *President and the Assassin*, 174.

105. Theodore Roosevelt, *Autobiography*, 146–47.

106. Grondahl, *I Rose Like a Rocket*, 288.

107. Ibid., 283.

108. Theodore Roosevelt, *Autobiography*, 150.

109. Grondahl, *I Rose Like a Rocket*, 297.

110. Platt, *Autobiography of Thomas Collier Platt*, 373, in Grondahl, *I Rose Like a Rocket*, 297.

111. Grondahl, *I Rose Like a Rocket*, 302.

112. Ibid., 357.

113. Eric Rauchway, *Murdering McKinley: The Making of Theodore Roosevelt's America* (New York: Hill & Wang, 2003), 10.

114. Grondahl, *I Rose Like a Rocket*, 325.

115. Theodore Roosevelt, *Autobiography*, 166.

116. Ibid., 166–67.

117. Ibid., 169.

118. John Milton Cooper, Jr., *The Warrior and the Priest*, 39.

119. Groundhog Day first became a reference in the 1840s, so they were accustomed to the context, but the concept of a recurring day stems from the 1993 film "Groundhog Day."

120. *Wheeling Daily Intelligencer* (W.Va.), November 22, 1899, Chronicling America: Historic American Newspapers, Library of Congress, http://chroniclingamerica.loc.gov/lccn/sn84026844/1899-11-22/ed-1/seq-1/.

121. *Anaconda Standard* (Mont.), November 22, 1899, p. 2, Chronicling America: Historic American Newspapers, Library of Congress, http://chroniclingamerica.loc.gov/lccn/sn84036012/1899-11-22/ed-1/seq-2/.

122. Kelter and Shellabarger, *Veeps*, 120.

123. Feerick, *From Failing Hands*, 152.

124. Andrew Noymer, "Life Expectancy in the USA, 1900–98," http://demog.berkeley.edu/~andrew /1918/figure2.html.

125. Kelter and Shellabarger, *Veeps*, 122.

126. Grondahl, *I Rose Like a Rocket*, 342. See also Feerick, *From Failing Hands*, 154—Feerick believes it would have gone to Root if he had wanted it.

127. Walter LaFeber, "Vice Presidential Nominee: Theodore Roosevelt," interview transcript, "America 1900," directed by David Grubin, *American Experience*, https://web.archive.org/web /20141115230252/http://www.pbs.org/wgbh/amex/1900/filmmore/reference/interview/lafeber_ vpnomineetr.html (archived copy of http://www.pbs.org/wgbh/amex/1900/filmmore/reference /interview/lafeber_vpnomineetr.html).

128. "Roosevelt Meets Platt: A Conference in New York Upon the Vice Presidency," *The Times* (Washington, D.C.), February 11, 1900, Chronicling America: Historic American Newspapers, Library of Congress, http://chroniclingamerica.loc.gov/lccn/sn85054468/1900-02-11/ed-1/seq -1/. See also Grondahl, *I Rose Like a Rocket*, 340.

129. Ibid. See also *Chariton Courier* (Keytesville, Chariton County, Mo.), February 16, 1900, Chronicling America: Historic American Newspapers, Library of Congress, http:// chroniclingamerica.loc.gov/lccn/sn88068010/1900-02-16/ed-1/seq-2/.

130. William Roscoe Thayer, *The Life and Letters of John Hay* (Boston: Houghton Mifflin, 1908), 2:342, in Scott Miller, *President and the Assassin*, 270.

131. William Roscoe Thayer, *Life and Letters of John Hay*, 342, in Scott Miller, *President and the Assassin*, 270. See also Grondahl, *I Rose Like a Rocket*, 346.

132. Grondahl, *I Rose Like a Rocket*, 346.

133. Stan M. Haynes, *President-Making in the Gilded Age: The Nominating Conventions of 1876–1900* (Jefferson, N.C.: McFarland, 2016), 243. See also Edmund Morris, *Rise of Theodore Roosevelt*, 763; and Scott Miller, *President and the Assassin*, 270–71.

134. Letter from Theodore Roosevelt to Lucius Nathan Littauer, from Albany, March 24, 1900, in Grondahl, *I Rose Like a Rocket*, 349–50.

135. Scott Miller, *President and the Assassin*, 270–71.

136. Ibid.

137. Grondahl, *I Rose Like a Rocket*, 341.

138. Theodore Roosevelt, *Autobiography*, 171.

139. Grondahl, *I Rose Like a Rocket*, 333.

140. Theodore Roosevelt, *The Autobiography of Theodore Roosevelt*, Wayne Andrews, ed. (New York: Octagon Books, 1958), 153, quoted in Feerick, *From Failing Hands*, 154.

141. Edmund Morris, *Rise of Theodore Roosevelt*, 756. See also Scott Miller, *President and the Assassin*, 270.

142. *The Call*, June 21, 1900, Chronicling America: Historic American Newspapers, Library of Congress, http://chroniclingamerica.loc.gov/lccn/sn85066387/1900-06-21/ed-1/seq-1/.

143. Morison et al., *Letters of Theodore Roosevelt*, 2:1337, in Grondahl, *I Rose Like a Rocket*, 352.

144. H. Wayne Morgan, *William McKinley and His America* (Syracuse, N.Y.: Syracuse University Press, 1963), 508, in Boller, *Presidential Campaigns*, 181.

145. Margaret Leech, *In the Days of McKinley* (Newtown, Conn.: American Political Biography Press, 1999; first published 1959 by Harper), 541, in Boller, *Presidential Campaigns*, 182.

146. Boller, *Presidential Campaigns*, 179.

147. James T. Woodward, "The United States, the Envy of the World," *New York Times*, January 1, 1900, in Scott Miller, *President and the Assassin*, 266.

148. Noel J. Kent, *America in 1900* (Armonk, N.Y.: M. E. Sharpe, 2002), 22. See also Scott Miller, *President and the Assassin*, 266.

149. Scott Miller, *President and the Assassin*, 289.

150. Ibid., 267.

151. Ibid.

152. Rauchway, *Murdering McKinley*, 6.

153. Noel F. Busch, *T. R.: The Story of Theodore Roosevelt and His Influence on Our Times* (New York: Reynal, 1963), 146–47, in Feerick, *From Failing Hands*, 155. See also Grondahl, *I Rose Like a Rocket*, 354; and Stefan Lorant, *Glorious Burden: The History of the Presidency and Presidential Elections from George Washington to James Earl Carter, Jr.*, rev. ed. (Lenox, Mass.: Authors Edition, 1976), 467, in Boller, *Presidential Campaigns*, 180.

154. Platt, *Autobiography of Thomas Collier Platt*, 397.

155. Ibid., 396.

156. Ibid., 397.

157. Cyrenus Cole, *I Remember, I Remember: A Book of Recollections* (Iowa City: State Historical Society of Iowa, 1936), 293, in Boller, *Presidential Campaigns*, 182.

158. Theodore Roosevelt, *American Ideals, The Strenuous Life, Realizable Ideals* (vol. 13, *The Works of Theodore Roosevelt*, Hermann Hagedorn, ed., New York: Charles Scribner's Sons, 1926), 138 and 142, in Rauchway, *Murdering McKinley*, 10.

159. Kelter and Shellabarger, *Veeps*, 125.

160. Sylvia Jukes Morris, *Edith Kermit Roosevelt: Portrait of a First Lady* (New York: Coward, McCann & Geoghegan, 1980), 209, in Grondahl, *I Rose Like a Rocket*, 359.

161. Theodore Roosevelt to Edward Bellamy and Maria Storer, April 17, 1901, Morison et al., *Letters of Theodore Roosevelt*, 3:57, in Rauchway, *Murdering McKinley*, 10–11.

162. Letter from Theodore Roosevelt to Endicott Peabody, May 7, 1901, Theodore Roosevelt Collection, Harvard University, in Grondahl, *I Rose Like a Rocket*, 361.

163. Arthur Wallace Dunn, *From Harrison to Harding*, 2 vols. (New York: G. P. Putnam's Sons, 1922), 1:335.

164. Edmund Morris, *Theodore Rex*, 6.

165. Letter from Theodore Roosevelt to Cecil Arthur Spring, March 16, 1901, in Ivie E. Cadenhead, *Theodore Roosevelt: The Paradox of Progressivism* (Woodbury, N.Y.: Barron's Educational Series, 1974), 73.

166. Scott Miller, *President and the Assassin*, 294.

167. Jay W. Murphy, *What Ails the White House: An Introduction to the Medical History of the American Presidency* (Overland Park, Kans.: Leathers Publishing, 2006), 69.

168. Scott Miller, *President and the Assassin*, 301. See also Rauchway, *Murdering McKinley*, 61–62.

169. "Acted as a Hero," *Washington Star*, September 7, 1901, 1, in Rauchway, *Murdering McKinley*, 62–63.

170. Charles S. Olcott, *The Life of William McKinley* (Boston: Houghton Mifflin, 1916), 2:316, in Scott Miller, *President and the Assassin*, 302.

171. Scott Miller, *President and the Assassin*, 312.

172. Jack C. Fisher, *Stolen Glory: The McKinley Assassination* (La Jolla, Calif.: Alamar Books, 2001), 69, in Scott Miller, *President and the Assassin*, 312–13.

173. Jay W. Murphy, *What Ails the White House*, 70.

174. "Official Report on the Case of President McKinley," 1030, in Scott Miller, *President and the Assassin*, 313–14.

175. Jay W. Murphy, *What Ails the White House*, 70.

176. Feerick, *From Failing Hands*, 156.

177. Scott Miller, *President and the Assassin*, 314. See also Grondahl, *I Rose Like a Rocket*, 366.

178. Rood, *Memories of the White House*, 264. See also Seale, *The President's House*, 1:618.

179. Jack Fisher, "McKinley's Assassination in Buffalo: Time to Put the Medical Controversy to Rest?" *Buffalo Physician* (Spring 2001), 12–19, in Rauchway, *Murdering McKinley*, 11.

180. Grondahl, *I Rose Like a Rocket*, 363.

181. Scott Miller, *President and the Assassin*, 247–49.

182. Walter Channing, "The Mental Status of Leon Czolgosz, the Assassin of President McKinley," *American Journal of Insanity* 59, no. 2 (1902), 22–23, in Scott Miller, *President and the Assassin*, 304. See also Rauchway, *Murdering McKinley*, 19.

183. Grondahl, *I Rose Like a Rocket*, 367.

184. Ibid., 368.

185. H. Wayne Morgan, *William McKinley and His America*, 518, in Feerick, *From Failing Hands*, 156.

186. Feerick, *From Failing Hands*, 157.

187. Facsimile telegram, Theodore Roosevelt Birthplace National Historic Site Archives, New York, in Edmund Morris, *Theodore Rex*, 3. See also Grondahl, *I Rose Like a Rocket*, 375–77; and Busch, *T. R.*, 151, in Feerick, *From Failing Hands*, 157.

188. Theodore Roosevelt, *Autobiography*, 193.

189. Morison et al., *Letters of Theodore Roosevelt*, 3:141–42, in Edmund Morris, *Theodore Rex*, 4.

190. Eloise C. Murphy, *Theodore Roosevelt's Night Ride to the Presidency* (Blue Mountain Lake, N.Y.: Adirondack Museum, 1977), 25, in Edmund Morris, *Theodore Rex*, 7.

191. Franklin Matthews, "The President's Last Days," *Harper's Weekly* 45, no. 2335 (September 21, 1901), 943, in Scott Miller, *President and the Assassin*, 319–20.

192. Busch, *T. R.*, 151, in Feerick, *From Failing Hands*, 157.

193. Edmund Morris, *Theodore Rex*, 7. See also Feerick, *From Failing Hands*, 157.

194. Edmund Morris, *Theodore Rex*, 7. See also Busch, *T. R.*, 151, in Feerick, *From Failing Hands*, 157.

195. *New York Herald*, September 15, 1901, in Grondahl, *I Rose Like a Rocket*, 381.

196. Ibid.

197. *New York Times*, September 15, 1901, in Edmund Morris, *Theodore Rex*, 14. See also Feerick, *From Failing Hands*, 157–58.

198. Busch, *T. R.*, 152, in Feerick, *From Failing Hands*, 158.

199. Theodore Roosevelt, *Autobiography*, 193–94.

200. Herman Henry Kohlsaat, *From McKinley to Harding* (New York: Charles Scribner's Sons, 1923), 98, in Rauchway, *Murdering McKinley*, 38. See also Edmund Morris, *Theodore Rex*, 30.

201. Kohlsaat, *From McKinley to Harding*, 30.

202. *Chicago Tribune*, September 17, 1901, in Edmund Morris, *Theodore Rex*, 39.

203. *Washington Post*, September 17, 1901, in Edmund Morris, *Theodore Rex*, 40.

204. Ibid.

205. *Bisbee Daily Review* (Ariz.), December 21, 1901, Chronicling America: Historic American Newspapers, Library of Congress, http://chroniclingamerica.loc.gov/lccn/sn84024827/1901-12-21/ed-1/seq-3/.

206. Seale, *The President's House*, 1:666.

207. Ibid., 1:667.

208. *Bisbee Daily Review*, December 21, 1901.

209. Seale, *The President's House*, 1:667.

210. Richard B. Jensen, *The Battle against Anarchist Terrorism: An International History, 1878–1934* (Cambridge, Mass.: Cambridge University Press, 2014), 251.

211. Seale, *The President's House*, 1:667. See also Jensen, *Battle against Anarchist Terrorism*, 251.

212. Jensen, *Battle against Anarchist Terrorism*, 251.

213. Ibid., 253.

214. Seale, *The President's House*, 1:667.

215. Ibid., 1:699.

216. Letter from Theodore Roosevelt to Booker T. Washington, Buffalo, N.Y., September 14, 1901, White House Historical Association, https://www.whitehousehistory.org/photos/a-letter-from -president-theodore-roosevelt-to-booker-t-washington. For discussion on Theodore Roosevelt and civil rights see Patricia O'Toole, *Theodore Roosevelt After the White House* (New York: Simon & Schuster, 2005), 194–197.

217. Dewey W. Grantham, "Dinner at the White House: Theodore Roosevelt, Booker T. Washington, and the South," *Tennessee Historical Quarterly* 17, no. 2 (June 1958), 112–30, https://www.jstor .org/stable/42621372, 114–15.

218. Frederick Douglass had been to the White House under both Lincoln and Johnson, but he didn't dine there. John Adams had invited Haiti's white representative and his Haitian wife to dine at the White House.

219. Grantham, "Dinner at the White House," 125–26.

220. Rauchway, *Murdering McKinley*, 68.

221. Clarence A. Bacote, "Negro Officeholders in Georgia under President McKinley," *Journal of Negro History* 44:3 (July 1959), 235, in Rauchway, 71.

222. Rauchway, *Murdering McKinley*, 72.

223. Jefferson Decker, "Anarchy in the U.S.A.," *In These Times*, November 24, 2003, http://inthe setimes.com/article/114/.

224. George E. Mowry, *Theodore Roosevelt and the Progressive Movement* (New York: Hill and Wang, 1960).

225. Cadenhead, *Theodore Roosevelt: Paradox of Progressivism*, 77.

226. Serge Ricard, "The Roosevelt Corollary," *Presidential Studies Quarterly* 36, no. 1, 2006, 17–26, JSTOR, www.jstor.org/stable/27552743; see also Henry William Brands, *T. R.: The Last Romantic* (New York: Basic Books, 1997).

227. John M. Blum, *The Republican Roosevelt* (Cambridge, Mass.: Harvard University Press, 1954), 70, in Boller, *Presidential Campaigns*, 184. See also John Milton Cooper, Jr., *The Warrior and the Priest*, 78–80.

228. Mark Sullivan, *Our Times: The United States, 1900–1925* (New York: Charles Scribner's Sons, 1927), 2:460.

229. Boller, *Presidential Campaigns*, 184–85.

230. Ibid., 183.

231. John Milton Cooper, Jr., *The Warrior and the Priest*, 70.

232. Theodore Roosevelt, *Autobiography*, 213.

233. Ibid., 214.

234. Ibid.

235. Ibid., 214–15.

236. Lorant, *Glorious Burden*, 486, in Boller, *Presidential Campaigns*, 185.

237. Theodore Roosevelt, *Autobiography*, 212.

CHAPTER SIX: AVERTING SCANDAL

1. Robert K. Murray, *The Harding Era: Warren G. Harding and His Administration* (Newtown, Conn.: American Political Biography Press, 2000; first published 1969 by University of Minnesota Press), 430.

2. *Cyclone and Record Republican* (Washington Court House, Ohio), May 14, 1890, in Samuel H.

Adams, *Incredible Era* (Boston: Houghton Mifflin, 1939), 42. See also Charles L. Mee, Jr., *The Ohio Gang: The World of Warren G. Harding* (New York: M. Evans and Company, 1981), 23.

3. Mee, *The Ohio Gang*, 23.

4. Ibid. See also Samuel H. Adams, *Incredible Era*, 86.

5. Samuel H. Adams, *Incredible Era*, 42.

6. Murray, *The Harding Era*, 434. See also Harry M. Daugherty in collaboration with Thomas Dixon, *The Inside Story of the Harding Tragedy* (New York: The Churchill Company, 1932), 247.

7. Mee, *The Ohio Gang*, 23. See also Murray, *The Harding Era*, 431.

8. Murray, *The Harding Era*, 431.

9. Mee, *The Ohio Gang*, 24.

10. Ibid., 32. See also Murray, *The Harding Era*, 431; Daugherty and Dixon, *Inside Story*, 68; and Edmund W. Starling, *Starling of the White House* (New York: Simon & Schuster, 1946), 172.

11. Mee, *The Ohio Gang*, 142.

12. John W. Dean, *Warren G. Harding*, The American Presidents (New York: Times Books, 2004), 142.

13. Daugherty and Dixon, *Inside Story*, 246–47.

14. Mee, *The Ohio Gang*, 144.

15. Eugene P. Trani and David L. Wilson, *The Presidency of Warren G. Harding* (Lawrence: Regents Press of Kansas, 1977), 179.

16. Daugherty and Dixon, *Inside Story*, 69. See also Murray, *The Harding Era*, 431.

17. Murray, *The Harding Era*, 431; and Daugherty and Dixon, *Inside Story*, 68–69.

18. Murray, *The Harding Era*, 299.

19. Mee, *The Ohio Gang*, 36–38. See also Samuel H. Adams, *Incredible Era*, 233–35; Francis Russell, *The Shadow of Blooming Grove* (New York: McGraw-Hill Book Co., 1968), 446–48.

20. Mee, *The Ohio Gang*, 38.

21. Ibid., 35.

22. Ibid. See also Russell, *Shadow of Blooming Grove*, 450.

23. Laton McCartney, *The Teapot Dome Scandal: How Big Oil Bought the Harding White House and Tried to Steal the Country* (New York: Random House, 2008), 63–64.

24. Mee, *The Ohio Gang*, 35.

25. Frederick L. Allen, *Only Yesterday: An Informal History of the 1920s* (New York: Harper Perennial, 2000; first published 1931 by Harper & Row), 111. See also McCartney, *Teapot Dome Scandal*, 63.

26. McCartney, *Teapot Dome Scandal*, 63–64.

27. Ibid.

28. Allen, *Only Yesterday*, 111.

29. Trani and Wilson, *Presidency of Warren G. Harding*, 181.

30. Ibid., 180. See also Dean, *Warren G. Harding*, 143, for bootlegging.

31. Ibid.

32. Roxy Stinson testimony, Hearings Before the Select Committee on Investigation of the Attorney General, United States Senate, 68th Congress, 1st Session, Pursuant to S. Res. 157, March 12–17, 1924, 4 vols. (Washington, D.C.: U.S. Government Printing Office, 1924); also Mee, *The Ohio Gang*, 142.

33. Murray, *The Harding Era*, 432.

34. Dean, *Warren G. Harding*, 143–44. See also Murray, *The Harding Era*, 434.

35. Daugherty and Dixon, *Inside Story*, 261.

36. Dean, *Warren G. Harding*, 144.

37. McCartney, *Teapot Dome Scandal*, 143.

38. Nathan Miller, *New World Coming: The 1920s and the Making of Modern America* (New York: Da Capo Press, 2004), 110. See also McCartney, *Teapot Dome Scandal*, 143.

39. McCartney, *Teapot Dome Scandal*, 143.

40. William A. Cook, *King of the Bootleggers: A Biography of George Remus* (Jefferson, N.C.: McFarland, 2008), 72. See also Mee, *The Ohio Gang*, 213.

41. Mee, *The Ohio Gang*, 213.

42. Daugherty and Dixon, *Inside Story*, 249.

43. Cook, *King of the Bootleggers*, 72. See also Mee, *The Ohio Gang*, 435.

44. Cook, *King of the Bootleggers*, 73. See also Mee, *The Ohio Gang*, 213 and 435; and Dean, *Warren G. Harding*, 144.

45. Cook, *King of the Bootleggers*, 73. See also McCartney, *Teapot Dome Scandal*, 144; Mee, *The Ohio Gang*, 435; and Daugherty and Dixon, *Inside Story*, 249.

46. McCartney, *Teapot Dome Scandal*, 144. See also Nathan Miller, *New World Coming*, 110.

47. Ibid.

48. Cook, *King of the Bootleggers*, 73–74. See also Nathan Miller, *New World Coming*, 110; Murray, *The Harding Era*, 436; and Daugherty and Dixon, *Inside Story*, 249.

49. Roxy Stinson's testimony; also Mee, *The Ohio Gang*, 214. See also Murray, *The Harding Era*, 437.

50. Mark Sullivan, *Our Times*, 6:236–37, in Murray, *The Harding Era*, 437. See also Mee, *The Ohio Gang*, 214.

51. Nathan Miller, *New World Coming*, 110.

52. Mee, *The Ohio Gang*, 214. See also Cook, *King of the Bootleggers*, 74; Murray, *The Harding Era*, 436; and Dean, *Warren G. Harding*, 144.

53. Seale, *The President's House*, 2:105.

54. Allen, *Only Yesterday*, 30. See also Samuel H. Adams, *Incredible Era*, 220–21.

55. Mee, *The Ohio Gang*, 102–3.

56. Trani and Wilson, *Presidency of Warren G. Harding*, 2.

57. Ibid., 14. See also "How Will You Vote," *The Nation* vol. 111 (September 4, 1920), 260, in Boller, *Presidential Campaigns*, 212.

58. Trani and Wilson, *Presidency of Warren G. Harding*, 14.

59. Mee, *The Ohio Gang*, 102–3.

60. Allen, *Only Yesterday*, 31.

61. The Fall and Hitchcock visit to the White House was nicknamed the "Smelling Committee" and would later be ridiculed for its bad form. Years later when Fall had been convicted and was awaiting sentencing, his lack of mercy for Woodrow Wilson would be remembered as many advocated he, too, should see no mercy. See David H. Stratton, *Tempest Over Teapot Dome: The Story of Albert Fall* (Norman: University of Oklahoma Press, 1998), 170–74 and 328–29. See also Ibid.

62. For an in-depth analysis on why the Democrats had no chance, see Karl Schriftgiesser, *This Was Normalcy: An Account of Party Politics During Twelve Republican Years, 1920–1932* (Boston: Little, Brown, 1948), 42–43.

63. James D. Robenalt, *The Harding Affair: Love and Espionage During the Great War* (New York: Palgrave MacMillan, 2009), 338. See also Samuel H. Adams, *Incredible Era*, 119.

64. Dean, *Warren G. Harding*, 50.

65. McCartney, *Teapot Dome Scandal*, 11. See also Schriftgiesser, *This Was Normalcy*, 5.

66. McCartney, *Teapot Dome Scandal*, 11–12.

67. Mee, *The Ohio Gang*, 70.

68. Schriftgiesser, *This Was Normalcy*, 33.

69. Mee, *The Ohio Gang*, 70.

70. Schriftgiesser, *This Was Normalcy*, 33.

71. Samuel H. Adams, *Incredible Era*, 86.

72. Murray, *The Harding Era*, 114–15.

73. Ibid., 41.

74. "Sees Harding as Compromise Choice," *New York Times*, February 21, 1920, 3, in Boller, *Presidential Campaigns*, 215–16. See also Murray, *The Harding Era*, 5, for a different quote: "We drew to a pair of deuces, and filled."

75. Schriftgiesser, *This Was Normalcy*, 21. See also Boller, *Presidential Campaigns*, 212–13.

76. Greenberg, *Calvin Coolidge*, The American Presidents (New York: Times Books, 2006), 30–32. See also Witcover, *American Vice Presidency*, 272; Willis Fletcher Johnson, *The Life of Warren G. Harding: From the Simple Life of the Farm to the Glamor and Power of the White House* (Philadelphia: John C. Winston, 1923), 6; Allen, *Only Yesterday*, 45–46; McCartney, *Teapot Dome Scandal*, 158; Schriftgiesser, *This Was Normalcy*, 156; and Samuel H. Adams, *Incredible Era*, 165.

77. Kelter and Shellabarger, *Veeps*, 147.

78. Clinton Gilbert, *Behind the Mirrors: The Psychology of Disintegration at Washington* (New York, G. P. Putnam's Sons, 1922), 145, in Murray, *The Harding Era*, 52–53. See also Dean, *Warren G. Harding*, 72.

79. Randolph C. Downes, *The Rise of Warren Gamaliel Harding, 1865–1920* (Columbus: Ohio State University Press, 1970), 557, in Dean, *Warren G. Harding*, 75.

80. Daugherty and Dixon, *Inside Story*, 59.

81. Murray, *The Harding Era*, 66.

82. Mee, *The Ohio Gang*, 107.

83. Dean, *Warren G. Harding*, 76.

84. Murray, *The Harding Era*, 66.

85. Alice Roosevelt Longworth, *Crowded Hours: Reminiscences of Alice Roosevelt Longworth* (New York: Charles Scribner's Sons, 1933), 325.

86. Ibid., 324.

87. Mee, *The Ohio Gang*, 111. See also Seale, *The President's House*, 2:99.

88. Murray, *The Harding Era*, 117.

89. Mee, *The Ohio Gang*, 38.

90. Seale, *The President's House*, 2:96.

91. McCartney, *Teapot Dome Scandal*, 137.

92. Longworth, *Crowded Hours*, 324. See also Mee, *The Ohio Gang*, 108.

93. For the most comprehensive account of Harding's affair with an alleged German spy, see Robenalt, *The Harding Affair*.

94. MacMahon and Curry, *Medical Cover-Ups*, 80.

95. Dean, *Warren G. Harding*, 135–36. See also Murray, *The Harding Era*, 418.

96. Murray, *The Harding Era*, 418.

97. Ibid., 419.

98. Nan Britton, *The President's Daughter* (New York: Elizabeth Ann Guild, 1927), 236.

99. Ibid., 238–39.

100. Ibid., 240.

101. Trani and Wilson, *Presidency of Warren G. Harding*, 171.

102. Ibid, 176. For detailed discussion of the Harding administration's relationship with the World Court, see Murray, *The Harding Era*, 368–73.

103. Seale, *The President's House*, 2:106.

104. Jay W. Murphy, *What Ails the White House*, 27–28. See also Bumgarner, *Health of the Presidents*, 190; Murray, *The Harding Era*, 438; and Dean, *Warren G. Harding*, 139.

105. MacMahon and Curry, *Medical Cover-Ups*, 82.

106. McCartney, *Teapot Dome Scandal*, 146–47.

107. Joe Mitchell Chapple, *Life and Times of Warren G. Harding: Our After-War President* (Boston: Chapple Publishing Company, 1924), 326–75, in Dean, *Warren G. Harding*, 148.

108. James E. Watson, *As I Knew Them* (New York: Bobbs-Merill, 1936), 231, in Murray, *The Harding Era*, 440. See also Starling, *Starling of the White House*, 196.

109. MacMahon and Curry, *Medical Cover-Ups*, 83. See also Murray, *The Harding Era*, 440–41.

110. Starling, *Starling of the White House*, 195–96, in Seale, *The President's House*, 2:106.

111. Dean, *Warren G. Harding*, 148.

112. Mee, *The Ohio Gang*, 218.

113. McCartney, *Teapot Dome Scandal*, 148.

114. Mee, *The Ohio Gang*, 218. See also Murray, *The Harding Era*, 442.

115. William A. White, *Autobiography of William Allen White* (New York: Easton Press, 1986; first published 1946 by Macmillan), 619, in Murray, *The Harding Era*, 436. See also Dean, *Warren G. Harding*, 141; Seale, *The President's House*, 2:105; McCartney, *Teapot Dome Scandal*, 147; and Russell, *Shadow of Blooming Grove*, 560.

116. Murray, *The Harding Era*, 447.

117. Mee, *The Ohio Gang*, 220.

118. Herbert Hoover, *The Memoirs of Herbert Hoover: Vol. 2: The Cabinet and the Presidency: 1920–1933* (New York: Macmillan, 1952), 49, https://hoover.archives.gov/sites/default/files/research/ebooks/b1v2_full.pdf.

119. June Allen, "A President's Ill-fated Trek to Alaska: What Did Kill Warren Harding?" *Stories in the News*, July 23, 2003, http://www.sitnews.net/JuneAllen/Harding/072303_warren_harding.html.

120. Ibid.

121. MacMahon and Curry, *Medical Cover-Ups*, 83.

122. Ibid.

123. Mee, *The Ohio Gang*, 220.

124. Ibid., 220.

125. MacMahon and Curry, *Medical Cover-Ups*, 83.

126. Gaston Means, *The Strange Death of President Harding* (New York: Guild Publishing, 1930), 222.

127. Mee, *The Ohio Gang*, 220. See also Bumgarner, *Health of the Presidents*, 191; Russell, *Shadow of Blooming Grove*, 586–87.

128. Murray, *The Harding Era*, 447. See also MacMahon and Curry, *Medical Cover-Ups*, 83; and Bumgarner, *Health of the Presidents*, 191.

129. Bumgarner, *Health of the Presidents*, 191. See also Murray, *The Harding Era*, 447.

130. Photograph of President Warren G. Harding golfing in Vancouver, British Columbia, July 26, 1923. The golfers in the photograph are identified (left to right) as F. W. Peters, General Superintendent, Canadian Pacific Railway; Chief Justice D. A. McDonald, British Columbia Court of Appeal; President Harding; and "the Hon. Dr. King." Ohio Historical Society, http://www.vancouverhistory.ca/archives_harding.htm.

131. Bumgarner, *Health of the Presidents*, 192. See also Jay W. Murphy, *What Ails the White House*, 30.

132. Murray, *The Harding Era*, 448.

133. Greg Lange, "President Harding Makes Final Speeches of his Life in Seattle on July 27, 1923," Historylink.org, February 10, 1999, http://www.historylink.org/File/878.

134. Trani and Wilson, *Presidency of Warren G. Harding*, 177.

135. Ibid.

136. Robert E. Ficken, "President Harding Visits Seattle," *Pacific Northwest Quarterly* 66, no. 3 (July 1975), 105–14, https://www.jstor.org/stable/40489403.

137. Russell, *Shadow of Blooming Grove*, 589.

138. MacMahon and Curry, *Medical Cover-Ups*, 84.

139. Carl S. Anthony, *Florence Harding: The First Lady, the Jazz Age, and the Death of America's Most Scandalous President* (New York: William Morrow, 1998), 436–37.

140. MacMahon and Curry, *Medical Cover-Ups*, 83.

141. Ibid., 84.

142. Murray, *The Harding Era*, 449. See also Dean, *Warren G. Harding*, 150.

143. MacMahon and Curry, *Medical Cover-Ups*, 83.

144. Gaston Means, *The Strange Death of President Harding*, 225.

145. Murray, *The Harding Era*, 449.

146. MacMahon and Curry, *Medical Cover-Ups*, 86.

147. Ibid., 87. See also Murray, *The Harding Era*, 450; and Dean, *Warren G. Harding*, 152.

148. Samuel Blythe, "A Calm Review of a Calm Man," *Saturday Evening Post* 196, no. 4 (January 28, 1923).

149. Starling, *Starling of the White House*, 198–99, in Murray, *The Harding Era*, 450. See also MacMahon and Curry, *Medical Cover-Ups*, 87; and Jeff Nilsson and Samuel Blythe, "Kind but Final Words for President Harding," *Saturday Evening Post*, August 14, 2015, http://www.saturdayeveningpost.com/2015/08/14/history/post-perspective/kind-but-final-words-for-president-harding.html.

150. Starling, *Starling of the White House*, 201, in Murray, *The Harding Era*, 450.

151. MacMahon and Curry, *Medical Cover-Ups*, 87.

152. Ibid., 89.

153. Calvin Coolidge, *The Autobiography of Calvin Coolidge* (New York: Cosmopolitan Book Corporation, 1929), 180, in Greenberg, *Calvin Coolidge*, 43.

154. Donald R. McCoy, *Calvin Coolidge: The Quiet President* (Newtown, Conn.: American Political Biography Press, 1998; first published 1967 by Macmillan), 148. His name was Erwin C. Geisser.

155. Greenberg, *Calvin Coolidge*, 44.

156. McCoy, *Calvin Coolidge*, 148.

157. Willis Fletcher Johnson, *Life of Warren G. Harding*, 236, in Feerick, *From Failing Hands*, 185.

158. McCartney, *Teapot Dome Scandal*, 155.

159. Willis Fletcher Johnson, *Life of Warren G. Harding*, 236, in Feerick, *From Failing Hands*, 185.

160. Claude M. Fuess, *Calvin Coolidge: The Man from Vermont* (Boston: Little, Brown, 1940), 307–11, in Murray, *The Harding Era*, 498.

161. Fuess, *Calvin Coolidge*, 311, in McCoy, *Calvin Coolidge*, 148.

162. Witcover, *American Vice Presidency*, 275.

163. McCartney, *Teapot Dome Scandal*, 155.

164. Ibid, 155–56.

165. Silva, *Presidential Succession*, 29.

166. McCartney, *Teapot Dome Scandal*, 155–56.

167. Merlo J. Pusey, *Charles Evans Hughes* (New York: Macmillan, 1951), 2:563–64, in McCoy, *Calvin Coolidge*, 149.

168. McCartney, *Teapot Dome Scandal*, 155–56.

169. Greenberg, *Calvin Coolidge*, 44.

170. Silva, *Presidential Succession*, 28. See also Witcover, *American Vice Presidency*, 275.

171. Greenberg, *Calvin Coolidge*, 44. See also McCoy, *Calvin Coolidge*, 6.

172. Charles C. Johnson, *Why Coolidge Matters: Leadership Lessons from America's Most Underrated President* (New York: Encounter Books, 2013), 113. See also Greenberg, *Calvin Coolidge*, 44; and Witcover, *American Vice Presidency*, 275; Fuess, *Calvin Coolidge*, 311.

173. Silva, *Presidential Succession*, 29. See also Daugherty and Dixon, *Inside Story*, 278–79.

174. Silva, *Presidential Succession*, 29. See also Daugherty and Dixon, *Inside Story*, 280.

175. Silva, *Presidential Succession*, 29; Judge Hoehling didn't confirm this until 1932.

176. Robenalt, *The Harding Affair*, 3.
177. Allen, *Only Yesterday*, 115.
178. Ibid., 116.
179. Seale, *The President's House*, 2:108. The Coolidges were living at the Willard Hotel, so I've written with the assumption that they prolonged their stay.
180. McCartney, *Teapot Dome Scandal*, 158.
181. "Introduction and Provenance," typescript, Warren G. Harding Papers, Library of Congress, in Seale, *The President's House*, 2:109; also Anthony, *Florence Harding*, 488. Anthony describes how Florence was able to ship a significant number of boxes to Friendship, which is where the McLeans resided. Once she left the White House, she destroyed the remainder of the boxes she had salvaged. This was not the first time the McLean's house had been used for book burning. In 1922, Gaston Means and Jess Smith burned boxes of William Chancellor's *The Illustrated Life of President Warren G. Harding*, which was a hit job on the President and attempted to "scientifically [address] his [black] ancestry." (Anthony, 361–362).
182. Calvin Coolidge, *Autobiography*, 147, in Greenberg, *Calvin Coolidge*, 23.
183. Greenberg, *Calvin Coolidge*, 23.
184. Irwin Hoover, *Forty-Two Years in the White House* (Boston: Houghton Mifflin, 1934), 13, in Greenberg, *Calvin Coolidge*, 58.
185. Witcover, *American Vice Presidency*, 269.
186. McCoy, *Calvin Coolidge*, 13.
187. Greenberg, *Calvin Coolidge*, 24.
188. Schriftgiesser, *This Was Normalcy*, 164.
189. Longworth, *Crowded Hours*, 337.
190. Harold Ickes to Henry Allen, November 24, 1923, box 29, Harold Ickes Papers, Library of Congress, in Greenberg, *Calvin Coolidge*, 45.
191. Kelter and Shellabarger, *Veeps*, 148.
192. Ibid.
193. Greenberg, *Calvin Coolidge*, 40–41.
194. George Wharton Pepper, *Philadelphia Lawyer: An Autobiography* (Philadelphia, 1944), 202, in McCoy, *Calvin Coolidge*, 146. See also Greenberg, *Calvin Coolidge*, 40–41; and Witcover, *American Vice Presidency*, 274; Boller, *Presidential Anecdotes*, 239–40.
195. McCartney, *Teapot Dome Scandal*, 158.
196. Fuess, *Calvin Coolidge*, 278, in Feerick, *From Failing Hands*, 182.
197. Louis C. Hatch and Earl L. Shoup, *A History of the Vice-Presidency of the United States* (New York: American Historical Society, 1934), 378, in McCoy, *Calvin Coolidge*, 123.
198. Fuess, *Calvin Coolidge*, 278, in Feerick, *From Failing Hands*, 182.
199. Daugherty and Dixon, *Inside Story*, 278, in Feerick, *From Failing Hands*, 182–83. See also Witcover, *American Vice Presidency*, 273–74; Charles C. Johnson, *Why Coolidge Matters*, 121; and McCoy, *Calvin Coolidge*, 131–32.
200. Robert E. Gilbert, *The Tormented President: Calvin Coolidge, Death, and Depression* (Westport, Conn.: Praeger, 2003), 106, in Witcover, *American Vice Presidency*, 273–74.
201. Robert Woods, *Preparation of Calvin Coolidge: An Interpretation* (New York: Houghton Mifflin, 1924), 225, in Charles C. Johnson, *Why Coolidge Matters*, 121.
202. Pusey, *Charles Evans Hughes*, 2:278, in McCoy, *Calvin Coolidge*, 137.
203. Seale, *The President's House*, 2:113.
204. Charles C. Johnson, *Why Coolidge Matters*, 118.
205. McCartney, *Teapot Dome Scandal*, 158.
206. Trani and Wilson, *Presidency of Warren G. Harding*, 186. See also McCartney, *Teapot Dome Scandal*, 207–08.

207. Robert H. Ferrell, *The Presidency of Calvin Coolidge* (Lawrence: University Press of Kansas, 1998), 18, in Witcover, *American Vice Presidency*, 275.

208. Mee, *The Ohio Gang*, 149. See also Mark Sullivan, *Our Times*, 6:238; and Samuel H. Adams, *Incredible Era*, 284.

209. Ibid.

210. Ibid.

211. Mee, *The Ohio Gang*, 153. See also Mark Sullivan, *Our Times*, 6:238; and Samuel H. Adams, *Incredible Era*, 284; and Murray, *The Harding Era*, 429.

212. Allen, *Only Yesterday*, 130.

213. Mee, *The Ohio Gang*, 154. See also Murray, *The Harding Era*, 429; and Schriftgiesser, *This Was Normalcy*, 112. Harding's doctor, Dr. Charles E. Sawyer provided Carolyn with some of the evidence of infidelity, which was in part motivated by hurting Forbes, who would not let him turn hospitals into homeopathic-medicine experiments.

214. "Reminiscences of James W. Wadsworth," 294, in Murray, *The Harding Era*, 429.

215. Allen, *Only Yesterday*, 130. See also Schriftgiesser, *This Was Normalcy*, 111; and M. R. Werner, *Privileged Characters* (New York: Arno Press, 1974; originally published 1935 by R. M. McBride).

216. Murray, *The Harding Era*, 430.

217. Mee, *The Ohio Gang*, 154–55. See also Greenberg, *Calvin Coolidge*, 50; Murray, *The Harding Era*, 430.

218. Dean, *Warren G. Harding*, 140.

219. *Investigation of Veterans Bureau, Hearings before the Select Committee*, U.S. Senate, 67th Congress, 4th Session (Washington, D.C., 1923), in Murray, *The Harding Era*, 459.

220. Murray, *The Harding Era*, 459.

221. Ibid., 461.

222. Allen, *Only Yesterday*, 118. See also Mee, *The Ohio Gang*, 159; McCartney, *Teapot Dome Scandal*, 28–29; and Dean, *Warren G. Harding*, 155.

223. Allen, *Only Yesterday*, 118–19.

224. Mee, *The Ohio Gang*, 162.

225. Ibid., 161. See also Allen, *Only Yesterday*, 119.

226. Mee, *The Ohio Gang*, 162–63.

227. Murray, *The Harding Era*, 462.

228. Ibid., 462–63.

229. *Leases upon Naval Oil Reserves: Hearings before the Committee on Public Lands and Surveys*, U.S. Senate, 68th Congress, 1st Session (Washington, D.C., 1924), 177–78, in Murray, *The Harding Era*, 463. See also Allen, *Only Yesterday*, 119; and Dean, *Warren G. Harding*, 156.

230. Murray, *The Harding Era*, 466.

231. Mee, *The Ohio Gang*, 163. See also McCartney, *Teapot Dome Scandal*, 140.

232. McCartney, *Teapot Dome Scandal*, 114.

233. Ibid., 115.

234. Ibid., 109.

235. Robert C. Byrd, ed., *The Senate, 1789–1989, V.1* (S. Doc.100-20, 100th Congress, 1st Session; Washington, D.C.: United States Government Printing Office, 1988). See also "Senate Investigates the 'Teapot Dome' Scandal," Art & History, United States Senate, http://www.senate.gov/artandhistory/history/minute/Senate_Investigates_the_Teapot_Dome_Scandal.htm.

236. Greenberg, *Calvin Coolidge*, 51. See also McCoy, *Calvin Coolidge*, 208.

237. Murray, *The Harding Era*, 471. See also Frederick L. Allen, *Only Yesterday*, 120; and Greenberg, *Calvin Coolidge*, 51.

238. Greenberg, *Calvin Coolidge*, 51. See also McCoy, *Calvin Coolidge*, 208; Murray, *The Harding Era*, 471; Frederick L. Allen, *Only Yesterday*, 120; and Greenberg, *Calvin Coolidge*, 51.

239. Murray, *The Harding Era*, 471–72.

240. William A. White, *A Puritan in Babylon: The Story of Calvin Coolidge* (Norwalk, Conn.: Easton Press, 1986; first published 1938 by Macmillan), 268–69, in Greenberg, *Calvin Coolidge*, 52.

241. Frederick L. Allen, *Only Yesterday*, 120.

242. Greenberg, *Calvin Coolidge*, 49.

243. Mee, *The Ohio Gang*, 201. See also Samuel H. Adams, *Incredible Era*, 237.

244. Mee, *The Ohio Gang*, 157.

245. Ibid., 138–40.

246. Greenberg, *Calvin Coolidge*, 51.

247. Murray, *The Harding Era*, 478–79.

248. Trani and Wilson, *Presidency of Warren G. Harding*, 181. See also Schriftgiesser, *This Was Normalcy*, 150–51; and Greenberg, *Calvin Coolidge*, 52.

249. William A. White, *Puritan in Babylon*, 268–69, in Greenberg, *Calvin Coolidge*, 52.

250. Greenberg, *Calvin Coolidge*, 53.

251. McCartney, *Teapot Dome Scandal*, 233–35. See also Daugherty and Dixon, *Inside Story*, 224–25.

252. *New York Times*, January 26, 1924, in Murray, *The Harding Era*, 482.

253. Frederick L. Allen, *Only Yesterday*, 134.

254. Charles C. Johnson, *Why Coolidge Matters*, 120.

255. Greenberg, *Calvin Coolidge*, 96–99.

256. Robert K. Murray, *The 103rd Ballot: The Legendary 1924 Democratic Convention that Forever Changed Politics* (New York: HarperCollins, 2016; originally published 1976 by Harper & Row), 252, in Boller, *Presidential Campaigns*, 220–21.

257. Frederick L. Allen, *Only Yesterday*, 162.

258. Ibid., 67–69.

259. Paul Johnson, *Modern Times: The World from the Twenties to the Nineties* (New York: Harper Perennial, 2001), 223, in Charles C. Johnson, *Why Coolidge Matters*, xix–xx.

260. Frederick L. Allen, *Only Yesterday*, 68–70.

261. Alben W. Barkley, *That Reminds Me* (New York: Doubleday, 1954), 124, in Charles C. Johnson, *Why Coolidge Matters*, 116.

262. Louis Untermeyer, *A Treasury of Laughter* (New York: Simon & Schuster, 1946), 85, in Boller, *Presidential Anecdotes*, 234.

263. Fuess, *Calvin Coolidge*, 300, in Greenberg, *Calvin Coolidge*, 10; Witcover, *American Vice Presidency*, 267.

264. Charles C. Johnson, *Why Coolidge Matters*, 116.

265. Untermeyer, *Treasury of Laughter*, 85, in Boller, *Presidential Anecdotes*, 234.

266. Greenberg, *Calvin Coolidge*, 7.

267. Ibid.

268. Ibid. See also McCoy, *Calvin Coolidge*, 55.

269. McCartney, *Teapot Dome Scandal*, 159.

270. Greenberg, *Calvin Coolidge*, 11.

271. Irwin Hoover, *Forty-Two Years in the White House*, 268, in Boller, *Presidential Anecdotes*, 244.

272. Allen, *Only Yesterday*, 143.

273. Ibid., 143–44.

274. Ibid., 144.

275. Greenberg, *Calvin Coolidge*, 67.

276. Murray, *The Harding Era*, 487. See also Britton, *President's Daughter*.

277. Silva, *Presidential Succession*, 29. For more detailed discussion, see Schriftgiesser, *This Was Normalcy*, 242–44.

278. H. L. Mencken, *On Politics: A Carnival of Buncombe*, Malcom Moos, ed. (New York: Vintage, 1960), 139, in Boller, *Presidential Anecdotes*, 234.

279. William Leuchtenburg, *The Perils of Prosperity, 1914–1932* (Chicago: University of Chicago Press, 1958), 243, in Greenberg, *Calvin Coolidge*, 146.

CHAPTER SEVEN: "THAT DAMN MULE!"

1. Most of my knowledge about the relationship between Vincent Astor and FDR comes from a collaboration with the FDR Presidential Library. As part of a philanthropic effort, a group of friends funded an Astor scholar to study this relationship for six months in 2017 and produce a report. Source material is in the author's possession. See William Villano, "Socialite, and Spy Master: Vincent Astor, FDR's Area Controller of Intelligence for New York," *FDR Presidential Library Blog*, November 16, 2016, https://fdr.blogs.archives.gov/2016/11/16/socialite-and-spy -master-vincent-astor-fdrs-area-controller-of-intelligence-for-new-york/.

2. "Part II: Vincent, the Astor Who Gave Away the Money," *New York Social Diary*, April 29, 2009, http://www.newyorksocialdiary.com/social-history/2009/part-ii-vincent-the-astor-who-gave -away-the-money.

3. Steven Lomazow and Eric Fettman, *FDR's Deadly Secret* (New York: PublicAffairs, 2009), 49.

4. There is a discrepancy on whether the trip was ten days or eleven: Frederick A. Storm, "Roosevelt Unhurt, But Chicago Mayor's Condition Critical," United Press International, February 16, 1933. See also Bob Crossland, "Fifteen Seconds of Terror," *Coronet*, February 1960, 107. See also Lomazow and Fettman, *FDR's Deadly Secret*, 49 (note: Lomazow says the trip was eleven days).

5. "Vincent, the Astor Who Gave Away the Money."

6. Lomazow and Fettman, *FDR's Deadly Secret*, 49.

7. Storm, "Roosevelt Unhurt, but Chicago Mayor's Condition Critical."

8. Ibid.

9. Interview with Vincent Astor, October 18, 1958, conducted by Sidney Shalett, Sidney Shalett Papers, "Interview with Vincent Astor re: the Attempted Assassination of FDR," reel B, side 1, courtesy of the FDR Presidential Library. The interview was originally embargoed until the publication of James Roosevelt and Sidney Shalett's book *Affectionately, F.D.R.: A Son's Story of a Lonely Man* in 1959. See also Hugh G. Gallagher, *FDR's Splendid Deception* (Arlington, Va.: Vandamere Press, 1999), 88.

10. Mel Ayton, *Hunting the President: Threats, Plots, and Assassination Attempts—From FDR to Obama* (Washington, D.C.: Regnery History, 2014), 7.

11. Interview with Vincent Astor. Courtesy of the FDR Presidential Library.

12. Gallagher, *FDR's Splendid Deception*, 88.

13. Feerick, *From Failing Hands*, 190. See also: Interview with Vincent Astor. Courtesy of the FDR Presidential Library.

14. Interview with Vincent Astor. Courtesy of the FDR Presidential Library.

15. Gallagher, *FDR's Splendid Deception*, 88.

16. Crossland, "Fifteen Seconds of Terror."

17. Blaise Picchi, *The Five Weeks of Giuseppe Zangara* (Chicago: Academy Chicago, 1998), 20–29, in Ayton, *Hunting the President*, 8.

18. Storm, "Roosevelt Unhurt, but Chicago Mayor's Condition Critical."

19. Gallagher, *FDR's Splendid Deception*, 88.

20. Picchi, *Five Weeks of Giuseppe Zangara*, 20–29, in Ayton, *Hunting the President*, 8.

21. Storm, "Roosevelt Unhurt, but Chicago Mayor's Condition Critical."

22. Crossland, "Fifteen Seconds of Terror."

23. Interview with Vincent Astor. Courtesy of the FDR Presidential Library.

24. Storm, "Roosevelt Unhurt, but Chicago Mayor's Condition Critical."

25. Ibid.

26. Interview with Vincent Astor. Courtesy of the FDR Presidential Library.

27. Interview with Vincent Astor. Courtesy of the FDR Presidential Library. See also Roosevelt and Libby, *My Parents*, 196–97.

28. Interview with Vincent Astor. Courtesy of the FDR Presidential Library.

29. Storm, "Roosevelt Unhurt, but Chicago Mayor's Condition Critical." See also Gallagher, *FDR's Splendid Deception*, 89; and Lomazow and Fettman, *FDR's Deadly Secret*, 49.

30. *New York Times*, February 17, 1933, in Jean E. Smith, *FDR*. New York: Random House, 2007, 297; See also Raymond Moley, *After Seven Years* (New York: Harper & Brothers, 1939), 149, in Gallagher, *FDR's Splendid Deception*, 89; James F. Simon, *FDR and Chief Justice Hughes: The President, the Supreme Court, and the Epic Battle Over the New Deal* (New York: Simon & Schuster, 2012), 226; and Lomazow and Fettman, *FDR's Deadly Secret*, 49.

31. Storm, "Roosevelt Unhurt, but Chicago Mayor's Condition Critical."

32. John Boettiger, "Maniac Fires on Roosevelt; Cermak Shot; Wound Grave," *Chicago Tribune*, February 16, 1933, https://chicagology.com/notorious-chicago/antoncermak/. See also "Assassin Fires at Roosevelt! Shoots Cermak and 4 Others!" *San Francisco Examiner*, February 16, 1933. For more detail, see Storm, "Roosevelt Unhurt, but Chicago Mayor's Condition Critical."

33. Leslie Heiter was a very close friend of Vincent Astor. It was through Astor that he cultivated a relationship with FDR. According to his grandson, Leslie Heiter went on six fishing cruises with Astor, of which this was the third. See Letter from W. Leslie Heiter to his father, February 16, 1933. provided by his son, Bill Heiter.

34. Letter from W. Leslie Heiter to his father, February 16, 1933. Provided by his son, Bill Heiter.

35. Moley, *After Seven Years*, 149, in Gallagher, *FDR's Splendid Deception*, 89. See also Roosevelt and Libby, *My Parents*, 197.

36. Interview with Vincent Astor. Courtesy of the FDR Presidential Library.

37. Jonathan Alter, *The Defining Moment: FDR's Hundred Days and the Triumph of Hope* (New York: Simon & Schuster, 2006), 170. See also Lomazow and Fettman, *FDR's Deadly Secret*, 49.

38. "Woman's Courage Foils Shots Assassin Aimed at Roosevelt," United Press International, February 16, 1933.

39. Ibid.

40. Storm, "Roosevelt Unhurt, but Chicago Mayor's Condition Critical."

41. "Woman's Courage Foils Shots Assassin Aimed at Roosevelt."

42. Ibid. See also Storm, "Roosevelt Unhurt, but Chicago Mayor's Condition Critical," in which the police are said to have corroborated this.

43. Storm, "Roosevelt Unhurt, but Chicago Mayor's Condition Critical."

44. Crossland, "Fifteen Seconds of Terror."

45. Ibid.

46. "Twentieth Amendment: U.S. Constitution: Commencement of the Terms of the President, Vice President, and Members of Congress, Etc.," FindLaw, http://constitution.findlaw.com/amendment20.html.

47. John C. Nagle, "A Twentieth Amendment Parable," *New York University Law Review* 72 (May 1997), 470, http://scholarship.law.nd.edu/law_faculty_scholarship/545.

48. Ibid.

49. Ibid., 481.

50. Garner would go on to loathe the vice presidency, perhaps more than any other man in history.

He famously lamented, "I gave up the second most important job in government for eight long years as Roosevelt's spare tire. Worst damn fool mistake I ever made." He also told LBJ that the vice presidency isn't "worth a bucket of warm piss." He fell out of favor with FDR after opposing his pursuit of a third term, remembering all too well the rancorous comments in his own home when Ulysses Grant considered another run at the presidency. Garner lived to the age of ninety-eight and, in an eerie twist of fate, received a phone call on his ninety-fifth birthday from President John F. Kennedy, who at the time was visiting Texas. In speaking to the president, Garner said, "You're my president and I love you. I hope you stay in there forever." Kennedy was shot dead two hours later.

51. Biographical information from official Senate biography: https://www.senate.gov/artandhistory/history/common/generic/VP_John_Garner.htm. See also Kelter and Shellabarger, *Veeps*, 164.

52. Alan Brinkley quoted in Adam Goodheart, "Ten Days that Changed History," *New York Times*, July 2, 2006.

53. "Oral History Interview with Edwin W. Pauley," interviewed by J. R. Fuchs, March 3, 1971. Harry S. Truman Presidential Library, https://www.trumanlibrary.org/oralhist/pauleye.htm. Pauley was particularly concerned about Wallace's pro-Soviet statements, saying, "I became concerned about Henry Wallace because he was the vice president. It seemed to me that he was making too many pro-Soviet statements, and his actions were such that I did not think that he would become, either by election or succession, a proper president of the United States." See also David M. Jordan, *FDR, Dewey, and the Election of 1944* (Bloomington: Indiana University Press, 2011), 489.

54. Alex Ross, "Uncommon Man: The Strange Life of Henry Wallace, the New Deal Visionary," *The New Yorker*, October 14, 2013. See also Robert H. Ferrell, *Choosing Truman: The Democratic Convention of 1944* (Columbia: University of Missouri Press, 1994), 66.

55. At Cairo, the leaders pledged to force Japan's unconditional surrender and promised no territorial aspirations of their own.

56. The journey to and from Tehran had been grueling, 17,742 miles by plane, car, and ship. See Robert H. Ferrell, *The Dying President: Franklin D. Roosevelt 1944–1945* (Columbia: University of Missouri Press, 1998).

57. Robert Nisbet, *Roosevelt and Stalin: The Failed Courtship* (Washington, D.C.: Regnery Gateway, 1988), 28.

58. *Stalin's Correspondence with Roosevelt and Truman, 1941–1945* (New York: Capricorn Books [a publication of the Ministry of Foreign Affairs of the USSR], 1965), 22–23, in Nisbet, *Roosevelt and Stalin*, 39.

59. Roosevelt to Stalin, December 2, 1942. Map Room Papers, Box 8, "Roosevelt to Stalin, May–December, 1942," *FDR Presidential Library*.

60. Roosevelt to Stalin, December 8, 1942. Map Room Papers, Box 8, "Roosevelt to Stalin, May–December, 1942," *FDR Presidential Library*.

61. Stalin to Roosevelt, November 5. Map Room Papers, Box 8, "Stalin to Roosevelt, October–December, 1943," *FDR Presidential Library*.

62. Kenneth R. Crispell and Carlos F. Gomez, *Hidden Illness in the White House* (Durham, N.C.: Duke University Press, 1988), 100, in Lomazow and Fettman, *FDR's Deadly Secret*, 100.

63. Doris Kearns Goodwin, *No Ordinary Time: Franklin & Eleanor Roosevelt: The Home Front in World War II* (New York: Simon & Schuster, 1994), 477.

64. This was the right-wing critique, which arose after Yalta and FDR's death and developed further in the 1950s.

65. Geoffrey Roberts, *Stalin's Wars: From World War to Cold War, 1939–1953* (New Haven: Yale University Press, 2006), 180–181. See also Bill Yenne, *Operation Long Jump: Stalin, Roosevelt,*

Churchill, and the Greatest Assassination Plot in History (New York: Regnery, 2015); also Nisbet, *Roosevelt and Stalin*, 44.

66. Frances Perkins, *The Roosevelt I Knew* (New York: Viking, 1946), 84. See also Virginia Cowles, *Winston Churchill: The Era and the Man* (London: Hamish Hamilton, Ltd., 1953), 343; and Nisbet, *Roosevelt and Stalin*, 49.

67. Charles McMoran Wilson and Baron Moran, *Churchill: Taken From the Diaries of Lord Moran: The Struggle for Survival, 1940–1965* (Boston: Houghton Mifflin, 1966), 150, quoted in James MacGregor Burns, *Roosevelt: The Soldier of Freedom, 1940–1945* (New York: Harcourt Brace Jovanovich, 1970), 409, in Lomazow and Fettman, *FDR's Deadly Secret*, 91. Per Burns and other advisors, Churchill's mood played a role in this statement. It is also worth noting that Churchill has been widely seen as a not always reliable narrator for these discussions. Politicized debate goes on, in many sources, about FDR at Tehran and at Yalta, and the degree to which illness may or may not have affected his judgment and purposes.

68. Baron Moran, *Churchill: The Struggle for Survival*, 150, quoted in Burns, *Roosevelt: Soldier of Freedom*, 409, in Lomazow and Fettman, *FDR's Deadly Secret*, 91.

69. Crispell and Gomez, *Hidden Illness in the White House*, 100, in Lomazow and Fettman, *FDR's Deadly Secret*, 100.

70. John Gunther, *Roosevelt in Retrospect* (New York: Harper, 1950), 365, in Feerick, *From Failing Hands*, 195.

71. Charles W. Robertson, "Some Observations on Presidential Illnesses," *Boston Medical Quarterly* 8, no. 3 (June 1957), 85, in Feerick, *From Failing Hands*, 195.

72. Ira Katznelson, *Fear Itself: The New Deal and the Origins of Our Time* (New York: W. W. Norton, 2013), 555 (description in chap. 6, note 1); See also David M. Jordan, *FDR, Dewey, and the Election of 1944* (Bloomington: Indiana University Press, 2011), 129.

73. Jim Bishop, *FDR's Last Year: April 1944–April 1945* (New York: William Morrow, 1974), 25–26. See also Ferrell, *Dying President*, 23.

74. Hugh E. Evans, *The Hidden Campaign: FDR's Health and the 1944 Election* (Armonk, N.Y.: M. E. Sharpe, 2002), 158. See also Ferrell, *Dying President*, 23.

75. Grace Tully, *F.D.R. My Boss* (New York: Charles Scribner's Sons, 1949), 273–74.

76. Ibid.

77. Howard Bruenn, "Clinical Notes on the Illness and Death of President Franklin D. Roosevelt," *Annals of Internal Medicine* 72, no. 4 (April 1970), 579–91, in Conrad Black, *Franklin Delano Roosevelt: Champion of Freedom* (New York: PublicAffairs, 2003), 932; for blood pressure, Roger Daniels, *Franklin D. Roosevelt: The War Years, 1939–1945* (Chicago: University of Illinois Press, 2016), 391. See also Gallagher, *FDR's Splendid Deception*, 180–81.

78. Gallagher, *FDR's Splendid Deception*, 180.

79. Howard Bruenn Papers; FDR-Medical Information; Box 1, FDR Presidential Library. See also Gallagher, *FDR's Splendid Deception*, 180–81.

80. Bruenn, "Clinical Notes on the Illness and Death of President Franklin D. Roosevelt."

81. Patricia O'Toole, *The Moralist: Woodrow Wilson and the World He Made* (New York: Simon & Schuster, 2018), 234–35 for during the war, 422–23 for during the campaign for the League of Nations.

82. Letter from Claude Bowers, U.S. ambassador to Chile, to James M. Cox, in which he relates a conversation with President Roosevelt about Woodrow Wilson's health, in James Middleton Cox, *Journey Through My Years* (Macon, Ga.: Macon University Press, 2004), 241–42. See also Frank Freidel, *Franklin D. Roosevelt: A Rendezvous with Destiny* (Boston: Little, Brown, 1990), 39, in Lomazow and Fettman, *FDR's Deadly Secret*, 22.

83. "Walker Voices Regret over GOP Attitude on Short Campaign," Associated Press, April 15,

1943, in Papers of the Democratic National Committee Party 1928–1948 ("Miscellaneous Papers, 1932–1948," "Secretaries of State 1939–1945, also Lt Governors Attorney General 1945," "Writers War Board—1944 Publicity Department," "Walker, Spangler [4th Term] Controversy"), FDR Presidential Library. See also "No Time for Politics," *Post*, April 13, 1943; and "Party Chiefs Tilt Verbally on 4th Term," *Times Herald*, April 13, 1943.

84. "Capital Stuff," *Times Herald*, April 12, 1943, in Papers of the Democratic National Committee Party 1928–1948, FDR Presidential Library.

85. Edward Pauley, memorandum to Jonathan Daniels, Robert E. Hannegan Papers, White House Central Files, Harry S. Truman Presidential Library, n.d. (probably 1950), in Evans, *The Hidden Campaign*, 66. See also "Oral History Interview with Edwin W. Pauley," interviewed by J. R. Fuchs, March 3, 1971. Harry S. Truman Presidential Library, https://www.trumanlibrary.org /oralhist/pauleye.htm.

86. Ibid.

87. MacMahon and Curry, *Medical Cover-Ups*, 97.

88. Ibid.

89. Bishop, *FDR's Last Year*, 109. See also Evans, *The Hidden Campaign*, 65.

90. Gallagher, *FDR's Splendid Deception*, 193.

91. Evans, *The Hidden Campaign*, 64. See also Gallagher, *FDR's Splendid Deception*, 193; and Bishop, *FDR's Last Year*, 22–23.

92. Joseph P. Lash, *A World of Love: Eleanor Roosevelt and Her Friends, 1943–1962* (Garden City, N.Y.: Doubleday, 1984), 130, in Goodwin, *No Ordinary Time*, 525.

93. Gallagher, *FDR's Splendid Deception*, 193.

94. Roosevelt to Robert E. Hannegan, July 10, 1944, Robert E. Hannegan Papers, Harry S. Truman Presidential Library, in Bishop, *FDR's Last Year*, 96–97. See also Evans, *The Hidden Campaign*, 62; and Goodwin, *No Ordinary Time*, 524.

95. Roosevelt made one exception to this during a campaign stop in New York, which was designed to show that he had the physical stamina to continue serving as president. The weather was horrendous with near perpetual rainfall throughout the visit.

96. David M. Kennedy, *Freedom from Fear: The American People in Depression and War, 1929–1945* (New York: Oxford University Press, 1999), 792.

97. Goodwin, *No Ordinary Time*, 530.

98. "The Political Mill," *The Star*, April 13, 1943, in Papers of the Democratic National Committee Party 1928–1948, FDR Presidential Library.

99. Ibid.

100. Margaret Truman, *Harry S. Truman* (New York: William Morrow, 1973), 169.

101. Letter from S. J. Mauhs, Chairman of the Schoharie County Democratic Committee, July 17, 1944 in Papers of the Democratic National Committee Party 1928–1948 ("Miscellaneous Papers, 1932–1948," "Secretaries of State 1939–1945, also: Lt Governors Attorney General 1945," "Writers War Board—1944 Publicity Department," "Vice President—Letters re Candidate—1944"), FDR Presidential Library.

102. Letter from E. V. Pease to Robert Hannegan, July 15, 1944 in Papers of the Democratic National Committee Party 1928–1948, FDR Presidential Library.

103. Letter from Benjamin Leurs to Robert Hannegan, July 15, 1944 in Papers of the Democratic National Committee Party 1928–1948, FDR Presidential Library.

104. Mary B. Mason to Robert Hannegan, July 15, 1944. See also Mary B. Mason to Robert Hannegan, July 15, 1944, both in Papers of the Democratic National Committee Party 1928–1948, FDR Presidential Library.

105. Tully, *F.D.R. My Boss*, 275.

106. Lash, *A World of Love*, 132, in Goodwin, *No Ordinary Time*, 530.

107. Tully, *F.D.R. My Boss*, 275.

108. Samuel I. Rosenman, *Working with Roosevelt* (New York: Harper, 1952), 439, in Goodwin, *No Ordinary Time*, 525.

109. Goodwin, *No Ordinary Time*, 525.

110. There were lots of names suggested: Judge Sherman Minton of Indiana, Sam Rayburn, Clark Gable, Senator Lister Hill of Alabama, James Farley, General Dwight Eisenhower, Wendell Willkie, John Winant, Wesley E. Disney, W. M. Clayton (Papers of the Democratic National Committee Party 1928–1948, FDR Presidential Library).

111. A. J. Baime, *The Accidental President: Harry S. Truman and the Four Months that Changed the World* (Boston: Houghton Mifflin Harcourt, 2017), 96. See also James F. Byrnes, *All in One Lifetime* (New York: Harper Collins, 1958), 224; also Ferrell, *Choosing Truman*, 7.

112. Ferrell, *Choosing Truman*, 27. See also "Oral History Interview with Samuel I. Rosenman," interviewed by Jerry N. Hess, October 15, 1968. Harry S. Truman Presidential Library, https://www.trumanlibrary.org/oralhist/rosenmn.htm.

113. A. G. Grayson, "North Carolina and Harry Truman, 1944–1948." *Journal of American Studies* 9, no. 3 (1975), 285–286. JSTOR, www.jstor.org/stable/27553190. See also Bishop, *FDR's Last Year*, 98. Bishop and Grayson both mention how Truman's work in the Senate investigating the industrial costs of the war was viewed as additive. For "northern" and "southern" see Samuel Lubell, *The Future of American Politics* (London: Hamish Hamilton, 1952), 8–21; and for "labor" and "industrialists" see Ferrell, *Choosing Truman*, 93.

114. Edward J. Flynn, *You're the Boss* (New York: Collier Books, 1962), 181, in Goodwin, *No Ordinary Time*, 527.

115. Ferrell, *Choosing Truman*, 93. See also A. G. Grayson, "North Carolina and Harry Truman, 1944–1948," 285.

116. Kennedy, *Freedom from Fear*, 791. Sam Rosenman argues that it was Truman's voting record in the Senate that made him most attractive. See "Oral History Interview with Samuel I. Rosenman," interviewed by Jerry N. Hess, October 15, 1968. Harry S. Truman Presidential Library, https://www.trumanlibrary.org/oralhist/rosenmn.htm.

117. A. G. Grayson, "North Carolina and Harry Truman, 1944–1948," 285.

118. Max Lowenthal diary, November 5, 1948, box C-272, Lowenthal Papers, in Ferrell, *Choosing Truman*, 58. See also "Oral History Interview with Tom L. Evans," interviewed by J. R. Fuchs, June 13, 1963. Harry S. Truman Presidential Library, https://www.trumanlibrary.org/oralhist/evans4.htm#331.

119. Ferrell, *Choosing Truman*, 60.

120. John C. Culver and John Hyde, *American Dreamer: A Life of Henry Wallace* (New York: W. W. Norton and Company, 2000), 331. See also Michael Janeway, *The Fall of the House of Roosevelt: Brokers of Ideas and Power from FDR to LBJ* (New York: Columbia University Press, 2004), 50, *see also* Goldsmith, *Conspiracy of Silence*, 232.

121. Edward L. Schapsmeier and Frederick H. Schapsmeier, *Prophet in Politics: Henry A. Wallace and the War Years, 1940–1945* (Ames: Iowa State University Press, 1950), 86, in Goldsmith, *Conspiracy of Silence*, 232. See also Ferrell, *Choosing Truman*, 18.

122. John C. Culver and John Hyde, *American Dreamer*, 339.

123. Margaret Truman, *Harry S. Truman*, 167.

124. FDR had the self-awareness to recognize his own soft spot for Wallace and felt that an initial conversation with Rosenman would make his inevitable conversation with Wallace easier to bear. See Bishop, *FDR's Last Year*, 99. See also Culver and Hyde, *American Dreamer*, 345–346; also Ferrell, *Choosing Truman*, 20.

125. "Wallace, Henry, 1945–1950," Rosenman Papers, FDR Presidential Library.

126. Rosenman quoting FDR's assessment of Wallace as a viable vice presidential candidate in Harold Ickes diary, July 16, 1944, in Ferrell, *Choosing Truman*, 21.

127. Ibid.

128. Accounts vary on whether Roosevelt volunteered to write the letter or whether Wallace made the request. Bishop, *FDR's Last Year*, 98 and 100–101. See also Ferrell, *Choosing Truman*, 22; and Culver and Hyde, *American Dreamer*, 345–346; and Black, *Franklin Delano Roosevelt: Champion of Freedom*, 970.

129. Wallace diary in Ferrell, *Choosing Truman*, 22.

130. Margaret Truman, "How Dad Fought Against His Own Nomination,"*Life Magazine* 73, no. 21 (November 24), 1972, 63.

131. Goldsmith, *Conspiracy of Silence*, 199. See also Margaret Truman, *Harry S. Truman*, 172.

132. Russell Lord, *The Wallaces of Iowa* (New York: Da Capo Press, 1972), 529. See also Bishop, *FDR's Last Year*, 100. Other sources quote FDR as saying, "I hope it will be the same old team."

133. "Oral History Interview with Edwin W. Pauley," interviewed by J. R. Fuchs, March 3, 1971. Harry S. Truman Presidential Library, https://www.trumanlibrary.org/oralhist/pauleye.htm.

134. Alfred Steinberg, *The Man from Missouri: The Life and Times of Harry S. Truman* (New York: Putnam, 1963), 201.

135. Letter from C. T. Ray to Robert E. Hannegan, July 12, 1944 in Papers of the Democratic National Committee Party 1928–1948, FDR Presidential Library.

136. Letter from Sam Hepburn to Robert Hannegan, July 15, 1944 in Papers of the Democratic National Committee Party 1928–1948, FDR Presidential Library.

137. John W. Partin, "Roosevelt, Byrnes, and the 1944 Vice-Presidential Nomination," *The Historian* 42, no. 1 (1979), 85–100. *JSTOR*, www.jstor.org/stable/24445289.

138. Ferrell, *Choosing Truman*, 11.

139. Kennedy, *Freedom from Fear*, 791–92.

140. Ferrell, *Choosing Truman*, 12.

141. Bishop, *FDR's Last Year*, 99. See also Ferrell, *Choosing Truman*, 13.

142. Ted Morgan, *FDR: A Biography* (New York: Simon & Schuster, 1985), 726, in Goldsmith, *Conspiracy of Silence*, 201. See also Goodwin, *No Ordinary Time*, 526–27. In *The Fall of the House of Roosevelt*, 44–66, Michael Janeway argues that Douglas was FDR's preferred choice.

143. Ted Morgan, *FDR: A Biography* (New York: Simon & Schuster, 1985), 726; See also Ferrell, *Choosing Truman*, 13.

144. According to Edwin Pauley, Boettinger retrieved the *Congressional Directory*, but nobody opened it. He claims to have personally put it back on the shelf and argues that had they opened it, Truman may not have been president, "not only because of the age, but because it would have opened up a whole new line of thought—county judge, etc." "Oral History Interview with Edwin W. Pauley," interviewed by J. R. Fuchs, March 3, 1971. Harry S. Truman Presidential Library, https://www.trumanlibrary.org/oralhist/pauleye.htm. See also Steinberg, *The Man from Missouri*, 205. See also Ferrell, *Choosing Truman*, 13; also Goodwin, *No Ordinary Time*, 527; also Bishop, *FDR's Last Year*, 99.

145. In discussions about what FDR wrote about Truman and when there are two events that are often conflated—the July 11 power dinner and the July 15 meeting with Hannegan in Chicago onboard the presidential train. Of the two notes that are debated—a shorthand note where FDR mentions Truman exclusively, and a longer note where he mentions Bill Douglas and Harry Truman together (backdated July 19)—the former should be discussed in the context of the July 11 event, while the latter belongs with the July 15 context.

146. Ferrell, *Choosing Truman*, 14. See also David McCullough, *Truman* (New York: Simon & Schuster, 1992), 301; and Morgan, *FDR: A Biography*, 728, in Goodwin, *No Ordinary Time*, 527.

Even for this version of the narrative, there are a number of different accounts. For example, some sources have "All right, Bob, start talking," referring to Harry Truman.

147. McCullough, *Truman*, 301. See also Margaret Truman, *Harry S. Truman*, 172. Additional detail related to the jacket comes from Ferrell, *Harry Truman: A Life*, 165.

148. Robert H. Ferrell, ed., *The Autobiography of Harry S. Truman* (Boulder: Colorado Associated University Press, 1980), 92.

149. McCullough, *Truman*, 301.

150. Byrnes to Burnet R. Maybank, July 19, 1944, Byrnes Papers in Jordan, *FDR, Dewey and the Election of 1944*, 146. See also Ferrell, *Autobiography of Harry S. Truman*, 89.

151. Ferrell, *Autobiography of Harry S. Truman*, 92, in Goldsmith, *Conspiracy of Silence*, 202. Truman became concerned with finding this note, even after he became president when he reached out to those present at the 1944 convention to confirm that he had in fact been FDR's choice. He even approached Hannegan's widow, asking for his papers, and instructed his secretary to engage the bosses who had presided over the convention. Truman's version has not been found. (Goldsmith, *Conspiracy of Silence*, 203).

152. Edwin Pauley with Richard English, "Why Truman is President" (memorandum), "President's Secretary's Files, Longhand Notes," Harry S. Truman Presidential Library, 20, in Ferrell, *Choosing Truman*, 14. Pauley later claimed that there was no note from this dinner, just a note from the July 15 meeting that Hannegan had with FDR during his train stop in Chicago right before the convention. In this same interview, he claims that while he and Hannegan had mixed up their jackets, they did not return upstairs. See "Oral History Interview with Edwin W. Pauley," interviewed by J. R. Fuchs, March 3, 1971. Harry S. Truman Presidential Library, https://www.trumanlibrary.org/oralhist/pauleye.htm.

153. Bishop, *FDR's Last Year*, 100. See also Goldsmith, *Conspiracy of Silence*, 208–9.

154. "The Presidency: The Waikiki Conference," *Time*, August 21, 1944, 21, in Evans, *The Hidden Campaign*, 74.

155. As late as July 13, Truman told Roy Roberts from the *Kansas City Star* that he was not in contention.

156. Byrnes, *All in One Lifetime*, 223.

157. Byrnes, *All in One Lifetime*, 224–25.

158. Ibid., 224–25, in David McCullough, *Truman*, 303. See also Ferrell, *Choosing Truman*, 32.

159. Byrnes, *All in One Lifetime*, 224.

160. FDR asked him, "Will you go on and run?" which Byrnes interpreted as being urged. Byrnes, *All in One Lifetime*, 224.

161. Byrnes, *All in One Lifetime*, 224.

162. Joseph Lelyveld, *His Final Battle: The Last Months of Franklin Roosevelt* (New York: Vintage, 2016), 169. See also Ferrell, *Choosing Truman*, 33.

163. Byrnes, *All in One Lifetime*, 225. See also Jordan, *FDR, Dewey and the Election of 1944*, 151.

164. Baime, *The Accidental President*, 93. See also Ferrell, *Choosing Truman*, 33.

165. Harry S. Truman, *Memoirs by Harry S. Truman: Year of Decisions* (Garden City, N.Y.: Doubleday, 1955), 190. For a supporting view that Byrnes attempted to manipulate Truman, see Jerry N. Hess interview with Judge Samuel I. Rosenman, October 15, 1968, and April 12, 1969. Harry Truman Presidential Library, https://www.trumanlibrary.org/oralhist/rosenmn.htm.

166. Robert H. Ferrell, *Harry S. Truman: A Life* (Columbia: University of Missouri Press, 1994), 167. See also Harry S. Truman, *Year of Decisions*, 191–92.

167. "Letter on the Vice-Presidential Nomination.," July 14, 1944, John Woolley and Gerhard Peters, The American Presidency Project, UC Santa Barbara, https://www.presidency.ucsb.edu/documents/letter-the-vice-presidential-nomination. See also Tully, *F.D.R. My Boss*, 275; and Bishop, *FDR's Last Year*, 100–101.

168. Jordan, *FDR, Dewey and the Election of 1944*, 151–52.

169. Tully, *F.D.R. My Boss*, 276.

170. McCullough, *Truman*, 306.

171. Description of the Ferdinand Magellan can be found in Edward G. Lengel, "Franklin D. Roosevelt's Train Ferdinand Magellan," The White House Historical Association, October 19, 2017, https://www.whitehousehistory.org/franklin-d-roosevelt-rsquo-s-train-ferdinand -magellan.

172. McCullough, *Truman*, 306.

173. "Letter Endorsing Truman or Douglas for the Vice-Presidential Nomination," July 19, 1944, John Woolley and Gerhard Peters, The American Presidency Project, UC Santa Barbara, https://www.presidency.ucsb.edu/documents/letter-endorsing-truman-or-douglas-for-the -vice-presidential-nomination. See also Tully, *F.D.R. My Boss*, 276; and Bishop, *FDR's Last Year*, 99.

174. Tully, *F.D.R. My Boss*, 276–77.

175. Discussion of the confusion and lack of clarity in Jim Bishop, *FDR's Last Year*, 104.

176. Ferrell, *Choosing Truman*, 50.

177. Goldsmith, *Conspiracy of Silence*, 218.

178. Ibid., 220.

179. Ferrell, *Choosing Truman*, 47. For a description of the setting in which FDR received the calls, see Bishop, *FDR's Last Year*, 104.

180. Kennedy, *Freedom from Fear*, 789.

181. Hannegan went to visit Truman one hour after the 6:45 p.m. phone call. Reverse engineering this, from the time the call ended, there had to be enough time within that hour for Crowley to talk to Byrnes and for Hannegan to talk to Truman.

182. Harry S. Truman, *Year of Decisions*, 191.

183. Truman interviews with Jonathan Daniels, August 30 and November 12, 1949, 3 and 66, Jonathan Daniels Papers, Harry S. Truman Presidential Library, Independence, Missouri, in Ferrell, *Choosing Truman*, 52–53.

184. Margaret Truman, *Harry S. Truman*, 168. See also Feerick, *From Failing Hands*, 194.

185. Margaret Truman, *Harry S. Truman*, 166. See also Kennedy, *Freedom from Fear*, 792.

186. Byrnes, *All in One Lifetime*, 229. See also Bishop, *FDR's Last Year*, 105.

187. Byrnes, *All in One Lifetime*, 230. See also Richard Rhodes, *The Making of the Atomic Bomb* (New York: Simon & Schuster, 1986), 619–20.

188. Ibid.

189. "Oral History Interview with Tom L. Evans," interviewed by J. R. Fuchs, June 13, 1963. Harry S. Truman Presidential Library, https://www.trumanlibrary.org/oralhist/evans4.htm#331. See also Ferrell, *Choosing Truman*, 58; also Sara L. Sale, *Bess Wallace Truman: Harry's White House "Boss,"* (Lawrence: University Press of Kansas, 2010), 30.

190. Margaret Truman, *Harry S. Truman*, 175.

191. *Official Proceedings of the Democratic National Convention*, National Document Publishers, 1944, in Goldsmith, *Conspiracy of Silence*, 235–36. John W. Partin, "Roosevelt, Byrnes, and the 1944 Vice-Presidential Nomination," *The Historian* 42, no. 1 (1979), 85–100. JSTOR, www.jstor .org/stable/24445289.

192. Ferrell, *Choosing Truman*, 80–85.

193. Ibid., 74.

194. Ferrell, *Choosing Truman*, 80–85. See also Jordan, *FDR, Dewey and the Election of 1944*, 168.

195. Ibid.

196. Ibid.

197. Ibid., 79. See also "Oral History Interview with Edwin W. Pauley," interviewed by J. R. Fuchs,

March 3, 1971. Harry S. Truman Presidential Library, https://www.trumanlibrary.org/oralhist /pauleye.htm.

198. Ibid.

199. Ibid.

200. "Oral History Interview with Neal Roach," interviewed by Jerry N. Hess, January 21–October 2, 1969, Harry S. Truman Presidential Library, https://www.trumanlibrary.org/oralhist/roachn. htm. See also "Oral History Interview with Edwin W. Pauley," interviewed by J. R. Fuchs, March 3, 1971. Harry S. Truman Presidential Library, https://www.trumanlibrary.org/oralhist/pauleye.htm.

201. Margaret Truman, *Harry S. Truman*, 178. See also Goldsmith, *Conspiracy of Silence*, 238.

202. Goldsmith, *Conspiracy of Silence*, 238. See also Baime, *The Accidental President*, 104; also Ferrell, *Choosing Truman*, 80.

203. Ferrell, *Choosing Truman*, 80. See also Goldsmith, *Conspiracy of Silence*, 238.

204. Jordan, *FDR, Dewey and the Election of 1944*, 173.

205. Ferrell, *Choosing Truman*, 80. See also Bob Considine, "On the Line: How FDR Ditched Wallace," *Van Wert Times-Bulletin* 119, no. 29, June 22, 1964.

206. McCullough, *Truman*, 314. See also Harry S. Truman, *Year of Decisions*, 192.

207. The best account of Truman resisting the nomination is found in Merle Miller, *Plain Speaking: An Oral Biography of Harry S. Truman* (New York: Putnam, 1974), 181.

208. Harry S. Truman, *Year of Decisions*, 192–93; Ferrell, *Choosing Truman*, 61; Kennedy, *Freedom from Fear*, 792. See also Margaret Truman, *Harry S. Truman*, 177. There is likely some revisionism in Truman's account. Other sources describe him as more panicked. George Elsey, one of FDR's and later Truman's top aides, recalled Truman's first reaction as, "Oh, shit. If that is the situation I'll have to say yes.": McCullough, *Truman*, 314. See also Robert Klara, *FDR's Funeral Train* (New York: Palgrave Macmillan, 2010), 89; and William H. Chafe, *The Unfinished Journey* (New York: Oxford University Press, 2015), 53. See also "Oral History Interview with Edwin W. Pauley," interviewed by J. R. Fuchs, March 3, 1971. Harry S. Truman Presidential Library, https://www.trumanlibrary.org/oralhist/pauleye.htm.

209. Goldsmith, *Conspiracy of Silence*, 242.

210. Conrad Black, *Franklin Delano Roosevelt: Champion of Freedom* (New York: Public Affairs, 2003), 975. See also Ferrell, *Choosing Truman*, 87.

CHAPTER EIGHT: "GIVE 'EM HELL HARRY!"

1. He had just a single one-on-one meeting with Truman, although they did see each other twice more before the inauguration (September 6, with Governor Coke Stevenson of Texas and a post-election reception). Harry Easley has an illuminating perspective on this reality in "Oral History Interview with Harry Easley," interviewed by J. R. Fuchs, August 24, 1967. Harry S. Truman Presidential Library, https://www.trumanlibrary.org/oralhist/easleyh.htm.

2. Evans, *The Hidden Campaign*, 73.

3. Margaret Truman, *Harry S. Truman*, 185.

4. Harry S. Truman, *Year of Decisions*, 193.

5. Arthur M. Schlesinger, Jr., *History of American Presidential Elections* (New York: McGraw-Hill, 1971), 4:3025, in Kennedy, *Freedom from Fear*, 792.

6. Harry S. Truman, *Year of Decisions*, 193.

7. This story is recounted in James Roosevelt and Bill Libby, *My Parents: A Differing View* (Chicago: Playboy Press, 1976), 281.

8. "Dates of U.S. Presidential Election Events: 1789 to the Present," TheGreenPapers.com, https://www.thegreenpapers.com/Hx/PresidentialElectionEvents.phtml.

9. Akhil Reed Amar, "Presidents, Vice Presidents, and Death: Closing the Constitution's Succession

Gap," *Arkansas Law Review* 48, no. 215 (1994), Faculty Scholarship Series, paper 978, p. 224, http://digitalcommons.law.yale.edu/fss_papers/978.

10. Ibid., 217–28 and 233.

11. Author interview with Akhil R. Amar, May 22, 2017, via email.

12. Three of the electors ended up casting their votes for the deceased Greeley.

13. Resa Willis, *FDR and Lucy: Lovers and Friends* (New York: Routledge, 2004), 139. See also Goldsmith, *Conspiracy of Silence*, 43.

14. Roosevelt and Sidney Shalett, *Affectionately, F.D.R.*, 354.

15. Roosevelt and Libby, *My Parents*, 281. After speaking to Ross McIntire, James also expressed concern to Lieutenant Commander George Fox, who was a long-time aide and assistant medic to his father.

16. Roosevelt and Shalett, *Affectionately, F.D.R*, 354, in Gallagher, *FDR's Splendid Deception*, 199.

17. Roosevelt and Libby, *My Parents*, 281.

18. Evans, *The Hidden Campaign*, 85.

19. This would not include Theodore Roosevelt's remarks upon assuming the presidency in 1901.

20. Evans, *The Hidden Campaign*, 84.

21. Gallagher, *FDR's Splendid Deception*, 200.

22. Kennedy, *Freedom from Fear*, 798.

23. MacMahon and Curry, *Medical Cover-Ups*, 91.

24. Goodwin, *No Ordinary Time*, 572–73. See also Roosevelt and Libby, *My Parents*, 283.

25. MacMahon and Curry, *Medical Cover-Ups*, 91.

26. Roosevelt and Libby, *My Parents*, 284. See also Roosevelt and Shalett, *Affectionately, F.D.R.*, 354, in Gallagher, *FDR's Splendid Deception*, 199.

27. Roosevelt and Libby, *My Parents*, 283–84.

28. Kennedy, *Freedom from Fear*, 807.

29. David Mayers, "The Great Patriotic War, FDR's Embassy Moscow, and Soviet–US Relations," *International History Review* 33, no. 2 (June 21, 2011), 299–333, http://doi.org/10.1080/07075332.2011.555448.

30. Kennedy, *Freedom from Fear*, 805.

31. Averell Harriman, *Special Envoy to Churchill and Stalin, 1941–1946* (New York: Random House, 1975), 170, in Nisbet, *Roosevelt and Stalin*, 74. Some of Roosevelt's own advisors feared this as well. Pauley recalled a fear that "Roosevelt was being fed a lot of bunk about Stalin's so-called cooperation." See "Oral History Interview with Edwin W. Pauley," interviewed by J. R. Fuchs, March 3, 1971. Harry S. Truman Presidential Library, https://www.trumanlibrary.org/oralhist/pauleye.htm.

32. Martin Gilbert, *Winston S. Churchill: Road to Victory, 1941–1945* (Boston: Houghton Mifflin, 1986), 1265.

33. Richard Rhodes, *Dark Sun: The Making of the Hydrogen Bomb* (New York: Simon & Schuster, 1995), 294.

34. Elliot Roosevelt, *As He Saw It* (New York: Greenwood Press, 1946), 117, in Nisbet, *Roosevelt and Stalin*, 73.

35. It is worth noting that Arthur Bryant, who was the editor of Brooke's diaries, was also vehemently anti-FDR and pro–Winston Churchill. This has led some historians to question the veracity of this quotation.

36. David Kennedy's *Freedom from Fear* offers a useful discussion of FDR turning a blind eye to Russia's territorial ambitions. He describes how "the most concrete—and among the most controversial—agreements reached at Yalta concerned Soviet entry into the war against Japan." Kennedy describes the extent of Stalin's territorial demands in Asia and how FDR more or less agreed to all of them. (Kennedy, 805–6).

37. Margaret Truman Daniel, telephone interview with Hugh Evans, October 21, 1999, in Evans, *The Hidden Campaign*, 73.

38. Harry S. Truman, *Year of Decisions*, 55.

39. Ibid., 195.

40. Ibid., 56.

41. Jeffrey Frank, "How FDR's Death Changed the Vice-Presidency," *New Yorker*, April 17, 2015.

42. Author interview with Henry Kissinger, July 28, 2015.

43. Frank, "How F.D.R.'s Death Changed the Vice-Presidency."

44. Margaret Truman, *Harry S. Truman*, 199.

45. Winston Churchill, *The Second World War* (Boston: Houghton Mifflin, 1951), 6:474, in Gallagher, *FDR's Splendid Deception*, 171.

46. Harry S. Truman, *Year of Decisions*, 56.

47. Churchill, *The Second World War*, 6:474, in Gallagher, *FDR's Splendid Deception*, 171.

48. William M. Rigdon and James Derieux, *White House Sailor* (New York: Doubleday and Company, 1962), 11, in Gallagher, *FDR's Splendid Deception*, 171.

49. Silva, *Presidential Succession*, 98.

50. David McCullough, "Looking Back at Harry Truman," *Chicago Tribune*, June 7, 1992, http://www.chicagotribune.com/news/ct-xpm-1992-06-07-9202200467-story.html.

51. Harry S. Truman, *Year of Decisions*, 1. Truman's subtle acknowledgment that he knew he would become president was not just something he recollected in his memoirs. In a defensive handwritten note to reporter Frank Kent, he wrote, "Your President [Truman] knew what he faced. Just eight days short of three months after he became Vice President, the blow fell." See Letter from President Harry S. Truman to Frank Kent, February 12, 1949, President's Secretary's Files—Longhand Notes, https://www.trumanlibrary.org/hstpaper/psf.htm#series30.

52. Harry S. Truman, *Year of Decisions*, 2.

53. Ibid.

54. Tully, *F.D.R. My Boss*, 354. See also Margaret Truman, *Harry S. Truman*, 202.

55. Harry S. Truman, "Memoirs First Draft," Post-Presidential Files, Memoirs File, box 16, Harry S. Truman Presidential Library, in Evans, *The Hidden Campaign*, 110.

56. "Address to Congress on the Yalta Conference," March 1, 1945, John Woolley and Gerhard Peters, The American Presidency Project, UC Santa Barbara, https://www.presidency.ucsb.edu/documents/address-congress-the-yalta-conference. For the reference about this being the first public acknowledgment, see McCullough, *Truman*, 337.

57. Tully, *F.D.R. My Boss*, 355.

58. Gunther, *Roosevelt in Retrospect*, 374, in Feerick, *From Failing Hands*, 196n.

59. Harry S. Truman, *Year of Decisions*, 2.

60. Margaret Truman, *Harry S. Truman*, 203.

61. Harry S. Truman, *Year of Decisions*, 3–4.

62. Goldsmith, *Conspiracy of Silence*, 42. See also William D. Hassett, *Off the Record with F.D.R., 1942–1945* (New Brunswick, N.J.: Rutgers University Press, 1958), 307.

63. "Oral History Interview with Harry Easley," August 24, 1967, by J. R. Fuchs, Harry S. Truman Presidential Library, https://www.trumanlibrary.org/oralhist/easleyh.htm, in Evans, *The Hidden Campaign*, 110.

64. Ibid., 111. See also Margaret Truman, *Harry S. Truman*, 190.

65. Evans, *The Hidden Campaign*, 73.

66. Harry S. Truman, *Year of Decisions*, 1–5.

67. Ibid., 4. See also Goldsmith, *Conspiracy of Silence*, 42. Truman recalls the departure on March 29.

68. Letter from Harry S. Truman to Hugh F. Williamson, April 6, 1945, FDR Presidential Library.

See also Margaret Truman, *Harry S. Truman*, who explains that this was the playful label he often assigned to the vice presidency, 202.

69. Edwin McDowell, "Roosevelt-Churchill Letters Depict Tensions," *New York Times*, July 11, 1984, https://www.nytimes.com/1984/07/11/books/roosevelt-churchill-letters-depict-tensions.html.

70. Correspondence between the Chairman of the Council of Ministers of the USSR and the President of the USA and the PM of Great Britain during the Great Patriotic War of 1941–1945, vols. 1 and 2, 2nd ed. (Salisbury, N.C.: Documentary Publications, 1978), in D. C. Sharma, "The Berne Incident," *Proceedings of the Indian History Congress* 51 (1990), 730–37, http://www.jstor.org/stable/44148323. See also Martin Gilbert, *Winston S. Churchill: Road to Victory*, 581.

71. Harry S. Truman, *Year of Decisions*, 4.

72. McCullough, *Truman*, 341. See also Harry S. Truman, *Memoirs*, 4, which makes no reference to "Jesus Christ and General Jackson." For discussion on this discrepancy, see Mary L. Scheer, ed., *Eavesdropping on Texas History* (Denton: University of North Texas Press, 2017), 233. She notes that the main references for this phone call are William White's *New York Times* story, Lewis Deschler's memoirs, Sam Rayburn's papers, and Truman's memoirs.

73. Goodwin, *No Ordinary Time*, 602–603.

74. Kennedy, *Freedom from Fear*, 808.

75. Harry S. Truman, *Year of Decisions*, 4.

76. Ibid.

77. Ibid., 5.

78. Ibid.

79. Author interview with George H. W. Bush, March 31, 2015, via email.

80. Author interview with Henry Kissinger, July 28, 2015.

81. Frank, "How FDR's Death Changed the Vice-Presidency."

82. Ibid.

83. Ibid.

84. Harry S. Truman, *Year of Decisions*, 13.

85. Ibid., 53.

86. Ibid.

87. Ibid.

88. Ibid., 22.

89. See also Feerick, *From Failing Hands*, 204.

90. Harry S. Truman, *Year of Decisions*, 22.

91. Ibid.

92. Ibid., 9.

93. Ibid.

94. Ibid., 10.

95. Ibid.

96. Ibid., 10–11.

97. Ibid., 11.

98. Ibid.

99. Ibid.

100. Ibid., 85–87.

101. Jennet Conant, *Man of the Hour*, 330–336. See also Ibid., 415. For detailed discussion of Truman and the Potsdam Conference see Byrnes, *Speaking Frankly*, 67–87.

102. Jennet Conant, *Man of the Hour*, 330–336.

103. Harry Truman diary entry, July 24, 1945, in Robert H. Ferrell, ed., *Off the Record: The Private Papers of Harry S. Truman* (Norwalk, Conn.: Easton Press, 1989; first published 1980 by Harper & Row), 55.

104. Harry Truman diary entry, July 24, 1945, in Ferrell, *Off the Record*, 55.

105. McCullough, *Truman*, 424–25.

106. Harry S. Truman, *Year of Decisions*, 416. See also Kennedy, *Freedom from Fear*, 843–44.

107. Robert W. Coakley, "World War II: The War against Japan," chap. 23, in Richard Stewart, ed., *American Military History: Vol. 2: The United States Army in a Global Era, 1917–2003* (Washington, D.C.: Center for Military History, United States Army, 1989), 499–528, https://history.army.mil/books/AMH/AMH-23.htm.

108. The number of casualties and deaths at Iwo Jima covers a range. Even estimating is difficult, given the varying citations in official and semiofficial sources. For instance, there were more than 2,600 battle fatigue deaths, which are often not counted as part of the 23,000 estimate for American casualties. The estimates in the text are drawn from various U.S. military websites. The numbers given to Truman at the time rivaled, but did not exceed Japanese casualties. In a June 18, 1945, meeting with President Truman, the joint staff cited 20,000 American casualties (killed, missing, wounded) and 25,000 Japanese (killed, missing, wounded) at Iwo Jima. See Minutes of Meeting held at the White House, June 18, 1945, Miscellaneous Historical Documents Collection, 736, in "Decision to Drop the Bomb," Truman Presidential Library, https://www.trumanlibrary.org/whistlestop/study_collections/bomb/large/.

109. Paul D. Walker, *Truman's Dilemma: Invasion or the Bomb* (Gretna, La.: Pelican, 2003), 131.

110. Kennedy, *Freedom from Fear*, 834. The Okinawa casualty numbers also vary from source to source: 13,000 American deaths, 36,000 Americans wounded, 70,000 Japanese soldiers killed, 100,000–150,000 Japanese civilians killed. See Jennet Conant, *Man of the Hour: James Conant, Warrior Scientist* (New York: Simon & Schuster, 2017), 327n. In the June 18, 1945, meeting with President Truman, the joint staff cited 51,000 (ground and Navy) American casualties (killed, missing, wounded) and 81,000 Japanese (killed, missing, wounded) at Okinawa. See Minutes of Meeting held at the White House, June 18, 1945, Miscellaneous Historical Documents Collection, 736, in "Decision to Drop the Bomb," Truman Presidential Library, https://www.trumanlibrary.org/whistlestop/study_collections/bomb/large/.

111. James D. Hornfischer, *The Fleet at Flood Tide: America at Total War in the Pacific, 1944–1945* (New York: Bantam Books, 2016), 341. See also Walker, *Truman's Dilemma*, 154. For detailed analysis of Operation Downfall plans, see *Reports of General MacArthur: The Campaigns of MacArthur in the Pacific*, vol. 1, 395–430.

112. Ibid, 342. For "650,000" see Walker, *Truman's Dilemma*, 152–56.

113. Walker, *Truman's Dilemma*, 156–57. See also Kennedy, *Freedom from Fear*, 829–37.

114. Walker, *Truman's Dilemma*, 161.

115. Memorandum, Herbert Hoover to Harry S. Truman, May 30, 1945, concerning Hoover's thoughts on how the war with Japan should be ended. Papers of Herbert Hoover: Post-Presidential Files-Individual, Harry Truman Presidential Library, https://www.trumanlibrary.org Hoover wrote Truman that 500,000 to 1,000,000 American lives could be lost in an invasion of Japan. General Douglas MacArthur later wrote Hoover to suggest that had Truman followed his course of action the war may have come to an earlier end. See Douglas MacArthur to Herbert Hoover, December 2, 1960, Herbert Hoover Presidential Library, Post-Presidential Papers, Individual File Series, box 129 G, Douglas MacArthur, 1953–1964, folder [3212 (3)], in Peter J. Kuznick, "The Decision to Risk the Future: Harry Truman, the Atomic Bomb and the Apocalyptic Narrative," *Asia-Pacific Journal* 5, no. 7 (July 3, 2007). According to Barton Bernstein's research, Hoover believed that the Japanese could have been brought to the negotiating table "as early as February." See Barton J. Bernstein, "The Struggle Over History: Defining the Hiroshima Narrative," in Philip Nobile, ed., *Judgment at the Smithsonian* (New York: Marlowe & Company, 1995), 142. See also Walker, 207.

116. Truman responded, "Thanks a lot for your memorandum. It will be very useful to me," adding a

postscript, "I appreciated very much your coming to see me. It gave me a lift." Harry S. Truman to Herbert Hoover, June 1, 1945, acknowledging Hoover's memoranda and thanking Hoover for his recent visit. Papers of Herbert Hoover: Post-Presidential Files-Individual, Harry Truman Presidential Library, http://www.trumanlibrary.org. See also Walker, *Truman's Dilemma*, 208.

117. Walker, *Truman's Dilemma*, 209–10. In minutes from the White House meeting the next day, on June 18, the general staff agreed that invading via Kyushu was the best option. Both Truman and the joint staff agreed that it "was practically creating another Okinawa closer to Japan." See Minutes of Meeting held at the White House, June 18, 1945, Miscellaneous Historical Documents Collection in "Decision to Drop the Bomb Collection," Truman Presidential Library, https://www.trumanlibrary.org/whistlestop/study_collections/bomb/large/.

118. Office of the Chief of Military History, *Japanese Monograph No. 17*, 65, in Major Mark P. Arens, USMCR, "V [Marine] Amphibious Corps Planning for Operation *Olympic* and the Role of Intelligence in Support of Planning," *Federation of American Scientists*. See also Walker, *Truman's Dilemma*, 167.

119. Walker, *Truman's Dilemma*, 157.

120. Ibid.,163.

121. Richard B. Frank, *Downfall: The End of the Japanese Imperial Empire* (New York: Random House, 1999), 300. See also Walker, *Truman's Dilemma*, 212.

122. C. Vann Woodward, *The Battle for Leyte Gulf: The Incredible Story of World War II's Largest Naval Battle* (New York: Skyhorse, 2017).

123. McCullough, *Truman*, 436–37. See also Walker, *Truman's Dilemma*, 167.

124. David M. Kennedy, *Freedom from Fear*, 845.

125. For analysis of the Japanese reaction to the Potsdam Proclamation, see Kazuo Kawai, "Mokusatsu, Japan's Response to the Potsdam Declaration," *Pacific Historical Review* 19, no. 4 (November 1950), 409–14, https://www.jstor.org/stable/3635822.

126. Kennedy, *Freedom from Fear*, 849.

127. Walker, *Truman's Dilemma*, 227–28. See also J. Boone Bartholomees, *The U.S. Army War College Guide to National Security Issues: National Security Policy and Strategy* (Strategic Studies Institute, July 2012), 2:374.

128. Leslie Groves, *Now It Can Be Told: The Story of the Manhattan Project* (Da Capo Press, 2009). See also Ray Monk, *Robert Oppenheimer: A Life Inside the Center* (New York: Anchor, 2012), 472.

129. Harry S. Truman, *Year of Decisions*, 419.

130. Roosevelt and Libby, *My Parents*, 169–70.

131. Author interview with Henry Kissinger, July 28, 2015.

132. Ibid.

133. Ibid.

134. Harry S. Truman, *Year of Decisions*, 26–27.

135. Ibid., 31.

136. Ibid., 15.

137. Eleanor Roosevelt Papers, "Correspondence, 1957–1962," FDR Presidential Library.

138. Letter from Harry Truman to Eleanor Roosevelt, December 21, 1945, in Eleanor Roosevelt Papers, "Correspondence, 1957–1962—Zab–Zaz," "Truman, Harry S.— Correspondence—1947," "Truman, Harry S.—Correspondence—1945–1946," folder 1, FDR Presidential Library. Truman's Nazi reference is to hate crimes against Japanese-Americans.

139. Eleanor Roosevelt writes about this incident in her My Day column, August 23, 1947, https://www2.gwu.edu/~erpapers/myday/displaydoc.cfm?_y=1947&_f=md000739.

140. Letter from Harry Truman to Eleanor Roosevelt, August 23, 1947 (about Jews "misbehaving"), Eleanor Roosevelt Papers, "Truman, Harry S.—Correspondence—1947," FDR Presidential Library.

141. Eleanor Roosevelt Papers, "Correspondence, 1957–1962," FDR Presidential Library.
142. Harry Truman to Eleanor Roosevelt, March 19, 1946 (tension and feud with Harold Ickes), Eleanor Roosevelt Papers, FDR Presidential Library.
143. Eleanor Roosevelt Papers, "Correspondence, 1957–1962," FDR Presidential Library.
144. Letter from Eleanor Roosevelt to Harry Truman, September 11, 1945, in Eleanor Roosevelt Papers, "Correspondence, 1957–1962, Zab–Zaz," "Truman, Harry S.— Correspondence—1947," "Harry Truman, 1945–1946," folder 1.
145. Letter from Eleanor Roosevelt to Harry Truman, May 14, 1945; response to Truman's letter of May 10, 1945, Eleanor Roosevelt Papers, FDR Presidential Library.
146. Ibid.
147. Ibid.
148. Harry S. Truman, *Year of Decisions*, 37–39.
149. Kennedy, *Freedom from Fear*, 802.
150. Harry S. Truman, *Year of Decisions*, 50.
151. Truman, *Year of Decisions*, 80–81. See also Byrnes, *Speaking Frankly* (New York: Harper and Brothers Publishing, 1947), 60–61.
152. Truman, *Year of Decisions*, 82.
153. Ibid., 86.
154. Ibid., 229.
155. Ibid.
156. Letter from Eleanor Roosevelt to Harry Truman, June 1, 1946 (critiquing U.S. Russia policy and urging Truman to reverse Stettinius's resignation), Eleanor Roosevelt Papers, FDR Presidential Library.
157. Ibid.
158. Letter from Harry Truman to Eleanor Roosevelt, June 4, 1946 (response to the above), Eleanor Roosevelt Papers, FDR Presidential Library.
159. Letter from Eleanor Roosevelt to Harry Truman, April 16, 1947 (concerning Greece–Turkey, Churchill), w/attachment offering her opinion on how FDR would have approached these issues differently, Eleanor Roosevelt Papers, "Truman, Harry S.—Correspondence—1947," FDR Presidential Library.
160. "The Truman Doctrine, 1947," United States Department of State, https://history.state.gov/milestones/1945-1952/truman-doctrine.
161. Letter from Harry Truman to Eleanor Roosevelt, May 7, 1947 (response to Eleanor Roosevelt critique of April 16, 1947), Eleanor Roosevelt Papers, "Truman, Harry S.—Correspondence—1947," FDR Presidential Library.
162. Ibid.
163. Ibid.
164. Ibid.
165. Letter from Harry Truman to Mary Jane Truman, November 14, 1947, in Ferrell, *Off the Record*, 118–19.
166. Harry S. Truman, *Memoirs by Harry S. Truman: Years of Trial and Hope* (Garden City, N.Y.: Doubleday, 1955), 277–85. See also Conant, *Man of the Hour*, 407 and 416.

CHAPTER NINE: THE LAST TIME

1. In the popular vote, Kennedy won 34,220,984 to Nixon's 34,108,157. The Electoral College vote was 303 to 219.
2. White House, *Warren Commission Report*, November 29, 1963, 57, in Ayton, *Hunting the President*, 56.

3. William Manchester, *The Death of a President* (New York: Harper and Row, 1967), 149, in Ayton, *Hunting the President*, 56.

4. Top-secret memo from J. Edgar Hoover to Marvin Watson, "Reaction of Soviet and Communist Party Officials to JFK Assassination," December 1, 1966, President John F. Kennedy Assassination Records Collection, National Archives, https://www.archives.gov/files/research/jfk /releases/docid-32204484.pdf.

5. Ibid.

6. Ibid.

7. I first heard this assertion in a phone interview with Tom Brokaw on July 26, 2017. As this was an assertion, I used this as background and subsequently found backing for it in Robert A. Caro, *Means of Ascent: The Years of Lyndon Johnson* (New York: Knopf, 1990). This is spotlighted in a review of Caro's book by Charles Trueheart, "LBJ Embellished War Record, New Bio Says," *Washington Post*, November 1, 1989, https://www.washingtonpost.com/archive/lifestyle/1989 /11/01/lbj-embellished-war-record-new-bio-says/7d1a36f6-d08a-4412-86c9-1a70d91cdf4c. See also discussion by Peter Roff focused on the sustained debate, "Commentary: A Late Look at LBJ's Medal," United Press International, July 9, 2001, https://www.upi.com/Archives/2001/07 /09/Commentary-A-late-look-at-LBJs-medal/5828994651200/.

8. Martin Tolchin, "How Johnson Won Election He'd Lost," *New York Times*, February 11, 1990, https://www.nytimes.com/1990/02/11/us/how-johnson-won-election-he-d-lost.html.

9. Caro, *Means of Ascent*, 506.

10. David Oshinsky, "Fear and Loathing in the White House: Why Couldn't LBJ and Bobby Kennedy Get Along?" *New York Times*, October 26, 1997, http://www.nytimes.com/books/97/10 /26/reviews/971026.26oshinkt.html.

11. Caro, *The Passage of Power*, 130–37.

12. Doris Kearns Goodwin, *Lyndon Johnson and the American Dream* (New York: St. Martin's Press, 1976), 200.

13. Joseph A. Califano, Jr., *The Triumph & Tragedy of Lyndon Johnson* (New York: Simon & Schuster, 1991), 296.

14. Author interview with Henry Kissinger, July 28, 2015.

15. Goodwin, *Lyndon Johnson and the American Dream*, 200.

16. Rowland Evans and Robert Novak, *Lyndon Johnson: The Exercise of Power—A Biography* (George Allen & Unwin, 1967), 280, in Goodwin, *Lyndon Johnson and the American Dream*, 161.

17. Goodwin, *Lyndon Johnson and the American Dream*, 161.

18. The text is printed in "United States–Vietnam Relations, 1945–1967," Book 11, 132–35, Kennedy Library, National Security Files, Viet-Nam Country Series; see "Foreign Relations of the United States, 1961–1963, Volume I, Vietnam, 1961: 48. Editorial Note," United States Department of State, https://history.state.gov/historicaldocuments/frus1961-63v01/d48.

19. United States Department of State, Central Files, 751K.5-MSP/5-1361, Secret, Priority. (Washington National Records Center, RG 84, Saigon Embassy Files: FRC 66 A 878, 361.1). Source: "Foreign Relations of the United States, 1961–1963, Volume I, Vietnam, 1961: 54. Telegram from the Embassy in Vietnam to the Department of State," United States Department of State, https://history.state.gov/historicaldocuments/frus1961-63v01/d54.

20. Ibid.

21. Robert Dallek, "Flawed Giant: Lyndon Johnson and His Times 1961–1973," chap. 1 excerpted in *New York Times*, 1998, http://www.nytimes.com/books/first/d/dallek-giant.html.

22. Author interview with Tom Brokaw, July 26, 2017.

23. Author interview with Richard "Dick" Cheney, Jackson Hole, Wyoming, January 5, 2016.

24. "Capital Buzzes Over Stories of Misconduct in High Places: The Bobby Baker Bombshell," *Life*, (November 8, 1963), 32–37.

25. Ibid.
26. Michael R. Beschloss, *Taking Charge: The Johnson White House Tapes, 1963–1964* (New York: Simon & Schuster, 1997), 158.
27. "Capital Buzzes Over Stories of Misconduct in High Places."
28. Ibid.
29. Beschloss, *Taking Charge*, 275.
30. Author interview with Tom Brokaw.
31. Ibid. Brokaw is referring to his impression that the comments were less than inspired.
32. Author's on-the-record dinner conversation with Jesse Jackson, June 21, 2017, Cannes, France.
33. The number of those reported injured varies depending on the source, ranging from fourteen to twenty-two. This fact is difficult to corroborate, so I've deliberately chosen general language to reflect this.
34. Author interview with Condoleezza Rice, September 26, 2017, via telephone.
35. Author's on-the-record dinner conversation with Jesse Jackson, June 21, 2017, Cannes, France.
36. W. Gardner Selby, "Lyndon Johnson Opposed Every Civil Rights Proposal Considered in His First 20 Years as Lawmaker," *Politifact*, April 14, 2014, http://www.politifact.com/texas /statements/2014/apr/14/barack-obama/lyndon-johnson-opposed-every-civil-rights-proposal/.
37. Memorandum from W. A. Branigan to W. C. Sullivan, "Subject: Lee Harvey Oswald," May 8, 1964, President John F. Kennedy Assassination Records Collection, https://www.archives.gov /files/research/jfk/releases/docid-32129399.pdf.
38. Author interview with Henry Kissinger, July 28, 2015.
39. Author interview with Tom Brokaw.
40. Robert F. Kennedy, Edwin O. Gotham, Jeffrey Shulman, *Robert Kennedy, In His Own Words: The Unpublished Recollections of the Kennedy Years* (New York: Bantam, 1988), 78–79.
41. Author interview with Tom Brokaw.
42. Author interview with Alphonso Jackson, October 7, 2017. Jackson served as Secretary of Housing and Urban Development under George W. Bush, but as a youth he was active in the civil rights movement and a protégé of Bernard Lewis. We know that the FBI had a dossier on Martin Luther King. While we don't have documentation confirming a secret deal, we do have evidence of spying on Dr. King: Secret FBI Report, "Martin Luther King, Jr., A Current Analysis," March 12, 1968, President John F. Kennedy Assassination Records Collection, https:// www.archives.gov/files/research/jfk/releases/104-10125-10133.pdf.
43. Author interview with Alphonso Jackson.
44. Ibid.
45. Author's on-the-record dinner conversation with Jesse Jackson.
46. Author interview with President George H.W., March 31, 2015. Via email.
47. Author interview with Condoleezza Rice.
48. Ibid.
49. Author's on-the-record dinner conversation with Jesse Jackson.
50. Author interview with Alphonso Jackson. Jackson recalls Bernard Lewis relaying Johnson's comments to him and other youth leaders following a meeting with the president.
51. Lyndon B. Johnson, "Radio and Television Address at the Signing of the 1964 Civil Rights Act," July 2, 1964.
52. Lyndon B. Johnson, "Remarks Before the National Convention Upon Accepting the Democratic Nomination," August 27, 1964.
53. Author interview with Alphonso Jackson.
54. More specifically, LBJ cited Appomattox as one turning point in a broader context including Lexington and Concord.
55. Lyndon B. Johnson, "Howard University Commencement Address," June 4, 1965.

56. Author's on-the-record dinner conversation with Jesse Jackson.

57. Unsent letter from Harry Truman to Jonathan Daniels, February 26, 1950, in Ferrell, *Off the Record*, 174.

58. John A. McCone "Memorandum for the Record," in Caro, *Passage of Power*, 212. According to Caro, McCone's memo did not specify "the scale" of the suggested air strike. He explains that Johnson was eventually swayed upon hearing that Dwight Eisenhower was supportive of the naval blockade.

59. Bruce L. Paisner, "Schlesinger Resigns to Write History of JFK Administration," *Harvard Crimson*, January 29, 1964, https://www.thecrimson.com/article/1964/1/29/schlesinger-resigns -to-write-history-of/.

60. Lyndon Johnson, conversation with Doris Kearns Goodwin, cited in Goodwin, *The Fitzgeralds and the Kennedys* (New York: Simon & Schuster, 1987), 780, in Tevi Troy, *Intellectuals and the American Presidency: Philosophers, Jesters, or Technicians?* (New York: Roman & Littlefield, 2002), 46.

61. Robert Dallek, *Flawed Giant: Lyndon Johnson and his Times, 1961–1973* (New York: Oxford University Press, 1998), 70.

62. Eric Goldman, *The Tragedy of Lyndon Johnson* (New York: Knopf, 1969), 523, in Troy, *Intellectuals and the American Presidency*, 48.

63. David Halberstam, *The Best and the Brightest* (New York: Random House, 1972), 263–305, in Dallek, *Flawed Giant*, 88.

64. Dallek, *Flawed Giant*, 89.

65. Doris Kearns Goodwin interview with George Reedy, 1974, quoted in Goodwin, *Lyndon Johnson and the American Dream*, 167.

66. Conversation with Henry Kissinger en route to Bilderberg, June 7, 2018.

67. Richard N. Goodwin, "President Lyndon Johnson: The War Within," *New York Times Magazine*, August 21, 1988, https://www.nytimes.com/1988/08/21/magazine/president-lyndon-johnson -the-war-within.html.

68. David Halberstam, *Best and Brightest* (Greenwich, CT: Fawcett Columbine, 1973), 372–73, and 53 in Dallek, *Flawed Giant*, 90.

69. Ibid.

70. Author interview with H. R. McMaster, July 18, 2018.

71. Troy, *Intellectuals and the American Presidency*, 49.

72. Richard Nelson obituary: "Richard H. Nelson '61," *Princeton Alumni Weekly*, https://paw .princeton.edu/memorial/richard-h-nelson-%E2%80%9961.

73. Troy, *Intellectuals and the American Presidency*, 49.

74. Ibid., 46.

75. Ibid., 58.

76. Doris Kearns Goodwin White House notes quoted in Goodwin, *Lyndon Johnson and the American Dream*, 178.

77. LBJ interview with Doris Kearns Goodwin in Andrew Johns, *Vietnam's Second Front: Domestic Politics, the Republican Party, and the War* (University of Kentucky Press, 2010), 45.

78. Author interview with Condoleezza Rice.

79. Halberstam, *Best and the Brightest*, 643.

80. Author interview with Henry Kissinger, July 28, 2015.

81. "Lyndon Johnson and McGeorge Bundy on 27 May 1964," tape WH 6405.10, citation no. 3522. *Presidential Recordings Digital Edition*, Toward the Great Society, vol. 6, Guian A. McKee, ed. (Charlottesville: University of Virginia Press, 2014), https://prde.upress.virginia.edu /conversations/9060284. See also Robert Dallek, "Three New Revelations About LBJ," *The Atlantic*, April 1998.

82. Where some, like Jay R. Galbraith, insist that JFK had made a formal decision to withdraw, others, from the left-wing author Rick Perlstein to Republican appointees like H. R. McMaster, Henry Kissinger, and Condoleezza Rice, express skepticism. See Rick Perlstein, "Kennedy Week: JFK's Uncertain Path in Vietnam," *The Nation*, November 21, 2013, https://www.thenation.com /article/kennedy-week-jfks-uncertain-path-vietnam/.

83. Author interview with Henry Kissinger, July 28, 2015.

84. Author interview with Condoleezza Rice.

85. Author interview with H. R. McMaster.

86. Paraphrased from an interview with H. R. McMaster.

87. Author interview with Condoleezza Rice.

88. Ibid.

89. Author interview with Henry Kissinger, July 28, 2015.

90. Author interview with Tom Brokaw.

CHAPTER TEN: CLOSE CALLS

1. Feerick, "Presidential Succession and Inability," 918.

2. Ibid.

3. Ibid.

4. Campbell, *Memorial Sketch of Lafayette S. Foster.*

5. Matthew Algeo, *The President is a Sick man: Wherein the Supposedly Virtuous Grover Cleveland Survives a Secret Surgery at Sea and Vilifies the Courageous Newspaperman who Dared Expose the Truth* (Chicago: Chicago Review Press, 2011), 81–97. See also "A Yacht, a Mustache: How a President Hid His Tumor," National Public Radio, July 6, 2011, https://www.npr.org/2011/07/06 /137621988/a-yacht-a-mustache-how-a-president-hid-his-tumor. See also Crispell and Gomez, *Hidden Illness in the White House*, 204.

6. Michael P. Riccards, "The Presidency in Sickness and in Health," *Presidential Studies Quarterly* 7, no. 4 (Fall 1977), 215–31. Center for the Study of the Presidency and Congress, in Crispell and Gomez, *Hidden Illness in the White House*, 205–6. For detailed description of Eisenhower's illnesses, medical episodes, impact on the 1956 campaign and his administration, see Robert E. Gilbert, *The Mortal Presidency: Illness and Anguish in the White House* (New York: Fordham University Press, 1998).

7. Edwin Weinstein, *Woodrow Wilson: A Medical and Psychological Biography* (Princeton: Princeton University Press, 1981), 357, in Crispell and Gomez, *Hidden Illness in the White House*, 70.

8. Cary Grayson, *Woodrow Wilson: An Intimate Memoir* (New York: Holt, Rinehart, and Winston, 1960), 114, in Crispell and Gomez, *Hidden Illness in the White House*, 72.

9. DeRose, *Presidents' War*, 17.

10. Michael Medved, *The American Miracle: Divine Providence in the Rise of the Republic* (New York: Crown Forum, 2016), 183.

11. DeRose, *Presidents' War*, 17.

12. Ibid., 17n.

13. Associated Press, "Strange Story Told of Plot to Assassinate Roosevelt," *St. Petersburg Times* (Fla.), December 4, 1943, 1, in Ayton, *Hunting the President*, 16–17.

14. "Franklin D. Roosevelt Day by Day: November 11th, 1943," Pare Lorentz Center, FDR Presidential Library, http://www.fdrlibrary.marist.edu/daybyday/daylog/november-11th-1943/, in Ayton, *Hunting the President*, 16–17.

15. Feerick, *From Failing Hands*, 202.

16. Letter from Harry Truman to Ethel Noland, November 17, 1950, in Ferrell, *Off the Record*, 198–99.

17. "Stay Calm, Says Truman of Dangers," *Herald-Journal*, November 2, 1961, 14, in Ayton, *Hunting the President*, 32–33.

18. Robin Erb, "Early Suicide Bomber," *Toledo Blade*, November 21, 2003.

19. Steve B. Davis, *Near Miss: The Attempted Assassination of JFK* (Lulu.com, 2014), 4 and 9. See also Erb, "Early Suicide Bomber"; and Philip Kerr, "JFK: The Assassin Who Failed," November 27, 2000, *New Statesman*, https://www.newstatesman.com/node/193790?page=18.

20. Erb, "Early Suicide Bomber." See also Steve B. Davis, *Near Miss*, 4.

21. Urbanus Edmund Baughman, *Secret Service Chief* (New York: Harper, 1962), 11, in Ayton, *Hunting the President*, 61. See also Erb, "Early Suicide Bomber."

22. Erb, "Early Suicide Bomber."

23. Ibid. See also Steve B. Davis, *Near Miss*, 5.

24. Frederick John, "Fate Foreshadowed: JFK Had Brush with Death in '60," *Deseret News*, November 19, 1989, http://archive.deseretnews.com/archive/print/74816/FATE-FORESHADOWED—JFK-HAD-BRUSH-WITH-DEATH-IN-60.html, in Ayton, *Hunting the President*, 61.

25. Steve B. Davis, *Near Miss*, 4–5.

26. Ibid. See also Ayton, *Hunting the President*, 61; and Erb, "Early Suicide Bomber."

27. Steve B. Davis, *Near Miss*, 4.

28. Jeff Greenfield, *If Kennedy Lived: The First and Second Terms of President John F. Kennedy: An Alternate History* (New York: G. P. Putnam's Sons, 2013), 17.

29. Steve B. Davis, *Near Miss*, 2.

30. Erb, "Early Suicide Bomber."

31. Ibid. See also Ayton, *Hunting the President*, 60.

32. Erb, "Early Suicide Bomber."

33. Baughman, *Secret Service Chief*, 11–12, in Ayton, *Hunting the President*, 60. See also Greenfield, *If Kennedy Lived*, 17; and Erb, "Early Suicide Bomber."

34. Steve B. Davis, *Near Miss*, 3. See also Greenfield, *If Kennedy Lived*, 17; Ayton, *Hunting the President*, 61; and Erb, "Early Suicide Bomber."

35. Gerald Blaine, *The Kennedy Detail* (New York: Gallery Books, 2010), 51, in Ayton, *Hunting the President*, 62.

36. Steve B. Davis, *Near Miss*, 3.

37. Blaine, *The Kennedy Detail*, 62.

38. Steve B. Davis, *Near Miss*, 3.

39. Blaine, *The Kennedy Detail*, 62.

40. Donna Rhodes, "Historians Re-visit Belmont Resident's Foiled Assassination Attempts Against JFK," *Salmon Press*, September 25, 2013, http://www.newhampshirelakesandmountains.com/Articles-Winnisquam-Echo-c-2013-09-25-158473.113119-Historians-revisit-Belmont-residents-foiled-assassination-attempts-against-JFK.html.

41. Blaine, *The Kennedy Detail*, 62.

42. Steve B. Davis, *Near Miss*, 3.

43. Erb, "Early Suicide Bomber."

44. Steve B. Davis, *Near Miss*, 5.

45. Ibid., 6. See also Donna Rhodes, "Historians Re-visit Belmont Resident's Foiled Assassination Attempts against JFK," *Salmon Press*, September 25, 2013, http://www.newhampshirelakesandmountains.com/Articles-Winnisquam-Echo-c-2013-09-25-158473.113119-Historians-revisit-Belmont-residents-foiled-assassination-attempts-against-JFK.html.

46. Erb, "Early Suicide Bomber." See also Steve B. Davis, *Near Miss*, 6.

47. Ibid., 15.

48. Ibid., 19.

49. *Look* magazine interview with Urbanus Baughman, January 1961 in Davis, *Near Miss*, 6–7.

50. Urbanus E. Baughman, *Secret Service Chief* (New York: Harper, 1962) in Harvey Sawler, *Saving Mrs. Kennedy: The Search for an American Hero* (Ontario, Canada: General Store Publishing House, 2005), 28.

51. Jim Bishop, *The Day Kennedy Was Shot* (New York: Gramercy, 1968), 28, in Ayton, *Hunting the President*, 55–56.

52. Greenfield, *If Kennedy Lived*, 18.

53. Ibid., 19.

54. Author interview with Richard "Dick" Cheney, Jackson Hole, Wyoming, January 5, 2016.

55. Ibid.

56. Ibid.

57. Blaine, *The Kennedy Detail*, 62, 357, and 358, in Ayton, *Hunting the President*, 139–40.

58. Ayton, *Hunting the President*, 146.

59. Ibid.

60. James S. Kunen, "Former Presidential Bodyguard Dennis McCarthy Tells of Life under Stress in the Line of Fire," *People*, October 28, 1985, in Ayton, *Hunting the President*, 146–47, https://people.com/archive/former-presidential-bodyguard-dennis-mccarthy-tells-of-life-under-stress-in-the-line-of-fire-vol-23-no-18/. For an eye witness account see Sam Donaldson, *Hold On, Mr. President!* (New York: Random House, 1987), 199–204. For political reaction see Richard Reeves, *President Reagan: The Triumph of Imagination* (New York: Simon & Schuster, 2005), 44–46.

61. Howell Raines, "Reagan Wounded in Chest By Gunman; Outlook 'Good' After 2-Hour Surgery; Aide And 2 Guards Shot; Suspect Held," *New York Times*, March 30, 1981, https://archive.nytimes.com/www.nytimes.com/learning/general/onthisday/big/0330.html#article. For more detailed description of Reagan's time in the hospital and the specifics of his wounds and surgery, see Robert E. Gilbert, *The Mortal Presidency*, 219-229.

62. Author interview with Condoleezza Rice.

63. Gina Pace, "Life for Grenade Toss at Bush Rally," CBS News, February 11, 2009, https://www.cbsnews.com/news/life-for-grenade-toss-at-bush-rally/, in Ayton, *Hunting the President*, 217–18.

64. Pace, "Life for Grenade Toss at Bush Rally, in Ayton, *Hunting the President*, 217–18.

65. Author interview with Dana Perino, June 30, 2018.

66. Jensen, *Battle against Anarchist Terrorism*, 253.

67. Leech, *In the Days of McKinley*, 584.

68. President's Commission on the Assassination of President Kennedy, *Hearings*, vol. 25, exhibit no. 2550 (Washington, D.C.: U.S. Government Printing Office, 1964), Frederick M. Kaiser, "Origins of Secret Service Protection of the President: Personal, Interagency, and Institutional Conflict," *Presidential Studies Quarterly* 18, no. 1, 1988, 112–14, https://www.jstor.org/stable/27550537; Richard B. Sherman, "Presidential Protection During the Progressive Era: The Aftermath of the McKinley Assassination," *The Historian* 46, no. 1 (November 1983), 6–13, in Jensen, *Battle against Anarchist Terrorism*, 253–54.

69. Author interview with Henry Kissinger, July 28, 2015.

70. Ibid.

71. Ibid.

72. Author interview with Richard "Dick" Cheney.

73. Ibid.

74. Gilbert King, "A Halloween Massacre at the White House," *Smithsonian*, October 25, 2012, https://www.smithsonianmag.com/history/a-halloween-massacre-at-the-white-house-92668509/.

75. Author interview with Henry Kissinger, July 28, 2015.

76. Crispell and Gomez, *Hidden Illness in the White House*, 213–16.

77. Ibid., 216–17. See also Robert E. Gilbert, *The Mortal Presidency*, 271.

78. Author interview with Richard "Dick" Cheney.

79. Ibid.

80. Ibid.

81. Ibid. For detailed discussion on what led Al Haig to say "I'm in control here," see Lou Cannon, *President Reagan: The Role of a Lifetime* (New York: Simon & Schuster, 1991), 197–99.

AFTERWORD

1. Author interview with Richard "Dick" Cheney.

Bibliography

BOOKS

Abbott, Philip. *Accidental Presidents: Death, Assassination, Resignation, and Democratic Succession.* New York: Palgrave Macmillan, 2008.

Ackerman, Kenneth D. *Dark Horse: The Surprise Election and Political Murder of President James A. Garfield.* Falls Church, Va.: Viral History Press, 2011.

Adams, John Quincy. *Memoirs of John Quincy Adams: Comprising Portions of His Diary from 1795 to 1848.* Edited by Charles Francis Adams. 12 vols. 1874–1877. Reprint, New York: AMS Press, 1970.

Adams, Samuel H. *Incredible Era.* Boston: Houghton Mifflin, 1939.

Alexander, DeAlva Stanwood. *A Political History of the State of New York.* 3 vols. New York: Henry Holt and Co., 1909.

Algeo, Matthew. *The President is a Sick Man: Wherein the Supposedly Virtuous Grover Cleveland Survives a Secret Surgery at Sea and Vilifies the Courageous Newspaperman who Dared Expose the Truth.* Chicago: Chicago Review Press, 2011.

Allen, Frederick L. *Only Yesterday: An Informal History of the 1920s.* New York: Harper Perennial Modern Classics, 1931. First published 1931 by Harper & Row.

Alter, Jonathan. *The Defining Moment: FDR's Hundred Days and the Triumph of Hope.* New York: Simon & Schuster, 2006.

Anthony, Carl S. *Florence Harding: The First Lady, the Jazz Age, and the Death of America's Most Scandalous President.* New York: William Morrow and Company, 1998.

Ayers, Edward. *Vengeance and Justice: Crime and Punishment in the 19th Century American South.* New York: Oxford University Press, 1984.

Ayre, F. K. *Beyond Tomorrow: The True-Life Story of America's Twenty-First President, Chester Alan Arthur.* Long Beach, Calif: Amayreka Publishing, 2002.

Ayton, Mel. *Hunting the President: Threats, Plots, and Assassination Attempts: From FDR to Obama.* Washington, D.C.: Regnery History, 2014.

Baime, A. J. *The Accidental President: Harry S. Truman and the Four Months that Changed the World.* Boston: Houghton Mifflin Harcourt, 2017.

Baker, Jean H. *Mary Todd Lincoln: A Biography.* New York: Norton, 2008.

Balch, William R., ed. *Garfield's Words: Suggestive Passages from the Public and Private Writings of James Abram Garfield.* Boston: Houghton, Mifflin, 1881.

Bancroft, Frederic, ed. *Speeches, Correspondence and Political Papers of Carl Schurz.* 6 vols. New York: G. P. Putnam's Sons, 1913.

Barkley, Alben W. *That Reminds Me.* New York: Doubleday, 1954.

Bartlett, Irving H. *Daniel Webster.* New York: Norton, 1978.

Basler, Roy P., ed. *The Collected Works of Abraham Lincoln.* 9 vols. New Brunswick, N.J.: Rutgers University Press, 1953–1955.

Bauer, K. Jack. *Zachary Taylor: Soldier, Planter, Statesman of the Old Southwest.* Baton Rouge: Louisiana State University Press, 1985.

Baughman, Urbanus Edmund. *Secret Service Chief.* New York: Harper, 1962.

Benton, Thomas Hart. *Thirty Years' View.* 2 vols. New York: D. Appleton and Company, 1886.

Beschloss, Michael R. *Taking Charge: The Johnson White House Tapes, 1963–1964.* New York: Simon & Schuster, 1997.

Bishop, Jim. *The Day Kennedy Was Shot.* New York: Gramercy, 1968.

———. *The Day Lincoln Was Shot.* New York: Harper, 1955.

———. *FDR's Last Year: April 1944–April 1945.* New York: William Morrow, 1974.

Black, Conrad. *Franklin Delano Roosevelt: Champion of Freedom.* New York: PublicAffairs, 2003.

Blaine, Gerald. *The Kennedy Detail.* New York: Gallery Books, 2010.

Blum, John M. *The Republican Roosevelt.* Cambridge, Mass.: Harvard University Press, 1954.

Boller, Paul F., Jr. *Presidential Anecdotes.* New York: Penguin, 1981.

———. *Presidential Campaigns.* Oxford: Oxford University Press, 1996.

Bowen, David W. *Andrew Johnson and the Negro.* Knoxville: University of Tennessee Press, 1989.

Brabson, Fay Warrington. *Andrew Johnson: A Life in Pursuit of the Right Course: 1808–1875.* Durham, N.C.: Seeman Printery, 1972.

Brands, Henry William. *T. R.: The Last Romantic.* New York: Basic Books, 1997.

Brisbin, James S. *The Early Life and Public Career of James A. Garfield.* Philadelphia: Hubbard Bros., 1880.

Britton, Nan. *The President's Daughter.* New York: Elizabeth Ann Guild, 1927.

Brooks, Noah. *Washington, D.C., in Lincoln's Time.* Chicago: Quadrangle, 1971.

Brown, Myers E., II. *Tennessee's Union Cavalrymen.* Mount Pleasant, S.C.: Arcadia, 2008.

Bumgarner, John R. *The Health of the Presidents.* Jefferson, N.C.: McFarland, 2004.

Burns, James MacGregor. *Roosevelt: The Soldier of Freedom, 1940–1945.* New York: Harcourt Brace Jovanovich, 1970.

Busch, Noel F. *T. R.: The Story of Theodore Roosevelt and His Influence on Our Times.* New York: Reynal, 1963.

Byrd, Robert C., ed. *The Senate, 1789–1989.* 2 vols. S. Doc.100-20, 100th Congress, 1st Session; Washington, D.C.: U.S. Government Printing Office, 1988.

Byrnes, Jim. *All in One Lifetime.* New York: Harper & Brothers, 1958.

———. *Speaking Frankly.* New York: Harper and Brothers Publishing, 1947.

Cadenhead, Ivie E. *Theodore Roosevelt: The Paradox of Progressivism.* Woodbury, N.Y.: Barron's Educational Series, 1974.

Califano, Joseph A., Jr. *The Triumph & Tragedy of Lyndon Johnson.* New York: Simon & Schuster, 1991.

Cannon, Lou. *President Reagan: The Role of a Lifetime.* New York: Simon & Schuster, 1991.

Caro, Robert A. *Means of Ascent: The Years of Lyndon Johnson.* New York: Knopf, 1990.

Carpenter, Francis B. *Six Months in the White House with Abraham Lincoln.* New York: Hurd and Houghton, 1866.

Castel, Albert. *The Presidency of Andrew Johnson.* Lawrence: Regents Press of Kansas, 1979.

Chafe, William H. *The Unfinished Journey.* New York: Oxford University Press, 2015.

Chambers, William N. *Old Bullion Benton: Senator from the New West: Thomas Hart Benton, 1782 to 1858.* New York: Little, Brown, 1956.

Chapple, Joe Mitchell. *Life and Times of Warren G. Harding: Our After-War President.* Boston: Chapple Publishing Company, 1924.

Chitwood, Oliver Perry. *John Tyler: Champion of the Old South.* Newtown, Conn.: American Political Biography Press, 1939.

Churchill, Winston. *The Second World War*. 6 vols. Boston: Houghton Mifflin, 1951.

Claiborne, J. F. H. *Life and Correspondence of John A. Quitman*. 2 vols. New York: Harper & Brothers, 1860.

Cleaves, Freeman. *Old Tippecanoe: William Henry Harrison and His Time*. Norwalk, Conn.: Easton Press, 1986.

Coakley, Robert W. "World War II: The War Against Japan." Chap. 23 in Richard Stewart, ed., *American Military History: Vol. 2: The United States Army in a Global Era, 1917–2003* (Washington, D.C.: Center for Military History, United States Army, 1989), 499–528, https://history.army.mil/books/AMH/AMH-23.htm.

Cole, Arthur C. *The Whig Party in the South*. Washington, D.C.: American Historical Association, 1913.

Cole, Cyrenus. *I Remember, I Remember: A Book of Recollections*. Iowa City: The State Historical Society of Iowa, 1936.

Coleman, Mrs. Chapman (Ann Mary Butler Crittenden), ed. *The Life of John J. Crittenden: With Selections from His Correspondences and Speeches*. 2 vols. Philadelphia: Lippincott, 1873.

Coleman, Elizabeth Tyler. *Priscilla Cooper Tyler and the American Scene: 1816–1889*. Tuscaloosa: University of Alabama Press, 2006.

Colman, Edna M. H. *White House Gossip from Andrew Johnson to Calvin Coolidge*. New York: Doubleday, 1927.

Colton, Calvin, ed. *The Private Correspondence of Henry Clay*. New York: A. S. Barnes, 1856.

———. *Works of Henry Clay: Comprising His Life, Correspondence, and Speeches*. 7 vols. New York: Henry Clay Publishing Company, 1897.

Conant, Jennet. *Man of the Hour: James B. Conant, Warrior Scientist*. New York: Simon & Schuster, 2017.

Conwell, Russell H. *The Life, Speeches, and Public Services of James A. Garfield*. Boston: B. B. Russell, 1881.

Cook, William A. *King of the Bootleggers: A Biography of George Remus*. Jefferson, N.C.: McFarland, 2008.

Coolidge, Calvin. *The Autobiography of Calvin Coolidge*. New York: Cosmopolitan Book Corporation, 1929.

Cooper, John Milton, Jr. *The Warrior and the Priest: Woodrow Wilson and Theodore Roosevelt*. Cambridge, Mass.: Belknap Press of Harvard University Press, 1983.

Cooper, William J., Jr. *The South and the Politics of Slavery, 1828–1856*. Baton Rouge: Louisiana State University Press, 1978.

Cortissoz, Royal. *The Life of Whitelaw Reid*. 2 vols. New York: Charles Scribner's Sons, 1921.

Cox, James Middleton. *Journey Through My Years*. Macon, Ga.: Macon University Press, 2004.

Cox, LaWanda, and John H. Cox. *Politics, Principle, and Prejudice, 1865–1886: Dilemma of Reconstruction America*. New York: Macmillan, 1969.

Crapol, Edward P. *John Tyler: The Accidental President*. Chapel Hill: University of North Carolina Press, 2006.

Crispell, Kenneth R., and Carlos F. Gomez. *Hidden Illness in the White House*. Durham, N.C.: Duke University Press, 1988.

Crook, W. H. Henry Rood, ed., *Memories of the White House: The Home Life of Our Presidents from Lincoln to Roosevelt*. Boston: Little, Brown, and Company, 1911.

Crowley, Richard. *Echoes from Niagara: Historical, Political, Personal*. Buffalo, N.Y.: C. W. Moulton, 1890.

Culver, John C., and John Hyde. *American Dreamer: A Life of Henry Wallace*. New York: W. W. Norton and Company, 2000.

Dallek, Robert. *Flawed Giant: Lyndon Johnson and His Times, 1961–1973*. New York: Oxford University Press, 1998.

Daniels, Roger. *Franklin D. Roosevelt: The War Years, 1939–1945.* Chicago: University of Illinois Press, 2016.

Daugherty, Harry M., in collaboration with Thomas Dixon. *The Inside Story of the Harding Tragedy.* New York: The Churchill Company, 1932.

Davies, Gareth, and Julian E. Zelizer. *America at the Ballot Box: Elections and Political History.* Philadelphia: University of Pennsylvania Press, 2015.

Davis, Jefferson. *The Rise and Fall of the Confederate Government.* 2 vols. New York: Thomas Yoseloff, 1958.

Davis, Steve B. *Near Miss: The Attempted Assassination of JFK.* Lulu.com, 2014.

Dean, John W. *Warren G. Harding.* The American Presidents. New York: Times Books, 2004.

DeGregorio, William A. *The Complete Book of U.S. Presidents: From George Washington to Bill Clinton.* New York: Wings Books, 1993.

DeRose, Chris. *The Presidents' War: Six American Presidents and the Civil War That Divided Them.* Guilford, Conn.: Lyons Press, 2014.

Dittenhoefer, Abram J. *How We Elected Lincoln: Personal Recollections of Lincoln and Men of His Time.* New York: Harper & Brothers, 1916.

Doenecke, Justus. *The Presidencies of James A. Garfield & Chester A. Arthur.* The American Presidency. Lawrence: University Press of Kansas, 1981.

Donald, David H. *Lincoln.* New York: Simon & Schuster, 1995.

Donaldson, Sam. *Hold On, Mr. President!* New York: Random House, 1987.

Douglass, Frederick. *The Life and Times of Frederick Douglass: From 1817–1882.* London: Christian Age, 1882.

Downes, Randolph C. *The Rise of Warren Gamaliel Harding, 1865–1920.* Columbus: Ohio State University Press, 1970.

Dunn, Arthur Wallace. *From Harrison to Harding.* 2 vols. New York: Reprint Services Corp. First published 1922 by G. P. Putnam's Sons.

Dyer, Brainerd. *Zachary Taylor.* Baton Rouge: Louisiana State University Press, 1946.

Ecelbarger, Gary. *The Great Comeback: How Abraham Lincoln Beat the Odds to Win the 1860 Republican Nomination.* New York: Thomas Dunne Books, 2009.

Eisenhower, John S. D. *Zachary Taylor.* New York: Times Books, 2008.

Ellet, E. F. *The Court Circles of the Republic.* New York: J. D. Dennison, 1869.

Encyclopedia of the American Civil War: A Political, Social, and Military History. David S. Heidler and Jeanne T. Heidler, eds. New York: Norton, 2000.

Evans, Hugh E. *The Hidden Campaign: FDR's Health and the 1944 Election.* Armonk, N.Y.: M. E. Sharpe, 2002.

Fanon, Frantz. *Black Skins, White Masks.* New York: Grove Press, 1967.

Farrand, Max, ed. *Records of the Federal Convention.* 3 vols. New Haven: Yale University Press, 1913.

Feerick, John D. *From Failing Hands: The Story of Presidential Succession.* New York: Fordham University Press, 1965.

Ferrell, Robert H. *Choosing Truman: The Democratic Convention of 1944.* Columbia: University of Missouri Press, 1994.

———. *Harry S. Truman: A Life.* Columbia: University of Missouri Press, 1994.

———. *The Dying President: Franklin D. Roosevelt, 1944–1945.* Columbia: University of Missouri Press, 1998.

———. *The Presidency of Calvin Coolidge.* Lawrence: University Press of Kansas, 1998.

Ferrell, Robert H., ed. *The Autobiography of Harry S. Truman.* Boulder: Colorado Associated University Press, 1980.

———. *Off the Record: The Private Papers of Harry S. Truman.* Norwalk, Conn.: Easton Press, 1989. First published 1980 by Harper & Row.

Finkelman, Paul. *Millard Fillmore*. The American Presidents. New York: Times Books, 2011.

Fisher, Jack C. *Stolen Glory: The McKinley Assassination*. La Jolla, Calif.: Alamar Books, 2001.

Flynn, Edward J. *You're the Boss*. New York: Collier, 1962.

Foote, Shelby. *The Civil War: A Narrative*. 3 vols. New York: Vintage Books, 1974.

Frank, Richard B. *Downfall: The End of the Japanese Imperial Empire*. New York: Random House, 1999.

Freidel, Frank. *Franklin D. Roosevelt: A Rendezvous with Destiny*. Boston: Little, Brown, 1990.

Fuess, Claude. *Calvin Coolidge: The Man from Vermont*. Boston: Little, Brown, 1940.

Gallagher, Hugh G. *FDR's Splendid Deception*. Arlington, Va.: Vandamere Press, 1999.

Gilbert, Clinton. *Behind the Mirrors: The Psychology of Disintegration at Washington*. New York: G. P. Putnam's Sons, 1922.

Gilbert, Martin. *Winston S. Churchill: Road to Victory, 1941–1945*. Boston: Houghton Mifflin, 1986.

Gilbert, Robert E. *The Mortal Presidency: Illness and Anguish in the White House*. New York: Fordham University Press, 1998.

———.*The Tormented President: Calvin Coolidge, Death, and Depression*. Westport, Conn.: Praeger, 2003.

Goldsmith, Harry S. *A Conspiracy of Silence: The Health and Death of Franklin D. Roosevelt*. New York: iUniverse, 2007.

Goodwin, Doris Kearns. *The Fitzgeralds and the Kennedys*. New York: Simon & Schuster, 1987.

———. *Lyndon Johnson and the American Dream*. New York: St. Martin's Press, 1976.

———. *No Ordinary Time: Franklin & Eleanor Roosevelt: The Home Front in World War II*. New York: Simon & Schuster, 1994.

———. *Team of Rivals: The Political Genius of Abraham Lincoln*. New York: Simon & Schuster, 2005.

Gosnell, Harold F. *Boss Platt and His New York Machine*. Chicago: AMS Press, 1924.

Graf, Leroy P., ed. *The Papers of Andrew Johnson*. 7 vols. Knoxville: University of Tennessee Press, 1986.

Grayson, Cary. *Woodrow Wilson: An Intimate Memoir*. New York: Holt, Rinehart, and Winston, 1960.

Green, F. M. *A Royal Life, or the Eventful History of James A. Garfield*. Chicago: Central Book Concern, 1882.

Greenberg, David. *Calvin Coolidge*. The American Presidents. New York: Times Books, 2006.

Greenberger, Scott S. *The Unexpected President: The Life and Times of Chester A. Arthur*. New York: Da Capo Press, 2017.

Greenfield, Jeff. *If Kennedy Lived: The First and Second Terms of President John F. Kennedy: An Alternate History*. New York: G. P. Putnam's Sons, 2013.

Grondahl, Paul. *I Rose Like a Rocket: The Political Education of Theodore Roosevelt*. New York: Free Press, 2004.

Guiteau, Charles J., and Henry G Hayes. *A Complete History of the Trial of Guiteau, Assassin of President Garfield*. Philadelphia: Hubbard Bros., Publishers, 1882.

Gunderson, *Log-Cabin Campaign*. Westport, Conn.: Greenwood Press, 1977.

Gunther, John. *Roosevelt in Retrospect*. New York: Harper, 1950.

Hagedorn, Hermann. *The Boy's Life of Theodore Roosevelt*. New York: Harper & Brothers, 1918.

Halberstam, David. *The Best and the Brightest*. New York: Random House, 1972.

Hamilton, Holman. *Prologue to Conflict: The Crisis & Compromise of 1850*. Lexington: University of Kentucky Press, 2005.

———. *Zachary Taylor: Soldier of the Republic*. Norwalk, Conn.: Easton Press, 1943.

Hamlin, Charles E. *The Life and Times of Hannibal Hamlin*. Cambridge, Mass.: Riverside Press, 1899.

Hanchett, William. *The Lincoln Murder Conspiracies*. Chicago: University of Illinois Press, 1983.

Harriman, Averell. *Special Envoy to Churchill and Stalin*. New York: Random House, 1975.

Hassett, William D. *Off the Record with F.D.R., 1942–1945*. New Brunswick, N.J.: Rutgers University Press, 1958.

Hatch, Louis C., and Earl L. Shoup. *A History of the Vice-Presidency of the United States*. New York: American Historical Society, 1934.

Headley, P. C. *Public Men of Today*. Hartford, Conn.: S. S. Scranton, 1882.

Hearn, Chester. *The Impeachment of Andrew Johnson*. Jefferson, N.C.: McFarland, 2000.

Henry, Lewis. *Humorous Anecdotes About Famous People*. Garden City, N.Y.: Halcyon House, 1948.

Hinman, Arthur. *How a British Subject Became President of the United States*. Madison: State Historical Society of Wisconsin, 1884.

Hoetink, Harmannus. *Slavery and Race Relations in the Americas: Comparative Notes on Their Nature and Nexus*. New York: Harper & Row, 1973.

Hofstadter, Richard. *The American Political Tradition and the Men Who Made It*. New York: Alfred A. Knopf, 1948.

Holland, Jesse. *The Invisibles: The Untold Story of African American Slaves in the White House*. Guilford, Conn.: Lyon's Press, 2016.

Holt, Michael F. *The Rise and Fall of the American Whig Party: Jacksonian Politics and the Onset of the Civil War*. Oxford: Oxford University Press, 1999.

Homfischer, James D. *The Fleet at Flood Tide: America at Total War in the Pacific, 1944–1945*. New York: Bantam Books, 2016.

Hoover, Herbert. *The Memoirs of Herbert Hoover: Vol. 2: The Cabinet and the Presidency: 1920–1933*. New York: Macmillan, 1952.

Hoover, Irwin. *Forty-Two Years in the White House*. Boston: Houghton Mifflin, 1934.

Howe, George F. *Chester A. Arthur: A Quarter-Century of Machine Politics*. Norwalk, Conn.: Easton Press, 1987. First published 1934 by Dodd, Mead.

Hoyt, Edwin P. *Zachary Taylor*. Chicago: Reilly & Lee, 1966.

Hudson, William C. *Random Recollections of an Old Political Reporter*. New York: Cupples & Leon, 1911.

Hunt, H. Draper. *Hannibal Hamlin of Maine: Lincoln's First Vice President*. Syracuse, N.Y.: Syracuse University Press, 1969.

Haynes, Stan M. *President-Making in the Gilded Age: The Nominating Conventions of 1876–1900*. Jefferson, N.C.: McFarland, 2016.

Janeway, Michael. *The Fall of the House of Roosevelt: Brokers of Ideas and Power from FDR to LBJ*. New York: Columbia University Press, 2004.

Jefferson, Thomas. *The Works of Thomas Jefferson*. Paul Leicester Ford, ed. New York: Knickerbocker Press, 1905.

Jensen, Richard B. *The Battle against Anarchist Terrorism: An International History, 1878–1934*. Cambridge, Mass.: Cambridge University Press, 2014.

Johns, Andrew. *Vietnam's Second Front: Domestic Politics, the Republican Party, and the War*. Lexington: University of Kentucky Press, 2010.

Johnson, Charles C. *Why Coolidge Matters: Leadership Lessons from America's Most Underrated President*. New York: Encounter Books, 2013.

Johnson, Paul. *Modern Times: The World from the Twenties to the Nineties*. New York: Harper Perennial, 2001.

Johnson, Willis Fletcher. *The Life of Warren G. Harding: From the Simple Life of the Farm to the Glamor and Power of the White House*. Philadelphia: John C. Winston, 1923.

Jordan, David M. *FDR, Dewey, and the Election of 1944*. Bloomington: Indiana University Press, 2011.

———. *Roscoe Conkling of New York: Voice in the Senate*. Ithaca, N.Y.: Cornell University Press, 1971.

Jortner, Adam. *Gods of Prophetstown: The Battle of Tippecanoe and the Holy War for the American Frontier*. Oxford: Oxford University Press, 2012.

Kaplan, Fred. *Lincoln: The Biography of a Writer*. New York: HarperCollins, 2008.

Karabell, Zachary. *Chester Alan Arthur.* The American Presidents. New York: Times Books, 2004.

Katznelson, Ira. *Fear Itself: The New Deal and the Origins of Our Time.* New York: W. W. Norton, 2013.

Kelter, Bill, and Wayne Shellabarger. *Veeps: Profiles in Insignificance: The American Vice Presidential Pantheon from Adams to Cheney.* Atlanta: Top Shelf Productions, 2008.

Kennedy, David M. *Freedom from Fear: The American People in Depression and War, 1929–1945.* New York: Oxford University Press, 1999.

Kent, Noel J. *America in 1900.* Armonk, N.Y.: M. E. Sharpe, 2002.

Kingsbury, Robert. *The Assassination of James A. Garfield.* New York: Rosen Publishing Group, 2002.

Klara, Robert. *FDR's Funeral Train.* New York: Palgrave Macmillan, 2010.

Kohlsaat, Herman Henry. *From McKinley to Harding.* New York: Charles Scribner's Sons, 1923.

Lamon, Ward Hill. *Recollections of Abraham Lincoln, 1847–1865.* Omaha: University of Nebraska Press, 1994.

Langguth, A. J. *After Lincoln: How the North Won the Civil War and Lost the Peace.* New York: Simon & Schuster, 2014.

Lash, Joseph P. *A World of Love: Eleanor Roosevelt and Her Friends, 1943–1962.* Garden City, N.Y.: Doubleday, 1984.

Leech, Margaret. *In the Days of McKinley.* Newtown, Conn.: American Political Biography Press, 1999. First published 1959 by Harper.

Lelyveld, Joseph. *His Final Battle: The Last Months of Franklin Roosevelt.* New York: Vintage, 2016.

Leuchtenburg, William. *The Perils of Prosperity, 1914–1932.* Chicago: University of Chicago Press, 1958.

Logan, Rayford W. *The Negro in American Life and Thought: The Nadir, 1877–1901.* New York: Dial Press, 1954.

Lomazow, Steven, and Eric Fettman. *FDR's Deadly Secret.* New York: PublicAffairs, 2009.

Long, John D. *Journal of John D. Long.* Margaret Long, ed. Rindge, N.H.: Richard R. Smith, 1956.

Longworth, Alice Roosevelt. *Crowded Hours: Reminiscences of Alice Roosevelt Longworth.* New York: Charles Scribner's Sons, 1933.

Lorant, Stefan. *Glorious Burden: The History of the Presidency and Presidential Elections from George Washington to James Earl Carter, Jr.* Revised edition. Lenox, Mass.: Authors Edition, 1976.

Lord, Russell. *The Wallaces of Iowa.* New York: Da Capo Press, 1972.

Lubell, Samuel. *The Future of American Politics.* London: Hamish Hamilton, 1952.

MacMahon, Edward B., and Leonard Curry. *Medical Cover-Ups in the White House.* Washington, D.C.: Farragut Publishing, 1987.

Manchester, William. *The Death of a President.* New York: Harper and Row, 1967.

Marx, Rudolph. *The Health of the Presidents.* New York: Putnam, 1960.

May, Gary. *John Tyler.* New York: Times Books, 2008.

McCabe, James D. *The Life and Public Services of Gen. James A. Garfield.* Cleveland, Ohio: C.C. Wick and Co., 1881.

McCartney, Laton. *The Teapot Dome Scandal: How Big Oil Bought the Harding White House and Tried to Steal the Country.* New York: Random House, 2008.

McDermott, Stacy Pratt. *Mary Lincoln: Southern Girl, Northern Woman.* New York: Routledge, 2015.

McClure, Alexander K. *Abraham Lincoln and Men of War-Times.* Philadelphia: Times Publishing Co., 1892.

McCoy, Donald R. *Calvin Coolidge: The Quiet President.* Newtown, Conn.: American Political Biography Press, 1998. First published 1967 by Macmillan.

McCulloch, Hugh. *Men and Measures of Half a Century.* New York: Charles Scribner's Sons, 1889.

McCullough, David. *Truman.* New York: Simon & Schuster, 1992.

McFeely, William S. *Grant: A Biography.* New York: Norton, 1982.

McPherson, Edward, ed. *The Political History of the United States of America During the Period of Reconstruction.* Washington, D.C.: Solomons & Chapman, 1875.

McPherson, James. *Abraham Lincoln.* Oxford: Oxford University Press, 2009.

Means, Gaston. *The Strange Death of President Harding.* New York: Guild Publishing, 1930.

Means, Howard. *The Avenger Takes His Place: Andrew Johnson and the 45 Days That Changed the Nation.* Orlando, Fla.: Harcourt, 2006.

Medved, Michael. *The American Miracle: Divine Providence in the Rise of the Republic.* New York: Crown Forum, 2016.

Mee, Charles L., Jr. *The Ohio Gang: The World of Warren G. Harding.* New York: M. Evans, 1981.

Melanson, Philip H. *The Secret Service: The Hidden History of an Enigmatic Agency.* New York: Carroll & Graf, 2002.

Mencken, Henry L. *On Politics: A Carnival of Buncombe.* Malcom Moos, ed. New York: Vintage, 1960.

Merk, Frederick. *Slavery and the Annexation of Texas.* New York: Alfred A. Knopf, 1972.

Millard, Candice. *Destiny of the Republic: A Tale of Madness, Medicine and the Murder of a President.* New York: Anchor, 2011.

Miller, Merle. *Plain Speaking: An Oral Biography of Harry S. Truman.* New York: Putnam, 1974.

Miller, Nathan. *New World Coming: The 1920s and the Making of Modern America.* New York: Da Capo, 2004.

Miller, Scott. *The President and the Assassin: McKinley, Terror, and Empire at the Dawn of the American Century.* New York: Random House, 2011.

Millis, Walter. *The Martial Spirit: A Study of Our War with Spain.* Boston: Houghton Mifflin, 1931.

Milton, George Fort. *Abraham Lincoln and the Fifth Column.* New York: Vanguard Press, 1942.

———. *The Age of Hate: Andrew Johnson and the Radicals.* New York: Coward-McCann, 1930.

Moley, Raymond. *After Seven Years.* New York: Harper & Brothers, 1939.

Monk, Ray. *Robert Oppenheimer: A Life Inside the Center.* New York: Anchor, 2012.

Monroe, Dan. *The Republican Vision of John Tyler.* College Station: Texas A&M University Press, 2003.

Montgomery, Henry. *The Life of Major General Zachary Taylor.* Buffalo, N.Y.: Derby & Hewson, 1847.

Morgan, H. Wayne. *From Hayes to McKinley.* Syracuse, N.Y.: Syracuse University Press, 1969.

———. *William McKinley and His America.* Syracuse, N.Y.: Syracuse University Press, 1963.

Morgan, James, *Our Presidents.* New York: Macmillan, 1935.

Morgan, Robert J. *A Whig Embattled: The Presidency under John Tyler.* Omaha: University of Nebraska Press, 1954.

Morgan, Ted. *FDR: A Biography.* New York: Simon & Schuster, 1985.

Morison, Elting E., John M. Blum, and John J. Buckley, eds. *The Letters of Theodore Roosevelt.* 2 vols. Cambridge, Mass.: Harvard University Press, 1951.

Morris, Edmund. *The Rise of Theodore Roosevelt.* New York: Random House, 1979.

———. *Theodore Rex.* New York: Random House, 2001.

Morris, Sylvia Jukes. *Edith Kermit Roosevelt: Portrait of a First Lady.* New York: Coward, McCann & Geoghegan, 1980.

Mowry, George E. *Theodore Roosevelt and the Progressive Movement.* New York: Hill & Wang, 1960.

Mudge, Zachariah Atwell. *The Forest Boy: A Sketch of the Life of Abraham Lincoln, for Young People.* New York: Carlton and Lanahan, 1867.

Murphy, Eloise C. *Theodore Roosevelt's Night Ride to the Presidency.* Blue Mountain Lake, N.Y.: Adirondack Museum, 1977.

Murphy, Jay W. *What Ails the White House: An Introduction to the Medical History of the American Presidency.* Overland Park, Kans.: Leathers Publishing, 2006.

Murray, Robert K. *The Harding Era: Warren G. Harding and His Administration.* Newtown, Conn.:

American Political Biography Press, 2000. First published 1969 by University of Minnesota Press.

———. *The 103rd Ballot: The Legendary 1924 Democratic Convention that Forever Changed Politics.* New York: HarperCollins, 2016. Originally published 1976 by Harper & Row.

Nathans, Sydney, *Daniel Webster and Jacksonian Democracy.* Baltimore: Johns Hopkins University Press, 1974.

Naylor, Natalie A., et al., eds. *Theodore Roosevelt: Many-Sided American.* Interlaken, N.Y.: Hearts of Lake Publishing, 1992.

Neill, Edward D. *Reminiscences of the Last Years of President Lincoln's Life.* St. Paul, Minn.: Pioneer Press, 1888.

Nicolay, John G., and John Hay, eds. *Complete Works of Abraham Lincoln.* 13 vols. Harrogate, Tenn.: Lincoln Memorial University, 1894.

Nisbet, Robert. *Roosevelt and Stalin: The Failed Courtship.* Washington, D.C.: Regnery Gateway, 1988.

Norton, Mary Beth, et al. *A People and a Nation.* Stamford, Conn.: Cengage Learning, 2015.

Ogilvie, J. S. *The Life and Death of James A. Garfield: From the Tow Path to the White House.* Cincinnati, Ohio: Cincinnati Publishing Co., 1882.

Olcott, Charles S. *The Life of William McKinley.* 2 vols. Boston: Houghton Mifflin, 1916.

O'Toole, Patricia. *The Moralist: Woodrow Wilson and the World He Made.* New York: Simon & Schuster, 2018.

———. *Theodore Roosevelt After the White House.* New York: Simon & Schuster, 2005.

Paul, James C. N. *Rift in the Democracy.* Philadelphia: University of Pennsylvania Press, 1951.

Pendel, Thomas F. *Thirty-Six Years in the White House.* Washington, D.C.: Neale, 1902.

Perkins, Frances. *The Roosevelt I Knew.* New York: Viking, 1946.

Pepper, George Wharton. *Philadelphia Lawyer: An Autobiography.* Philadelphia: Lippincott, 1944.

Peskin, Allan. *Garfield.* Kent, Ohio: Kent State University Press, 1978.

Peterson, Norma Lois. *The Presidencies of William Henry Harrison and John Tyler.* Lawrence: University Press of Kansas, 1989.

Picchi, Blaise. *The Five Weeks of Giuseppe Zangara.* Chicago: Academy Chicago, 1998.

Platt, Thomas Collier. *The Autobiography of Thomas Collier Platt.* Lewis J. Lang, ed. New York: B. W. Dodge & Company, 1910.

Poage, George R. *Henry Clay and the Whig Party.* Chapel Hill: University of North Carolina Press, 1936.

Poling, Jim, Sr. *Tecumseh: Shooting Star, Crouching Panther.* Toronto, Calif.: Dundurn Press, 2009.

Poore, Benjamin Perley. *Perley's Reminiscences of Sixty Years in the National Metropolis.* 2 vols. Philadelphia: Hubbard Bros, 1886.

Poore, Benjamin Perley, ed. *The Conspiracy Trial for the Murder of the President, and the Attempt to Overthrow the Government by the Assassination of Its Principal Officers.* 3 vols. Boston: J. E. Tilton, 1865.

Pringle, Henry F. *Theodore Roosevelt: A Biography.* New York: Charles Scribner's Sons, 1958.

Pusey, Merlo J. *Charles Evans Hughes.* 2 vols. New York: Macmillan, 1951.

Putnam, Carleton. *Theodore Roosevelt, Vol. I: The Formative Years, 1858–1886.* New York: Scribner's, 1958.

Rauchway, Eric. *Murdering McKinley: The Making of Theodore Roosevelt's America.* New York: Hill & Wang, 2003.

Rayback, Robert. *Millard Fillmore: Biography of a President.* Norwalk, Conn.: Easton Press, 1989. First published 1959 by the Buffalo Historical Society by H. Stewart.

Reck, W. Emerson. *A. Lincoln: His Last 24 Hours.* Columbia: University of South Carolina Press, 1994. First published 1987 by McFarland and Company.

Reeves, Richard. *President Reagan: The Triumph of Imagination.* New York: Simon & Schuster, 2005.

Reeves, Thomas C. *Gentleman Boss*. Newtown, Conn.: American Political Biography Press, 1975.

Remini, Robert V. *Henry Clay: Statesman for the Union*. New York: Norton, 1991.

Renehan, Edward. *The Monroe Doctrine: The Cornerstone of American Foreign Policy*. New York: Chelsea House Publishing, 2007.

Rhodes, Richard. *Dark Sun: The Making of the Hydrogen Bomb*. New York: Simon & Schuster, 1995.

———. *The Making of the Atomic Bomb*. New York: Simon & Schuster, 1986.

Richardson, James D., ed. *The Messages and Papers of the Presidents*. 20 vols. New York: Bureau of National Literature, 1914.

———. *A Compilation of the Messages and Papers of the Presidents*. 10 vols. Washington, D.C.: U.S. Government Printing Office, 1897.

Rickover, H. G. *How the Battleship Maine Was Destroyed*. Washington, D.C.: Naval History Division, Department of the Navy, 1976.

Ridpath, John C. *The Life and Work of James A. Garfield, Twentieth President of the United States*. Cincinnati: Forshee & McMakin, 1881.

Ridpath, John C., and Selden Connor. *Life and Work of James G. Blaine*. Philadelphia: Historical Publishing Company, 1893.

Rigdon, William M., and James Derieux. *White House Sailor*. New York: Doubleday and Company, 1962.

Robenalt, James D. *The Harding Affair: Love and Espionage During the Great War*. New York: Palgrave Macmillan, 2009.

Roberts, Geoffrey. *Stalin's Wars: From World War to Cold War, 1939–1953*. New Haven: Yale University Press, 2006.

Rood, Henry, ed. *Memories of the White House: The Home Life of Our Presidents from Lincoln to Roosevelt, Being Personal Recollections of Colonel W. H. Crook*. Boston: Little, Brown, 1911.

Roosevelt, Elliott. *As He Saw It*. New York: Greenwood Press, 1946.

Roosevelt, James, and Bill Libby. *My Parents: A Differing View*. Chicago: Playboy Press, 1976.

Roosevelt, James, and Sidney Shalett. *Affectionately, F.D.R.: A Son's Story of a Lonely Man*, New York: Harcourt, Brace, 1959.

Roosevelt, Theodore. *American Ideals, The Strenuous Life, Realizable Ideals*. vol. 13, *The Works of Theodore Roosevelt*. Hermann Hagedorn, ed. 20 vols. New York: Charles Scribner's Sons, 1926.

———. *The Autobiography of Theodore Roosevelt*. Seven Treasures Publications, 2009. First published 1913 by Macmillan.

Rosenberg, Charles E. *The Trial of the Assassin Guiteau: Psychiatry and Law in the Gilded Age*. Chicago and London, University of Chicago Press, 1968.

Rosenman, Samuel I. *Working with Roosevelt*. New York: Harper, 1952.

Royall, Margaret Shaw. *Andrew Johnson: Presidential Scapegoat*. New York: Exposition Press, 1958.

Russell, Francis. *The Shadow of Blooming Grove*. New York: McGraw-Hill, 1968.

Sale, Sara L. *Bess Wallace Truman: Harry's White House "Boss."* Lawrence: University Press of Kansas, 2010.

Sargent, Mildred Crow. *Andrew and Eliza Johnson*. Philadelphia: Clibris Corporation, 2009.

Sargent, Nathan. *Public Men and Events*. 2 vols. Philadelphia: Lippincott, 1875.

Sawler, Harvey. *Saving Mrs. Kennedy: The Search for an American Hero*. Ontario, Canada: General Store Publishing House, 2005.

Schapsmeier, Edward L., and Frederick H. Schapsmeier. *Prophet in Politics: Henry A. Wallace and the War Years, 1940–1945*. Ames: Iowa State University Press, 1950.

Scheer, Mary L., ed. *Eavesdropping on Texas History*. Denton: University of North Texas Press, 2017.

Schlesinger, Arthur M., Jr. *The History of American Presidential Elections*. 4 vols. New York: McGraw-Hill, 1971.

Schriftgiesser, Karl. *This Was Normalcy: An Account of Party Politics During Twelve Republican Years, 1920–1932.* Boston: Little, Brown, 1948.

Schurz, Carl. *Life of Henry Clay:* American Statesman. 2 vols. Cambridge, Mass.: Riverside Press, 1887.

Scroggins, Mark. *Hannibal: The Life of Abraham Lincoln's First Vice-President.* New York: Rowman & Littlefield, 1994.

Seager, Robert, II. *And Tyler Too: A Biography of John and Julia Gardiner Tyler.* Norwalk, Conn.: Easton Press, 1989. First published 1963 by McGraw-Hill.

Seale, William. *The President's House.* 2 vols. Washington, D.C.: White House Historical Association, 1986.

Sellers, Charles. *James K. Polk: Continentalist.* Princeton, N.J.: Princeton University Press, 1966.

Seigenthaler, John. *James K. Polk.* New York: Times Books, 2003.

Seward, Frederick W. *Seward at Washington as Senator and Secretary of State.* New York: Derby and Miller, 1891.

Sherman, John. *Recollections of Forty Years in the House, Senate and Cabinet: An Autobiography.* 2 vols. Chicago: Werner, 1895.

Shlaes, Amity. *Coolidge.* New York: HarperCollins, 2013.

Silbey, Joel H. *Storm over Texas: The Annexation Controversy and the Road to Civil War.* Oxford: Oxford University Press, 2005.

Silva, Ruth. *Presidential Succession.* New York: Greenwood Press, 1968.

Simon, James F. *FDR and Chief Justice Hughes: The President, the Supreme Court, and the Epic Battle Over the New Deal.* New York: Simon & Schuster, 2012.

Singleton, Esther. *The Story of the White House.* 2 vols. New York: McClure, 1907.

Smith, Elbert B. *The Presidencies of Zachary Taylor & Millard Fillmore.* Lawrence: University of Kansas Press, 1988.

Smith, Jean E. *FDR.* New York: Random House, 2007.

Smith, Jeffrey K. *The Loyalist: The Life and Times of Andrew Johnson.* North Charleston, S.C.: CreateSpace, 2012.

Smith, Theodore Clarke. *The Life and Letters of James A. Garfield.* 2 vols. New Haven, Conn.: Yale University Press, 1925.

Speer, John. *Life of General James H. Lane.* Garden City, Kans.: John Speer, 1896.

Starling, Edmund W. *Starling of the White House.* New York: Simon & Schuster, 1946.

Steinberg, Alfred. *The Man from Missouri: The Life and Times of Harry S. Truman.* New York: Putnam, 1963.

Stewart, David O. *Impeached: The Trial of President Andrew Johnson and the Fight for Lincoln's Legacy.* New York: Simon & Schuster, 2009.

Stratton, David H. *Tempest Over Teapot Dome: The Story of Albert Fall.* Norman: University of Oklahoma Press, 1998.

Strode, Hudson. *Jefferson Davis: American Patriot, 1808–1861.* 3 vols. New York: Harcourt, Brace, 1955.

Stryker, Lloyd P. *Andrew Johnson: A Study in Courage.* New York: Macmillan, 1929.

Sugden, John. *Tecumseh: A Life.* New York: Henry Holt and Company, 1997.

Sullivan, Mark. *Our Times: 1900–1925.* 6 vols. New York: Charles Scribner's Sons, 1936.

Summers, Mark Wahlgren. *Party Games: Getting, Keeping, and Using Power in the Gilded Age Politics.* Chapel Hill: University of North Carolina Press, 2004.

Swanson, James L. *Manhunt: The Twelve-Day Chase for Lincoln's Killer.* New York: Harper Perennial, 2007.

Tarbell, Ida. *The Life of Abraham Lincoln.* 2 vols. New York: Lincoln Memorial Association, 1917.

Thayer, William M. *From Log-Cabin to White House.* Boston: James H. Earle, 1881.

Thayer, William Roscoe. *The Life and Letters of John Hay*. 2 vols. Boston: Houghton Mifflin, 1908.

———. *Theodore Roosevelt: An Intimate Biography*. Boston and New York: Houghton Mifflin, 1919.

Thomas, Hugh. *The Slave Trade: The Story of the Atlantic Slave Trade: 1440–1870*. New York: Simon & Schuster, 1997.

Thomas, Lately. *The First President Johnson: The Three Lives of the Seventeenth President of the United States of America*. New York: William Morrow, 1968.

Townsend, George Alfred. *Life of Hon. Levi P. Morton*. Philadelphia: Hubbard Bros, 1888.

Trani, Eugene P., and David L. Wilson. *The Presidency of Warren G. Harding*. Lawrence: Regents Press of Kansas, 1977.

Trefousse, Hans L. *Andrew Johnson: A Biography*. Norwalk, Conn.: Easton Press, 1996. First published 1989 by Norton.

———. *Ben Butler: The South Called Him Beast!* New York: Twayne Publishers, 1957.

Troy, Tevi. *Intellectuals and the American Presidency: Philosophers, Jesters, or Technicians?* New York: Rowman & Littlefield, 2002.

Truman, Harry S. *Memoirs by Harry S. Truman: Year of Decisions*. Garden City, N.Y.: Doubleday, 1955.

———. *Memoirs by Harry S. Truman: Years of Trial and Hope*. Garden City, N.Y.: Doubleday, 1955.

Truman, Margaret. *Harry S. Truman*. New York: William Morrow, 1973.

Tully, Grace. *F.D.R. My Boss*. New York: Charles Scribner's Sons, 1949.

Turner, Justin G., and Linda Levitt Turner. *Mary Todd Lincoln: Her Life and Letters*. New York: Alfred A. Knopf, 1972.

Tuturow, Norman E. *Texas Annexation and the Mexican War: A Political Study of the Old Northwest*. Palo Alto, Calif.: Chadwick House, 1978.

Tyler, Lyon Gardiner. *The Letters and Times of the Tylers*. New York: Da Capo, 1970. First published 1884–1896 by Whittet & Shepperson.

Untermeyer, Louis. *A Treasury of Laughter*. New York: Simon & Schuster, 1946.

Van Deusen, Glyndon G. *The Life of Henry Clay*. New York: Little, Brown, 1963.

Walker, Paul D. *Truman's Dilemma: Invasion or the Bomb*. Gretna, La.: Pelican Publishing, 2003.

Walters, Kerry. *The 1844 Calamity Aboard the USS Princeton*. Charleston, S.C.: The History Press, 2006.

War of the Rebellion, series 3, vol. 4, serial no. 125.

Watson, James E. *As I Knew Them*. New York: Bobbs-Merrill, 1936.

Waugh, John C. *On the Brink of Civil War: The Compromise of 1850 and How It Changed the Course of American History*. Wilmington, Del.: Scholarly Resources Books, 2003.

———. *Reelecting Lincoln: The Battle for the 1864 Presidency*. New York: Crown, 1997.

Wead, Doug. *All the Presidents' Children: Triumph and Tragedy in the Lives of America's First Families*. New York: Atria, 2003.

Webster, Daniel. *Letters of Daniel Webster from Documents Owned Principally by the New Hampshire Historical Society*. C. H. Van Tyne, ed. New York: McClure, Phillips & Co., 1902.

———. *The Private Correspondence of Daniel Webster*. Fletcher Webster, ed. 2 vols. Boston: Little, Brown, 1857.

Weinstein, Edwin. *Woodrow Wilson: A Medical and Psychological Biography*. Princeton, N.J.: Princeton University Press, 1981.

Werner, M. R. *Privileged Characters*. New York: Arno Press, 1974. Originally published 1935 by R. M. McBride.

White, Ronald C., Jr. *A. Lincoln: A Biography*. New York: Random House, 2009.

———. *Lincoln's Greatest Speech: The Second Inaugural*. New York: Simon & Schuster, 2002.

White, William A. *Autobiography of William Allen White*. New York: Macmillan, 1946.

———. *A Puritan in Babylon: The Story of Calvin Coolidge*. Norwalk, Conn.: Easton Press, 1986. First published 1938 by Macmillan.

Whitney, David C. *The Graphic Story of the American Presidents.* Garden City, N.Y.: J. G. Ferguson Publishing Company, 1967.

Williams, Charles R., ed. *Diary and Letters of Rutherford B. Hayes, Nineteenth President of the United States, Vol. 1: 1834–1860.* Columbus: Ohio State Archaeological and Historical Society, 1922.

Willis, Resa. *FDR and Lucy: Lovers and Friends.* New York: Routledge, 2004.

Wilson, Charles McMoran, Lord Moran. *Churchill: Taken from the Diaries of Lord Moran: The Struggle for Survival, 1940–1965.* Boston: Houghton Mifflin, 1966.

Wilson, Henry. *Rise and Fall of the Slave Power in America.* 2 vols. Boston: J. R. Osgood, 1872.

Winston, Robert W. *Andrew Johnson: Plebeian and Patriot.* Norwalk, Conn.: Easton Press, 1987. First published 1928 by Henry Holt and Company.

Wise, John. *Recollections of Thirteen Presidents.* New York: Doubleday, Page and Company, 1906.

Witcover, Jules. *The American Vice Presidency: From Irrelevance to Power.* Washington, D.C.: Smithsonian Books, 2014.

Wolff, Wendy, ed. *The Senate, 1789–1989.* 4 vols.. Washington, D.C.: U.S. Government Printing Office, 1995.

Wolraich, Michael. *Unreasonable Men: Theodore Roosevelt and the Republican Rebels Who Created Progressive Politics.* New York: Palgrave, 2014.

Woods, Robert. *Preparation of Calvin Coolidge: An Interpretation.* New York: Houghton Mifflin, 1924.

Woodward, C. Vann. *The Battle for Leyte Gulf: The Incredible Story of World War II's Largest Naval Battle.* New York: Skyhorse, 2017.

Young, John Russell. *Men and Memories.* New York: Coward-McCann, 1931.

Zornow, William F. *Lincoln and the Party Divided.* Norman: University of Oklahoma Press, 1954.

ARTICLES

Achenbach, Joel. "The Election of 1864 and the Last Temptation of Abraham Lincoln." *Washington Post*, September 11, 2014.

Anderson, Ross. "The Bug That Poisoned the President." *Food Safety News*, February 21, 2011, https://www.foodsafetynews.com/2011/02/the-bug-that-poisoned-the-president/.

"Assassination of Presidents." *New York Times*, August 29, 1881, https://timesmachine.nytimes.com/timesmachine/1881/08/29/98918603.html?pageNumber=8.

Bacote, Clarence A. "Negro Officeholders in Georgia under President McKinley." *Journal of Negro History* 44, no. 3 (July 1959), 217–39.

Binkley, William C. "The Question of Texan Jurisdiction in New Mexico under the United States, 1848–1850." *Southwestern Historical Quarterly* 26 (1920–21), 24–35, https://www.jstor.org/stable/30234791.

Blackman, Ann. "Fatal Cruise of the Princeton." *Navy History*, September 2005, http://www.military.com/NewContent/1,13190,NH_0905_Cruise-P1,00.html.

Blythe, Samuel. "A Calm Review of a Calm Man." *Saturday Evening Post* 196, no. 4 (January 28, 1923).

Brauer, Kinley J. "Hannibal Hamlin of Maine: Lincoln's First Vice-President (review)." *Civil War History* 16, no. 2 (June 1970), 176–77, https://doi.org/10.1353/cwh.1970.0072.

Bruenn, Howard. "Clinical Notes on the Illness and Death of President Franklin D. Roosevelt." *Annals of Internal Medicine* 72, no. 4 (April 1970), 579–91.

Butler, Benjamin F. "Vice-Presidential Politics in '64." *North American Review* 141, no. 347 (October 1885), 331–34, http://www.jstor.org/stable/25118532.

Channing, Walter. "Mental Status of Leon Czolgosz, the Assassin of President McKinley." *American Journal of Insanity* 59, no. 2 (1902).

Connery, T. B. "Secret History of the Garfield-Conkling Tragedy." *The Cosmopolitan* 23, no. 2 (June 1897).

———. "Secret History of the Garfield-Conkling Tragedy," *Watson's Magazine* 26, no. 4 (Thomson, Georgia: The Jeffersonian Publishing Company (February and March 1913).

Crossland, Bob. "Fifteen Seconds of Terror." *Coronet*, February 1960.

Dallek, Robert. "Three New Revelations About LBJ." *The Atlantic*, April 1998.

Davis, Damani. "Slavery and Emancipation in the Nation's Capital: Using Federal Records to Explore the Lives of African American Ancestors," *Prologue Magazine* 42, no. 1 (Spring 2010), https://www.archives.gov/publications/prologue/2010/spring/dcslavery.html.

Dinnerstein, Leonard. "The Accession of John Tyler to the Presidency." *Virginia Magazine of History and Biography* 70, no. 4 (October 1962), 447–58, http://www.jstor.org/stable/4246893.

Dudley, Harold M. "The Election of 1864." *Mississippi Valley Historical Review* 18, no. 4 (March 1932), 500–518, https://wwwjstor.org/stable/1898560.

Dunning, William A., and Charles P. Bowditch. "November Meeting, 1905. A Little More Light on Andrew Johnson; Treatment of Negro Seamen at the South." *Proceedings of the Massachusetts Historical Society* 19 (1905), 395, https://wwwjstor.org/stable/25079929.

Edmunds, George F. "Ex-Senator Edmunds on Reconstruction and Impeachment." *Century Magazine* 85 (November 1912 to April 1913), 863–64.

Erb, Robin. "Early Suicide Bomber." *Toledo Blade* November 21, 2003.

Feerick, John D. "Presidential Succession and Inability: Before and After the Twenty-Fifth Amendment." *Fordham L. Rev.* 79, no. 3 (2011), 907–49, http://ir.lawnet.fordham.edu/flr/vol79/iss3/8.

Ficken, Robert E. "President Harding Visits Seattle." *Pacific Northwest Quarterly* 66, no. 3 (July 1975), 105–14, https://www.jstor.org/stable/40489403.

Fisher, Jack. "McKinley's Assassination in Buffalo: Time to Put the Medical Controversy to Rest?" *Buffalo Physician* Spring 2001.

Frank, Jeffrey. "How FDR's Death Changed the Vice-Presidency." *New Yorker*, April 17, 2015.

Freeman, Joanne B. "When Congress Was Armed and Dangerous," *New York Times*, January 11, 2011, https://www.nytimes.com/2011/01/12/opinion/12freeman.html.

Grantham, Dewey W. "Dinner at the White House: Theodore Roosevelt, Booker T. Washington, and the South." *Tennessee Historical Quarterly* 17, no. 2 (June 1958), 112–30, https://wwwjstor.org/stable/42621372.

Grayson, A. G. "North Carolina and Harry Truman, 1944–1948." *Journal of American Studies* 9, no. 3 (1975), 283–300, www.jstor.org/stable/27553190.

"From Mentor to Elberon." *Century Magazine*, vol. 23 (January 1882).

Hamlin, Charles S. "The Presidential Succession Act of 1886." *Harvard Law Review* 18, no. 3 (January 1905).

Harrison, Eric. "Zachary Taylor Did Not Die of Arsenic Poisoning, Tests Indicate." *Los Angeles Times*, June 27, 1991, http://articles.latimes.com/1991-06-27/news/mn-2064_1_zachary-taylor.

Hatfield, Mark O., with the Senate Historical Office. *Vice Presidents of the United States, 1789–1993* (Washington: U.S. Government Printing Office, 1997), 137–46, http://www.senate.gov/artandhistory/history/resources/pdf/john_tyler.pdf, https://www.gpo.gov/fdsys/pkg/CDOC-104sdoc26/pdf/CDOC-104sdoc26.pdf.

Jackson, E. Hilton. "The Trial of Guiteau." *The Virginia Law Register* 9, no. 12 (April 1904), 1023–35, http://www.jstor.org/stable/1100203.

Kaiser, Frederick M. "Origins of Secret Service Protection of the President: Personal, Interagency, and Institutional Conflict." *Presidential Studies Quarterly* 18, no. 1 (1988), 101–27, https://wwwjstor.org/stable/27550537.

Kawai, Kazuo. "Mokusatsu, Japan's Response to the Potsdam Declaration." *Pacific Historical Review* 19, no. 4 (November 1950), 409–14, https://wwwjstor.org/stable/3635822.

Kelly, Niall. "The Forgotten Tragedy: The 1844 Explosion on the USS Princeton Shook the Presidency of John Tyler." Fredericksburg.com, September 24, 2005, fredericksburg.com/town_ and_countymiscellaneous/the-forgotten-tragedy-the-explosion-on-the-uss-princeton-shook /article_58a55481-ebdf-56f9-b5fb-b82fd2d894b6.html.

King, Gilbert. "A Halloween Massacre at the White House." *Smithsonian*, October 25, 2012, https:// www.smithsonianmag.com/history/a-halloween-massacre-at-the-white-house-92668509/.

Kleber, Louis C. "John Tyler." *History Today* 25, no. 10 (October 1975), 699.

Kunen, James S. "Former Presidential Bodyguard Dennis McCarthy Tells of Life Under Stress in the Line of Fire." *People*, October 28, 1985, https://people.com/archive/former-presidential -bodyguard-dennis-mccarthy-tells-of-life-under-stress-in-the-line-of-fire-vol-23-no-18/.

Letter, James R. Doolittle to John B. Henderson. *Century Magazine* 85 (November 1912 to April 1913).

Lynch, William O. "Zachary Taylor as President." *Journal of Southern History* 4, no. 3 (1938), 279–94, https://wwwjstor.org/stable/2191290.

Marriott, Michel. "President Zachary Taylor's Body to Be Tested for Signs of Arsenic." *New York Times*, June 15, 1991, https://www.nytimes.com/1991/06/15/us/president-zachary-taylor-s-body -to-be-tested-for-signs-of-arsenic.html.

Matthews, Franklin. "The President's Last Days." *Harper's Weekly* 45, no. 2335 (September 21, 1901).

Mayers, David. "The Great Patriotic War, FDR's Embassy Moscow, and Soviet–US Relations." *International History Review* 33 (June 21, 2011), 299–333, https://doi.org/10.1080/070753 32.2011.555448.

McHugh, Jane and Philip A. Mackowiak. "What Really Killed William Henry Harrison?" *New York Times*, March 31, 2014, http://www.nytimes.com/2014/04/01/science/what-really-killed-william -henry-harrison.html.

Nagle, John C. "A Twentieth Amendment Parable." *New York University Law Review* 72 (May 1997), 470–94.

Nilsson, Jeff, and Samuel Blythe. "Kind but Final Words for President Harding." *Saturday Evening Post* 196, no. 4 (January 28, 1923).

Oshinsky, David. "Fear and Loathing in the White House: Why Couldn't LBJ and Bobby Kennedy Get Along?" *New York Times*, October 26, 1997, http://www.nytimes.com/books/97/10/26/ reviews/971026.26oshinkt.html.

"Outrage upon Colored Persons" and "Legal Rights Vindicated." *Frederick Douglass' Paper*, July 8, 1854.

Partin, John W. "Roosevelt, Byrnes, and the 1944 Vice-Presidential Nomination." *The Historian* 42, no. 1 (1979), 85–100, www.jstor.org/stable/24445289.

"President Zachary Taylor's Body to Be Tested for Signs of Arsenic." *New York Times*, June 15, 1991.

Reeves, Thomas C. "The Mystery of Chester Alan Arthur's Birthplace." *Vermont History* 38, no. 3 (Summer 1970), 291–304.

Resnick, Brian. "This *New York Times* Reporter Was Not Impressed with Lincoln's Second Inaugural." *National Journal*, January 22, 2013.

Riccards, Michael P. "The Presidency in Sickness and in Health." *Presidential Studies Quarterly* 7, no. 4 (Fall 1977), 215–31, Center for the Study of the Presidency and Congress.

Richardson, Joe M. "The Florida Excursion of President Chester A. Arthur." *Tequesta* 24, no. 1 (1964), 46.

Robertson, Charles W. "Some Observations on Presidential Illnesses." *Boston Medical Quarterly* 8, no. 3 (June 1957), 76–86.

Roff, Peter. "Commentary: A Late Look at LBJ's Medal." United Press International, July 9, 2001,

https://www.upi.com/Archives/2001/07/09/Commentary-A-late-look-at-LBJs-medal
/5828994651200/

Ross, Alex. "Uncommon Man: The Strange Life of Henry Wallace, the New Deal Visionary," *The New Yorker,* October 14, 2013.

Sherman, Richard B. "Presidential Protection During the Progressive Era: The Aftermath of the McKinley Assassination." *The Historian* 46, no 1 (November 1983), 6–13.

Searles, Harry. "Compromise of 1850." American History Central, http://www.americanhistorycentral .com/entries/compromise-of-1850/.

Selby, W. Gardner. "Lyndon Johnson Opposed Every Civil Rights Proposal Considered in His First 20 Years as Lawmaker." Politifact, April 14, 2014, http://www.politifact.com/texas/statements/2014 /apr/14/barack-obama/lyndon-johnson-opposed-every-civil-rights-proposal/.

Sioussat, George L., ed. "The Accident on Board the U.S.S. Princeton, February 28, 1844: A Contemporary News-Letter." *Pennsylvania History: A Journal of Mid-Atlantic Studies* 4, no. 3 (July 1937), 161–89, https://journals.psu.edu/phj/article/viewFile/21070/20839.

Sterner, Kenneth L. "President Kennedy and the Escalation of the Vietnam War." History Capstone Research Papers, Cedarville University, 2015. http://digitalcommons.cedarville.edu/history_ capstones/1.

Storer, Mrs. Bellamy. "How Theodore Roosevelt Was Appointed Assistant Secretary of the Navy: A Hitherto Unrelated Chapter of History." *Harper's Weekly* no. 2893 (July 1, 1912).

Storm, Frederick A. "Roosevelt Unhurt, but Chicago Mayor's Condition Critical." United Press International, February 16, 1933.

Swansburg, John. "The Self-Made Man." *Slate,* September 29, 2014, http://www.slate.com/articles /news_and_politics/history/2014/09/the_self_made_man_history_of_a_myth_from_ben_ franklin_to_andrew_carnegie.html.

Taylor, Stephen J. "When Theodore Roosevelt Was Hospitalized at St. Vincent's." Hoosier State Chronicles: Indiana Historic Newspapers, September 22, 2015, http://blog.newspapers.library .in.gov/theodore-roosevelt-hospitalized-at-st-vincents/.

Tolchin, Martin. "How Johnson Won Election He'd Lost," *New York Times,* February 11, 1990, https://www.nytimes.com/1990/02/11/us/how-johnson-won-election-he-d-lost.html.

Trueheart, Charles. "LBJ Embellished War Record, New Bio Says." *Washington Post.* November 1, 1989, https://www.washingtonpost.com/archive/lifestyle/1989/11/01/lbj-embellished-war -record-new-bio-says/7d1a36f6-d08a-4412-86c9-1a70d91cdf4c.

Tucker, Nathaniel Beverley. "Address of Beverley Tucker, Esq. to the People of the United States, 1865." James Harvey Young, ed. Ser. 5, no. 1. Atlanta: Emory University, 1948.

Varon, Elizabeth R. "Andrew Johnson: Campaigns and Elections." The Miller Center, University of Virginia, https://millercenter.org/president/johnson/campaigns-and-elections.

"Vincent, the Astor Who Gave Away the Money." 3 parts. *New York Social Diary,* April 28–30, 2009, http://www.newyorksocialdiary.com/social-diary/2009/vincent-astor-the-man-who-gave -away-the-money, http://www.newyorksocialdiary.com/social-history/2009/part-ii-vincent -the-astor-who-gave-away-the-money, and http://www.newyorksocialdiary.com/social-history /2009/part-iii-vincent-the-astor-who-gave-away-the-money.

"Women's Courage Foils Shots Assassin Aimed at Roosevelt." United Press International, February 16, 1933.

Woodward, James T. "The United States the Envy of the World." *New York Times,* January 1, 1900.

"A Yacht, a Mustache: How a President Hid His Tumor." National Public Radio, July 6, 2011, https:// www.npr.org/2011/07/06/137621988/a-yacht-a-mustache-how-a-president-hid-his-tumor.

Yannielli, Joseph. "The Assassination of Zachary Taylor." Digital Histories @ Yale, November 22, 2013, http://digitalhistories.yctl.org/2013/11/22/the-assassination-of-zachary-taylor/.

CONGRESSIONAL RECORDS

Congressional Globe, 28th Congress, 2nd Session; 31st Congress, 1st Session.

Horace Mann, of Massachusetts. On Slavery and the Slave-trade in the District of Columbia, Delivered in the House of Representatives of the United States, February 23, 1849. Published by Pennsylvania Anti-Slavery Society, December 31, 1849.

House Executive Document, 25th Congress, 1st Session, no. 40.

House Report 7, 40th Congress, 1st Session (1867).

Investigation of Veterans Bureau, Hearings before the Select Committee, U.S. Senate, 67th Congress, 4th Session. Washington, D.C., 1923.

Leases upon Naval Oil Reserves: Hearings before the Committee on Public Lands and Surveys, U.S. Senate, 68th Congress, 1st Session, vol. 1. Washington, D.C., 1924.

Reports of Committees: 30th Congress, 1st Session–48th Congress, 2nd Session.

Senate Documents, 28th Congress, 1st Session (Series 435), no. 341.

Senate Journal, 31st Congress, 1st Session, 443.

AUDIO AND VIDEO

Interview with Vincent Astor. October 18, 1958. Conducted by Sidney Shalett. "Interview with Vincent Astor re: the Attempted Assassination of FDR," reel B, side 1, Sidney Shalett Papers. Courtesy of the FDR Presidential Library.

Christopher Klein, "The 24-Hour President." History Channel, February 28, 2013, https://www.history.com/news/the-24-hour-president.

Interview with Harrison Tyler, Jr. "Life Portrait of John Tyler." C-SPAN, aired May 17, 1999, http://www.c-span.org/video/?123380-1/life-portrait-john-tyler.

"Oral history interview with Neal Roach," interviewed by Jerry N. Hess, January 21–October 2, 1969. Harry S. Truman Presidential Library, https://www.trumanlibrary.org/oralhist/roachn.htm.

"Oral History Interview with Edwin W. Pauley," interviewed by J. R. Fuchs, March 3, 1971. Harry S. Truman Presidential Library, https://www.trumanlibrary.org/oralhist/pauleye.htm

"Oral History Interview with Harry Easley," interviewed by J. R. Fuchs, August 24, 1967. Harry S. Truman Presidential Library, https://www.trumanlibrary.org/oralhist/easleyh.htm.

"Oral History Interview with Tom L. Evans," interviewed by J. R. Fuchs, June 13, 1963. Harry S. Truman Presidential Library, https://www.trumanlibrary.org/oralhist/evans4.htm#331.

"Oral History Interview with Samuel I. Rosenman," interviewed by Jerry N. Hess, October 15, 1968 and April 12, 1969. Harry S. Truman Presidential Library, https://www.trumanlibrary.org/oralhist/rosenmn.htm.

Walter LaFeber, "Vice Presidential Nominee: Theodore Roosevelt," America 1900: American Experience, Film, http://www.pbs.org/wgbh/amex/1900/filmmore/reference/interview/lafeber_vpnomineetr.html.Index.

AUTHOR INTERVIEWS

Akhil R. Amar, May 22, 2017, via email.

Tom Brokaw, July 26, 2017, via telephone.

George H. W. Bush, March 31, 2015, via email.

Richard "Dick" Cheney, Jackson Hole, Wyoming, January 5, 2016.

Alphonso Jackson, October 7, 2017, via telephone.

Jesse Jackson (on-the-record dinner conversation), June 21, 2017, Cannes, France.

Henry Kissinger, July 28, 2015; June 7, 2018, en route to Bilderberg.

Paul McCartney, New York, July 12, 2017.

Thomas "Mack" McLarty, September 4, 2014, via telephone.

H. R. McMaster, July 18, 2018, via telephone.

Dana Perino, June 30, 2018, via email.

Condoleezza Rice, September 26, 2017, via telephone.

REPORTS, TESTIMONIES, DIARIES, AND PAPERS

Benjamin B. French, *Inventory of the White House*, May 26, 1865, commissioner's miscellaneous correspondence.

Brodie Herndon diaries.

Chester Arthur III Papers, Library of Congress.

Chester A. Arthur, Scrapbooks, Columbia University.

Civil Service Commission, *Second Annual Report*.

Diary of Lucretia Garfield.

Harold Ickes Papers, Library of Congress.

James A. Garfield Papers, 1775–1889, Library of Congress.

James K. Polk, *The Diary of James K. Polk: During his Presidency 1845 to 1849*, Milo Milton Quaife, ed., 4 vols. Chicago: A.C. McClurg and Co., 1910.

John Nicolay Papers.

Jonathan Daniels Papers, Harry S. Truman Presidential Library.

Joseph Stanley-Brown, "Memorandum Concerning Joseph Stanley-Brown's Relations with General Garfield." June 24, 1924, Stanley-Brown Papers, Library of Congress.

Max Lowenthal Papers, Harry S. Truman Presidential Library.

The New York Court of Appeals Report of the Lemmon Slave Case. New York: Horace Greely and Co., 1861.

Official Proceedings of the Republican National Convention Held at Chicago, Illinois. Chicago, 1990.

"Official Report on the Case of President McKinley."

Papers of John Sherman, Library of Congress.

Papers of the Democratic National Committee Party 1928–1948, FDR Presidential Library.

Robert E. Hannegan Papers, Harry S. Truman Presidential Library.

Roxy Stinson testimony, Hearings Before the Select Committee on Investigation of the Attorney General, United States Senate, 68th Congress, 1st Session, Pursuant to S. Res. 157, March 12–17, 1924, 4 vols. (Washington, D.C.: U.S. Government Printing Office, 1924).

Sam Houston, *The Writings of Sam Houston, 1813–1863*. 8 vols. Austin: University of Texas Press, 1939.

Sidney Shalett Papers, FDR Presidential Library.

Theodore Roosevelt Birthplace National Historic Site Archives, New York.

Theodore Roosevelt Collection, Harvard University.

Thurlow Weed Papers, River Campus Libraries, University of Rochester.

The Papers of Willie Person Mangum. Henry Thomas Shanks, ed. 5 vols. Philadelphia: Lippincott, 1875.

The United States News National Political Campaign of 1944 Proceedings of Democratic National Convention Chicago, July 19–21.

United States v. Charles J. Guiteau, New York: Arno Press, 1973.   Warren G. Harding Papers, Library of Congress.

Welles, Gideon. *Diary of Gideon Welles*. Howard K. Beale, ed. 3 vols. New York: Norton, 1960.

Welles Papers, Rare Books and Manuscripts Division, New York Public Library.

Index

About the Author

Jared Cohen is the founder and CEO of Jigsaw at Alphabet Inc. He also serves as an adjunct senior fellow at the Council on Foreign Relations. Prior to working at Alphabet, he was director of Google Ideas and chief advisor to Google's executive chairman. From 2006 to 2010 he served as a member of the secretary of state's Policy Planning Staff and as a close advisor to both Condoleezza Rice and Hillary Clinton.

Cohen is the *New York Times* bestselling author of four books, including *Children of Jihad, One Hundred Days of Silence: America and the Rwanda Genocide,* and *The New Digital Age: Transforming Nations, Business, and Our Lives,* which he coauthored with Eric Schmidt. His writing has appeared in the *New York Times, Wall Street Journal, Foreign Affairs, Los Angeles Times, Washington Post, Time* magazine, and *Foreign Policy.*

He has been named to the "*Time* 100" list, *Foreign Policy*'s "Top 100 Global Thinkers," and *Vanity Fair*'s "Next Establishment." Cohen serves on several advisory boards, including those of Allianz, Stanford University's Freeman Spogli Institute, Fluid Market, ASAPP, and the National Counterterrorism Center.

Cohen received his BA from Stanford University and his MPhil in International Relations from the University of Oxford, where he studied as a Rhodes Scholar. He speaks fluent Swahili. He lives in New York with his wife and two daughters.